Frommer's

W9-BHY-226

POSTCARDS
FROM
COSTA RICA

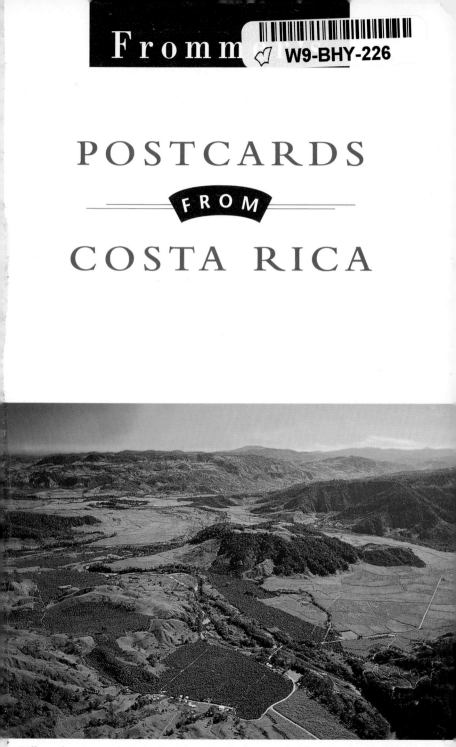

Coffee and sugarcane thrive in the rich, verdant volcanic soil of the Central Valley. You can visit a coffee farm as a side trip from San José. See chapter 4. ©Nicholas DeVore III/Bruce Coleman Inc.

Scarlet macaw. Carara Biological Reserve is a good place to spot one. See chapter 7. They're also abundant in Corcovado National Park. See chapter 8. © Art Wolfe/Tony Stone Images

You'll find this flower, the heliconia marginata, throughout the country.
© Margarette Mead/Image Bank

Male resplendent quetzal guarding his nest. Visible in Monteverde Cloud Forest (see chapter 6), Los Angeles Cloud Forest (see chapter 4), Cerro de La Muerte (see chapter 7), and Chirripó National Park (see chapter 7). © Michael Fogden/Bruce Coleman Inc.

Squirrel monkey. These guys live around Manuel Antonio National Park (see chapter 7) and the Osa Peninsula (see chapter 8). © Norman Owen Tomalin/Bruce Coleman, Inc.

White-faced capuchin monkeys abound in Manuel Antonio National Park. See chapter 7.
© Wolfgang Kaehler

It's not unusual to see iguanas scurrying about throughout all of Costa Rica. © Russell
Mittermeir/Bruce Coleman Inc.

Recently hatched green turtle. These turtles nest and hatch in Tortuguero National Park. See chapter 9. © Kevin Schafer/Tony Stone Images

Exhausted leatherback turtle heading back to the sea after laying her eggs on the beach. Playa Grande in Playa Tamarindo is a popular nesting spot. See chapter 5. © M.R. Borland/Bruce Coleman Inc.

Visitors look on as a leatherback turtle lays her eggs in Playa Grande near Playa Tamarindo. See chapter 5. © Roy Morsch/Bruce Coleman Inc.

Yellow-banded poison frog. ©*Tom Brakefield/Bruce Coleman Inc.*

Red-eyed treefrog. © *James Carmichael/Image Bank*

Red and blue poison arrow frog. © *Kenneth Deitcher/The Wildlife Collection*

Monteverde Cloud Forest Preserve. See chapter 6. © Drew Thate/Bruce Coleman Inc.

Praying mantis. ©*James Carmichael/ Image Bank*

Tropical land crab. © *Margarette Mead/Image Bank*

Workers gathering coffee—one of Costa Rica's most important crops. Coffee farms dot the San José area. See chapter 4. © J-C Carton/Bruce Coleman Inc.

Tabacón Hot Springs at the base of Arenal Volcano. See chapter 6. © Robert Winslow/Vesti Collection, Inc.

Beach at Manuel Antonio National Park. See chapter 7. © Len Kaufman Photography

Waterfall inside Monteverde Cloud Forest Preserve. See chapter 6. ©*Janis Burger/Bruce Coleman Inc.*

Steaming geyser at crater of Poás Volcano in Poás Volcano National Park near San José. This is said to be the second largest crater in the world. See chapter 4. © Janis Burger/Bruce Coleman, Inc.

This beach in Corcovado National Park is one of many beaches that line Costa Rica's Pacific coast. See chapter 8. © Dave G. Houser.

Arenal Volcano. See chapter 6. © Macduff Everton/Image Bank

When should I travel to get the best airfare?
Where do I go for answers to my travel questions?
What's the best and easiest way to plan and book my trip?

www.frommers.travelocity.com

Frommer's, the travel guide leader, has teamed up with **Travelocity.com**, the leader in online travel, to bring you an in-depth, easy-to-use resource designed to help you plan and book your trip online.

At **www.frommers.travelocity.com**, you'll find free online updates about your destination from the experts at Frommer's plus the outstanding travel planning and purchasing features of Travelocity.com. Travelocity.com provides reservations capabilities for 95 percent of all airline seats sold, more than 47,000 hotels, and over 50 car rental companies. In addition, Travelocity.com offers more than 2,000 exciting vacation and cruise packages. Travelocity.com puts you in complete control of your travel planning with these and other great features:

> **Expert travel guidance from Frommer's** - over 150 writers reporting from around the world!
>
> **Best Fare Finder** - an interactive calendar tells you when to travel to get the best airfare
>
> **Fare Watcher** - we'll track airfare changes to your favorite destinations
>
> **Dream Maps** - a mapping feature that suggests travel opportunities based on your budget
>
> **Shop Safe Guarantee** - 24 hours a day / 7 days a week live customer service, and more!

Whether traveling on a tight budget, looking for a quick weekend getaway, or planning the trip of a lifetime, Frommer's guides and Travelocity.com will make your travel dreams a reality. You've bought the book, now book the trip!

Frommer's® 2001

Costa Rica

by Eliot Greenspan

IDG Books Worldwide, Inc.
An International Data Group Company
Foster City, CA • Chicago, IL • Indianapolis, IN • New York, NY

ABOUT THE AUTHOR

Eliot Greenspan is a poet, journalist, and travel writer who took his backpack and type-writer the length of Mesoamerica before settling in Costa Rica in 1992. Since then he has worked steadily for the *Tico Times* and other local media, and continued his travels in the region. He is also the author of Frommer's *Costa Rica and Belize from $35 a Day.*

IDG BOOKS WORLDWIDE, INC.

An International Data Group Company
919 E. Hillsdale Blvd.
Suite 400
Foster City, CA 94404

Find us online at **www.frommers.com**

Copyright © 2000 by IDG Books Worldwide, Inc.
Maps copyright © 2000 by IDG Books Worldwide, Inc.

All rights reserved. No part of this book may be reproduced or transmitted in any form or by any means, electronic or mechanical, including photocopying, recording, or by any information storage and retrieval system, without permission in writing from the Publisher.

FROMMER'S is a registered trademark of Arthur Frommer. Used under license.

ISBN: 0-02-863745-3
ISSN: 1077-890X

Editor: John Rosenthal/Dog-Eared Pages
Production Editor: Jenaffer Brandt
Photo Editor: Richard Fox
Design by Michele Laseau
Staff Cartography: John Decamillis, Roberta Stockwell, and Elizabeth Puhl
Page Creation by IDG Books Indianapolis Production Department

SPECIAL SALES

For general information on IDG Books Worldwide's books in the United States, please call our Consumer Customer Service department at 1-800-762-2974. For reseller information, including discounts, bulk sales, customized editions, and premium sales, please call our Reseller Customer Service department at 1-800-434-3422.

Manufactured in the United States of America

5 4 3 2 1

Contents

7 The Central Pacific Coast: Where the Mountains Meet the Sea 240

8 The Southern Zone 287

9 The Caribbean Coast 313

Appendix A: Costa Rica in Depth 344

Appendix B: Glossary of Spanish Terms & Phrases 355

Index 358

List of Maps

ACKNOWLEDGMENTS

I'd like to thank Ana Domb for too many things to list here, but most of all for putting up with me as the deadline approached. Jim Shapiro gets a big nod for his help on the road and on the phone. I'd also like to thank my parents, Marilyn and Warren Greenspan, who showed unwavering love, support, and encouragement (well, one out of three ain't bad) as I pursued words and world wandering over a more stable and lucrative career. Jody and Ted Ejnes (my sister and brother-in-law) deserve a mention, they risked life and limb (literally) leading to two important tips that may help you save yours. Finally, Anne Becher and Joe Richey were instrumental in getting me this gig—*muchas gracias.*

An Invitation to the Reader

In researching this book, we discovered many wonderful places—hotels, restaurants, shops, and more. We're sure you'll find others. Please tell us about them, so we can share the information with your fellow travelers in upcoming editions. If you were disappointed with a recommendation, we'd love to know that, too. Please write to:

Frommer's Costa Rica 2001
IDG Books Worldwide, Inc.
909 Third Avenue
New York, NY 10022

An Additional Note

Please be advised that travel information is subject to change at any time—and this is especially true of prices. We therefore suggest that you write or call ahead for confirmation when making your travel plans. The authors, editors, and publisher cannot be held responsible for the experiences of readers while traveling. Your safety is important to us, however, so we encourage you to stay alert and be aware of your surroundings. Keep a close eye on cameras, purses, and wallets, all favorite targets of thieves and pickpockets.

What the Symbols Mean

✪ Frommer's Favorites

Our favorite places and experiences—outstanding for quality, value, or both.

The following abbreviations are used for credit cards:

AE	American Express	EURO	Eurocard
CB	Carte Blanche	JCB	Japan Credit Bank
DC	Diners Club	MC	MasterCard
DISC	Discover	V	Visa
ER	enRoute		

Find Frommer's Online

www.frommers.com offers up-to-the-minute listings on almost 200 cities around the globe—including the latest bargains and candid, personal articles updated daily by Arthur Frommer himself. No other Web site offers such comprehensive and timely coverage of the world of travel.

The Best of Costa Rica

For years, Costa Rica was the well-kept secret of a few biologists, backpackers, and beachcombers, but that's all changed. Today, the country is a major international vacation and adventure-travel destination. Tourism has become the nation's number-one source of income, but it seems like the country is just beginning to get popular. Despite the boom in vacationers, Costa Rica remains a place rich in natural wonders and biodiversity, but relatively poor in infrastructure and luxurious beach resorts and hotels. Here, you can still find unsullied beaches that stretch for miles, small lodgings that haven't attracted hordes of tourists, jungle rivers for rafting and kayaking, and spectacular cloud and rain forests with ample opportunities for bird-watching and hiking.

This is my fifth year putting this book together, and the "best of" experiences keep racking up. Some of my personal highlights include watching the sun rise on the first day of a new year from the top of the Irazú Volcano, camping alone on a deserted beach in Guanacaste, battling a feisty snook in the Golfo Dulce, soaking in some newly discovered hot springs alongside a jungle river as a sun bittern majestically stalks its dinner, conducting a half-hour-long photo session with a remarkably calm eyelash viper, swimming in a pristine pool formed by a jungle waterfall, finding myself in the midst of a school of hammerhead sharks in the waters off Cocos Island, swooping from treetop platform to treetop platform on a canopy tour, seeing both the Pacific Ocean and Caribbean Sea at the same time from the summit of Mount Chirripó, and finally learning how to surf.

In this chapter, I've selected the very best of what this unique country has to offer. I'll show you where to find all of my favorite things in Costa Rica, as well as some personal bests of your own. Most of these unmissable places and experiences are covered in greater detail elsewhere in the book; this chapter is merely meant to give you an overview of the highlights so you can start planning your own adventure.

1 The Best of Natural Costa Rica

- **Rincón de la Vieja National Park** (northeast of Liberia, in Guanacaste): This is an area of rugged beauty and high volcanic activity. The Rincón de la Vieja Volcano rises to 6,159 feet, but the thermal activity is spread out along its flanks where numerous geysers, vents, and fumaroles let off its heat and steam. This is a

The Best of Costa Rica

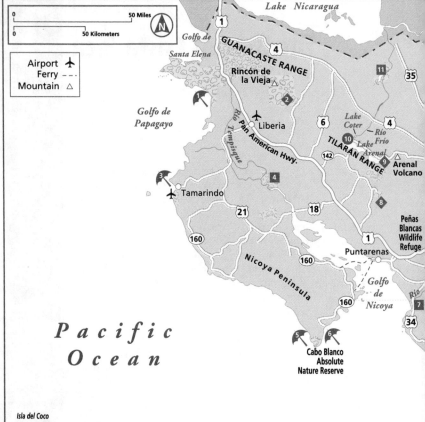

THE BEST OF NATURAL COSTA RICA
Arenal Volcano/Tabacón Hot Springs 9
Braulio Carrillo National Park 13
Manuel Antonio 21
Monteverde Cloud Forest Preserve 8
Osa Peninsula 24
Rincón de la Vieja National Park 2
The Rió Sarapiquí Region 14
Tortuguero Village and Jungle Canals 16

THE BEST BEACHES
Malpais 5
Manuel Antonio 21
Playa Montezuma 6
Playa Tamarindo 3
Punta Uva & Manzanillo 18
Punta Uvita 22
Santa Rosa National Park 1

THE BEST ACTIVE VACATIONS
Diving off Isla del Coco 27
Hiking Mount Chirripó 23
Kayaking in Golfo Dulce 25
Mountain Biking Around Lake Arenal 10
Surfing Pavones 26
Windsurfing Lake Arenal 10
Rafting the Upper Reventazon River 15

THE BEST BIRD WATCHING
Aviarios del Caribe 17
Caño Negro Wildlife Refuge 11
Carara Biological Reserve 7
Cerro de la Muerte 20
La Selva Biological Station 12
Palo Verde National Park 4
Parque del Este 19

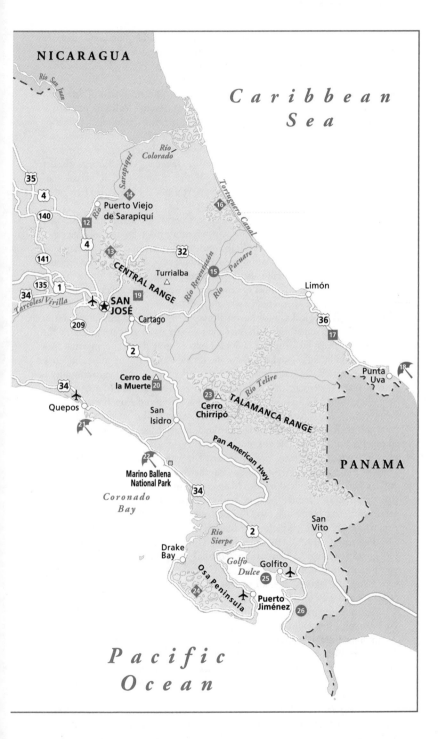

NICARAGUA

Caribbean Sea

Río San Juan

Río Sarapiquí

Río Colorado

35

4

140

14

Puerto Viejo de Sarapiquí

12

4

13

141

135

1

34

Tarcoles/Virilla

209

CENTRAL RANGE

Turrialba △

32

15

Río Reventazón

Pacuare

Río

Tortuguero Canal

16

Limón

19

SAN JOSÉ

Cartago

2

36

17

Cerro de la Muerte 20 △

34

Quepos

21

San Isidro

23 △

Cerro Chirripó

Río Telire

TALAMANCA RANGE

Río

Pan American Hwy.

Punta Uva

18

PANAMA

22

Marino Ballena National Park

34

Coronado Bay

2

San Vito

Río Sierpe

Drake Bay

Golfo Dulce

Golfito

25

Osa Peninsula

24

Puerto Jiménez

26

Pacific Ocean

great place to hire a guide and a horse for a day of rugged exploration. There are waterfalls and mud baths, hot springs and cool jungle swimming holes. You'll pass through pastureland, scrub savannah, and moist secondary forest; the bird-watching is excellent. See chapter 5.

- **Arenal Volcano/Tabacón Hot Springs** (near La Fortuna, northwest of San José): When the skies are clear and the lava is flowing, **Arenal Volcano** provides a thrilling light show accompanied by an earthshaking rumble that defies description. All this can be more than a bit exciting, which is why it's nice to have a natural hot spring to soak in immediately afterward. Or do both at the same time, while having a drink at the swim-up bar at **Tabacón Hot Springs Resort** (☎ **506/256-1500;** www.tabacon.com). If the rushing torrent of volcano-heated spring water isn't therapeutic enough, you can get a massage here at an incredibly inexpensive price. See chapter 6.

- **The Río Sarapiquí Region** (north of San José between Guanacaste in the west and the Caribbean coast in the east): This is a prime place for an ecolodge experience. Protected tropical forests climb from the Caribbean coastal lowlands up into the central mountain, affording you a glimpse of a plethora of life zones and ecosystems. **Braulio Carrillo National Park** borders several other private reserves here, and there is a host of ecolodges in a range of price categories from which to choose. See chapter 6.

- **Monteverde Biological Cloud Forest Preserve** (in the mountains northwest of San José): There's something both eerie and majestic about walking around in the early morning mist with the sound of bird calls all around and the towering trees hung heavy in broad bromeliads, flowering orchids, and hanging moss and vines. The preserve itself has a well-maintained network of trails, and the community is truly involved in conservation. Not only that, but in and around Monteverde and Santa Elena you'll find a whole slew of related activities and attractions, including canopy tours (see "The Best Active Vacations," below), which allow you to swing from treetop to treetop while hanging from a skinny cable. See chapter 6.

- **Manuel Antonio** (near Quepos on the central Pacific coast): There's a reason this place is so popular and renowned: Monkeys! The national park here is full of them, even the endangered squirrel monkeys. But there's plenty to see and do outside the park as well. The road leading into Manuel Antonio provides numerous lookouts that consistently produce postcard-perfect snapshots—even with a throwaway Instamatic. Steep jungle hills meet the sea. Uninhabited islands lie just off the coast. And the beaches here are perfect crescents of soft white sand. See chapter 7.

- **Osa Peninsula** (in southern Costa Rica): This is Costa Rica's most remote and biologically rich region. **Corcovado National Park,** the largest remaining patch of virgin lowland tropical rain forest in Central America, takes up much of the Osa Peninsula. Jaguars, crocodiles, and scarlet macaws all call this place home. Whether you stay in a luxury nature lodge in Drake Bay or outside of Puerto Jiménez, or camp in the park itself, you will be surrounded by some of the lushest and most intense jungle this country has to offer. See chapter 8.

- **Tortuguero Village & Jungle Canals** (on the Caribbean coast, north of Limón): Tortuguero Village is a small collection of rustic wood shacks on a narrow spit of land between the Caribbean Sea and a dense maze of jungle canals. It's been called Costa Rica's Venice, but it actually has more in common with the South American Amazon. You can fly into the small airstrip, but it's better to take one of the slow boats that ply the river and canal route. On the way you'll see a wide variety of herons and other waterbirds, three types of monkeys, three-toed sloths, and huge American crocodiles. If you come between June and October, you may be treated to the awe-inspiring spectacle of a green turtle nesting—the small stretch of Tortuguero beach is the last major remaining nesting site of this endangered animal. See chapter 9.

2 The Best Beaches

With more than 750 combined miles of shoreline on its Pacific and Caribbean coasts, Costa Rica offers beachgoers an embarrassment of riches.

- **Playa Tamarindo:** On the verge of becoming a little too overdeveloped, crowded, and chaotic, Tamarindo is still hanging on to its place on this list. Tamarindo has ample lodgings to suit every budget and excellent restaurants at almost every turn. The beach here is long and broad, with sections calm enough for swimmers and others just right for surfers. Located about midway along the beaches of Guanacaste province, Tamarindo makes a good base for exploring other nearby stretches of sand. There are plenty of surfers here, as well as one of the liveliest nightlife scenes on this coast. See chapter 5.

- **Playa Montezuma:** This tiny beach town at the southern tip of the Nicoya Peninsula has weathered fame and infamy and yet retains a funky sense of individuality. European backpackers, vegetarian yoga enthusiasts, and UFO seekers choose Montezuma's beach over any other in Costa Rica. The waterfalls are what set it apart from the competition, but the beach stretches for miles, with plenty of isolated spots to plop down your towel or mat. Nearby are the Cabo Blanco and Curu Wildlife preserves. See chapter 5.

- **Malpais:** If you're looking to visit Costa Rica's newest hot spot before the throngs discover it, head out to Malpais. If your car survives the road, you'll find miles of nearly deserted beaches, great surf, and just a smattering of lodges, surf camps, and simple cabinas. The **Cabo Blanco Reserve** is right here. If Malpais is too crowded for you, head farther on down the road to Santa Teresa, Playa Hermosa, and Manzanillo. See chapter 5.

- **Santa Rosa National Park:** If you really want to get away from it all, the beaches here in the northwest corner of Costa Rica are a good bet. You'll have to four-wheel-drive or hike 8 miles (13km) from the central ranger station to reach the beach. And once you get there, you'll find only the most basic of camping facilities: outhouse latrines and cold-water showers. But you will probably have the place almost to yourself. In fact, the only time it gets crowded is in October, when thousands of olive Ridley sea turtles nest in one of their yearly *arribadas* (arrivals). See chapter 5.

- **Manuel Antonio:** The first beach destination to become popular in Costa Rica, it still retains its charms, despite burgeoning crowds and mushrooming hotels. The beaches inside the park are idyllic, and the views from the hills approaching the park are enchanting. This is one of the few remaining habitats for the endangered squirrel monkey. Rooms with views tend to be a bit expensive, but many a satisfied guest will tell you they're worth it. See chapter 7.

- **Punta Uvita:** Part of the Ballena Maritime National Park, this is a wide beach with calm water and plenty of trees for shade. At low tide, a sandbar connects the mainland to a small offshore island. Most people visit for the day and stay in nearby Dominical, although small hotels and cabinas are starting to pop up closer by. You'll find several more glorious and practically undiscovered beaches south of Playa Uvita. See chapter 7.

- **Punta Uva & Manzanillo:** Below Puerto Viejo, the beaches of Costa Rica's Atlantic coast take on true Caribbean splendor, with turquoise waters, coral reefs, and palm-lined stretches of nearly deserted white-sand beach. Punta Uva and Manzanilloare the two most sparkling gems of this coastline. Tall coconut palms line the shore, providing shady respite for those who like to spend a full day on the sand, and the water is usually quite calm and good for swimming. See chapter 9.

3 The Best Active Vacations

- **Swinging Through the Treetops on a Canopy Tour:** This unique new adventure is becoming quite the rage. In most cases, after a strenuous climb using ascenders, you strap on a harness and zip from treetop to treetop while dangling from a cable. There are canopy tours all around Costa Rica. **The Original Canopy Tours** (☎ and fax **506/257-5149;** www.canopytour.com; E-mail: canopy@racsa.co.cr) runs dependable operations in several locations. See chapter 3.
- **Mountain Biking Around Lake Arenal** (near Tilarán and Arenal Volcano): This huge artificial lake, with the majestic Arenal Volcano as a backdrop, has trails all around its shores and into neighboring forests and pasturelands. There is a variety of rides of all difficulty levels. The setting is spectacular, and there are hot springs nearby for sore muscles. Contact either **Desafio Raft** (☎ **506/ 479-9464;** E-mail: desafio@racsa.co.cr) or **Aguas Bravas** (☎ **506/479-9025;** E-mail: info@aguas-bravas.co.cr). See chapters 3 and 6.
- **Diving off the Shores of Isla del Coco** (off Guanacaste in the Pacific): Legendary among treasure seekers, pirate buffs, and scuba divers, this small island is consistently rated one of the 10 best dive sites in the world. A protected national park, Isla del Coco is surrounded by clear Pacific waters, and its reefs are teeming with life (divers regularly encounter large schools of hammerhead sharks, curious manta rays, and docile whale sharks). Since the island is so remote and has no overnight facilities for visitors, the most popular way to visit is on 10-day excursions on a live-aboard boat, where guests live, eat, and sleep onboard—with nights spent anchored in the harbor. See chapters 3 and 7.
- **Battling a Billfish off the Pacific Coast:** Billfish are plentiful all along Costa Rica's Pacific coast, and boats operate from Playa del Coco to Playa Zancudo. Costa Rican anglers hold world records for both blue marlin and Pacific sailfish. Go to Quepos (just outside Manuel Antonio) for the best après-fish scene, or head down to Drake Bay if you want some isolation. **Americana Fishing Services** (☎ **888/651-6999** in the U.S., or 506/223-4331 in Costa Rica) or **Costa Rica Outdoors** (☎ **800/308-3394** in the U.S., or 506/282-6743) can help you find a good charter skipper or specialized fishing lodge. See chapters 3, 5, and 8.
- **Rafting the Upper Reventazón River** (near Turrialba): The Class V "Guayabo" section of this popular river is serious white water. Only experienced and gutsy river runners need apply. If you're not quite up to that, try a 2-day Pacuare River trip, which passes through primary and secondary forests and a beautiful steep gorge that, sadly, may be dammed soon. Get there quick! **Aventuras Naturales** (☎ **800/514-0411** in the U.S., or 506/225-3939 in Costa Rica; www. toenjoynature.com) or **Ríos Tropicales** (☎ **506/233-6455;** www.riostropicales. com) can arrange either of the above tours. See chapters 3 and 4.
- **Surfing & Four-Wheeling Guanacaste Province:** This northwestern province has dozens of respectable beach and reef breaks from Witch's Rock at Playa Naranjo near the Nicaraguan border to Playa Nosara more than 62 miles (100km) away. Rent a four-by-four with a roof rack, pile on the boards, and explore. See chapter 5.

- **Windsurfing Lake Arenal:** With steady gale-force winds and stunning scenery, the northern end of Lake Arenal (see above) has become a major international windsurfing hot spot. If you're an avid boardsailor, be sure to check in with Norm at **Rock River Lodge** (☎ **506/695-5644;** E-mail: rokriver@racsa.co.cr). See chapter 6.
- **Hiking Mount Chirripó** (near San Isidro de El General on the central Pacific coast): The highest mountain in Costa Rica, Mount Chirripó is one of the few places in the world where (on a clear day) you can see both the Atlantic and the Pacific oceans at the same time. Hiking to Chirripó's 12,412-foot summit will take you through a number of distinct bio-regions, ranging from lowland pastures and a cloud forest to a high-altitude *páramo,* a tundralike landscape with stunted trees and morning frosts. See chapter 7.
- **Kayaking Around the Golfo Dulce:** Slipping through the waters of the Golfo Dulce by kayak gets you intimately in touch with the raw beauty of this underdeveloped region. Spend several days poking around in mangrove swamps, fishing in estuaries, and watching dolphins frolic in the bay. **Escondido Trex** (☎ **506/735-5210;** www.escondidotrex.com; E-mail: osatrex@racsa.co.cr) provides multiday custom kayaking trips out of Puerto Jiménez on the Osa Peninsula. See chapter 8.
- **Surfing Pavones** (on the south Pacific coast): Just 8 miles (13km) from the Panamanian border at the southern reaches of Costa Rica's Pacific coast, Pavones is reputed to have one of the longest ridable waves in the world. When this left-point break is working, surfers enjoy rides of almost a mile in length. Much more can be said about this experience, but if you're a surfer, you've heard it all before. Contact **Casa Impact** (☎ **506/775-0637**), a long-standing budget hotel popular with surfers, for current wave reports and other surfing information. See chapter 8.

4 The Best Day Hikes & Nature Walks

- **Lankester Botanical Gardens:** If you want a really pleasant but not overly challenging day hike, consider a walk among the hundreds of distinct species of flora on display here. Lankester Gardens (☎ **506/552-3247** or 506/552-3151) is just 17 miles (27.4km) from San José and makes a wonderful day's expedition. The trails meander from areas of well-tended open garden to shady natural forest. See chapter 4.
- **Los Angeles Cloud Forest:** This private cloud forest reserve is close enough to San José for a day trip, but pristine enough to be a suitable home for the Resplendent Quetzal and hundreds of other bird species. **Villablanca Hotel** (☎ **506/228-4603;** www.villablanca-costarica.com. E-mail: info@villablanca-costarica.com) runs day trips from San José and allows walk-in visitors to explore the 6.8 miles (11km) of trails here with advance reservations. See chapters 4 and 6.
- **Rincón de la Vieja National Park:** This park has a number of wonderful trails through a variety of ecosystems and natural wonders. My favorite hike is down to the Blue Lake and Cangrejo Falls. It's 3.2 miles (5.1km) each way, and you'll want to spend some time at the base of this amazing lake, so plan on spending at least 5 hours on the outing, and bring along lunch and plenty of water. You can also hike up to two craters and a crater lake here, and there's the Las Pailas loop for those seeking a less strenuous hike. This remote volcanic national park is located about an hour north of Liberia (it's only 15^{1}/$_{2}$ miles/25km, but the road is quite rough), or about 5 hours from San José. See chapter 5.

- **La Selva Biological Station:** This combination research facility and rustic nature lodge has an extensive and well-marked network of trails. You'll have to reserve in advance (☎ 506/766-6565) and take the guided tour if you aren't a guest at the lodge. But the hikes are led by very informed naturalists, so you might not mind the company. The Biological Station is located north-northeast on the Caribbean slope of Costa Rica's central mountain range. It'll take you about 1¹/₂ hours to drive from San José via the Guápiles Highway. See chapter 6.
- **Monteverde Biological Cloud Forest Preserve:** In the morning rush of high season, when groups and tours line up to enter the preserve, you'd think the sign says CROWD FOREST. Still, the guides here are some of the most professional and knowledgeable in the country. Take a tour in the morning to familiarize yourself with the forest, then spend the late morning or afternoon (your entrance ticket is good for the whole day) exploring the preserve. Once you get off the main thoroughfares, Monteverde reveals its rich mysteries with stunning regularity. Walk through the gray mist and look up at the dense tangle of epiphytes and vines. The only noises you'll hear are the rustlings of birds or monkeys and the occasional distant rumble of Arenal Volcano. The trails are well marked and regularly tended. It's about 3¹/₂ hours by bus or car to Monteverde from San José. See chapter 6.
- **Corcovado National Park:** This large swath of dense lowland rain forest is home to Costa Rica's second-largest population of scarlet macaws. The park has a well-designed network of trails, ranger stations, and camping facilities. Most of the lodges in Drake Bay and Puerto Jiménez offer day hikes through the park, but if you really want to experience it, you should hike in and stay at one or more of the campgrounds. This is strenuous hiking, and you will have to pack in some gear and food, but the reward is some of Costa Rica's most spectacular and unspoiled scenery. Because strict limits are placed on the number of visitors allowed into the park, you'll always be far from the madding crowd. See chapter 8.
- **Cahuita National Park:** The trails here are flat, well-maintained paths through thick lowland forest. Most of the way they parallel the beach, which is usually no more than 90 meters (100 yd.) away, so you can hike out on the trail and back along the beach, or vice versa. White-faced and howler monkeys are quite common here, as are brightly colored land crabs. See chapter 9.

5 The Best Bird-Watching

- **Observing Oropendula & Blue-Crowned Motmot at Parque del Este:** A boon for city bird-watchers, this San José park rambles through a collection of lawns, planted gardens, and harvested forest, but it also includes second-growth scrub and dense woodland. Oropendula and blue-crowned motmot are common species here. Take the San Ramón/Parque del Este bus from Calle 9 between Avenida Central and Avenida 2. See chapter 4.
- **Spotting Hundreds of Marsh & Stream Birds Along the Río Tempisque Basin:** Hike around the Palo Verde Biological Station, or take a boat trip down the Bebedero River with **TAM Tours** (☎ and fax **506/668-1028**) or **Safaris Corobici** (☎ and fax **506/669-1091**; E-mail: safaris@racsa.co.cr). This area is an important breeding ground for gallinules, jacanas, and limpkins, as well as a common habitat for numerous heron and kingfisher species. Palo Verde is about a 3¹/₂-hour drive from San José. See chapter 5.
- **Looking for More Than 300 Species of Birds in La Selva Biological Station:** With an excellent trail system through a variety of habitats, from dense primary

rain forest to open pasturelands and cacao plantations, this is one of the finest places for bird-watching in Costa Rica. With such a variety of habitats, the number of species spotted runs to well over 300. Contact the **Organization for Tropical Studies** (☎ **506/240-6696;** www.ots.duke.edu; E-mail: reservas@ots.ac.cr), or see chapter 6.

- **Sizing Up a Jabiru Stork at Wildlife Refuge:** Caño Negro Lake and the Río Frío that feeds it are incredibly rich in wildlife and a major nesting and gathering site for aquatic bird species. These massive birds are getting less and less common in Costa Rica, but this is still one of the best places to see one. **Tilajari Hotel Resort** (☎ **506/469-9091;** www.tilajari.com; E-mail: tilajari@tilajari. com) makes a good base for exploring this region. The Caño Negro Refuge is way up north near the Nicaraguan border. The most popular entry point is by boat from Los Chiles, which is about 4 hours from San José. See chapter 6.
- **Catching a Scarlet Macaw in Flight over Carara Biological Reserve:** Home to Costa Rica's largest population of scarlet macaws, Carara Biological Reserve is a special place for devoted bird-watchers and recent converts. Macaws are noisy and colorful birds that spend their days in the park but choose to roost in the evenings near the coast. They arrive like clockwork every morning and then head for the coastal mangroves around dusk. These daily migrations give birders a great chance to see these magnificent birds in flight. The reserve is located about 2 hours from San José along the central Pacific coast. See chapter 7.
- **Looking for a Resplendent Quetzal in the Cerro de la Muerte:** Don't let the name (Hill of Death) scare you away from the opportunity to see this spectacular bird, revered by the ancient Aztecs and Mayas. Serious bird-watchers won't want to leave Costa Rica without crossing this bird off their life lists, and neophytes may be hooked for life after seeing one of these iridescent green wonders fly overhead, flashing its brilliant red breast and trailing 2-foot-long tail feathers. **Savegre Lodge** (☎ and fax **506/771-1732**) can almost guarantee a sighting. The Cerro de la Muerte is a high mountain pass located along the way to San Isidro de El General about 1½ hours from San José. See chapter 7.
- **Taking Advantage of the Caribbean's Best Birding at Aviarios del Caribe:** In just a few short years, Aviarios del Caribe (☎ **506/382-1335**) has established itself as the prime bird-watching resort on the Caribbean. If it flies along this coast, chances are good you'll spot it here; more than 310 species of birds have been spotted so far. Located on the Caribbean coast, Aviarios del Caribe is about a 3-hour drive from San José. See chapter 9.

6 The Best Family-Vacation Experiences

- **San José:** If your family is like mine, you'll want to spend your nights in San José, far away from the traffic and street chaos of downtown. The best place for all of you to experience Costa Rica's capital city (and still get a decent night's sleep) is the **Meliá Cariari Conference Center and Golf Resort** (☎ **800/336-3542** in the U.S. and Canada, or 506/239-0022 in Costa Rica). With facilities that include several large pools, an 18-hole golf course, 11 tennis courts, and a game room (not to mention baby-sitting service), there's something here for everyone. If you're traveling with teens, they'll feel right at home at the new Mall Cariari, which has a multiplex theater, indoor skating rink, and, of course, a food court. Located just 15 minutes from downtown, it's well situated for exploring all of the city's sights and attractions. See chapter 4.

- **Hotel Hacienda La Pacífica** (north of Cañas; ☎ **506/669-0266;** E-mail: pacifica@racsa.co.cr): This hotel is set on expansive grounds with marked trails and trees. There's a small neighboring zoo, and a variety of tours and activities are close at hand. The gentle Corobicí River is a good river float for all ages, and there are bicycles for rent, bird-watching guides, and educational tours to a nearby historic ranch. See chapter 5.
- **Playa Hermosa, Guanacaste:** The protected waters of this Pacific beach make it a family favorite. However, just because the waters are calm doesn't mean it's boring here. Check in at **Aqua Sport** (☎ **506/672-0050**), where you can rent sea kayaks, sailboards, paddleboats, beach umbrellas, and bicycles. See chapter 5.
- **Monteverde:** Located about 100 miles (160km) northwest of San José, this area hosts not only the country's most famous cloud forest, but it also sports a wide variety of related attractions and activities. After hiking through the preserve, you should be able to keep most kids happy and occupied riding horses, squirming at the local serpentarium, or visiting the butterfly farm and hummingbird gallery. See chapter 6.
- **Playa de Jacó:** On the central Pacific coast, this is Costa Rica's liveliest and most developed beach town. The streets are lined with souvenir shops, ice-cream stands, and inexpensive eateries; there's even a miniature-golf course. This is a good place for a family to rent a few mopeds for an afternoon cruise. Older children can rent a boogie board, though everyone should be careful with the rough surf here. **Hotel Club del Mar** (☎ and fax **506/643-3194;** www.jacobeach. com) is situated at the calm southern end of the beach. The hotel has a small pool and some shady grounds and is accommodating to families traveling with small children. See chapter 7.
- **Manuel Antonio:** Manuel Antonio has a little bit of everything: miles of gorgeous beaches, tons of wildlife (with an almost guaranteed monkey sighting), and plenty of active tour options. There's a load of lodging options, but **Hotel Sí Como No** (☎ **506/777-0777;** www.sicomono.com), with its large villas, water slide, and poolside bar and grill, is probably your best bet. See chapter 7.

7 The Most Scenic Towns & Villages

Earthquakes and isolation have deprived Costa Rica of the architectural splendor found in neighboring nations. San José isan unremarkable city, rapidly becoming a textbook example of what a hectic pace of poorly planned urban development can do to a third-world city. Most of the towns and villages in the country are very simple farming communities, with few attractions for traditional tourists. Still, there are towns and villages both on and off the beaten track that are worth the trip.

- **Cartago:** Located 15 miles (24km) southeast of San José, Cartago was the country's first capital and contains the most traces of the country's Spanish Catholic colonial past. Churches—some still standing, others in ruins—dominate this small city. The Basilica de Nuestra Señora de los Angeles is the most striking example of an active church and is the site of a massive annual pilgrimage. A public park now occupies what was once the site of a large unfinished church, destroyed in the wake of the 1910 earthquake. Just outside the city are the ruins of the Ujarrás church. Built in 1693, it is the country's oldest church. Cartago makes an easy and interesting day trip out of San José. See chapter 4.
- **Guayabo:** Costa Rica's oldest known city, Guayabo is nestled amid the lush forests of the mountainous Turrialba region, about 45 miles (72.5km) east of San José. Today, it has the distinction of being the country's only major archaeological site.

Although it lacks the ornate majesty of such Mayan cities as Tikal, Chichén Itzá, and Copán, it has a wonderfully homey, lived-in feel. Its residents were probably Olmecs fleeing Aztec persecution more than 3,000 years ago. Excavations have revealed that the ancient city had a well-designed water system, clearly defined living areas, and a stone-paved "highway" running through the city center. Today, visitors can experience this Indian past by walking among building foundations, marveling at the still-working aqueducts, viewing carved petroglyphs, and touring burial sites. Guayabo National Monument is best visited as a day trip from San José. See chapter 4.

- **Liberia:** The capital and commercial hub of the northern province of Guanacaste, Liberia still retains much of its classic Spanish colonial architecture. Walk around town and admire the plentiful adobe buildings with ornate wooden doors, heavy beams, central courtyards, and faded, sagging, red-tile roofs. Liberia is the only major city in Costa Rica not situated in the temperate Central Valley; instead, it's located on a hot and dry lowland savannah, surrounded by cattle land and distant foothills. There are plenty of lodging options, and Liberia makes a good base for exploring the beaches and national parks of Guanacaste. See chapter 5.

- **Golfito:** The hub of Costa Rica's southern Pacific zone, Golfito is 210 miles (338km) south of San José. Steep jungle hills meet the water, where you'll find the town spread out along one main road that hugs the winding coastline of the Golfo Dulce (Sweet Gulf). Golfito was once the largest base for United Fruit Company's banana operations. United Fruit pulled out, but left behind their company housing; many of these old wooden homes with gingerbread trim and manicured lawns have been turned into comfortable budget lodgings. You won't want to stay in Golfito too long—parts of it are quite seedy—but if you'll be exploring the Osa Peninsula or the Golfo Dulce, or visiting the Wilson Botanical Gardens, it makes a good base. See chapter 8.

- **Tortuguero:** Little more than a collection of wooden shacks built on stilts and connected by footpaths, this isolated little village on the Caribbean coast is charming, laid-back, and friendly. Although the influx of tourists is having an effect, Tortuguero retains the feel of a tiny fishing and turtling village. If you tire of the town, head out into the lush jungle canals that surround it. See chapter 9.

8 The Best Places to Shop

Shopping can be difficult in Costa Rica. Coffee is the best buy and probably the most "Costa Rican" thing you can bring home. Costa Rica doesn't have a strong handcraft and artisan tradition. Most of the crafts and colorful textiles come from Guatemala, Panama, and Ecuador. While these may be cheap, they are obviously more expensive than they'd be in their countries of origin. The hottest new item on the market is Cuban cigars, which you'll see for sale at a variety of outlets.

- **Boutique Annemarie** (San José; ☎ **506/221-6063**): This bilevel store is actually part of the Hotel Don Carlos in San José; it sells a broad selection of crafts and clothing. Here you can buy a clay or silver reproduction of some pre-Columbian figure. Most items are similar to those you'll see on the streets or in other stores, but they're all under one roof here, and the atmosphere is friendlier and more relaxed. See chapter 4.

- **Central Market (Mercado Central)** (San José): No trip to the city is complete without a tour of this indoor labyrinth of shops, stalls, and restaurants. Everything from crafts and clothing to fresh butchered meats is sold here. The surrounding streets host a daily farmers market. This is a good place to stock up on fresh-roasted whole-bean coffee. Be careful in this area, as tourists are easy targets for pickpockets and other scamsters. See chapter 4.

- **Atmosfera** (San José; ☎ **506/222-4322**): It's a little pricey, but this three-story gallery-cum-gift-shop has some very classy crafts and legitimate pieces of art. You'll find everything here, from small gifts and fine jewelry to large silk screens and oil paintings by prominent Costa Rican artists. See chapter 4.
- **Sarchí** (Central Valley): This small city outside of San José has long served as the headquarters for Costa Rica's modest craft industry. Woodwork is the most developed and available craft, with traditional painted oxcarts coming in a wide range of styles and sizes. See chapter 4.

9 The Best Luxury Hotels & Resorts

"Luxury" is a relative term in Costa Rica. To date, no hotel I've found hits truly high standards across the board. Magnificent settings abound, but service and food can sometimes fall short. They may not be perfect, but there are a few places that at least try to treat you like a king or queen.

- **Marriott Hotel and Resort** (San Antonio de Belén, San José area; ☎ **800/ 228-9290** in the U.S. and Canada, or 506/298-0844 in Costa Rica; E-mail: costaric@marriott.co.cr): Of all the contenders in the upscale urban market, the Marriott seems to be doing the best job. It might just be that it's the newest, but everything is in great shape, the service is bend-over-backward, the restaurants are excellent, and there are all the facilities and amenities for which one could hope. See chapter 4.
- **Meliá Playa Conchal** (on the northern Pacific coast; ☎ **888/336-3542** in the U.S., or 506/654-4123; E-mail: mconchal@racsa.co.cr): If you're looking for a large and luxurious resort with all the trappings, including an 18-hole Robert Trent Jones golf course, this is the only game in town. As a bonus, it's located on one of the nicest beaches in Costa Rica, the seashell-strewn wonder of Playa Conchal. See chapter 5.
- **Hotel Punta Islita** (on the Pacific coast in central Guanacaste; ☎ **800/525-4800** in the U.S., or 506/231-6122 in Costa Rica; www.hotelpuntaislita.com; E-mail: info@hotelpuntaislita.com): This is a great getaway. Perched on a high, flat bluff overlooking the Pacific Ocean, Punta Islita is popular with honeymooners, and rightly so. The rooms are large and comfortable, the food is excellent, and the setting is stunning. If you venture beyond your room and the hotel's inviting hillside pool, there's a long, almost-always deserted beach for you to explore, as well as a wealth of activities for the more adventurous. See chapter 5.
- **Hotel Sí Como No** (Manuel Antonio; ☎ **506/777-0777**; www.sicomono.com; E-mail: information@sicomono.com): Although there are fancier and more posh places in Costa Rica, the large modern villas and rooms, spectacular views, attentive service, and first-rate facilities here earn this small resort a spot on this list. See chapter 7.
- **Villa Caletas** (north of Jacó; ☎ **506/257-3653;** www.hotelvillacaletas.com; E-mail: caletas@racsa.co.cr): Spread out over a steep hillside, high above the Pacific Ocean, these individual villas have a Mediterranean feel. The Greek Doric amphitheater follows the same motif. Carved into the steep hillside, the theater frequently features evening concerts of jazz or classical music. The "infinity pool" here was one of the first in Costa Rica and is still the most interesting. Sitting in a lounge chair at the pool's edge, you'll swear it joins the sea beyond. See chapter 7.

10 The Best Moderately Priced Hotels

- **Hotel Le Bergerac** (San José; ☎ **506/234-7850;** E-mail: bergerac@racsa.co.cr): This classy little hotel has been pleasing diplomats, dignitaries, and other discerning travelers for years. Ask for one of the garden rooms, or get the old master bedroom with its small private balcony. See chapter 4.
- **Hotel Grano de Oro** (San José; ☎ **506/255-3322;** E-mail: granoro@racsa. co.cr): San José boasts dozens of old homes that have been converted into hotels, but few offer the luxurious accommodations or professional service that can be found at the Grano de Oro. Throughout all the guest rooms, you'll find attractive hardwood furniture, including old-fashioned wardrobes in some rooms. When it comes time to relax, you can soak in a hot tub or have a drink in the rooftop lounge while taking in the commanding view of San José. See chapter 4.
- **Villa del Sueño** (Playa Hermosa; ☎ and fax **506/672-0026;** www. villadelsueno.com; E-mail: delsueno@racsa.co.cr): It's not right on the beach (you'll have to walk about 91m/100 yd.), but everything else about this place is right on the money. Clean, comfortable rooms, a nice refreshing pool, and an excellent restaurant. You can't do better in Playa Hermosa. See chapter 5.
- **Amor de Mar** (Playa Montezuma; ☎ **506/642-0262;** E-mail: shoebox@racsa. co.cr): This hotel has brightly varnished woodwork, immaculate rooms, hammocks strung under shady mango trees, a wide grass lawn overlooking the Pacific Ocean, and a swimming-pool–size tide pool carved into the adjoining rocky shore. They could charge much more than they do. See chapter 5.
- **El Sano Banano** (Playa Montezuma; ☎ and fax **506/642-0068;** www. elbanano.com; E-mail: elbanano@racsa.co.cr): Isolated, private cabins with outdoor showers set amid lush grounds a stone's throw from the Pacific Ocean all add up to my idea of a tropical paradise. See chapter 5.
- **El Sapo Dorado** (Monteverde; ☎ **506/645-5010;** E-mail: elsapo@racsa. co.cr): Spacious wooden cabins with fireplaces and private porches are spread across an open hillside planted with fruit trees and tropical flowers. The hotel has an excellent restaurant and is a great place to enjoy some of the best sunsets in town. See chapter 6.
- **Hotel Club del Mar** (Playa de Jacó; ☎ and fax **506/643-3194**): This is a great bet and a good bargain in Playa de Jacó. The rooms are clean and comfortable, the service is friendly, and it's right on the beach. See chapter 7.

11 The Best Ecolodges & Wilderness Resorts

The term "ecotourism" is fast becoming ubiquitous within the travel industry, particularly in Costa Rica. Ecolodge options in Costa Rica range from tent camps with no electricity, cold-water showers, and communal buffet-style meals to some of the most luxurious accommodations in the country. Generally, outstanding ecolodges and wilderness resorts are set apart by an ongoing commitment (financial or otherwise) to minimizing their effect on surrounding ecosystems and to supporting residents of local communities. They should also be able to provide naturalist guides and plentiful information. All of the following do.

- **Arenal Observatory Lodge** (near La Fortuna; ☎ **506/257-9489;** www. arenal-observatory.co.cr; E-mail: info@arenal-observatory.co.cr): Originally a research facility, this lodge has upgraded quite a bit over the years and now features comfortable rooms with impressive views of the Arenal Volcano. There are also excellent trails to nearby lava flows and a nice waterfall. Toucans frequent the trees near the lodge, and howler monkeys provide the wake-up calls. See chapter 6.

- **La Selva Biological Station** (south of Puerto Viejo; ☎ **506/240-6696;** www. ots.duke.edu; E-mail: reservas@cro.ots.ac.cr): Sure, this place is geared more toward researchers than tourists, but that (and the surrounding rain forest and extensive trail system) is what makes this one of the best ecotourism spots in the country. See chapter 6.

- **La Paloma Lodge** (Drake Bay; ☎ **506/239-2801;** www.lapalomalodge.com; E-mail: lapaloma@lapalomalodge.com): If your idea of the perfect nature lodge is one where your front porch provides some prime-time viewing of flora and fauna, this place is for you. If you decide to leave the comfort of your porch, the Osa Peninsula's lowland rain forests are just outside your door. See chapter 8.

- **Bosque del Cabo Wilderness Lodge** (Osa Peninsula; ☎ and fax **506/ 735-5206;** www.bosquedelcabo.com. E-mail: boscabo@racsa.co.cr): Large and comfortable private cabins perched on the edge of a cliff overlooking the Pacific Ocean and surrounded by lush rain forest make this one of my favorite spots in the country. There's plenty to do and there are always great guides here. See chapter 8.

- **Lapa Ríos** (Osa Peninsula; ☎ **506/735-5130;** www.laparios.com; E-mail: info@laparios.com): Situated at the southern tip of the Osa Peninsula, this is the most luxurious ecolodge in Costa Rica. The 14 bungalow rooms all have spectacular views and are set into a lush forest. A lot of care went into the design and construction of this hotel. There is a host of tours available for guests, and the guides are usually local residents who are intimately familiar with the environment. See chapter 8.

- **Corcovado Lodge Tent Camp** (Playa Carate; ☎ **506/257-0766;** www. costaricaexpeditions.com; E-mail: costaric@expeditions.co.cr): Located right on the border of Corcovado National Park, these accommodations are in spacious individual tents set within walking distance of the crashing surf. The whole operation is run by the very dependable and experienced Costa Rica Expeditions. See chapter 8.

- **Selva Bananito Lodge** (in the Talamanca Mountains south of Limón; ☎ and fax **506/253-8118;** www.selvabananito.com; E-mail: conselva@racsa.co.cr): This is one of the few lodges providing direct access to the southern Caribbean lowland rain forests. There's no electricity here, but that doesn't mean it's not plush. Hike along a riverbed, ride horses through the rain forest, climb 100 feet up a ceiba tree, or rappel down a jungle waterfall. There is fabulous bird-watching here, and the Caribbean beaches are nearby. See chapter 9.

- **Cabinas Chimuri** (Puerto Viejo; ☎ **506/750-0428;** E-mail: atecmail@ racsa.co.cr): These rustic Bribri-style A-frame cabins are built out of local materials and are owned and managed by Mauricio Salazar, a local Bribri Indian. The tours, setting, and surroundings make this the perfect way to really get to know the people, customs, and ecology of the Talamanca region. Mauricio will take you to visit the nearby reservation and show you some of the secrets of jungle herbology and bush medicine. The accommodations are basic, but you'll have a mosquito net and a porch to sit on, and you can watch the Caribbean birds pass by. See chapter 9.

12 The Best Bed-and-Breakfasts & Small Inns

- **Finca Rosa Blanca Country Inn** (Santa Bárbara de Heredia; ☎ **506/ 269-9392;** www.finca-rblanca.co.cr; E-mail: info@finca-rblanca.co.cr): If the cookie-cutter rooms of international resorts leave you cold, then perhaps the unique rooms of this unusual inn will be more your style. Square corners seem to have been prohibited here in favor of turrets and curving walls of glass, arched windows, and a semicircular built-in couch. It's set into the lush hillsides just 20 minutes from San José. See chapter 4.

- **Vista del Valle Plantation Inn** (near Grecia; ☎ 506/450-0900; www. vistadelvalle.com; E-mail: mibrejo@racsa.co.cr): This is a great choice for those who want something close to the airport but have no need for San José. The separate cabins are influenced by traditional Japanese architecture, with lots of polished woodwork and plenty of light. The gardens are also meticulously tended, and the chef is excellent. There's a nice tile pool and Jacuzzi that look out over a deep river canyon. See chapter 4.
- **Sueño del Mar** (Playa Tamarindo; ☎ and fax 506/653-0284; www.tamarindo. com; E-mail: suenodem@racsa.co.cr): You may think you're dreaming here. The rooms feature African dolls on the windowsills, Kokopeli candleholders, and open-air showers with sculpted angelfish, hand-painted tiles, and lush tropical plants. The fabrics are from Bali and Guatemala. Somehow, all this works well together. Add in the requisite hammocks under shade trees right on the beach, a new small pool, and you really have something. The breakfasts here are earning local renown; yours comes with the price of your room. See chapter 5.
- **Arco Iris Lodge** (Monteverde; ☎ 506/645-5067; E-mail: arcoiris@racsa.co.cr): This small lodge is right in Santa Elena and it's by far the best deal in the Monteverde area. The owners are extremely knowledgeable and helpful. See chapter 6.
- **Los Cocos** (Playa Zancudo; ☎ and fax 506/776-0012; E-mail: loscocos@racsa. co.cr): If you've ever dreamed about chucking it all and setting up shop in a simple house right on the beach, you should come here and give it a trial run first. See chapter 8.
- **Shawandha Lodge** (Playa Chiquita; ☎ 506/750-0018; E-mail: shawanda@ racsa.co.cr): Spacious, individual bungalows set amid flowering gardens and thick jungle make this the most comfortable lodge on the Caribbean coast. Artistic touches abound. See chapter 9.
- **Casa Verde** (Puerto Viejo; ☎ 506/750-0015; E-mail: casaver@hotmail.com): This is my favorite budget lodging along the Caribbean coast. The rooms are clean and airy and have comfortable beds with mosquito nets. The owner is friendly and is always doing some work in the gardens or around the grounds. See chapter 9.

13 The Best Restaurants

- **Café Mundo** (San José; ☎ 506/222-6190): This elegant little restaurant is my favorite place in downtown San José for a casual meal. The pizzas are excellent, the salads and main dishes are fresh and creative (Chef Ray Johnson prepares daily specials), and the desserts are some of the best in the country. If the weather's nice, you should grab a table in the lush patio garden, beside the small tile fountain under large shade trees. See chapter 4.
- **La Peña de Cantares** (Santa Ana; ☎ 506/282-5441): Great Tico cuisine served up in a historic 200-year old home, and live music most weekends to boot. On the menu the dishes all feature poetic descriptions, and the preparation is almost as creative. See chapter 4.
- **Tin Jo** (San José; ☎ 506/221-7605): In a city with hundreds of Chinese restaurants, this place stands head-and-shoulders above the competition. In addition to

an extensive selection of Szechuan and Cantonese classics, there are Japanese, Thai, Indian, and Malaysian dishes on the menu. Tin Jo has the most adventurous Asian cuisine in Costa Rica. See chapter 4.

- **La Meridiana** (Tamarindo; ☎ and fax **506/653-0230**): I'm not sure that a surfer town deserves such fine Italian food, but it's got it. The gnocchi here are delicate and served as small medaillons, not dumplings. If you don't want to lose sight of the fact that you're at the beach, have a fresh fillet of fish, or the home-made ravioli stuffed with lobster. This is a family-run establishment, and even the grappa is brewed by an uncle back in the homeland. See chapter 5.

- **Playa de los Artistas** (Montezuma; no phone): This place is the perfect blend of refined cuisine and beachside funkiness. There are only a few tables here, so make sure you get here early. Fresh grilled seafood is served in oversized ceramic bowls and on large wooden slabs lined with banana leaves. See chapter 5.

- **El Gran Escape** (Quepos; ☎ **506/777-0395**): The prices are right, the portions are generous, and the fish is always fresh and expertly prepared. What more could you ask for from a seafood restaurant in a popular port town? Well, since you asked, there's even an adjunct new sushi restaurant upstairs. See chapter 7.

- **Restaurant Edith** (Cahuita; ☎ **506/755-0248**): Miss Edith cooks up some of the best and most authentic Caribbean cuisine. Service is slow, but you can spend your time chatting with other hungry travelers at the large communal tables packed into this humble open-air affair. See chapter 9.

14 The Best After-Dark Fun

- **El Cuartel de la Boca del Monte** (San José; ☎ **506/221-0327**): This is where San José's young, restless, and beautiful congregate. From Wednesday through Saturday the place is jam-packed. Originally a gay and bohemian hangout, it is now decidedly yuppie. There's frequently live music here. See chapter 4.

- **La Esmeralda** (San José; ☎ **506/221-0530**): This restaurant serves as a meeting place and central dispatch center for scores of local mariachi bands, some of which even print the restaurant's pay-phone number on their business cards. Hire your own combo for a song or two, or just enjoy the cacophony as the bands battle it out through the night. See chapter 4.

- **San Pedro** (San José): This is San José's university district, and at night its streets are filled with students strolling among a variety of bars and cafes. If you'd like to join them, keep in mind that **La Villa** (☎ **506/225-9612**) caters to artists and bohemians; **Mosaikos** (☎ **506/280-9541**) is popular with young Tico rockers; **Omar Khayyam** (☎ **506/253-8455**) is a great place to grab an outdoor table and watch the crowds walk by; and **Pizza Caccio** (☎ **506/283-2809**) seems to attract a good share of the U.S. students studying here. All of the spots listed above are located in a 3-block stretch that begins 200 meters (218 yd.) east of the San Pedro Church and heads north. If you head straight 500 meters (545 yd.) east from the church, you'll come to **Jazz Café** (☎ **506/253-8933**), which as its name indicates often features live jazz. See chapter 4.

- **Mar y Sombra** (Manuel Antonio; ☎ **506/777-0510**): Located on the beach a couple of hundred yards from the national park entrance, this is the most happening spot in the Manuel Antonio area. There's a large, open-air dance floor and plenty of tables set in the sand. If the dancing gets too intense, you can always cool your feet in the ocean. See chapter 7.

- **San Clemente Bar & Grill** (Dominical; ☎ **506/787-0055**): This is a quintessential surfers' joint, but whether you hang 10 or not, this is where you'll want to hang out in Dominical at night. The fresh seafood and Tex-Mex specialties are hearty, tasty, and inexpensive. And there are pool, Ping-Pong, and foosball tables, as well as televised sporting events and surf videos. See chapter 7.

- **Johnny's Place** (Puerto Viejo; no phone): Picture yourself sipping a cold beer at a candlelit table set in the sand with the Caribbean lapping at your feet. Could you ask for more? If so, a few steps away there's a steamy dance floor that lets loose to loud reggae. See chapter 9.

15 The Best Views

- **The Summit of Irazú Volcano** (near San José): On a very clear day you can see both the Pacific Ocean and the Caribbean Sea from this vantage point. Even if visibility is low and this experience eludes you, you will have a view of the volcano's spectacular landscape, the Meseta Central, and the Orosi Valley. See chapter 4.
- **Iguanazul Hotel** (Playa Junquillal; ☎ and fax **506/653-0123;** www.iguanazul.com; E-mail: info@iguanazul.com): Located on a high bluff above Playa Junquillal, this hotel has a wonderful view of the Pacific and the windswept coastline in either direction. It gets best around sunset, and better yet if you can commandeer one of the hammocks set in a little palapa on the hillside itself. See chapter 5.
- **Tabacón Resort** (near Arenal Volcano; ☎ **506/256-1500;** www.tabacon.com; E-mail: info@tabacon.com): It seems so close, you'll swear you can reach out and touch the volcano. Unlike on Irazú Volcano (see above), when *this* volcano rumbles and spews, you may have the urge to run for cover. Most rooms here have spectacular views from—sheltered—private patios or balconies. See chapter 6.
- **La Mariposa** (Quepos; ☎ **506/777-0456;** www.lamariposa.com; E-mail: htlmariposa@msn.com): This place has arguably the best view in Manuel Antonio, and that's saying a lot. Come for breakfast or a sunset drink, because unfortunately I've had bad luck with dinner here. See chapter 7.
- **The Outdoor Restaurant at Villa Caletas** (Playa Hermosa de Jacó; ☎ **506/257-3653**): You'll have a view over the Golfo de Nicoya and the Pacific Ocean beyond. Sunsets here are legendary, but it's beautiful during the day as well. See chapter 7.
- **The Summit of Mount Chirripó** (near San Isidro): What more can one say: At 12,412 feet, this is the highest spot in Costa Rica. On a clear day you can see both the Pacific Ocean and Caribbean Sea from here. Even if it isn't clear, you can catch some pretty amazing views and scenery. See chapter 7.

16 The Best Drives

Driving in Costa Rica can be unpleasant, to say the least. Routes are rarely marked, roads resemble bombing ranges, and the famously peaceful Ticos become downright homicidal once they climb behind the wheel of a car. Nevertheless, renting a car provides freedom and independence, and there are some drives that are noteworthy for their scenery.

- **Irazú Volcano & the Orosi Valley:** This makes an excellent day tour and drive from San José. Start out early to reach the peak of the volcano while the skies are clearest, then spend the afternoon touring the Orosi Valley, with scenic ⋯rs at both Orosi and Ujarrás. See chapter 4.
- **Braulio Carrillo National Park:** Any trip to the Caribbean coast w' through this vast national park of mountainous cloud and rain fc

elephant-ear plants line the steep jungle roadside. Broad vistas open up to reveal a number of waterfalls cascading out of the forested mountains. A bridge crosses over the juncture of the clear General River and the sulfuric yellow Río Sucio (Dirty River). Be careful about stopping, and don't leave your car parked here for long: Robberies have been reported along this stretch of highway. Alternatively, you can make a loop heading out of San José and through Braulio Carrillo, then up to Puerto Viejo de Sarapiquí, returning via La Virgen and passing by the La Paz waterfall and Poás Volcano. Be careful here, while this is spectacular in nice weather, it's equally treacherous when it's rainy or foggy, which is often. See chapter 6.

• **La Fortuna–Tiláran–Monteverde:** This route connects two of the country's prime visitors' destinations: Arenal Volcano and Monteverde Cloud Forest. Along the way you can marvel at the beauty of Lake Arenal and stop at the wonderful Arenal Botanical Gardens. While the scenery along the way is stunning, the drive itself, especially the section between Tiláran and Monteverde, is, to put it mildly, rugged. You'll have to negotiate crater-size potholes all along this bone-rattling 22 miles. A four-wheel-drive vehicle is highly recommended for this route. See chapter 6.

• **The Rocky Coast South of Dominical:** This has often been compared to Big Sur, California. For years this stretch of road was the definition of rugged, but recent improvements have made it into an enjoyable ride. All along the way there are informal lookouts where you can pull over and watch the waves crash on the rocks below. On the inland side of the road are dense lowland rain forests with side roads that lead to hiking trails and mountain waterfalls. Be sure to stop for a break at Playa Piñuelas. See chapter 7.

Planning Your Trip: The Basics

2

Costa Rica is one of the fastest-growing tourist destinations in the Americas, and as the number of visitors increases, so does the need for pretrip planning. When is the best time to go to Costa Rica? The cheapest time? Should you rent a car (or will you need four-wheel drive) and what will it cost? Where should you go in Costa Rica? What are the hotels like? How much should you budget for your trip? These are just a few of the important questions that this chapter will answer so you can be prepared when you arrive in Costa Rica.

1 The Regions in Brief

Costa Rica rightfully should be called Costas Ricas since it has two coasts, one on the Pacific Ocean and one on the Caribbean Sea. These two coasts are as different from each other as are the Atlantic and Pacific coasts of North America.

Costa Rica's Pacific coast, which can be divided into three distinct regions (Guanacaste and the Nicoya Peninsula, the central coast, and the southern coast), is characterized by a rugged, though mostly accessible, coastline, where mountains often meet the sea. There are some spectacular stretches of coastline and most of the country's top beaches. This coast varies from the dry, sunny climate of the northwest to the hot, humid rain forests of the south.

The **Caribbean coast** can be divided into two roughly equal stretches, one of which is accessible only by boat or small plane. The remote northeast coastline is a vast flat plane laced with rivers and covered with rain forest. Farther south, along the stretch of coast accessible by car, there are uncrowded beaches and even a bit of coral reef.

Bordered by Nicaragua in the north and Panama in the southeast, Costa Rica (19,530 square miles) is only slightly larger than Vermont and New Hampshire combined. Much of the country is mountainous, with three major ranges running northwest to southeast. Among these mountains are several volcanic peaks, some of which are still active. Between the mountain ranges are fertile valleys, the largest and most populated of which is the Central Valley. With the exception of the dry Guanacaste region, much of Costa Rica's coastal area is hot and humid and covered with dense rain forests.

SAN JOSÉ & THE CENTRAL VALLEY The Central Valley is characterized by rolling green hills that rise to heights between 3,000 and 4,000 feet above sea level. The climate here is mild and springlike year-round. It's Costa Rica's primary agricultural region, with coffee farms making with up the majority of landholdings. The rich volcanic soil of this region makes it ideal for growing almost anything. The country's earliest settlements were in this area, and today the Central Valley (which includes San José) is a densely populated area with decent roads, dotted with small towns. Surrounding the Central Valley are high mountains, among which are four volcanic peaks. Two of these, **Poás** and **Irazú,** are still active and have caused extensive damage during cycles of activity in the past two centuries. Many of the mountainous regions to the north and to the south of the capital of San José have been declared national parks (Tapantí, Juan Castro, and Braulio Carrillo) to protect their virgin rain forests against logging.

GUANACASTE & THE NICOYA PENINSULA   The northwestern corner of the country near the Nicaraguan border is the site of many of Costa Rica's sunniest and most popular **beaches.** Because many Americans have chosen to build beach houses and retirement homes here, Guanacaste in particular is experiencing quite a bit of new development. While Cancún-style high-rise hotels are far from the norm, condos, luxury resorts, and golf courses are springing up like gold-plated mushrooms. That's not to say you'll be towel-to-towel with thousands of strangers. On the contrary; you can still find long stretches of deserted sands. But maybe not for long. When the new international airport in Liberia is up and running for real, it will be possible to get here from North America without so much as a stopover in San José.

With about 65 inches of rain a year, this region is by far the driest in the country and has been likened to west Texas. Guanacaste province sits at the border of Nicaragua and is named after the shady trees that still shelter the herds of cattle that roam the dusty savannah here. In addition to cattle ranches, Guanacaste boasts semiactive volcanoes, several lakes, and one of the last remnants of tropical dry forest left in Central America (dry forest once stretched all the way from Costa Rica up to the Mexican state of Chiapas).

THE NORTHERN ZONE   This region lies to the north of San José and includes rain forests, cloud forests, the country's two most active volcanoes (**Arenal** and **Rincón de la Vieja**), **Braulio Carrillo National Park,** and numerous remote lodges. Because this is one of the few regions of Costa Rica without any beaches, it primarily attracts people interested in nature and active sports. **Lake Arenal** boasts some of the best windsurfing in the world, as well as several good mountain-biking trails along its shores. The **Monteverde Cloud Forest,** perhaps Costa Rica's most internationally recognized attraction, is another top draw in this region.

THE CENTRAL PACIFIC COAST   Because it's the most easily accessible coastline in Costa Rica, the central Pacific coast boasts the greatest number of beach resorts and hotels. **Playa de Jacó** is the most popular destination here, a beach within a few hours' drive of San Jose that attracts a large number of Canadian and German charter groups and plenty of Tico tourists on weekends. **Manuel Antonio,** the name of a popular coastal name national park as well as the resort area that surrounds it, caters to people seeking a bit more tranquillity and beauty. At the same time, this region is also home to the highest peak in Costa Rica—**Mount Chirripó**—where frost is common.

THE SOUTHERN ZONE   This hot, humid region is one of Costa Rica's most remote and undeveloped regions. It is characterized by dense rain forests

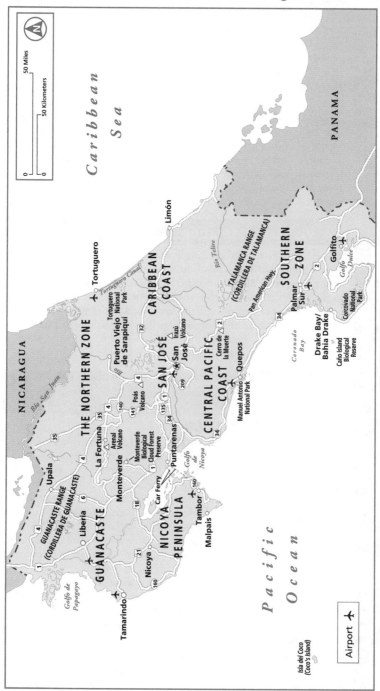

Caribbean Sea

PANAMA

NICARAGUA

Limón

Tortuguero

THE NORTHERN ZONE

Puerto Viejo de Sarapiquí

Tortuguero National Park

CARIBBEAN COAST

TALAMANCA RANGE (CORDILLERA DE TALAMANCA)

Río Telire

Pan American Hwy

SOUTHERN ZONE

Golfito

Golfo Dulce

Palmar Sur

SAN JOSÉ

Irazú Volcano

San José

Poás Volcano

La Fortuna

Arenal Volcano

Monteverde Biological Cloud Forest Preserve

Upala

Cerro de la Muerte

CENTRAL PACIFIC COAST

Quepos

Drake Bay/ Bahía Drake

Caño Island Biological Reserve

Corcovado National Park

Coronado Bay

Manuel Antonio National Park

Puntarenas

Golfo de Nicoya

Car Ferry

GUANACASTE RANGE (CORDILLERA DE GUANACASTE)

Liberia

GUANACASTE

Nicoya

NICOYA PENINSULA

Tambor

Malpaís

Tamarindo

Golfo de Papagayo

Pacific Ocean

Isla del Coco (Coco's Island)

Río San Juan

Río Reventazón

Tortuguero Canal

Airport ✈

50 Miles

50 Kilometers

and rugged coastlines. Much of the area is protected in **Corcovado** and **La Amistad** national parks. There are a wealth of wonderful nature lodges spread around the shores of the **Golfo Dulce** and along the **Osa Peninsula.** There's a lot of solitude to be found here, due in no small part to the fact that it's hard to get here (and to get around while you're here). But if you like your eco-tourism challenging, you'll find plenty here.

THE CARIBBEAN COAST Most of the Caribbean coast is a wide, steamy lowland laced with rivers and blanketed with rain forests and banana plantations. The culture here is predominantly black, with many residents speaking English or Caribbean patois. The northern section of this coast is accessible only by boat or small plane and is the site of **Tortuguero National Park,** which is known for its nesting sea turtles and riverboat trips. The towns of **Cahuita, Puerto Viejo,** and **Manzanillo,** on the southern half of the Caribbean coast, are increasingly popular destinations. The coastline here boasts many beautiful beaches and, as yet, few large hotels. However, this area can be rainy, especially between December and April.

2 Visitor Information

In the United States, you can get a basic packet of information on Costa Rica by contacting the **Costa Rican Tourist Board** (ICT, or Instituto Costarricense de Turismo) at ☎ **800/343-6332.** Much of the same information is available at their Web site, **www.tourism-costarica.com**.

If you have a computer and access to the World Wide Web, you will be able to find a wealth of information on Costa Rica just by sitting at your terminal. See "Top Web Sites for Costa Rica", in our online directory (page 000), for some helpful suggestions on where to begin your online search.

3 Passport Information, Entry Requirements & Customs

PASSPORT INFORMATION

FOR RESIDENTS OF THE UNITED STATES For general information, call the **National Passport Agency** (☎ 202/647-0518). If you're applying for a first-time passport, you need to do it in person at one of 13 passport offices throughout the United States; a federal, state, or probate court; or a major post office (though not all post offices accept applications; call the number below to find the ones that do). To find your regional passport office, call the **National Passport Information Center** (☎ 900/225-5674; http://travel.state.gov). You'll need to present a certified birth certificate as proof of citizenship, and it's wise to bring along your driver's license, state or military ID, and social security card as well.

You can renew your passport by mail. Just pick up a form at any post office. Allow up to 3 weeks (especially during spring and summer) to receive your new passport. You'll need two identical passport-size photos (2 in. by 2 in.), taken at any corner photo shop (not one of the strip photos, however, from a photo-vending machine).

FOR RESIDENTS OF CANADA You can pick up a passport application at one of 28 regional passport offices or most travel agencies. Children under 16 may be included on a parent's passport but need their own to travel unaccompanied by the parent. Applications, which must be accompanied by two identical passport-size photographs and proof of Canadian citizenship, are available at travel agencies throughout Canada or from the central **Passport Office, Department of Foreign Affairs and International Trade,** Ottawa, Ontario K1A 0G3 (☎ **800/567-6868;** www.dfait-maeci.gc.ca/passport).

FOR RESIDENTS OF THE UNITED KINGDOM To pick up an application for a regular 10-year passport (the Visitor's Passport has been abolished), visit your nearest passport office, major post office, or travel agency. You can also contact the **London Passport Office** at ☎ **0171/271-3000** or search its Web site at www.open.gov.uk/ukpass/ukpass.htm.

DOCUMENTS

Citizens of the United States, Canada, Great Britain, and most European nations may visit Costa Rica for a maximum of 90 days. No visa is necessary, but you must have a valid passport. (U.S. citizens can enter with just a valid photo ID and a copy of their birth certificate, but I still recommend bringing a passport.) Citizens of Australia and New Zealand can enter the country without a visa and stay for 30 days. Citizens of the Republic of Ireland need a visa, a valid passport, and a round-trip ticket in order to enter.

If you overstay your visa or entry stamp, you will have to pay around $45 for an exit visa and a nominal fee for each extra month you've stayed. If you need to get an exit visa, a travel agent in San José can usually get one for you for a small fee and save you the hassle of dealing with Immigration. If you want to stay longer than the validity of your entry stamp or visa, the easiest thing to do is cross the border into Panama or Nicaragua for 72 hours and then re-enter Costa Rica on a new entry stamp or visa. However, be careful. Periodically, the Costa Rican government has cracked down on "perpetual tourists," and if they notice a continued pattern of exits and entries designed simply to support an extended stay, they may deny you re-entry.

If you need a visa or have other questions about Costa Rica, you can contact any of the following Costa Rican embassies: in the **United States,** 2112 S St. NW, Washington, DC 20008 (☎ **202/234-2945**); in **Canada,** 135 York St., Suite 208, Ottawa, Ontario K1N 5T4 (☎ **613/562-2855**); in **Great Britain,** 14 Lancaster Gate, London, England W2 3LH (☎ **71-706-8844**). In the United States, Costa Rica also maintains consulates in New York (☎ **212/509-3066**), Atlanta (☎ **770/951-7025**), New Orleans (☎ **504/ 581-6800**), Chicago (☎ **312/263-2772**), Denver (☎ **303/696-8211**), Houston (☎ **713/266-0484**), Los Angeles (☎ **213/380-6031**), and Miami (☎ **305/871-7485**).

Lost Documents

If you lose your passport or need special assistance once inside Costa Rica, contact your embassy, listed in "Fast Facts: Costa Rica," below. Most embassies can replace your passport and help you get an exit visa in about 24 hours. If your embassy won't get your exit visa for you, see a local travel agent or **OTEC Viajes,** Edificio Ferencz, 2nd floor, Calle 3 between avenidas 1 and 3, 275 meters (300 yd.) north of the National Theater (☎ **506/256-0633**). If you try to deal with Immigration yourself, you will face long lines, long waits, and endless frustration. Local travel agents and agencies regularly deal with Immigration and will charge you about $10 to $15 for the service (sometimes free if you ticket with them).

CUSTOMS

Visitors entering Costa Rica are entitled to bring in 500 grams of tobacco, 3 liters of liquor, and $400 in merchandise. Cameras, computers, and electronic equipment for personal use are also permitted. Customs officials in Costa Rica rarely check tourists' luggage.

IMPORT RESTRICTIONS   To the United States   Returning citizens who have been away for 48 hours or more are allowed to bring back, once every 30 days, $400 worth of merchandise duty-free. You'll be charged a flat rate of 10% duty on the next $1,000 worth of purchases. Be sure to have your receipts handy. On gifts, the duty-free limit is $100. You cannot bring fresh foodstuffs into the United States; canned foods, however, are allowed. You can also bring coffee home with you. For more information, contact the **U.S. Customs Service,** 1301 Constitution Ave. (P.O. Box 7407), Washington, DC 20044 (☎ **202/927-6724**), and request the free pamphlet *Know Before You Go.* It's also available on the Web at **www.customs.ustreas.gov/travel/ kbygo.htm**.

To the United Kingdom   There's a Customs allowance of 200 cigarettes; 50 cigars; 250 grams of smoking tobacco; 2 liters of still table wine; 1 liter of spirits or strong liqueurs (over 22% volume); 2 liters of fortified wine, sparkling wine, or other liqueurs; 60 cubic centimeters (ml) of perfume; 250 cubic centimeters (ml) of toilet water; and £145 worth of all other goods, including gifts and souvenirs. People under 17 can't bring in tobacco or alcohol. For more information, contact HM Customs & Excise, Passenger Enquiry Point, 2nd Floor, Wayfarer House, Great South West Road, Feltham, Middlesex TW14 8NP (☎ **0181/910-3744;** from outside the U.K., ☎ 44/181-910-3744), or consult their Web site at **www.hmce.gov.uk**.

To Canada   For a clear summary of Canadian rules, write for the booklet *I Declare,* issued by **Revenue Canada,** 2265 St. Laurent Blvd., Ottawa, Ontario K1G 4KE (☎ **613/993-0534;** www.ccra-adrc.gc.cc). Canada allows its citizens a $500 exemption, and you're allowed to bring back duty-free 200 cigarettes, 2.2 pounds of tobacco, 40 imperial ounces of liquor, and 50 cigars. In addition, you're allowed to mail gifts to Canada from abroad at the rate of C$60 a day, provided they're unsolicited and don't contain alcohol or tobacco (write on the package "unsolicited gift, under $60 value"). All valuables should be declared on the Y-38 form before departure from Canada, including serial numbers of valuables you already own, such as expensive foreign cameras. *Note:* The $500 exemption can only be used once a year and only after an absence of 7 days.

4 Money

CASH & CURRENCY

The unit of currency in Costa Rica is the colón. In early 2000, there were approximately 300 colones to the American dollar, but because the colón has been in a constant state of devaluation, you can expect this rate to change. Because of this devaluation and accompanying inflation, this book lists prices in U.S. dollars only.

The colón is divided into 100 centimos. There are currently two types of coins in circulation. The older and larger nickel alloy coins come in denominations of 10, 25, and 50 centimos and 1, 2, 5, 10, and 20 colones; however, because of their evaporating value, you will rarely see or have to handle

The Colón, the U.S. Dollar & the British Pound

Colones	U.S.$	U.K.£	Colones	U.S.$	U.K.£
5	.016	0.01	1,000	3.33	2.10
10	.03	0.02	5,000	16.67	10.50
25	.08	0.052	10,000	33.33	21.00
50	.166	0.105	25,000	83.33	52.50
75	.25	0.158	50,000	166.67	105.00
100	.333	0.21	75,000	250.00	158.00
200	.666	0.42	100,000	333.33	210.00
300	1	0.63	200,000	666.67	420.00
400	1.33	0.84	300,000	1,000.00	630.00
500	1.67	1.05	500,000	1,666.67	1,050.00
750	2.5	1.58	1,000,000	3,333.33	2,100.00

centimos. In 1997, the government introduced new gold-hued 5-, 10-, 25-, 50-, and 100-colón coins. They are smaller and heavier than the older coins, and they will slowly phase out the other currency. There are paper notes in denominations of 50, 100, 500, 1,000, 2,000, 5,000, and 10,000 colones. You might also encounter a special-issue 5-colón bill that is a popular gift and souvenir. It is valid currency, although it sells for much more than its face value. You may hear people refer to a *rojo* or *tucan*, which are slang terms for the 1,000- and 5,000-colón bills, respectively. One-hundred colón denominations are called *tejas*, so *cinco tejas* would be 500 colones. The 2,000 and 10,000 bills are relatively new and I've yet to encounter a slang equivalent for them. In recent years forged bills have become increasingly common. When **receiving change** in colones it's a good idea to check the larger denomination bills, which should have protective bands or hidden images that appear when held up to the light.

EXCHANGING MONEY

You can change money at all state-owned banks. However, the service at these banks is slow and tedious. This simple transaction can often take more than an hour and cause unnecessary confusion and anxiety. I don't recommend it.

Fortunately, you don't have to rely on the state's banks. In late 1996, Costa Rica passed a law opening up the state's banking system. Accordingly, private banks have been opening up around San José and in some of the larger provincial towns and cities. So far, these private banks are kicking the state banks' butts, providing fast service at reasonable commissions, with small or no lines. Hotels will often exchange money and cash traveler's checks as well; there usually isn't much of a line, but they may shave a few colones off the exchange rate.

Be very careful about exchanging money on the streets; it's extremely risky. In addition to forged bills and short counts, street money changers frequently work in teams that can leave you holding neither colones nor dollars.

TRAVELER'S CHECKS

These days, traveler's checks seem less necessary because most cities and major tourist destinations have 24-hour ATMs that allow travelers to withdraw small amounts of cash as needed—and thus avoid the risk of carrying a fortune around an unfamiliar environment. Many banks, however, impose a fee every time a card is used at an ATM in a different city or bank. If you're withdrawing money every day, you might be better off with traveler's checks—provided that you don't mind showing identification every time you want to cash a check.

You can get traveler's checks at almost any bank. **American Express** offers denominations of $10, $20, $50, $100, $500, and $1,000. You'll pay a service charge ranging from 1% to 4%. You can also get American Express traveler's checks over the phone by calling ☎ **800/221-7282;** by using this number, AMEX gold and platinum cardholders are exempt from the 1% fee. AAA members can obtain checks without a fee at most AAA offices.

Visa offers traveler's checks at Citibank locations nationwide, as well as several other banks. The service charge ranges between 1.5% and 2%; checks come in denominations of $20, $50, $100, $500, and $1,000. **MasterCard** also offers traveler's checks. Call ☎ **800/223-9920** for a location near you.

ATMS

While ATMs are still mostly found at bank offices and major shopping centers in and around San José, they're popping up at many major tourist destinations around the country.

ATMs are linked to a national network that most likely includes your bank at home. **Cirrus** (☎ **800/424-7787;** www.mastercard.com/atm) and **Plus** (☎ **800/843-7587;** www.visa.com) are the two most popular networks; check the back of your ATM card to see which network your bank belongs to. Use the toll-free numbers to locate ATMs in your destination. Before traveling to Costa Rica, ask your bank for a list of ATMs. Be sure to check the daily withdrawal limit before you depart, and ask whether you need a new personal ID number. I recommend you think of your ATM as a backup measure, since machines are not nearly as readily available or dependable as you might expect and you may encounter compatibility problems. So, it is always a good idea to carry some cash with you.

CREDIT CARDS

Credit cards are invaluable when traveling, and they are becoming widely accepted in Costa Rica (primarily American Express, MasterCard, and Visa). They are a safe way to carry money and provide a convenient record of all your expenses. You can also withdraw cash advances from your credit cards at any bank (though you'll start paying hefty interest on the advance the moment you receive the cash, and you won't receive frequent-flyer miles on an airline credit card). At most banks, you don't even need to go to a teller; you can get a cash advance at the ATM if you know your PIN. If you've forgotten your PIN or didn't even know you had one, call the phone number on the back of your credit card and ask the bank to send it to you. It usually takes 5 to 7 business days, though some banks will provide the number over the phone if you tell them your mother's maiden name or pass some other security clearance.

Since credit-card purchases are dependent upon phone verifications, some hotels and restaurants in more remote destinations do not accept them. Moreover, many add on a 5% to 10% surcharge for credit-card payments. Always check in advance if you're heading to a more remote corner of Costa Rica.

THEFT Almost every credit-card company has an emergency toll-free number that you can call if your wallet or purse is stolen. However, in Costa Rica, since it's difficult to dial direct to toll-free numbers in the United States, these numbers aren't too helpful. In the event of a lost or stolen credit card, see the

What Things Cost in San José	U.S. $
Taxi from airport to the city center	13.00
Local telephone call	.05
Double at Marriott Hotel & Resort (expensive)	140.00
Double at Hotel Grano de Oro (moderate)	72.00
Double at Pension de la Cuesta (inexpensive)	26.00
Lunch for one at Café Mundo (moderate)	7.00
Lunch for one at Soda Coppelia (inexpensive)	3.50
Dinner for one, without wine, at La Peña de Cantares (moderate)	10.00
Dinner for one, without wine, at Manolo's Restaurante (inexpensive)	6.00
Bottle of beer	.90
Coca-Cola	.85
Cup of coffee	.50
Roll of ASA 100 Kodacolor film, 24 exposures	7.00
Admission to the Gold Museum	4.00
Ticket at Teatro Melico Salazar	4.00–15.00

"Fast Facts" section below for a local service number. Once you contact your bank or issuing company, they may be able to wire you a cash advance off your credit card immediately, and in many places, they can deliver an emergency credit card in a day or two. Odds are that if your wallet is gone, the police won't be able to recover it for you. But your credit-card company or insurer may require a police report number, so you may want to call the police anyway (after you cancel your credit cards).

Remember: If you opt to carry traveler's checks, be sure to keep a record of their serial numbers, separately from the checks of course, so you're ensured a refund in just such an emergency.

5 When to Go

Costa Rica's high season for tourism runs from late November to late April, which coincides almost perfectly with the northern winter and major holiday travel periods. The high season is also the dry season. If you want some unadulterated time on a tropical beach and a little less rain during your rain-forest experience, this is the time to come. During this period you will find tourism in full tilt—prices are higher, attractions are more crowded, and reservations need to be made in advance.

In recent years local tourism operators have begun calling the tropical rainy season (May through mid-November) the "green season." The adjective is appropriate. At this time of year, even brown and barren Guanacaste province becomes lush and verdant. I love traveling around Costa Rica during the rainy season. It's easy to find or at least negotiate reduced rates, there are far fewer fellow travelers, and the rain is often limited to a few hours each afternoon (although you can occasionally get socked in for a week at a time). One other drawback: Some of the country's rugged roads become downright impassable without four-wheel drive during the rainy season.

CLIMATE

Costa Rica is a tropical country and has distinct wet and dry seasons. However, some regions are rainy all year and others are very dry and sunny for most of the year. Temperatures vary primarily with elevation, not with season: On the coasts it's hot all year, while up in the mountains it can be cool at night any time of year. At the highest elevations (10,000 to 12,000 ft.), frost is common.

Average Daytime Temperatures & Rainfall in San José

	Jan	Feb	Mar	Apr	May	June	July	Aug	Sept	Oct	Nov	Dec
Temp. (°F)	66	66	69	71	71	71	70	70	71	69	68	67
Temp. (°C)	19	19	20.5	21.5	21.5	21.5	21	21	21.5	20.5	20	19.5
Days of rain	1	0	1	4	17	20	18	19	20	22	14	4

Generally speaking, the **rainy season** (or "green season") is from **May to mid-November.** Costa Ricans call this wet time of year their winter. The **dry season,** considered summer by Costa Ricans, is from **mid-November through April.** In **Guanacaste,** the dry northwestern province, the dry season lasts several weeks longer than in other places. Even in the rainy season, days often start sunny, with rain falling in the afternoon and evening. On the **Caribbean coast,** especially south of Limón, you can count on rain year-round, although this area gets less rain in September and October than the rest of the country.

In general, the best time of year to visit is in December and January, when everything is still green from the rains, but the sky is clear.

HOLIDAYS

Because Costa Rica is a Roman Catholic country, most of its holidays and celebrations are church-related. The major celebrations of the year are Christmas, New Year's, and Easter, which are all celebrated for several days. Keep in mind that Holy Week (Easter Week) is the biggest holiday time in Costa Rica and many families head for the beach (this is the last holiday before school starts). Also, there is no public transportation on Holy Thursday or Good Friday. Government offices and banks are closed on official holidays, transportation services are reduced, and stores and markets may also close.

Official holidays in Costa Rica include **January 1** (New Year's Day), **March 19** (St. Joseph's Day), Thursday and Friday of Holy Week, **April 11** (Juan Santamaría's Day), **May 1** (Labor Day), **June 29** (Saints Peter and Paul's Day), **July 25** (annexation of the province of Guanacaste), **August 2** (Virgin of Los Angeles's Day), **August 15** (Mother's Day), **September 15** (Independence Day), **October 12** (Discovery of America/Día de la Raza), **December 8** (Immaculate Conception of the Virgin Mary), **December 24 and 25** (Christmas), **December 31** (New Year's Eve).

Costa Rica Calendar of Events

Some of the events listed here might be considered more of a *happening* than an event, so there's not, for instance, a Virgin of Los Angeles PR Committee that readily dispenses information. If I haven't listed a contact number, your best bet is to call the Costa Rican Tourist Board (ICT) at ☎ **800/343-6332** in the United States, or 506/223-1733 in Costa Rica.

January

- **Copa del Café** (Coffee Cup), San José. An international event on the junior tennis tour. Matches are held at the Costa Rica Country Club (☎ 506/228-9333). First week in January.
- **Fiesta of Santa Cruz,** Santa Cruz, Guanacaste. A religious celebration honoring the Black Christ of Esquipulas (a famous Guatemalan statue), featuring folk dancing, marimba music, and bullfights. Mid-January.

February

- ✪ **Fiesta of the Diablitos,** Rey Curré village near San Isidro de El General. Boruca Indians wearing wooden devil and bull masks perform dances representative of the Spanish conquest of Central America; there are fireworks displays and an Indian handcrafts market. Date varies.

March

- ✪ **Día del Boyero** (Oxcart Drivers' Day), San Antonio de Escazú. Colorfully painted oxcarts parade through this suburb of San José, and local priests bless the oxen. Second Sunday.
- ✪ **National Orchid Show,** San José. Orchid growers the world over gather to show their wares, trade tales and secrets, and admire the hundreds of species on display. Exact location and date change from year to year.

April

- **Holy Week** (week before Easter). Religious processions are held in cities and towns throughout the country. Dates vary from year to year (between late March and early April).
- **Juan Santamaría Day,** Alajuela. Costa Rica's national hero is honored with parades, concerts, and dances. April 11.

May

- **Carrera de San Juan.** The country's biggest marathon runs through the mountains, from the outskirts of Cartago to the outskirts of San José. May 17.

July

- ✪ **Fiesta of the Virgin of the Sea,** Puntarenas. A regatta of colorfully decorated boats carrying a statue of Puntarenas's patron saint marks this festival. A similar event is held at Playa de Coco. Saturday closest to July 16.
- **Annexation of Guanacaste Day,** Liberia. Tico-style bullfights, folk dancing, horseback parades, rodeos, concerts, and other events celebrate the day when this region became part of Costa Rica. July 25.

August

- ✪ **Fiesta of the Virgin of Los Angeles,** Cartago. This is the annual pilgrimage day of the patron saint of Costa Rica. Many people walk from San José 15 miles to the basilica in Cartago. August 2.
- **Día de San Ramón,** San Ramón. More than two dozen statues of saints from various towns are brought to San Ramón, where they are paraded through the streets. August 31.

September

- **Costa Rica's Independence Day.** Celebrated all over the country. Most distinctive are the nighttime parades of children. September 15.
- **International Beach Clean-Up Day.** A good excuse to chip in and help clean up the beleaguered shoreline of your favorite beach. Third Saturday in September.

October

- **Fiesta del Maíz,** Upala. A celebration of corn with local beauty queens wearing outfits made from corn plants. October 12.
- ✪ **Limón Carnival/Día de la Raza,** Limón. A smaller version of Mardi Gras, complete with floats and dancing in the streets, commemorates Columbus's discovery of Costa Rica. Week of October 12.

November

- **All Soul's Day/Día de los Muertos,** celebrated countrywide. Although not as elaborate or ritualized as in Mexico, most Costa Ricans take some time this day to remember the dead with flowers and trips to the cemeteries. November 2.

December

- **Día de la Polvora,** San Antonio de Belen and Jesus Maria de San Mateo. Fireworks displays to honor Our Lady of the Immaculate Conception. December 8.
- **Fiesta de los Negritos,** Boruca. Boruca Indians celebrate the feast day of their patron saint, the Virgin of the Immaculate Conception, with costumed dances and traditional music. December 8.
- **Fiesta de la Yeguita,** Nicoya. A statue of the Virgin of Guadalupe is paraded through the streets accompanied by traditional music and dancing. December 12.
- **Las Posadas.** A countrywide celebration during which children and carolers go door-to-door seeking lodging in a reenactment of Joseph and Mary's search for a place to stay. Begins December 15.
- ✪ **Festejos Populares,** San José. Bullfights, a horseback parade (El Tope), and a carnival with street dancing, floats, and a pretty impressive bunch of carnival rides all take place at the fairgrounds in Zapote. On the night of December 31, there is a dance in the Parque Central. Last week of December.

6 Health & Insurance Information

HEALTH INFORMATION

Staying healthy on a trip to Costa Rica is predominantly a matter of being a little cautious about what you eat and drink, and using common sense. Know your physical limits and don't overexert yourself in the ocean, on hikes, or in athletic activities. Respect the tropical sun and protect yourself from it. I recommend buying and drinking bottled water or soft drinks, but the water in San José and in most of the heavily visited spots is safe to drink. The sections below deal with specific health concerns in Costa Rica.

TROPICAL DISEASES   Your chances of contracting any serious tropical disease in Costa Rica are slim, especially if you stick to the beaches or traditional spots for visitors. However, malaria, dengue fever, and leptospirosis all exist in Costa Rica, so it's a good idea to know what they are.

Malaria is found in the lowlands on both coasts and in the northern zone. Although it's rarely found in urban areas, it's still a problem in remote wooded regions and along the Atlantic coast. Malaria prophylaxes are available, but several have side effects and others are of questionable effectiveness. Consult your doctor as to what is currently considered the best preventive treatment for malaria. Be sure to ask whether a recommended drug will cause you to be hypersensitive to the sun. It would be a shame to come down here for the beaches and then have to hide under an umbrella the whole time. Because malaria-carrying mosquitoes usually come out at night, you should do as much as possible to avoid being bitten after dark. If you are in a malarial area, wear long pants and long sleeves, use insect repellent, and either sleep under a mosquito net or burn mosquito coils (similar to incense but with a pesticide).

Of greater concern may be **dengue fever,** which has had periodic outbreaks in Latin America since 1993. Dengue fever is similar to malaria and is spread by an aggressive daytime mosquito. This mosquito seems to be most common in lowland urban areas, and Liberia and Limón have been the worst-hit cities in Costa Rica. Dengue is also known as "bone-break fever," because it is usually accompanied by severe body aches. The first infection with dengue fever will make you very sick but should cause no serious damage. However, a second infection with a different strain of the dengue virus can lead to internal hemorrhaging and may be life-threatening.

Many people are convinced that taking B-complex vitamins daily will help prevent mosquitoes from biting you. I don't think the AMA has endorsed this idea yet, but I've run across it in enough places to think there may be something to it.

One final tropical fever I think you should know about (just because I got it) is **leptospirosis.** There are more than 200 strains of leptospirs, which are animal-borne bacteria transmitted to humans via contact with drinking, swimming, or bathing water. This bacterial infection is easily treated with antibiotics; however, it can quickly cause very high fever and chills, and should be treated promptly.

If you develop a high fever accompanied by severe body aches, nausea, diarrhea, or vomiting during or shortly after a visit to Costa Rica, it's a good idea to consult a physician as soon as possible.

Costa Rica has been relatively free from the cholera epidemic that has spread through much of Latin America in recent years. This is largely due to an extensive public awareness campaign that has promoted good hygiene and increased sanitation. Your chances of contracting cholera while you're here are very slight.

AMOEBAS, PARASITES, DIARRHEA, & OTHER INTESTINAL WOES
While the water in San José and most popular destinations is generally safe, and even though you've bought bottled water, ordered *frescos en leche* (i.e., fruit shakes made with milk, rather than water), and drunk your soda warm (without ice cubes—which are made from water, after all), you still may encounter some intestinal difficulties. Most of this is just due to tender northern stomachs coming into contact with slightly more aggressive Latin-American intestinal flora. In extreme cases of diarrhea or intestinal discomfort it's worth taking a stool sample to a lab for analysis. The results will usually pinpoint the amoebic or parasitic culprit, which can then be readily treated with available over-the-counter medicines.

Except in the most established and hygienic of restaurants, it's also advisable to avoid *ceviche,* a raw seafood salad, especially if it has any shellfish in it. It could be home to any number of bacterial critters.

TROPICAL SUN   Limit your exposure to the sun, especially during the first few days of your trip and, thereafter, from 11am to 2pm. Use a sunscreen with a high protection factor and apply it liberally. Remember that children need more protection than adults do.

RIPTIDES   Many of Costa Rica's beaches have riptides: strong currents that can drag swimmers out to sea. A riptide occurs when water that has been dumped on the shore by strong waves forms a channel back out to open water.

These channels have strong currents. If you get caught in a riptide, you can't escape the current by swimming toward shore; it's like trying to swim upstream in a river. To break free of the current, swim parallel to shore and use the energy of the waves to help you get back to the beach.

BEES & SNAKES   Although Costa Rica has Africanized bees (the notorious "killer bees" of fact and fable) and several species of venomous snakes, your chances of being bitten are minimal, especially if you refrain from sticking your hands into hives or under rocks in the forest. If you know that you're allergic to bee stings, consult your doctor before traveling. Snake sightings, much less snake bites, are very rare. Moreover, the majority of snakes in Costa Rica are nonpoisonous. If you do encounter a snake, stay calm, don't make any sudden movements, and do not try to handle it. As recommended above, avoid sticking your hand under rocks, branches, and fallen trees. If you really want to see a fer-de-lance or eyelash viper, it might be best to visit one in San José's Serpentarium (see chapter 4).

WHAT TO DO IF YOU GET SICK AWAY FROM HOME

In addition to the advice listed above, try to take proper precautions the week before you depart, to avoid falling ill while you're away from home. Amid the last-minute frenzy that often precedes a vacation break, make an extra effort to eat and sleep well, especially if you feel an illness coming on.

If you worry about getting sick away from home, you may want to consider **medical travel insurance** (see the section on travel insurance later in this chapter). In most cases, however, your existing health plan will provide all the coverage you need. Be sure to carry your identification card in your wallet.

If you suffer from a chronic illness, consult your doctor before your departure. For conditions like epilepsy, diabetes, or heart problems, wear a **Medic Alert Identification Tag** (☎ 800/432-5378; www.medicalert.org), which will immediately alert doctors to your condition and give them access to your records through Medic Alert's 24-hour hot line. Membership is $35, plus a $15 annual fee.

Pack prescription medications in your carry-on luggage. Bring enough to last the duration of your trip, since certain scripts may be difficult to refill in Costa Rica. If there's a medication you can't live without, bring along a copy of your prescription in case you lose your pills. If you wear contact lenses, pack an extra pair in case you lose one.

Contact the **International Association for Medical Assistance to Travelers (IAMAT)** (☎ 716/754-4883 or 416/652-0137; www.sentex.net/~iamat). This organization offers tips on travel and health concerns in the countries around the world, and lists many local English-speaking doctors. The U.S. **Centers for Disease Control and Prevention** (☎ 877/394-8747; www.cdc.gov) provides up-to-date information on necessary vaccines and health hazards by region or country (by mail, their booklet is $20; on the Internet, it's free).

When you're in Costa Rica, any local consulate can provide a list of area doctors who speak English. The local English-language newspaper, the *Tico Times,* is another good resource. If you can't find a doctor who can help you right away and you're in San José, try the emergency room at the **Hospital Clínica Bíblica** (☎ 800/911-0800 in Costa Rica, or 506/257-0466). Most state-run hospitals and walk-in clinics around the country have emergency rooms that can treat most conditions, although I highly recommend the private hospital listed above if the condition is not life-threatening.

INSURANCE

There are three kinds of travel insurance: trip cancellation, medical, and lost-luggage coverage. **Trip cancellation insurance** is a good idea if you have paid a large portion of your vacation expenses up front. The other two types don't make sense for most travelers. Rule number one: Check your existing policies before you buy any additional coverage.

Your existing health insurance should cover you if you get sick while on vacation (though if you belong to an HMO, you should check to see whether you are fully covered when away from home). If you need hospital treatment, most health insurance plans and HMOs will cover out-of-country hospital visits and procedures, at least to some extent. However, most make you pay the bills up front at the time of care, and you'll get a refund after you've returned and filed all the paperwork. Members of **Blue Cross/Blue Shield** can now use their cards at select hospitals in most major cities worldwide (☎ 800/810-BLUE or www.bluecares.com/blue/bluecard/wwn for a list of hospitals). For independent travel health-insurance providers, see below.

Your **homeowner's insurance** should cover stolen luggage. The airlines are responsible for a surprisingly small sum if they lose your luggage, and the claims process can be trying and tedious. Try to keep your most valuable items (cameras, computers, and most importantly prescription medication) in your carry-on bag.

Some credit cards (American Express and certain gold and platinum Visa and MasterCards, for example) offer automatic flight insurance against death or dismemberment in case of an airplane crash.

If you do require additional insurance, try one of the companies listed below. But don't pay for more than you need. For example, if you need only trip-cancellation insurance, don't purchase coverage for lost or stolen property. Trip-cancellation insurance costs approximately 6% to 8% of the total value of your vacation.

Among the reputable issuers of **travel insurance** are **Access America,** P.O. Box 90315, Richmond, VA 23286 (☎ 800/284-8300; www.accessamerica.com); **Travel Guard International,** 1145 Clark St., Stevens Point, WI 54481 (☎ 800/826-1300); **Travel Insured International, Inc.,** P.O. Box 280568, East Hartford, CT 06128 (☎ 800/243-3174); and **Travelex Insurance Services,** P.O. Box 9408, Garden City, NY 11530-9408 (☎ 800/ 228-9792; www.travelex-insurance.com).

ACCIDENT & MEDICAL CARE   Medicare only covers U.S. citizens traveling in Mexico and Canada. For Blue Cross/Blue Shield coverage abroad, see above. Companies specializing in accident and medical care include:

MEDEX International, P.O. Box 5375, Timonium, MD 21094-5375 (☎ 888/MEDEX-00 or 410/453-6300; fax 410/453-6301; www.medexassist.com)

Travel Assistance International (Worldwide Assistance Services, Inc.), 1133 15th St NW, Suite 400, Washington, DC 20005 (☎ 800/821-2828 or 202/828-5894; fax 202/828-5896)

Divers Alert Network (DAN) (☎ 800/446-2671 or 919/684-2948; www.diversalertnetwork.org) insures scuba divers.

7 Tips for Travelers with Special Needs

TRAVELERS WITH DISABILITIES

Although Costa Rica does in fact have a law mandating Equality of Opportunities for People with Disabilities, and facilities are beginning to be adapted for those with disabilities, in general there are relatively few handicapped-accessible buildings in Costa Rica. In San José, sidewalks are crowded and uneven. Few hotels offer handicapped-accessible accommodations, and there are no public buses. In short, it is difficult for a person with disabilities to get around in Costa Rica.

However, there are two local agencies that specialize in tours for travelers with disabilities and restricted ability. **Vaya Con Silla de Ruedas,** Apdo. 1146-2050, San Pedro Montes de Oca, Costa Rica (☎ **506/225-8561;** fax 506/253-0931; E-mail: vayacon@racsa.co.cr), has a ramp and elevator-equipped van and knowledgeable bilingual guides. They charge very reasonable prices and can provide anything from simple airport transfers to complete multiday tours.

Kosta Roda Foundation, Apdo. 217-8000, San Isidro de El General, Costa Rica (☎ and fax **506/771-7482;** E-mail: chabote@racsa.co.cr), is a nonprofit organization dedicated to helping the Costa Rican tourist industry remove barriers (architectural and societal). They can provide assistance and information for travelers with disabilities.

GAY & LESBIAN TRAVELERS

Costa Rica is a Catholic, conservative, macho country where public displays of same-sex affection are rare and somewhat shocking. In 1998, the archbishop of San José publicly denounced homosexuality. There followed two prominent protests in the tourist destinations of Manuel Antonio and Playa Hermosa, Guanacaste, that resulted in quite some inconvenience for the organizers and participants of openly gay and lesbian group tours. However, gay and lesbian tourism to Costa Rica is quite robust, and gay and lesbian travelers are generally treated with respect and should not experience any harassment.

La Asociación Triángulo Rosa (☎ **506/258-0214;** fax 506/258-0736; E-mail: atrirosa@racsa.co.cr) is a local human rights organization that can provide up-to-date information and tips for gay and lesbian travelers. Two local travel agencies that specialize in gay and lesbian travel are **Tiquicia Travel** (☎ **506/236-7446;** fax 506/236-7447; www.tiquicia.ibiznet.net; E-mail: tiquicia@racsa.co.cr) and **Maguines Travel** (☎ and fax **506/283-4510;** E-mail: manfredg@racsa.co.cr). You might also check out **www.gaycostarica. com,** although the site is mostly in Spanish.

General gay and lesbian travel agencies include **Above and Beyond Tours** (☎ **800/397-2681;** www.abovebeyond.com), which caters mostly to gay men, and **Family Abroad** (☎ **800/999-5500** or 212/459-1800; www. familyabroad.com), which arranges trips for both gay men and lesbians.

GENERAL INFORMATION Two good, biannual English-language guidebooks focus on gay men and include information for lesbians. You can get the *Spartacus International Gay Guide* or *Odysseus* at most gay and lesbian bookstores, or order them from Giovanni's Room (☎ **215/923-2960**) or A Different Light Bookstore (☎ **800/343-4002** or 212/989-4850). Both lesbians and gays may want to pick up a copy of *Gay Travel A to Z* ($16). The **Ferrari Guides** (**www.q-net.com**) is yet another very good series of gay and lesbian guidebooks.

Out and About, 8 W. 19th St., #401, New York, NY 10011 (☎ 800/929-2268 or 212/645-6922; www.outandabout.com), offers guidebooks and a monthly newsletter packed with good information on the global gay and lesbian scenes. A year's subscription to the newsletter costs $49. *Our World,* 1104 N. Nova Rd., Suite 251, Daytona Beach, FL 32117 (☎ 904/441-5367; www.pimps.com/ourworld), is a slicker monthly magazine promoting and highlighting travel bargains and opportunities. An annual subscription costs $35 ($45 outside the U.S.).

SENIORS

Don't be shy about asking for discounts, but always carry some kind of identification, such as a driver's license, that shows your date of birth. Also, mention the fact that you're a senior citizen when you first make your travel reservations. For example, many hotels and airlines offer seniors discounts. In most cities, people over the age of 60 qualify for reduced admission to theaters, museums, and other attractions, and discounted fares on public transportation.

Members of the **American Association of Retired Persons (AARP),** 601 E St. NW, Washington, DC 20049 (☎ 800/424-3410 or 202/434-2277; www.aarp.org), get discounts not only on hotels but on airfares and car rentals, too. Most of the major hotel chains—Marriott, Best Western, Holiday Inn in Costa Rica—offer AARP discounts. It's usually around 10%. For more details, check out their Web site at www.aarp.org. AARP also offers members a wide range of special benefits, including *Modern Maturity* magazine and a monthly newsletter.

The **National Council of Senior Citizens,** 8403 Colesville Rd., Suite 1200, Silver Spring, MD 20910 (☎ 301/578-8800; www.ncscinc.org), a nonprofit organization, offers a newsletter six times a year (partly devoted to travel tips) and discounts on hotel and auto rentals; annual dues are $13 per person or couple.

Mature Outlook, P.O. Box 9390, Des Moines, IA 50306 (☎ 800/336-6330), began as a travel organization for people over 50, though it now caters to people of all ages. Members receive discounts on hotels and receive a bimonthly magazine. Annual membership is $19.95, which entitles members to discounts and, often, free coupons for discounted merchandise from Sears.

Mature Traveler, a monthly 12-page newsletter on senior-citizen travel, is a valuable resource. It is available by subscription ($30 a year) from **GEM Publishing Group,** Box 50400, Reno, NV 89513-0400. GEM also publishes *The Book of Deals,* a collection of more than 1,000 senior discounts on airlines, lodging, tours, and attractions around the country; it's available for $9.95 by calling ☎ 800/460-6676. Another helpful publication is *101 Tips for the Mature Traveler,* available from **Grand Circle Travel,** 347 Congress St., Suite 3A, Boston, MA 02210 (☎ 800/221-2610 or 617/350-7500; fax 617/346-6700; www.gct.com).

Grand Circle Travel is also one of the hundreds of travel agencies specializing in vacations for seniors. Many of these packages, however, are of the tour-bus variety, with free trips thrown in for those who organize groups of 10 or more. Seniors seeking more independent travel should probably consult a regular travel agent. **SAGA International Holidays,** 222 Berkeley St., Boston, MA 02116 (☎ 800/343-0273; www.sagaholidays.com), offers inclusive tours and cruises for those 50 and older. SAGA also sponsors the more substantial "Road Scholar Tours" (☎ 800/621-2151), which are fun-loving but with an educational bent.

If you want something more than the average vacation or guided tour, try **Elderhostel** (☎ 877/426-8056; www.elderhostel.org) or the University of New Hampshire's **Interhostel** (☎ 800/733-9753; www.learn.unh.edu/interhostel), both variations on the same theme: educational travel for senior citizens. On these escorted tours, the days are packed with seminars, lectures, and field trips, and the sightseeing is led by academic experts. **Elderhostel** runs regular educational trips to Costa Rica for those age 55 and over (and a spouse or companion of any age). Most tours last about 3 weeks and many include airfare, accommodations in student dormitories or modest inns, meals, and tuition. Write or call for a free catalog, which lists upcoming courses and destinations. **Interhostel** takes travelers 50 and over (with companions over 40), and offers 2- and 3-week trips, mostly international. The courses in both these programs are ungraded, involve no homework, and often focus on the liberal arts. They're not luxury vacations, but they're fun and fulfilling.

Although all the specialty books on the market are U.S.-focused, three do provide good general advice and contacts for the savvy senior traveler. Thumb through *The 50+ Traveler's Guidebook* (St. Martin's Press), *The Seasoned Traveler* (Country Roads Press), or *Unbelievably Good Deals and Great Adventures That You Absolutely Can't Get Unless You're Over 50* (Contemporary Books). Also check out your newsstand for the quarterly magazine *Travel 50 & Beyond.*

Due to its temperate climate, stable government, low cost of living, and friendly *pensionado* program, Costa Rica is popular with retirees from North America. There are excellent medical facilities in San José and plenty of community organizations to help retirees feel at home. If you would like to learn more about applying for residency and retiring in Costa Rica, contact the **Association of Residents of Costa Rica** in San José (☎ 506/233-8068; www.arcr.org; E-mail: arcrsacc@racsa.co.cr).

FAMILIES

Hotels in Costa Rica often give discounts for children under 12 years old, and children under 3 or 4 years old are usually allowed to stay for free. Discounts for children and the cut-off ages vary according to hotel, but in general, don't assume that your kids can stay in your room for free.

Many hotels, villas, and cabinas come equipped with kitchenettes or full kitchen facilities. These can be a real money-saver for those traveling with children.

The highly regarded *Family Travel Times* newsletter is published six times a year by Travel with Your Children, or TWYCH, 40 Fifth Ave., 7th Floor, New York, NY 10011 (☎ 888/822-4388 or 212/477-5524). Subscriptions are $40 a year. A free publication list and a sample issue are available on request.

Syndicated columnist Eileen Ogintz's book *Are We There Yet?: A Parent's Guide to Fun Family Vacations* (HarperCollins) is available at most U.S. bookstores.

A Note for Female Travelers

For lack of better phrasing, Costa Rica is a typically "macho" Latin-American nation. Single women can expect a nearly constant stream of catcalls, hisses, whistles, and car horns. The best advice is to ignore the unwanted attention, rather than try to come up with a witty or antagonistic rejoinder. Women should also be careful walking alone at night, both in San José and in other more remote destinations. I definitely don't recommend hitchhiking.

STUDENTS

Costa Rica is the only country in Central America with a network of hostels affiliated with the International Youth Hostel Federation. Ask at the **Toruma Youth Hostel,** Avenida Central between calles 29 and 31, San José (☎ **506/ 224-4085;** E-mail: recajhi@racsa.co.cr), for information on hostels at Rara Avis, La Fortuna, Lake Arenal, San Isidro, Jacó Beach, Liberia, and Rincón de la Vieja National Park.

In San José, there are now two student travel agencies: **OTEC** (☎ **506/ 256-0633;** fax 506/233-2321; www.gotec.com; E-mail: otec@gotec.com) is located at Edificio Ferencz, 2nd floor, Calle 3 between avenidas 1 and 3, 275 meters (300 yd.) north of the National Theater; **Sin Límites** (☎ **506/ 280-5182;** fax 506/225-9325; www.ucitworld.com) is located on Calle 35 and Avenida Central, 200 meters (218 yd.) east of the Kentucky Fried Chicken in Los Yoses. If you already have an **international student identity card,** you can use it to get discounts on airfares, hostels, national and international tours and excursions, car rentals, and store purchases. If you don't have one, stop by either the OTEC or Sin Límites office with proof of student status, two passport photos, and a passport or other identification that shows you are under 35 years old; for about $10, you can get an ID card.

In terms of pretrip planning, the best resource for students is the **Council on International Educational Exchange (CIEE).** You can get an ID card here, and the travel branch, **Council Travel Service** (☎ **800/226-8624;** www.ciee.org), is the biggest student travel agency operation in the world. It can get you discounts on plane tickets, hotels, tours, and the like. From CIEE you can obtain the student traveler's best friend, the $18 **International Student Identity Card (ISIC).** It's the only officially acceptable form of student identification, good for cut rates on accommodations, plane tickets, and other discounts. It also provides you with basic health and life insurance and a 24-hour help line. If you're no longer a student but are still under 26, you can get a **GO 25 card** from the same people, which will get you the insurance and some of the discounts (but not student admission prices in museums).

In Canada, **Travel CUTS,** 200 Ronson St., Suite 320, Toronto, Ontario M9W 5Z9 (☎ **800/667-2887** or 416/614-2887; www.travelcuts.com), offers similar services. **Campus Travel,** 52 Grosvenor Gardens, London SW1W 0AG (☎ **0870/240-1010;** www.campustravel.co.uk), opposite Victoria Station, is Britain's leading specialist in student and youth travel.

8 Getting There

BY PLANE

It takes between 3 and 7 hours to fly to Costa Rica from most U.S. cities, and as Costa Rica becomes more and more popular with North American travelers, more flights are available into San José's **Juan Santamaría International Airport.** Costa Rica keeps threatening to open a new international airport in Liberia, gateway to the beaches of the Guanacaste region and the Nicoya Peninsula, but at press time, it still wasn't able to handle international flights.

THE MAJOR AIRLINES There is a host of airlines flying into Costa Rica. Be warned that the smaller Latin-American carriers tend to make several stops (sometimes unscheduled) en route to San José, thus increasing flying time. In fact, Aviateca, Lacsa, and Taca are actually operating under a single parent company, and they practice code-sharing, so the flight you book on one of these airlines may in fact fly under another name. The following airlines

Tips for Getting the Best Airfares

Pricing is so volatile that almost every passenger on a given aircraft may have paid a different price. Fares change constantly, varying from airline to airline and even from day to day on the same airline. Flexibility is costly—last-minute travelers pay the premium rate, or full fare—and getting a good deal usually means booking well in advance and agreeing to many restrictions. The lowest-priced fares are often nonrefundable, require advance purchase of 1 to 3 weeks and a certain length of stay, and carry penalties for changing travel dates.

Try to travel on weekdays during the busy summer season and to avoid major holiday periods, when fares go up. Staying over a Saturday night usually means a lower price. Call around, or ask your travel agent to call around, as far in advance as possible. And be flexible if you can—shifting by a day or two can sometimes mean great savings, but you have to ask, because many airlines won't volunteer this information.

Here are a few ways to save:

1. Check newspapers for advertised discounts, or call the airlines directly and ask if any **promotional rates** or special fares are available.

2. **Consolidators,** also known as bucket shops, are a good place to find low fares. Consolidators buy seats in bulk and sell them at prices below even the airlines' discounted rates. Their small ads usually run in the Sunday travel section at the bottom of the page. Before you pay, ask the consolidator for a confirmation number, then call the airline to confirm your seat—and be prepared to book your ticket with a different consolidator if the airline can't confirm your reservation. Also be aware that bucket-shop tickets are usually nonrefundable or carry stiff cancellation penalties, often as high as 50% to 75% of the ticket price. **Council Travel** (☎ **800/226-8624;** www.counciltravel.com) and **STA Travel** (☎ **800/781-4040;** www.statravel.com) cater to young travelers, but their bargains are available to people of all ages. **Travel Bargains** (☎ **800/AIR-FARE;** www.1800airfare.com) was formerly owned by TWA but now offers the deepest discounts on many other airlines, with a 4-day advance purchase. Other reliable consolidators include **1-800-FLY-CHEAP** (www.1800flycheap.com) and **TFI Tours International** (☎ **800/745-8000** or 212/736-1140), which

currently serve Costa Rica from the United States, using the gateway cities listed. **American Airlines** (☎ **800/433-7300;** www.aa.com) has daily flights from Miami and Dallas/Fort Worth. **Continental** (☎ **800/525-0280;** www. continental.com) offers flights daily from Houston and from Newark International. **Delta** (☎ **800/221-1212;** www.delta-air.com) offers flights from Atlanta. **Lacsa** (Costa Rican; ☎ **800/225-2272**) has service from Dallas, New York, Miami, Orlando, New Orleans, Los Angeles, and San Francisco. **Mexicana** (☎ **800/531-7921;** www.mexicana.com) offers flights from Montréal, Toronto, Chicago, Los Angeles, New York, Denver, Miami, Dallas/Fort Worth, San Antonio, San Jose (Calif.), and San Francisco. **Grupo Taca** (☎ **800/535-8780;** www.grupotaca.com) is a conglomeration of the Central American airlines, Aviateca, Taca, and Lacsa. Flights and connections travel to and from Los Angeles, San Francisco, Houston, New Orleans, New York, serves as a clearinghouse for unused seats. "Rebaters" such as **Travel Avenue** (☎ **800/333-3335** or 312/876-1116; www.travelavenue.com) and the **Smart Traveller** (☎ **800/448-3338** in the U.S., or 305/448-3338) rebate part of their commissions to you.

3. Surf the Web for the best deals. In addition to the Web sites for the consolidators above, check out fare-finders like **Expedia** (**www.expedia.com**) or **Yahoo's Roundtrip Flight Search** (**www.yahoo.com**), which can give you the lowest available price for any itinerary, as well as suggest some even cheaper alternatives on different airlines, days, or both. See the online directory on page 58 for details on how to make these sites work for you.

4. Book a seat on a **charter flight.** Discounted fares have pared the number available, but they can still be found. Most charter operators advertise and sell their seats through travel agents, so the local professionals are your best source. Before deciding to take a charter, check and double-check the restrictions—expect there to be many for you and few for the tour operator. Summer charters fill up quickly and are almost sure to fly, but if you decide on a charter flight at any time, seriously consider cancellation insurance. Check with the Better Business Bureau before you pay to make sure that the company is reliable.

5. Look into **courier flights.** Companies that hire couriers use your luggage allowance for their business baggage; in return, you get a deeply discounted ticket. Flights are often offered at the last minute, and you may have to arrange a pretrip interview to make sure you're right for the job. **Now Voyager,** open Monday to Friday from 10am to 5:30pm and Saturday from noon to 4:30pm (☎ **212/431-1616**), flies from New York. Now Voyager also offers noncourier discounted fares, so call the company even if you don't want to fly as a courier.

6. Join a travel club such as **Moment's Notice** (☎ **718/234-6295;** www.moments-notice.com) or **Sears Discount Travel Club** (☎ **800/433-9383,** or 800/255-1487 to join), which supply unsold tickets at discounted prices. You pay an annual membership fee to get the club's hot-line number.

Miami, and Washington. **United Airlines** (☎ **800/241-6522;** www.ual.com) has daily flights from Los Angeles and Washington, with one stop either in Mexico or Guatemala. From Europe, you can take any major carrier to a hub city such as Miami or New York and then make connections to Costa Rica. Alternately, **Iberia** (☎ **800/772-4642;** www.iberia.com) from Spain, **Condor Airways** (www.condor.de) from Germany, and **Martin Air** (☎ **800/ 627-8462;** www.martinair.com) from Holland have established routes to San José, stopping in Miami.

REGULAR AIRFARES In recent years airfares to Costa Rica have been very unstable. Fares vary seasonally, and price wars flare up unexpectedly. Such instability makes it very difficult to quote an airline ticket price. **APEX** (advance-purchase excursion) fares are often similar from airline to airline, but the cost of a first-class ticket can vary greatly. At press time, an APEX or a coach ticket from New York or Los Angeles to San José was running between $550 and $950. First-class fares from these same destinations run between $1,200 and $1,800.

BY BUS

Bus service runs regularly from both Panama City, Panama, and Managua, Nicaragua. It's always better to get a direct bus, rather than one that stops along the way. I've heard that some of the Panama buses have bathrooms, but they are often out of order. From Panama City it's a 20-hour, 558-mile (900km) trip. The one-way fare is around $18. **Tracopa** has a daily bus leaving Panama City at 12:30pm, while **Tica Bus** has a daily bus leaving Panama City at 11am. Call Tracopa (☎ **506/221-4214**) or Tica Bus Company (☎ **506/221-8954**) for further information. From Managua, it's 11 hours and 279 miles (450km) to San José. Tica Bus leaves Managua daily at 6 and 7am and noon; the one-way fare is around $10. None of these bus companies will reserve a seat by telephone, so buy your ticket in advance—several days in advance if you plan to travel on weekends or holidays.

BY CAR

It's possible to travel to Costa Rica by car, but it can be difficult, especially for U.S. citizens. After leaving Mexico, the Interamerican Highway (also known as the Pan American Highway) passes through Guatemala, El Salvador, Honduras, and Nicaragua before reaching Costa Rica. All of these countries can be problematic for travelers for a variety of reasons, including internal violence, crime, and visa formalities. If you do decide to undertake this adventure, take the **Gulf coast route** from the border crossing at Brownsville, Texas, as it involves traveling the fewest miles through Mexico. Those planning to travel this route should look through *Driving the Pan-Am Highway to Mexico and Central America* by Audrey and Raymond Pritchard, available from **Costa Rica Books,** Suite 1, SJO 981, P.O. Box 025216, Miami, FL 33102 (☎ **800/ 365-2342** in the U.S., or ☎ and fax 506/232-5613 in Costa Rica).

CAR DOCUMENTS   You will need a current driver's license, as well as your vehicle's registration and the original title (no photocopies), in order to enter the country.

CENTRAL AMERICAN AUTO INSURANCE   Contact **Sanborn's Insurance Company,** 2009 S. 10th St., McAllen, TX 78505 (☎ **800/222-0158** or 956/686-3601; www.sanbornsinsurance.com; E-mail: info@sanbornsinsurance. com), located about 1¹/₂ hours from Brownsville, Texas; agents are at various border towns in the United States. These folks have been servicing this niche for over 50 years. They can supply you with trip insurance for Mexico and Central America (you won't be able to buy insurance after you've left the United States), driving tips, and an itinerary.

CAR SAFETY   Along the way, it's advisable not to drive at night because of the danger of being robbed by bandits. Also, drink only bottled beverages along the way, to avoid any unpleasant microbes that might be lurking in the local tap water.

BY CRUISE SHIP

More than 200 cruise ships stop each year in Costa Rica, calling at Limón on the Caribbean coast, and at Puerto Caldera and Puntarenas on the Pacific coast. Cruise lines that offer stops in Costa Rica include **Cunard** (☎ 800/ 7-CUNARD;** www.cunard.com), **Holland America** (☎ 877/ 724-5425; www.hollandamerica.com), **Princess** (☎ 800/421-0522; www. princesscruises. com), **Royal Caribbean** (☎ 800/398-9819; www.rccl.com), and **Radisson Seven Seas Cruises** (☎ 800/285-1835; www.rssc.com). Contact these companies directly or visit a travel agent to find out more information about cruising to Costa Rica. Most cruise travel is wholesale, and the best bargains can often be obtained from such wholesalers and consolidators as **Cruise World** (☎ 800/588-7447), **Cruises, Inc.** (☎ 800/596-5529; www. cruisesinc. com), **Cruise Web** (☎ 800/377-9383; www.cruiseweb.com), and **Forever Cruising** (☎ 800/338-8005).

PACKAGE TOURS

This book contains all the information and resources you need to design and book a wonderful trip, tailored to your particular interests and budget. Moreover, package tours are still a budding industry in Costa Rica, and do not offer the kinds of amazing bargains as those to Cancún or the Caribbean. In fact, many come with hidden charges and costs, so shop carefully. Still, some folks feel best buying a complete package. What you lose in adventure, you may gain in time and money saved when you book accommodations, and maybe even food and entertainment, along with your flight.

Packages vary widely. Some offer a better class of hotels than others. Some offer the same hotels for lower prices. Some offer flights on scheduled airlines, while others book charters. In some packages, your choice of accommodations and travel days may be limited. Some packages let you choose between escorted vacations and independent vacations; others will allow you to add on just a few excursions or escorted day trips (also at lower prices than you could locate on your own) without booking an entirely escorted tour.

FINDING A PACKAGE DEAL

The airlines themselves are one of the best sources of packages to Costa Rica. When you buy your package through the airline, moreover, you can be pretty sure that the company will still be in business when your departure date arrives. (Fly-by-night packagers are uncommon, but they do exist.) Among the airline packagers who fly to Costa Rica, your options include **American Airlines FlyAway Vacations** (☎ 800/321-2121) and **Delta Dream Vacations** (☎ 800/872-7786).

The larger hotel chains, casinos, and resorts in Costa Rica also offer package deals. If you already know where you want to stay, call the resort itself and ask if they can offer land/air packages. In the end, if you decide to opt for a package, remember that there's a multitude of both tour operators and packagers, with various specialties, so it's best to work with a travel agent to select the tour or package that's right for you.

There are scores of companies offering package tours to Costa Rica; most specialize in adventure or light adventure tourism. For a more complete listing of tour companies servicing Costa Rica, see section 1 in chapter 3, "Organized Adventure Trips."

Before you book your package through a tour company, remember that with a few phone calls and E-mails, you can often organize the same thing on your own without having to pay the sometimes hefty service fee.

Planning Basics

BY PLANE

Flying is one of the best ways to get around Costa Rica. Because the country is quite small, flights are short and not too expensive. The domestic airlines of Costa Rica are **Sansa** (☎ **506/221-9414;** fax 506/255-2176; E-mail: reservations@flysansa.com), which offers a free shuttle bus from its downtown office to the airport, and **Travelair** (☎ **506/220-3054;** fax 506/220-0413; www.travelair-costarica.com; E-mail: reservations@travelair-costarica.com), which charges slightly more for flights to the same destinations, but is popular because it is more reliable.

I personally highly recommend Travelair over Sansa. Sansa has an unfriendly and unwieldy reservation system, they frequently overbook flights, and they have been known to change schedules with short or little notice. The one thing Sansa has going for it is that it flies out of the main airport, so it is possible, albeit risky, to make same-day connections with international flights. Flight times are generally between 20 minutes and a little over an hour. Sansa operates from San José's Juan Santamaría International Airport, while Travelair operates from **Tobís Bolaños International Airport** in Pavas, 4 miles (6.4km) from San José. The ride from downtown to Pavas takes about 10 minutes, and a metered taxi fare should cost $6 to $8. The ride from the airport to downtown is a different story—most taxis refuse to use their meter, and the standard fee is set at double the metered rate, around $10 to $12.

In the high season (late November to late April), be sure to book reservations well in advance. For Sansa flights, you don't have to call Costa Rica to make reservations—you can book flights through **Grupo Taca** (☎ 800/535-8780). But *be careful:* I've heard horror stories of ticket vouchers issued in the United States not being accepted in Costa Rica; always reconfirm once you arrive. You can book flights on Travelair via the Web or E-mail. If you plan to return to San José, buy a round-trip ticket—it's always nice to have a confirmed seat, and with Travelair you'll save a little money.

What Travel Agents Don't Tell You

You don't have to spend the night in San José. Travel agents will encourage you to do this so that they can stick you with unnecessary and outrageous airport transfer fees—twice. But don't listen to them. If your flight arrives in San Jose early in the day, you should consider heading straight to your first destination. It's easy to catch a domestic flight to Liberia or Tamarindo from the domestic terminal at the San Jose airport. Note, however, that you'll have to carry your bags the 250 yards between terminals (or take a cab), and you'll also have to use the cheaper but less reliable carrier Sansa, rather than Travelair, for your domestic flight (Travelair flights leave from an entirely different airport). But if this doesn't cause you any grief, you can leave the United States in the morning and be on the beach before sunset (and in some cases, by lunchtime).

You can also drive to your first destination if you arrive early enough. However, if the thought of doing a 4-hour drive immediately after your 5-hour flight seems exhausting, my best advice is to grab your rental car and head to a hotel like Vista del Valle Plantation Inn, which is 20 minutes from the airport toward Guanacaste, Monteverde, and Arenal. You'll cut lots of time off your drive the next day.

BY BUS

This is by far the most economical way to visit most of Costa Rica. Buses are inexpensive and relatively well maintained, and they go nearly everywhere. There are three types: **Local buses** are the cheapest and slowest; they stop frequently and are generally a bit dilapidated. **Express buses** run between San José and most beach towns and major cities; they sometimes operate only on weekends and holidays. A few **luxury buses** and minibuses drive to destinations frequented by foreign travelers. For details on how to get to various destinations from San José, see the "Getting There" sections of the regional chapters that follow.

BY CAR

Renting a car in Costa Rica is no idle proposition. The roads are riddled with potholes, most rural intersections are unmarked, and for some reason, sitting behind the wheel of a car seems to turn peaceful Ticos into homicidal maniacs. But unless you want to see the country from the window of a bus (inconvenient) or pay exorbitant amounts for private transfers (expensive), renting a car is still your best option for independent exploring. Four-wheel drives are particularly useful in the rainy season (May to mid-November) and for navigating the bumpy, poorly paved roads year-round.

Be forewarned, however: although rental cars no longer bear special license plates, they are still readily identifiable to thieves and frequently targeted. (Nothing is ever safe in a car in Costa Rica, although parking in guarded parking lots helps.) Transit police also seem to target tourists. Never pay money directly to a police officer who stops you for any traffic violation. Before driving off with a rental car, be sure that you inspect the exterior and point out to the rental-company representative every tiny scratch, dent, tear, or any other damage. It's a common practice with many Costa Rican car-rental companies to claim that you owe payment for minor dings and dents the company finds when you return the car. Also, if you get into an accident, be sure the rental company doesn't try to bill you for a higher amount than the deductible on your rental contract.

These caveats aren't meant to scare you off from driving in Costa Rica. Thousands of tourists rent cars here every year, and the large majority of them suffer no ill consequences. Just keep your wits about you.

Note: It's sometimes cheaper to reserve a car in your home country, rather than book when you arrive in Costa Rica. If you know you will be renting a car, it is always wise to reserve a car well in advance for the high season, as the rental fleet still can't match demand.

Avis Rent A Car (☎ **800/331-1212** in the U.S., 506/442-1321 at the airport, or 506/232-9922 in downtown San José; www.avis.com); **Budget Rent A Car** (☎ **800/527-0700** in the U.S., 506/441-4444 at the airport, or 506/223-3284 in downtown San José; www.budget.co.cr); **Elegante Rent A Car** (☎ **800/582-7432** in the U.S., 506/441-9366 at the airport, or 506/257-0026 in downtown San José; www.eleganterentacar.com); **Hertz Rent A Car** (☎ **800/654-3131** in the U.S., 506/441-0097 at the airport, or 506/221-1818 in downtown San José; www.hertz.com); **National Car Rental** (☎ **800/328-4567** in the U.S., 506/441-6533 at the airport, or 506/290-8787 in downtown San José; www.natcar.com); and **Thrifty Car Rental** (☎ **800/367-2277** in the U.S., 506/442-8585 at the airport, or 506/257-3434 in downtown San José) are some of the larger rental companies in Costa Rica. All of the above companies maintain toll-free numbers in the

While it's preferable to use the coverage provided by your home auto-insurance policy or credit card, check carefully to see if the coverage really holds in Costa Rica. Many policies exclude four-wheel-drive vehicles and off-road driving. Much of Costa Rica can in fact be considered off-road. While it's possible at some car-rental agencies to waive the insurance charges, you will have to pay all damages before leaving the country if you're in an accident. If you do take the insurance, you can expect a deductible of between $500 and $1,250. At some agencies, you can buy additional insurance to lower the deductible. To rent a car in Costa Rica, you must be at least 21 years old and have a valid driver's license and a major credit card in your name. See the "Getting Around" section of chapter 4 for details on renting a car in San José. You can also rent cars in Quepos, Jacó, Liberia, Playa Conchal, Tamarindo, and Limón.

United States. For more listings of Costa Rican car-rental agencies, see "By Car" under "Getting Around," in chapter 4.

GASOLINE   Gasoline is sold as "regular" and "super"; both are unleaded. "Super" is just higher octane. Diesel is available at almost every gas station as well. Most rental cars run on "super," but always ask your rental agent what type of gas your car takes. When going off to remote places, try to leave with a full tank of gas since gas stations can be hard to find. If you need to gas up in a small town, you can sometimes get gasoline from enterprising families who sell it by the liter from their houses. Look for hand-lettered signs that say GASOLINA.

ROAD CONDITIONS   The awful road conditions in San José and throughout the country are legendary, and deservedly so. Despite constant promises to fix the problem, the hot sun, hard rain, and rampant corruption have continued to outpace any progress made toward improving the condition. Even paved roads are often badly potholed, so stay alert. Road conditions get especially tricky during the rainy season, when heavy rains and runoff can destroy a stretch of pavement in the blink of an eye.

Route numbers are rarely used on road signs in Costa Rica, though there are frequent signs listing the number of kilometers to various towns or cities. In recent years, the Transportation Ministry began placing helpful markers at major intersections and turnoffs, but your best bets for on-road directions are still billboards and advertisements for hotels located at your destination.

DEMYSTIFYING RENTER'S INSURANCE   Before you drive off in a rental car, be sure you're insured. Hasty assumptions about your personal auto insurance or a rental agency's additional coverage could end up costing you tens of thousands of dollars—even if you are involved in an accident that was clearly the fault of another driver.

If you already hold a **private auto-insurance** policy, you are most likely covered in the United States for loss of or damage to a rental car, and liability in case of injury to any other party involved in an accident. Coverage doesn't always extend outside the United States, however. Be sure to find out whether you are covered in Costa Rica, whether your policy extends to all persons who will be driving the rental car, how much liability is covered in case an outside party is injured in an accident, and whether the type of vehicle you are renting is included under your contract. (Rental trucks, sport utility vehicles, and four-wheel-drive vehicles may not be covered.)

Most **major credit cards** provide some degree of coverage as well—provided they were used to pay for the rental. Again, terms vary widely, so be sure to call your credit-card company directly before you rent. If you are **uninsured or driving abroad,** your credit card provides primary coverage as long as you decline the rental agency's insurance. This means that the credit card will cover damage or theft of a rental car for the full cost of the vehicle. If you already have insurance, your credit card will provide secondary coverage—which basically covers your deductible.

Credit cards **will not cover liability** or the cost of injury to an outside party and/or damage to an outside party's vehicle. If you do not hold an insurance policy, or if you are driving outside the United States, you may seriously want to consider purchasing additional liability insurance from your rental company. Be sure to check the terms, however: Some rental agencies only cover liability if the renter is not at fault; even then, the rental company's obligation varies from state to state.

Bear in mind that each credit-card company has its own peculiarities. Most **American Express Optima** cards, for instance, do not provide any insurance. American Express does not cover vehicles valued at over $50,000 when new, luxury vehicles, or vehicles built on a truck chassis. **MasterCard** does not provide coverage for loss, theft, or fire damage, and only covers collision if the rental period does not exceed 15 days. Call your own credit-card company for details.

The basic insurance coverage offered by most car-rental companies, known as the **Loss/Damage Waiver (LDW)** or **Collision Damage Waiver (CDW),** can cost as much as $20 per day. It usually covers the full value of the vehicle with no deductible if an outside party causes an accident or other damage to the rental car. Liability coverage varies according to the company policy. If you are at fault in an accident, however, you will be covered for the full replacement value of the car but not for liability. Most rental companies will require a police report in order to process any claims you file, but your private insurer will not be notified of the accident.

MAPS   Car-rental agencies and the ICT information centers (see "Visitor Information" at the beginning of this chapter) at the airport and in downtown San José have adequate road maps. Other sources in San José are **Seventh Street Books,** Calle 7 between avenidas Central and 1 (☎ 506/256-8251); **Libreria Lehmann,** Avenida Central between calles 1 and 3 (☎ 506/223-1212); and **Librería Universal,** Avenida Central between calles Central and 1 (☎ 506/222-2222).

DRIVING RULES   A current foreign driver's license is valid for the first 3 months you are in Costa Rica. Seat belts are required for the driver and front-seat passengers. Motorcyclists must wear a helmet. Highway police use radar, so keep to the speed limit (usually between 60 and 90kmph/37 and 56 m.p.h.) if you don't want to get pulled over. Maybe it just seems this way, but the police seem to target rental cars. Never give the police any money. Speeding tickets can be charged to your credit card for up to a year after you leave the country if they are not paid before departure.

BREAKDOWNS   Be warned that emergency services, both vehicular and medical, are extremely limited once you leave San José, and their availability is directly related to the remoteness of your location at the time of breakdown. You'll find service stations spread over the entire length of the Interamerican Highway, and most of these have tow trucks and mechanics. The major towns of Puntarenas, Liberia, Quepos, San Isidro, Palmar, and Golfito all have hospitals, and most other moderately sized cities and tourist destinations have some sort of clinic or health-services provider.

If you're involved in an accident, you should contact the **National Insurance Institute (INS)** at ☎ **800/800-8000.** You should probably also call the **Transit Police** (☎ **506/222-9330** or 506/222-9245); if they have a unit close by, they'll send one. An official transit-police report will greatly facilitate any insurance claim. If you can't get help from any of these, try to get written statements from any witnesses. Finally, you can also call ☎ **911** and they should be able to redirect your call to the appropriate agency.

If the police do show up, you've got a 50/50 chance of finding them helpful or downright antagonistic. Many officers are unsympathetic to the problems of what they perceive to be rich tourists running around in fancy cars with lots of expensive toys and trinkets. Success and happy endings run about equal with horror stories.

If you don't speak Spanish, expect added difficulty in any emergency or stressful situation. Don't expect that rural (or urban) police officers, hospital personnel, service-station personnel, or mechanics will speak English.

Lastly, a little tip: If your car breaks down and you're unable to get well off the road, check to see if there are reflecting triangles in the trunk. If there are, place them as a warning for approaching traffic, arranged in a wedge that starts at the shoulder about 100 feet back and nudges gradually toward your car. If your car has no triangles, try to create a similar warning marker using a pile of leaves or branches.

BY FERRY

There are four different ferries operating across the Gulf of Nicoya. Three are car ferries: one across the Río Tempisque, one from Puntarenas to Playa Naranjo, and one from Puntarenas to Paquera; and one is a passenger ferry that runs from Puntarenas to Paquera.

HITCHHIKING

Although buses go to most places in Costa Rica, they can be infrequent in the remote regions, and so local people often hitchhike to get to their destination sooner. If you're driving a car, people will frequently ask you for a ride. In rural areas, a hitchhiker carrying a machete is not necessarily a great danger, but use your judgment. Hitchhiking is not recommended on major roadways or in urban areas. In rural areas it's usually pretty safe. However, women should be extremely cautious about hitchhiking anywhere in Costa Rica. If you choose to hitchhike, keep in mind that if a bus doesn't go to your destination, there probably aren't too many cars going there, either. Good luck.

Suggested Itineraries

If You Have 1 Week

Day 1 Visit the museums and the National Theater in San José.

Day 2 Make an excursion to the Orosi Valley, Lankester Gardens, and Irazú Volcano.

Days 3 and 4 Travel to Monteverde (or another cloud-forest region) and spend a day exploring the cloud forest.

Days 5 and 6 Head to one of the many Pacific coast beaches. I'd recommend Manuel Antonio for its accessibility and range of accommodations and activities.

Day 7 Return to San José.

Day 1   Visit the museums and the National Theater in San José.

Days 2 and 3   Make an excursion to the Orosi Valley, Lankester Gardens, and Irazú Volcano one day and go river rafting on the other day.

Days 4 and 5   Travel to Lake Arenal to see the eruptions of Arenal Volcano, soak in some hot springs, and maybe go to Caño Negro National Wildlife Refuge.

Days 6 and 7   Travel to Monteverde (or another cloud-forest region) and explore the cloud forest.

Day 8   Explore Rincón de la Vieja or Santa Rosa National Park.

Days 9, 10, 11, and 12   Spend these days relaxing on a beach in Guanacaste, or perhaps explore a more remote location on the Osa Peninsula or along the Caribbean coast.

Days 13 and 14   Fly to Tortuguero National Park and spend a night there, returning the next day by boat and bus.

10 Spanish-Language Programs

As more and more people travel to Costa Rica with the intention of learning Spanish, the number of options continues to increase. Courses are of varying lengths and intensiveness and often include cultural activities and day excursions. Many of these schools have reciprocal relationships with U.S. universities and often college credit can be arranged. Most Spanish schools can also arrange for homestays with a middle-class Tico family for a total-immersion experience. Classes are often small, or even one-on-one, and can last anywhere from 2 to 8 hours a day. Listed below are some of the larger and more established Spanish-language schools, with approximate costs. As you'll see, most are located in San José; however, there are listings here for schools in Heredia, Monteverde, Manuel Antonio, and Tamarindo, and all things being equal, I'd certainly rather spend 2 weeks or a month in one of these spots than in San José. Contact the schools for the most current price information.

Central American Institute for International Affairs (ICAI), Apdo. 10302-1000, San José, Costa Rica (☎ **506/233-8571;** fax 506/221-5238; E-mail: icai@expreso.co.cr), offers a 4-week Spanish-language immersion program, along with a homestay, for $1,200. In the United States, contact the **Language Studies Enrollment Center,** 13948 Hemlock Dr., Penn Valley, CA 95946 (☎ **916/432-7690;** fax 916/432-7615).

Centro Cultural Costarricense Norteamericano, Apdo. 1489-1000, San José, Costa Rica (☎ **506/225-9433;** fax 506/224-1480; www.ccncr.com; E-mail: acccnort@racsa.co.cr), is an extension of the U.S. embassy and government programs in Costa Rica. Its facilities are the most extensive of any language school in the country. A 2-week intensive course with 4 hours of instruction per day costs $450. Homestays are also available for $130 per week.

Centro Lingüístico Conversa, Apdo. 17-1007, Centro Colón, San José, Costa Rica (☎ **800/354-5036** in the U.S. and Canada, or 506/221-7649 in Costa Rica; fax 506/233-2418; www.conversa.co.cr; E-mail: conversa@racsa.co.cr), has classes in both San José and Santa Ana (a suburb of the capital city). A 2-week course here with 4 hours of classes each day, including room and board with a Costa Rican family, costs between $750 and $1,300 for one person, depending on which campus you choose and the level of luxury you're looking for.

✪ **Centro Panamericano de Idiomas (CPI),** Apdo. 151-3007, San Joaquín de Flores, Heredia, Costa Rica (☎ and fax **506/265-6213;** www.

cpi-edu.com; E-mail: info@cpi-edu.com). This school has three campuses: one in the quiet suburban town of Heredia, another in Monteverde, and a new facility in Playa Flamingo. A 4-week program, with 4 hours of classes per day and a homestay, costs $1,220.

Costa Rican Language Academy, Apdo. 336-2070, San José, Costa Rica (☎ 800/854-6057 in the U.S., or 506/233-8914; fax 506/233-8670; www.learn-spanish.com; E-mail: crlang@racsa.co.cr), has intensive programs with classes only on Monday through Thursday, to give students a chance to make longer weekend excursions. They also integrate Latin dance and Costa Rican cooking classes into the program. A 2-week class with 4 hours of class per day, plus homestay, costs $550.

Costa Rica Spanish Institute (COSI), Apdo. 1366-2050, San Pedro, Costa Rica (☎ 506/253-9272; fax 506/253-2117; www.cosi.co.cr; E-mail: office@cosi.co.cr), offers small classes in the San Pedro neighborhood of San José, as well as a program at the Pacific beach of Manuel Antonio. The cost is $295 per week with a homestay in San José; at the beach it's $350, with room and board extra.

✪ **Forester Instituto Internacional,** Apdo. 6945-1000, San José, Costa Rica (☎ 506/225-3155, 506/225-0135, or 506/225-1649; fax 506/225-9236; www.fores.com; E-mail: forester@racsa.co.cr), is located 75 meters (82 yd.) south of the Automercado in the Los Yoses district of San José. I've received glowing reports from satisfied customers here. The cost of a 4-week language course with a homestay and excursions is approximately $1,360.

✪ **Institute for Central American Development Studies (ICADS),** Apdo. 3-2070 Sabanilla, San José, Costa Rica (Dept. 826, P.O. Box 025216, Miami, FL 33102-5216, in the U.S.; ☎ 506/225-0508; www.icadscr.com; E-mail: icads@netbox.com). In addition to having one of the best and most extensive field-work and volunteer programs in Costa Rica, this institution runs quality Spanish-language immersion programs. A 4-week course with homestay costs $1,500.

✪ **Instituto Britanico,** Apdo. 8184-1000, San José, Costa Rica (☎ 506/225-0256 or 506/234-9054; fax 506/253-1894; www.instbrit.com; E-mail: instbrit@racsa.co.cr). This venerable institution has installations in the Los Yoses neighborhood of San José. A bit more attention seems to be paid to teacher training and selection here than at other institutions around town. A 2-week course with 4 hours of classes per day and homestay costs $600.

Instituto Interamericano de Idiomas (Intensa), Calle 33 between avenidas 1 and 3 (Apdo. 8110-1000), San José, Costa Rica (☎ 506/224-6353; fax 506/253-4337; www.intensa.com; E-mail: intensa@racsa.co.cr), offers 2- to 4-week programs. A 4-week, 4-hour-per-day program with a homestay costs $1,300.

✪ **La Escuela Idiomas D'Amore,** Apdo. 67, Quepos, Costa Rica (☎ and fax 414/367-8598 in the U.S., ☎ and fax 506/777-1143 in Costa Rica; www.escueladamore.com; E-mail: damore@racsa.co.cr), is situated in the lush surroundings of Manuel Antonio National Park. Four weeks of classes, 4 hours per day, costs $1,340; with a homestay, the cost rises to $1,590. Fifteen percent of your tuition is donated to the World Wildlife Fund. This is a much nicer environment than San José for learning Spanish (for most everything else too, in fact).

Pura Vida Instituto, Avenida 3 between calles 8 and 10 (Apdo. 275-3000), Heredia, Costa Rica (☎ and fax 506/237-0387; www.costaricaspanish.com; E-mail: puravida@costaricaspanish.com). For $370, you receive 5 days of classroom instruction and 7 days of lodging (room and board) with a Costa Rican family.

Wayra Instituto de Español (☎ and fax **506/653-0359;** www.spanish-wayra.co.cr; E-mail: spanishw@racsa.co.cr). This place is located in the beach town of Tamarindo. A week of classes, 4 hours per day, will run you $200. Wayra doesn't offer any homestays in Tamarindo, but can help arrange accommodations in Tamarindo, or a homestay in a nearby village.

11 Tips on Accommodations

Tourism insiders had been predicting it for years, and despite the ever-increasing number of visitors, tough times and fierce competition have hit Costa Rican hoteliers. When the tourist boom hit Costa Rica in the late 1980s, hotels began popping up like mushrooms after a few days of rain. In recent years Costa Rica has seen the opening of the first true mega-resorts, and several more are under construction and near completion. There is a hotel glut, and this is good news for travelers and bargain hunters. A weeding-out period has apparently begun, and hotels that want to survive are being forced to reduce their rates and provide better service.

Glut notwithstanding, there are still few hotels or resorts here offering the sort of luxurious accommodations you'll find in Hawaii or the Caribbean. Sure, there are hotels that meet international standards, but Costa Rica is not yet a luxury resort destination. One item you're likely to want to bring with you is a beach towel. Your hotel might not provide one at all, and even if it does, it might be awfully thin.

ROOM RATES

I've separated hotel listings throughout into several broad categories: **Very Expensive,** $125 and up; **Expensive,** $80 to $125; **Moderate,** $40 to $80; and **Inexpensive,** under $40 double. These rates do not include the **16.3% room taxes.** These taxes will add considerably to the cost of your room. Also note that with rooms at the beach that cost under $20, you usually don't get hot water.

HOTEL OPTIONS

The country's strong suit is its **moderately priced hotels.** In the $40-to-$80 price range, you'll find comfortable, and sometimes outstanding, accommodations almost anywhere in the country. However, room size and quality vary quite a bit within this price range, so don't expect the kind of uniformity you find in the United States.

The Best Room in the House

Somebody has to get the best room in the house. It might as well be you. Always ask for a corner room. They're usually larger, quieter, and they often have more windows and light than standard rooms, and they don't always cost more. Inquire, too, about the location of the restaurants, bars, and discos in the hotel—these could all be a source of irritating noise. If you aren't happy with your room when you arrive, talk to the front desk. If they have another room, they should be happy to accommodate you, within reason. Or, if you arrive early enough, you might ask to see a few rooms and choose the best one, before actually checking in.

Planning Basics

If you are booking direct (either by phone/fax or E-mail), remember that most hotels are accustomed to paying as much as 20% in commission to agents and wholesalers. It never hurts to ask if they'll pass some of that on to you. Don't be afraid to bargain.

If you're even more budget- or bohemian-minded, there are quite a few good deals for less than $40 per double room. But beware: Budget-oriented lodgings often feature shared bathrooms, and either cold-water showers or showers heated by electrical heat-coil units mounted at the shower head. These are affectionately known as "suicide showers." If you find your hotel has one, do not try to adjust it while the water is running. Unless specifically noted, all the rooms I've listed in this guide have a private bathroom.

Bed-and-breakfasts have also been proliferating. Though the majority of these are in the San José area, you will now find B&Bs (often gringo owned and operated) throughout the country. Another welcome hotel trend in the San José area is the renovation and conversion of old homes into small hotels. Most of these hotels are in the **Barrio Amón** district of downtown San José, which means you'll have to put up with noise and exhaust fumes, but these establishments have more character than any other hotels in the country. You'll find similar hotels in the **Paseo Colón** and **Los Yoses** districts.

Costa Rica has been riding the ecotourism wave, and there are now small nature-oriented **ecolodges** throughout the country. These lodges offer opportunities to see wildlife (including sloths, monkeys, and hundreds of species of birds) and learn about tropical forests. They range from Spartan facilities catering primarily to scientific researchers to luxury accommodations that are among the finest in the country. Keep in mind that though the nightly room rates at these lodges are often quite moderate, the price of a visit starts to climb when you throw in transportation (often on chartered planes), guided excursions, and meals. Also, just because your travel agent can book a reservation at most of these lodges doesn't mean they're not remote. Make sure to find out how you will be getting to and from your ecolodge and just what tours and services are included in your stay. Then think long and hard about whether you really want to put up with hot, humid weather (cool and wet in the cloud forests), biting insects, rugged transportation, and strenuous hikes to see wildlife.

A couple of uniquely Costa Rican accommodation types you may encounter are the *apartotel* and the *cabina*. An apartotel is just what it sounds like: an apartment hotel, where you'll get a full kitchen and one or two bedrooms, along with daily maid service. Cabinas are Costa Rica's version of cheap vacation lodging. They're very inexpensive and very basic—often just cinderblock buildings divided into small rooms. Occasionally you'll find a cabina where the units are actually cabins, but these are a rarity. Cabinas often have clothes-washing sinks or *pilas,* and some come with kitchenettes, since they cater primarily to Tico families on vacation.

12 Tips on Dining

Simply put, Costa Rican cuisine is unmemorable. San José remains the unquestioned gastronomic capital of the country, and here you can find the cuisines of the world served with formal service at moderate prices. At the most expensive restaurant in San José, you'll have to drink a lot of wine to spend more than $40 per person on dinner. It gets even cheaper outside of the city. There are several excellent French and Italian restaurants around the San José area, as well as Peruvian, Japanese, Swiss, and Spanish establishments. Costa Rica is a major producer and exporter of beef, and consequently, San José has plenty of steak houses. Unfortunately, quantity doesn't mean quality. Unless you go to one of the better restaurants or steak houses, you will probably be served rather tough steaks, cut rather thin.

One recent development is worth noting, and it is slowly making my opening caveat untrue: With the increase in international tourism and the need to please a more sophisticated palate, local chefs have begun to create a "nouvelle Costa Rican cuisine," updating time-worn recipes and using traditional ingredients in creative ways. Unlike most visitors to Costa Rica, however, this phenomenon hasn't traveled far outside of downtown San José.

Outside of the capital, your options get very limited, and quickly. In fact, many beach resorts are so remote that you have no choice but to eat in the hotel's dining room. Even on the more accessible beaches, the only choices aside from the hotel dining rooms are cheap local places or overpriced tourist traps serving indifferent meals. At remote jungle lodges, the food is usually served buffet or family style and can range from bland to inspired, depending on who's doing the cooking at the moment, and turnover is high.

If you're looking for cheap eats, you'll find them in little restaurants known as *sodas,* which are the equivalent of diners in the United States. At a soda you'll have lots of choices: rice and beans with steak, rice and beans with fish, rice and beans with chicken, or, for vegetarians, rice and beans. You get the picture. Rice and beans are standard Tico fare, and are served at all three meals a day. Also, though there is plenty of seafood available throughout the country, at sodas it's all too often served fried.

Costa Ricans love to eat, and they love to have a view when they eat. Almost anywhere you go in the country, if there's a view, there will be a restaurant taking advantage of it. These restaurants are often called *miradores.* If you are driving around the country, don't miss an opportunity to dine with a view at some little roadside restaurant. The food may not be fantastic, but the scenery will be.

COST OF DINING I have separated restaurant listings throughout this book into three price categories based on the average cost per person of a meal, including tax and service charge but not including beer or wine. The categories are **Expensive,** more than $15; **Moderate,** $8 to $15; and **Inexpensive,** less than $8. (Note, however, that individual items in the listings—entrees, for instance—do not include the sales or service taxes.) Keep in mind that there is an additional 13% sales tax, as well as a 10% service charge. Ticos rarely tip, but that doesn't mean you shouldn't. If the service was particularly good and attentive, you should probably leave a little extra.

13 Tips on Shopping

FOOD FADS Buy coffee. Even if you're not a coffee drinker, you're bound to know someone who is, and coffee is the best buy in Costa Rica. **Café Britt** is the most common brand, sold in hotels and souvenir shops all over the country. Sure, it's good coffee, but it's also a little overpriced. If you go into the Central Market in downtown San José or a grocery store anywhere in the country, you'll find coffee at much lower prices. If you're in **Manuel Antonio,** pick up your coffee at Cafe Milagro (see chapter 7), and if you're in **Monteverde,** you can get some fresh roasted beans at CASEM (see chapter 6). Just be sure you're buying whole beans (*grano entero*) and not ground (*molido*). Packaged Costa Rican grinds are much finer than U.S. grinds and often have sugar mixed right in with the coffee.

Costa Rica also produces its own coffee liqueur (**Café Rica**), and a creme liqueur (**Salicsa**), both of which are quite inexpensive. These are best purchased in a liquor store or a grocery store. In fact, grocery stores are where I do my best gift shopping.

If you'd like to add a little spice to your life, **Tipica Tropical Sauce** produces a line of spicy salsas made from mango, pineapple, passion fruit, and tamarind. A small bottle costs around 75¢ and makes a great gift. **Salsa Lizano,** a flavorful green sauce used the same way we use steak sauce in the United States, is another condiment worth bringing home with you.

HANDCRAFTS   Costa Rica is not known for its handcrafts, though it does have a town, **Sarchí,** that's filled with handcraft shops. Sarchí is best known as the home of the colorfully painted Costa Rican oxcart, reproductions of which are manufactured in various scaled-down sizes. These make excellent gifts. (Larger oxcarts can be easily disassembled and shipped to your home.) There's also a lot of furniture made here. So scant are the country's handcraft offerings that most tourist shops sell Guatemalan clothing, Panamanian appliquéd textiles, El Salvadoran painted wood souvenirs, and Nicaraguan rocking chairs. The small town of Guaitíl, in central Guanacaste, is famous for its pottery. You can find examples of this low-fired simple ceramic work in many gift shops. There's quite a bit of wood carving being done in the country, but it is, for the most part, either tourist-souvenir wooden bowls, napkin holders, and the like, or elegant and expensive art pieces. One exception is the work of **Barry Biensanz,** whose excellent hardwood creations are sold at better gift shops around the country.

COSTA RICAN SPECIALTIES   A few other items worth keeping an eye out for include reproductions of pre-Columbian gold jewelry and carved-stone figurines. The former are available either in solid gold, silver, or gold-plated. The latter, though interesting, are extremely heavy.

On the streets of San José you'll see a lot of hammocks for sale. I personally find the Costa Rican hammocks a little crude and unstable. The same vendors usually have single-person hanging chairs, which are strung similarly to the full-size hammocks and are a better bet.

Finally, one new item you'll see at gift shops around the country is Cuban cigars. Although these are illegal to bring into the United States, they are perfectly legal and readily available in Costa Rica.

Fast Facts: Costa Rica

Business Hours   Banks are usually open Monday through Friday from 9am to 3pm, though many have begun to offer extended hours. Offices are open Monday through Friday from 8am to 5pm (many close for an hour at lunch). Stores are generally open Monday through Saturday from 9am to 6pm (many close for an hour at lunch). Stores in modern malls generally stay open until 8 or 9pm and don't close for lunch. Most bars are open until 1 or 2am.

Cameras/Film   Most types of film are available, as are developing services. However, prices are higher than in the United States, so I recommend bringing plenty of film with you and waiting until you get home for processing. For camera repair in San José, head to **Equipos Fotograficos Canon,** on Avenida 3 between calles 3 and 5 (☎ **506/ 233-0176**). You could also try **Dima,** Avenida Central between calles 3 and 5 (☎ **506/222-3969**).

Climate   See "When to Go," earlier in this chapter.

Currency   See "Money," earlier in this chapter.

Documents Required   See "Passport Information, Entry Requirements, & Customs," earlier in this chapter.

Driving Rules   See "Getting Around," earlier in this chapter.

Drug Laws   Drug laws in Costa Rica are strict, so stay away from marijuana and cocaine. Many prescription drugs are sold over the counter here, but often the names are different from those in the United States and Europe. It's always best to have a prescription from a doctor.

Electricity   The standard in Costa Rica is the same as in the United States: 110 volts AC (60 cycles). However, three-pronged outlets can be scarce, so it's helpful to bring along an adapter.

Embassies/Consulates   The following embassies and consulates are located in San José: **United States Embassy,** in front of Centro Commercial, on the road to Pavas (☎ **506/220-3939**); **Canadian Consulate,** Oficentro Ejecutivo La Sabana, Edificio 5 (☎ **506/296-4149**); **British Embassy,** Paseo Colón between calles 38 and 40 (☎ **506/ 258-2025**).

Emergencies   In case of an emergency, dial ☎ **911** (which should have an English-speaking operator); for an ambulance, call ☎ **128;** to report a fire, call ☎ **118;** if 911 doesn't work, you can contact the police at ☎ **506/222-1365** or 506/221-5337 and hopefully they can find someone who speaks English.

Holidays   See "When to Go," earlier in this chapter.

Information   See "Visitor Information" and "Passport Information, Entry Requirements, & Customs," earlier in this chapter. Also see individual city sections for local information offices.

Internet Cafes   Staying connected on the road is getting easier. (It's best to set up a free Web-based mail account with someone like Hotmail, Yahoo, Netscape, etc., before you leave for Costa Rica). Many hotels allow guests to send and receive E-mail. If not, you have a number of options: **Racsa,** Avenida 5 and Calle 1 (☎ **506/287-0087;** www.racsa.co.cr); **Cybercafe** at the Las Arcadas shopping center next to the Gran Hotel Costa Rica (☎ **506/233-3310**); **Internet Café** in Plaza San Pedro (☎ **506/224-7295;** www.internetcafecr.com; open 24 hr.), with another office in the Centro Colón, on Paseo Colón; and **Browsers Coffee & Internet** (☎ **506/228-7190**), in the Plaza Colonial in Escazú, all allow Web and E-mail access. Rates run between $2 and $10 per hour.

Language   Spanish is the official language of Costa Rica. *Berlitz Latin-American Spanish Phrasebook and Dictionary* (Berlitz Guides, 1992) is probably the best phrase book to bring with you. However, in most tourist areas, you'd be surprised by how well Costa Ricans speak English.

Laundry   Laundromats are few and far between in Costa Rica—more common are hotel laundry services, which can sometimes be expensive. For listings of Laundromats, see individual city and town sections.

Liquor Laws   Alcoholic beverages are sold every day of the week throughout the year, with the exception of the 2 days before Easter and the 2 days before and after a presidential election. The legal drinking age is 18, though it's almost never enforced.

Lost or Stolen Credit/Charge Cards   Credomatic (☎ **506/ 257-0155** main office, or 506/257-4744 to report lost or stolen cards 24 hours) is the local representative of most major credit cards: American Express, MasterCard, and Visa. They have an office in San José across from the Banco de San José on Calle Central between avenidas 3 and 5. It's open Monday through Friday from 8am to 7pm, and Saturday from 9am to 1pm. This office also serves as a traditional **American Express Travel Services** office, issuing traveler's checks and providing other standard services. You can call the number above to report all lost or stolen cards. To report a lost or stolen American Express card from inside Costa Rica, you can also call ☎ **0-800-012-3211.** To report a lost or stolen **Diners Club** card from inside Costa Rica, call ☎ **506/287-8801,** or call collect ☎ **001-303-799-1504.**

To report lost or stolen American Express traveler's checks within Costa Rica, call ☎ **0-800-011-0080.**

Mail   Mail to the United States usually takes a little over a week to reach its destination. Postage for a postcard is around 18¢; for a letter, 23¢. A post office is called a *correo* in Spanish. You can get stamps at the post office and at some gift shops in large hotels. If you are sending mail to Costa Rica, it generally takes between 10 and 14 days to reach San José, although it can take as much as a month to get to the more remote corners of the country. Plan ahead. Also, note that many hotels and ecolodges have mailing addresses in the United States. Always use these addresses when writing from North America or Europe. Never send cash, checks, or valuables through the Costa Rican mail system.

Maps   The **Costa Rican Tourist Board** (ICT; see "Visitor Information," earlier in this chapter) can usually provide you with good maps of both Costa Rica and San José. See "By Car" under "Getting Around," above, for names of bookstores that sell good maps.

Newspapers/Magazines   There are six Spanish-language dailies in Costa Rica and one English-language weekly, the *Tico Times.* There is also a multilingual tourist weekly, *Central America Weekly.* In addition, you can get *Time, Newsweek,* and several U.S. newspapers at some hotel gift shops and a few of the bookstores in San José. If you understand Spanish, *La Nación* is the paper of record. Its "Viva" section lists what's going on in the world of music, theater, dance, and more.

Passports   See "Passport Information, Entry Requirements, & Customs," earlier in this chapter.

Police   In most cases, you should dial ☎ **911** for the police, and you should be able to get someone who speaks English on the line. Other numbers for the **Judicial Police** are ☎ **506/222-1365** and 506/221-5337. The numbers for the **Traffic Police (Policia de Transito)** are ☎ **506/222-9330** and 506/222-9245.

Radio/TV   There are about 10 local TV channels; cable and satellite TV from the United States are also common. There are scores of radio stations on the AM and FM dials. 107.5 FM is my favorite English-language station, with a wide range of musical programming, as well as news and some talk shows.

Rest Rooms   These are known as *sanitarios, servicios sanitarios,* or *baños.* They are marked *damas* (women) and *hombres* or *caballeros* (men). Public rest rooms are hard to come by. You will almost never find a public rest room in a city park or downtown area. There are usually public rest rooms at most national-park entrances, and much less frequently inside the national park (there are usually plenty of trees and bushes). In the towns and cities it gets much trickier. One must count on the generosity of some hotel or restaurant. Same goes for most beaches. However, most restaurants, and to a lesser degree hotels, will let you use their facilities, especially if you buy a Coke or something. Bus and gas stations often have rest rooms, but in many cases these are quite disgusting.

Safety   Though most of Costa Rica is safe, crime has become much more common in recent years. San José is known for its pickpockets, so never carry a wallet in your back pocket. A woman should keep a tight grip on her purse (keep it tucked under your arm). Thieves also target gold chains, cameras and video cameras, prominent jewelry, and nice sunglasses. Be sure not to leave valuables in your hotel room. Don't park a car on the street in Costa Rica, especially in San José; there are plenty of public parking lots around the city.

Rental cars generally stick out, and they are easily spotted by thieves, who know that such cars are likely to be full of expensive camera equipment, money, and other valuables. Don't ever leave anything of value in a car parked on the street, not even for a moment. Public intercity buses are also frequent targets of stealthy thieves. Never check your bags into the hold of a bus if you can avoid it. If this can't be avoided, keep your eye on what leaves the hold. If you put your bags in an overhead rack, be sure you can see the bags at all times. Try not to fall asleep.

For safety tips while swimming, see "Riptides" under "Health Information," above.

Taxes   All hotels charge 16.3% tax. Restaurants charge 13% tax and also add on a 10% service charge, for a total of 23% more on your bill. There is an airport departure tax of $17.

The **departure tax** is actually a separate little piece of paper that you must fill out (name, passport number, etc.) and that has a few official governmental stamps on the back. The tax/piece of paper is turned in to Immigration after check-in, as you enter the gate area. You must pay this tax prior to departure. You can buy the stamps and little piece of paper at several desks inside the airport, and at some of the individual airline check-in counters. You can also buy them at most travel agencies in San José. I no longer recommend purchasing them from the independent agents roaming around passenger drop-off points at the airport. Although generally safe, there have been instances where they have sold already-canceled stamps, which were then not accepted inside the airport, and the unwitting traveler has had to pay the tax twice.

Taxis   Taxis are common and inexpensive in San José but harder to find and more expensive in rural areas. In San José, taxis are supposed to charge metered fares. Outside of the city and on longer rides, be sure to agree on a price beforehand. For more information on taxis in San José, see "By Taxi" under "Getting Around," in chapter 4.

Telegrams/Wiring Money   Western Union (☎ **800/777-7777** in Costa Rica, or 506/283-6336) has numerous offices around San José and in several major towns and cities around the country. It offers a secure and rapid, although pricey, money wire service, as well as telegram service. A $100 wire will cost around $15, and a $1,000 wire will cost around $50. **Radiográfica** (☎ **506/287-0087**), at Calle 1 and Avenida 5 in San José, also has telegram service.

Telephones/Faxes   Costa Rica has an excellent phone system, with a dial tone similar to that heard in the United States. All phone numbers in Costa Rica have seven digits. For information, dial ☎ **113.** A pay phone costs around 10 colones (3¢) per minute. Pay phones will either take a calling card, or 5-, 10-, or 20-colón coins. Calling cards are becoming more and more prominent, and you can purchase them in a host of gift shops and pharmacies. However, there are several competing calling-card companies and certain cards only work with certain phones. Others work with complicated touch-tone dialing sequences. Moreover, pay phones are generally hard to find and frequently unreliable. It is often best to call from your hotel, although you will likely be charged around 100 colones per call.

For making international calling-card and collect calls, you can reach an **AT&T** operator by dialing ☎ **0-800-011-4114, MCI** by dialing ☎ **0-800-012-2222, Sprint** by dialing ☎ **0-800-013-0123, Canada Bell** by dialing ☎ **0-800-015-1161, British Telephone** by dialing ☎ **0-800-044-1044,** and a **Costa Rican international operator** by dialing ☎ **116** (pay phones may sometimes require a coin deposit). The Costa Rican telephone system allows direct international dialing, but it's expensive. To get an international line, dial 00 followed by the country code (1 for the U.S.) and number.

You can make international phone calls, as well as send faxes, from the **ICE office,** Avenida 2 between calles 1 and 3, in San José (☎ **506/255-0444**). The office is open daily from 7am to 10pm. Faxes cost around $2 per page to the United States. (Many hotels will also offer the same service for a fee.) **Radiográfica** (☎ **506/287-0087**), at Calle 1 and Avenida 5 in San José, also has fax service.

To call Costa Rica from the United States, dial the international access code, 011, followed by the country code 506, then the local number.

Time   Costa Rica is on central standard time (same as Chicago and St. Louis), 6 hours behind Greenwich mean time. Costa Rica does not use daylight saving time, so the time difference is an additional hour from April through October.

Tipping   Tipping is not necessary in restaurants, where a 10% service charge is always added to your bill (along with a 13% tax). If service was particularly good, you can leave a little at your own discretion, but it's not mandatory. Porters and bellhops get around 75¢ per bag. You don't need to tip a taxi driver unless the service has been superior—a tip is not usually expected.

Useful Telephone Numbers   For directory assistance, call ☎ **113;** for international directory assistance, call ☎ **124;** for the exact time, call ☎ **112.**

Visas See "Passport Information, Entry Requirements & Customs," earlier in this chapter.

Water Though the water in San José is said to be safe to drink, water quality varies outside of the city. Because many travelers get sick within a few days of arriving in Costa Rica, I recommend playing it safe and sticking to bottled drinks as much as possible and avoiding ice.

Planning Your Trip: An Online Directory

This Online Directory will help you take better advantage of the travel planning information available online. Section 1 lists general Internet resources that can make any trip easier, such as sites for obtaining the best possible prices on airline tickets. In section 2 you'll find some top online guides specifically for Costa Rica.

Recognition is given to sites based on their content value and ease of use. Inclusion is not paid for—unlike some Web-site rankings, which are based on payment. Finally, remember this is a press-time snapshot of leading Web sites; some undoubtedly will have evolved, changed, or moved by the time you read this.

1 Top Travel-Planning Web Sites

by Lynne Bairstow

Lynne Bairstow is the co-author of *Frommer's Mexico,* and the editorial director of *e-com* magazine.

WHY BOOK ONLINE?

Online agencies have come a long way over the past few years, now providing tips for finding the best fare, and giving you suggested dates or times to travel that yield the lowest price if your plans are at all flexible. Other sites even allow you to establish the price you're willing to pay, and they check the airlines' willingness to accept it. However, in some cases, these sites may not always yield the best price. Unlike a travel agent, for example, they may not have access to charter flights offered by wholesalers.

Online booking sites aren't the only places to reserve airline tickets—all major airlines have their own Web sites and often offer incentives (bonus frequent-flyer miles or Net-only discounts, for example) when you buy online or buy an E-ticket.

The new trend is toward conglomerated booking sites. By mid-2000, a consortium of U.S. and European-based airlines is planning to launch an as-yet unnamed Web site that will offer fares lower than those available through travel agents. United, Delta, Northwest, and Continental have initiated this effort, based on their success at selling airline seats on their own sites.

The best of the travel-planning sites are now highly personalized; they store your seating preferences, meal preferences, tentative

Check Out Frommer's Site

We highly recommend **Arthur Frommer's Budget Travel Online** (**www.frommers.com**) as an excellent travel-planning resource. Of course, we're a little biased, but you'll find indispensable travel tips, reviews, monthly vacation giveaways, and online booking. Among the most popular features of this site are the regular "Ask the Expert" bulletin boards, which feature Frommer's authors answering your questions via online postings.

Subscribe to Arthur Frommer's Daily Newsletter (**www.frommers. com/newsletters**) to receive the latest travel bargains and inside travel secrets in your E-mailbox every day. You'll read daily headlines and articles from the dean of travel himself, highlighting last-minute deals on airfares, accommodations, cruises, and package vacations.

Search our Destinations archive (**www.frommers.com/destinations**) of more than 200 domestic and international destinations for great places to stay and dine, and tips on sightseeing. Once you've researched your trip, the online reservation system (**www.frommers.com/ booktravelnow**) takes you to Frommer's favorite sites for booking your vacation at affordable prices.

itineraries, and credit-card information, allowing you to quickly plan trips or check agendas.

In many cases, booking your trip online can be better than working with a travel agent. It gives you the widest variety of choices, control, and the 24-hour convenience of planning your trip when you choose. All you need is some time—and often a little patience—and you're likely to find the fun of online travel research will greatly enhance your trip.

WHO SHOULD BOOK ONLINE?

Online booking is best for travelers who want to know as much as possible about their travel options, for those who have flexibility in their travel dates, and for bargain hunters.

One of the biggest successes in online travel for both passengers and airlines is the offer of last-minute specials, such as American Airlines' weekend deals or other Internet-only fares that must be purchased online. Another advantage is that you can cash in on incentives for booking online, such as rebates or bonus frequent-flyer miles.

Business and other frequent travelers also have found numerous benefits in online booking, as the advances in mobile technology provide them with the ability to check flight status, change plans, or get specific directions from handheld computing devices, mobile phones, and pagers. Some sites will even E-mail or page a passenger if their flight is delayed.

Online booking is increasingly able to accommodate complex itineraries, even for international travel. The pace of evolution on the Net is rapid, so you'll probably find additional features and advancements by the time you visit these sites. The future holds ever-increasing personalization and customization for online travelers.

Online Directory

TRAVEL-PLANNING & -BOOKING SITES

The following sites offer domestic and international flight, hotel, and rental-car bookings, plus news, destination information, and deals on cruises and vacation packages. Free (one-time) registration is required for booking.

Cheap Tickets. www.cheaptickets.com

Cheap Tickets has exclusive deals that aren't available through more mainstream channels. One caveat about the Cheap Tickets site is that it will offer fare quotes for a route, and later show this fare is not valid for your dates of travel—most other Web sites, such as Expedia, consider your dates of travel before showing what fares are available. Despite its problems, Cheap Tickets can be worth the effort because its fares can be lower than those offered by its competitors.

✪ Expedia. expedia.com

Expedia is known as the fastest and most flexible online travel planner for booking flights, hotels, and rental cars. It offers several ways of obtaining the best possible fares: **Flight Price Matcher** service allowsyour preferred airline to match an available fare with a competitor; a comprehensive **Fare Compare** area shows the differences in fare categories and airlines; and **Fare Calendar** helps you plan your trip around the best possible fares. Its main limitation is that like many online databases, Expedia focuses on the major airlines and hotel chains, so don't expect to find too many budget airlines or one-of-a-kind B&Bs here.

Personalized features allow you to store your itineraries, and receive weekly fare reports on favorite cities. You can also check on the status of flight arrivals and departures, and through MileageMinder, track all of your frequent-flyer accounts.

Expedia also offers packages, cruises, and information on specialized travel (like casino destinations, and adventure, ski, and golf travel). There are also special features for travelers accessing information on mobile devices.

Note: In early 2000, Expedia bought travelscape.com and vacationspot.com, and incorporated these sites into expedia.com.

Travelocity (incorporates Preview Travel). www.travelocity.com; www.previewtravel.com

Travelocity uses the SABRE system to offer reservations and tickets for more than 400 airlines; you can also reserve and purchase from more than 45,000 hotels and 50 car-rental companies. An exclusive feature of the SABRE system is their **Low Fare Search Engine,** which automatically searches for the three lowest-priced itineraries based on a traveler's criteria. Last-minute deals and consolidator fares are included in the search. If you book with Travelocity, you can select specific seats for your flights with online seat maps, and also view diagrams of the most popular commercial aircraft. Their hotel finder provides street-level location maps and photos of selected hotels.

Travelocity features an inviting interface for booking trips, though the wealth of graphics involved can make the site somewhat slow to load, and any adjustment in your parameters means you'll need to completely start over.

This site also has some very cool tools. With the **Fare Watcher** E-mail feature, you can select up to five routes for which you'll receive E-mail notices when the fare changes by $25 or more. If you own an alphanumeric pager with national access that can receive E-mail, Travelocity's **Flight Paging** can alert you if your flight is delayed. You can also access real-time departure and arrival information on any flight within the SABRE system.

Online Directory

More people still look online than book online, partly due to fear of putting their credit-card numbers out on the Net. Secure encryption, and increasing experience buying online, has removed this fear for most travelers. In some cases, however, it's simply easier to buy from a local travel agent who can deliver your tickets to your door (especially if your travel is last-minute or if you have special requests). You can find a flight online and then book it by calling a toll-free number or contacting your travel agent, though this is somewhat less efficient. To be sure you're in secure mode when you book online, look for a little icon of a key (in Netscape) or a padlock (in Internet Explorer) at the bottom of your Web browser.

Note to AOL Users: You can book flights, hotels, rental cars, and cruises on AOL at keyword: Travel. The booking software is provided by Travelocity/Preview Travel and is similar to the Internet site. Use the AOL "Travelers Advantage" program to earn a 5% rebate on flights, hotel rooms, and car rentals.

TRIP.com. www.trip.com

TRIP.com began as a site geared for business travelers, but its innovative features and highly personalized approach have broadened its appeal to leisure travelers as well. It is the leading travel site for those using mobile devices to access Internet travel information.

TRIP.com provides the average and lowest fare for the route requested, in addition to the current available fare. An on-site "newsstand" features breaking news on airfare sales and other travel specials. Among its most popular features are Flight TRACKER and intelliTRIP. **Flight TRACKER** allows users to track any commercial flight en-route to its destination anywhere in the United States, while accessing real-time FAA-based flight monitoring data. **IntelliTRIP** allows you to identify the best airline, hotel, and rental-car fares in less than 90 seconds.

In addition, TRIP.com offers E-mail notification of flight delays, plus city resource guides, currency converters, and a weekly E-mail newsletter of fare updates, travel tips, and traveler forums.

Yahoo Travel. www.travel.yahoo.com

Yahoo is currently the most popular of the Internet information portals, and its travel site is a comprehensive mix of online booking, daily travel news, and destination information. Their **Best Fares** area offers what it promises, and provides feedback on refining your search if you have flexibility in travel dates or times. There is also an active section of Message Boards for discussions on travel in general, and to specific destinations.

LAST-MINUTE DEALS & OTHER ONLINE BARGAINS

There's nothing airlines hate more than flying with lots of empty seats. The Net has enabled airlines to offer last-minute bargains to entice travelers to fill those seats. Most of these are announced on Tuesday or Wednesday and are valid for travel the following weekend, but some can be booked weeks or months in advance. You can sign up for weekly E-mail alerts at the airlines' own sites (see "Getting There," in "Planning Your Trip: The Basics") or check sites that compile lists of these bargains, such as **Smarter Living** or **WebFlyer** (see below). To make it easier, visit a site that will round up all the deals and send them in one convenient weekly E-mail.

Airline Web Sites

Below are the Web sites for the major airlines serving Costa Rica's international airport. These sites offer schedules, flight booking, and most have pages where you can sign up for alerts on weekend deals.

American Airlines: www.aa.com

Continental Airlines: www.flycontinental.com

Delta Airlines: www.delta-air.com

Grupo Taca (includes Lacsa, Taca, and Aviateca): www.grupotaca.com/ing

Mexicana: www.mexicana.com

United Airlines: www.ual.com

Also popular are services that let you name the price you're willing to pay for an air seat or vacation package, and travel auction sites.

Bid for Travel. www.bidfortravel.com
Bid for Travel is another of the travel auction sites, similar to Priceline (see below), which are growing in popularity. In addition to airfares, Internet users can place a bid for vacation packages and hotels.

LastMinuteTravel.com. www.lastminutetravel.com
Suppliers with excess inventory come to this online agency to distribute unsold airline seats, hotel rooms, cruises, and vacation packages. It's got great deals but an excess of advertisements and slow-loading graphics.

Moment's Notice. www.moments-notice.com
As the name suggests, Moment's Notice specializes in last-minute vacation deals. You can browse for free, but if you want to purchase a trip you have to join Moment's Notice, which costs $25.

✪ 1travel.com. www.1travel.com
Here you'll find deals on domestic and international flights and hotels. 1travel. com's **Saving Alert** compiles last-minute air deals so you don't have to scroll through multiple E-mail alerts. A feature called "Drive a little using low-fare airlines" helps map out strategies for using alternate airports to find lower fares. And **Farebeater** searches a database that includes published fares, consolidator bargains, and special deals exclusive to 1travel.com. *Note:* The travel agencies listed by 1travel.com have paid for placement.

✪ Priceline.com. travel.priceline.com
Priceline lets you "name your price" for domestic and international airline tickets and hotel rooms. You select a route and dates, guarantee it with a credit card, and make a bid for what you're willing to pay. If one of the airlines in Priceline's database has a fare lower than your bid, your credit card will automatically be charged for a ticket.

But you can't say when you want to fly—you have to accept any flight leaving between 6am and 10pm on the dates you selected, and you may have to make a stopover. No frequent-flyer miles are awarded, and tickets are nonrefundable and can't be exchanged for another flight. So if your plans change, you're out of luck. Priceline can be good for travelers who have to take off on short notice (and who are thus unable to qualify for advance-purchase discounts). But be sure to shop around first, because if you overbid, you'll be required to purchase the ticket—and Priceline will pocket the difference between what it paid for the ticket and what you bid.

Priceline says that over 35% of all reasonable offers for domestic flights are being filled on the first try, with much higher fill rates on popular routes (New York to San Francisco, for example). They define "reasonable" as not more than 30% below the lowest generally available advance-purchase fare for the same route.

SkyAuction.com. www.skyauction.com
An auction site with categories for airfare, travel deals, hotels, and much more.

Smarter Living. www.smarterliving.com
Best known for its E-mail dispatch of weekend deals on 20 airlines, Smarter Living also keeps you posted about last-minute bargains.

Travelzoo.com. www.travelzoo.com
At this Internet portal, more than 150 travel companies post special deals. It features a Top 20 list of the best deals on the site, selected by its editorial staff each Wednesday night. This list is also available via an E-mailing list, free to those who sign up.

WebFlyer. www.webflyer.com
WebFlyer is a comprehensive online resource for frequent flyers and also has an excellent listing of last-minute air deals. Click on "Deal Watch" for a round-up of weekend deals on flights, hotels, and rental cars from domestic and international suppliers.

HANDY ONLINE TOOLS

CDC Travel Information. www.cdc.gov/travel/index.htm
Health advisories and recommendations for inoculations from the U.S. Centers for Disease Control. The CDC site is good for an overview, but it's best to consult your personal physician to get the latest information on required vaccinations or other health precautions.

✪ Foreign Languages for Travelers. www.travlang.com
Learn basic terms in more than 70 languages and click on any underlined phrase to hear what it sounds like. (*Note:* free audio software and speakers are required.) They also offer hotel and airline finders with excellent prices and a simple system to get the listings you are looking for.

Intellicast. www.intellicast.com
CNN Interactive. www.cnn.com
The Weather Channel. www.weather.com
Weather forecasts for destinations around the world.

Universal Currency Converter. www.xe.net/currency
X-rates. www.x-rates.com
See what your dollar or pound is worth in more than a hundred other countries.

U.S. State Department Travel Warnings. travel.state.gov/travel_warnings. html
Reports on places where health concerns or unrest might threaten U.S. travelers. Keep in mind that these warnings can be somewhat dated and conservative. You can also sign up to receive State Department briefings via E-mail.

Check Your E-mail While You're on the Road

You don't have to be out of touch just because you don't carry a laptop while you travel. Web browser–based free E-mail programs make it much easier to stay in E-touch.

Just open a free-mail account at a browser-based provider, such as **MSN Hotmail** (**hotmail.com**) or **Yahoo! Mail** (**mail.yahoo.com**). AOL users should check out AOL Netmail, and USA.NET (www.usa.net) comes highly recommended for functionality and security. You can find hints, tips, and a mile-long list of free-mail providers at **www.emailaddresses.com**.

Be sure to give your free-mail address to the family members, friends, and colleagues with whom you'd like to stay in touch while you're in Costa Rica. All you'll need to check your free-mail account while you're away from home is a Web connection, easily available at Net cafes. After logging on, just point the browser to **www.hotmail.com**, **www.yahoo.com**, or the address of any other service you're using. Enter your user name and password, and you'll have access to your mail, both for receiving and sending messages to friends and family back home, for just a few dollars an hour. From these sites, you can download all of your E-mail (even from office accounts); there will be a section generally called "check other mail" that allows you to add the names of other E-mail servers.

Many hotels in Costa Rica allow guests to send and receive E-mail. If not, you have a number of options in San José: **Racsa**, Avenida 5 and Calle 1 (☎ 506/287-0087; www.racsa.co.cr); **Cybercafe**, at the Las Arcadas shopping center next to the Gran Hotel Costa Rica (☎ 506/233-3310); **Internet Café**, in Plaza San Pedro (☎ 506/224-7295; www.internetcafecr.com; open 24 hours), with another office in the Centro Colón, on Paseo Colón; and **Browsers Coffee & Internet,** in the Plaza Colonial in Escazú (☎ 506/228-7190), all allow Web and E-mail access. In Manuel Antonio, try **Surf's Up Net Café**, in front of Hotel Sí Como No (☎ 506/777-0777), open daily from 7am to 8pm. Rates at most Internet cafes run between $2 and $10 per hour.

Online Directory

Visa ATM Locator. **www.visa.com/pd/atm/**
MasterCard ATM Locator. **www.mastercard.com/atm**
Find ATMs in hundreds of cities in the United States and around the world. Both include maps for some locations and both list airport ATM locations, some with maps.

2 Top Web Sites for Costa Rica

by Eliot Greenspan

GENERAL GUIDES

Bienvenido a Costa Rica. **www.cr**
A general-interest and tourism site in Spanish.

Costa Rica Accommodations. www.accommodations.co.cr
A well-rounded tourism site, with a list of more than 350 lodging options with separate pages, and sometimes direct links to each hotel. The starred hotels here lead you directly into their own booking system.

Costa Rica Naturally. www.tourism.co.cr
This guide, run by the Costa Rica National Chamber of Tourism, includes a section on adventure travel (mainly surfing, diving, and fishing), bird-watching, and specialty tours (from coffee excursions to helicopter flights). You'll find some listings for rental cars and hotels and a map showing national-park locations.

✪ Costa Rica Supersite: Visitor Center. incostarica.net/centers/visitor
This is an extensive tourism site from *La Nación,* Costa Rica's leading newspaper. It includes basics such as hotels (online booking is available) and rental cars, as well as attractions by region. The "Adventure" section includes pages on rock climbing, diving, surfing, paragliding, and more. Small images are woven into the site and the descriptions usually include E-mail addresses to enable you to easily contact outfitters. The site's search feature can help you narrow your search.

Costa Rica Travel Net. www.centralamerica.com
A solid, basic site with information on hotel, rental cars, tours, and flights within Costa Rica, as well as sections on national parks and the country's 1,000 species of butterflies. The butterfly pages include a virtual tour of Costa Rica's butterfly farm.

Costa Rica Travel Web. www.crica.com
A well-designed, easy-to-use site listing hotels, car rentals, tours, fishing excursions, and other adventures. Although this site doesn't include a comprehensive list of hotels and activities, it does provide nice images and intuitive navigation. Booking is available through an online form or via E-mail. At press time, a note on the site promised a more direct booking solution soon.

Costa Rica Tourism Board. www.tourism-costarica.com
A decent all-around guide to Costa Rica, including slides of its natural wonders, planning information for hotels and car rentals, and tips for enjoying white-water rafting and other adventures. Consider the information on activities an overview—at press time these pages did not have links to outfitters' sites. Also, many of the pages on this site have little to do with travel.

Gay & Lesbian Guide to Costa Rica. hometown.aol.com/GayCRica/ guide.html
This is an extensive guide to gay-friendly establishments and attractions around the country.

✪ Latin America Network Information Center (LANIC). info.lanic. utexas.edu
Hosted by the University of Texas Latin American Studies Department, this site houses a vast collection of diverse information about Costa Rica There are helpful links to a wide range of tourism and general-information sites.

Talamanca Discovery. www.greencoast.com
If you're looking for information on hotels, activities, and attractions along Costa Rica's Caribbean coast, from Puerto Viejo to Manzanillo and the Panamanian border, this is the site.

AOL's Costa Rica area includes updates from Reuters, entry rules and safety tips from the U.S. State Department, and a sound bite of the Costa Rican national anthem. You'll also find a collection of relevant Web sites and AOL access numbers for Costa Rica in case you want to log on while traveling. Perhaps the best part of AOL's Costa Rica resource center is that you can post to the message board or chat live with other members to learn more about the country. Log in to AOL International: Costa Rica, or **AOL Keyword:** Costa Rica.

Tico Travel. www.ticotravel.com
We don't usually include wholesalers, but this site does more than try to hawk tours. The surf map is an excellent resource, and Tico Travel includes fishing trips and other adventures, such as mountain biking up Irazú Volcano.

✪ **Yellow Web Costa Rica. www.yellowweb.co.cr**
The best all-around information site and online guide to Costa Rica that I've found. Information is organized into helpful categories and is quite extensive. This site is tied to www.hotels.co.cr.

NEWSPAPERS & MAGAZINES

La Nación Digital. www.nacion.co.cr
Find out the latest news from Costa Rica's national newspaper's site. Most of the site is in Spanish. They do maintain a small summary of major news items in English, although this section tends to run about a week behind the current events.

La Republica (Spanish). www.larepublica.net
Costa Rica's second leading daily. Entirely in Spanish.

Spiritual Naturalist E-Magazine. www.spiritualnaturalist.com
A new online magazine, featuring articles on indigenous culture, healing arts and retreats, and other New Age topics. Linked to an in-house travel agency.

✪ **The Tico Times. www.ticotimes.co.cr**
The English-language *Tico Times* makes it easy for norteamericanos (and other English speakers) to see what's happening in Costa Rica. There's a travel section here, which publishes selections from their weekly print edition.

ADVENTURE TOURS & OUTFITTERS

Aggressor Fleet. www.aggressor.com
This site has good information about the company's luxury dive tours to Costa Rica's most pristine dive spot, Coco Island.

Canopy Tours. www.canopytour.co.cr
Explore the rain forest from treetop levels. The site includes information on five canopy tours, with some good high-tech graphics that "almost" give you the feel of gliding from tree to tree.

Coast-to-Coast Adventures. www.ctocadventures.com
Learn how you can join a trip going from one coast to the other—without motorized transport. The group also offers valley explorations and kayak schools.

Costa Rica Connection. www.crconnect.com
Offering sample 10-day tours and single-day excursions, this agency can help you plan your Costa Rica vacation. You'll also find information on hotels, rental cars, and short-hop flights within the country.

Costa Rica Expeditions. www.costaricaexpeditions.com
A smorgasbord of natural adventures, from river rafting to birding, as well as photos of the fine hotels that this organization owns.

Horizontes. www.horizontes.com
This is the home of one of Costa Rica's more reputable tour agencies. Tours that let you get up-close and personal with nature are featured here.

International Expeditions. www.ietravel.com/destcentcostanathis.html
In addition to descriptions of its natural-history tours, IE's site offers detailed information on national parks, wildlife, and geography.

Mountain Travel Sobek. www.mtsobek.com
Renowned for its trailblazing trips and superb guides, MTS offers several trips to Costa Rica, but you can't search solely for Costa Rica trips. Try searching by region (Latin America) and the type of activities you enjoy, and see what the search engine turns up.

✪ **Rain-Forest Aerial Tram. www.rainforesttram.com**
Learn about this 90-minute tram ride through the jungle canopy, which helps promote conservation in Costa Rica. The site has terrific images, including QuickTime panoramas (free software required). You can also find visitor information and book tickets online.

Ríos Tropicales. www.riostro.com
Learn about white-water rafting and sea-kayak tours on the country's most exciting rivers. Includes descriptions, images, prices, and river reports.

Selva Mar. www.chirripo.com
Great information on climbing Mount Chirripó and exploring Chirripó National Park, including trail maps, 3-D maps, and elevation maps. Selva Mar runs guided trips to the top of the mountain and around the southern Pacific region.

Serendipity Adventures. www.serendipityadventures.com
Focusing on small group adventures, Serendipity offers challenges for mind and body in trips ranging from kayaking to mountain biking.

Tam Travel. www.tamtravel.com
This is the home of another long-standing and reputable Costa Rican travel agency. A broad selection of tours, to rain forests, volcanoes, and beaches, as well as a host of day trips from San José.

EDUCATIONAL & VOLUNTEER TRAVEL

For more details and listings of Spanish Language schools and their Web sites, see "Spanish Language Programs" in chapter 2. For more information on volunteer and ecological study programs, see "Ecologically Oriented Volunteer & Study Programs" in chapter 3.

AmeriSpan Unlimited. www.amerispan.com
Organizes both study and volunteer programs in Costa Rica and other Latin-American countries.

Online Directory

Eco Teach. **www.ecoteach.com**

Works arranging educational travel to Costa Rica with an ecological focus for teachers, students, and groups. They also organize volunteer projects and place volunteers within the Costa Rican school system.

Global Volunteers. **www.globalvolunteers.org**

This group offers short-term service projects, such as a 2-week construction project in the Monteverde cloud-forest area.

Spanish-Language Schools in Costa Rica. **www.westnet.com/costarica/ education.html**

This site lists about two dozen schools with links to each of the schools' own Web sites.

Vida. **www.vida.org**

Working in conjunction with the organization Youth Service International, Vida places volunteers in several of Costa Rica's national parks.

TRAVELOGUES

Sometimes a perception is worth a thousand facts. The following two sites host a variety of travelogues written by fellow travelers who have visited Costa Rica.

Nuevo Mundo. **www.nvmundo.com/travelogues**

Rec. Travel Library. **www.travel-library.com**

The Active Vacation Planner **3**

Although it's possible to come to Costa Rica and stay clean and dry, most visitors want to spend some time getting their hair wet, their feet muddy, and their adrenaline pumping. To many, tropical rain forests and cloud forests are the stuff of myth and legend. Partly because evolution is a slow process, and partly because much of the country's natural landscape is protected in national parks and bioreserves, Costa Rica's primary forests, which are open to adventurous travelers, are still in much the same state as when early explorers such as Columbus found them. Along the coasts and just offshore, there is an equal number of options for the active traveler.

As awareness of the value of tropical forests and interest in visiting them have grown, dozens of lodges and tour companies have sprung up to cater to travelers interested in enjoying the natural beauties of Costa Rica. These lodges are usually situated in out-of-the-way locations, sometimes deep in the heart of a forest and sometimes on a farm with only a tiny bit of natural forest. However, they all have one thing in common: They cater to environmentally aware people with an interest in nature and offer such activities as bird-watching, rafting, kayaking, horseback riding, and hiking. For detailed listings of these lodges, many of which offer special packages, see the "Accommodations" and "Dining" sections of the regional chapters that follow (chapters 4 through 9).

There are myriad approaches to planning an active vacation in Costa Rica. This chapter lays out your options, from tour operators who run multiactivity package tours that often include stays at ecolodges, to the best places in Costa Rica to pursue active endeavors (with listings of tour operators, guides, and outfitters that specialize in each), to an overview of the country's national parks and bioreserves, with suggestions on how to plan your itinerary. After a few tips on health and safety in the wilderness, the chapter closes with a list of educational and volunteer travel options for those with a little more time on their hands and a desire to actively assist Costa Rica in the maintenance and preservation of its natural wonders.

1 Organized Adventure Trips

Since many travelers have limited time and resources, organized eco-tourism or adventure travel packages, arranged by tour operators in the United States or Costa Rica, are a popular way of combining several activities. Bird-watching, horseback riding, rafting, and hiking can be teamed with, say, visits to Monteverde Biological Cloud Forest Preserve and Manuel Antonio National Park.

Traveling with a group has several advantages over traveling independently: Your accommodations and transportation are arranged, and most (if not all) of your meals are included in the cost of a package. If your tour operator has a reasonable amount of experience and a decent track record, you should proceed to each of your destinations quickly without the snags and long delays that those traveling on their own can face. You'll also have the opportunity to meet like-minded souls who are interested in nature and active sports. Of course, you'll pay more for the convenience of having all your arrangements handled in advance.

In the best cases, group size is kept small (between 10 and 20 people), and tours are escorted by knowledgeable guides who are either naturalists or biologists. Be sure to ask about difficulty levels when you're choosing a tour. While most companies offer "soft-adventure" packages that those in moderately good, but not phenomenal, shape can handle, others focus on more hard-core activities geared toward only seasoned athletes or adventure travelers. For more information, see "Package Tours" under "Getting There," in chapter 2.

U.S.-BASED ADVENTURE TOUR OPERATORS

These agencies and operators specialize in well-organized and coordinated tours that cover your entire stay. Many travelers prefer to have everything arranged and confirmed before arriving in Costa Rica, and this is a good idea for first-timers and during the high season. Be warned: Most of these operators are not cheap, with 10-day tours generally costing a little over $2,000 per person, not including airfare to Costa Rica.

Abercrombie & Kent, 1520 Kensington Rd., Oak Brook, IL 60521 (☎ 800/ 323-7308; fax 630/954-3324; www.abercrombiekent.com), is a premier luxury tour company that has added several tours of Costa Rica to its menu. One interesting option offered by this outfitter is the 10-day family vacation, which hits San José, Arenal, Monteverde, and Manuel Antonio. In addition to a naturalist guide, the trip carries a children's activity coordinator and offers baby-sitting at all of the hotels visited. The cost is $3,250 per adult, $2,600 per child.

Costa Rica Connections, 975 Oso St., San Luis Obispo, CA 93401 (☎ 800/ 345-7422 or 805/543-8823; www.crconnect.com; E-mail: crconnec@crconnect.com), specializes in natural-history tours of major national parks. There is a complete range of independent packages and scheduled group departures for fishing, ecotourism, kayaking/rafting, and dive trips, plus a special family-oriented package.

International Expeditions, 1 Environs Park, Helena, AL 35080 (☎ 800/ 633-4734 or 205/428-1700; www.ietravel.com; E-mail: nature@ietravel.com), specializes in independent programs and 10-day natural-history group tours.

Journeys International, 4011 Jackson Rd., Ann Arbor, MI 48103 (☎ 800/ 255-8735 or 734/665-4407; www.journeys-intl.com; E-mail: info@journeys-intl.com), offers small-group (no more than 4 to 12 people) natural-history tours guided by Costa Rican naturalists. Eight-day, 10-day, and 3-week itineraries are available.

Mountain Travel-Sobek, 6420 Fairmount Ave., El Cerrito, CA 94530 (☎ 888/ MTSOBEK or 510/527-8100; fax 510/525-7718; www.mtsobek.com; E-mail: info@ mtsobek.com), offers natural-history tours with naturalist guides. Ten-day itineraries can include visits to Corcovado and Tortuguero national parks, Monteverde, and Arenal Volcano; activities include jungle walks, boat rides, snorkeling, and swimming. You'll spend your nights in nature lodges or out camping, with the exception of the first and last nights of each itinerary, which are spent in hotels in San José.

Overseas Adventure Travel, 625 Mount Auburn, Cambridge, MA 02138 (☎ 800/493-6824; www.oattravel.com; info@oattravel.com), offers natural-history and "soft-adventure" 10- and 12-day itineraries, with optional 3-day add-on excursions. Tours are limited to no more than 16 people and are guided by naturalists. All accommodations are in small hotels, lodges, or tent camps. Itineraries include visits to most major national parks and private nature reserves.

Wilderness Travel, 1102 Ninth St., Berkeley, CA 94710 (☎ 800/368-2794 or 510/558-2488; www.wildernesstravel.com; E-mail: webinfo@wildernesstravel.com), specializes in 14-day natural history and bird-watching group tours. The cost of the trip goes down as the size of the group goes up (minimum 6 people, maximum 15). Tours include visits to Corcovado and Tortuguero national parks, Monteverde, Arenal Volcano, and Caño Negro National Wildlife Refuge, among other destinations.

In addition to these companies, many environmental organizations, including the **Sierra Club** (☎ 415/977-5500; www.sierraclub.org; E-mail: information@ sierraclub.org), the **Nature Conservancy** (☎ 800/628-6860; www.tnc.org), the **Smithsonian Institute** (☎ 202/357-2700; www.si.edu), and the **National Audubon Society** (☎ 800/274-4201 or 212/979-3000; www.audubon.org), regularly offer organized trips to Costa Rica.

COSTA RICAN TOUR AGENCIES

Since many U.S.-based companies subcontract portions of their tours to established Costa Rican companies, some travelers like to set up their tours directly with these companies, thereby cutting out the middleman. While that means these packages are often less expensive than those offered by U.S. companies, it doesn't mean they are cheap. You're still paying for the convenience of having all your arrangements handled for you.

There are scores of agencies in San José that offer a plethora of adventure options. These agencies can arrange everything from white-water rafting to sightseeing at one of the nearby volcanoes or a visit to a butterfly farm. While it's generally quite easy to arrange a day trip at the last minute, other tours are offered only when there are enough interested people or on set dates. It pays to contact a few of the companies before you leave the United States and find out what they might be doing when you arrive.

Costa Rica Expeditions, Dept. 235, P.O. Box 025216, Miami, FL 33102 (☎ 506/257-0766 or 506/222-0333; fax 506/257-1665; www.costaricaexpeditions. com; E-mail: costaric@expeditions.co.cr), offers everything from 10-day tours covering the whole country, to 3-day/2-night and 2-day/1-night tours of Monteverde Biological Cloud Forest Preserve, Tortuguero National Park, and Corcovado National Park, where they run their own lodges. They also offer 1- to 2-day white-water rafting trips and other excursions. All excursions include transportation, meals, and lodging. Their tours are some of the most expensive in the country, but they are the most consistently reliable outfitter as well (and their customer service is excellent). If you want to go out on your own, Costa Rica Expeditions can supply you with just transportation from place to place.

Costa Rica Sun Tours, Apdo. 1195-1250, Escazú, Costa Rica (☎ 506/255-3418; fax 506/255-3529; E-mail: suntours@racsa.co.cr), specializes in multiday tours that include stays at small country lodges for nature-oriented travelers. Destinations include Arenal Volcano, with stays at the Arenal Observatory Lodge; Monteverde Cloud Forest, with stops in Poás and Sarchí; and Corcovado and Manuel Antonio national parks, with overnight stays at Tiskita Jungle Lodge, Corcovado Tent Camp, Lapa Ríos, and Drake Bay Wilderness Lodge, among other accommodations.

Coast to Coast Adventures, Apdo. 2135-1002, San José, Costa Rica (☎ **506/ 225-6055;** fax 506/225-7806; www.ctocadventures.com; E-mail: info@ctocadventures. com), has a unique excursion in which no motor vehicles are involved. The company's namesake 2-week trip spans the country, traveling on horses and rafts, by mountain bikes, and on foot. Custom-designed trips (with a minimum of motorized transport) of shorter duration are also available.

Ecole Travel, Calle 7 between avenidas Central and 1, San José, Costa Rica (☎ **506/223-2240;** fax 506/223-4128; E-mail: ecolecr@racsa.co.cr), offers a range of economical tours and day trips around the country. This operator works primarily with student and European travelers. While they often use their own guides for longer trips, many of their day trips are subcontracted out. Their tours are most popular with students and European travelers, including a fair amount of backpackers.

Fantasy Tours, Apdo. 962-1000, San José, Costa Rica (☎ **800/272-6654** in the U.S., 800/453-6654 in Canada, or 506/220-2126 in Costa Rica; fax 506/220-2393; www.fantasy.co.cr; E-mail: info@fantasy.co.cr), is not a specifically adventure-oriented operator. They do offer a comprehensive list of full-day tours to destinations that include Arenal Volcano and Tabacón Hot Springs, Poás and Irazú volcanoes, Manuel Antonio National Park, Carara Biological Reserve, and Bosque de Paz, a private biological reserve. White-water rafting expeditions, fishing trips, island cruises, and multiday tours are also available. Some of their tours, however, have a cattle-car feel to them.

✪ **Horizontes,** Calle 28 between avenidas 1 and 3 (☎ **506/222-2022;** fax 506/ 255-4513; www.horizontes.com; E-mail: horizont@racsa.co.cr), again, not a specifically adventure-oriented operator, offers a wide range of individual, group, and package tours and generally hire responsible and knowledgeable guides.

OTEC Viajes, Apdo. 323-1002, San José, Costa Rica (☎ **506/256-0633;** fax 506/ 233-2321; www.gotec.com; E-mail: otec@gotec.com), offers a range of tour options and specializes in student and discount travel.

Serendipity Adventures, Apdo. 76 CATIE, Turrialba, Costa Rica (☎ **800/ 635-2325** and fax 734/426-5026 in the U.S., or 506/556-2592; fax 506/556-2593; www.serendipityadventures.com; E-mail: costarica@serendipityadventures.com), an adventure travel operator, offers everything from ballooning to mountain biking, sea kayaking to canyoning, as well as most of the popular white-water rafting trips.

Sin Límites, Calle 35 and Avenida Central, 200 meters (218 yd.) east of the Kentucky Fried Chicken in Los Yoses (☎ **506/280-5182;** fax 506/225-9325), specializes in student and discount travel.

2 Activities A to Z

Each listing in this section describes the best places to practice a particular sport or activity and lists tour operators and outfitters. If you want to focus on only one active sport during your Costa Rican stay, these companies are your best bets for quality equipment and knowledgeable service.

BIKING

There are several significant regional and international touring races in Costa Rica each year, but as a general rule the major roads are dangerous and inhospitable for cyclists. They're narrow, there's usually no shoulder, and most drivers show little care or consideration for those on two wheels. The options are much more appealing for mountain bikers and off-track riders, however. Fat-tire explorations are relatively new to Costa Rica but growing fast. If you plan to do a lot of biking and are very attached to your rig, bring your own. However, several companies in San José and elsewhere rent bikes, and the quality of the equipment is improving all the time. See the regional chapters for rental listings.

The area around **Lake Arenal** and **Arenal Volcano** wins my vote as the best place for mountain biking in Costa Rica. The scenery's great, with primary forests, waterfalls, and plenty of trails. And nearby Tabacón Hot Springs is a perfect place for those with aching muscles to unwind at the end of the day. (See chapter 6.)

TOUR OPERATORS & OUTFITTERS

Aguas Bravas, P.O. Box 1504-2100, Costa Rica (☎ **506/292-2072;** fax 506/229-4837; www.aguas-bravas.co.cr; E-mail: info@aguas-bravas.co.cr), has a range of mountain-biking trips and is a particularly good bet in La Fortuna.

Coast to Coast Adventures, Apdo. 2135-1002, San José, Costa Rica (☎ **506/225-6055;** fax 506/225-7806; www.ctocadventures.com; E-mail: info@ctocadventures.com), offers mountain-biking itineraries among its many tour options.

Experience Plus/Specialty Tours, 415 Mason Ct. #1, Ft. Collins, CO 80524 (☎ **800/685-4565;** www.xplus.com; E-mail: tours@xplus.com), offers guided group and assisted individual bike tours around the country. This is the only company I know of to use touring bikes. They also offer guided group hiking tours.

Frontiers Spirited Adventures, P.O. Box 8070, St. Paul, MN 55108 (☎ **877/603-1989;** www.spiritedadventures.com; E-mail: frontiers@spiritedadventures.com), runs guided multiday mountain-biking trips around Costa Rica.

Serendipity Adventures, Apdo. 76 CATIE, Turrialba, Costa Rica (☎ **800/635-2325** and fax 734/426-5026 in the U.S., or 506/556-2592; fax 506/556-2593; www.serendipityadventures.com; E-mail: costarica@serendipityadventures.com), offers several mountain-biking trips among its many other expeditions.

BIRD-WATCHING

With more than 850 species of resident and migrant birds identified throughout the country, Costa Rica abounds with great bird-watching sites. Lodges with the best bird-watching include **Savegre Lodge,** in Cerro de la Muerte, off the road to San Isidro de El General (quetzal sightings are almost guaranteed); **La Paloma Lodge** in Drake Bay (where you can sit on the porch of your cabin as the avian parade goes by); **Villablanca** in San Ramón (on the edge of a cloud-forest reserve where quetzals are often seen); **Arenal Observatory Lodge** on the flanks of Arenal Volcano; **La Selva Biological Station** in Puerto Viejo de Sarapiquí; **Aviarios del Caribe** just north of Cahuita; **Lapa Ríos** and **Bosque del Cabo** on the Osa Peninsula; **Rainbow Adventures** on Playa Cativa along the Golfo Dulce; **La Laguna del Lagarto Lodge** up by the Nicaraguan border; and **Tiskita Lodge** down by the Panamanian border.

Some of the best parks and preserves to visit are **Monteverde Biological Cloud Forest Preserve** (for resplendent quetzals and hummingbirds); **Corcovado National Park** (for scarlet macaws); **Caño Negro Wildlife Refuge** (for wading birds, including jabiru storks); **Wilson Botanical Gardens** and the **Las Cruces Biological Station,** near San Vito (the thousands of flowering plants here are bird magnets); **Guayabo, Negritos,** and **Pájaros islands biological reserves** in the Gulf of Nicoya (for magnificent frigate birds and brown boobies); **Palo Verde National Park** (for ibises, jacanas, storks, and roseate spoonbills); **Tortuguero National Park** (for great green macaws); and **Rincón de la Vieja National Park** (for parakeets and curassows). Rafting trips down the Corobicí and Bebedero rivers near Liberia, boat trips to or at Tortuguero National Park, and hikes in any cloud forest also provide good bird-watching.

A Bird-Watcher's Bible

Any serious bird-watcher will find *A Guide to the Birds of Costa Rica,* by F. Gary Stiles and Alexander Skutch (Comstock Publishing Associates, a Division of Cornell University Press; Ithaca, NY, 1994), to be essential. For more casual enthusiasts, there's a series of laminated plates covering specific regions, which you'll find for sale at many local bookstores and some gift shops.

U.S. TOUR OPERATORS

Field Guides, 9433 Bee Cave Rd., Building 1, Suite 150, Austin, TX 78733 (☎ 800/728-4953 or 512/263-7295; fax 512/263-0117; www.fieldguides.com; E-mail: fgileader@aol.com), is a specialty bird-watching travel operator. The 16-day tour of Costa Rica costs $3,200, not including airfare. Group size is limited to 14 participants.

Wings, 1643 N. Alvernon Way, Suite 105, Tucson, AZ 85712 (☎ **520/320-9868;** fax 520/320-9373; www.wingsbirds.com; E-mail: wings@wingsbirds.com), is also a specialty bird-watching travel operator with more than 27 years of experience in the field. The 17-day Costa Rica trip covers all the major bird-watching zones in the country and costs around $3,500, not including airfare. Trip size is usually between 6 and 18 people.

COSTA RICAN TOUR AGENCIES

In addition to the agencies listed below, check in with the **Birding Club of Costa Rica** (☎ **506/267-7197**), which runs regular outings and provides you with the opportunity to connect with local birders.

Both **Costa Rica Expeditions,** Dept. 235, P.O. Box 025216, Miami, FL 33102 (☎ **506/257-0766** or 506/222-0333; fax 506/257-1665; www.costaricaexpeditions. com; E-mail: costaric@expeditions.co.cr), and **Costa Rica Sun Tours,** Apdo. 1195-1250, Escazú, Costa Rica (☎ **506/255-3418;** fax 506/255-3529; E-mail: suntours@ racsa.co.cr), are well-established companies with very competent and experienced guides who offer a variety of tours to some of the better birding spots in Costa Rica.

BUNGEE JUMPING & BALLOONING

Both of these sports are new to Costa Rica, so as yet there's only one operator who specializes in each activity. The price you'll pay is generally cheaper than in the United States, and the scenery is certainly more lush.

Tropical Bungee, A.P. 1247-1007, San José, Costa Rica (☎ **506/232-3956;** www.bungee.co.cr; E-mail: bungee@bungee.co.cr), will let you jump off a 265-foot bridge over the Río Colorado for $45; if you want to do it twice, the cost is $70. They are physically located on a small bridge over the Rio Colorado about 23 miles northwest of San Jose, just off the Pan American Highway. There are obvious and well-placed signs on the highway. Someone will be there from 9am to 3pm every day

Serendipity Adventures, Apdo. 76 CATIE, Turrialba, Costa Rica (☎ **800/ 635-2325** and fax 734/426-5026 in the U.S., or 506/556-2592; fax 506/556-2593; www.serendipityadventures.com; E-mail: costarica@serendipityadventures.com), will take you up, up, and away in a hot-air balloon on a variety of single- or multiday tours, either in Turrialba, Naranjo, or near Arenal Volcano. A basic flight costs $900 for up to five people or 800 pounds.

Where to See the Resplendent Quetzal

Revered by pre-Columbian cultures throughout Central America, the Resplendent Quetzal has been called the most beautiful bird on earth. Ancient Aztec and Maya Indians believed that the robin-size quetzal protected them in battle. The males of this species have brilliant red breasts; iridescent emerald green heads, backs, and wings; and white tail feathers complemented by a pair of iridescent green tail feathers that are nearly 2 feet long.

The belief that these endangered birds live only in the dense cloud forests cloaking the higher slopes of Central America's mountains was instrumental in bringing many areas of cloud forest under protection as quetzal habitats; since then, researchers have recently discovered that the birds do not in fact spend their entire lives here. After nesting, between March and July, Resplendent Quetzals migrate down to lower slopes in search of food. These lower slopes have not been preserved in most cases, and now conservationists are trying to salvage enough lower-elevation forests to help the quetzals survive. It is hoped that enough land will soon be set aside to ensure the perpetuation of this magnificent species.

Though for many years **Monteverde Biological Cloud Forest Preserve** was *the* place to see quetzals, throngs of people crowding the preserve's trails now make the pursuit more difficult. Other places where you can see quetzals are in the **Los Angeles Cloud Forest Reserve** near San Ramón, in **Tapantí National Wildlife Refuge**, and in **Chirripó National Park.** Perhaps the best place to spot a quetzal is at one of the specialized lodges located along the Cerro de la Muerte between San José and San Isidro de El General.

CAMPING

Heavy rains, difficult access, and limited facilities make camping a real challenge in Costa Rica. Nevertheless, a backpack and tent will get you far from the crowds and into some of the most pristine and undeveloped nooks and crannies of the country. Those who relish sleeping out on a beach but wouldn't mind a bit more luxury (beds, someone to prepare meals for you, and running water) might want to consider staying in one of the tent camps on the **Osa Peninsula** (Drake Bay Wilderness Resort or Corcovado Lodge Tent Camp) or down in **Manzanillo** (Almendros and Corales Tent Camp). See chapters 8 and 9 for details. Camping is forbidden in some national parks, so read through the descriptions for each park carefully before you pack a tent.

If you'd like to participate in an organized camping trip, contact **Coast to Coast Adventures,** Apdo. 2135-1002, San José, Costa Rica (☎ **506/225-6055;** fax 506/225-7806; www.ctocadventures.com; E-mail: info@ctocadventures.com), or **Serendipity Adventures,** Apdo. 76 CATIE, Turrialba, Costa Rica (☎ **800/635-2325** and fax 734/426-5026 in the U.S., or 506/556-2592; fax 506/556-2593; www.serendipityadventures.com; E-mail: costarica@serendipityadventures.com).

Another option is to hook up with a **Green Tortoise** (☎ **800/867-8647** or 415/956-7500 in the U.S.; E-mail: info@greentortoise.com) tour of Costa Rica. This bus tour/camping outfit runs around five trips each year to Costa Rica, with a 15-day tour of the country costing around $520, not including transportation to Costa Rica.

In my opinion, the best place to pop up a tent on the beach is in **Santa Rosa National Park,** or at the Puerto Vargas campsite in **Cahuita National Park.** The best camping trek is, without a doubt, a hike through **Corcovado National Park,** or a climb up **Mount Chirripó.**

CANOPY TOURS

Canopy tours are taking off in Costa Rica, largely because they are such a unique way to experience tropical rain forests. It's estimated that some two-thirds of a typical rain forest's species live in the canopy (the uppermost, branching layer of the forest). From the relative luxury of Aerial Tram's high-tech funicular to the rope-and-climbing-gear rigs of more basic operations, a trip into the canopy will give you a bird's-eye view of a neotropical forest. There are now canopy tour facilities in Monteverde, Aguas Zarcas (near San Carlos), Villablanca, Playa Hermosa, and Rincón de la Vieja, as well as on Tortuga Island, around the Osa Peninsula, and at the Iguana Park.

With the exception of the Aerial Tram, most canopy tours involve strapping yourself into a climbing harness and being winched up to a platform some 100 feet above the forest floor, or doing the work yourself. Many of these operations have a series of treetop platforms connected by taut cables. Once up on the first platform, you click your harness into a pulley and glide across the cable to the next (slightly lower) platform, using your hand (protected by a thick leather glove) as a brake. When you reach the last platform, you usually rappel back down to the ground (don't worry, they'll teach even the most nervous neophyte).

Be careful, canopy tours are quite the rage and there is no regulation on the activity. Some of the tours being set up are quite fly-by-night operations. Obviously, I haven't listed any of those. But please make sure you feel comfortable and confident with the operator, and be sure to ask around and check them out first. The most reputable operator is **The Original Canopy Tours** (see below), but there are other safe, well-run operations around the country. My favorite canopy tour is the Original Canopy Tour's operation in **Monteverde,** where the ascent goes up the inside of a strangler fig, in the space where the host tree once lived. Before you sign on to any tour, ask whether you have to hoist yourself to the top under your own steam, then make your decision accordingly.

Aerial Tram, Apdo. 1959-1002, San José, Costa Rica (☎ **506/257-5961;** fax 506/257-6053; www.rainforesttram.com; E-mail: info@rainforesttram.com), is located 50 minutes from San José. For $49.50 (transportation extra), this modern tram takes you on a 90-minute trip through the rain-forest canopy in the comfort and safety of an enclosed cab. The entrance fee includes an additional guided hike.

The Original Canopy Tours, Interlink 227, P.O. Box 025635, Miami, FL 33152 (☎ and fax **506/257-5149** or 506/256-7626; www.canopytour.com; E-mail: canopy@racsa.co.cr), is the largest canopy-tour), operator, with sites in Monteverde, Aguas Zarcas, Rincón de la Vieja, and Iguana Park.

CRUISING

Cruising options in Costa Rica range from transient cruisers setting up a quick charter business to converted fishing boats taking a few guests out to see the sunset. For information on the major cruise lines that ply the waters off of Costa Rica, see "By Cruise Ship" under "Getting There," in chapter 2.

One popular cruise is a day trip from San José (the boats actually leave from Puntarenas) to Isla Tortuga in the Nicoya Gulf (see "Side Trips from San José" in chapter 4). Alternately, you can book a cruise to Tortuga from Playa Montezuma at the tip of the Nicoya Peninsula (see chapter 5 for details). It's much cheaper from here (around $35 per person), but the excursion doesn't include the gourmet lunch that's usually featured on cruises leaving from San José.

Beach Blanket, Bingo

If you plan on spending time at the beach, make sure to pack your own beach towel or blanket. Your hotel is unlikely to provide one for you.

___

One interesting recent entry into the Costa Rican cruising scene is the **Windstar Cruise** line's (☎ **800/258-7245;** www.windstarcruises.com) 148-passenger, four-masted sail-assist cruise ship, *Wind Song,* which leaves out of Caldera on weeklong trips. A weeklong cruise runs between $2,500 and $3,500 per person.

Another option is to take a cruise on the *Temptress.* This small cruise ship plies the waters off Costa Rica's Pacific coast from Santa Rosa National Park in the north to Corcovado National Park in the south. The ship has no pool or casino, but it does usually anchor in remote, isolated, and very beautiful spots. Each day you can choose between a natural-history tour or a recreational and cultural tour. For information, contact **Temptress Cruises,** 140 E. 56th St., New York, NY, 10022 (☎ **800/255-3585** in the U.S.; 506/220-1679 in Costa Rica; www.temptresscruises.org; E-mail: sales@temptresscruises.org). Weeklong cruises run between $1,600 and $2,700 per person.

If diesel fumes and engine noise bother you, the best places to charter a sailboat are in Playa del Coco, Playa Hermosa, and Playa Flamingo in Guanacaste province (see chapter 5); Playa Herradura and Quepos, along the central Pacific coast (see chapter 7); and Golfito, along the southern Pacific coast (see chapter 8). You can get information about sailboat rides at any one of the larger lodgings in these areas. If you're at Flamingo Beach, head to the marina, where you should be able to find a captain who will take you out. My favorite place to charter a sailboat is **Golfito.** From here, it's a pleasant, peaceful day's sail around the Golfo Dulce (see chapter 8).

DIVING & SNORKELING

Many islands, reefs, caves, and rocks lie off the coast of Costa Rica, providing excellent spots for underwater exploration. Visibility varies with season and location. Generally, heavy rainfall tends to swell the rivers and muddy the waters, even well offshore. Banana plantations and their runoff have destroyed most of the Caribbean reefs, although there's still good diving at Isla Uvita, just off the coast of Limón, and in Manzanillo, down near the Panamanian border. Most divers choose Pacific dive spots like Caño Island, Bat Island, and the Catalina Islands, where you're likely to spot manta rays, moray eels, white-tipped sharks, and plenty of smaller fish and coral species. But the ultimate in Costa Rican dive experiences is a week to 10 days spent on a chartered boat, diving off the coast of Coco Island.

Snorkeling is not incredibly common or rewarding in Costa Rica. The rain, runoff, and wave conditions that drive scuba divers well offshore tend to make coastal and shallow water conditions less than optimum. If the weather is calm and the water is clear, you might just get lucky. Ask at your hotel or check the different beach listings to find snorkeling options and operators up and down Costa Rica's coasts.

SCUBA-DIVING OUTFITTERS & OPERATORS

In addition to the companies listed below, check the listings at specific beach and port destinations in the regional chapters.

Aggressor Fleet Limited, P.O. Box 1470, Morgan City, LA 70381-1470 (☎ **800/348-2628** or 504/385-2628; fax 504/384-0817; www.aggressor.com; E-mail: divboat@aol.com), runs the 120-foot *Okeanos Aggressor* on regular trips out to Coco Island.

Diving Safaris de Costa Rica, Apdo. 121-5019, Playa del Coco, Costa Rica (☎ **800/779-0055** in the U.S., or 506/672-0012; fax 506/672-0231; www. costaricadiving.net; E-mail: diving@racsa.co.cr), is perhaps the largest, most professional, and best-established dive operation in the country. Based out of the Sol Playa Hermosa Hotel in Playa Hermosa, this outfitter is also a local pioneer in nitrox diving.

Mundo Aquatico, Apdo. 7875-1000, San José, Costa Rica (☎ **506/224-9729;** fax 506/234-2982; E-mail: mundoac@racsa.co.cr), offers equipment rental, certification classes, and tours. Tours go to Catalina and Bat islands, as well as to Isla del Caño.

Undersea Hunter, Undersea Hunter, A.P. 310-1260, Plaza Colonial, Escazú, Costa Rica (☎ **800/203-2120** in the U.S., or ☎ 506/228-6613 in Costa Rica; www.underseahunter.com; E-mail: info@underseahunter.com), offers the *Undersea Hunter* and its sister ship the *Sea Hunter,* two pioneers of the live-aboard diving excursions to Coco Island.

FISHING

Anglers in Costa Rican waters have landed more than 65 world-record catches, including blue marlin, Pacific sailfish, dolphin, wahoo, yellowfin tuna, guapote, and snook. Whether you want to head offshore looking for a big sail, wrestle a tarpon near a Caribbean river mouth, or choose a quiet spot on Arenal Lake to cast for guapote, you'll find it here. You can land a marlin anywhere along the Pacific coast.

Many of the Pacific port and beach towns—Quepos, Puntarenas, Playa del Coco, Tamarindo, Flamingo, Golfito, Drake Bay, Zancudo—support large charter fleets and have hotels that cater to anglers; see chapters 5, 7, and 8 for recommended boats, captains, and lodges. Costs for fishing trips usually range between $400 and $1,500 per day (depending on the size of the boat) for boat, captain, tackle, drinks, and lunch.

Richard Krug writes a fishing column for the *Tico Times* and offers a wide body of knowledge about fishing. He can arrange and book tours, as well as provide useful advice. Ask for Richard at **Americana Fishing Services,** SJO 795, P.O. Box 025216, Miami, FL 33102 (☎ **888/651-6999** in the U.S., or 506/223-4331 in Costa Rica; fax 506/221-0096; E-mail: rkrug@costarica.net).

Costa Rica Outdoors, SJO 2316, P.O. Box 025216, Miami, FL 33102 (☎ **800/ 308-3394** in the U.S., or 506/282-6743; fax 506/282-7241; E-mail: jruhlow@ racsa.co.cr), is another well-established operation, run by longtime resident, fisherman, and outdoor writer, Jerry Ruhlow.

FISHING LODGES

For more detailed information about these lodges, see their full listings in chapters 8 and 9.

✪ **Aguila De Osa Inn** (mailing address in the U.S.: Isla Fantasma, Interlink #898, P.O. Box 025635, Miami, FL 33102; ☎ and fax **506/296-2190** or 506/232-7722; www.aguiladeosa.com; E-mail: reserve@aguiladeosa.com), is a luxury lodge catering to anglers in Drake Bay. See chapter 8.

Río Colorado Lodge, P.O. Box 5094-1000, San José (☎ **800/243-9777** in the U.S. and Canada, or 506/232-4063 in Costa Rica; fax 506/231-5987; www. riocoloradolodge.com; E-mail: tarpon@racsa.co.cr). Located at the Barra del Colorado National Wildlife Refuge. See chapter 9.

Roy's Zancudo Lodge, Apdo. 41, Playa Zancudo, Golfito (☎ **800/515-7697** in the U.S., or 506/776-0008; fax 506/776-0011; www.royszancudo.com; E-mail: rroig@ golfito.net), is located in Playa Zancudo. See chapter 8.

✪ **Silver King Lodge** (mailing address in the U.S.: Interlink 399, P.O. Box 02-5635, Miami, FL 33102; ☎ **800/847-3474,** or 800/309-8125 in the U.S., or

506/381-1403 in Costa Rica; fax 506/381-0849; www.silverkinglodge.com; E-mail: slvrkng@racsa.co.cr) is a luxury lodge at Barra del Colorado. See chapter 9.

GOLF

Costa Rica is not one of the world's great golfing destinations. Not yet, anyway. There are currently four regulation 18-hole courses open to the public and/or visitors, but several others are either under construction or in the planning stages, with a potential boom shaping up in Guanacaste. Very shortly, there should be new courses in operation just south of Playa Tamarindo, and near the port of Caldera at La Roca Resort.

The **Meliá hotel chain** runs two courses, with the Meliá Cariari course (☎ **800/ 336-3542** in the U.S. and Canada, or 506/239-0022 in Costa Rica; fax 506/ 239-0285; E-mail: cariari@racsa.co.cr) just outside of San José. Greens fees here are $60. The hotel chain also runs the **Meliá Playa Conchal** (☎ **506/654-4123;** E-mail: mconchal@racsa.co.cr) up in Guanacaste. Greens fees here are $90, including cart. This course is currently open, with advance notice and depending on available tee times, to guests at other hotels in the region. The Cariari course is officially open only to guests of the Cariari and Herradura hotels, but they will sometimes accept guests staying at other hotels. Another option for golfers staying in the metropolitan area is the new 18-hole course **Parque Valle del Sol** (☎ **506/282-9222**) in the western suburb of Santa Ana.

The newest major course to open is at the **Los Sueños Marriott Beach & Golf Resort** in Playa Herradura (☎ **800/228-9290** in the U.S., 506/630-9000 in Costa Rica). Greens fees, including cart, run around $95 for guests of the hotel, $145 for the general public.

Another course in operation is **Rancho Las Colinas** (☎ and fax **506/654-4089;** E-mail: rlc@compusource.net), near Playa Grande, also in Guanacaste. Greens fees there are $45 ($20 for a cart).

Golfers interested in a package deal or potentially playing a variety of courses should contact **Golf Costa Rica Adventures,** Interlink 854, P.O. Box 02-5635, Miami, FL 33102 (☎ **888/261-6645** in the U.S., or ☎ and fax 506/293-9785; www. golfcr.com; E-mail: info@golfcr.com).

HORSEBACK RIDING

Costa Rica's rural roots are evident in the continued use of horses for real work and transportation throughout the country. Visitors will find that horses are easily available for riding, whether you want to take a sunset trot along the beach, ride through the cloud forest, or take a multiday trek through the northern zone.

While most travelers simply saddle up for a couple of hours, as part of their broader itinerary, those looking for a more specifically equestrian-based visit should check in with the following folks.

T'ai Chi in Paradise

For the past 11 years, ta'i chi master and two-time U.S. national champion Chris Luth has been leading weeklong retreats to Costa Rica, combining intensive classes in this ancient Chinese martial art with rain-forest hikes, river rafting, and just enough beach time. For more information, contact the Pacific School of T'ai Chi (☎ **800/266-5803** in the U.S., or 619/259-1401).

Coast to Coast Adventures, Apdo. 2135-1002, San José, Costa Rica (☎ **506/ 225-6055;** fax 506/225-7806; www.ctocadventures.com; E-mail: info@ctocadventures. com), specializes in 2-week trips spanning the country via horseback, raft, mountain bike, and on foot, with no motor vehicles involved. Other trips are also available.

Nature Lodge Finca Los Caballos, Apdo. 22, Cóbano de Puntarenas (☎ and fax **506/642-0124;** E-mail: naturelc@racsa.co.cr), has the healthiest horses in the Montezuma area. See chapter 5.

Rancho Savegre Horseback Tours, Rancho Savegre, c/o Hotel Sirena, Quepos, Costa Rica (☎ **506/777-0528;** fax 506/777-0165), offers 1-day and multiday horseback tours based out of their rustic ranch near Quepos. See chapter 7.

Serendipity Adventures, Apdo. 76 CATIE, Turrialba, Costa Rica (☎ **800/ 635-2325** and fax 734/426-5026 in the U.S., or 506/556-2592; fax 506/556-2593; www.serendipityadventures.com; E-mail: costarica@serendipityadventures.com), offers many activities including horseback treks and tours.

SPAS & YOGA RETREATS

While Costa Rica still doesn't have any world-class spas, the conditions here are ripe and some early attempts are beginning to mature and flourish. I expect the trend to boom here in the coming years.

✪ **El Tucano Resort and Spa,** Apdo. 114-1017, San José, Aguas Calientes de San Carlos (☎ **506/460-6000** or 506/460-3141; fax 506/460-1692; E-mail: tucano@racsa. co.cr), the oldest and most established full-service spa facility in Costa Rica, offers a wide range of treatments in a lush forested setting, with natural hot springs. See chapter 6.

Hotel Martino Med-Spa & Resort, La Garita de Alajuela (☎ **506/433-8382;** fax 506/433-9052; www.hotelmartino.com; E-mail: martino@racsa.co.cr), is a new hotel that has a top-notch modern spa facility with tons of equipment.

Nosara Retreat, Nosara (☎ **888/803-0580** in the U.S., or 506/682-0071; www.nosarayoga.com; E-mail: yogacr@racsa.co.cr), is a small, upscale yoga retreat run by former instructors at the Kripalu Yoga center. See chapter 5.

Pura Vida Retreat, Pavas de Carrizal, Alajuela (mailing address in the U.S.: P.O. Box 3029, San Rafael, CA 94912; ☎ **888/767-7375,** in the U.S., or 506/483-0033; fax 506/493-0041; www.puravidaspa.com; E-mail: info@puravidaspa.com), is primarily a yoga retreat, hosting a steady stream of visiting teachers and groups practicing a wide range of styles and meditations. It's located in a lovely setting in the hills above Alajuela.

✪ **Samasati,** Puerto Viejo de Talamanca (☎ **506/224-1870;** fax 506/224-5032; www.samasati.com; E-mail: samasati@samasati.com), is a small new yoga retreat in some dense forest on a hillside above the Caribbean Sea. See chapter 9.

Tabacón Resort, Tabacón, (P.O. Box 181-1007, Centro Colón, San José; ☎ **506/ 256-1500;** fax 506/221-3075; www.tabacon.com; E-mail: info@tabacon.com), has the setting and potential to become the country's premiere spa. As of press time, the spa services and facilities were on the brink of a big expansion. Spectacular hot springs and volcano view. See chapter 6.

Tara Resort Hotel and Spa, Apdo. 1459-1250, Escazú (☎ **506/228-6992;** fax 506/228-9651; www.tararesort.com; E-mail: taraspa@racsa.co.cr), is a small hotel and spa located in the hills above Escazú, just 20 minutes from downtown San José. Modern equipment and a wide range of treatments are available. See chapter 4.

SURFING

When *Endless Summer II,* the sequel to the all-time surf classic, was filmed, the production crew brought its boards and cameras to Costa Rica. Point and beach breaks that work almost year-round are located all along Costa Rica's immense coastline. **Playas Hermosa, Jacó,** and **Dominical,** on the central Pacific coast, and **Tamarindo,**

In Search of Turtles

Few places in the world have as many sea-turtle nesting sites as Costa Rica. Along both coasts, five species of these huge marine reptiles come ashore at specific times of the year to dig nests in the sand and lay their eggs. Sea turtles are endangered throughout the world due to overhunting, accidental deaths in fishing nets, development on beaches formerly used as nesting areas, and the collection and sale (often illegally) of their eggs. International trade in sea-turtle products is already prohibited by most countries (including the U.S.), but sea-turtle numbers continue to dwindle.

Among the species of sea turtles that nest on Costa Rica's beaches are **olive Ridley** (known for their mass egg-laying migrations, or *arribadas*), **leatherback, hawksbill, green,** and **Pacific green turtles.** Excursions to see nesting turtles have become common, and they are fascinating, but please make sure that you and/or your guide do not disturb the turtles. Any light source (other than red-tinted flashlights) can confuse female turtles and cause them to return to the sea without laying their eggs. In fact, as more and more development takes place on the Costa Rican coast, hotel lighting may cause the number of nesting turtles to drop. Luckily, many of the nesting beaches have been protected as national parks.

Here are the main places to see nesting sea turtles: **Santa Rosa National Park** (near Liberia), **Las Baulas National Marine Park** (near Tamarindo), **Ostional National Wildlife Refuge** (near Playa Nosara), and **Tortuguero National Park** (on the northern Caribbean coast).

See the regional chapters for a description of the resident turtles and their respective nesting seasons, as well as listings of local tour operators and companies that arrange trips to see sea turtles nesting.

in Guanacaste, are becoming mini–surf meccas. **Salsa Brava** in Puerto Viejo has a habit of breaking boards, but the daredevils keep coming back for more. Crowds are starting to gather at the more popular breaks, but you can still stumble onto secret spots on the **Osa** and **Nicoya peninsulas** and along the northern Guanacaste coast. Costa Rica's signature wave is still found at **Playa Pavones,** which is reputed to have one of the longest lefts in the world. The cognoscenti, however, also swear by places like **Playa Grande, Playa Negra, Matapalo, Malpais,** and **Witch's Rock.**

If you're looking for an organized surf vacation, contact **Tico Travel** (☎ 800/493-8426 in the U.S., or 506/221-3912; www.ticotravel.com; E-mail: info@ticotravel. com). For more general surf information, live wave-cams, and a great links pages, check out the Web sites **www.surf-the-earth.com** and **www.surfline.com.**

WHITE-WATER RAFTING, KAYAKING & CANOEING

Whether you're a first-time rafter or a world-class kayaker, Costa Rica's got some white water suited to your abilities. Rivers rise and fall with the rainfall, but you can get wet and wild here even in the dry season. The best white-water-rafting ride is still the scenic **Pacuare River,** though unfortunately it may be dammed soon. If you're just experimenting with river rafting, stick to Class II and III rivers, like the **Reventazón, Sarapiquí, Peñas Blancas,** and **Savegre.** If you already know which end of the paddle goes in the water, there are plenty of Class IV and V sections to run. Die-hard river rats should pick up a copy of *The Rivers of Costa Rica,* by Michael W. Mayfield and Rafael E. Gallo (Menasha Ridge Press, 1988), which is loaded with technical data and route tips on every rideable river in the country.

Aguas Bravas, P.O. Box 1504-2100, Costa Rica (☎ **506/292-2072;** fax 506/229-4837; www.aguas-bravas.co.cr; E-mail: info@aguas-bravas.co.cr), specializes in trips on the Sarapiquí and Peñas Blancas rivers, although they also run the Reventazón and Pacuare rivers.

✪ **Aventuras Naturales,** P.O. Box 107360-1000, San José, Costa Rica (☎ **800/ 514-0411** in the U.S., or 506/225-3939; fax 506/253-6934; www.toenjoynature.com; E-mail: avenat@racsa.co.cr), is a major rafting operator running daily trips on the most popular rivers in Costa Rica. Their Pacuare Jungle Lodge is a great place to spend the night on one of their 2-day rafting trips.

✪ **Costa Rica White Water,** Dept. 235, P.O. Box 025216, Miami, FL 33102 (☎ **506/257-0766** or 506/222-0333; fax 506/257-1665; www.costaricaexpeditions.com; E-mail: costaric@expeditions.co.cr), was the first building block in the Costa Rica Expeditions empire. It remains one of the better-run rafting operations.

Canoe Costa Rica, PMB 567, P.O. Box 917729, Longwood, FL 32791 (☎ and fax **732/350-3963** in the U.S., or ☎ 506/282-3579 in Costa Rica; www.canoecostarica.com; E-mail: gegrant@aol.com). The only outfit I know of to specialize in canoe trips. Works primarily with custom-designed tours and itineraries.

Escondido Trex, Apdo. 9, Puerto Jiménez, Osa Peninsula, Costa Rica (☎ and fax **506/735-5210;** www.escondidotrex.com; E-mail: osatrex@racsa.co.cr): If you're out on the Osa Peninsula, these are the folks to see.

Iguana Tours, Apdo. 227, Quepos, Costa Rica (☎ and fax **506/777-1262;** www.iguanatours.com; E-mail: info@iguanatours.com), is based in Quepos/Manuel Antonio and specializes in rafting on the Savegre and Naranjo rivers, as well as ocean and mangrove kayak trips.

Rancho Leona Kayak Tours, Rancho Leona, La Virgen de Sarapiquí, Heredia, Costa Rica (☎ **506/761-1019;** www.rancholeona.com; E-mail: rleona@racsa.co.cr). This small hostel-like roadside hotel caters to both experienced and beginning kayakers looking to ply the Río Sarapiquí. See chapter 6.

✪ **Ríos Tropicales,** Apdo. 472-1200, Pavas, Costa Rica (☎ **506/233-6455;** fax 506/255-4354; www.riostropicales.com; E-mail: info@riostropicales.com), is one of the major operators in Costa Rica, running most of the runnable rivers. Lodgings include a very comfortable lodge on the banks of the Río Pacuare for the 2-day trips.

WINDSURFING

Windsurfing is still not very popular on the high seas here, where winds are fickle and rental options are limited, even at beach hotels. However, **Lake Arenal** is considered one of the top spots in the world for high-wind boardsailing. During the winter months, many of the regulars from Washington's Columbia River Gorge take up residence around the nearby town of Tilarán. Small boards, water starts, and fancy gibes are the norm. The best time for windsurfing on Lake Arenal is between December and March. The same winds that buffet Lake Arenal make their way down to **Bolaños Bay,** near Santa Cruz, Guanacaste, where you can also get some good windsurfing in. See chapters 5 and 6 for more information.

3 Costa Rica's National Parks & Bioreserves

Costa Rica has 32 national parks protecting more than 12% of the country and ranging in size from the 530-acre Guayabo National Monument to the 474,240-acre La Amistad National Park. Many of these national parks are undeveloped tropical forests, with few services or facilities available for visitors. Others, however, offer easier access to their wealth of natural wonders.

After several years of fee hikes, scaled pricing, green passes, and heated controversy, national-park fees seem to have settled on a flat $6-per-person per-day fee for any foreigner. Costa Ricans and foreign residents continue to pay just $1. At parks where camping is allowed, there is an additional charge of $2 per person per day.

The following section is not a complete listing of all of Costa Rica's national parks and protected areas but rather a selective list of those parks that are of greatest interest and accessibility. They're popular, but they're also among the best. You'll find detailed information about food and lodging options near some of the individual parks in the regional chapters that follow. As you'll see from the descriptions, Costa Rica's national parks vary greatly in terms of attractions, facilities, and accessibility. If you're looking for a camping adventure or an extended stay in one of the national parks, I recommend **Santa Rosa, Rincón de la Vieja, Chirripó, Corcovado,** or **Cahuita.** Any of the others are better suited for day trips, guided hikes, or in combination with your travels around the country.

For more information, call the national parks office at ☎ **506/257-0922** from the United States, or by dialing ☎ **192** from Costa Rica. You can also stop by the **National Parks Foundation office** (☎ **506/257-2239**) in San José, which is located between Calle 23 and Avenida 15. Both offices are open Monday through Friday from 9am to 5pm.

SAN JOSÉ/CENTRAL VALLEY AREA

GUAYABO NATIONAL MONUMENT   This is the country's only significant pre-Columbian archaeological site. It's believed that Guayabo supported a population of about 10,000 people some 3,000 years ago. The park is set in a forested area rich in flora and fauna. **Location:** 12 miles (19km) northeast of Turrialba, which is 33 miles (53km) east of San José. See chapter 4.

IRAZÚ VOLCANO NATIONAL PARK   Irazú Volcano is the highest (11,260 ft.) of Costa Rica's four active volcanoes and a popular day trip from San José. A paved road leads right up to the crater, and the lookout also allows you a view of both oceans on a clear day. The volcano last erupted in 1963—the same day President John F. Kennedy visited the country. There's an information center, picnic tables, rest rooms, and a parking area here. **Location:** 34 miles (55km) east of San José. See chapter 4.

POÁS VOLCANO NATIONAL PARK   Poás is the other active volcano close to San José. The main crater is more than 1 mile wide, and it is constantly active with fumaroles and hot geysers. The area around the volcano is lush, but much of the growth is stunted due to the gasses and acid rain. The park sometimes closes when the gasses get too feisty. There are nature trails, picnic tables, rest rooms, and an information center. **Location:** 23 miles (37km) northwest of San José. See chapter 4.

GUANACASTE & THE NICOYA PENINSULA

BARRA HONDA NATIONAL PARK   Costa Rica's only underground national park, Barra Honda features a series of limestone caves that were once part of a coral reef, some 60 million years ago. Today the caves are home to millions of bats and impressive stalactite and stalagmite formations. Only Terciopelo Cave is open to the public. There's a camping area, rest rooms, and an information center here, as well as trails through the surrounding tropical dry forest. **Location:** 208 miles (335km) northwest of San José. See chapter 5.

PALO VERDE NATIONAL PARK   A must for bird-watchers, Palo Verde National Park is one of Costa Rica's best-kept secrets. This part of the Tempisque River lowlands

Costa Rica's National Parks & Bioreserves

Airport ✈
Ferry - - -
Mountain △

Arenal National Park ⑦
Barra Honda National Park ⑤
Braulio Carrillo National Park ⑩
Cahuita National Park ⑰
Caño Negro National Wildlife Refuge ⑧
Carara Biological Reserve ⑬
Chirripó National Park ⑮
Corcovado National Park ⑯
Guanacaste National Park ②
Guayabo National Monument ⑪

Irazú Volcano National Park ⑫
Manuel Antonio National Park ⑭
Monteverde Biological Cloud
    Forest Preserve ⑥
Palo Verde National Park ④
Poás Volcano National Park ⑨
Rincón de la Vieja National Park ③
Santa Rosa National Park ①
Tortuguero National Park ⑱

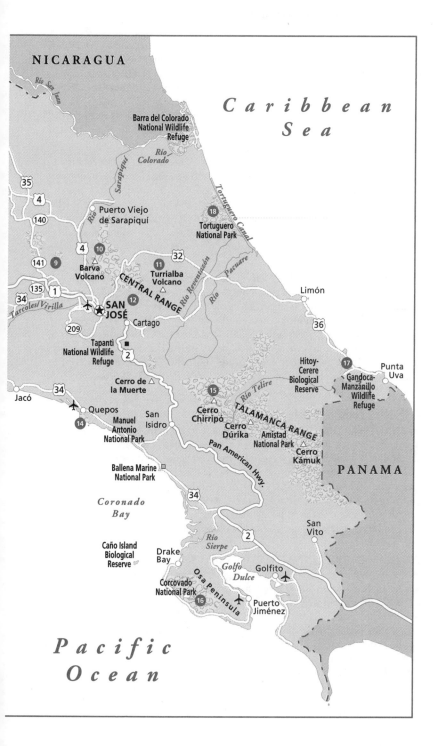

NICARAGUA

*Caribbean
Sea*

Río San Juan

Barra del Colorado
National Wildlife
Refuge

*Río
Colorado*

35

4

140

Río Sarapiquí

Puerto Viejo
de Sarapiquí

4

10

Tortuguero Canal

18

Tortuguero
National Park

141

9

Barva
Volcano

CENTRAL RANGE

32

11

Turrialba
Volcano

Río Reventazón

Río Pacuare

Río

Limón

135

1

34

Tárcoles/Virilla

SAN
JOSÉ

12

209

Cartago

36

Tapanti
National Wildlife
Refuge

2

Hitoy-
Cerere
Biological
Reserve

17

Punta
Uva

Cerro de
la Muerte

15

Río Telire

Gandoca-
Manzanillo
Wildlife
Refuge

34

Jacó

34

Quepos

14

Manuel
Antonio
National Park

San
Isidro

Cerro
Chirripó

Cerro
Dúrika

TALAMANCA RANGE

Amistad
National Park

Cerro
Kámuk

PANAMA

Pan American Hwy.

Ballena Marine
National Park

34

*Coronado
Bay*

2

San
Vito

Caño Island
Biological
Reserve

Drake
Bay

*Río
Sierpe*

*Golfo
Dulce*

Golfito

Corcovado
National Park

Osa Peninsula

16

Puerto
Jiménez

*Pacific
Ocean*

supports a population of more than 50,000 waterfowl and forest bird species. Various ecosystems here include mangroves, savannah brush lands, and evergreen forests. There are camping facilities, an information center, and some nice new accommodations at the Organization for Tropical Studies (OTS) research station here. **Location:** 125 miles (200km) northwest of San José. Be warned, the park entrance is 17¹/₂ miles (28km) off the highway down a very rugged dirt road. It is another 5¹/₂ miles (9km) to the OTS station and campsites. For more information, call the OTS (☎ **506/240-6696;** E-mail: reservas@cro.ots.ac.cr). See chapter 5.

RINCÓN DE LA VIEJA NATIONAL PARK   This is a large tract of parkland that experiences high volcanic activity. There are numerous fumaroles and geysers, as well as hot springs, cold pools, and mud pots. There are also excellent hikes to the upper craters, as well as to several waterfalls. You should hire a guide for any hot-spring or mud-bath expeditions, because inexperienced visitors have been burned. Camping is permitted at two separate sites, each of which has an information center, picnic area, and rest rooms. **Location:** 165 miles (266km) northwest of San José. See chapter 5.

SANTA ROSA NATIONAL PARK   Occupying a large section of Costa Rica's northwestern Guanacaste province, Santa Rosa contains the country's largest area of tropical dry forest, as well as important turtle nesting sites and the historically significant La Casona monument. There are also caves for exploring. The beaches here are pristine and have basic camping facilities, and the waves make them quite popular with surfers. An information center, picnic area, and rest rooms are located at the main campsite and entrance. **Location:** 160 miles (258km) northwest of San José. For more information, you can call the park office at ☎ **506/666-5051.** See chapter 5.

THE NORTHERN ZONE

ARENAL NATIONAL PARK   This new park, created to protect the ecosystem that surrounds Arenal Volcano, has few services or attractions. Basically, the government has set up a toll booth on the access road leading to an up-close view of the volcano's lava flows. Most travelers and tour operators choose to forgo the entrance fee and watch the volcano from spots along the dirt road leading to the Arenal Observatory Lodge, or from the road to Tabacón, where the view is just as good as it is inside. However, there are several excellent hiking trails inside the park that explore cooled off lava flows and the neighboring rain forest. **Location:** 80 miles (129km) northwest of San José. See chapter 6. .

BRAULIO CARRILLO NATIONAL PARK   This park, which occupies a large area of the nation's central mountain range, is the park you pass through on your way from San José to the Caribbean coast. A deep rain forest, Braulio Carrillo receives an average of 177 inches of rain per year. There are beautiful rivers, majestic waterfalls, and more than 6,500 species of plants and animals. The park has an information center, picnic tables, rest rooms, and hiking trails. Camping is allowed, but not very common or recommended. Be careful here. Make sure you park your car in, and base your explorations from, the park's main entrance, not just anywhere along the highway. There have been several robberies and attacks against visitors reported at trails leading into the park from the highway. This park also seems to have the highest incidence of lost hikers. **Location:** 14 miles (22km) north of San José. See chapter 6.

CAÑO NEGRO NATIONAL WILDLIFE REFUGE A lowland swamp and drainage basin for several northern rivers, Caño Negro is excellent for bird-watching. There are a few basic cabinas and lodges in this area, but the most popular way to visit is on a combined van and boat trip from the La Fortuna/Arenal area. **Location:** 12$^1/_2$ miles (20km) south of Los Chiles, near the Nicaraguan border. See chapter 6.

MONTEVERDE CLOUD FOREST PRESERVE This private reserve might be the most famous patch of forest in Costa Rica. It covers some 26,000 acres of primary forest. Most of it is midelevation cloud forest, with a rich variety of flora and fauna. Epiphytes thrive in the cool misty climate. The most famous resident here is the spectacular Resplendent Quetzal. There is a well-maintained trail system, as well as some of the best-trained and most experienced guides in the country. Nearby, you can visit both the Santa Elena and Sendero Tranquilo reserves. **Location:** 103 miles (167km) NW of San José. See chapter 6.

CENTRAL PACIFIC COAST

CHIRRIPÓ NATIONAL PARK Home to Costa Rica's tallest peak, 12,536-foot Mount Chirripó, Chirripó National Park is a hike, but on a clear day you can see both the Pacific Ocean and Caribbean Sea from its summit. There are a number of interesting climbing trails here, and camping is allowed. **Location:** 94 miles (151km) southeast of San José. See chapter 7.

MANUEL ANTONIO NATIONAL PARK The grande dame of Costa Rican national parks, Manuel Antonio supports the largest number of hotels and resorts of any national park. This lowland rain forest is home to a healthy monkey population, including the endangered squirrel monkey. The park is best known for its splendid beaches. **Location:** 80 miles (129km) south of San José. See chapter 7.

THE SOUTHERN ZONE

CORCOVADO NATIONAL PARK As the largest single block of virgin lowland rain forest in Central America, Corcovado National Park receives more than 200 inches of rain per year. One of Costa Rica's increasingly popular national parks, it's still largely a remote area (it has no roads; only dirt tracks lead into it). Scarlet macaws live here, as do countless other neotropical species, including two of the country's largest cats, the puma and endangered jaguar. There are camping facilities and trails throughout the park. **Location:** 208 miles (335km) south of San José, on the Osa Peninsula. See chapter 8. .

CARIBBEAN COAST

CAHUITA NATIONAL PARK A combination land and marine park, Cahuita National Park protects one of the few remaining living coral reefs in the country. The topography here is lush lowland tropical rain forest. Monkeys and numerous bird species are common. Camping is permitted, and there are basic facilities at the Puerto Vargas entrance to the park. If you want to visit for only the day, however, enter from Cahuita village, because as of press time, the local community had taken over that entrance and was asking for only a voluntary donation. **Location:** On the Caribbean coast, 26 miles (42km) south of Limón. See chapter 9.

TORTUGUERO NATIONAL PARK Tortuguero National Park has been called the Venice of Costa Rica due to its maze of jungle canals that meander through a dense lowland rain forest. Small boats, launches, and canoes carry visitors through these

Monkey Business

No trip to Costa Rica would be complete without at least one monkey sighting. Home to four distinct species of primates, inhabiting the forests along both coasts as well as those in between, Costa Rica offers the opportunity for one of the world's most gratifying wildlife-watching experiences. Just listen for the deep guttural call of a howler or the rustling of leaves overhead, telltale signs that monkeys are in your vicinity.

Costa Rica's most commonly spotted monkey is the white-faced or **capuchin monkey** (*mono cara blanca* in Spanish), which you may recognize as the infamous culprit from the film *Outbreak*. Contrary to that film's plot, however, these monkeys are native to the New World tropics and do not exist in Africa. Capuchins are agile, medium-size monkeys that make good use of their long prehensile tails. They inhabit a diverse collection of habitats, ranging from the high-altitude cloud forests of the central region to the lowland mangroves of the Osa Peninsula. It's almost impossible not to spot capuchins at Manuel Antonio (see chapter 7), where the resident white-faced monkeys have become a little too dependent on fruit and junk-food feedings by tourists. Please do not feed wild monkeys (and try to keep your food away from them; they're notorious thieves), and boycott establishments that try to attract both monkeys and tourists with daily feedings.

Howler monkeys (*mono congo* in Spanish) are named for their distinct and eerie call. Large and mostly black, these monkeys can seem ferocious because of their physical appearance and deep, resonant howls that can carry for more than a mile, even in dense rain forest. Biologists believe that male howlers mark the bounds of their territories with these deep guttural sounds. In the presence of humans, however, howlers are actually a little timid and tend to stay higher up in the canopy than their white-faced cousins. Howlers are fairly common and easy to spot in the dry tropical forests of coastal Guanacaste and the Nicoya Peninsula (see chapter 5).

Even more elusive are **spider monkeys** (*mono araña* in Spanish). These long, slender monkeys are dark brown to black and prefer the high canopies of primary rain forests. Spiders are very adept with their prehensile tails but actually travel through the canopy with a hand-over-hand motion frequently imitated by their less graceful human cousins on playground monkey bars around the world. I've had my best luck spotting spiders along the edges of Tortuguero's jungle canals (see chapter 9), where howlers are also quite common.

The rarest and most endangered of Costa Rica's monkeys is the tiny **squirrel monkey** (*mono titi* in Spanish). These small brown monkeys have dark eyes surrounded by large white rings, white ears, white chests, and very long tails. In Costa Rica, squirrel monkeys can be found only in Manuel Antonio (see chapter 7) and the Osa Peninsula (see chapter 8). These seemingly hyperactive monkeys are predominantly fruit eaters and often feed on bananas and other fruit trees near hotels in both of the above-mentioned regions. Squirrel monkeys usually travel in large bands, so if you do see them, you'll likely see quite a few. .

waterways, where caimans, manatees, and numerous bird and mammal species are common. The extremely endangered great green macaw lives here. On the beaches, green sea turtles nest here every year between June and October. The park has a small but helpful information office and some well-marked trails. **Location:** 160 miles (258km) from San José. See chapter 9.

4 Tips on Health, Safety & Etiquette in the Wilderness

Much of what is discussed below is common sense. For more detailed information, see "Health & Insurance Information" in chapter 2.

While most tours and activities are extremely safe, there are risks involved in any adventure activity. Know and respect your own physical limits before undertaking any strenuous activity. Be prepared for extremes in temperature and rainfall and for wide fluctuations in weather. A sunny morning hike can quickly become a cold and wet ordeal, so it's usually a good idea to carry along some form of rain gear when hiking in the rain forest, or to have a dry change of clothing waiting at the end of the trail. Make sure to bring along plenty of sunscreen when you're not going to be covered by the forest canopy.

If you do any backcountry packing or camping, remember that it really is a jungle out there. Don't go poking under rocks or fallen branches. Snakebites are very rare, but don't do anything to increase the odds. If you do encounter a snake, stay calm, don't make any sudden movements, and *do not* try to handle it. Also, avoid swimming in major rivers unless a guide or local operator can vouch for their safety. Though white-water sections and stretches in mountainous areas are generally pretty safe, most mangrove canals and river mouths in Costa Rica support healthy crocodile and caiman populations.

Bugs and bug bites will probably be your greatest health concern in the Costa Rican wilderness, and even they aren't as big a problem as you might expect. Mostly, bugs are an inconvenience, although mosquitoes can carry malaria or dengue (see chapter 2 for more information). A strong repellent and proper clothing will minimize both the danger and inconvenience. On the beaches you will probably be bitten by sand fleas, or *pirujas*. These nearly invisible insects leave an irritating welt. Try not to scratch, as this can lead to open sores and infections. Pirujas are most active at sunrise and sunset, so you might want to cover up or avoid the beaches at these times.

And remember: Whenever you enter and enjoy nature, you should tread lightly and try not to disturb the natural environment. There's a popular slogan well known to most campers that certainly applies here: "Leave nothing but footprints, take nothing but memories." If you must take home a souvenir, take photos. Do not cut or uproot plants or flowers. Pack out everything you pack in, and *please* do not litter.

5 Ecologically Oriented Volunteer & Study Programs

Below are some institutions and organizations that are working on ecology and sustainable development projects.

Asociación de Voluntarios para el Servicio en las Areas Protegidas (ASVO), Apdo. 113384-1000, San José, Costa Rica (☎ and fax **506/233-4989;** E-mail: asvo89@racsa.co.cr), organizes volunteers to work in Costa Rican national parks. A 30-day minimum commitment is required, as are several letters of recommendation and a basic ability to converse in Spanish. Housing is provided at a basic ranger station, and there is a $10-per-day fee to cover food, which is basic Tico fare.

Costa Rica Rainforest Outward Bound School, PO Box 243, Quepos, Costa Rica (mailing address in the U.S.: SJO 829, P.O. Box 025216, Miami, FL 33102-5216; ☎ and fax **506/777-1222;** www.crrobs.org; E-mail: info@crrobs.org), is the local branch of this well-respected international adventure-based outdoor-education organization. Courses range from 2 weeks to a full semester and cover everything from surfing, kayaking, and tree-climbing to learning Spanish.

Eco Teach, P.O. Box 73, Suquamish, WA 98392 (☎ and fax **360/598-1543;** www.ecoteach.com; E-mail: info@ecoteach.com), works primarily in facilitating educational trips for high school and college student groups. Trips focus on Costa Rican ecology and culture. Costs run around $1,900 per person for a 10-day trip, including airfare, lodging, meals, classes, and travel.

Global Volunteers, 375 Little Canada Rd., St. Paul, MN 55117 (☎ **800/487-1074** or 651/407-6100; www.globalvolunteers.com; E-mail: info@globalvolunteers.com), is a U.S.-based organization that offers a unique opportunity to travelers who've always wanted a Peace Corps–like experience but couldn't make a 2-year commitment. For 2 to 3 weeks, you can join one of their working vacations in Costa Rica. A certain set of skills, such as engineering or agricultural knowledge, is helpful but by no means necessary. Each trip is undertaken at a particular community's request, to complete a specific project. However, be warned, these "volunteer" experiences do not come cheap. You must pay for your transportation as well as a hefty program fee, around $1,600 for a 2-week program.

Institute for Central American Development Studies (ICADS), Apdo. 3-2070 Sabanilla, San José, Costa Rica (Dept. 826, P.O. Box 025216, Miami, FL 33102-5216, in the U.S.; ☎ **506/225-0508;** fax 506/234-1337; www.icadscr.com; E-mail: icads@netbox.com), offers internship and research opportunities in the areas of environment, agriculture, human rights, and women's studies. An intensive Spanish-language program can be combined with work-study or volunteer opportunities.

Monteverde Institute, Apdo. 69-5655, Monteverde de Puntarenas, Costa Rica (☎ **506/645-5053;** fax 506/645-5219; mvi.cea.edu; E-mail: mviimv@racsa.co.cr), offers study programs in Monteverde and also has a volunteer center that helps in placement and training of volunteers.

Organization for Tropical Studies, Apdo. 676, San José, Costa Rica (☎ **506/ 240-6696;** www.ots.ac.cr; E-mail: reservas@cro.ots.ac.cr), represents several Costa Rican and U.S. universities. This organization's mission is to promote research, education, and the wise use of natural resources in the tropics. Research facilities include La Selva Biological Station near Braulio Carrillo National Park and Palo Verde and the Wilson Botanical Gardens near San Vito. Housing is provided at one of the research facilities. A wide variety of programs is offered, ranging from full-semester undergraduate programs (at around $11,000) to specific graduate courses (of varying duration), to their recently added straight tourist programs (these are generally being sponsored/run by established operators such as Costa Rica Expeditions, Elderhostel, and others). These range in duration from 3 to 10 days, and costs vary greatly. Entrance requirements and competition for some of these courses can be demanding.

Vida, Apdo. 7-350-1000, San José (☎ **506/233-7203;** fax 506/222-3620; E-mail: info@vida.org), is a local nongovernmental organization working on sustainable development and conservation issues, that can often place volunteers.

San José 4

At first blush, San José may seem little more than a chaotic jumble of cars, buses, buildings, and people. The central downtown section of San José is an urban planner's nightmare, where once-quiet streets are now burdened by traffic and in a near-constant state of gridlock. Antiquated buses spewing diesel and leaded fuels and a lack of emission controls have given San José a brown cloud. Below the cloud, the city bustles, but it is not particularly hospitable to travelers. Sidewalks are poorly maintained and claustrophobic, and street crime is a problem. Most visitors quickly seek the sanctuary of their hotel room and the first chance to escape the city.

Still, San José is the most cosmopolitan city in Central America. Costa Rica's stable government and the Central Valley's climate have, over the years, attracted people from all over the world. There's a large diplomatic and international business presence here. As a result, there has been a proliferation of small, elegant hotels in renovated historic buildings, as well as a diverse variety of innovative new restaurants serving a wide range of international cuisines. Together, these hotels and restaurants provide visitors with one of the greatest varieties of options found anywhere between Mexico City and Bogotá.

San José will invariably serve as a default hub or transfer point for all visitors to Costa Rica (at least until the Liberia airport gets more flights). This chapter will help you plan your time in the capital and help ease your way through the pitfalls inherent in such a rough-and-tumble little city.

IT'S IN THE BEANS   San José was built on the profits of the coffee-export business. Between the airport and downtown, you'll pass by working coffee farms. Glance up from almost any street in the city and on the surrounding volcanic mountains and you'll see a patchwork quilt of farm fields, most of which are planted with the *grano de oro* (golden bean), as it's known here. San José was a forgotten backwater of the Spanish empire until the first shipments of the local beans made their way to sleepy souls in Europe late in the 19th century. Soon, San José was riding high. Coffee planters, newly rich and craving culture, imposed a tax on themselves in order to build the Teatro Nacional, San José's most beautiful building. Coffee profits also built the city a university. Today, you can wake up and smell the coffee roasting as you wander the streets near the Central Market (Mercado Central), and in any cafe or restaurant you can get a hot cup of sweet, milky *café con leche* to remind you of the bean that built San José.

Why does coffee grow so well around the city? It's the climate. The Central Valley, in which the city sits, has a perfect climate. At 3,750 feet above sea level, San José enjoys springlike temperatures year-round. This pleasant climate, and the beautiful views of lush green mountainsides, make San José a memorable city to visit. All you have to do is glance up at those mountains to know that this is one of the most beautifully situated capitals in Central America. And if a glance isn't enough for you, you'll find that it's extremely easy to get out into the countryside. Within an hour or two, you can climb a volcano, go white-water rafting, hike through a cloud forest, and stroll through a butterfly garden—among many, many other activities.

1 Orientation

ARRIVING

BY PLANE   Juan Santamaría International Airport (☎ **506/443-2942** for 24-hour airport information) is located near the city of Alajuela, about 20 minutes from downtown San José. A taxi into town will cost between $12 and $15, and a bus is only 55¢. The Alajuela–San José buses run frequently and will drop you off anywhere along Paseo Colón, or at a station near the Parque de la Merced (downtown, between calles 12 and 14 and avenidas 2 and 4). There are two separate lines: **Tuasa** buses are red; **Station Wagon** buses are beige/yellow. At the airport you'll find the bus stop directly in front of the main terminal. Make sure to ask if the bus is going to San José, or you'll end up in Alajuela. If you have a lot of luggage, you should probably take a cab.

There are quite a few car-rental agencies with desks and offices at the airport, although if you're planning on spending a few days in San José, a car is a liability. (If you're heading off immediately to the beach, though, it's much easier to pick your car up here than at a downtown office.) The car-rental agencies are currently in limbo awaiting completion of an airport remodeling (see below), so make sure to contact them first to confirm that they will have an agent and/or an office at the airport when you arrive.

At press time, the airport was in the midst of a major renovation and expansion. Hopefully by the time you read this, the awkward and uncomfortable international arrivals and customs set-up will have been modified, making the whole thing more user-friendly. Unlike the chaos and confusion that greeted arriving passengers in the past, I expect there will be a little bit more room and order granted them in the new airport. In the past, you literally had to fight off people offering to carry your bags. Most porters or skycaps wear a uniform identifying them as such, but sometimes "improvised" porters will try to earn a few dollars here. Either way, make sure you keep a very watchful eye on your bags, as thieves have historically preyed on newly arrived passengers and their luggage. You should tip porters about 50¢ per bag.

You have several options for **exchanging money** when you arrive at the airport. There's an official state bank inside the main terminal. It's open Monday through Friday from 9am to 4pm. When the bank is closed (and even when it's open), there are usually official money changers (with badges) working both inside and outside the terminal. Outside the terminal, you may be approached by unofficial money changers. Three things to note: (1) Though black-market money changing is illegal, it's quite common; (2) there's never much variance between the official bank rate and the street exchange rate; (3) the airport is one of the safer places to try black-market exchange, though you should be careful wherever and whenever you decide to change money. See "Exchanging Money" in chapter 2 for more details.

If for some reason you arrive in San José via Travelair, private aircraft, or another small commuter or charter airline, you may find yourself at the **Tobías Bolaños International Airport** in Pavas. This small airport is located on the western side of downtown San José, about 10 minutes by car from the center. There are no car-rental desks here, however, so unless you have a car and/or driver waiting for you here, you will have to take a cab into town, which should cost between $10 and $15.

BY BUS   If you're coming to San José by bus, where you disembark depends on where you're coming from. (The different bus companies have their offices, and thus their drop-off points, all over downtown San José. When you buy your ticket, ask where you'll be let off.) Buses arriving from Panama pass first through Cartago and San Pedro before letting passengers off in downtown San José; buses arriving from Nicaragua generally enter the city on the west end of town, on Paseo Colón. If you're staying here, you can ask to be let off before the final stop.

BY CAR   For those of you intrepid readers arriving by car, you will be entering San José via the Interamerican Highway. If you arrive **from Nicaragua and the north,** you will find that the highway brings you to the western edge of the downtown, right at the end of Paseo Colón, where it hits the Parque Sabana. This area is well marked with large road signs, which will either direct you to the downtown (CENTRO) or the western suburbs of Rhomerser, Pavas, and Escazú. If you're heading toward downtown, just follow the flow of traffic and turn left on Paseo Colón.

For those of you entering **from Panama and the south,** things get a little more complicated. The Interamerican Highway first passes through the city of Cartago, and then through the San José suburbs of Curridabat and San Pedro, before reaching downtown. This route is relatively well marked, and if you stick with the major flow of traffic, you should find San José without any problem.

VISITOR INFORMATION

There's an **ICT (Instituto Costarricense de Turismo)** office at Juan Santamaría International Airport, where you can pick up maps and brochures before you head into San José. It's not clear where they'll set up shop once the remodeling is complete, but expect this office to be open Monday through Friday from 8am to 4pm. If you're looking for the **main ICT visitor information center** in San José, it's located below the Plaza de la Cultura, at the entrance to the Gold Museum, on Calle 5 between Avenida Central and Avenida 2 (☎ **506/223-1733,** or 506/222-1090). The people here are very helpful, although the information they have to offer is rather limited. This office is open Monday through Friday from 9am to 5pm.

CITY LAYOUT

Downtown San José is laid out on a grid. *Avenidas* (avenues) run east and west, while *calles* (streets) run north and south. The center of the city is at **Avenida Central** and **Calle Central.** To the north of Avenida Central, the avenidas have odd numbers beginning with Avenida 1; to the south, they have even numbers beginning with Avenida 2. Likewise, calles to the east of Calle Central have odd numbers, and those to the west have even numbers. The main downtown artery is **Avenida 2,** which merges with Avenida Central on either side of the downtown area. West of downtown, Avenida Central becomes **Paseo Colón,** which ends at Sabana Park and feeds into the highway to Alajuela, the airport, and the Pacific coast. East of downtown, Avenida Central leads to San Pedro and then to Cartago and the Interamerican Highway heading south. **Calle 3** will take you out of town to the north and put you on the Guápiles Highway out to the Caribbean coast.

San José

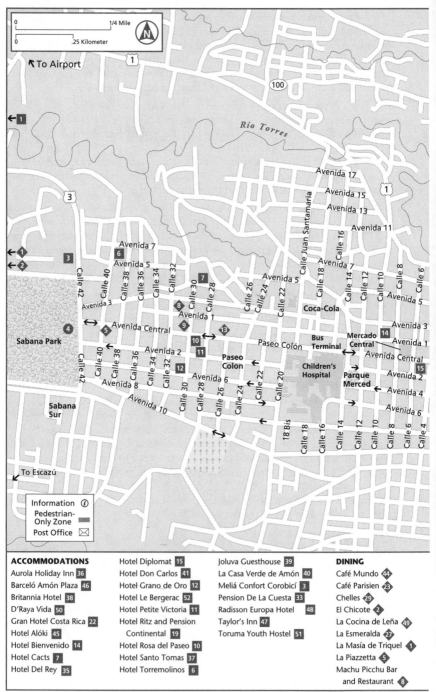

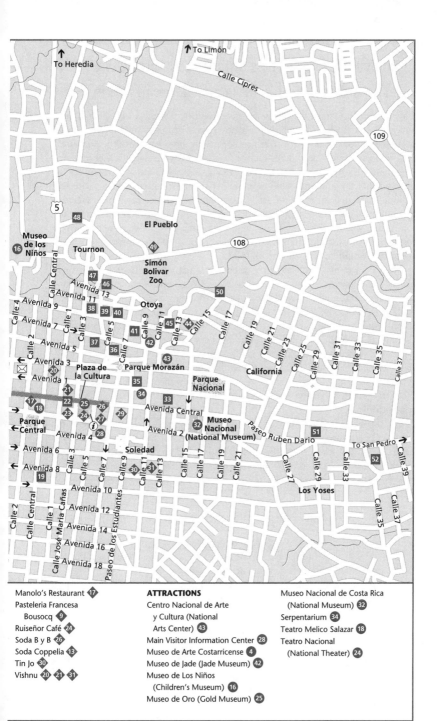

Manolo's Restaurant **17**
Pasteleria Francesa
  Bousocq **9**
Ruiseñor Café **24**
Soda B y B **26**
Soda Coppelia **13**
Tin Jo **30**
Vishnu **20** **21** **31**

ATTRACTIONS
Centro Nacional de Arte
  y Cultura (National
  Arts Center) **43**
Main Visitor Information Center **28**
Museo de Arte Costarricense **4**
Museo de Jade (Jade Museum) **42**
Museo de Los Niños
  (Children's Museum) **16**
Museo de Oro (Gold Museum) **25**

Museo Nacional de Costa Rica
  (National Museum) **32**
Serpentarium **34**
Teatro Melico Salazar **18**
Teatro Nacional
  (National Theater) **24**

"I know there's got to be a number here somewhere . . .":
The Arcane Art of Finding an Address in San José

This is one of the most confusing aspects of visiting Costa Rica in general, and San José in particular. Though there are often street addresses and building numbers for locations in downtown San José, they are almost never used. Addresses are given as a set of coordinates such as "Calle 3 between Avenida Central and Avenida 1." It's then up to you to locate the building within that block, keeping in mind that the building could be on either side of the street. Many addresses include additional information, such as the number of meters or *varas* (an old Spanish measurement roughly equal to a yard) from a specified intersection or some other well-known landmark. These landmarks are what become truly confusing for visitors to the city because they are often simply restaurants, bars, and shops that would be familiar only to locals.

Things get even more confusing when the landmark in question no longer exists. The classic example of this is "the Coca-Cola," one of the most common landmarks used in addresses in the blocks surrounding San José's main market. Trouble is, the Coca-Cola bottling plant it refers to is no longer there; the edifice is long gone, and one of the principal downtown bus depots stands in its place. Old habits die hard, though, and the address description remains. You may also try to find someplace near the *antiguo higuerón* ("old fig tree") in San Pedro. This tree was felled years ago. In outlying neighborhoods, addresses can become long directions such as "50 meters south of the old church, then 100 meters east, then 20 meters south." Luckily for the visitor, most downtown addresses are more straightforward.

Oh, if you're wondering how letter carriers manage, well, welcome to the club. Some folks actually get their mail delivered this way, but most people and businesses in San José use a post-office box. This is called an *apartado,* and is abbreviated "Apdo." or "A.P." on mailing addresses.

The Neighborhoods in Brief

San José is sprawling. Today it's divided into dozens of neighborhoods known as *barrios.* Most of the listings in this chapter fall within the main downtown area, but there are a few outlying neighborhoods you'll need to know about.

Downtown   In San José's busiest area, you'll find most of the city's museums. There are also many tour companies, restaurants, and hotels here. Unfortunately, traffic noise and exhaust fumes make this one of the least pleasant parts of the city. Streets and avenues are usually bustling and crowded with pedestrians and vehicular traffic, and street crime is most rampant here.

Barrio Amón/Barrio Otoya   These two neighborhoods, just north and east of downtown, are the site of the greatest concentration of historic buildings in San José. In the past few years some enterprising entrepreneurs have been renovating the old buildings and turning them into hotels. If you're looking for character and don't mind the noise and exhaust fumes, this neighborhood makes a good base for exploring the city.

La Sabana/Paseo Colón   Paseo Colón, a wide boulevard west of downtown, is an extension of Avenida Central and ends at La Sabana Park. It has several good, small hotels and numerous excellent restaurants. This is also where many of the city's car-rental agencies have their in-town offices.

San Pedro/Los Yoses   Located east of downtown San José, Los Yoses is an upper-middle-class neighborhood that is home to many diplomatic missions and embassies. San Pedro is a little farther east and is the site of the University of Costa Rica. There are numerous college-type bars and restaurants all around the edge of the campus and several good restaurants and small hotels in both neighborhoods.

Escazú/Santa Ana   Located in the hills west of San José, Escazú and Santa Ana are two fast-growing suburbs. Although the area is only 15 minutes from San José by taxi, it feels much farther away because of its relaxed atmosphere. This area has a large expatriate community, with so many bed-and-breakfast establishments located here.

2 Getting Around

BY BUS   Bus transportation around San José is cheap—the fare is usually somewhere around 15¢ (though the Alajuela–San José buses that run in from the airport cost 55¢). The most important buses are those running east along Avenida 2 and west along Avenida 3. The **Sabana/Cementerio** bus runs from Sabana Park to downtown and is one of the most convenient buses to use. You'll find a bus stop for the outbound Sabana/Cementerio bus near the main post office on Avenida 3 near the corner of Calle 2, and another one on Calle 11 between Avenida Central and Avenida 1. This bus also has stops all along Avenida 2. **San Pedro** buses leave from Avenida Central between Calle 9 and Calle 11, in front of the Cine Capri, and will take you out of downtown heading east. **Escazú**-bound buses leave from the Coca-Cola bus station, as well as from Avenida 6 and Calle 2, while buses for **Santa Ana** leave only from the Coca-Cola bus station.

Board buses from the front. The bus drivers can make change, although they don't like to receive large bills. Be especially mindful of your wallet, purse, or other valuables, since pickpockets often work the crowded buses.

BY TAXI   Although taxis in San José have meters (*marías*), the drivers sometimes refuse to use them, particularly with foreigners, so you'll occasionally have to negotiate the price. Always try to get them to use the meter first (say *"ponga la maría, por favor"*). The official rate at press time is around 80¢ for the first kilometer (0.6 miles) and around 40¢ for each additional kilometer. If you have a rough idea of how far it is to your destination, you can estimate how much it should cost from these figures. After 10pm, taxis are legally allowed to add a 20% surcharge. Some of the meters are programmed to include the extra charge automatically, but be careful: Some drivers will use the evening setting during the daytime, or (at night) try to charge an extra 20% on top of the higher meter setting. **Tipping** taxi drivers is not expected. It's not uncommon for passengers to sit in the front seat with the driver.

Depending on your location, the time of day, and the weather (rain places taxis at a premium), it's relatively easy to hail a cab downtown. You'll always find taxis in front of the Teatro Nacional (albeit at high prices) and around the Parque Central at Avenida Central and Calle Central. Taxis in front of hotels and the El Pueblo tourist complex usually charge more than others, although this is technically illegal. Most hotels will gladly call you a cab, either for a downtown excursion or for a trip back out to the airport. You can also get a cab by calling **Coopetaxi** (☎ **506/235-9966**), **Coopetico** (☎ **506/224-7979**), **Coopeirazu** (☎ **506/254-3211**), or **Coopeguaria** (☎ **506/226-1366**).

ON FOOT   Downtown San José is very compact. Nearly every place you might want to go is within a 15-by-4-block area. Because of the traffic congestion, you'll often find it faster to walk than to take a bus or taxi. Be careful when walking the streets any time of day or night. Flashy jewelry, loosely held handbags or backpacks, and expensive camera equipment tend to attract thieves. You should also watch your step: Between the earthquakes, wear and tear, and negligence, the sidewalks in San José have become veritable obstacle courses and the cause of more than one sprained ankle.

Avenida Central is a pedestrian-only street for several blocks around Calle Central toward the Cultural Plaza. It has recently been redone with interesting paving stones and the occasional fountain in an attempt to create a comfortable pedestrian mall.

BY CAR   It will cost you between $35 and $65 per day to rent a car in Costa Rica. The higher prices are for four-wheel-drive vehicles. Many of the car-rental agencies have offices at the airport. If not, they will usually either pick you up or deliver the car to any San José hotel. If you decide to receive your rental car in downtown San José, be prepared for some very congested streets.

The following companies have desks at Juan Santamaría International Airport, as well as offices downtown: **Ada Rent A Car** (☎ **506/441-9961** at the airport, or 506/233-7733 in downtown San José; www.adarentacar.com); **Adobe Rent A Car** (☎ **506/442-2422** at the airport, or 506/221-5425 in downtown San José; www.adobecar.com); **Avis Rent A Car** (☎ **800/331-1212** in the U.S., 506/442-1321 at the airport, or 506/232-9922 in downtown San José; www.avis.com); **Budget Rent A Car** (☎ **800/527-0700** in the U.S., 506/441-4444 at the airport, or 506/223-3284 in downtown San José; www.budget.co.cr); **Elegante Rent A Car** (☎ **800/582-7432** in the U.S., 506/441-9366 at the airport, or 506/257-0026 in downtown San José; www.eleganterentacar.com); **Hertz Rent A Car** (☎ **800/654-3131** in the U.S., 506/441-0097 at the airport, or 506/221-1818 in downtown San José; www.hertz.com); **National Car Rental** (☎ **800/328-4567** in the U.S., 506/441-6533 at the airport, or 506/290-8787 in downtown San José; www.natcar.com); **Prego Rent A Car** (☎ **506/443-2336** at the airport; or 506/257-1158 in San José; www.pregorentacar.com); **Thrifty Car Rental** (☎ **800/367-2277** in the U.S., 506/442-8585 at the airport, or 506/257-3434 in downtown San José); **Tropical Rent A Car** (☎ **506/442-8000**); and **Toyota Rent A Car** (☎ **506/441-1411** at the airport or 506/223-2250 in downtown San José; www.toyotarent.com).

There are dozens of other car-rental agencies in San José, and most of them will arrange for airport or hotel pickup or delivery. Two of the more dependable agencies are **American Rent A Car,** 425 meters (463 yd.) north of the Toyota dealership on Paseo Colón (☎ **506/221-5353**); and **Hola! Rent A Car,** west of Hotel Irazú, La Uruca, San José (☎ **506/231-5666;** www.hola.net).

During the high season, I highly recommend reserving your car in advance, as the car-rental fleet is often smaller than the demand.

Rental-Car Advice

If you know you will be renting a car, it is wise to reserve it in advance from home. All of the major international agencies and many of the local companies have toll-free numbers and Web sites. Sometimes you can even save a bit on the cost by reserving in advance. Costa Rica's car-rental fleet is not sufficient to meet demand during the high season and rental cars run at a premium. Sometimes this allows the agencies here on the ground to gouge last-minute rental-car shoppers.

To rent a car in Costa Rica, you must be at least 21 years old and have a valid driver's license and a major credit card in your name. For more information about renting a car in Costa Rica see the "Getting Around" section in chapter 2.

Fast Facts: San José

Airport   See "Arriving," earlier in this chapter.

Bookstores   **Seventh Street Books,** Calle 7 between avenidas 1 and Central (☎ **506/256-8251**), has a wide range of new and used books in English, with an excellent selection of tropical biology, bird, and flora books; it's open daily from 9am to 7pm. For a wide selection of new books in English and Spanish, you can also check out **Libreria Internacional,** located 300 meters west of the Taco Bell in San Pedro (☎ **506/253-9553**). It's open Monday through Saturday from 9:30am to 7pm. Libreria International also has a store in the Multiplaza mall in Escazú (☎ **506/288-1138**).

Camera Repair   **Equipos Fotograficos Canon,** Avenida 3 between calles 3 and 5 (☎ **506/233-0176**), specializes in Canon but may be able to repair other brands. You could also try **Dima,** Avenida Central between calles 3 and 5 (☎ **506/222-3969**).

Car Rentals   See "Getting Around," earlier in this chapter.

Climate   See "When to Go" in chapter 2.

Country Code   The telephone country code for Costa Rica is **506;** there are no city or area codes.

Credit Cards   **Credomatic** (☎ **506/257-0155** main office or 506/257-4744 to report lost or stolen cards 24 hours) is the local representative of most major credit cards: American Express, MasterCard, and Visa. They have an office in San José across from the Banco de San José on Calle Central between avenidas 3 and 5. It's open Monday through Friday from 8am to 7pm, and Saturday from 9am to 1pm. This office also serves as a traditional **American Express Travel Services** office, issuing traveler's checks and providing other standard services. You can call the number above to report all lost or stolen cards. To report lost or stolen American Express traveler's checks within Costa Rica, call ☎ **0-800-011-0080.** To report a lost or stolen American Express card from inside Costa Rica, you can also call **0-800-012-3211.** To report a lost or stolen Diners Club card from inside Costa Rica, call ☎ **506/287-8801,** or call collect ☎ **001-303-799-1504.**

Currency Exchange   Most state-run banks will change money, although the lines and bureaucracy can be daunting. The best thing to do is to exchange money at your hotel. If they can't do this for you, or if they are giving a very poor rate of exchange, have them direct you to a private bank or exchange house (*casa de cambio*) where you won't have to stand in line for hours. Avoid exchanging money on the street.

Dentists   If you need a dentist while in San José, your best bet is to call your embassy, which will have a list of recommended dentists. Many bilingual dentists also advertise in the *Tico Times.* Because treatments are so inexpensive in Costa Rica, dental tourism has become a popular option for people needing extensive work.

Doctors   Contact your embassy for information on doctors in San José.

Drugstores   There are countless pharmacies and drugstores in San José. Many of them will deliver at little or no extra cost. The pharmacy at the **Hospital Clinica Biblica** (Avenida 14 between Calle Central and Calle 1; ☎ 506/257-5252) is open 24 hours every day of the year. **Farmacia Fischel,** Avenida 3 and Calle 2, is across from the main post office (☎ 506/257-7979). It's open Monday through Saturday from 8am to 7pm.

Embassies/Consulates   See "Fast Facts: Costa Rica" in chapter 2.

Emergencies   In case of fire, dial ☎ 118; for the police, an ambulance, or general emergencies, dial ☎ 911.

Express Mail Services   Many international courier and express-mail services have offices in San José, including: **DHL,** on Paseo Colón between calles 30 and 32 (☎ 506/290-3020; www.dhl.com); **EMS Courier,** with desks at the principal metropolitan post offices (☎ 506/233-2762); **Fed Ex,** represented by the Aerocasillas office at the Yaohan shopping center across from the Hotel Corobicí (☎ 506/255-4567); and **United Parcel Service,** in Pavas (☎ 506/257-7447; www.ups.com). *Beware:* Despite what you may be told, packages sent overnight to U.S. addresses tend to take 3 to 4 days to reach their destination.

Eyeglasses   Look for the word *optica.* **Optica Jiménez** (☎ 506/257-4658 or 506/233-4475) and **Optica Vision** (☎ 506/255-2266) are two dependable chains, with stores around San José. They can do everything from eye exams to repairs.

Faxes   Many hotels will send and receive faxes for a fee. You can make international phone calls as well as send faxes from the **ICE office** at Avenida 2 between calles 1 and 3 (☎ 506/255-0444). Faxes cost around $2 per page to the United States.

Holidays   See "When to Go" in chapter 2.

Hospitals   **Clinica Biblica,** Avenida 14 between Calle Central and Calle 1 (☎ 506/257-5252 or, for emergencies, 506/257-0466), is conveniently located close to downtown and has several English-speaking doctors.

Information   See "Visitor Information," earlier in this chapter.

Internet Cafes   Staying connected on the road is getting easier. Many hotels allow guests to send and receive E-mail. If not, you have a number of options: **Racsa,** Avenida 5 and Calle 1 (☎ 506/287-0087; www.racsa.co.cr); **Cybercafe,** at the Las Arcadas shopping center next to the Gran Hotel Costa Rica (☎ 506/233-3310); **Internet Café,** in Plaza San Pedro (☎ 506/224-7295; www.internetcafecr.com; open 24 hours), with another office in the Centro Colón, on Paseo Colón; and **Browsers Coffee & Internet,** in the Plaza Colonial in Escazú (☎ 506/228-7190), all allow Web and E-mail access. Rates run between $2 and $10 per hour.

Laundry/Dry Cleaning   **Sixaola,** Avenida 2 between calles 7 and 9 (☎ 506/221-2111), open Monday through Friday from 7am to 6pm and Saturday from 8am to 1pm, is a dependable place downtown to get clothes cleaned. Unfortunately, their prices are quite high. **Cybercafe,** at the Las Arcadas shopping center next to the Gran Hotel Costa Rica (☎ 506/233-3310), is a popular Internet café that has recently added a self-serve Laundromat.

Luggage Storage/Lockers   Most hotels will store luggage for you while you're traveling around the country. Sometimes there is a charge for this service.

Maps   The Costa Rican Tourist Board (ICT) (see "Visitor Information," earlier in this chapter) can usually provide you with good maps of both Costa Rica and San José. Other sources in San José are **Seventh Street Books,** Calle 7 between avenidas Central and 1 (☎ **506/256-8251**); **Librería Lehmann,** Avenida Central between calles 1 and 3 (☎ **506/223-1212**); and **Librería Universal,** Avenida Central and calles Central and 1 (☎ **506/222-2222**).

Newspapers/Magazines   The *Tico Times* is Costa Rica's principal English-language weekly paper and serves both the expatriate community and visitors. You may also see *Central America Weekly,* a multilingual tabloid (English, Spanish, German, and Italian) geared toward visitors, which has almost no news. You can also get the *International Herald Tribune, Miami Herald, New York Times, USA Today, Time,* and *Newsweek,* as well as other English-language publications. You'll find these publications in hotel gift shops and in bookstores that sell English-language books. If you understand Spanish, *La Nación* is the leading daily paper. Their "Viva" section has an extensive listing of current cultural events.

Photographic Needs   Film is expensive in Costa Rica, so bring as much as you will need from home. In a pinch, you can buy film and other photographic equipment at several places around town. I recommend that you wait to have your film processed at home, but if you must develop your prints down here, try **Fuji Foto,** Avenida Central between Calle 1 and Calle Central (☎ **506/222-2222**). For more serious photographic needs (equipment, repairs, etc.), try **Dima,** Avenida Central between calles 3 and 5 (☎ **506/222-3969**).

Police   Dial ☎ **911** for the police. They should have someone who speaks English.

Post Office   The main post office (*correo*) is on Calle 2 between avenidas 1 and 3 (☎ **506/223-9766**), and is open Monday through Friday from 7:30am to 6pm and Saturday from 7:30am to noon. At press time, it costs 70 colones (23¢) to mail a letter to the United States; 90 colones (30¢) to Europe; 55 colones (18¢) for a postcard. Given the Costa Rican postal service's track record, I recommend paying an extra 165 colones (55¢) to have anything of any value certified.

Radio/TV   There are about 10 local TV channels, plus local cable and satellite TV from the United States. There are dozens of AM and FM radio stations in San José.

Religious Services   The *Tico Times* has a listing of churches in San José. You can also ask at the tourist office for a list of the city's churches, or ask at your hotel. The following are suggestions for English-language services. Call for locations. **Episcopal:** Church of the Good Shepherd (☎ **506/222-1560**); **Reform Judaism:** B'nai Israel (☎ **506/257-1785**); **Roman Catholic:** the International Chapel of St. Mary at the Hotel Herradura complex (☎ **506/293-4457**); **Baptist:** International Baptist Church (☎ **506/237-7569**); **Quaker:** Call ☎ **506/233-6168** for information; **Unitarian:** Unity Church (☎ **506/228-6051;** www.unitycostarica.org).

Rest Rooms   These are known as *sanitarios* or *servicios sanitarios.* You may also see or hear them called *baños.* They are marked *damas* (women) and *hombres* or *caballeros* (men). Public rest rooms are rare to nonexistent, but most big hotels and public restaurants will let you use their bathrooms. If you're downtown, there are public bathrooms at the entrance to the Gold Museum.

Safety   Pickpockets and purse slashers are rife in San José, especially on public buses, in the markets, on crowded sidewalks, and near hospitals. Leave your passport, money, and other valuables in your hotel safe and carry only as much as you really need when you go out. It's a good idea to make a photocopy of your passport's opening pages and carry that with you. If you do carry anything valuable with you, keep it in a money belt or special passport bag around your neck. Day packs are a prime target of brazen pickpockets throughout the city. Stay away from the red-light district northwest of the Central Market. Also, be advised that the Parque Nacional is not a safe place for a late-night stroll.

Other precautions include walking around corner vendors, not between the vendor and the building. The tight space between the vendor and the building is a favorite spot for pickpockets. Never park a car on the street, and never leave anything of value in a car, even if it's in a guarded parking lot. Don't even leave your car unattended by the curb in front of a hotel while you dash in to check on your reservation. With these precautions in mind, you should have a safe visit to San José. Also, see "Safety" in "Fast Facts: Costa Rica," in chapter 2.

Taxes All hotels charge 16.3% tax. Restaurants charge 13% tax and also add on a 10% service charge, for a total of 23% more on your bill. There is an airport departure tax of $17.

Taxis See "Getting Around," earlier in this chapter.

Telegrams/Telexes You can send telegrams and telexes from the **ICE office** on Avenida 2 between calles 1 and 3 (open daily from 7am to 10pm). **Radiográfica,** at Calle 1 and Avenida 5 in San José (☎ **506/287-0600**), and **Western Union** (☎ **800/777-7777** or 506/283-6336), with numerous offices around the country, also have telegram services.

Telephones See "Telephones/Faxes" in "Fast Facts: Costa Rica," in chapter 2.

Time Zone San José is on central standard time (same as Chicago and St. Louis), 6 hours behind Greenwich mean time.

Useful Telephone Numbers For directory assistance, call ☎ **113;** for international directory assistance, call ☎ **124;** for the exact time, call ☎ **112.**

Water The water in San José is perfectly fine to drink. Nonetheless, travelers sometimes experience stomach discomfort during their first few days of drinking it. If you want to be cautious, drink bottled water and *frescos* made with milk instead of water. *Sin hielo* means "no ice," and this is what you'll want to say if you're nervous about the water—just because it's frozen doesn't mean it's not water.

Weather The weather in San José (including the Central Valley) is usually temperate, never getting extremely hot or cold. May to November is the rainy season, though the rain usually falls only in the afternoon and evening.

3 Accommodations

Just a few years back, hotels were popping up all over downtown San José, but in recent years the boom has not only stopped; there is, in fact, a distinct glut of accommodations. This can be good for you, the visitor, as it's created a healthy degree of competition—it pays to shop around and ask if anyone's offering special packages or promotions when you plan to visit. Nevertheless, there has also been a significant weeding out process, and the better-run establishments (and those recommended here) are often booked well in advance during the high season.

Of the many hotels in San José, your choices range from luxury resorts to budget pensions charging only a few dollars a night. However, these two extremes are the exceptions, not the norm. The vast number of accommodations, and the best deals, are to be found in the $40-to-$90 price range. Within this moderate bracket, you'll find restored homes that have been turned into small hotels and bed-and-breakfasts, modern hotels with swimming pools and exercise rooms, and older downtown business hotels. When considering where to stay in San José, you should take into consideration how long you plan to stay, what you expect to do while you're here, and whether you want to be in the heart of the city or out in the suburbs.

Downtown hotels, many of which are in beautifully restored homes, are convenient to museums, restaurants, and shopping, but can be noisy. Many people are also bothered by the exhaust fumes that permeate downtown streets. If you want clean air and a peaceful night's sleep, consider staying out in the suburbs. **Escazú** is quiet and has great views, while **Los Yoses** is fairly close to downtown yet still quiet. If you've rented a car, make sure your hotel provides secure parking, or you'll have to find (and pay for) a nearby lot. If you plan to take some day tours, you can just as easily arrange these from a hotel situated outside the downtown area.

If you're heading out to Guanacaste, the central Pacific, or the northern zone, you might consider a hotel or bed-and-breakfast either near or beyond the airport. Sure, you give up proximity to downtown, but you can cut as much as an hour off your travel time to any of these destinations. Many car-rental companies will even deliver or pick up cars at these establishments.

ALTERNATIVES TO HOTELS   In the past few years, dozens of bed-and-breakfast inns have opened up around the San José area. Most are in residential neighborhoods that are quieter, though less convenient, than downtown locations. You can find out about many bed-and-breakfasts, both in San José and around the country, by contacting the **Costa Rica Bed and Breakfast Group** (☎ **506/223-4168;** fax 506/223-4157; E-mail: rayavida@hotels.co.cr).

If you plan to be in town for a while or are traveling with family or several friends, you may want to consider staying in an *apartotel*. As the name implies, this is a cross between an apartment and a hotel. You can rent by the day, week, or month, and you get a furnished apartment with a full kitchen, plus housekeeping and laundry service. Options to choose from include **Apartotel El Sesteo** (☎ **506/296-1805;** fax 506/296-1865; E-mail: sesteo@racsa.co.cr); **Apartotel La Sabana** (☎ **506/220-2422;** fax 506/231-1786; E-mail: lasabana@racsa.co.cr); **Apartotel Don Carlos** (☎ **506/221-6707;** fax 506/ 255-0828; www.doncarlos.co.cr; E-mail: hotel@doncarlos.co.cr); and **Apartotel Los Yoses** (☎ **506/ 225-0033;** fax 506/225-5595; www.apartotel.com; E-mail: losyoses@racsa.co.cr).

DOWNTOWN SAN JOSÉ/BARRIO AMÓN
VERY EXPENSIVE

Aurola Holiday Inn. Avenida 5 and Calle 5 (Apdo. 7802-1000), San José. ☎ **506/222-2424.** Fax 506/222-0603. www.aurola-holidayinn.com. E-mail: auroven@racsa.co.cr. 200 units. A/C TV TEL. $110–$140 double, $150 junior suite, $250–$450 suite. AE, DC, MC, V. Free parking.

Situated directly across the street from the attractive Parque Morazán, this is San José's only high-rise deluxe hotel. The rooms are everything you might expect in this price range—but nothing more. The hotel has been around for quite a few years, and the age is starting to show. Moreover, I've found the service can be somewhat hit-or-miss. However, if you get one of the upper-floor rooms on the north side, you'll have one of the best views in the city.

Dining/Diversions: The Mirador, up on the 17th floor, is the Aurola's top restaurant and serves good continental and international fare—and the view is one of the best in San José. There's also a casino on this same floor. Just off the lobby is the more casual Tropicana, which serves an impressive, though pricey, breakfast buffet. Bar La Palma overlooks the lobby and Parque Morazán. There is also a snack bar adjacent to the pool.

Amenities: Room service, laundry service, car-rental desk, travel agency, tour desk, indoor pool, hot tub, saunas, exercise room, gift shop, executive center.

Radisson Europa Hotel. Calle Blancos, behind La República building (Apdo. 538-2120), San José. ☎ **800/333-3333** in the U.S., or 506/257-3257. Fax 506/257-8221. E-mail: eurohot@sol.racsa.co.cr. 107 units. A/C MINIBAR TV TEL. $160–$180 double, $250 junior suite, $700 presidential suite. AE, DC, MC, V. Free parking.

This hotel is geared primarily to business travelers, but it's a good choice for anyone looking for a big, dependable luxury hotel close to downtown San José. Wooden head-boards and angular window nooks and other small architectural details give these rooms a slight edge over those in the Aurola Holiday Inn. For an extra $20 you can ask for an executive room, which is basically a standard room with a coffeemaker, scale, terry-cloth bathrobes, and an extra telephone in the bathroom. The junior suites are called CEO Club rooms here and are in an isolated wing with its own comfortable lounge and honor bar. They come with all the above amenities, as well as a desk and chair, in-room fax machine, and small balcony.

Dining: There are two restaurants here: an informal cafe for breakfast and lunch, and the more formal Acuarelas, serving up a varied plate of international fare in a more elegant setting.

Amenities: Pool, small gym, casino, gift shop, art gallery, tour desk, and car-rental agency. Business travelers will find a full-service business center, as well as ample conference facilities.

EXPENSIVE

Barceló Amón Plaza. Avenida 11 and Calle 3 bis (Apdo. 4192-1000), San José. ☎ **800/575-1253** in the U.S., or 506/257-0191. Fax 506/257-0284. www.barcelo.com. E-mail: amonpark@racsa.co.cr. 90 units. A/C TV TEL. $104 double, $136–$220 suite. AE, DC, MC, V. Free parking.

Located on the north edge of the Barrio Amón historic neighborhood, this hotel stands out in size and luxury from most of the area's smaller hotels. Moreover, in terms of service, location, and price, this hotel gets my nod over the nearby Holiday Inn. The rooms are spacious and up to international standards.

Dining: The Park Plaza restaurant is the hotel's most formal dining option, serving well-prepared international and nouvelle Costa Rican cuisine. There is also a more casual 24-hour lobby restaurant and the Tamesis Bar.

Amenities: The hotel also has a small gym, tour desk, and gift shop.

✪ Britannia Hotel. Calle 3 and Avenida 11 (Apdo. 3742-1000), San José. ☎ **800/263-2618** in the U.S., or 506/223-6667. Fax 506/223-6411. www.centralamerica.com. E-mail: britania@racsa.co.cr. 24 units. TV TEL. $89–$117 double. AE, MC, V. Parking nearby.

Of the many hotels that have been created from restored old houses in downtown San José, this is the most luxurious. The big pink building, with its wraparound veranda, is unmistakable and is certainly one of the most attractive old houses in the neighborhood. In the lobby, tile floors, stained-glass large picture windows, a brass chandelier, and reproduction Victorian decor all help set a tone of tropical luxury. Along with restoring the old home, the owners have built a four-story addition, which is separated from the original building by a narrow atrium. Rooms in the orig-inal home have hardwood floors and furniture, and high ceilings and fans help keep them cool. In the deluxe rooms and junior suites, you get air-conditioning. Though the street-side rooms have double glass, light sleepers will still want to avoid them. The quietest rooms are those toward the back of the new addition.

Dining: In what was once the wine cellar, you'll find a casual restaurant. The buffet breakfast is served in the adjacent skylit room. Afternoon tea and happy-hour drinks are also served.

Amenities: There are room service and laundry services, and the hotel will store luggage and arrange tours.

Hotel Alóki. 949 Calle 13 between avenidas 9 and 11 (Apdo. 1040-2050), San José. ☎ **506/ 222-6702.** Fax 506/221-2533. www.traveltocostarica.com. E-mail: haloki@racsa.co.cr. 7 units. TV TEL. $90 double, $140 suite. Rates include full breakfast. MC, V. Parking nearby.

Formerly the Hotel L'Ambiance, this small hotel is located in a beautifully restored stucco building with a large central courtyard. The building is on a quiet street only a few blocks from the heart of downtown San José, so you get both the convenience of the city and the quiet of a suburban location. Tile floors in the halls and on the veranda surrounding the courtyard provide a touch of old Costa Rica, while European and North American antiques add a bit of international flavor. Guest rooms have high ceilings and either hardwood floors or carpeting. There is a mix of antique and modern furnishings, and though there is no air-conditioning, overhead fans manage to keep the rooms cool. Rooms vary in size.

Dining: Wrought-iron tables are spread around the covered central patio, which serves as the hotel's restaurant. Well-prepared continental dinners are served here by candlelight. There's also a quiet bar located in the back of the building with an open picture window overlooking the Simón Bolívar Zoo.

Amenities: Concierge and laundry service available.

MODERATE

D'raya Vida. Apdo. 2209-2100, San José (mailing address in the U.S.: P.O. Box 025216-1638, Miami, FL 33102-5216). ☎ **506/223-4168.** Fax 506/223-4157. E-mail: rayavida@hotels.co.cr. 4 units. Nov–Apr $85 double; May–Oct $65 double. Rates include full breakfast. MC, V. Free parking.

This little bed-and-breakfast is so secluded that it seems to be in a world all its own, yet it's in downtown San José. To find the inn, go east on Avenida 9 (following it as it jogs slightly north on Calle 15) until you reach the main entrance to the Calderon Guardia Hospital. Go 1 block east beyond the hospital entrance and turn left on Calle 19 and go 1 block north. Turn left again and go 2 blocks west on Avenida 11, until you see the hotel's sign and a small road on your right. Follow this road to the dead-end at the inn's front gate.

Behind the gate, in a shady old garden, is a miniature villa. The restored old stucco home is furnished with the owners' eclectic collection of crafts from around the world, and in the living room you'll find a grand piano and fireplace. Guest rooms are all different. My favorite rooms are the two downstairs. One is decorated with masks from around the world, and the other has Indian art and a fountain just outside. D'raya Vida offers free airport pickup and drop-off.

Gran Hotel Costa Rica. Avenida 2 between calles 1 and 3, San José. ☎ **506/221-4000.** Fax 506/221-3501. E-mail: granhcr@racsa.co.cr. 110 units. TV TEL. $71 double, $78 triple, $104–$199 suite. AE, DC, MC, V. Free parking.

Though the Gran Hotel Costa Rica can claim the best location of any downtown hotel (bordering the National Theater and the Plaza de la Cultura), it does not, unfortunately, offer rooms to match the prestigious location or name. Though most of the guest rooms here are fairly large, they have not been well maintained over the decades, giving them an adequate but rather run-down feel, especially in the bathrooms.

The Café Parisien is the hotel's greatest attribute, and it's memorable not so much for its food as for its atmosphere. The restaurant is an open-air patio that overlooks the National Theater, street musicians, and all the activity of the Plaza de la Cultura. On the opposite side of the lobby, there's a small and very casual casino. The hotel also maintains a tour desk and gift shop, and it offers 24-hour room service and laundry service.

Hotel Del Rey. Avenida 1 and Calle 9 (Apdo. 6241-1000), San José. ☎ **506/257-7800.** Fax 506/221-0096. www.hoteldelrey.com. E-mail: delrey@ticonet.co.cr. 103 units. A/C TV TEL. $68–$75 double, $75–$85 triple, $125 suite. AE, MC, V. Parking nearby.

You can't miss the Del Rey; it's a massive pink corner building with vaguely colonial styling. The lobby continues the facade's theme with pink-tile floors and stone columns. Inside, every guest room is marked by a carved hardwood door. The rooms vary in size and comfort: There are quiet interior rooms that have no windows, and larger rooms with windows (but also street noises). Try for a sixth-floor room with a balcony. The hotel's only restaurant is the Del Rey Cafe, which serves respectable U.S.-style deli sandwiches and light meals. Much of the first floor is taken up with a lively casino and the neighboring Blue Marlin Bar, which is very popular with sports fans and prostitutes. The hotel has full-service tour and sportfishing desks.

✪ **Hotel Don Carlos.** 779 Calle 9 between avenidas 7 and 9, San José (mailing address in the U.S.: SJO 1686, P.O. Box 025216, Miami, FL 33102). ☎ **506/221-6707.** Fax 506/255-0828. www.doncarlos.co.cr. E-mail: hotel@doncarlos.co.cr. 36 units. TV. $60–$70 double. Rates include continental breakfast. AE, MC, V. Free parking.

If you're looking for a small hotel that is unmistakably Costa Rican and hints at the days of the planters and coffee barons, this is the place for you. Located in an old residential neighborhood, only blocks from the business district, the Don Carlos is popular with both vacationers and businesspeople. A large reproduction of a pre-Columbian carved-stone human figure stands outside the front door of this gray inn, which was a former president's mansion. Inside, you'll find many more such reproductions, as well as orchids, ferns, palms, and parrots. After a day of exploring the capital, there's nothing like settling down in the lounge, the small courtyard, or the sunny deck, where the wicker furniture, bubbling fountain, and tropical breezes will make you think you're Hope or Crosby on the road to somewhere. The rooms are all distinct and vary greatly in size, so be specific when you reserve, or ask to see a few if possible when you check in.

The newest additions here include a 10-person Jacuzzi, and an outdoor orchid garden and atrium where breakfast is served. There's also another restaurant and the comfortable pre-Columbian lounge. The gift shop here is one of the largest in the country, and the paintings hung throughout the hotel are also for sale. There's a helpful in-house tour company, and the hotel allows guests to send and receive E-mail free of charge.

✪ **Hotel Santo Tomas.** Avenida 7 between calles 3 and 5, San José. ☎ **506/255-0448.** Fax 506/222-3950. www.hotelsantotomas.com. E-mail: info@hotelsantotomas.com. 20 units. TV TEL. $70–$100 double. Rates include continental breakfast. MC, V. Parking nearby.

Even though it's on a nondescript street, this converted mansion is a real jewel inside. Built 100 years ago by a coffee baron, the house has been lovingly restored and maintained by its owner, Thomas Douglas. The first thing you see when you walk through the front door is the beautiful carved-wood desk that serves as the reception area. In the guest rooms you'll find similar pieces of exquisitely crafted antique reproductions, made here in Costa Rica from rare hardwoods. Keeping with the theme, the hardwood floors throughout most of the hotel are original and were made from a type of tree that has long since become almost impossible to find. The rooms vary in size, but most are fairly large and have a small table and chairs. Skylights in some bathrooms will brighten your morning, and queen-size beds will provide a good night's sleep. Maps of Costa Rica hang on the walls of all the guest rooms so you can get acquainted with the country.

There are a couple of patio areas, as well as a TV lounge and combination breakfast room and outdoor bar. Laundry service and a baggage-storage room are available. The staff and management are extremely helpful with tour arrangements and any other needs or requests. The hotel has bought a neighboring property and plans to add a swimming pool, Jacuzzi, conference room, and gift shop.

La Casa Verde de Amón. Calle 7 and Avenida 9, no. 910, San José (mailing address in the U.S.: Dept. 1701, P.O. Box 025216, Miami, FL 33102-5216). ☎ and fax **506/223-0969.** www.zurqui.com. E-mail: casaverd@racsa.co.cr. 8 units. TV TEL. $65–$96 double. Rates include continental breakfast. AE, MC, V. Parking nearby.

This tropical Victorian house was built around 1910 and was completely renovated between 1989 and 1992. There are beautiful old-tile and polished-hardwood floors throughout the building, which give the house a patrician air. Off the lobby, there's a small patio and open-air breakfast room. Up on the second floor, there's a large high-ceilinged central seating area with a 110-year-old baby grand piano and large stained-glass picture windows that bathe the room in a beautiful blue light. Rooms are all different, but most are furnished with antiques. Some have their original porcelain fixtures and brass faucets; you may find a bathtub or only a shower in your bathroom. The Don Carlos suite is huge, with a high ceiling, king-size beds, and a separate seating area. All the rooms have clock radios, but unfortunately, it's likely that traffic noises will wake you in the morning if you have a room on the street side of the hotel. You shouldn't have any trouble finding this hotel, especially if you remember that *casa verde* translates as "green house"—this one is painted a prominent green.

Taylor's Inn. Avenida 13 between Calle 3 and 3 bis (Apdo. 531-1000), San José. ☎ **506/ 257-4333.** Fax 506/221-1475. www.catours.co.cr. E-mail: taylor@catours.co.cr. 12 units. TV. $60 double; slightly lower in the off-season. Rates include buffet breakfast. AE, MC, V.

This is yet another lovely converted home turned bed-and-breakfast. The rooms are all arranged around the interior courtyard, which features a small garden of flowering ginger and other tropical flora—a perfect place for eating breakfast. Most rooms have one single and one double bed, although a few have sleeping lofts and are good for families. All are very clean and feature artwork from prominent Costa Rican artists. The suite is a bit bigger, with a 20-inch television. Don't expect a sense of hermetic privacy here, though—most of the rooms open onto the courtyard, and the old wooden construction guarantees that you hear every footfall and conversation of other guests passing by your door. The hotel has a helpful tour desk.

INEXPENSIVE

Hotel Bienvenido. Calle 10 between avenidas 1 and 3, San José. ☎ **506/233-2161.** Fax 506/221-1872. 51 units. $18 double, $27 triple. AE, MC, V. Parking nearby.

This very basic hotel is one of the most popular in the city for travelers on a tight budget. The rooms are clean, though a bit dark, and there is always ample hot water. The hotel was created from an old movie theater, and there are still a few architectural details remaining from this incarnation. They recently opened a simple restaurant serving simple and inexpensive meals. The place fills up by early afternoon in the high season, so call ahead for a reservation and ask for a quiet room in the back.

Hotel Diplomat. Calle 6 between Avenida Central and Avenida 2 (Apdo. 6606-1000), San José. ☎ **506/221-8133.** Fax 506/233-7474. 29 units. TEL. $30 double. AE, MC, V. Parking nearby.

It's easy to miss the entrance to this hotel. Watch for it on the east side of the street. The place is what you might expect from a worn yet perennially popular downtown budget hotel. The lobby is narrow, and the front door is fairly nondescript. The carpeted rooms are rather small, and the appointments have seen better days, but they're comfortable nonetheless, and some rooms on the upper floors even have nice views of the mountains. The tiled baths are clean, and the water is hot. The hotel's restaurant is a dark, attractive room with pink tablecloths, flowers on every table, and pastel walls. For those seeking an intimate dinner, try one of the tiny booths for two.

Hotel Ritz and Pension Continental. Calle Central between avenidas 8 and 10 (Apdo. 5343-1000), San José. ☎ **506/222-4103.** Fax 506/222-8849. 25 units, 5 with bathroom. $15–$20 double without bathroom, $25 double with bathroom. AE, MC, V. Parking nearby.

These two side-by-side budget hotels are under the same management and together have rooms to fit most budget travelers' needs. There is even a travel agency and tour company on the first floor, so you can arrange all of your travels around Costa Rica without leaving the hotel. Rooms vary greatly in size and comfort levels and can be dark and a bit musty. Bathrooms are old, and those showers that do have hot water use showerhead heaters that barely work. If the first room you see isn't to your liking, just ask to see another, or make a small jump up in price category. The current owners are Swiss, so you'll probably meet quite a few Swiss travelers if you stay here. The hotel is in a bit of a bad neighborhood, so be careful walking around, especially if you're carrying a pack on your back.

Joluva Guesthouse. 936 Calle 3B between avenidas 9 and 11, San José. ☎ **800/298-2418** in the U.S., or 506/223-7961. Fax 506/257-7668. www.joluva.com. E-mail: joluva@racsa.co.cr. 7 units, 6 with bathroom. TV. $27 double without bathroom, $37–$47 double with bathroom. Rates include continental breakfast. AE, MC, V. Parking nearby.

Though you can find a less expensive hotel, there are few in this price range that offer the old-fashioned architectural detail of the Joluva—old tile and hardwood floors throughout and high ceilings (in one room, beautiful plasterwork on the ceiling). However, the rooms are small and a bit dark, and only two have windows that open onto the small courtyard. The breakfast room has skylights, which help brighten it a bit. This hotel caters to a gay clientele, but guests of all types are welcome.

Pension de la Cuesta. 1332 Cuesta de Nuñez, Avenida 1 between calles 11 and 15, San José. ☎ and fax **506/255-2896.** www.arweb.com/lacuesta. E-mail: ggmnber@racsa.co.cr. 9 units, none with bathroom. $26 double, $34 triple. Rates include continental breakfast. AE, MC, V. Parking nearby.

If you don't mind a clean collective bathroom down the hall from your room, this little bed-and-breakfast is a real bargain and definitely worth considering. It was once the home of Otto Apuy, a well-known Costa Rican artist, and original artwork abounds. The building itself is a classic example of a tropical wood-frame home and has been painted an eye-catching pink with blue-and-white trim. Some of the rooms can be a bit dark and are very simply furnished, but there's a very sunny and cheery sunken lounge/courtyard area in the center of the house. Most of the rooms have one double and a set of bunk beds. Overall, the place feels a lot like a hostel. The owners give you free run of the kitchen and are even offering free use of their Internet connection. If that's not enough free stuff, there's no charge for children under 12. You'll find this hotel on the hill leading up to the Parque Nacional.

HOTELS IN LA SABANA/PASEO COLÓN
VERY EXPENSIVE

Meliá Confort Corobicí. Autopista General Cañas, Sabana Norte (Apdo. 2443-1000), San José. ☎ **888/485-2676** in the U.S., or 506/232-8122 in Costa Rica. Fax 506/231-5834. www.solmelia.es. E-mail: corobici@racsa.co.cr. 198 units. A/C MINIBAR TV TEL. $135 double, $150–$450 suite. Rates include breakfast buffet. AE, MC, V. Free parking.

Located just past the end of Paseo Colón and on the edge of Parque La Sabana, the Corobicí offers all the amenities you would expect at a large airport hotel, with one added bonus—it's much closer to downtown. The lobby is a vast expanse of marble floor faced by blank walls, though the art-deco furnishings lend a bit of character. Guest rooms are quite modern and comfortable, with good beds and walls of glass through which, on most floors, you get good views of the valley and surrounding mountains. Joggers will enjoy the nearby Parque La Sabana.

Dining/Diversions: Perhaps the hotel's greatest attributes are its restaurants. Fuji serves authentic Japanese meals amid equally authentic surroundings; La Gondola serves good Italian food. These two restaurants are open for lunch and dinner only. At El Tucan Coffee Shop, you can get an inexpensive meal throughout the day. The Guacamaya is a quiet lobby bar, while the Pub Bar is a bit more lively and features karaoke music. There's also a casino.

Amenities: The Corobicí claims to have the largest health spa in Central America. Here you'll find a well-equipped exercise room, sauna, hot tub, and aerobics classes. The hotel also offers 24-hour room service, a valet/laundry service, a downtown shuttle, a tour desk, a car-rental desk, an outdoor pool, conference rooms, a beauty parlor, and a gift shop.

MODERATE

✪ **Hotel Grano de Oro.** Calle 30, no. 251, between avenidas 2 and 4, 150m (164 yd.) south of Paseo Colón (Apdo. 1157-1007, Centro Colón), San José (mailing address in the U.S.: SJO 36, P.O. Box 025216, Miami, FL 33102). ☎ **506/255-3322.** Fax 506/221-2782. www.hotelgranodeoro.com. E-mail: granoro@racsa.co.cr. 35 units. MINIBAR TV TEL. $75–$105 double, $130–$200 suite. AE, MC, V. Free parking.

San José boasts dozens of old homes that have been converted into hotels, but few offer the luxurious accommodations or professional service that can be found at the Grano de Oro. Located on a quiet side street off of Paseo Colón, this small hotel offers a variety of room types to fit most budgets and tastes. Personally, I prefer the patio rooms, which have French doors opening onto private patios. However, if you want a room with plenty of space, ask for one of the deluxe rooms, which have large, modern, tiled baths with big tubs.

Throughout all the guest rooms, you'll find attractive hardwood furniture, including old-fashioned wardrobes in some rooms. For additional luxuries, you can stay in one of the suites, which have whirlpool tubs. The Vista de Oro suite is the hotel's crowning jewel, with its own private staircase and wonderful views of the city and surrounding mountains. If you don't grab a suite, you still have access to the hotel's two rooftop Jacuzzis. The hotel's patio garden restaurant serves excellent international cuisine and some of the best desserts in the city.

Hotel Rosa del Paseo. 2862 Paseo Colón (Apdo. 287-1007, Centro Colón), San José. ☎ **506/257-3213** or 506/257-3258. Fax 506/223-2776. www.online.co.cr. E-mail: rosadelp@racsa.co.cr. 14 units. TV TEL. $65–$70 double, $90 suite; lower in the off-season. Rates include continental breakfast. AE, MC, V. Limited free parking.

This hotel is housed in one of San José's most beautiful old stucco homes, right on busy Paseo Colón. However, the rooms are all located away from the street and are well insulated against the noise. Built more than 110 years ago, this old home underwent a complete renovation and modernization a few years ago and is now richly appointed and surprisingly evocative of 19th-century Costa Rica. The rooms are all quite comfortable; the master suite even comes with its own balcony and Jacuzzi. There are beautiful details throughout the hotel: transoms, ornate stucco door frames, polished hardwood floors. Reproduction antique and wicker furnishings evoke both the tropics and the past century.

The restaurant here serves international cuisine, with a nice selection of Peruvian dishes. You'll also find 24-hour bar/beverage service, laundry service, airport transportation, a craft shop, and an art gallery.

Hotel Torremolinos. Calle 40 and Avenida 5 bis (Apdo. 434-1150, La Uruca), San José. ☎ **506/222-9129.** Fax 506/255-3167. www.solmelia.es. E-mail: torrehtl@racsa.co.cr. 84 units. TV TEL. $70 double, $80–$90 suite. Rates include breakfast. AE, MC, V. Free parking.

If you want to be close to downtown, have some of the trappings of a modern business-class hotel, and not spend a fortune, this is your best choice. Located at the west end of Paseo Colón, the Torremolinos is on a fairly quiet street and is built around a colorful and well-tended garden that makes the hotel's pool a wonderful place to while away an afternoon. The rooms are simply furnished and have plenty of space. There's a moderately priced restaurant serving international dishes, a lobby bar, conference room, tour desk, downtown shuttle bus, and room service.

INEXPENSIVE

Hotel Cacts. 2845 Avenida 3 bis, between calles 28 and 30 (Apdo. 379-1005), San José. ☎ **506/221-2928** or 506/221-6546. Fax 506/221-8616. www.tourism.co.cr. E-mail: hcacts@racsa.co.cr. 30 units. $42–$60 double, $53–$65 triple. Rates include breakfast buffet. AE, MC, V. Free parking.

This is one of the most interesting and unusual budget hotels I've ever seen, housed in an attractive tropical contemporary home on a business and residential street. The original building is a maze of rooms and hallways on several levels (the house is built on a slope). The newer rooms all come with telephones and televisions. My favorite room is the huge bilevel family room with a high-beamed ceiling. There's a third-floor open terrace that serves as the breakfast area. The hotel has even recently added a swimming pool and Jacuzzi. Hotel Cacts has its own tour desk and gift shop. The staff here is very helpful, and the hotel will receive mail and faxes, change money, and store baggage for guests.

Hotel Petite Victoria. Paseo Colón, Frente a la Sala Garbo (Apdo. 357-1007), San José. ☎ and fax **506/233-5193.** 16 units. TV. $35 double, $45 triple. Rates include continental breakfast. No credit cards. Free parking.

One of the oldest houses in San José, this tropical Victorian home was once the election campaign headquarters for Oscar Arias Sánchez, Costa Rica's Nobel Prize–winning former president. Today, after extensive remodeling and restoration, it's an interesting little hotel that offers a historic setting at inexpensive rates. The big covered patio is perfect for sitting and taking in the warm sun, and it doubles as the hotel's restaurant. Guest rooms have medium to large tiled bathrooms and high ceilings and fans to keep the air cool. Inside, walls are made of wood, so noise can be a bit of a problem, but this is a small price to pay for such old-fashioned elegance. Tour arrangements and laundry service are also offered.

SAN PEDRO/LOS YOSES
MODERATE

✪ **Hotel Le Bergerac.** 50 S. Calle 35 (Apdo. 1107-1002), San José. ☎ **506/234-7850.** Fax 506/225-9103. www.bergerac.com. E-mail: bergerac@racsa.co.cr. 18 units. TV TEL. $68–$88 double; corporate rates available. Rates include full breakfast. AE, MC, V. Free parking.

With all the sophistication and charm of a small French inn, the Hotel Le Bergerac has ingratiated itself with business travelers and members of various diplomatic missions. What these visitors have found is a tranquil environment in a quiet suburban neighborhood, spacious and comfortable accommodations, personal service, and gourmet meals. The owners have a total of 32 years of hotel experience, which accounts for the professionalism with which Le Bergerac is operated.

The hotel is composed of three houses with courtyard gardens in between. Almost all of the rooms are quite large, and each is a little different. My favorite rooms are those with private patio gardens. Some rooms have king-size beds and refrigerators, and in the old master bedroom you'll find a little balcony. In the evenings, candlelight and classical music set a relaxing and romantic mood. The long-standing **L'Ile de France restaurant** has recently set up shop here, and gourmet French and continental dinners are available for guests and by reservation. The hotel also has a helpful tour desk and provides a wide range of business services to guests.

INEXPENSIVE

D'galah Hotel. Apdo. 85-2350 (in front of the University of Costa Rica's School of Pharmacy), San José. ☎ and fax **506/280-8092.** E-mail: dgalah@racsa.co.cr. 25 units. TV TEL. $38–$48 double. Rates include full breakfast. AE, MC, V. Free parking.

If you want to be close to downtown but away from the smog and traffic, this budget hotel is a good choice. Directly across the street from the hotel is the University of Costa Rica, which is an oasis of greenery that attracts many species of birds, especially among the bamboo groves. Rooms are a bit old-fashioned and dark. But, if you aren't too demanding, for the most part they're quite spacious and acceptable. The largest rooms have kitchenettes and sleeping lofts; the newest rooms have carpets and small private patios. Amenities include a small swimming pool, a sauna, and a breakfast room.

Toruma Youth Hostel. Avenida Central between calles 29 and 31 (Apdo. 1352-1002), San José. ☎ **506/224-4085.** E-mail: recajhi@racsa.co.cr. 95 beds, all with shared bathroom. $11 per person per night with an IYHF card, $13 with student ID, $14 general public. Rates include continental breakfast. MC, V. Free parking.

This attractive old building, with its long veranda, is the largest hostel in Costa Rica's system of official youth hostels. Although it's possible to find other accommodations around town in this price range, none would likely be as clean. The atmosphere here is convivial and will be familiar to anyone who has hosteled in Europe. There's a large lounge in the center of the building with a high ceiling and a great deal of light. The dorms have four to six beds per room. The staff here can help you arrange stays at other hostels and trips around the country, and you can store luggage for 25¢ per day.

ESCAZÚ & SANTA ANA

Located about 15 minutes west of San José and about the same distance from the international airport, these affluent suburbs have experienced rapid growth in recent years, as the metropolitan area continues its urban sprawl. Both Escazú and Santa Ana are popular with North American retirees and expatriates, and quite a few little B&Bs have sprung up to cater to the needs of their visiting friends. If you're interested in staying at one of these, you might contact the **Costa Rica Bed and Breakfast Group** (☎ 506/223-4168; fax 506/223-4157). It's also easy to commute between Escazú and downtown via bus or taxi. Taxi fare should run around $9 (each way). A bus costs around 30¢.

VERY EXPENSIVE

Camino Real Inter-Continental. Autopista Própero Fernández, across from the Multiplaza shopping complex, Escazú. ☎ **506/289-7000.** Fax 506/289-8930. www.interconti.com. E-mail: sanjose@interconti.com. 260 units. A/C MINIBAR TV TEL. $230 double, $450–$800 suite. AE, MC, V. Free parking.

This is the newest large-scale resort hotel to open in the metropolitan area. The hotel has three five-story wings radiating off of a central hub. The large open lobby has a flagstone and mosaic floor. The rooms are all well appointed, with either one king or two double beds, a working desk, sitting chair and ottoman, and large armoire housing a 25-inch television. For an extra $35 you can stay on the Club Intercontinental floor and enjoy personalized concierge and butler services, separate check-in area, on-floor buffet breakfast, as well as an assortment of refreshments, sweets, hors d'oeuvres and drinks, throughout the day. This floor is where the junior and master suites are located. Overall, the Camino Real offers many of the same features and amenities as the Marriott, although the latter gets the nod in terms of service, restaurants, and ambiance.

Dining/Diversions: The hotel's Mirage restaurant serves upscale French and international cuisine. Azulejos is a more casual option, serving buffet and à la carte continental cuisine daily from 6am to midnight. There's also the Scenario Lobby bar, which has a small menu, as well as the poolside Bananas Bar. The hotel's Casino Real is open nightly from 7pm until the last bettor calls it quits.

Amenities: The hotel has a large free-form pool, gym and spa facilities, a tennis court, beauty salon, car-rental and tour desks, several gift shops, business center, conference and banquet facilities. The hotel is just across from a large, modern shopping-mall complex.

Hotel Alta. Old road to Santa Ana (mailing address in the U.S.: Interlink 964, P.O. Box 02-5635, Miami, FL 33102). ☎ **888/388-2582** in the U.S., or 506/282-4160. Fax 506/282-4162. www.altatravelplanners.com. E-mail: hotlalta@racsa.co.cr. 23 units. A/C MINI-BAR TV TEL. $215 double, $275–$450 suite, $1,400 penthouse; lower in the off-season. AE, MC, V. Free parking.

This new boutique hotel is infused with old-world charm. Curves and high arches abound. My favorite touch is the winding interior alleyway that snakes down from the reception through the hotel. Most of the rooms here have wonderful views of the Central Valley from private balconies. Those that don't have nice garden patios. The rooms are all up to modern resort standards, although some have cramped bathrooms. The suites are considerably larger, with a separate sitting room with its own television, as well as large Jacuzzi-style tubs (although without the jets) in spacious bathrooms. The penthouse is a three-bedroom full-floor extravaganza, with massive living room and stunning open-air rooftop patio.

Dining/Diversions: The hotel's **La Luz** restaurant is one of the most elegant and creative in the Central Valley. Just off the restaurant you'll find a quiet leather-saddled bar.

Amenities: The hotel has a nice-size oval tiled pool, Jacuzzi, and small gym. There's a banquet/conference room, tour desk, and small gift shop. Room service during restaurant hours.

Tara Resort Hotel and Spa. Apdo. 1459-1250, Escazú. ☎ **506/228-6992.** Fax 506/228-9651. www.tararesort.com. E-mail: taraspa@racsa.co.cr. 14 units. TV TEL. $130 double, $200 bungalow, $160–$250 suite. AE, MC, V. Free parking.

Located in San Antonio de Escazú, 600 meters (654 yd.) south of the cemetery (once you hit Escazú—just follow the numerous signs)—Tara is perched high on a mountainside overlooking the entire Central Valley and surrounding volcanic peaks. The view is breathtaking and so is the setting. The owner has a fixation on *Gone With the Wind,* and everything at this spa/resort follows the theme, from the O'Hara Dining Hall down to one of Rhett's Vitality Baths. It's rich in antebellum Southern grandeur, not local color.

The suites are all part of the main house, and each has its own balcony (try to get one overlooking the valley). The penthouse suite is on the third floor, and has high ceilings, private Jacuzzi, and 360° views. Villas and bungalows vary in size, but in the larger rooms you might find a seating area, a big bathroom with two sinks, a tub, a heat lamp, and perhaps even two balconies. Furnishings are traditional American styles that fit right in with the architecture. My biggest complaint is that service seems to run the gamut from excellent to inattentive to gruff.

Dining: The Atlanta Dining Gallery is an elegant setting for fine meals; unfortunately, the windows do not do justice to the view. Meals are sometimes served on the large back patio, which has an unobstructed view of the valley. of

Amenities: Full assortment of spa treatments, including massage, facials, and aromatherapy, outdoor swimming pool, hot tub, sauna, small gym, various lawn and indoor games, conference facilities, and a tour desk.

MODERATE

Costa Verde Inn. Apdo. 1610, Escazú (mailing address in the U.S.: SJO 1313, Box 025216, Miami, FL 33102). ☎ **506/228-4080.** Fax 506/289-8591. www.hotelcostaverde.com. E-mail: costainn@amnet.co.cr. 14 units. $55 double, $65 triple, $70 apt; lower in the off-season. Rates include continental breakfast. AE, MC, V. Free parking.

This sprawling, converted modern home is one of the many nice smaller hotels in Escazú. It incorporates flagstone and stone walls throughout and has a vaguely colonial feel. My favorite rooms are the two by the tennis court, one of which has a sunken, stone-floored shower. You'll find king-size beds in all the rooms, and 25-inch televisions in most. The apartments have complete kitchens. The gardens are lush and overgrown and there's even a postage-stamp pool here. Common areas include a large living room with fireplace and a wide tiled patio that overlooks the garden. You can also find out about various excursions around the country; airport pickups are available, too. The inn is located 100 meters (109 yd.) west and 300 meters (327 yd.) south of the cemetery in Escazú (follow the signs). After you go the 100 meters west of the first cemetery, there's actually another smaller one. Don't let it throw you.

Hotel Mirador Pico Blanco. Apdo. 900 (half a mile/1km south of the church in San Antonio de Escazú), Escazú. ☎ **506/289-6197.** Fax 506/289-5189. 25 units. $45–$65 double. AE, MC, V. Free parking.

There's nothing fancy about the rooms here, but most offer absolutely fabulous views. Some rooms have high ceilings, creating an appearance of spaciousness, and almost all of them have balconies (albeit small ones) and television sets with cable. A few resident macaws fly around the hillsides during the day but come home here each evening. The restaurant is a popular and inexpensive spot, probably the cheapest "view" restaurant in the valley, and the bar has been getting bigger and more popular over the years as well. A hotel shuttle from the airport will cost you about $15 (per trip, not per person); it holds up to 10 people, so this is a good choice for families or big groups.

Villa Escazú. Apdo. 1401-1250, Escazú. ☎ and fax **506/289-7971.** www.hotels.co.cr. E-mail: villaescazu@yellowweb.co.cr. 6 units, all with shared bathroom. $60 double; lower in the off-season. Rates include full breakfast. No credit cards.

If you're looking for a quiet little inn with a homey feel, this converted private home fits the bill. Service is friendly and personable. The rooms are large and immaculate, with plenty of varnished wood. The upstairs rooms have balconies, and the shared bathroom features a tub. The complimentary breakfasts are extensive and creative. The hotel has well-tended grounds and gardens, with quiet sitting areas. There is a new studio for rent by the week or month. To find the place, first get yourself to the Banco Nacional in Escazú. (Most any road into Escazu will lead you onto the one-way street along the western edge of the town's central park.) Follow this road uphill (south) until you see the bank on your right. Turn right. Then go 600 meters (654 yd.) west, follow the severe dogleg 300 meters (327 yd.) south, and watch for the sign marking the driveway. of

HEREDIA/ALAJUELA/AIRPORT AREA

Alajuela and Heredia are two colonial-era cities that lie much closer to the airport than San José. Alajuela is the closest city to the airport, with Heredia lying about midway between Alajuela and the capital. These are two great places to find small, distinct, and charming hotels. If you'd like to learn more about either of these cities, look under "Side Trips from San José," later in this chapter. If your plans are to get yourself to a remote beach or rain-forest lodge as quickly as possible and use San José and the Central Valley purely as a transportation hub, or you just detest urban clutter, noise, and pollution, you might do well to choose one of the hotels listed below.

VERY EXPENSIVE

✪ **Finca Rosa Blanca Country Inn.** Santa Bárbara de Heredia (mailing address in the U.S.: SJO 1201, P.O. Box 025216, Miami, FL 33102-5216). ☎ **506/269-9392.** Fax 506/269-9555. www.finca-rblanca.co.cr. E-mail: info@finca-rblanca.co.cr. 7 units, 2 villas. MINIBAR TEL. $150–$235 double. Extra person $25. Rates include breakfast. AE, MC, V. Free parking.

If the cookie-cutter rooms of international resorts leave you cold, then perhaps the fascinatingly unique rooms of this unusual inn will be more your style. Finca Rosa Blanca is an eclectic architectural confection set amid the lush green hillsides of a coffee plantation. Square corners seem to have been prohibited in the design of this beautiful home. There are turrets and curving walls of glass, arched windows, and a semicircular built-in couch. Everywhere the glow of polished hardwood blends with blindingly white stucco walls and brightly painted murals. The best way I can describe the architecture of this inn is 21st-century pueblo.

Inside, there's original artwork everywhere, and each room is decidedly different and unique. There's the black-and-white room with a patio and bed made from coffee-tree wood. Another room has a bed built into a corner and a handmade tub with windows on two sides. The view is fabulous. If breathtaking bathrooms are your idea of the ultimate luxury, then consider splurging on the master suite, which has a stone waterfall that cascades into a tub in front of a huge picture window. This suite also has a spiral staircase that leads to the top of the turret. The two separate villas have the same sense of eclectic luxury, with small kitchenettes, and quite a bit of space and privacy.

Dining/Diversions: A four-course gourmet dinner served in the small dining room will run you $25 per person. Be sure to reserve early because there's limited seating. In a tiny space off of the living room, there's an honor bar tucked into a reproduction of a typical Costa Rican oxcart.

Amenities: There's a free-form swimming pool outdoors set in the hillside, as well as a hot tub in the main building. Car rentals and guide services can be arranged through the hotel, as well as transportation to and from the airport.

Hotel Herradura. Autopista General Cañas, Ciudad Cariari (Apdo. 7-1880), San José. ☎ **800/245-8420** in the U.S. and Canada, or 506/239-0033 in Costa Rica. Fax 506/239-0210. www.costasol.co.cr. E-mail: hherradu@racsa.co.cr. 234 units. A/C TV TEL. $140–$180 double, $220–$750 suite. AE, DC, MC, V. Free parking.

Big and sprawling, the Herradura still possesses San José's largest and most flexible conference facilities, and so it's often bustling with businesspeople and assorted convention traffic. However, despite the crowds, service here never seems to falter. The superior rooms (there are no standard rooms) are all up to snuff, although the bathrooms in these rooms are small, and most have no view. The deluxe rooms, on the other hand, are very attractive and luxurious. The walls of glass let in plenty of light and usually a good view (pool-view rooms cost $30 extra). The balconies boast marble-topped cafe tables, while the bathrooms feature green-marble counters, phones, and hair dryers.

Dining/Diversions: For quiet dining, there is Sakura, a Japanese restaurant with an indoor garden setting, sushi bar, and table-side teppanyaki preparations. The Sancho Panza Restaurant specializes in formal Spanish meals. Casual meals, including buffets, are available at the 24-hour Tiffany's Restaurant coffee shop. Bambolleo offers nightly piano music and light snacks. Gamblers can spend their time at the elegant Casino Krystal, which is also open 24 hours.

Amenities: The Herradura's wealth of facilities makes it a favorite with families. The main swimming pool (there are three) is one of the largest and most attractive in San José, with a beachlike patio, a swim-up bar, tiled cafe tables in the water, and attractive landscaping around the edges of the pool. Guests have access to the neighboring Meliá Cariari's 18-hole golf course, not to mention its 11 tennis courts, pro shop, and health club. The Herradura also offers 24-hour room service, city and airport shuttle, car-rental desk, tour desk, and baby-sitting. Other facilities include extensive conference and banquet facilities, and a gift shop.

✪ **Marriott Hotel and Resort.** San Antonio de Belén (Apdo. 502-4005). ☎ **800/228-9290** in the U.S. and Canada, or 506/298-0844 in Costa Rica. Fax 506/298-0844. www.marriott.com. E-mail: costaric@marriott.co.cr. 252 units. A/C MINIBAR TV TEL. $140–$200 double, $450 master suite. Rates include breakfast buffet. AE, DC, MC, V. Free parking.

For my money, the Marriott is still the only luxury resort hotel in the San José area to be hitting on all cylinders. Amenities are plentiful, and service here reaches a level and attention to detail uncommon in Costa Rica. The hotel is designed in a mixed colonial style, with hand-painted Mexican tiles, antique red clay roof tiles, weathered columns, and heavy wooden doors, lintels, and trim. The centerpiece is a large open-air interior patio, which somewhat replicates Old Havana's Plaza de Armas. The rooms are all comfortable and well appointed, with either a king-size or two double beds, two telephones, a working desk, an elegant wooden armoire holding the large television, plenty of closet space, a comfortable sitting chair and ottoman, and a small "Juliet" balcony. The bathrooms are up to par but might seem slightly small at this price.

Dining/Diversions: There are several dining options here. The most elegant restaurant is La Isabela, housed in a re-created wine cellar, which has an extensive menu of creative international fare. For more intimacy, you can reserve La Cava, a private room off of Isabela's main dining room. For more casual dining, the Villa Hermosa restaurant serves "nouvelle Costa Rican" and continental dishes, and there also are the outdoor Casa del Sol grill and the Casa del Café coffeehouse. The lobby bar features daily piano music and weekend nights of jazz, as well as a tapas bar, a cigar bar, and both indoor and patio seating.

Amenities: The two pools are adjacent but on separate levels of the large outdoor patio area. There is a small but well-appointed health club, outdoor Jacuzzi, saunas, three tennis courts, hiking and jogging trails, golf driving range, golf pro shop, conference rooms, car-rental and tour desks, beauty salon, private chapel, casino, two gift shops, a concierge, room service, laundry service, newspaper delivery, nightly turndown, and express checkout. In-room massage, baby-sitting, and secretarial services are available, and there's a regular shuttle to the airport.

☉ Meliá Cariari Conference Center and Golf Resort. Autopista General Cañas, Ciudad Cariari (Apdo. 737-1007, Centro Colón), San José. ☎ **800/336-3542** in the U.S. and Canada, or 506/239-0022 in Costa Rica. Fax 506/239-2803. www.solmelia.es. E-mail: cariari@racsa.co.cr. 220 units. A/C MINIBAR TV TEL. $150–$170 double, $170–$490 suite. AE, DC, MC, V. Free parking.

Located about halfway into San José from the airport, the Cariari is the only resort hotel in the Central Valley with its own golf course, and as such is a must for golfers vacationing in San José. With its use of stone walls, an open-air lobby, and lush garden plantings, the Cariari also has more of a tropical feel than the city's other luxury hotels. However, the landscaping is not as impeccably manicured as that at the Herradura, nor is the hotel as elegant as the Marriott. But since the Cariari has come under the management of the large Meliá chain, many of the guest rooms have been remodeled, and all now have plenty of space. The basic rooms have either one king-size or two double beds, and small bathrooms. The suites are more spacious and better appointed. All in all, the rooms lack the sort of quality furnishings and styling that you would expect in this price range. Try to get an upper-floor room; those on the lower floor tend to be a bit dark.

Dining/Diversions: Los Vitrales is the hotel's most formal restaurant and serves well-prepared French and continental fare. For more casual meals, you can try Las Tejas Coffee Shop, which offers a breakfast buffet. For seafood and cocktails, there's the tropical, open-air atmosphere of Los Mariscos, which also has live Latin and jazz music in the evenings. More entertainment is provided by the hotel's casino, which is open nightly until 2am.

Amenities: The large pool is surrounded by plenty of patio space and lots of lounge chairs, and has a swim-up bar. In addition to the 18-hole golf course, there are 11 tennis courts, a pro shop, and a health club with saunas, whirlpool tubs, an exercise room, a game room, and an Olympic-size swimming pool. Other facilities include a gift shop, beauty parlor, and barbershop. Services include 24-hour room service, concierge, complimentary city shuttle, tour desk, car-rental desk, golf lessons and club rentals, baby-sitting, and massage.

Xandari Plantation. Apdo. 1485-4050, Alajuela (mailing address in the U.S.: Box 1449, Summerland, CA 93067). ☎ **506/443-2020.** Fax 506/442-4847. www.xandari.com. E-mail: paradise@xandari.com. 16 villas. MINIBAR TEL. $150–$215 villa; lower in the offseason. Rates include full breakfast. AE, MC, V.

Xandari Plantation is yet another architecturally stunning small hotel not far from the airport. Set on a high hilltop above the city of Alajuela, Xandari Plantation commands wonderful views of the surrounding coffee farms and the Central Valley below. The villas are huge private affairs with high-curved ceilings, stained-glass windows, and handmade fine furniture. All come with both an outdoor patio with a view and private covered palapa, as well as a smaller interior terrace with chaise lounges. Most have king-size beds, the rest have two queens. There are spacious living rooms with rattan sofas and chairs, as well as small kitchenettes. The owners are artists, and their original works and innovative design touches abound.

Dining: The hotel's restaurant serves well-prepared continental cuisine in the main lodge and breakfasts on a large terrace. If you tire of the views from the restaurant, you can have breakfast delivered to your villa.

Amenities: There are two lap pools, a Jacuzzi, and a small outdoor gym. The hotel grounds contain several miles of trails that pass by at least five jungle waterfalls, as well as lush gardens and fruit orchards. There's also a central TV room with a video library, a regular lending library, and a small gift shop. The hotel provides free airport transfers.

EXPENSIVE

Hampton Airport Inn. Autopista General Cañas, by the airport (Apdo. 195-4003), San José. ☎ **800/426-7866** in the U.S., or 506/443-0043. Fax 506/442-9532. www.hamptonhotel. co.cr. E-mail: hampton@racsa.co.cr. 100 units. A/C TV TEL. $90 double. Rates include continental breakfast. AE, DC, MC, V. Free parking.

If familiarity, basic comfort, and proximity to the airport are important to you, then the Hampton Airport Inn is your best bet. The rooms are what you'd expect from a well-known chain, and since the hotel is new, they don't show much wear and tear. There's an outdoor swimming pool, free parking, airport shuttle, and free local phone calls. Although they do serve breakfast, there are no other restaurant or dining options right on the premises. This is a good choice if your plane arrives very late or leaves very early and you don't plan on spending any time in San José.

✪ **Vista del Valle Plantation Inn.** Apdo. 185-4003, Alajuela. ☎ **506/450-0900,** 506/450-0800, or ☎ and fax 506/451-1165. www.vistadelvalle.com. E-mail: mibrejo@racsa.co.cr. 10 units. $110–$145 double; lower in the off-season. Rates include full breakfast. V.

If you have little need for—or interest in—San José and would like a comfortable base for exploring the rest of Costa Rica, you should consider this fine little country inn. Originally a converted private home, the owners have been adding elegant little cottages around their grounds, which command an impressive view over the Rio Grande and its steep-walled canyon. The architecture here has a strong Japanese influence. Most of the accommodations are in independent cottages or bungalows. The cottages are open and airy, with lots of windows letting in lots of light. You'll also find plenty of varnished woodwork, small kitchenettes (in some), and comfortable wraparound decks. The grounds are wonderfully landscaped, with several inviting seating areas set among a wealth of flowering tropical plants. The hotel is located 20 minutes north of the Juan Santamaría Airport, and staying here can cut as much as an hour off your travel time to the Pacific coast beaches, Arenal Volcano, and Monteverde Cloud Forest.

Dining: Meals are served on the poolside terrace's dining area. The dinner menu varies nightly, featuring fine continental cuisine prepared with fresh local ingredients.

Amenities: The tile pool has an interesting little fountain/waterfall, and there's an inviting Jacuzzi here, too. There is also a tennis court, horse stable, and an athletic trail down to a 300-foot waterfall.

MODERATE

✪ **Hotel Bougainvillea.** Apdo. 69-2120 (in Santo Tomás de Santo Domingo de Heredia, 150m (164 yd.) west of the Escuela de Santo Tomás), San José. ☎ **506/244-1414.** Fax 506/244-1313. www.bougainvillea.co.cr. E-mail: info@bougainvillea.co.cr. 86 units. TV TEL. $75 double. AE, MC, V. Free parking.

The Hotel Bougainvillea is an excellent choice and great value if you're looking for a hotel in a quiet residential neighborhood not far from downtown. It offers most of the amenities of the more-expensive resort hotels around the Central Valley, but charges considerably less. The views across the valley from this hillside location are wonderful, and the gardens are beautifully designed and well tended. Rooms are carpeted and have small triangular balconies oriented to the views. Though there is no air-conditioning, there are fans, and temperatures rarely get too hot here. The hotel's dining room features continental dishes, with several preparations of the local sea bass, *corvina,* anchoring the menu. Prices are quite reasonable. There is also a quiet bar just off the lobby, and room service. A complimentary hourly downtown shuttle bus will take you in and out of town. The hotel's swimming pool is in its own private walled garden and is quite attractive. There are also tennis courts, a sauna, a jogging trail, and conference facilities.

Orquideas Inn. Apdo. 394, Alajuela. ☎ **506/433-9346.** Fax 506/433-9740. www.hotels.co.cr. E-mail: orchid@racsa.co.cr. 20 units. $65 double, $120–$130 suite. Rates include breakfast buffet. AE, MC, V.

This small country inn is just 10 minutes from the airport on the road heading up to the Poás Volcano. The rooms are all spacious and comfortable, with tile floors, private bathrooms, and colorful Guatemalan bedspreads. There are a few larger minisuites located around the small pool, as well as a separate geodesic dome, with a king-size bed in a loft reached by a spiral staircase, a large sunken tub in the bathroom, and a full kitchen and living-room area. The entire grounds are lush and tropical. The Marilyn Monroe bar serves up good drinks, *bocas,* and some seriously spicy buffalo wings. A wide range of tours is available.

4 Dining

For decades, Costa Rican cuisine has been dismissed and disparaged. Rice and beans are served at nearly every meal, the selection of other dishes is minimal, and Ticos generally don't go for spicy food—or so the criticism goes. In recent years, though, some contemporary and creative chefs have been trying to educate and enlighten the Costa Rican palate, particularly in San José, and the early results are promising. Still, most visitors to the capital city quickly tire of Tico fare, even in its more chichi incarnation, and start seeking out the many local restaurants serving international cuisines. They are richly rewarded.

San José has a rather amazing variety of restaurants serving cuisines from all over the world, and you'll never pay much even at the best restaurants. In fact, you really have to work at it to spend more than $40 per person for an extravagant six- or seven-course meal (not including liquor). Most restaurants fall into the moderately priced range. However, service can be indifferent at many restaurants, since the gratuity is already tacked on to the check, and tipping is not common among locals.

LOCAL CUISINE If you'd really like to sample the local flavor, head to a *soda,* the equivalent of a diner in the United States, where you can get good, cheap, and filling Tico food. Rice and beans are the staples here and show up at breakfast, lunch, and dinner (when mixed together, they're called *gallo pinto*). For breakfast, they're garnished with everything from fried eggs to steak. At lunch and dinner, rice and beans are the main components of a *casado* (which means "married"), the Costa Rican equivalent of a "blue-plate special." A casado generally is served with a salad of cabbage and tomatoes, fried bananas, and steak, chicken, or fish. A plate of gallo pinto might cost $2, and a casado might cost $2.50 to $4, usually with a *fresco* (a fresh fruit drink) thrown into the bargain.

You Paid What?

47,000 hotels, 700 airlines,
50 rental car companies. And a few
million ways to save money.

Travelocity.com
A Sabre Company

Go Virtually Anywhere.

AOL Keyword: Travel

Travelocity® and Travelocity.com are trademarks of Travelocity.com LP and Sabre® is a trademark of an affiliate of Sabre Inc.
© 2000 Travelocity.com LP. All rights reserved.

Will you have enough stories to tell your grandchildren?

Yahoo! Travel

While in Costa Rica, be sure to taste a few of these frescos. They're a bit like a fresh-fruit milkshake without the ice cream, and when made with mangoes, papayas, bananas, or any of the other delicious tropical fruits of Costa Rica, they're pure ambrosia. Frescos can be made with water (*con agua*) or with milk (*con leche*), and preferences vary. Certain fruits like *carambola* (star fruit), *maracuyá* (a type of passion fruit), and *cas* (you'll just have to try it) are used only with water. But remember, while the water in Costa Rica is generally very safe to drink, those with tender stomachs and/or intestinal tracts should stick to frescos made with milk.

STREET FOOD & LATE-NIGHT BITES   On almost every street corner in downtown San José you'll find a fruit vendor. If you're lucky enough to be in town between April and June, you can sample more varieties of mangoes than you ever knew existed. I like buying them already cut up in a little bag; they cost a little more this way, but you don't get nearly as messy. Be sure to try a green mango with salt and chili peppers. That's the way they seem to like mangoes best in the steamy tropics—guaranteed to wake up your taste buds. Another common street food that you might be wondering about is called *pejibaye*, a bright orange palm nut about the size of a plum. They're boiled in big pots on carts, you eat them in much the same way you eat an avocado, and they taste a bit like squash.

San José has quite a few **all-night restaurants,** including La Esmeralda and Café Parisien, all of which are described below. There's also a new **Denny's** (☎ 506/231-3500), located at the Best Western Irazú, on the highway out to the airport. Another popular place, which is quite a bit seedier, is Chelles, on Avenida Central and Calle 9 (see "San José After Dark," below, for more information).

DOWNTOWN SAN JOSÉ
MODERATE

✪ **Café Mundo.** Calle 15 and Avenida 9, 200m (218 yd.) east and 100m (109 yd.) north of the INS building. ☎ **506/222-6190.** Main courses $7–$15. AE, MC, V. Mon–Thurs 11am–11pm, Fri 11am–midnight, Sat 5pm–midnight. INTERNATIONAL.

This is one of the only places in San José to successfully create an ambiance of casual elegance. Wood tables and art-deco wrought-iron chairs are spread spaciously around several rooms in this former colonial mansion. There's additional seating on the open-air veranda and in the small garden. The tables and chairs here are just plastic lawn furniture, but the lush tropical foliage and small tile fountain make the tradeoff worth-while, especially during the day.

Chef Ray Johnson has a passion for fresh local ingredients prepared with a balanced mix of adventurous creativity and classical finesse. The appetizers include vegetable tempura and fried clam cakes alongside more traditional Tico standards like patacones and fried yucca. There's a long list of pastas and pizzas, as well as more substantial main courses. The nightly special on my last visit was a macadamia-nut–crusted corvina fillet with a mint-papaya chutney. Desserts here are high art, and the chocolate cake may just be the best I've ever tasted. One room here is a lively bar with colorful wall murals by Costa Rican artist Miguel Cassafonte that has become the popular hangout for a broad mix of San José's gay, bohemian, theater, arts, and university crowds.

Café Parisien. Gran Hotel Costa Rica, Avenida 2 between calles 1 and 3. ☎ **506/221-4011.** Sandwiches $2–$4, main courses $5–$20. AE, DC, MC, V. Daily 24 hours. INTERNATIONAL.

The Gran Hotel Costa Rica is hardly the best hotel in San José, but it does have a pic-turesque patio cafe right on the Plaza de la Cultura. A wrought-iron railing, white columns, and arches create an old-world atmosphere, while on the plaza in front of the cafe, a marimba band performs and vendors sell handcrafts. It's open 24 hours a day and is one of the best spots in town to people-watch. Stop by for the breakfast buffet ($7) and watch the plaza vendors set up their booths, peruse the *Tico Times* over coffee while you have your shoes polished, or simply bask in the tropical sunshine while you sip a beer. Lunch and dinner buffets are also offered for around $9. This is one of the best spots in town on a sunny afternoon, or just before or after a show at the National Theater.

La Cocina de Leña. Centro Comercial El Pueblo. ☎ **506/255-1360** or 506/223-3704. Main courses $6–$25. AE, MC, V. Daily 11am–11pm. COSTA RICAN.

Located in the El Pueblo shopping, dining, and entertainment center, La Cocina de Leña (The Wood Stove) is designed to have a rustic feel to it. There are stacks of firewood on shelves above the booths, long stalks of bananas hanging from pillars, tables suspended from the ceiling by heavy ropes, and, most unusual of all, menus printed on paper bags. If you're adventurous, you could try some of the more unusual dishes—perhaps oxtail stew served with yucca and plátano might appeal to you; if not, there are plenty of steaks and seafood dishes on the menu. *Chilasuilas* are delicious tortillas filled with fried meat. Black-bean soup with egg is a Costa Rican standard and is mighty fine here; the corn soup with pork is equally satisfying. For dessert, there's tres leches cake as well as the more unusual sweetened *chiverre*, which is a type of squash that looks remarkably like a watermelon.

✪ **Tin Jo.** Calle 11 between avenidas 6 and 8. ☎ **506/221-7605.** Fax 506/222-3942. Main courses $4–$12. AE, MC, V. Mon–Sat 11:30am–3pm and 5:30–10:30pm, Sun 11:30am–10pm. CHINESE/THAI/PAN-ASIAN.

San José has hundreds of Chinese restaurants, but most simply serve up tired takes on chop suey, chow mein, and fried rice. In contrast, Tin Jo has a wide and varied menu, with an assortment of Cantonese and Szechuan staples as well as a few Thai, Japanese, and Malaysian dishes, and even some Indian food. This is as close to an elegant pan-Asian restaurant as you'll find in these latitudes. The mu shu is so good that you'll forgive the fact that the pancakes are actually thin flour tortillas. Some of the dishes are served in edible rice-noodle bowls, and the pineapple shrimp in coconut milk curry is served in the hollowed-out half of a fresh pineapple. Other dishes not to miss include the pepper shrimp, beef teriyaki, and Thai curries. Tin Jo is also a great option for vegetarians. For dessert, try the sticky rice with mango, or banana tempura. The waiters here are some of the most attentive in Costa Rica. The decor features artwork and textiles from across Asia, and you'll have real tablecloths and cloth napkins. The restaurant has recently expanded quite a bit, and there's a comfortable new bar and lounge area.

INEXPENSIVE

Café Britt. Teatro Nacional, Avenida 2 between calles 3 and 5. ☎ **506/221-3262.** Sandwiches $2–$4, main courses $4–$6. AE, MC, V. Mon–Sat 9am–6pm. CONTINENTAL/ COFFEEHOUSE.

The folks at Café Britt recently took over the in-house restaurant at the Teatro Nacional, to good effect. Even if there's no show on during your visit, you can enjoy a light meal, sandwich, dessert, and/or a cup of coffee here, while soaking up the neoclassical atmosphere. The theater was built in the 1890s from the designs of European architects, and the art-nouveau chandeliers, ceiling murals, and marble floors and tables are pure Parisian. There are changing art exhibits by local artists to complete the chic cafe atmosphere. There's a daily selection of about three lunch items, as well as sandwiches, quiches, and salads. There are also plenty of desserts and a wide range of coffee drinks. The ambiance is classic French cafe, but the marimba music drifting in from outside the open window will remind you that you're still in Costa Rica. On sunny days, there's outdoor seating at wrought-iron tables on the side of the theater.

✪ **La Esmeralda.** Avenida 2 between calles 5 and 7. ☎ **506/221-0530.** Main courses $4–$22. AE, MC, V. Mon–Sat 11:30am–5am. COSTA RICAN.

No one should visit San José without stopping in at La Esmeralda at least once—and the later at night, the better. This is much more than just a restaurant serving Tico food: It's Grand Central Station for Costa Rican mariachi bands. In fact, mariachis and other bands from throughout Central America and Mexico hang out here every night waiting for work. While they wait they often serenade diners in the cavernous open-air dining hall of the restaurant. Friday and Saturday nights are always the busiest, but you'll probably hear lots of excellent music any night of the week. A personal concert will cost you anywhere from $5 to $10 per song, depending on the size of the group, but if you're on a tight budget you will still be able to hear just fine eavesdropping on your neighbors. The classic Tico food is quite good. Try the coconut flan for dessert.

Manolo's Restaurante. Avenida Central between Calle Central and Calle 2. ☎ **506/ 221-2041.** All items $3–$10. AE, MC, V. Daily 11:30am–10pm upstairs; 24 hours downstairs. COSTA RICAN.

This roomy restaurant, spread out over three floors on a busy corner on Avenida Central, is popular with Ticos and travelers alike. You can grab a first-floor table to view the action passing by on the street, or catch the live folk-dance performances that are staged nightly upstairs. The open kitchen serves up steaks and fish, but there is also a popular buffet that includes several typical Costa Rican dishes, such as plátanos-and-black-bean soup, for about $5. The ground floor has the feel of a diner. It's a good place for a quick sandwich or one of the fried dough *"churros"* and a cup of coffee—or espresso. There's another Manolo's located on Avenida Central and Calle 11.

Soda B y B. Calle 5 and Avenida Central. ☎ **506/222-7316.** Breakfast $1.50–$3, sandwiches $2.50–$4, main courses $3–$5. AE, MC, V. Mon–Thurs 8:30am–10pm, Fri–Sat 9am–10pm. COSTA RICAN.

Located on the corner across from the Tourist Information Center on the Plaza de la Cultura, this spot is popular with downtown shoppers and office workers. It's not a B-and-B and you don't have to BYOB—"B y B" stands for Billy Boy, and beer is available here. Service is prompt, prices (and noise level) are low, and the food is surprisingly good for a sandwich shop. Slide into a high-backed wooden booth and order the *chalupa de pollo B y B*—it's a sort of toasted sandwich piled high with chicken salad and drenched with sour cream and guacamole.

Vishnu. Avenida 1 between calles 1 and 3. ☎ **506/222-2549.** Reservations not accepted. Main courses $1.25–$3. No credit cards. Daily 7:30am–9:30pm. VEGETARIAN.

Vegetarians will most certainly find their way here. There are booths for two or four people and photo murals on the walls. At the cashier's counter, you can buy natural cosmetics, honey, and bags of granola. However, most people just come for the filling *plato de día* that includes soup, salad, veggies, an entree, and dessert for around $2. There are also bean burgers and cheese sandwiches on whole-wheat bread. This restaurant is part of the Vishnu chain; there are six sister restaurants spread over the city.

IN LA SABANA/PASEO COLÓN
EXPENSIVE

✪ **La Masía de Triquel.** Sabana Norte, 50m (55 yd.) west and 175m (191 yd.) north of the Burger King in La Sabana. ☎ **506/296-3528** or 506/232-3584. Reservations recommended. Main courses $10–$17. AE, MC, V. Mon–Sat 11:30am–2pm and 6:30–10:30pm. SPANISH.

Only in the Central Valley:
Dining Under the Stars on a Mountain's Edge

While there are myriad unique experiences to be had in Costa Rica, one of my favorites is dining on the side of a volcano, with the lights of San José shimmering below. These hanging restaurants, called *miradores,* are a resourceful response to the city's topography. Because San José is set in a broad valley surrounded on all sides by volcanic mountains, people who live in these mountainous areas have no place to go but up—so they do, building roadside cafes vertically up the sides of the volcanoes.

While the food at most of these establishments is not usually spectacular, the views often are, particularly at night, when the whole wide valley sparkles in a wash of lights. The town of **Aserri,** 6 miles (10km) south of downtown San José, is the king of miradores, and **Mirador Ram Luna** (☎ **506/230-3060**) is the king of Aserri. Grab a window seat and, if you've got the fortitude, order a plate of *chicharrones* (fried pork rinds). There's often live music. You can hire a cab for around $9 or take the Aserri bus at Avenida 6 between Calle Central and Calle 2. Just ask the driver where to get off.

There are also miradores in the hills above Escazú and in San Ramón de Trés Ríos and Heredia. One of the best of this bunch is **Le Monestère** (☎ **506/ 289-4404**), an elegant converted church serving fine French and Belgian cuisine, in a spectacular setting above the hills of Santa Ana. The Bar La Cava here is also quite popular and often features live music.

Despite relocation, a healthy field of competitors, and the death of founding chef Francisco Triquel, La Masía de Triquel is still San José's finest Spanish restaurant. Francisco Triquel Jr. has seen to that. Service is extremely formal, and the regular clientele includes most of the city's upper crust. Although Costa Rica is known for its beef, here you'll also find wonderfully prepared lamb, quail, and rabbit. Seafood dishes include the usual shrimp and lobster, but also squid and octopus. However, there is really no decision to be made when perusing the menu: Start with a big bowl of gazpacho and then spend the rest of the evening enjoying all the succulent surprises you'll find in a big dish of paella.

La Piazzetta. Paseo Colón near Calle 40 (opposite Banco de Costa Rica). ☎ **506/222-7896.** Reservations recommended. Main courses $6–$20. AE, MC, V. Mon–Sat noon–2:30pm and 6:30–11pm. ITALIAN.

With an amazingly long menu and service by waiters in suits and bow ties, this restaurant harks back to the Italian restaurants of old in the United States, when southern Italian cooking was still an exotic ethnic cuisine. The menu includes quite a few risotto dishes, which is a surprise, since most Italian restaurants in Costa Rica stick to spaghetti. Some other unexpected dishes also make appearances here, including several lobster dishes, and veal scaloppine in a truffle sauce. Salads are colorful and artistically arranged. If you're in no danger of a coronary, try the *baugna cauda*—anchovies and peppers in an olive-oil–based broth. For dessert, sample a classic chocolate mousse, or tiramisu.

MODERATE

El Chicote. Avenida Las Américas, 400m (436 yd.) west of the ICE building, Sabana Norte. ☎ **506/232-0936** or 506/232-3777. Fax 506/231-1742. E-mail: chicote@racsa.co.cr. Reservations recommended. Main courses $8–$22 (most dishes around $10). AE, MC, V. Daily 11am–midnight. COSTA RICAN/STEAK HOUSE.

This is San José's premiere steak house. The large room is divided up by half-walls planted with tropical flora and a bevy of hanging ferns. There are heavy wooden beams and plenty of varnished-wood accents all around. True meat aficionados should order the imported rib-eye, or pound-and-a-half T-bone. There's an extensive selection of fish and poultry dishes, as well. Everything comes with a choice of baked or mashed potatoes, black beans, and fresh tortillas. The wine list features a broad range of Italian, Spanish, French, and California wines. Waiters wear black jackets, white shirts, and black bow ties. There's a formal feel to the service, which is uncommon in Costa Rica.

Machu Picchu Bar and Restaurant. Calle 32 between avenidas 1 and 3, 150m (164 yd.) north of the Kentucky Fried Chicken on Paseo Colón. ☎ **506/222-7384.** Main courses $4–$12. AE, DC, MC, V. Mon–Sat 11am–3pm and 6–10pm. PERUVIAN/CONTINENTAL.

Located just off Paseo Colón near the Kentucky Fried Chicken, Machu Picchu is an unpretentious little restaurant that has become one of the most popular places in San José. The menu is primarily seafood (especially sea bass), and consequently most dishes tend toward the upper end of the menu's price range. Also, many of these fish dishes come in thick cream sauces. You're better off sticking with the two-person seafood sampler, combined with different appetizers. One of my favorite entrees is the *causa limeña,* lemon-flavored mashed potatoes stuffed with shrimp. The ceviche here is excellent, as is the *aji de gallina,* a dish of chopped chicken in a fragrant cream sauce, and octopus with garlic butter. Be sure to ask for a pisco sour, a Peruvian specialty drink made from grape brandy.

INEXPENSIVE

Pasteleria Francesa Boudsocq. Calle 30 at Paseo Colón. ☎ **506/222-6732.** Pastries $1.05–$2.75, breakfast $3.50–$4.50, lunch $4–$5.50. AE, MC, V. Mon–Sat 7am–7pm. PASTRIES/FRENCH.

Pastry shops abound in San José, but this little place on Paseo Colón is worth seeking out. Boudsocq recently celebrated their 20th anniversary, so they must be doing something right. Savory meat-filled pastries make good lunches; unusual sweets are great afternoon snacks. There are only a couple of tables here, so most folks get their goodies to go.

Soda Coppelia. Paseo Colón between calles 26 and 28. ☎ **506/223-8013.** Reservations not necessary. Most items $1.75–$5. No credit cards. Daily 7am–8pm. COSTA RICAN.

If you're looking for a filling, cheap, and quick breakfast in the Paseo Colón area, I recommend this *soda.* You'll find it near the Universal movie theater. The wooden booths and a few tables on the (rather noisy) covered walkway are frequently full of local businesspeople because the meals are so reasonably priced. A thin steak will run you just over $2. For lighter fare, try the burgers, sandwiches, or some of the good-looking pastries such as flaky empanadas or carrot bread.

SAN PEDRO/LOS YOSES

In addition to the restaurants listed below, my vegetarian friends swear that the best vegetarian restaurant in San José is the little **Restaurante El Vegetariano San Pedro** (☎ 506/224-1163), located 125 meters (136 yd.) north of the San Pedro Church.

EXPENSIVE

Le Chandelier. 100m (109 yd.) west and 100m south of the ICE office in San Pedro. ☎ **506/225-3980.** Reservations recommended. Main courses $15–$25, fixed-price lunch $20, fixed-price dinner $40. AE, MC, V. Mon–Fri 11:30am–2pm; Mon–Sat 6:30–11pm. FRENCH.

Located in a large old house in a quiet residential neighborhood east of downtown San José, Le Chandelier is one of the most elegant restaurants in town. The neighborhood, landscaping, and architectural styling give it the feel of an older Hollywood or Beverly

Hills restaurant. The menu includes delicious renditions of French classics such as onion soup, escargots bourguignonne, and chicken à l'orange. There are also some unexpected and less familiar dishes, such as tenderloin with cranberry sauce, carpaccio with smoked salmon and palmito, and roast duck in green-pepper sauce. The set dinner is a true feast and might start with an appetizer of carpaccio, followed by langostinos Newburg, sorbet, tournedos in cabernet sauvignon and green pepper, cheese and fruit, and a dessert of crème brûlée.

MODERATE

Ambrosia. Centro Comercial Calle Real. ☎ **506/253-8012.** Reservations not necessary. Sandwiches and salads $3.50–$5, main courses $5–$12. AE, DC, MC, V. Daily 11:30am–3pm; Mon–Sat 6–10:30pm. CONTINENTAL.

This elegant little restaurant is a good choice for lunch or dinner. Greek and Latin mythology are the dominant menu theme here, with Ulysses, Circe, and Poseidon all having seafood dishes named after them; Zeus, Apollo, and Orion providing namesakes for the different steaks; and the pasta selections anchored by Ravioli Romulus. Behind the mythology, what you will find are well-prepared meals made with fresh ingredients and interesting spices. The Crepe Aphrodite is a delicate crepe filled with chunks of fish and shrimp in a Gouda cheese sauce. The Corvina Cassiopeia is a grilled sea-bass fillet topped with a light almond sauce. The ambiance is relaxed, and the service can be a bit inattentive. There's a small bar at the center of the restaurant, and live piano music is sometimes offered in the evenings.

✪ **Il Ponte Vecchio.** San Pedro, 75m (82 yd.) east and 10m (11 yd.) north of the Salón de Patines Music. ☎ **506/283-1810.** Main courses $5–$12. AE, MC, V. Mon–Sat noon–2:30pm and 6–10:30pm. ITALIAN.

Everyone should have a favorite neighborhood Italian restaurant, and this is mine. Not too formal, but no simple pasteria, Il Ponte Vecchio is consistent, comfortable, and personal. Chef Tony D'Alaimo has years of experience, having cut his teeth in New York's Little Italy before settling in San José. There's a small bar just as you enter, then three separate rooms with tables draped in linen tablecloths and set with glass-lanterned candles. The service is attentive and professional but never overbearing. My favorite dish is the chicken Valdostana, a delicate breast fillet rolled around some fresh mozzarella, Italian prosciutto, and porcini mushrooms, covered in tangy pomodoro sauce and baked in the oven. You should also check out the homemade ravioli in a cream sauce, with hints of nutmeg.

Shiraz. 100m (109 yd.) east of the Fuente de la Hispanidad, San Pedro. ☎ **506/280-4703.** Main courses $7–$12. AE, MC, V. Daily 7am–1am. INTERNATIONAL.

This stylish new restaurant offers up creative international cuisine in a comfortable, unpretentious atmosphere. In fact, there are several atmospheres here, including a covered patio cafe, a casual wine and tapas bar, and the main restaurant. The menu changes nightly, but you're sure to find a wide selection of dishes made with fresh ingredients. Possibilities include mahimahi with a tamarind ginger sauce, or Chilean salmon with cilantro pesto. The desserts are sinfully delicious and the restaurant has one of the most extensive (and reasonably priced) wine lists in the country. There's even a small gourmet deli featuring fresh breads, cakes, and pastries.

ESCAZÚ
EXPENSIVE

Atlanta Dining Gallery. Tara Resort Hotel, 600m (654 yd.) south of the San Antonio de Escazú cemetery. ☎ **506/228-6992.** Reservations recommended. Main courses $7–$22. AE, MC, V. Daily 6am–10:30pm. CONTINENTAL.

Located in a reproduction antebellum mansion, this place is straight out of the Deep South, except for the view of the Central Valley. Elegant dark-wood furnishings and a hardwood floor set the tone, but it's the view that keeps grabbing your attention. Scarlett O'Hara never had it so good. Most nights of the week the view is accompanied by such dishes as filet mignon in a Gorgonzola sauce, shrimp scampi, chicken with a mango-and-avocado sauce, and corvina with a red-pepper–and-wine sauce. A tempting assortment of desserts accompanies a choice of after-dinner aperitifs and cognacs.

✪ **La Luz.** On the old road to Santa Ana, inside Hotel Alta. ☎ **506/282-4160.** Fax 506/282-4162. Reservations recommended. Main courses $6–20. AE, DC, MC, V. Daily 7am–3pm and 6–10pm. CALIFORNIAN/PACIFIC RIM/FUSION.

La Luz serves up some of the most adventurous food in Costa Rica. Mixing fresh local ingredients with the best of a whole host of international ethnic cuisines, this restaurant is quickly making its mark on the local restaurant scene. The fiery garlic prawns are sautéed in ancho-chili oil and sage and served over a roasted garlic potato. Then the whole thing is served with a garnish of fried leeks and a tequila-lime-butter-and-cilantro-oil sauce. There's also a pan-seared veal chop stuffed with a cilantro cashew pesto. On top of all this there are nightly specials, such as fresh baked rolls and breads, and a wide selection of inventive appetizers and desserts. The glass-walled dining room is one of the most elegant in town, with a view of the city lights. The wait staff is attentive and knowledgeable, and the chef makes the rounds most nights. La Luz is also open for breakfast and lunch.

MODERATE

✪ **La Peña de Cantares.** Santa Ana. ☎ **506/282-5441.** Reservations accepted. Main courses $3–$15. AE, MC, V. Mon–Thurs 11:30am–11pm, Fri–Sun 11:30am–1am. COSTA RICAN.

Housed in the Casa Quitirrisí, a 200-year-old home constructed of wild cane and adobe, with a red-tile roof, this restaurant serves up great traditional Costa Rican cooking in a classic setting. Heavy wooden tables are spread through several rooms in this old house and around a large covered patio. The menu features all the Tico staples: ceviche, gallos, chicharron, gallo pinto, and chorreados. Most carry playful and poetic names and descriptions. If you want something really unique, try the Flor de Itabo, which are flowers of the Itabo tree, battered in egg and fried. *Peña* translates roughly as "jam session," and there is almost always live music here on weekends, either featuring the owners, the musical group Cantares, or visiting artists.

5 Seeing the Sights

Most visitors to Costa Rica try to get out of the city as fast as possible so they can spend more time on the beach or off in the rain forests. But the country's main metropolis has enough attractions here to keep you busy for a while. Some of the best and most modern museums in Central America are here, with a wealth of fascinating pre-Columbian artifacts. Recent additions include a modern and expansive Children's Museum, as well as a centrally located National Arts Center, featuring yet another museum and several performing-arts spaces. There are also several great things to see and do just outside San José in the Central Valley. If you start doing day trips out of the city, you can spend quite a few days in this region.

ORGANIZED TOURS   There really isn't much reason to take a tour of San José. It's so compact, you can easily visit all the major sites on your own (see below). However, if you want to take a city tour, which will run you between $15 and $20, here are some companies: **Otec Tours,** Edificio Ferencz, Calle 3 between avenidas 1 and 3

(Apdo. 323-1002), San José (☎ **506/256-0633;** www.gotec.com); **TAM,** Calle Central between Avenida Central and Avenida 1 (☎ **506/256-0203**); **Horizontes Travel,** Calle 32 between avenidas 3 and 5 (☎ **506/222-2022;** www.horizontes.com); **Ecole Travel,** Calle 7 between Avenida Central and 1 (☎ **506/223-2240**); and **Swiss Travel Service** (☎ **506/282-4898**). These same companies also offer a whole range of day trips out of San José (see "Side Trips from San José," later in this chapter). Almost all of the major hotels have tour desks, and most of the smaller hotels will also help arrange tours and day trips.

Suggested Itineraries

If You Have 1 Day

Start your day on the Plaza de la Cultura. Visit the Gold Museum and see if you can get tickets for a performance that night at the Teatro Nacional. From the Plaza de la Cultura, stroll up Avenida Central to the Museo Nacional. After lunch, head over to the neighboring National Arts Center (if you have the energy for another museum). After all this culture, a stroll through the chaos of the Mercado Central is in order. Try dinner at either Café Mundo or La Cocina de Leña before going to the Teatro Nacional. After the performance you absolutely must swing by La Esmeralda for some live mariachi music before calling it a night.

If You Have 2 Days

On Day 2, visit the Serpentarium, the Children's Museum (a must if you've brought the kids along), or the Spyrogyra Butterfly Garden, do a bit of shopping, and then head out on Paseo Colón to the Museo de Arte Costarricense and La Sabana Park. Alternately, you could take one of the day trips outside of San José described below.

If You Have 3 Days

On Day 3, head out to Irazú Volcano, Orosi Valley, Lankester Gardens, and Cartago. Start your day at the volcano and work your way back toward San José. If you prefer less strenuous activities, try a cruise around the Gulf of Nicoya or a trip to the Rain Forest Aerial Tram.

If You Have 4 Days or More

Get out of San José. Do a 1- or 2-night trip to Tortuguero, Monteverde, or Arenal. You can go white-water rafting, hiking in a cloud forest, horseback riding near a volcano, or cruising through jungle canals.

THE TOP ATTRACTIONS

✪ **Centro Nacional de Arte y Cultura (National Arts Center).** Calle 13 between avenidas 3 and 5. ☎ **506/257-7202** or 506/257-9370. Admission $1.50. Museum hours: Tues–Sun 10am–5pm. Any downtown bus.

Occupying a full city block, this was once the National Liquor Factory (FANAL). Now it houses the offices of the Cultural Ministry, several performing-arts centers, and the Museum of Contemporary Art and Design. The latter has featured several impressive traveling international exhibits since its inception, including large retrospectives by Mexican painter José Cuevas and Ecuadoran painter Oswaldo Guayasamin. If you're looking for modern dance, experimental theater, or a lecture on Costa Rican video, this is the place to be.

Museo de Arte Costarricense. Calle 42 and Paseo Colón, Parque La Sabana Este. ☎ **506/ 222-7155.** Admission $1.50 adults, free for children and students. Tues–Sun 10am–4pm. Sabana-Cementerio bus.

This small museum at the end of Paseo Colón in Parque La Sabana was formerly an airport terminal. Today, however, it houses a collection of works in all media by Costa Rica's most celebrated artists. On display are some exceptionally beautiful pieces in a wide range of artistic styles, demonstrating how Costa Rican artists have interpreted and imitated the major European artistic movements over the years. In addition to the permanent collection of sculptures, paintings, and prints, there are regular temporary exhibits. If the second floor is open during your visit, be sure to go up and have a look at the conference room's unusual bas-relief walls, which chronicle the history of Costa Rica from pre-Columbian times to the present with evocative images of its people.

Museo de Los Niños (Children's Museum). Calle 4 and Avenida 9. ☎ **506/233-2734.** Admission $2 adults, $1.50 students and children under 18. Tues–Fri 8am–4pm, Sat–Sun 10am–5pm. Any downtown bus.

This museum is located a few blocks north of downtown, on Calle 4. It's within easy walking distance, but you might want to take a cab, as you'll have to walk right through the worst part of the red-light district.

Recently converted from use as a prison, the museum houses an extensive collection of exhibits designed for the edification and entertainment of children of all ages. Experience a simulated earthquake, or make music by dancing across the floor. Many of the exhibits encourage hands-on play. If you're traveling with children, you'll definitely want to come here, and you may want to visit even if you don't. This museum sometimes features limited shows of "serious" art, and is also the home of the new National Auditorium. Be careful, though: The museum is large and spread out, and it's easy to lose track of a family member or friend.

✪ Museo de Oro Banco Central (Gold Museum). Calle 5 between Avenida Central and Avenida 2, underneath the Plaza de la Cultura. ☎ **506/223-0528.** Admission $4 adults, $1.50 students, 75¢ children under 12. Tues–Sun 10am–4:30pm. Any downtown bus.

Located directly beneath the Plaza de la Cultura, this unusual underground museum houses one of the largest collections of pre-Columbian gold in the Americas. On display are more than 20,000 troy ounces of gold in more than 2,000 objects. The sheer number of small pieces can be overwhelming and seem redundant; however, the unusual display cases and complex lighting systems show off every piece to its utmost. This museum complex also includes a gallery for temporary art exhibits, separate numismatic and philatelic museums (coins and stamps, for the lay reader), and a modest gift shop.

Museo Nacional de Ciencias Naturales "La Salle." Across from the southwest corner of Parque La Sabana. ☎ **506/232-1306.** Admission $1.50 adults, 75¢ children. Mon–Sat 8am–4pm, Sun 9am–4pm. Any Escazú, Pavas, or Sabana bus.

Before heading out to the wilds of the Costa Rican jungles, you might want to stop by this natural-history museum and find out more about the animals you will encounter. There are stuffed and mounted anteaters, monkeys, tapirs, and many others from Costa Rica and from around the world as well. There are also 1,200 birds, 12,500 insects, and 13,500 seashells displayed.

Museo Nacional de Costa Rica. Calle 17 between Avenida Central and Avenida 2, on the Plaza de la Democracia. ☎ **506/257-1433.** Admission $1 adults, free for students and children under 10. Tues–Sun 9am–4:30pm. Closed Dec 25 and 31. Any downtown bus.

Costa Rica's most important historical museum is housed in a former army barracks that was the scene of fighting during the civil war of 1948. You can still see hundreds of bullet holes on the turrets at the corners of the building. Inside this traditional Spanish-style courtyard building, you will find displays on Costa Rican history and culture from pre-Columbian times to the present. In the pre-Columbian rooms, you'll see a 2,500-year-old jade carving that is shaped like a seashell and etched with an image of a hand holding a small animal.

Among the most fascinating objects unearthed at Costa Rica's numerous archaeological sites are many *metates,* or grinding stones. This type of grinding stone is still in use today throughout Central America; however, the ones on display here are more ornately decorated than those that you will see anywhere else. Some of the metates are the size of a small bed and are believed to have been part of funeral rites. A separate vault houses the museum's collection of pre-Columbian gold jewelry and figurines. In the courtyard, you'll be treated to a wonderful view of the city and see some of Costa Rica's mysterious stone spheres.

Parque Zoológico Simón Bolívar. Avenida 11 and Calle 7, in Barrio Amón. ☎ 506/ **233-6701.** Admission $1.50 adults, free for children under 3. Daily 9am–4:30pm. Any downtown bus, then walk.

This zoo has received some upkeep and renovation in recent years. And while it no longer suffers from an overwhelming sense of neglect and despair, the whole thing is still slightly desultory. Instead, I recommend heading out into the forests and jungles. You won't see the great concentrations of wildlife available in one stop here at the zoo, but you'll see the animals in their natural habitats, not yours. The zoo is really geared toward locals and school groups, with a collection that includes Asian, African, and Costa Rican animals. There's a new children's discovery area, snake-and-reptile house, and gift shop.

Serpentarium. Avenida 1 between calles 9 and 11. ☎ 506/255-4210. Admission $5 adults, $1.50 children under 13. Mon–Fri 9am–6pm, Sat–Sun 10am–5pm. Any downtown bus.

Reptiles and amphibians abound in the tropics, and the Serpentarium is an excellent introduction to all that slithers and hops through the jungles of Costa Rica. The live snakes, lizards, and frogs are kept in beautiful large terrariums that simulate their natural environments. Poisonous snakes make up a large part of the collection, with the dreaded fer-de-lance pit viper eliciting the most gasps from enthralled visitors. Also fascinating to see are the tiny, brilliantly colored poison arrow frogs. Iguanas and Jesus Christ lizards are two of the more commonly spotted of Costa Rica's reptiles, and both are represented here. Also on display is an Asian import: a giant Burmese python, which is one of the largest I've ever seen. This little museum is well worth a visit, especially if you plan to go bashing about in the jungles: It will help you identify the numerous poisonous snakes you'll want to avoid. If you show up around 3pm, you may catch them feeding the piranhas and perhaps some of the snakes.

OUTSIDE SAN JOSÉ

Butterfly Farm. In front of Los Reyes Country Club, La Guácima de Alajuela. ☎ 506/ **438-0400.** www.butterflyfarm.co.cr. E-mail: info@butterflyfarm.co.cr. Admission $14 adults, $9 students, $7 children 4 to 12, free for children under 4. Daily 9am–5pm. San Antonio/Ojo de Agua bus on Avenida 1 between calles 20 and 22.

At any given time, you may see around 30 of the 80 different species of butterflies raised at this butterfly farm south of Alajuela. The butterflies live in a large enclosed garden similar to an aviary and flutter about the heads of visitors during tours of the gardens. You should be certain to spot glittering blue morphos and a large butterfly that mimics the eyes of an owl. The admission includes a 2-hour guided tour. In the demonstration room you'll see butterfly eggs, caterpillars, and pupae. There are cocoons trimmed in a shimmering gold color and cocoons that mimic a snake's head in order to frighten away predators. The last guided tour of the day begins at 3pm.

If you reserve in advance, the Butterfly Farm has three daily bus tours that stop at many major San José hotels for $20, including round-trip transportation and the tour of the garden. Buses pick up passengers at more than 20 different hotels in the San José area. For a full-day excursion (including lunch and transportation), check out the "Perfect Combination Tour," which takes you first to the Butterfly Farm and then to Café Britt coffee farm (see below), for $60 per person.

Café Britt Farm. North of Heredia on the road to Barva. ☎ **506/261-0707.** www.coffeetour.com. Admission $25 per person, including transportation from downtown San José; $20 walk-in. Three tours daily: 9am, 11am, and 3pm. Tours Nov–Feb during the harvest season; store open daily 8:30am–5pm year-round.

Though bananas are the main export of Costa Rica, most people are far more interested in the country's second most important export crop: coffee. Café Britt is one of the leading brands of coffee here, and the company has put together an interesting tour and stage production at its farm, which is 20 minutes outside of San José. Here, you'll see how coffee is grown. You'll also visit the roasting plant to learn how a coffee "cherry" is turned into a delicious roasted bean. Tasting sessions are offered for visitors to experience the different qualities of coffee. There is also a restaurant, and a store where you can buy very reasonably priced coffee and coffee-related gift items. For a full-day tour, you can visit both the coffee farm and the Butterfly Farm (see above) for $60 per person, including transportation and lunch.

✪ **Lankester Gardens.** Paraíso de Cartago. ☎ **506/552-3247** or 506/552-3151. Admission $4 adults, 50¢ children. Daily 8:30am–3:30pm. Closed on all national holidays. Cartago bus from San José, then the Paraíso bus from the south side of the Parque Central in Cartago (ride takes 30–40 min.)

There are more than 1,200 varieties of orchids in Costa Rica, and no fewer than 800 species are on display at this botanical garden in Cartago province. Created in the 1940s by English naturalist Charles Lankester, the gardens are now administered by the University of Costa Rica. The primary goal of the gardens is to preserve the local flora, with an emphasis on orchids and bromeliads. Paved trails wander from open, sunny gardens into shady forests. In each environment, different species of orchids are in bloom. There's an information center, and the trails are well tended and well marked.

✪ **Zoo Ave.** La Garita, Alajuela. ☎ **506/433-8989.** Admission $9 adults, $1 children under 12. Daily 9am–5pm. Catch one of the frequent Alajuela buses on Avenida 2 between calles 12 and 14. In Alajuela, transfer to a bus for Atenas and get off at Zoo Ave. before you get to La Garita. The fare is 55¢.

Dozens of scarlet macaws, reclusive owls, majestic raptors, several different species of toucans, and a host of brilliantly colored birds from Costa Rica and around the world make this one exciting place to visit. Bird-watching enthusiasts will be able to get a closer look at birds they may have seen in the wild. There are also large iguana, deer, and monkey exhibits—and look out for the 12-foot-long crocodile. Zoo Ave. houses only injured, donated, or confiscated animals.

The **Juan Santamaría Historical Museum,** Avenida 3 between Calle Central and Calle 2 (☎ **506/441-4775**), isn't worth a trip of its own, but if you're looking to make an afternoon of it in Alajuela, you might want to make a stop here before or after

Zoo Ave. The museum commemorates Costa Rica's national hero, who gave his life defending the country against a small army led by William Walker, a U.S. citizen who invaded Costa Rica in 1856, attempting to set up a slave state. The museum is open Tuesday through Sunday from 10am to 6pm; admission is free.

6 Outdoor Activities & Spectator Sports

Due to the chaos and pollution, you'll probably want to get out of the city before undertaking any strenuous or aerobic activity. But, if you want to brave the elements, activities exist in and around San José.

La Sabana Park (at the western end of Paseo Colón), formerly San José's international airport, is the city's center for active sports and recreation. Here you'll find everything from jogging trails, soccer fields, and a few public tennis courts to the National Stadium. All the facilities are free and open to the public. Families gather for picnics, people fly kites, and there's even an outdoor sculpture garden. If you really want to experience the local culture, try getting into a pickup soccer game here. However, be careful in this park, especially at dusk or after dark: because it is so expansive, it has become a favorite haunt for youth gangs and muggers.

For information on horseback riding, hiking, and white-water rafting trips from San José, see "Side Trips from San José," at the end of this chapter.

BIRD-WATCHING   While serious birders will certainly want to head out of San José, it is still possible to see quite a few species in the metropolitan area. Two of the best spots for urban bird-watching are the campus at the **University of Costa Rica** in the eastern suburb of San Pedro, and **Parque del Este,** located a little further east on the road to San Ramón de Tré Ríos. To get to the University Campus, take any San Pedro bus from Avenida Central between Calle 9 and Calle 11. To get to Parque del Este, take the San Ramón/Parque del Este bus from Calle 9 between Avenida Central and Avenida 2.

BULLFIGHTING   Although I hesitate to call it a sport, **Las Corridas a la Tica** (Costa Rican bullfighting) is a popular and frequently comic stadium event. Instead of the blood-and-gore/life-and-death confrontation of traditional bullfighting, Ticos just like to tease the bull. In a typical corrida, anywhere from 50 to 150 *toreadores improvisados* (literally, improvised bullfighters) stand in the ring waiting for the bull. What follows is a slapstick scramble to safety whenever the bull heads toward a crowd of bullfighters. The braver bullfighters try to slap the bull's backside as the beast chases down one of his buddies.

You can see a bullfight during the Festejos Populares in Zapote, a suburb east of San José. The corridas run all day and well into the night during Christmas week and the first week in January. Admission is $2 to $5. Take the Zapote bus from Calle 1 between avenidas 4 and 6. If you're in Costa Rica during the holidays but can't make it out to the stadium, don't despair—the local TV stations show nothing but live broadcasts from Zapote.

GOLF & TENNIS   If you want to play tennis or golf in San José, your options are limited. Your best bet is to stay at either the Hotel Meliá Cariari or Hotel Herradura. Tennis players looking for a real local experience, on some rough concrete courts, can take a racket and some balls down to **Parque La Sabana.** Golfers have a new option with the opening of the new 18-hole course **Parque Valle del Sol** (☎ **506/282-9222**) in the western suburb of Santa Ana. The course at the Meliá Cariari is not technically open to the public, but if there's room, they'll generally let guests at other hotels tee off with advance notice.

JOGGING   Try **La Sabana Park** mentioned above, or head to **Parque del Este,** which is east of town, in the foothills above San Pedro. Take the San Ramón/Parque del Este bus from Calle 9 between Avenida Central and Avenida 2. It's never a good idea to jog at night, on busy streets, or alone. Women should be particularly careful about jogging alone. And remember, Tico drivers are not accustomed to sport joggers on residential streets, so don't expect drivers to give you much berth.

SOCCER/FÚTBOL   Ticos take their *fútbol* seriously. Although not up to European or World Cup standards, Costa Rican professional soccer is some of the best in Central America. The soccer season runs from September through June, with the finals spread out over several weeks in late June and early July. You don't need to buy tickets in advance. Tickets generally run between $2.50 and $12.50. It's worth paying a little extra for *sombra numerado* (reserved seats in the shade). Other options include *sombra* (general admission in the shade), *palco* and *palco numerado* (general admission and reserved mezzanine), and *sol general* (general admission in full sun). The main San José team is Saprissa (affectionately called *El Monstro,* or The Monster). **Saprissa's stadium** is in Tibás (take any Tibás bus from Calle 2 and Avenida 5). Games are usually held on Sunday at 11am, but occasionally they are scheduled for Saturday afternoon or Wednesday evening. Check the local newspapers for game times and locations.

SWIMMING   If you aren't going to get to the beach anytime soon and your hotel doesn't have a pool, check out **Ojo de Agua** (☎ **506/441-2808**), which is on the road between the airport and San Antonio de Belén. The spring-fed waters are cool and refreshing, and even if it seems a bit chilly in San José, it's always several degrees warmer out here. This place is very popular with Ticos and can get quite crowded on weekends. Unfortunately, you do have to keep an eye on your valuables here. Admission is $4.50. Buses leave almost hourly for Ojo de Agua from Avenida 1 between calles 18 and 20.

7 Shopping

Serious shoppers will be disappointed in Costa Rica. Aside from coffee and oxcarts, there isn't much that's distinctly Costa Rican. To compensate for its own relative lack of goods, Costa Rica does a brisk business in selling crafts and clothes imported from Guatemala, Panama, and Ecuador.

THE SHOPPING SCENE   San José's central shopping corridor is bounded by avenidas 1 and 2, from about Calle 14 in the west to Calle 13 in the east. For several blocks west of the Plaza de la Cultura, Avenida Central is a pedestrian-only street mall where you'll find store after store of inexpensive clothes for men, women, and children. Depending on the mood of the police that day, you may find a lot of street vendors as well.

Most shops in the downtown district are open Monday through Saturday from about 8am to 6pm. Some shops close for lunch, while others remain open (it's just the luck of the draw for shoppers). When you do purchase something, you'll be happy to find that the sales and import taxes have already been figured into the display price.

International laws prohibit trade in endangered wildlife, so don't buy any plants or animals, even if they're readily for sale. The Audubon Society does not tolerate sales of any kind of sea-turtle products (including jewelry); wild birds; lizard, snake, or cat skins; corals; or orchids (except those grown commercially).

It's especially hard to capture the subtle shades and colors of the rain and cloud forests, and many a traveler has gone home thinking his or her undeveloped film contained the full beauty of the jungle, only to return from the photo developer with 36 bright green blurs. To avoid this heartache, you might want to buy one of the picture books on Costa Rica mentioned in the "Recommended Books" section of appendix A. Or pick up some postcards of the sights you want to remember forever and send them to yourself.

MARKETS　There are several markets near downtown, but by far the largest is the ✪ **Mercado Central,** which is located between Avenida Central and Avenida 1 and calles 6 and 8. Although this dark maze of stalls is primarily a food market, inside you'll find all manner of vendors, including a few selling Costa Rican souvenirs, crude leather goods, and musical instruments. Be especially careful about your wallet or purse and any prominent jewelry, because this area is frequented by very skilled pickpockets. All the streets surrounding the Mercado Central are jammed with produce vendors selling from small carts or loading and unloading trucks. It's always a hive of activity, with crowds of people jostling for space on the streets. In the hot days of the dry season, the aromas can get quite heady. If you have a delicate constitution, don't eat any fruit you don't peel yourself (oranges, bananas, mangoes, etc.).

There is also a daily street market on the west side of the **Plaza de la Democracia.** Here you'll find two long rows of temporary stalls selling T-shirts, Guatemalan and Ecuadoran handcrafts and clothing, small ceramic *ocarinas* (a small musical wind instrument), and handmade jewelry. You may be able to bargain the price down a little bit, but bargaining is not a traditional part of the vendor culture here, so you'll have to work hard to save a few dollars.

SHOPPING A TO Z
ART GALLERIES

Arte Latino. Calle 5 and Avenida 1. ☎ **506/258-3306.** Mon–Sat 9am–7pm, Sun 10am–5pm. AE, MC, V.

This gallery carries original artwork in a variety of media featuring predominantly Central American themes. Some of it is pretty gaudy, but this is a good place to find Nicaraguan and Costa Rican "primitive" paintings. The gallery also has storefronts in the Multiplaza Mall in Escazú and at the Mall Cariari, which is located on the Interamerican Highway, about halfway between the airport and downtown, across the street from the Hotel Herradura.

Galería Andromeda. Calle 9 at Avenida 9. ☎ **506/223-3529.** Mon–Fri 10am–7pm, Sat 2–6pm. AE, MC, V.

This small, personal gallery features contemporary national artists of good quality. There are usually prints and paintings by several artists on display, and prices are very reasonable.

✪ **Galería 11-12.** Avenida 15 and Calle 35. Casa 3506, in Barrio Escalante (from the Farolito, 200m/218 yd. east, 100m/109 yd. north). ☎ **506/280-8441.** www.galeria11-12.com. E-mail: galearte@racsa.co.cr. Mon–Sat 9am–7pm, Sun by appointment. AE, V.

This gallery deals mainly in high-end Costa Rican art, from neoclassical painters like Teodorico Quirós to modern masters like Francisco Amighetti and Paco Zuñiga to current stars like Rafa Fernandez, Fernando Carballo, and Fabio Herrera.

Galería Jacobo Karpio. Paco Shopping Center, on the old road to Santa Ana, Escazú. ☎ **506/228-7862.** Tues–Sat 10am–7pm, Sun 10am–4pm. MC, V.

This gallery handles some of the more adventurous modern art to be found in Costa Rica. Karpio has a steady stable of prominent Mexican, Cuban, and Argentine artists, as well as some local talent. There's another branch of this gallery downtown, on Avenida 1, between calles 11 and 13.

Joe to Go

Two words of advice: Buy coffee. Lots of it.

Coffee is the best shopping deal in all of Costa Rica. Although the best Costa Rican coffee is supposedly shipped off to North American and European markets, it's hard to beat the coffee that's roasted right in front of you here. Best of all is the price: One pound of coffee sells for between $2 and $3. It makes a great gift and keeps for a long time in your refrigerator or freezer.

Café Britt is the big name in Costa Rican coffee. These folks have the largest export business in the country, and while high-priced, their blends are very dependable. My favorites, however, are the coffees roasted and packaged in Manuel Antonio and Monteverde, by Café Milagro and Café Monteverde, respectively. If you're going to either of these places, definitely pick up their beans. For good flavor and value, you can visit Café Trebol, on Calle 8 between Avenida Central and Avenida 1. Be sure to ask for whole beans; Costa Rican grinds are often too fine for standard coffee filters. They'll pack the beans for you in whatever size bag you want. If you should happen to buy prepackaged coffee in a supermarket in Costa Rica, the whole beans will be marked either *grano* (grain) or *grano entero* (whole bean). If you opt for ground varieties (*molido*), be sure the package is marked *puro;* otherwise, it will likely be mixed with a good amount of sugar, the way Ticos like it.

One good coffee-related gift to bring home is a coffee sock and stand. This is the most common mechanism for brewing coffee beans in Costa Rica. It consists of a simple circular stand, made out of wood or wire, which holds a sock. Put the ground beans in the sock, place a pot or cup below, and pour boiling water through. You can find the socks and stands at most supermarkets and in the Mercado Central. In fancier craft shops, you'll find them made out of ceramics. Depending on its construction, a stand will cost you between $1.50 and $15; socks run around 30¢, so buy a few spares.

COFFEE

The best place to buy coffee is in any supermarket. Why pay more at a specialty shop? You can also try **Café Trebol,** on Calle 8 between Avenida Central and Avenida 1 (on the western side of the Central Market; ☎ **506/221-8363**). They're open Monday through Saturday from 7am to 6:30pm, Sunday from 8am to 2pm.

HANDCRAFTS

As I've said, the quality of Costa Rican handcrafts is generally very low, and the offerings are limited. The most typical items you'll find are hand-painted wooden oxcarts. These come in a variety of sizes, and the big ones can be shipped to your home for a very reasonable price.

One notable exception is the fine wooden creations of **Barry Biesanz** (☎ **506/ 228-1811;** www.biesanz.com). His work is sold in many of the finer gift shops around, but beware: Biesanz's work is often imitated, so make sure what you buy is the real deal (he generally burns his signature into the bottom of the piece). **Lil Mena** is a local artist, who specializes in working with and painting on handmade papers and rough fibers. You'll find her work in a number of shops around San José. You may also run across **carved masks** made by the indigenous Boruca people of southern Costa

Rica. These full-sized balsa wood masks come in a variety of styles, both painted and unpainted, and run anywhere from $10 to $70, depending on the quality of workmanship.

You'll find a collection of shops at the **Artisans Plaza** across from the Mall San Pedro. If you want to stick to downtown San José, try the outdoor market on the **Plaza de la Democracia,** though prices here tend to be high and bargaining can be difficult. If you prefer to do your craft shopping in a flea-market atmosphere, head over to **La Casona** on Calle Central between Avenida Central and Avenida 1.

Scores of shops around San José sell a wide variety of crafts, from the truly tacky to the divinely inspired. Here are some that sell more of the latter and fewer of the former.

Angie Theologos's Gallery. San Pedro (call for appointment and directions). ☎ **506/225-6565.**

Angie makes sumptuous handcrafted jackets from handwoven and embroidered Guatemalan textiles. Her work also includes bolero jackets, plus T-shirts made with Panamanian *molas* (appliquéd panels).

✪ **Atmosfera.** Calle 5 between avenidas 1 and 3. ☎ **506/222-4322.** Mon–Sat 9am–6pm, Sun 10am–6pm. AE, DC, MC, V.

This place sells high-quality Costa Rican arts and crafts, from primitivist paintings and sculpture to skillfully made turned-wood bowls. It consists of several small rooms spread over three floors, so be sure you explore every nook and cranny—you'll see stuff here that's not available anywhere else in town.

✪ **Biesanz Woodworks.** Bello Horizonte, Escazú. ☎ **506/228-1811.** www.biesanz.com. Mon–Fri 9am–5pm (call for directions and off-hour appointments). AE, MC, V.

Biesanz makes a wide range of high-quality items, including bowls, jewelry boxes, humidors, and some wonderful sets of wooden chopsticks. The showroom is adjoined to the artist's house. Biesanz Woodworks is actively involved in reforestation, so you can even pick up a hardwood seedling here.

✪ **Boutique Annemarie.** Calle 9 between avenidas 7 and 9. ☎ **506/221-6063.** Daily 9am–7pm. AE, MC, V.

Now occupying two floors at the Hotel Don Carlos, this shop has an amazing array of wood products, leather goods, papier-mâché figurines, paintings, books, cards, posters, and jewelry. You'll see most of this stuff at the other shops but not in such a relaxed and pressure-free environment. Don't miss this shopping experience.

✪ **Galería Namu.** Avenida 8 between calles 5 and 7. ☎ **506/256-3412.** www.galerianamu.com. E-mail: befrench@racsa.co.cr. Mon–Sat 9:30am–6:30pm. AE, MC, V.

This shop has some very high-quality arts and crafts, including excellent Boruca and Huetar carved masks, and "primitive" paintings, many painted by rural women. They also carry a good selection of the ceramic work of "Pefi" Figueres.

Las Garzas Handicraft Market. In Moravia, 100m (109 yd.) south and 50m (55 yd.) east of the Red Cross Station. ☎ **506/236-0037.** Daily 9am–6pm. AE, MC, V. Ask a taxi driver to take you to Las Garzas Mercado de Artesenia en Moravia.

This is the most appealing artisans' market close to San José (it's a short ride out of town). It includes more than 25 shops selling wood, metal, and ceramic crafts, among a large variety of other items. There's a huge selection, and you can get some really good buys here.

Madera Magia. Calle 5 between avenidas 1 and 3. ☎ **506/233-2630.** Mon–Fri 9am–6pm, Sat 9am–2pm. MC, V.

Almost everything is made of wood (*madera* is Spanish for wood). The shop is filled with elegant thin bowls of native hardwood, a big selection of wooden boxes, mirrors framed in wood, and very handsome handmade furniture. All items are of high quality, created by skilled artisans under the guidance of designer J. Morrison. These folks also have a large showroom in the suburb of Santa Ana.

Maya-Quiche. Avenida Central between calles 5 and 7, Locale #147. ☎ **506/223-5030.** Mon–Sat noon–6pm. AE, MC, V.

Located in the Galería Central Ramírez Valido shopping mall, this shop sells handcrafts from Central American countries, including gaily painted animals, boxes, and wooden letters from El Salvador, and *molas* from Panama.

Suraska. Calle 5 and Avenida 3. ☎ **506/222-0129.** Mon–Sat 9am–5pm. AE, V.

Among the selections here are ceramics, mobiles, and jewelry. This store tends to carry higher-quality items than most gift shops downtown. Be warned, however, that the prices here are accordingly more expensive.

JEWELRY

Esmeraldas y Diseños. Sabana Norte. From the Restaurante Chicote, go 100m (109 yd.) north, 25m (27 yd.) west, and 150m (164 yd.) north again. ☎ **506/231-4808** or 506/231-5428. Mon–Sat 8am–6pm. AE, MC, V.

Notice the location given above for this jewelry store—it's truly a classically complicated San José address. Once you find it, however, you'll uncover copies of pre-Columbian jewelry designs in gold, plus jewelry featuring semiprecious stones from Brazil and emeralds from Colombia.

LEATHER GOODS

Malety. Avenida 1 between calles 1 and 3. ☎ **506/221-1670.** Mon–Fri 9am–6pm, Sat 9am–5pm. AE, MC, V.

The quality of leather products found in Costa Rica is not as good as in North America, and prices are high, but take a look and see for yourself. This is one of the outlets in San José where you can shop for locally produced leather bags, briefcases, purses, wallets, and other such items. A second store is located on Calle 1 between Avenida Central and Avenida 2.

LIQUOR

Café Rica, similar to Kahlúa, and **Salicsa,** a cream liqueur, are two delicious coffee liqueurs made in Costa Rica. You can buy them in most supermarkets, liquor stores, and tourist shops, but the best prices I've seen are at the supermarket chain Mas X Menos. There is a **Mas X Menos outlet** on Paseo Colón and another on Avenida Central at the east end of town, just below the Museo Nacional de Costa Rica.

8 San José After Dark

In order to keep up with the tourism boom and steady urban expansion, San José has made strides to meet the nocturnal needs of visitors and residents alike. You'll find plenty of interesting clubs and bars, a wide range of theaters, and some very lively discos and dance salons.

To find out what's going on in San José while you're in town, pick up a copy of the *Tico Times* (English) or *La Nación* (Spanish). The former is a good place to find out where local expatriates are hanging out; the latter's "Viva" and "Tiempo Libre" sections have extensive listings of discos, movie theaters, and live music.

THE PERFORMING ARTS

Theater is very popular in Costa Rica, and downtown San José is studded with small theaters. However, tastes tend toward the burlesque, and the crowd pleasers are almost always simplistic sexual comedies. The **National Theater Company** (☎ 506/ 257-8305) is one major exception, tackling works from Lope de Vega to Lorca to Mamet. Almost all of the theater offerings are in Spanish, though the Little Theater Group is a long-standing amateur group that periodically stages works in English. Check the *Tico Times* to see if anything is running during your stay.

Costa Rica has a strong modern dance scene. Both the University of Costa Rica and the National University have modern-dance companies that perform regularly in San José. Two independent companies—**Los Denmedium** and **Diquis Tiquis**—are excellent. Sadly, however, you're almost more likely to catch these troupes performing in New York or Caracas than in San José.

The **National Symphony Orchestra** (☎ 506/236-5396) is a respectable orchestra by regional standards, though their repertoire tends to be rather conservative. The symphony season runs from March through November, with concerts roughly every other weekend at the **Teatro Nacional,** Avenida 2 between calles 3 and 5 (☎ 506/221-1329), and the new **Auditorio Nacional,** located at the **Children's Museum** (see above). Tickets cost between $3 and $15 and can be purchased at the box office.

Visiting artists also stop in Costa Rica from time to time. Recent concerts have featured Spanish pop diva Ana Belen, Argentine legend Mercedes Sosa, Salsa legends Celia Cruz and Ruben Blades, and Cuban jazz great Chuchu Valdes. Revival tours of aging pop rockers are also popular, with recent visits by America, Yes, and Jethro Tull topping the bill. Many of these concerts and guest performances take place in San José's two historic theaters, the Teatro Nacional and the **Teatro Melico Salazar,** Avenida 2 between Calle Central and Calle 2 (☎ 506/222-2653), as well as at the new Auditorio Nacional. Really large shows are sometimes held at soccer stadiums, or at the amphitheater at the Hotel Herradura.

Costa Rica's cultural panorama changes drastically every March, when the country hosts large arts festivals. In odd-numbered years, **El Festival Nacional de las Artes** reigns supreme, featuring purely local talent. In even-numbered years, the monthlong fete is **El Festival Internacional de las Artes** (**www.festivalcostarica.org**), which offers a nightly smorgasbord of dance, theater, music, and monologue from around the world. Most nights of the festival you will have between 4 and 10 shows to choose from. Many are free, and the most expensive ticket is $5. For exact dates and details of the program, you can contact the Ministry of Youth, Culture and Sports (☎ 506/255-3188), though you might have trouble getting any info if you don't speak Spanish.

THE CLUB, MUSIC & DANCE SCENE

If you like to dance, you'll find plenty of places to get down in San José. Salsa and merengue are the main beats that move people here, and many of the dance clubs, discos, and salons feature live music on the weekends. You'll find a pretty limited selection, though, if you're looking to catch some small-club jazz, rock, or blues.

The daily "Viva" and Thursday's "Tiempo Libre" sections of *La Nación* newspaper have weekly performance schedules. A couple of dance bands to watch for are Marfil and Los Brillanticos. El Parque, Ghandi, and Bruno Porter are popular local rock groups, Expresso is a good cover band, and both Blues Machine and the Blind Pig Blues Band are electric blues outfits. If you're looking for jazz, check out Jazz Garbo, Editus, El Sexteto de Jazz Latino, or pianist Manuel Obregon. Two very good local bands that don't seem to play that frequently are Cantoamerica and Adrian Goizueta's Grupo Experimental.

A good place to sample a range of San José's nightlife is in **El Pueblo,** a shopping, dining, and entertainment complex done up like an old Spanish village. It's just across the river to the north of town. The best way to get there is by taxi; all the drivers know El Pueblo well. Within the alleyways that wind through El Pueblo are a dozen or more bars, clubs, and discos; there's even a roller-skating rink. **Cocoloco** (☎ **506/222-8782**) features nightly "fiestas," **Discoteque Infinito** (☎ **506/221-9134**) has three different environments under one roof, and **Friends** (☎ **506/233-5283**) is a lively party spot. Across the street you'll find **La Plaza** (☎ **506/222-5143**), one of my favorite dance spots.

Most of the places listed below charge a nominal cover charge; sometimes it includes a drink or two.

✪ **El Tobogan.** 200m (218 yd.) north and 100m (109 yd.) east of the La República main office, off the Guápiles Hwy. ☎ **506/257-3396.** Fri–Sat 8pm–2am. AE, MC, V.

The dance floor in this place is about the size of a football field, and yet it still fills up. This is a place where Ticos come with their loved ones and dance partners. There's always a live band here, and sometimes it's very good.

✪ **La Plaza.** Across from the El Pueblo shopping center. ☎ **506/222-5143.** Daily 7pm–4am. AE, DC, MC, V.

This large, open, upscale disco seems to be the favored dance venue for the young and beautiful of San José. The interior is designed to resemble a colonial plaza. This place gets a younger crowd than many of the other spots around town. Admission is around $3.

Las Tunas. Sabana North, 500m (545 yd.) west of the ICE office. ☎ **506/231-1802.** Daily 6pm–2am. AE, MC, V.

This happening place serves Mexican food and barbecue throughout the day, but it's the nightly bar and discotheque that're really cookin'. Live Costa Rican pop music is featured periodically.

Salsa 54. Calle 3 between avenidas 1 and 3. ☎ **506/233-3814.** Daily 7pm–4am. MC, V.

This is the place to go to watch expert salsa dancers and to try some yourself. You can take formal Latin dance classes here, or you might learn something just by watching.

THE BAR SCENE

There seems to be something for every taste here. Lounge lizards will be happy in most hotel bars in the downtown area, while students and the young at heart will have no problem mixing in at the livelier spots around town. Sports fans can find plenty of places to catch the most important games of the day, and there are even a couple of brew pubs drastically improving the quality and selection of the local suds.

The best part of the varied bar scene in San José is something called a *boca,* the equivalent of a *tapa* in Spain: a little dish of snacks that arrives at your table when you order a drink. In most bars, the bocas are free, but in some, where the dishes are more sophisticated, you'll have to pay for the treats. You'll find drinks reasonably priced, with beer costing around $1.50 to $2 and mixed drinks $2 to $4.

Beatle Bar. Calle 9 between Avenida Central and Avenida 1. ☎ **506/256-9085.** Daily 11am–2am. MC, V.

Photos of the Fab Four line the walls here, and the music is a mix of Beatles and other sixties and seventies rock classics. Sit at the bar, or take a turn on the dance floor. There are even a couple of outdoor tables at the front of the bar. The location is one of the liveliest in the downtown area.

Cabeza Grande. Paseo Colón between calles 22 and 24. ☎ **506/256-6589.** Mon–Sat 5pm–2am. MC, V.

This brew pub serves up a wide range of homemade beers. There's some indoor seating near the bar and in plain view of the brewing tanks, but I'd opt for an outdoor table on the large covered patio overlooking Paseo Colón.

Chelles. Avenida Central and Calle 9. ☎ **506/221-1369.** Daily 24 hours. MC, V.

This classic downtown bar and restaurant makes up for it's lack of ambiance with plenty of tradition and its diverse and colorful clientele. The lights are bright, the chairs surround simple Formica-topped card tables, and mirrors adorn most of the walls. Simple sandwiches and meals are served, and pretty good bocas come with the drinks.

◯ El Cuartel de la Boca del Monte. Avenida 1 between calles 21 and 23 (50m/55 yd. west of the Cine Magaly). ☎ **506/221-0327.** Daily 6pm–1am. AE, DC, MC, V.

This popular bar began life as an artist-and-bohemian hangout, and over the years it's evolved into the leading meat market for the young and well heeled. However, artists still come, as do foreign-exchange students, visitors, and, for some reason, many of the river-rafting guides, so there's always a diverse mix. There's usually live music here on Monday, Wednesday, and Friday nights, and when there is, the place is packed shoulder to shoulder.

Key Largo. Calle 7 between avenidas 1 and 3. ☎ **506/221-0277.** Daily 6pm–4am. V.

Housed in a beautiful old building just off Parque Morazán in downtown San José, Key Largo is the best-known nightclub in Costa Rica. It's worth a visit just to see the interior of the building, but be warned: This is San José's number-one prostitute pickup spot. There's a $4 cover charge for men.

✪ La Esmeralda. Avenida 2 between calles 5 and 7. ☎ **506/221-0530.** Mon–Sat 11am–5am. AE, DC, MC, V.

A sort of mariachi Grand Central Station, La Esmeralda is a cavernous open-air restaurant and bar that stays open 24 hours a day. In the evenings, mariachi bands park their vans out front and wait to be hired for a moonlight serenade or perhaps a surprise party. While they wait, they often fill the restaurant with loud trumpet blasts and the sound of the big bass *guitarón.* If you've never been serenaded at your table before, this place is a must. A song will cost you anywhere from $3 to $10, depending on the size of the group you hire.

Rio. Avenida Central, Los Yoses. ☎ **506/225-8371.** Daily noon–3am. AE, DC, MC, V.

This bar and restaurant is close to the University of Costa Rica, and consequently attracts a younger clientele. At night, Rio is always packed to overflowing with the wealthy and the wanna-bes of San José.

Risa's Bar. Calle 1 between Avenida Central and Avenida 1. ☎ **506/223-2803.** Mon–Sat 11:30am–3am. V.

This popular restaurant and bar now occupies all four floors of this beautiful old building in the heart of downtown San José. Yet another renovation has created a large disco occupying much of the first two floors, with a variety of different environments spread around the rest of the building. Overall, there are six different bars and a good typical restaurant in this complex.

Shakespeare Bar. Avenida 2 and Calle 28. ☎ **506/257-1288.** Daily 5pm–1am. V.

Located next to the Sala Garbo movie theater, this quiet and classy little spot is a good place to meet after a movie or a show at the Sala Garbo or Laurence Olivier Theater next door.

HANGING OUT IN SAN PEDRO

The 2-block stretch of ✪ **San Pedro** just south of the University of Costa Rica is the closest thing to Paris's Left Bank or New York's East Village you'll find here. Bars and cafes are mixed in with bookstores and copy shops. It's one of the few places in town where you can sit calmly at an outdoor table or walk the streets without constantly looking over your shoulder and checking if your wallet's still with you. You can just stroll the strip until someplace strikes your fancy—you don't need a travel guide to find **Omar Khayyam** (☎ **506/253-8455**) or **Pizza Caccio** (☎ **506/283-2809**)— or you can trust me and try one of the following.

   You can get here by heading out (east) on Avenida 2, following the flow of traffic. You will first pass through the neighborhood of Los Yoses before reaching a big traffic circle with a big fountain in the center (La Fuente de la Hispanidad). The Mall San Pedro is located on this traffic circle. Heading straight through the circle (well, going around it and continuing on what would have been a straight path), you will come to the Church of San Pedro about 4 blocks east of the circle. The church is the major landmark in San Pedro. You can also take a bus here from downtown.

All-Star Bar & Grill. Centro Comercial Cocorí, in front of the Fuente de la Hispanidad, San Pedro. ☎ **506/225-0838.** Daily 11am–2am. AE, MC, V.

This is the closest thing to a U.S.-style sports bar in San José. There's at least one television, and usually more, visible from every seat in the house, as well as one mammoth screen anchoring the main room. There are framed sports jerseys and covers of *Sports Illustrated* on the walls. Upstairs you'll find some billiard and foosball tables. The menu features excellently prepared hamburgers, hot dogs, and cheese-steak subs. What else would you expect? On weekends they sometimes have live music and charge a minimal cover.

✪ **Jazz Café.** Next to the Banco Popular on Avenida Central. ☎ **506/253-8933.** Daily 6pm–2am. MC, V.

Opened by one of the former owners of the popular, but now defunct, La Maga, this has quickly become one of the more happening spots in San Pedro. Wrought-iron chairs, sculpted busts of famous jazz artists, and creative lighting give the place ambiance. There's live music here most nights, and visiting artists have included Chucho Valdes and Tony Perez.

Mosaikos. 200m (218 yd.) east and 150m (164 yd.) north of the Church in San Pedro. ☎ **506/280-9541.** Mon–Fri 11am–2am, Sat–Sun 4pm–2am. No credit cards.

The entrance to this popular nightspot is a long, narrow corridor/bar that is generally packed solid. In the back there's a slightly larger room, with another bar, some tables, a couple of televisions, and some funky art. Unlike most bars in San Pedro, these folks actually know how to make a couple of mixed drinks.

Planet Mall. In the San Pedro Mall. ☎ **506/280-4693.** Thurs–Sat 8pm–2am. AE, MC, V.

This new place is on the fourth floor of the Mall San Pedro. There are a couple of quiet nooks and corners here, but most of the action takes place under the neon lights on and around the immense dance floor, which sometimes features live music.

✪ **La Villa.** 200m (218 yd.) east and 125m (136 yd.) north of the Church in San Pedro. ☎ **506/225-9612.** Mon–Sat 11am–1am, Sun 7pm–1am. AE, MC, V.

This converted Victorian house holds the ghosts of Che Guevara and Camilo Cienfuegos—or so you'd think from the posters of these and other Latin-American revolutionaries on the walls. Around the tables you'll find poets and painters mixing with a new generation of student activists, all in a lively atmosphere. There's even a foosball table in the far back. Consistent with the revolutionary ethos, everything is priced reasonably.

THE GAY & LESBIAN SCENE

Because Costa Rica is such a conservative Catholic country, the gay and lesbian communities here are rather discreet. Homosexuality is not generally under attack, but many gay and lesbian organizations guard their privacy, and the club scene is not entirely stable. For a general overview of the current situation, news of any special events or meetings, and up-to-date information, gay and lesbian travelers should check in with **La Asociación Triángulo Rosa** (☎ 506/258-0214; fax 506/258-0635; E-mail: atrirosa@racsa.co.cr). This is a local human rights organization that is usually able to provide information and orientation to visitors.

The most established and happening gay and lesbian bars and dance clubs in San José are **Déjà Vu,** Calle 2 between avenidas 14 and 16 (☎ 506/223-3758), and **La Avispa,** Calle 1 between avenidas 8 and 10 (☎ 506/223-5343). The former is predominantly a guys' bar, while the latter is popular with both men and women, although they sometimes set certain nights of the week or month aside for specific persuasions. There's also **Buenas Vibraciones** (☎ 506/223-4573) out on Paseo de los Estudiantes and **Bochinche** on Calle 11 between avenidas 10 and 12. In San Pedro, you'll find **La Tertulia** (☎ 506/225-0250), **Faces,** and **Los Bigotitos.** As you'll notice above, some of these places don't advertise their phone numbers, but you can call **Triángulo Rosa** (see above) for directions and more specific information.

CASINOS

Gambling is legal in Costa Rica, and there are casinos at virtually every major hotel. However, as in Tico bullfighting, there are some idiosyncrasies involved in *gambling a la Tica.* If blackjack is your game, you'll want to play "rummy." The rules are almost identical, except the house doesn't pay double on blackjack—instead it pays double on any three of a kind or three-card straight flush. If you're looking for roulette, what you'll find here is a bingolike spinning cage of numbered balls. The betting is the same, but some of the glamour is lost. You'll also find a version of five-card draw poker, but the rule differences are so complex that I advise you to sit down and watch for a while and then ask some questions before joining in. That's about all you'll find. There are no craps tables or baccarat.

There's some controversy over slot machines—one-armed bandits are currently outlawed—but you will be able to play electronic slots and poker games. Most of the casinos here are quite casual and small by international standards. You may have to dress up slightly at some of the fancier hotels, but most are accustomed to tropical vacation attire.

9 Side Trips from San José

San José makes an excellent base for exploring the beautiful Central Valley and the surrounding mountains. For first-time visitors, the best way to make the most of these excursions is usually on guided tours, but if you rent a car you'll have greater independence. There are also some day trips that can be done by public bus.

GUIDED TOURS & ADVENTURES

A number of companies offer a wide variety of primarily nature-related day tours out of San José. The most reputable include **Costa Rica Expeditions** (☎ **506/257-0766;** www.costaricaexpeditions.com), **Costa Rica Sun Tours** (☎ **506/255-3418;** www.crsuntours.com), **Ecole Travel** (☎ **506/223-2240**), **Fantasy Tours** (☎ **800/ 272-6654** in the U.S., 800/463-6654 in Canada, or 506/220-2126), **Horizontes Tours** (☎ **506/222-2022;** www.horizontes.com), **Otec Tours** (☎ **506/256-0633;** www.gotec.com), **Swiss Travel Service** (☎ **506/282-4898**), and **TAM** (☎ **506/ 256-0203;** www.tamtravel.com).

Before signing on for a tour of any sort, find out how many fellow travelers will be accompanying you, how much time will be spent in transit and eating lunch, and how much time will actually be spent doing the primary activity. I've had complaints about tours that were rushed, that spent too much time in a bus or on secondary activities, or that had a cattle-car, assembly-line feel to them.

The tours below are arranged by type of activity. In addition to these, there are many other tours, some of which combine two or three different activities or destinations.

BUNGEE JUMPING   There's nothing unique about bungee jumping in Costa Rica except for the price—it's a little bit less expensive here than elsewhere. If you've always had the bug, **Tropical Bungee** (☎ **506/232-3956;** www.bungee.co.cr) will let you jump off a 265-foot bridge for $45; two jumps cost $70. Transportation is $7 each way.

CRUISES   Several companies offer cruises to the lovely Tortuga Island in the Gulf of Nicoya. The original and most dependable company running these trips is **Calypso Tours** (☎ **506/256-2727;** www.calypsotours.com). The cruise costs $99 per person and includes transportation from San José to Puntarenas and back, a basic continental breakfast during the bus ride to the boat, all drinks on the cruise, and an excellent lunch on the beach at the island. Calypso Tours also conducts cruises to a private nature reserve at Punta Coral. Alternately, you could try **Seascape** (☎ **506/ 289-3333**), which has a 1-day tour to Isla Tortuga for just $80.

HIKING   Most of the tour agencies listed above offer 1-day guided hikes to a variety of destinations. In general, I recommend taking guided hikes, to really see and learn about the local flora and fauna.

If you don't plan to visit Monteverde or one of Costa Rica's other cloud-forest reserves (see chapter 6), consider doing a day tour to the ✪ **Los Angeles Cloud Forest Reserve.** This full-day excursion and guided walk through the cloud forest is operated by **Villablanca Hotel** (☎ **506/228-4603**). The cost is $75, which includes transportation, breakfast, and lunch. They also offer horseback riding and canopy-tour options.

HORSEBACK RIDING   Costa Rica is a country with a strong agricultural tradition and horseback riding is a popular activity. While options are nearly endless outside of San José, it gets a little bit more difficult to find a place to saddle up in the metropolitan area. The **Valle de Yos-Oy Riding Center** (☎ **506/282-6934** or 506/282-7850) is located in Santa Ana and offers riding classes as well as guided trail rides.

MOUNTAIN-BIKING   The best bicycle riding is well outside of San José—on dirt roads where you're not likely to be run off the highway by a semi, or run head-on into someone coming around a blind curve in the wrong lane. **Velero del Rey Tours** (☎ 506/235-4982), **Costa Rica Sun Tours** (☎ 506/255-3418; www.crsuntours.com), and **Aguas Bravas** (☎ 506/292-2072) all run a variety of mountain-biking tours, including descents of Irazú Volcano. A 1-day trip should cost between $70 and $90 per person.

Another company offering mountain-biking trips is **BiCosta Rica** (☎ 506/446-7585). You might also contact **Coast to Coast Adventures** (☎ 506/225-6055), which, in addition to its 2-week namesake adventure, will also design customized mountain-biking trips of shorter duration.

PRE-COLUMBIAN RUINS   Though Costa Rica lacks the kind of massive pre-Columbian archaeological sites that can be found in Mexico, Guatemala, or Honduras, it does have **Guayabo National Monument,** a small excavated town, which today is just a collection of building foundations and cobbled streets. **Costa Rica Sun Tours** (☎ 506/255-3418; www.crsuntours.com) offers a day trip here for around $110 per person. If you have a car, or are an intrepid bus hound, you can do this tour on your own—you can usually find a guide at the entrance for $5. See the section on Turrialba, later in this chapter.

RAFTING, KAYAKING & RIVER TRIPS   Cascading down Costa Rica's mountain ranges are dozens of tumultuous rivers, several of which have become very popular for white-water rafting and kayaking. If I had to choose just one day trip to do out of San José, it would be a white-water rafting trip. For between $65 and $90, you can spend a day rafting through lush tropical forests; longer trips are also available. Some of the more reliable rafting companies are **Aventuras Naturales** (☎ 800/514-0411 in the U.S., or 506/225-3939), **Costa Rica White Water** (☎ 506/257-0766), **Ríos Tropicales** (☎ 506/233-6455), and **Aguas Bravas** (☎ 506/292-2072).

These companies all ply a number of rivers of varying difficulties, including the popular Pacuare and Reventazón rivers. For more information see "White-Water Rafting, & Canoeing" in chapter 3.

The Sarapiquí River is also a popular waterway for day trips out of San José. **Costa Rica Fun Adventures** (☎ 506/290-6015) and **Ecoscapes Highlights Tour** (☎ 506/297-0664), both run jam-packed trips up here that combine a stop at the La Paz waterfall, a visit to a banana plantation, a rain-forest hike, and a boat ride on the river for around $75 to $80 per person, including round-trip transportation and lunch.

Perhaps the best-known river tours are those that go up to **Tortuguero National Park.** Though it's possible to do this tour as a day trip out of San José, it's a long, tiring, and expensive day. You're much better off doing it as a 1- or 2-night trip. See chapter 9 for details.

RAIN-FOREST AERIAL TRAM   When you first see the Aerial Tram (☎ 506/257-5961; www.rainforesttram.com; E-mail: info@rainforesttram.com), you may wonder where the ski slopes are. Built on a private reserve bordering Braulio Carillo National Park, the tramway is the brainchild of rain-forest researcher Dr. Donald Perry, whose cable-car system through the forest canopy at Rara Avis helped establish him as an early expert on rain-forest canopies. The tramway takes visitors on a 90-minute ride through the treetops, where they have the chance to glimpse the complex web of life that makes these forests unique. There are also well-groomed trails through the rain forest and a restaurant on site, so a trip here can easily take up a full day.

The Central Valley: Side Trips from San José

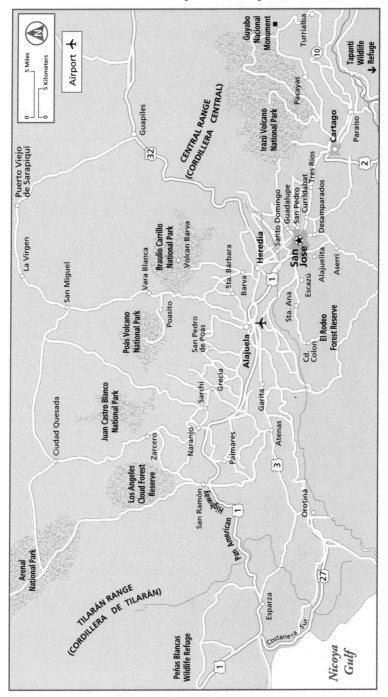

Holy Smoke! Choosing the Volcano Trip That's Right for You

Poás, Irazú, and Arenal volcanoes are three of Costa Rica's most popular destinations, and the first two are easy day trips from San José (see below). Although numerous companies offer day trips to Arenal, I don't recommend them because there's at least 3¹/₂ hours of travel time in each direction. You usually arrive when the volcano is hidden by clouds and leave before the night's darkness shows off its glowing eruptions. For more information on Arenal Volcano, see chapter 6.

Tour companies offering trips to Poás and Irazú include **Costa Rica Expeditions** (☎ 506/257-0766), **Costa Rica Sun Tours** (☎ 506/255-3418), **Horizontes** (☎ 506/222-2022), **Otec Tours** (☎ 506/256-0633), **TAM** (☎ 506/256-0203), and **Swiss Travel Service** (☎ 506/282-4898). Prices range from $25 to $35 for a half-day trip and from $50 to $90 for a full-day trip.

The 11,260-foot-tall ✪ **Irazú Volcano** is historically one of Costa Rica's more active volcanoes, although it's relatively quiet these days. It last erupted on March 19, 1963, on the day that President John F. Kennedy arrived in Costa Rica. There's a good paved road right to the rim of the crater, where a desolate expanse of gray sand nurtures few plants and the air smells of sulfur. The landscape here is often compared to that of the moon. There are magnificent views of the fertile Meseta Central and Orosi Valley as you drive up from Cartago, and if you're very lucky you may be able to see both the Pacific Ocean and Caribbean Sea. Clouds usually descend by noon, so get here as early in the day as possible.

There's a new visitor center up here with information on the volcano and natural history. A short trail leads to the rim of the volcano's two craters, their walls a maze of eroded gullies feeding onto the flat floor far below. This is a national park, with an admission fee of $6 charged at the gate. Dress in layers. This may be the tropics, but it can be cold up at the top if the sun's not out. The park restaurant, at an elevation of 10,075 feet, with walls of windows looking out over the valley far below, claims to be the highest restaurant in Central America.

The cost for tours, including transportation from San José and either breakfast or lunch, is $78.50. Alternately, you can drive or take one of the frequent Guápiles buses—they leave every half hour and cost $2—from Calle 12 between avenidas 7 and 9. Ask the driver to let you off in front of the "teleferico." If driving, head out on the Guápiles Highway as if driving to the Caribbean coast. Watch for the tram's roadside welcome center—it's hard to miss. For walk-ins, the entrance fee is $49.50. Students and anyone under 18 pay $25.

CARTAGO & THE OROSI VALLEY

These two regions southeast of San José can easily be combined into one day trip. You might also squeeze in a visit to the Irazú Volcano (see "Holy Smoke!: Choosing the Volcano Trip That's Right for You").

CARTAGO

Located about 15 miles (24km) southeast of San José, ✪ **Cartago** is the former capital of Costa Rica. Founded in 1563, it was Costa Rica's first city, and was in fact its

Getting There: Buses leave for Irazú Volcano Saturday, Sunday, and holidays at 8am from Avenida 2 between calles 1 and 3 (in front of the Gran Hotel Costa Rica). The fare is $5 round-trip, with the bus leaving the volcano at 3pm. To make sure the buses are running, call ☎ **506/272-0651**. If you're driving, head northeast out of Cartago toward San Rafael, then continue driving uphill toward the volcano, passing the turnoffs for Cot and Tierra Blanca en route.

Poás Volcano is 23 miles (37km) from San José on narrow roads that wind through a landscape of fertile farms and dark forests. As at Irazú, there's a paved road right to the top. The volcano stands 8,800 feet tall and is located within a national park, which preserves not only the volcano but also dense stands of virgin forest. Poás's crater, said to be the second-largest in the world, is over a mile across. Geysers in the crater sometimes spew steam and muddy water 600 feet into the air, making this the largest geyser in the world. There's an information center where you can see a slide show about the volcano, and there are marked hiking trails through the cloud forest that rings the crater. About 20 minutes from the parking area, along a forest trail, is an overlook onto beautiful Botos Lake, which has formed in one of the volcano's extinct craters.

Be prepared when you come to Poás: This volcano is often enveloped in dense clouds. If you want to see the crater, it's best to come early, and during the dry season. Moreover, it can get cool up here, especially when the sun isn't shining, so dress appropriately. Admission to the national park is $6 at the gate.

Getting There: There is a daily bus (☎ **506/222-5325**) from Calle 12 and avenidas 2 and 4, leaving at 8:30am and returning at 2:30pm. The fare is $3.50 for the round-trip. The bus is usually crowded, so arrive early. If you're driving, head for Alajuela and continue on the main road through town and follow signs for Fraijanes. Just beyond Fraijanes, you will connect with the road between San Pedro de Poás and Poasito, turn right toward Poasito and continue to the rim of the volcano.

only city for almost 150 years. Irazú Volcano rises up from the edge of town, and although it's quiet these days, it has not always been so peaceful. Earthquakes have damaged Cartago repeatedly over the years, so today there are few of the old colonial buildings left standing. In the center of the city, a public park winds through the ruins of a large church that was destroyed in 1910, before it could be finished. Construction was abandoned after the quake, and today the ruins are a neatly manicured park, with quiet paths and plenty of benches.

Cartago's most famous building, however, is the **Basilica de Nuestra Señora de los Angeles** (the Basilica of Our Lady of the Angels), which is dedicated to the patron saint of Costa Rica and stands on the east side of town. Within the walls of this Byzantine-style church is a shrine containing the tiny figure of **La Negrita,** the Black Virgin, which is nearly lost amid its ornate altar. Legend has it that La Negrita first revealed herself on this site to a peasant girl in 1635. Miraculous healing powers have been attributed to La Negrita, and over the years thousands of pilgrims have come to the shrine seeking cures for their illnesses and difficulties. The walls of the shrine are covered with a fascinating array of tiny silver images left as thanks for cures affected by La Negrita. Amid the plethora of diminutive silver arms and legs, there are also hands, feet, hearts, lungs, kidneys, eyes, torsos, breasts, and—peculiarly—guns, trucks, beds, and planes. There are even dozens of sports trophies that I assume were left in thanks for helping teams win big games. Outside the church, vendors sell a wide selection of these trinkets, as well as little candle replicas of La Negrita. August 2 is the day dedicated to La Negrita, and on this day tens of thousands of people walk to Cartago from San José and elsewhere in the country, in devotion to this powerful statue.

A little over a mile (1.6km) east of Cartago, on the road to Paraíso, you'll find **Lankester Gardens** (☎ **506/552-3247** or 506/552-3151), a botanical garden known for its orchid collection. (See "Outside San José," above, for details.)

GETTING THERE   Buses (☎ **506/233-5350**) for Cartago leave San José every 10 minutes between 5am and midnight from Calle 5 between avenidas 18 and 20. You can also pick one up en route at any of the covered little bus stops along Avenida Central in Los Yoses and San Pedro. The length of the trip is 45 minutes; the fare is about 45¢.

OROSI VALLEY

The Orosi Valley, southeast of Cartago and visible from the top of Irazú on a clear day, is generally considered one of the most beautiful valleys in Costa Rica. The Reventazón River meanders through this steep-sided valley until it collects in the lake formed by the Cachí Dam. There are scenic overlooks near the town of Orosi, which is at the head of the valley, and in Ujarrás, which is on the banks of the lake. Near Ujarrás are the ruins of Costa Rica's oldest church (built in 1693), whose tranquil gardens are a great place to sit and gaze at the surrounding mountains.

Across the lake is a popular recreation center, called **Charrara** (☎ **506/574-7557**), where you'll find a picnic area, swimming pool, hiking trails, and a camping area. In the town of Orosi there is yet another colonial church, built in 1743. A small museum here displays religious artifacts. Near the town of Cachí, you'll find **La Casa del Soñador** (The House of the Dreamer; ☎ **506/533-3297**), which is the home and gallery of the late sculptor Macedonio Quesada, and his sons, who carry on the family tradition.

GETTING THERE   It would be difficult to explore this whole area by public bus, since this is not a densely populated region. However, there are buses from Cartago to the town of Orosi. During the week, these buses run every hour and leave from a spot 1 block east and 25 meters (27 yd.) south of the church ruins in Cartago. Saturday and Sunday, the bus runs roughly every 45 minutes from the same block and will drop you at the Orosi lookout point. The trip takes 30 minutes, and the fare is 35¢. If you're driving, take the road to Paraíso from Cartago, head toward Ujarrás, continue around the lake, then pass through Cachí and on to Orosi. From Orosi, the road leads back to Paraíso. There are also guided day tours of this area from San José (call any of the companies listed under "Guided Tours & Adventures," above).

TURRIALBA

This attractive little town 33 miles (53km) east of San José is best known as the starting point and home base for many popular white-water-rafting trips. However, it's also worth a visit if you have an interest in pre-Columbian history or tropical botany.

✪ **Guayabo National Monument** is one of Costa Rica's only pre-Columbian sites that has been excavated and open to the public. It's located 12 miles (19km) northeast of Turrialba and preserves a town site that dates from between 1000 B.C. and

A.D. 1400. Archaeologists believe that Guayabo may have supported a population of as many as 10,000 people, but there is no clue yet as to why the city was eventually abandoned only shortly before the Spanish arrived in the New World. Excavated ruins at Guayabo consist of paved roads, aqueducts, stone bridges, and house and temple foundations. There are also grave sites and petroglyphs. The monument is open daily from 8am to 4pm. This is a national park, and admission is $6 at the gate. For more information, see "Costa Rica's National Parks & Bioreserves" in chapter 3.

Botanists and gardeners will want to pay a visit to the **Center for Agronomy Research and Development (CATIE),** which is located 3 miles (5km) southeast of Turrialba on the road to Siquerres. This center is one of the world's foremost facilities for research into tropical agriculture. Among the plants on CATIE's 2,000 acres are hundreds of varieties of cacao and thousands of varieties of coffee. The plants here have been collected from all over the world. In addition to trees used for food and other purposes, there are plants grown strictly for ornamental purposes. CATIE is open Monday through Friday from 7am to 4pm. Guided tours are available with advance notice for $25 per person. Call ☎ **506/556-6431** for reservations.

While you're in the area, don't miss an opportunity to spend a little time at **Turrialtico** (☎ **506/556-1111**), a lively open-air restaurant and small hotel high on a hill overlooking the Turrialba Valley. The view from here is one of the finest in the country, with lush greenery far below and volcanoes in the distance. Meals are quite inexpensive; a room will cost you $35. This place is popular with rafting companies that bring groups here for meals and for overnights before, during, and after multiday rafting trips. You'll find Turrialtico about 6 miles (10km) out of Turrialba on the road to Siquierres.

If you're looking for some luxury in this area, check out **Casa Turire** (☎ **506/ 531-1111;** fax 506/531-1075; www.hotelcasaturire.com; E-mail: info@hotelcasaturire. com), where well-appointed rooms and suites in an elegant country mansion run between $140 and $220.

GETTING THERE   Buses (☎ **506/556-0073**) leave hourly for Turrialba throughout the day from Calle 13 between avenidas 6 and 8. The fare is $1.50. If you're driving, take the road from Cartago to Paraíso, then through Juan Viñas and on to Turrialba. It's pretty well marked. (Alternately you can head toward the small town of Cot, on the road to Volcan Irazú, then through the town of Pacayas on to Turrialba, another well-marked route.) Turrialba itself is a bit of a jumble and you will probably have to ask directions to get to locations out of town. Guayabo is about 12½ miles (20km) beyond Turrialba on a road that is paved the entire way except for the last 2 miles (3km). There are also around three buses daily to Guayabo from the main bus terminal in Turrialba.

HEREDIA, GRECIA, SARCHÍ & ZARCERO

All of these cities and towns are northwest of San José and can be combined into a long day trip (if you have a car), perhaps in conjunction with a visit to Poás Volcano. The scenery here is rich and verdant, and the small towns and scattered farming communities are truly representative of Costa Rica's agricultural heartland and campesino tradition. If you're relying on buses, you'll be able to visit any of the towns listed below, but probably just one or two per day.

The road to Heredia turns north off the highway from San José to the airport. If you're going to Sarchí, take the highway west toward Puntarenas. Turn north to Grecia and then west to Sarchí. There'll be plenty of signs.

HEREDIA

Set on the flanks of the impressive Barva Volcano, this city was founded in 1706. Heredia is affectionately known as "The City of Flowers." A colonial church inaugurated in 1763 stands in the central park. The stone facade leaves no questions as to the age of the church, but the altar inside is decorated with neon stars and a crescent moon surrounding a statue of the Virgin Mary. In the middle of the palm-shaded park is a music temple, and across the street, beside several tile-roofed municipal buildings, is the tower of an old Spanish fort. Of all the cities in the Meseta Central, Heredia has the most colonial feel to it—you'll still see adobe buildings with Spanish tile roofs along narrow streets.

In the center of town you'll find the small **Museo de Cultura Popular** (☎ **506/260-1619**), which is open daily from 8am to 4pm. Heredia is also the site of the **National Autonomous University,** so you'll find some nice coffee shops and bookstores near the school. Surrounding Heredia are a bevy of picturesque villages and towns, including Santa Barbara, Santo Domingo, Barva, and San Joaquín de Flores. The newest attraction up here is the **InBio Park** (☎ **506/244-4730**). Located on 5 hectares (12 acres) in Santo Domingo de Heredia, this place is part museum, part educational center, and part nature park. In addition to watching a 15-minute informational video, visitors can tour two large pavilions explaining Costa Rica's biodiversity and natural wonders, and hike on trails that re-create the ecosystems of a tropical rain forest, dry forest, and premontane forest. Admission is $18 for adults, $9 for children 12 and under.

Buses leave for Heredia almost every 10 minutes from Calle 12 and Avenida 2, and from Calle 1 between avenidas 7 and 9. Bus fare is 40¢.

GRECIA

The picturesque little town of Grecia is noteworthy for its unusual metal church, which is painted a deep red and has white gingerbread trim. Just off the central park, next to the Palacio Municipal, you'll find the humble **Grecia Regional Museum** (☎ **506/494-6767**), which has some simple exhibits and information about the town's history. About 1¹/₂ miles (1km) outside of Grecia, on the old road to Alajuela, you will find **The World of Snakes** (☎ **506/494-3700**). Open daily from 8am to 4pm, this serpentarium has over 150 snakes representing over 50 species. Admission is $11 and includes a guided tour. Buses leave hourly for Grecia from the Coca-Cola bus station at Calle 16 between avenidas 1 and 3. The road to Sarchí is to the left as you face the church in Grecia, but due to all the one-way streets you'll have to drive around it.

SARCHÍ

✪ **Sarchí** is Costa Rica's main artisan town. It's here that the colorfully painted miniature oxcarts you see all over the country are made. Oxcarts such as these were once used to haul coffee beans to market. Today, though you may occasionally see oxcarts in use, most are purely decorative. However, they remain a well-known symbol of Costa Rica. In addition to miniature oxcarts, many carved wooden souvenirs are made here with rare hardwoods from the nation's forests. There are dozens of shops in town, and all have similar prices. Aside from handcrafts, the other reason to visit Sarchí is to see its **unforgettable church.** Built between 1950 and 1958, the church is painted pink with aquamarine trim and looks strangely like a child's birthday cake. Buses leave for Grecia every 30 minutes between 7am and 7pm, from the Coca-Cola bus station, at Calle 16 and avenidas 1 and 3. In Grecia they connect with the Alajuela-Sarchí buses, which leave every 30 minutes from Calle 8 between Avenida Central and Avenida 1 in Alajuela. The fare is 75¢.

ZARCERO

Beyond Sarchí, on picturesque roads lined with cedar trees, you'll find the town of Zarcero. In a small park in the middle of town is a **menagerie of sculpted shrubs** that includes a monkey on a motorcycle, people and animals dancing, an ox pulling a cart, a man wearing a top hat, and a large elephant. Behind all the topiary is a wonderful rural church. It's worth the drive just to see this park. Zarcero is also a good stop on the way to La Fortuna and Arenal Volcano. Buses (☎ **506/255-4318**) for Zarcero leave from San José hourly from the Atlantico del Norte bus station at Avenida 9 and Calle 12. This is actually the Ciudad Quesada–San Carlos bus. Just tell the driver you want to get off in Zarcero and keep an eye out for the topiary.

5 Guanacaste & the Nicoya Peninsula: The Gold Coast

Guanacaste province is Costa Rica's hottest and driest region. The rainy season starts later and ends earlier here, and overall it's more dependably sunny than in other parts of the country. Combine this climate with a coastline that stretches from the Nicaraguan border to the southern tip of the Nicoya Peninsula, and you have an equation that yields beach bliss. Beautiful beaches abound along this coastline. Some are pristine and deserted, some are dotted with luxury resort hotels, and still others are backed by little villages where you can still get a clean double room for less than $30 a night. These beaches vary from long, straight stretches of sand to tiny coves bordered by rocky headlands. Whatever your passion in beaches, you're likely to find something that comes close to perfection.

This is Costa Rica's most coveted vacation region and the site of its greatest tourism development. The change is dramatic and ongoing. Large resorts have sprung up, and more are in the works. So far, two regulation golf courses have opened up, and several more are under construction. The long-awaited international airport in Liberia is finally getting on its feet, and while charter flights still make up the lion's share of the traffic here, it will soon be possible to fly from major international hubs directly in and out of Liberia—and on to any one of the numerous beaches below—without having to go through San José.

There is one caveat: During the dry season (from mid-November through April), when sunshine is most reliable, the hillsides in Guanacaste turn browner than the chaparral of southern California. Dust from dirt roads blankets the trees in many areas, and the vistas are far from tropical. Driving these dirt roads without air-conditioning and hermetically sealed windows can be extremely unpleasant. But, if you can't tolerate the least bit of rain on your holiday in the sun, the beaches up here are where you'll want to be.

On the other hand, if you happen to visit this area in the **rainy season** (May to mid-November), the hillsides are a beautiful rich green, and the sun usually shines all morning, giving way to an afternoon shower—just in time for a nice siesta.

Guanacaste is also Costa Rica's "Wild West," a dry landscape of cattle ranches and cowboys, who are known here as *sabaneros,* a name that derives from the Spanish word for "savannah" or "grassland." This is big country, with big views and big sky. If it weren't for those rainforest–clad volcanoes in the distance, you might swear you were in

TIMBUKTU   KALAMAZOO

AT&T Direct® Service

The easy way to call home from anywhere.

Global | **AT&T**
connection | direct
with the AT&T | service
Network |

For the easy way to call home, take the attached wallet guide.

www.att.com/traveler

AT&T Calling Card, AT&T Corporate Card, AT&T Universal Card, MasterCard®, American Express®, Diners Club®, and Discover® cards accepted. Credit card calling subject to availability. Payment terms subject to your credit card agreement. ©2000 AT&T

Make Learning Fun & Easy

With IDG Books Worldwide

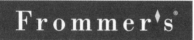

Available at your local bookstores

Guanacaste & the Nicoya Peninsula

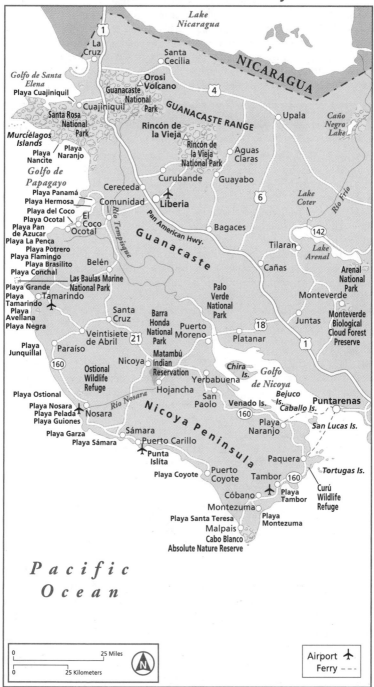

Texas. However, Guanacaste hasn't always looked this way. At one time this land was covered with a dense, though fairly dry, forest that was cut for lumber and to create pasturelands for grazing cattle. Today, that dry tropical forest exists only in remnants preserved in several national parks. Up in the mountains, in **Rincón de la Vieja National Park,** you'll find not only forests and wildlife, but also hot springs and bubbling mud pots similar to those in Yellowstone National Park in the United States.

1 Liberia

134¹/₂ miles (217km) NW of San José; 82 miles (132km) NW of Puntarenas

Founded in 1769, ❸ **Liberia** is the capital of Guanacaste province, and though it can hardly be considered a bustling city, it does have the distinction of having a more colonial atmosphere than almost any other city in the country. Narrow streets are lined with charming old adobe homes, many of which have ornate stone accents on their facades, carved wooden doors, and aged red-tile roofs. Many have beautiful, large shuttered windows (some don't even have iron bars for protection) that open onto the narrow streets.

Liberia is best looked upon as a base for exploring this region, or as an overnight stop as part of a longer itinerary. From here it's possible to do day trips to nearby beaches and three national parks, although only two of them have facilities for visitors. Several moderately priced hotels are located on the outskirts of Liberia at the intersection of the Interamerican Highway and the road to the Nicoya Peninsula and its many beaches.

ESSENTIALS

GETTING THERE & DEPARTING   By Plane   The airstrip in Liberia has been cleared to accept commercial international flights for a couple of years now. But so far, the traffic still remains predominantly charter flights. No major airline has regularly scheduled flights to Liberia, although as I've been writing for years, this is expected to change. Check with your travel agent.

Sansa (☎ 506/221-9414; fax 506/255-2176; E-mail: reservations@flysansa.com) has daily flights to Liberia leaving at 7:15 and 11:30am, and 2:10 and 5:30pm from San José's Juan Santamaría International Airport. Return flights depart for San José at 8:35am and 12:40, 3:15, and 7pm. The one-way fare is $61; duration, 50 minutes.

Travelair (☎ 506/220-3054; fax 506/220-0413; E-mail: reservations@travelaircostarica.com) has a daily flight to Liberia at 8:20am from Tobías Bolaños International Airport in Pavas. This flight stops first in Tamarindo. The return flight leaves Liberia at 9:30am. Fares are $92 one-way; $152 round-trip.

If you plan on flying here and renting a car to continue on to one of the nearby beaches and explore the region, contact the following agencies: **Ada Rent A Car** (☎ 506/668-1111), **Alamo Rent A Car** (☎ 506/666-2998), **Budget Rent A Car** (☎ 506/668-1024), **Economy Rent A Car** (☎ 506/666-2816), **Toyota Rent A Car** (☎ 506/666-8190), and **Sol Rent A Car** (☎ 506/666-2222). You can also reserve with these companies via their San José and international offices (see chapter 4).

By Bus   Express buses (☎ 506/222-1650 or 506/666-0458) leave **San José** roughly every hour between 6am and 8pm from Calle 14 between avenidas 1 and 3. The ride is 4 hours. A one-way fare costs $3.50. Buses leave **Puntarenas** for Liberia periodically; it's best to check for a current schedule in town. The ride takes 2¹/₂ hours. A one-way fare costs $2.

For the Birds

The Río Tempisque Basin is one of the best places in the country to spot marsh and stream birds by the hundreds. This area is an important breeding ground for gallinules, jacanas, and limpkins, as well as a common habitat for numerous heron and kingfisher species. Several tour operators offer excursions and a wide range of tours in the region from Liberia. Try **TAM Tours** (☎ and fax **506/668-1028**), **Swiss Travel Services** (☎ and fax **506/668-1020**), or **Safaris Corobicí** (☎ and fax **506/669-1091;** www.nicoya.com; E-mail: safaris@racsa.co.cr). One of the more popular tours is a boat tour down the Bebedero River to **Palo Verde National Park,** which is south of Cañas and is best known for its migratory bird populations. Some of the best bird-watching requires no more than a little walking around the Biological Station in the park.

Buses depart for San José from the Liberia bus station on the edge of town, 200 meters (218 yd.) north and 100 meters (109 yd.) east of the main intersection on the Interamerican Highway. Express buses for San José leave roughly every hour between 5am and 8pm. To reach **Monteverde,** take any Puntarenas or San José bus leaving before 1pm. Get off at the Río Lagarto Bridge, walk to the dirt road that leads to Santa Elena, and flag down the Puntarenas/Santa Elena bus, which passes here at approximately 3:15pm. For information on getting to various beaches, see the sections below. The ride takes around 2$^1/_2$ to 3 hours.

By Car   Take the Interamerican Highway west from San José and follow the signs for Nicaragua and the Guanacaste beaches. It takes approximately 4 hours to get to Liberia.

EXPLORING RINCÓN DE LA VIEJA NATIONAL PARK

This national park begins on the flanks of the Rincón de la Vieja Volcano and includes this volcano's active crater. Down lower, you'll find an area of geothermal activity similar to Yellowstone National Park in the United States. Fumaroles, geysers, and hot pools cover this small area, creating a bizarre, otherworldly landscape. In addition to hot springs and mud pots, you can explore waterfalls, a lake, and volcanic craters. The bird-watching here is excellent, and the views across the pasturelands to the Pacific Ocean are stunning.

The main entrance is 15$^1/_2$ miles (25km) northeast of Liberia, down a badly rutted dirt road. The park entrance fee is $6 per person per day. Camping will cost you an extra $2 per person per day. There are actually two entrances and camping areas here, the **Santa María** and **Las Espuelas** ranger stations. The latter is by far the more popular and accessible, and it's closer to the action. Here you'll find two small camping areas near each other. I recommend the one closer to the river, although the bathroom and shower facilities are 91 meters (100 yd.) away, at the other site. For those seeking a less rugged tour of the park, there are several lodges located around the perimeter of the park; all offer guided hikes and horseback rides into the park.

GETTING THERE   To reach the Las Espuelas entrance, drive about 3 miles (5km) north of Liberia and turn right on the dirt road to the park. The turnoff is well marked. In about 7$^1/_2$ miles (12km) you'll pass through the small village of Curubandé. Continue on this road for another 3$^1/_2$ miles (6km), until you reach the Hacienda Lodge Guachipelin. The lodge is private property and the owners have been charging vehicles a $2 toll to pass through their gate and continue on to the park. I'm not sure if this is legal or mandatory, but it's not worth the hassle to protest. Pay the toll, pass through the lodge's gate, and continue for another 2^1/$_2$ miles (4km) until you reach the park entrance.

There are two routes to the **Santa Maria entrance.** The principal route heads out of the northeastern end of Liberia toward the small village of San Jorge. This route is about 15^1/$_2$ miles (25km) long and takes roughly 45 minutes. A four-wheel-drive vehicle is required. Alternately, you can reach the Santa Maria entrance from a turnoff in the Interamerican Highway at Bagaces. From here, head north through Guayabo, Aguas Claras, and Colonia Blanca. The road is paved up to Colonia Blanca, but again, a four-wheel-drive vehicle is required for the final, very rough, 6 miles (10km) of gravel road.

HIKING IN THE PARK   There are several excellent trails inside the Rincón de la Vieja National Park. More energetic hikers can tackle the 5 miles (8km) up to **the summit** and explore the several craters and beautiful lakes up here. On a clear day, you'll be rewarded with a fabulous view of the plains of Guanacaste and the Pacific Ocean below. The easiest hiking is the gentle **Las Pailas loop.** This 2-mile (3km) trail is just off Las Espuelas park entrance and passes by several bubbling mud pots and steaming fumaroles. This trail crosses a river, so you'll either have to take off your shoes or get them wet. The whole loop takes around 2 hours.

My favorite hike here is to the **Blue Lake and La Cangrejo Waterfall.** This 3-mile (5km) trail passes through several different life zones, including dry forest, transitional moist forest, and open savannah. A variety of birds and mammals are commonly sighted. Pack a lunch; at the end of your 2-hour hike in, you can picnic at the aptly named Blue Lake, where a 100-foot waterfall empties into the small pond, whose crystal blue hues are amazing.

NEARBY RAFTING TRIPS   Leisurely raft trips (with little white water) are offered by **Safaris Corobicí** (☎ and fax **506/669-1091;** www.nicoya.com; E-mail: safaris@racsa.co.cr), about 25 miles (40km) south of Liberia. They have 2-hour ($37), 3-hour ($45), and half-day ($60) trips that are great for families and bird-watchers. Along the way you may see many of the area's more exotic animal residents: howler monkeys, iguanas, caimans, coatimundis, otters, toucans, parrots, motmots, trogons, and many other species of birds. Aside from your binoculars and camera, a bathing suit and sunscreen are the only things you'll need. Safaris Corobicí is based on the main highway, just before the Hotel Hacienda La Pacífica (see below). They also run trips on the Bebedero River.

ACCOMMODATIONS
IN TOWN

Best Western El Sitio. Apdo. 134-5000, Liberia, Guanacaste. ☎ **506/666-1211.** Fax 506/666-2059. www.bestwestern.co.cr. E-mail: htlsitio@racsa.co.cr. 52 units. A/C TV TEL. $65 double, $75 triple, $85 quad. Rates include continental breakfast. AE, MC, V.

Located about 73 meters (80 yd.) west of the main intersection on the road to Santa Cruz and the beaches, this hotel follows the same basic Spanish-influenced hacienda style as the Best Western Las Espuelas and offers similar amenities, although I prefer this one. El Sitio just feels more open and modern than its sister, and it's even slightly less expensive. Throughout the hotel, there are cool tile floors and original paintings of local Guanacaste scenes. There's even one of the famous pre-Columbian stone spheres in the garden (see "Those Mysterious Stone Spheres," page 291). Beside the large shady pool (a welcome relief from the strong Guanacaste sun), there's a rancho-style bar/restaurant. Other amenities and services include horseback riding, a children's play area, a whirlpool tub, a small gym, casino, tour arrangements, and a car-rental desk.

Best Western Las Espuelas. Apdo. 88-5000, Liberia, Guanacaste. ☎ **506/666-0144.** Fax 506/666-2441. www.bestwestern.co.cr. E-mail: espuelas@racsa.co.cr. 44 units. A/C TV TEL. $70 double, $85 triple. AE, DC, MC, V.

This hotel is located on the Interamerican Highway, 1¼ miles (2km) south of Liberia. The name means "spurs" and is a reference to this being cowboy country, but despite the rugged epithet, this is still one of the most luxurious hotels in Liberia. The open-air lobby and adjacent dining room and bar all have the feel of a modern hacienda. Spacious gardens shaded by huge old guanacaste trees surround the hotel. The guest rooms are attractive, though a bit small, and have polished tile floors. The restaurant serves moderately priced international and Costa Rican meals. Las Espuelas has a tour desk, conference facilities, a small swimming pool, and a new Jacuzzi.

Hotel Guanacaste. Apdo. 251-5000 (25m/27 yd. west of the bus station), Liberia, Guanacaste. ☎ **506/666-0085.** Fax 506/666-2287. E-mail: htlguana@racsa.co.cr. 30 units. $15 double, $25 triple, $35 quad. Discounts for students and those holding a valid hostel ID. MC, V.

This economical little hotel is primarily a hostel catering to young travelers on a tight budget. In addition to the simply furnished rooms, there's a basic *soda* serving cheap Tico meals. The management here can help arrange trips to nearby national parks and tell you about other interesting budget accommodations, including campgrounds, in the area. In fact, you can even camp here for $5 per person. The two newest rooms are doubles with air-conditioning and they cost slightly more. You'll find this basic hotel around the corner from Hotel Bramadero.

Nuevo Hotel Boyeros. Apdo. 85-5000, Liberia, Guanacaste. ☎ **506/666-0722** or 506/666-0809. Fax 506/666-2529. www.hotelboyeros.com. E-mail: hboyeros@racsa.co.cr. 70 units. A/C TEL. $38–$45 double. AE, MC, V.

This economical hotel isn't as attractively landscaped as other hotels in town, but it's good in a pinch (especially at these prices). Arches with turned wooden railings and a red-tile roof give this two-story, motel-style building a Spanish feel. In the courtyard of the hotel are two pools—one for adults and one for children—and a rancho bar/snack bar. All the rooms have a private balcony or patio overlooking the pool. The best and coolest rooms are on the second floor of the east wing. The small restaurant is open 24 hours and serves meals ranging from $4 to $10.

✪ **Posada del Tope.** Calle Real, (Apdo. 26-5000) Liberia, Guanacaste. ☎ and fax **506/666-3876.** E-mail: hottope@racsa.co.cr. 18 units, 4 with bathroom. $10–$15 double, $15–$22 triple. Rates include breakfast. AE, MC, V.

This humble little pension is nothing fancy, but the rooms and shared bathrooms are clean, the owners are friendly and helpful, and it's a real bargain. Only a couple of rooms have double beds; the rest have either one, two, or three single beds. The nicest thing about Posada del Tope is that it's housed in a wonderfully restored traditional colonial home, with high ceilings, big shuttered windows facing the street, and hefty wooden trim all around. The hotel has a simple restaurant serving inexpensive Tico cuisine. There's safe parking out back and the hotel even offers Internet access. You'll find this place 1½ blocks south of the central park.

NEAR CAÑAS

✪ **Hotel Hacienda La Pacífica.** Apdo. 8-5700, Cañas, Guanacaste. ☎ **506/669-0050.** Fax 506/669-0555. E-mail: pacifica@racsa.co.cr. 33 units. $70 double, $80 triple, $90 quad. AE, DC, MC, V. The hotel is located right on the Interamerican Hwy. a couple of miles north of Cañas, which is 25 miles (40km) south of Liberia.

If you want a central location for exploring the national parks or a good stopover to break up the long drive to the Guanacaste beaches, there are few better choices than the Hacienda La Pacífica. Originally started as a research facility and wild-animal rehabilitation center, La Pacífica is now a spacious mini-resort hotel with attractive grounds, organized tours and activities, marked trails, and an inviting pool. The hotel is located near the banks of the gentle Corobicí River, which is a good place for bird-watching or trail walking.

Rooms vary in size, though all have tile floors and a patio of some sort. The larger ones have private sun patios as well as small courtyardlike walled-in patios accessed through sliding glass doors that make the rooms quite bright. High ceilings keep them cool. The open-air restaurant is shady and cool and serves moderately priced meals. The lodge offers a number of services, including horseback riding ($10 per hr.), bike rentals ($3 per hr.), guided walks ($15), rafting trips ($35 for 2 hr.), and tours to the different national parks.

NEAR RINCÓN DE LA VIEJA NATIONAL PARK

Hacienda Lodge Guachipelin. Apdo. 636-4050, Alajuela. ☎ **506/256-6995** or 506/284-2049. Fax 506/256-6995. www.guachipelin.com. E-mail: tbatalla@racsa.co.cr. 20 units. $48 double. MC, V. Follow the directions/signs to Curubandé and Rincón de la Vieja National Park. A 4-wheel-drive vehicle is required in the rainy season (May to mid-Nov) and strongly recommended at other times.

Located $14^1/_4$ miles (23km) northeast of Liberia on the edge of Rincón de la Vieja National Park, this rustic lodge is housed in a 19th-century ranch house. Although they received some sprucing up recently, the rooms are still pretty basic. The ranch is still in operation today; you can ride horses on the property, or just commune with the pigs, dairy cows, and beef cattle. It isn't easy to get to the lodge, so plan on taking all your meals here and going on a few guided tours. A horseback tour with a bilingual guide will cost around $35 per person for a half-day ride.

This is one of the closest lodges to the thermal springs (6.2 miles/10km) and bubbling mud pots (3 miles/5km) of Rincón de la Vieja National Park. Horseback rides can be arranged to the geothermal areas, as well as to various lakes, the top of a nearby dormant volcano, and some beautiful waterfalls. These folks work together with the Original Canopy Tour and their neighboring Kazam Canyon attraction ($45 per person), in which you strap on a climbing harness and ride back and forth over a deep canyon while hanging from a cable.

Rincón de la Vieja Mountain Lodge. Apdo. 114-5000, Liberia, Guanacaste. ☎ **506/ 256-8206** or 506/695-5553. Fax 506/256-7290. www.guanacaste.co.cr. E-mail: rincon@ racsa.co.cr. 50 units. $67 double; student and off-season rates available. AE, MC, V.

This is the closest lodge to the Las Pailas mud pots and the Azufrale hot springs. Located in a remote spot at the end of a rough road, it's surrounded by grasslands that conjure up images of the African savannah. Rooms vary in size, but most have hammocks on their verandas, and several back up to a small stream. Camping is permitted, but it's best to reserve space in advance. Meals, which are simple but hearty Tico fare, will cost you around $30 per day. The lodge offers numerous daylong tours either on foot or on horseback. They also run an extensive canopy tour, which takes you on a high-wire ride over a dozen different treetop platforms, beginning with a manual ascent up a towering ceiba tree. The hotel has an interesting insect collection as well as a small serpentarium.

If you're driving, follow the directions to the Hacienda Lodge Guachipelin and continue driving on this dirt road for another $4^1/_4$ miles (7km), bearing right at the turnoff for the park entrance. Transportation from Liberia can be arranged for around $25.

DINING

There are plenty of standard Tico dining choices in Liberia. In town, the most popular alternatives are **Pizzeria Pronto,** which is located 100 meters (109 yd.) north of the visitor information center (☎ **506/666-2098**), and **Pizzeria da Beppe,** located near the highway on the road that leads into central Liberia (☎ **506/666-0917**). Both serve a wide range of pizzas and assorted pasta dishes. Another alternative is to choose one of the *sodas* around the central park. The best of these is **Restaurante Paseo Real** (☎ **506/666-3455**). Other choices include:

Restaurante Pókopí. 100m (109 yd.) west of the main intersection in Liberia on the road to Santa Cruz. ☎ **506/666-1036.** Fax 506/666-1528. Main courses $5–$15. AE, MC, V. Sun–Wed 11am–10pm, Thurs–Sat 11am–midnight. CONTINENTAL.

It doesn't look like much from the outside, but this tiny restaurant has a surprising amount of class. An even more pleasant surprise is the unusual (for rural Costa Rica) variety of continental dishes on the menu. Order a delicious daiquiri while you peruse the menu, which is on a wooden cutting board. You have your choice of mahimahi prepared five different ways, pizza, chicken cordon bleu, chicken in wine sauce, and other equally delectable dishes. However, for a real surprise, order the chateaubriand. It comes to your table with great flair, surrounded by succulent fresh vegetables and a tomato stuffed with peas. Be sure to dine early if you want a quiet meal; attached to the restaurant is a disco that swings into action most nights at 9pm. If you want to milk the local nightlife, you can combine dinner and disco. And you thought you were out in the sticks.

Restaurant Rincón Corobicí. Interamerican Hwy., 3 miles (5km) north of Cañas. ☎ **506/669-1234.** Reservations accepted. Main courses $4–$25. AE, DC, MC, V. Daily 8am–9pm. COSTA RICAN/INTERNATIONAL.

The food here is decidedly mediocre, but the setting, particularly during the day, sort of makes up for it. While there's plenty of covered seating in the main open-air dining room, you'll want to choose a table on the wooden deck, which overlooks a beautiful section of the Corobicí River. The sound of rushing water tumbling over the rocks in the riverbed is a soothing accompaniment to the simple but filling meals. The whole fried fish is your best choice here, though you can also have steaks, lobster, shrimp, and sandwiches. This restaurant makes an ideal lunch stop if you're heading to or coming from Liberia, or have just done a rafting trip on the Corobicí River. Be sure to try the fried yucca chips—you may never go back to french fries.

2 La Cruz

172 miles (277km) NW of San José; 37 miles (59km) NW of Liberia; 12 miles (20km) S of Peñas Blancas

La Cruz is a tiny hilltop town near the Nicaraguan border. The town itself has little to offer beyond a fabulous view of Bahía Salinas, but it does serve as a gateway to the nearly deserted beaches down below, a few mountain lodges bordering the nearby Santa Rosa and Guanacaste national parks, and the Nicaraguan border crossing at Peñas Blancas.

ESSENTIALS

GETTING THERE & DEPARTING   **By Plane**   The nearest airport with regularly scheduled service is in Liberia.

By Bus   Buses (☎ 506/222-3006) leave San José daily for **Peñas Blancas** at 4:30, 5, 7, 7:45, and 10am and 1:30 and 4pm from Calle 14 between avenidas 3 and 5. These buses stop in La Cruz and will also let you off at the entrance to Santa Rosa National Park. The ride to La Cruz takes 6 hours. A one-way fare costs $5.

Buses leave Liberia for Peñas Blancas at 5:30, 8:30, and 11am and 2 and 4:30pm. The ride takes about 1 hour to La Cruz and costs $1.75.

Buses depart for San José from Peñas Blancas daily at 5, 7:15, 10:30am, noon, 1:30, 2:45, and 3:30pm, passing through La Cruz about 20 minutes later. Buses leave Liberia for San José roughly every hour between 5am and 8pm.

By Car   Take the Interamerican Highway west from San José and follow the signs for Nicaragua and the Guanacaste beaches. When you reach Liberia, head straight through the major intersection, following signs to Peñas Blancas and the Nicaraguan border. It takes approximately 5 hours to get from San José to La Cruz.

ORIENTATION   The highway passes slightly to the east of town. You'll pass the turnoffs to Santa Rosa National Park, Playa Caujiniquil, and Los Inocentes Lodge before reaching the town. To reach the beaches of Bahía Salinas, head into La Cruz to El Mirador Ehecatl and then follow the signs down to the water.

EXPLORING SANTA ROSA NATIONAL PARK

Best known for its remote, pristine beaches (reached by several kilometers of hiking trails or a four-wheel-drive vehicle), Santa Rosa National Park is a fine place to ramble, surf, or just watch sea turtles nest. Located 18¹/₂ miles (30km) north of Liberia and 13 miles (21km) south of La Cruz on the Interamerican Highway, Costa Rica's first national park blankets the Santa Elena Peninsula. Unlike other national parks, it was founded not to preserve the land but to save a building, known as **La Casona,** which played an important role in Costa Rican independence. It was here, in 1856, that Costa Rican forces fought the decisive Battle of Santa Rosa, forcing the U.S.-backed soldier of fortune William Walker and his men to flee into Nicaragua. Inside the restored ranch house you'll find relics from and representations of that historic battle. This small museum and monument is open daily from 8am until 4pm.

It costs $6 per person to enter the park. Camping is allowed at several sites within the park. At times, especially during high season, you must reserve in advance (☎ 506/666-5051). A campsite costs $2 per person per day. There's camping near the entrance and principal ranger station, as well as at La Casona, and down by Playas Naranjo and Nancite.

○ **THE BEACHES**   Five miles (8km) west of La Casona down a rugged road that is impassable during the rainy season is **Playa Naranjo.** Even during the dry season, this road is rough on four-wheel-drive vehicles. Two and a half miles (4km) north of Playa Naranjo along a hiking trail that follows the beach you'll find **Playa Nancite. Playa Blanca** is 13 miles (21km) down a dirt road from Caujiniquil, which itself is 12¹/₂ miles (20km) north of the park entrance.

Playa Nancite is known for its *arribadas* ("arrival"; grouped egg-layings) of olive Ridley sea turtles, which come ashore to nest by the tens of thousands each year in October. Playa Naranjo is legendary for its perfect surfing waves. In fact, this spot is quite popular with day-trippers who come in by boat from the Playa del Coco area to ride the waves that break around Witches Rock, which lies just offshore.

On the northern side of the peninsula is **Playa Blanca,** a beautiful, remote white-sand beach with calm waters. This beach is reached by way of the small village of Caujiniquil and is accessible only during the dry season. However, if you reach Caujiniquil and then head north for a few kilometers, you will come to a small annex to the national park system at Playa Junquillal (not to be confused with the more-developed beach of the same name farther south in Guanacaste). This is a lovely little beach that is also often good for swimming. You'll have to pay the park entrance fee ($6) to use the beach, and $2 more to camp here. There are basic bathroom and shower facilities.

WHAT TO DO IN LA CRUZ

There's not really much to do in La Cruz except catch a sunset and some ceviche at the **El Mirador Ehecatl** (☎ **506/679-9104**). This humble little restaurant holds a commanding view of Bahía Salinas and serves up hearty Tico standards at only slightly inflated prices. Similarly, there's not really much reason to stay in La Cruz, but if you must, check out **Amalia's Inn** (☎ and fax **506/679-9181**), which is a simple little hotel with a small pool and good views of the bay.

ACCOMMODATIONS NEAR LA CRUZ

✪ **Los Inocentes Lodge.** Apdo. 228-3000, Heredia. ☎ and fax **506/265-5484,** or 506/679-9190. Fax 506/265-4385. www.arweb.com/orosi. E-mail: orosina@racsa.co.cr. 11 units, 12 cabins. $74 per person, including 3 meals daily, a daily tour, and taxes. AE, V.

Set on a ranch 8½ miles (14km) from La Cruz, near the Nicaraguan border and bordering Guanacaste National Park, Los Inocentes is popular with naturalists interested in exploring the nearby dry and transitional forests. Horseback riding through the ranch ($18 for 3 hr. with guide) is the most popular activity; the ranch does a brisk business in day trips by visitors from various Guanacaste beaches.

The rooms are located in the main lodge building, which dates back to 1890. Some have high ceilings, and most open onto large verandas with hammocks and wicker rocking chairs. Each room has access to a private bathroom, but most are not attached to the room and some folks on the second floor even have to go downstairs to their bathroom on the first floor. The cabins, which are located about 91 meters (100 yd.) away from the main lodge, are two-bedroom affairs better suited for families and small groups. Meals are simple but filling. There are nature trails, a swimming pool, and a new Jacuzzi. There's a great view of Orosi Volcano from the lodge, and the bird-watching here is excellent.

Three Corners Bolaños Bay. Apdo. 1686-1250, Escazú. ☎ **506/289-5561.** Fax 506/228-4205. www.threecorners.com. E-mail: 3cornco@racsa.co.cr. 72 units. $50 per person all inclusive (rates include food, drinks, lodging, activities, and taxes). AE, MC, V. From La Cruz, take the dirt road that passes to the right of the popular El Mirador Ehecatl restaurant (as you face the water) and then follow the signs to the hotel. You can arrange pickup in La Cruz, or you can take a cab from the bus station, which should cost around $10.

This new hotel occupies a beautiful spot in front of Isla Bolaños on Bahía Salinas. But as a destination, it appeals primarily to windsurfers, due to the fact that strong, steady winds buffet the bay throughout the Guanacaste dry season and periodically during the rainy season. When these winds are really howling, it makes most other activities here impossible or uncomfortable—even reading quietly by the pool can be quite a challenge. The rooms are acceptable, but uninspired. Eighteen of them have ocean views; all have small patios. The bathrooms have bidets.

The restaurant is located under one of the hotel's two immense peaked thatch roofs, and the reception, gift shop, and tour desk are under the other. Food and service here are inconsistent at best. In addition to full-service windsurfing and scuba-diving centers, the hotel can arrange a wide range of tours and activities, including trips to Nicaragua.

3 Playa Hermosa & Playa Panamá

160 miles (258km) NW of San José; 25 miles (40km) SW of Liberia

Playa Hermosa means "beautiful beach," which is an appropriate name for this crescent of sand. Surrounded by dry, rocky hills, this curving gray-sand beach is long and wide and rarely crowded, despite the presence of the Costa del Cacique condo development and the Sol Playa Hermosa Hotel on the hill at the north end of the beach. Fringing the beach is a swath of trees that stays surprisingly green right through the dry season. The shade provided by these trees is a big part of the beach's appeal. Rocky headlands jut out into the surf at both ends of the beach, and at the base of these rocks you'll find fun tide pools to explore.

Beyond Playa Hermosa, you'll find **Playa Panamá** and the calm waters of **Bahía Culebra.** Once one of the most remote and underdeveloped spots in Guanacaste, this area now hosts not one, but two large resort hotels. In addition, the lack of facilities and misuse by campers and day visitors has turned this once pristine beach into one of the worst garbage dumps on the coast.

ESSENTIALS

GETTING THERE & DEPARTING   By Plane   The nearest airport with regularly scheduled service is in Liberia. From here you can arrange a taxi to bring you the rest of the way. The ride takes about 45 minutes and should cost around $20.

By Bus   Express buses (☎ **506/666-0042**) leave San José daily at 3:10pm from Calle 12 between avenidas 5 and 7, stopping first at Playa Hermosa and next at Playa Panamá, 2 miles (3km) farther north. One-way fare for the 5-hour trip is $4.

Alternately, you can take a bus from San José to Liberia (see "Liberia," above, for details) and then take a bus from Liberia to Playa Hermosa and Playa Panamá. Buses (☎ **506/666-1249**) leave Liberia for these two beaches daily at 5, 7, and 11:30am and 1, 3:30, 5:30, and 7pm. The trip lasts 45 minutes. The one-way fare costs $1.25. During the high season, extra buses from Liberia are sometimes added. Alternately, you can take a bus to Playa del Coco, from which these beaches are a quick taxi ride away. Taxi fare should run between $5 and $6.

One direct bus departs for San José daily at 5am from Playa Panamá, with a stop in Playa Hermosa along the way. Buses to Liberia leave Playa Panamá at 6 and 10am, and 2, 4 and 5pm, stopping in Playa Hermosa a few minutes later. Ask at your hotel where to catch the bus.

By Car   Follow the directions for getting to Liberia, then head west toward Santa Cruz. Just past the village of Comunidad, turn right. In about 7 miles (11km) you'll come to a fork in the road. Take the right fork. These roads are relatively well marked, and a host of prominent hotel billboards should make it easy enough to find the beach. It takes about 5 hours from San José.

ORIENTATION   There are no real towns here, just a few houses and hotels on and near the beach. You'll come to Playa Hermosa first, followed by Playa Panamá a few kilometers farther along the same road. The road ends at the Blue Bay Village Beach Resort.

Playa Hermosa is about a 457-meter-long (500 yd.) stretch of beach, with all the hotels laid out along this stretch. From the main road, which continues on to Playa Panamá, there are about three access roads heading off toward the beach. All the hotels are well marked, with signs pointing guests down the right access road.

VISITOR INFORMATION & EQUIPMENT RENTAL   In the middle of Playa Hermosa, you'll find **Aqua Sport** (☎ **506/672-0050**), which is both the visitor information center and water-sports equipment rental center for Playa Hermosa. Kayaks, sailboards, canoes, bicycles, beach umbrellas, snorkel gear, and parasails are all available for rental at fairly reasonable rates. This is also where you'll find the local post office, public phones, a small supermarket, and a restaurant (see "Dining & After Dark," below).

OUTDOOR PURSUITS

Both beaches are usually good for swimming, although Playa Panamá is slightly more protected. If you want to do some diving while you're here, check in with **Diving Safaris de Costa Rica** (☎ **800/779-0055** in the U.S., or 506/672-0012; fax 506/672-0231; www.costaricadiving.net; E-mail: diving@racsa.co.cr) at the Sol Playa Hermosa Hotel at the north end of the beach. Formerly Bill Beard's Diving Safaris, this is a long-established and respected dive operation. It's got a large shop and offers a wide range of trips to numerous dive spots and also offers night dives, multiday packages, certification classes, and Nitrox dives. Alternately, you can check out the Costa Smeralda Hotel or Blue Bay Village Beach Resort, which also have dive operations. A two-tank dive should run between $70 and $120 per person.

Since Playa Hermosa is generally flat, **surfers** should look into boat trips to nearby Witch's Rock and Ollie's Point. **Hotel Finisterra** (☎ **506/672-0227**) and **Aqua Sport** (☎ **506/672-0050**) both offer trips for up to six surfers for between $200 and $250, including lunch. Both of these places offer fishing trips for between $200 and $400.

You can charter the 44-foot *Jessica Anne* (☎ **506/672-0012**), for full-day ($50 per person) or sunset ($45 per person) cruises.

Both **Tam** (☎ **506/256-0203**) and **Swiss Travel Services** (☎ and fax **506/668-1020**) run a wide range of trips to Santa Rosa or Rincón de la Vieja national parks. They'll pick you up at any hotel in either Playa Hermosa or Playa Panamá.

ACCOMMODATIONS
VERY EXPENSIVE

Blue Bay Village Resort. Playa Arenilla, Guanacaste. ☎ **800/BLUE-BAY** in the U.S., or 506/672-0130. Fax 506/672-0139. www.bluebayresorts.com. E-mail: costarica@bluebayresorts.com. 160 units. A/C TV TEL. $190 double; children under 12 are $50 per day. Rates are all-inclusive (including food, drinks, activities, and taxes). Rates slightly higher during peak weeks, lower in the off-season. AE, DC, MC, V.

This was the first all-inclusive resort in the Guanacaste region. It has changed its name and management at least twice, but seems to have settled down now as a Blue Bay resort. Most of the independent villas can be separated into two rooms or shared by a family or two couples. Inside, one room is equipped with a king-size bed, the other with two queen-size beds. All rooms have marble floors, pine ceilings, large bathrooms, and small private patios or balconies. The resort is quite spread out, so if you don't want to do a lot of walking or wait for the minivan shuttles, ask for a room near the main pool and restaurants. If you want a good view, ask for one on the hill overlooking the bay. For those seeking more isolation, there are rooms located in the dry forest behind the resort. The hotel has a host of organized sports and activities, including daily programs for children. All nonmotorized sports equipment, activities, and classes are included. The hotel has its own small crescent-shaped swath of beach, which is very calm and protected for swimming.

Dining/Diversions: The hotel's most formal restaurant is **Da Vinci,** serving northern Italian cuisine in an elegant indoor setting. Reservations and proper attire are required. Breakfasts and more casual meals can be taken at the open-air **El Papagayo**

restaurant, overlooking the pool. There's also a poolside bar and a snack bar down at the spa. **Extasis** is the hotel's new dinner theater and disco complex, which offers up nightly entertainment reviews and late-night dancing.

Amenities: Three-tiered main pool, a small lap pool, and a resistance lap pool; well-equipped fitness center, with Nautilus machines, free weights, Jacuzzis, a steam room, sauna, health bar, and daily classes. There's also a tennis court, volleyball courts, water-sports equipment, nature trails, children's programs, conference center, tour desk, beauty salon, boutique, laundry service, and valet parking.

EXPENSIVE

Sol Playa Hermosa Hotel and Villas. Playa Hermosa, Guanacaste. ☎ **800/572-9934** or 506/257-0607. Fax 506/223-3036. www.solmelia.es. E-mail: hermosol@racsa.co.cr. 54 units, 74 villas. A/C TV TEL. Dec 1–Apr 15 $125 double, $236–$278 villa; Apr 16–Nov 30 $94 double, $177–$206 villa. AE, DC, MC, V.

This is the oldest and most established resort in the area. Set on a steep hillside at the north end of the beach, the Sol Playa Hermosa was built with Mediterranean styling. The hotel is at the top of the hill, about 274 meters (300 yd.) from the beach—you'll need to be in good shape to stay here. Luckily, the two pools are both at the top of the hill. The villas are new units located just off the entrance. All have kitchens, satellite TVs, and modern furnishings. Almost half of them have their own small swimming pool or Jacuzzi, although only a few of the newest villas, built high on the hill, have really worthwhile views. The hotel rooms are all well maintained and quite standard for this price range; most have excellent views.

Just so you don't get too confused, this whole complex was formerly the Condovac Hotel and Villas. However, the Sol chain has divorced itself from the older villas, which are spread along the hillside below the main hotel, and now only operates the new villas near the entrance.

Dining/Diversions: The hotel has numerous dining options. **El Roble** is the hotel's most formal dining room and specializes in steaks and northern Italian cuisine. **Las Gaviotas** is a casual buffet that is open throughout the day. **Heliconias** is a snack bar by the pool at the villas. Bars include **Frutas y Flores,** the lobby bar, and **Las Lapas,** the hotel's beach bar.

Amenities: There are two freshwater swimming pools, a tennis court, a dive shop, a tour desk, a minimarket, and a gift shop. Services include diving-equipment rentals, scuba classes, dive trips, and jet-ski rentals.

MODERATE

El Velero Hotel. Playa Hermosa, Guanacaste. ☎ **506/672-0036.** Fax 506/672-0016. www.costaricahotel.net. E-mail: elvelerocr@yahoo.com. 22 units. A/C. $72 double; lower in the off-season. AE, MC, V.

This small hotel is the best choice right on the beach in Playa Hermosa. White walls and polished tile floors give El Velero a Mediterranean flavor. The guest rooms are large, and those on the second floor have high ceilings. The furnishings are simple, though, and some of the bathrooms are a bit small. All the rooms have air-conditioning, but the fans alone are usually enough to keep things cool. The hotel has its own popular little restaurant, which offers a good selection of meat, fish, and shrimp dishes in the $6-to-$15 range. There's even a small pool down by the restaurant. Various tours, horseback riding, and fishing trips can be arranged through the hotel; however, the most popular excursions are the full-day and sunset cruises on the hotel's 38-foot sailboat.

Hotel Finisterra. Playa Hermosa, Guanacaste. ☎ and fax **506/670-0293,** or 506/ 672-0227. www.finisterra.net. E-mail: finisterra@hotmail.com. 10 units. $65 double, $75 triple; lower in the off-season. Rates include full breakfast. MC, V.

This new hillside hotel offers clean, spacious accommodations on the southern end of Playa Hermosa. The rooms are all located on the second floor and come with either one queen or two double beds. Large picture windows face out onto either a forested hillside or the Pacific Ocean. A large open-air restaurant and lounge takes up most of the first floor, and there's a refreshing little pool with great views. The restaurant here serves a nightly mix of fresh seafood, steaks, and chicken prepared with fusion flare. The owners have a van for beach transfers (the beach is about 274m/300 yd. away, down the steep driveway), as well as a couple of boats for fishing and tours.

✪ **Villa del Sueño.** Playa Hermosa, Guanacaste (Interlink 2059, P.O. Box 025635, Miami, FL 33102). ☎ and fax **506/672-0026.** www.villadelsueno.com. E-mail: delsueno@racsa. co.cr. 15 units. $55–$80 double; lower in the off-season. AE, MC, V.

Although this hotel is not right on the beach (it's located about 91m/100 yd. from the sand), its well-groomed lawns and gardens feel like an oasis in the dust and heat of a Guanacaste dry season. Villa del Sueño offers clean and comfortable rooms at a good price, and the restaurant here is one of the best in Playa Hermosa. All the rooms have cool tile floors, high hardwood ceilings, ceiling fans, and well-placed windows for cross ventilation. The second-floor superior rooms have more space, larger windows, and air-conditioning. There's a small pool and open-air bar in the center courtyard. Meals are served in the main building's open-air restaurant, which even has a stage and features live music during much of the high season. The folks here manage a neighboring condominium development, which has additional apartment and efficiency units available for nightly and weekly rental. They can also help with a variety of tour arrangements, and have a small gift shop.

INEXPENSIVE

Cabinas Playa Hermosa. Playa Hermosa, Guanacaste. ☎ and fax **506/672-0046,** or 506/672-0019. 22 units. $40 double, $50 triple, $60 quad; lower in the off-season. No credit cards.

This little hotel, tucked away under shady trees, is a sprawling beachfront spread at the south end of Playa Hermosa. Each large room has a pair of Adirondack chairs on its front porch, and the beach is only a few steps away. Rooms 1 through 4 directly face the ocean, but they're also very close to the restaurant and bar and can be noisy. The rest are located in several low buildings that run perpendicular to the beach. Even though most of the rooms are rather dark and can feel run-down, they're large, with two double beds and lots of closet space. The open-air restaurant has a rustic tropical feel to it, with unfinished tree trunks holding up the roof. Seafood and homemade pasta are the specialties. Menu prices range from $5 to $10; service can be quite slow and inattentive. To find the hotel, turn left at the first road into Playa Hermosa. The hotel's white archway gate is about half a mile (1km) down this dirt road.

DINING & AFTER-DARK FUN

In addition to the place listed below, you'll find the best restaurants in Playa Hermosa at the hotel **Villa del Sueño** (☎ 506/672-0026) and **Hotel Finisterra** (☎ 506/ 670-0293). Neither restaurant has a fixed menu, but the nightly selections of blackboard specials will please most palates.

For nightlife, check out **Monkey Bar** (☎ 506/672-0267), which is inland, off the main road to Playa Panamá, and has a pool table, satellite TV, and serves U.S.-style bar food, or **Puerta del Sol** (no phone), a casual place on the beach, near the Sol Playa Hermosa. Also, find out if there's any live music at **Villa del Sueño.**

Aqua Sport. On the beach in Playa Hermosa. ☎ **506/672-0050.** Reservations not necessary. Main courses $4–$17. AE, MC, V. Daily 9am–10pm (noon–9pm in the rainy season). CONTINENTAL.

Part of the Aqua Sport market and equipment-rental shop is a small open-air restaurant with tables of polished hardwood. The beach is only steps away, the atmosphere is very casual, and the food is much better than you'd expect from such a place. The focus is on seafood—grilled lobster for $16, shrimp à la diabla for $7, and huge paella or assorted seafood platters that feed four and cost $45 and $50, respectively.

4 Playa del Coco & Playa Ocotal

157 miles (253km) NW of San José; 21^1/$_2$ miles (35km) W of Liberia

Playa del Coco is one of the most easily accessible beaches in Guanacaste, with a paved road right down to the water, and has been a longtime popular destination with middle-class Ticos and weekend revelers from San José. It's also a prime scuba diving spot. The beach, which has grayish-brown sand, is quite wide at low tide and almost nonexistent at high tide. In between high and low, it's just right. The crowds that come here like their music loud and constant, so if you're in search of a quiet retreat, stay away from the center of town. Still, if you're looking for a beach with a wide range of inexpensive hotels, lively nightlife, and plenty of cheap food and beer close at hand, you'll enjoy Playa del Coco.

Better still, if you have a car, head over to **Playa Ocotal,** which is a couple of kilometers to the south, down a dirt road. This tiny pocket cove features a small salt-and-pepper beach bordered by high bluffs, and is quite beautiful. When it's calm, there's good snorkeling around some rocky islands close to shore here.

ESSENTIALS
GETTING THERE & DEPARTING　By Plane　The nearest airport with regularly scheduled flights is in Liberia. From there you can take a bus or arrange for a taxi to take you to Playa del Coco or Playa Ocotal, which is about a 45-minute drive.

By Bus　Express buses (☎ **506/222-1650**) leave San José for Playa del Coco at 8am and 2pm daily from Calle 14 between avenidas 1 and 3. Allow 5 hours for the trip. A one-way ticket is $5. From Liberia, buses to Playa del Coco leave at 5:30am and 12:30, 2, and 4:30pm. A one-way ticket for the 45-minute trip costs $1.50.

The direct bus for San José leaves Playa del Coco daily at 8am and 2pm. Buses for Liberia leave at 7 and 9:15am and 2 and 6pm.

Depending on demand, the Playa del Coco buses sometimes go as far as Playa Ocotal; it's worth checking beforehand if possible. Otherwise, a taxi should cost around $5.

By Car　From Liberia, head west toward Santa Cruz. Just past the village of Comunidad, turn right. In about 7 miles (11km) you'll come to a fork in the road. Take the left fork. It takes about 5 hours from San José. .

ORIENTATION　Playa del Coco is a small but busy beach town. Most of its hotels and restaurants are either on the water, on the road leading into town, or on the road that heads north from San Francisco Treats. Playa Ocotal, which is south of Playa del Coco on a dirt road that leaves the main road about 183 meters (200 yd.) before the beach, is a small collection of vacation homes, condos, and a couple of hotels. It has one bar and one restaurant on the beach.

FUN ON & OFF THE BEACH

There are plenty of boats anchored here at Playa del Coco, and that means plenty of opportunities to go fishing, diving, or sailing. However, the most popular activities, especially among the hordes of Ticos who come here, are hanging out on the beach, hanging out in the *sodas* and bars, and cruising the discos at night. If you're interested, you might be able to join a soccer match (the soccer field is in the middle of town). It's also possible to arrange horseback rides; ask at your hotel.

SCUBA DIVING Scuba diving is the most popular water sport in the area, and dive shops abound. **Mario Vargas Expeditions** (☎ and fax **506/670-0351;** www. diveexpeditions.com; E-mail: mvexped@racsa.co.cr) and **Rich Coast Diving** (☎ **506/670-0176;** www.richcoastdiving.com; E-mail: diva@richcoastdiving.com) are the most established and offer equipment rentals and dive trips. A two-tank dive, with equipment, should cost between $55 and $90 per person. Both also offer PADI certification courses. Mario Vargas offers Nitrox diving. Rich Coast offers multiday trips aboard a 35-foot trimaran. A 3-day/2-night excursion, with food, equipment, and diving, costs $350 to $500 per person, depending on the size of your group and the dive destinations. This trimaran is also available for the surf or fishing excursions described below.

SPORTFISHING & SAILBOAT CHARTERS Full- and half-day sportfishing excursions can be arranged through **Papagayo Sportfishing** (☎ and fax **506/670-0354**) or **Agua Rica Yacht Charters** (☎ **506/670-0805;** www.aguaricacharters. com; E-mail: jimgray@racsa.co.cr). A half day of fishing, with boat, captain, food, and tackle, should cost between $200 and $400; a full day should run between $450 and $800. Papagayo also arranges trips to ferry surfers up to Witches Rock. A boat that carries six surfers for a full day, including lunch and beer, will run around $300. If you're more interested in wind power, you can take a 6-hour cruise on the catamaran *Spanish Dancer* (☎ **506/385-2260;** E-mail: dancer@racsa.co.cr). The cost is $50 per person, including lunch and drinks.

ACCOMMODATIONS
EXPENSIVE

Ocotal Beach Resort. Apdo. 1, Playa del Coco, Guanacaste. ☎ **506/670-0321.** Fax 506/670-0083. www.ocotalresort.com. E-mail: elocotal@racsa.co.cr. 50 units, 12 bungalows, 9 suites. A/C TV TEL. $88 double, $114 bungalow, $155 suite; higher during peak weeks and lower in the off-season. AE, DC, MC, V.

This is the most luxurious hotel in the Playa del Coco area. The guest rooms vary in size, styling, and age. The older rooms are closest to the beach, while the six spacious duplex bungalows are strung along the hillside that climbs toward the reception. The rooms with the best views and greatest comfort are at the top of the hill, overlooking a dramatic stretch of rocky coastline. These feature lively pastel-wash painted walls and colorful floral bedspreads. Be forewarned, it's a steep, vigorous hike from top to bottom. Scuba diving and sportfishing are the main draws here, and package tours are available. Diminutive Playa Ocotal is one of the prettiest little beaches along this stretch of coast and offers good swimming. Unfortunately, service has consistently been the Achilles' heel here.

Dining: El Ocotal's primary restaurant is one of its greatest assets. The large open-air dining room opens onto an expansive, multilevel deck that has a stunning view of Playa Ocotal and miles of coastline. Seafood is the specialty, and the prices are moderate. El Ocotal also runs the Father Rooster restaurant on the beach, with more casual meals and service.

Amenities: Scuba classes, rentals, and trips are some of the hotel's most popular services. There are also boat excursions, fishing charters, surfing excursions, a car-rental desk, and a tour desk. The hotel's main swimming pool is quite attractive and has a little artificial waterfall. Thatch ranchos beside the pool provide shady shelter when the sun gets too strong. There are also three other pools, tennis courts, a couple of Jacuzzis, a small gym, and a dive shop.

MODERATE

Hotel Coco Verde. Apdo. 61, Playa del Coco, Guanacaste. ☎ **506/670-0494.** Fax 506/670-0555. www.cocoverde.com. E-mail: cocoverd@racsa.co.cr. 33 units. A/C. $65 double; lower in the off-season. Rates include breakfast. V.

This new two-story hotel is the biggest thing in Playa del Coco and a good bet if you're looking for a clean, comfortable, modern room close to the beach and all the action. The rooms are all identical in size, but come equipped with a variety of bedding options for singles, couples, and families. They all share a common veranda, which gets blasted by the hot afternoon Guanacaste sun. But there's a pool for cooling off, as well as a popular restaurant and bar, small boutique, tour desk, and dive shop. You can't miss this green-and-white building on your right, on the main road into Playa del Coco, about 183 meters (200 yd.) before you hit the beach.

Hotel La Flor de Itabo. Apdo. 32, Playa del Coco, Guanacaste. ☎ **506/670-0292** or 506/670-0003. www.flordeitabo.com. E-mail: info@flordeitabo.com. 33 units, 8 apts. $45–$80 double, $100 apt for 1–4 people. AE, MC, V.

This is the largest hotel in Playa del Coco with most of the trappings of a resort, although that's not saying an awful lot, and it's not on the beach. Still, the pool is large and the grounds are lushly planted. Toucans and parrots squawk and talk amid the flowers, adding their own bright colors to an already colorful garden. Stone reproductions of pre-Columbian statues provide a touch of the mysterious. The hotel has been expanding and renovating over the past couple of years. The most inexpensive rooms are in four bungalows, with screened windows and fans. The standard rooms are more spacious, have air-conditioning and cable television, and are attractively decorated with wood carvings and Guatemalan textiles. The apartments are located a little bit away from the main building. They're larger than the standard bungalow rooms and have air-conditioning and kitchenettes, but they're nevertheless Spartan.

Italian dishes are the specialty of the restaurant, with main courses ranging from $6 to $15. The bar is decorated with flags from all over the world and is a popular hangout with sport fishers. There's even a small casino here.

✪ **Hotel Villa Casa Blanca.** Playa Ocotal (Apdo. 176-5019), Playa del Coco, Guanacaste. ☎ **506/670-0518.** Fax 506/670-0448. www.ticonet.co.cr/casablanca. E-mail: vcblanca@racsa.co.cr. 15 units. $66 double, $77 triple, $88–$96 suite. Rates include breakfast buffet. AE, MC, V.

With friendly, helpful owners, beautiful gardens, and attractive rooms, this bed-and-breakfast inn is my favorite spot in the area. Located about 500 meters (545 yd.) inland from the beach at Playa Ocotal, it is built in the style of a Spanish villa. All the guest rooms have their own distinct characters, and though some are a tad small, others are quite roomy. One room has a canopy bed and a beautiful bathroom with a step-up bathtub. The suites are higher up and have ocean views. My favorite has a secluded patio with lush flowering plants all around. A little rancho serves as an open-air bar and breakfast area, and beside this is a pretty little lap pool with a bridge over it. Another separate rancho serves as a sort of recreation area and has a satellite television.

There's an inviting hot tub set amidst the gardens. Villa Casa Blanca also manages several rental houses and condos in the area, so if you plan to stay for a week or more, or need lots of room, ask about these.

Villa del Sol B&B. Playa del Coco, Guanacaste. ☎ and fax **506/670-0085.** www.villadelsol. com. E-mail: villasol@racsa.co.cr. 7 units, 5 with bathroom. $40–$55 double; lower in the off-season. MC, V.

This small bed-and-breakfast, located half a mile (1km) north of Playa del Coco village, is a friendly family-run joint, with four rooms upstairs and three downstairs. All are spacious and clean and receive plenty of light. The most interesting room has a round queen-size bed, high ceilings, and views of the gardens. There's an inviting small pool with a covered barbecue area. A continental breakfast is included in the rates, and tasty dinners are prepared nightly for guests from a small menu of European-influenced dishes. There's plenty of protected parking, and the hotel can arrange a wide variety of tours, diving, and fishing options. For me, the hotel's greatest attribute is its location on the quiet northern end of Playa del Coco. To find the hotel, just turn onto the dirt road just beyond the Hotel Coco Verde, before you hit the beach.

INEXPENSIVE

La Luna Tica. Playa del Coco, (Apdo. 67) Guanacaste. ☎ **506/670-0127.** Fax 506/670-0459. 31 units. $20 double, $30 triple, $35 quad; lower in the off-season. V.

This is your best budget choice if you want to be real close to the beach. It's located just south of the soccer field, and the 15 oldest rooms are located right on the beach. These are very basic, have polished concrete floors, and are kept very clean. The newer rooms are in the annex just across the street. The nicest rooms are on the second floor; each has hardwood floors and is flanked by a cool veranda. La Luna Tica also houses the **Las Olas restaurant,** serving Tico standards, Tex-Mex, Creole cuisine, and fish dishes at very reasonable prices.

DINING

There are dozens of cheap open-air *sodas* at the traffic circle in the center of El Coco village. These restaurants serve Tico standards, with an emphasis on fried fish. Prices are quite low, and so is the quality for the most part. For views, you can't beat the restaurant at **El Ocotal Beach Resort.** In addition to the places listed below, you can get excellent Italian food at the new hotel/restaurant **La Puerta del Sol** (☎ 506/670-0195), located 200 meters (218 yd.) north and 100 meters (109 yd.) east of the main road at the turnoff just beyond the Hotel Coco Verde, before you hit the beach.

Helen's. 100m (109 yd.) south of the ice factory. ☎ **506/670-0121.** Reservations not accepted. Main courses $4.50–$12. No credit cards. Daily 10am–11pm. COSTA RICAN/SEAFOOD.

This is a local favorite, and because Helen's husband is a fisherman, the seafood is always absolutely fresh. The ceviche comes in a big bowl and is enough for a meal. Be sure to try the lobster soup if it's on the menu.

L'Angoletto di Roma. 800m (872 yd.) before the beach on the main road. ☎ **506/670-0145.** Reservations not necessary. Main courses $3–$8. V. Fri–Wed 6–10pm. ITALIAN/PASTA.

This small Italian-run restaurant is part of the Pato Loco Inn and serves up the best pasta in these parts. Choose spaghetti, penne, linguine, or fettuccine in one of their innumerable fresh sauces, or opt for the nightly special. If you're lucky, they might have some fresh homemade ravioli in a creamy ricotta sauce. If not, the penne *melanzana* (with eggplant) on the regular menu is a standout. Service is friendly and informal at the six tables spread out underneath the exposed red-tile roof. You'll even find a good selection of Italian wines at fair prices here.

✪ **Papagayo Seafood.** 200m (218 yd.) before the beach on the main road. ☎ **506/ 670-0882.** Reservations recommended. Main courses $5–$18. AE, MC, V. Daily 11am–10pm. SEAFOOD/CAJUN.

This simple seafood joint is a definite notch above the rest of the options in town. There are just a dozen or so plastic tables and a couple of crude plywood booths built against one wall, but they fill up fast in the high season. The place doubles as a seafood market, so you know the fish is fresh. In addition to the daily catch cooked to order, you can get seared yellowfin tuna with a ginger-sesame sauce, blackened mahimahi, or broiled grouper with green peppercorn sauce. There are also several types of jambalaya, some pasta dishes and a full compliment of meat and poultry selections. The owner and chef also runs **Tequila Bar & Grill,** a Mexican joint, and **Pacific Café,** a casual restaurant. All are quite good.

PLAYA DEL COCO AFTER DARK

Playa del Coco is one of Costa Rica's liveliest beach towns after dark. **Coconuts** (no phone) is the main disco in town and is located just off the little park right on the beach. If these directions don't get you there, just follow the loud music. Alternately, you can head across the park to the **Zebra Bar** (☎ 506/670-0272), a lively nightspot with a crowded dance floor. On the road into town, you'll find **Banana's Bar and Garden Restaurant** (☎ 506/670-0605), a comfortable second-floor affair with good bocas and some outdoor tables on the veranda overlooking Coco's main street. Finally, if you want to test your luck, head to the casino at **La Flor de Itabo** (see "Accommodations," above).

5 Playas Flamingo, Potrero, Brasilito & Conchal

173 miles (280km) NW of San José; 41 miles (66km) SW of Liberia

These beaches were among the first in Costa Rica to attract international attention, and are the heart of Guanacaste's "Gold Coast." The Meliá Playa Conchal Beach & Golf Resort is still the premiere large-scale luxury resort in Costa Rica. Still, with attention and development shifting toward the Papagayo Gulf a little farther north, along with an amazing boom in Tamarindo to the south, this has become a great place to find desolate stretches of beautiful beach and isolated hotels in a wide-range of price categories.

Playa Conchal is the first in a string of beaches that work their way north along this coast. In 1997, the 310-room Meliá Playa Conchal opened here, and forever changed the face of what had been a semiprivate haunt of a few beach cognoscenti. The unique beach here is made up primarily of soft crushed shells. Nearly every place you walk, turn, or lay your towel down is shell-collectors' heaven. Unfortunately, as Conchal's popularity has spread, unscrupulous builders have been bringing in dump trucks to haul away the namesake seashells for landscaping and construction, and the impact is noticeable.

All beaches in Costa Rica are public property. But the land behind the beaches is not, and the Meliá company owns almost all of it in Playa Conchal, so the only public access is along the soft-sand road that follows the beach south from Brasilito (see below). Before the road reaches Conchal, you'll have to ford a small river and then climb a steep rocky hill, so four-wheel drive is recommended.

Just beyond Playa Conchal to the north, you'll come to **Playa Brasilito,** a tiny beach town and one of the few real villages in the area. The soccer field is the center of the village, and around its edges you'll find a couple of little *pulperías* (general stores). There's a long stretch of beach, and though it's of gray sand, it still has a quiet, undiscovered feel to it (at least on weekdays). However, Playa Brasilito is rapidly becoming popular both with Ticos and budget travelers from abroad, and there are a few hotels and a couple of campsites here.

For many years **Playa Flamingo** was *the* beach resort in this neck of the woods. Playa Flamingo is on a long spit of land that forms part of Potrero Bay. On the ocean side of the peninsula, there's the long white-sand beach, behind which is a dusty road and then a mangrove swamp. At the end of the sand spit is a fortresslike rock outcropping upon which most of Playa Flamingo's hotels and vacation homes are built. There are great views from this rocky hill. In addition to several luxury hotels, Flamingo has a full-service marina, private airstrip, and a bevy of vacation homes and condo developments. However, whether it's despite or because of, the attention and development all around, Playa Flamingo has a forgotten feel to it. Still, I wouldn't count Flamingo out. The beach here is a beautiful stretch of white sand. In fact, the old name for this beach was Playa Blanca, which made plenty of sense. When the developers moved in, they needed a more romantic name than "White Beach," so it became Playa Flamingo, even though there are no flamingos. If you're not staying on Playa Flamingo, you should know that there are (unprotected) parking spots all along the beach road where you can park your car for the day. There isn't much shade on the beach, so be sure to use plenty of sunscreen and bring an umbrella if you can.

If you continue along the road from Brasilito without taking the turn for Playa Flamingo, you'll soon come to **Playa Potrero.** The sand here is a brownish gray, but the beach is long, clean, deserted, and quite calm for swimming. You can see the hotels of Playa Flamingo across the bay. Drive a little farther north and you'll find the still-underdeveloped **Playa La Penca** and, finally, **Playa Pan de Azúcar (Sugar Beach).**

ESSENTIALS

GETTING THERE & DEPARTING   By Plane   The nearest airports with regularly scheduled flights are in Liberia and Tamarindo. From either of these places you can arrange for a taxi to drive you to any one of these beaches. Playa Brasilito and Conchal are about 45 minutes from Liberia and 25 from Tamarindo (add about 5 more min. for Flamingo and 10 for Potrero). A taxi from Liberia should cost around $30; $25 from Tamarindo.

By Bus   Express buses (☎ 506/221-7202) leave San José daily at 8 and 10am from the corner of Calle 20 and Avenida 3, stopping at Playas Brasilito, Flamingo, and Potrero, in that order. The ride takes 6 hours. A one-way ticket costs $7.

Alternately, you could take the same company's bus to Santa Cruz and connect with either the 6am, 11am, noon, or 3pm bus from Santa Cruz to Playa Potrero. Buses depart San José for Santa Cruz roughly every hour between 7am and 6pm from Calle 20 between avenidas 1 and 3. Trip duration is around 5 hours; fare, $4. From Santa Cruz, the ride is about 90 minutes; fare, $1.50.

Express buses depart **Playa Potrero** for San José at 9am and 2pm, stopping a few minutes later in Playas Flamingo and Brasilito. Ask at your hotel where to catch the bus. Buses to **Santa Cruz** leave Potrero at 9am, 11am, 2pm, and 5pm and take about 90 minutes. If you're heading north toward Liberia, get off the bus at Belén and wait for a bus going north. Buses leave Santa Cruz regularly for San José.

By Car   There are two major routes to these beaches. The most direct route is by way of the **Tempisque River Ferry** (☎ 506/661-8105). Take the Interamerican Highway west from San José. Twenty-nine miles (47km) past the turnoff for Puntarenas, turn left for the ferry. The ferry operates continually (at about 20-min. intervals), 24 hours a day. The fare is $3 per car, with an additional fee of 35¢ per passenger. The ferries that ply this crossing are quite small, and on busy days you may have to wait for several crossings before making it onboard. After crossing the Tempisque River, follow the signs for Nicoya, continuing north to Santa Cruz. About 10 miles (16km) north of Santa Cruz, just before the village of Belén, take the turnoff for Playas Flamingo, Brasilito, and Potrero. After another 12¹/₂ miles (20km), at the town of Huacas, take the right fork to reach these beaches. The drive takes about 6 hours.

Alternately, you can drive here via Liberia. When you reach Liberia, turn west and follow the signs for Santa Cruz and the various beaches. Just beyond the town of Belén, take the turnoff for Playas Flamingo, Brasilito, and Potrero, and continue following the directions given above. This route also takes around 6 hours.

ORIENTATION   These beaches are strung out over several miles of deeply rutted dirt roads. Playa Flamingo is by far the most developed. It's located down a side road, while the villages of Brasilito and Potrero are right on the main road.

GETTING AROUND   Economy Rent A Car has an office in Playa Flamingo (☎ 506/654-4543); **Budget Rent A Car** has an office at the Meliá Playa Conchal Resort (☎ 506/654-4381).

FUN ON & OFF THE BEACH

Though **Playa Flamingo** is the prettiest beach in this area, **Playa Potrero** has the gentlest surf and therefore is the best swimming beach. **Playa Conchal,** which is legendary for its crushed seashells, is beautiful, but the drop-off is quite steep, making it notorious for its strong riptides. The water at **Playa Brasilito** is often fairly calm, which makes it another good swimming choice. However, my favorites for a full day of swimming and sunbathing are **Playa La Penca** and **Playa Pan de Azúcar (Sugar Beach),** both of which are just north of Playa Potrero

SCUBA DIVING   Scuba diving is quite popular here. The **Edge Adventure Company** (☎ 506/654-4946) and **Costa Rica Diving** (☎ and fax **506/654-4148;** www. costarica-diving.com; E-mail: coridive@racas.co.cr) both have shops on the roads into Flamingo. These companies offer trips out to the Catalina and Bat islands for between $65 and $125. Both also offer PADI certification courses, as well as multiday packages. Alternately, you can check in at the **Flamingo Marina Resort Hotel and Club** (see below).

SPORTFISHING & SAILBOAT CHARTERS   You have plenty of sportfishing options here. The choices are many and competition is fierce here, so shop around to

---

Driving Tip

It's often slightly quicker, particularly on Friday and Saturday when beach traffic is heavy, to drive north all the way to Liberia and then come back south, thus avoiding the lines of cars waiting to take the Tempisque River ferry. This also applies if you're heading back to San José on a Sunday. After you reach Liberia, follow the directions for Playa Hermosa but continue on the main road past the town of Filadelfia, until the village of Belén. Turn right here until you reach Huacas, where there will be signs pointing you toward Playa Flamingo. The ride from Liberia should take about an hour.

find the boat, skipper, and price that best fit your needs. At the **Marina Flamingo Yacht Club** (☎ **506/654-4203;** www.marflam.com), you can hook up with a variety of boats based along the docks. A full-day fishing excursion can cost between $475 and $1,300, depending on the size of the boat. Half-day trips cost between $275 and $650.

Alternately, you can contact the **Bahía Potrero Resort Hotel and Club** (☎ **506/654-4183**) or the **Flamingo Marina Resort Hotel and Club** (☎ **506/654-4141**).

If you're looking for a full- or half-day sail or sunset cruise, check in at the Marina Flamingo (see above), or try to track down the **52-foot cutter *Shannon*** (☎ **506/654-4537**). Prices range from around $45 to $90 per person, depending on the length of the cruise. Multiday trips are also available.

HORSEBACK RIDING You can arrange a horseback ride with **Costa Rica Riding Adventures** (☎ **506/654-4106**), **Bo-Mar Tours** (☎ **506/654-4469**), or **Brasilito Excursions** (☎ **506/654-4237**). This last place works out of the Hotel Brasilito. Depending on the size of your group, it should cost between $10 and $20 per person per hour.

MOUNTAIN BIKING & OTHER ADVENTURE TOURS You can rent a mountain bike from the **Edge Adventure Company** (☎ **506/654-4946**). This company can also arrange multiday biking tours to other parts of Costa Rica, as well as kayaking, hiking, and rafting trips. Alternately, check in with the tour desk at the **Flamingo Marina Resort Hotel and Club** (☎ **506/654-4141**).

ACCOMMODATIONS

If you plan to be here for a while or are coming down with friends or a large family, you might want to consider renting a condo or house. They rent for anywhere between $100 and $1,200 (depending on size and luxury) per day in the high season (slightly less during the low season). For information and reservations, contact **Sea View Rentals** (☎ **506/654-4007;** fax 506/654-4009), or the **Marina Trading Post** (☎ and fax **506/654-4004;** E-mail: tpostcr@racsa.co.cr).

VERY EXPENSIVE

✪ **Meliá Playa Conchal.** Apdo. 232-5150, Santa Cruz, Guanacaste. ☎ **888/336-3542** in the U.S., or 506/654-4123. Fax 506/654-4181. www.meliaplayaconchal.com. E-mail: mconchal@racsa.co.cr. 310 suites. A/C MINIBAR TV TEL. $200–$265 suite, $700 master suite; lower in the off-season and higher during Christmas and Easter weeks. AE, MC, V.

This sprawling hotel is the largest and most luxurious resort in Costa Rica. And while this is far from the norm for tourism here, if you're looking for a big-resort vacation in Costa Rica, this is a great option. From the massive open-air reception building down to the free-form swimming pool (the largest in Central America), everything here has been done on a grand scale. There's a small village feel to the layout; guest rooms are located in 30 separate low-slung buildings, reached by way of the constantly circulating shuttles. All of the rooms come with either one king or two double beds in a raised bedroom nook. Down below, there's a comfortable sitting area, with a couch, coffee table, and chairs with ottomans. The bathrooms are large and modern, with marble tiles, full tubs, bidets, and even a telephone. Each has a garden patio or a small balcony. Only three of the bungalows are actually oceanfront, and two of these contain the master suites, which have double the living area of the standard suites and slightly more luxurious appointments.

Because of the golf course and its ponds and wetlands, there's good bird-watching here, with healthy populations of parrots, roseate spoonbills, and wood storks. Because the hotel owns so much land behind Playa Conchal, you'll have almost exclusive access to this crushed-seashell beach.

Dining/Diversions: Guests generally take all their meals here, and there is a variety of options. The large generic international buffet restaurant seats 400 and has the most extensive hours. Off of this you'll find an open-air bar and large lounge where nightly entertainment revues are staged. There's also an outdoor grill, a poolside snack bar, the **Spirula Steak House,** and **La Faisanela,** a semi-fancy Italian restaurant. Up on a high bluff you'll find the hotel's most formal restaurant, **Astrea,** whose meals and service, unfortunately, don't live up to expectations. In the same building, you'll find the hotel's casino and disco.

Amenities: Aside from the massive pool and its scattered Jacuzzis, there's a regulation 18-hole golf course designed by Robert Trent Jones, a pro shop, four lighted tennis courts, water-sports equipment, a dive shop, and a small gym with exercise equipment. There's also a conference facility, a small shopping arcade with an assortment of gift shops and galleries, a car-rental desk, a tour desk, a concierge, 24-hour room service, laundry service, and valet parking.

EXPENSIVE

Flamingo Marina Resort Hotel and Club. Playa Flamingo (Apdo. 321-1002, Paseo de los Estudiantes, San José), Guanacaste. ☎ **506/290-1858** or 506/654-4141. Fax 506/ 231-1858. www.FlamingoMarina.com. E-mail: TickledPink@FlamingoMarina.com. 35 units, 25 apts. A/C TV TEL. $70–$90 double, $100–$135 suite, $180–$240 apt; rates slightly higher during peak periods. AE, DC, MC, V.

Located up the hill from the beach, the Flamingo Marina Hotel offers one of the most attractive settings at Flamingo Beach. The open-air lobby overlooks both the swimming pool and the bay. Standard rooms have tile floors and lots of wood accents, while suites have wet bars in the seating area, mini-fridges, and private whirlpool tubs. All the rooms have patios or balconies, and most have bay views.

Dining: The Sunrise Cafe serves reasonably priced continental dishes with an emphasis on seafood.

Amenities: There's a tennis court here, as well as four swimming pools, one with a popular swim-up bar. You'll also find a tour desk, offering up a wide range of tours around the region, as well as sportfishing charters, sea kayaking, and boogie-board rentals. There's a dive shop, offering snorkeling and diving trips as well as certification classes.

Hotel Aurola Playa Flamingo Holiday Inn. Playa Flamingo (Apdo. 7802-1000, San José), Guanacaste. ☎ **506/654-4010.** Fax 506/654-4060. 88 units. A/C TV TEL. $110–$130 double, $240 suite; lower in the off-season. AE, DC, MC, V.

This hotel, right across the road from the beach at Playa Flamingo, has long been a favorite of vacationing gringos. The hotel is constructed in a horseshoe shape around a large pool and opens out on the ocean. Half the rooms have clear views of the ocean, across a narrow dirt road. All the rooms are clean and cool, with tile floors, modern bathrooms, and many amenities. The pool- and beach-view rooms are slightly nicer, and you'll pay more for them. The suites each have a sitting room, wet bar, and VCR. The hotel also rents some slightly less expensive rooms in a new annex.

Dining/Diversions: The most popular meeting and eating place here is the poolside **Arenas** bar and restaurant. The second-floor **Catalinas** restaurant is for those seeking a little more formal setting and air-conditioning.

Amenities: There's a modest gym, a large game room, and a children's playroom.

Hotel Fantasias Flamingo. Playa Flamingo (Apdo. 12270-1000, San José), Guanacaste.
☎ **506/654-4350** or 506/231-5086. Fax 506/220-4405. www.fantasiasflamingo.com.
E-mail: flamingo@racsa.co.cr. 42 units. A/C TEL. $79–$99 double. AE, MC, V.

This new hotel is located up on the bluff, a little bit beyond the Flamingo Marina
Hotel and Club. The rooms are all identical, with wall-to-wall carpeting, two double
beds, large dressers and plenty of closet space, and private bathrooms with tubs. The
nicest rooms enjoy a view of Potrero Bay and have large sliding glass doors that open
onto either a private patio or a balcony. Several of these patios adjoin the swimming
pool and have stairs leading down into the water.

   Dining/Diversions: There's only one restaurant here, located on the second floor
with stunning views of Bahía Potrero. Breakfast, lunch, and dinner are served—
pretty standard continental fare, at reasonable prices. Your best bet is usually the catch
of the day. Just off the restaurant, you'll find the hotel's small bar and casino.

   Amenities: The free-form pool has a swim-up bar and a footbridge over it, and even
adjoins several of the rooms. Tour desk, laundry service.

Hotel Sugar Beach. Playa Pan de Azúcar (Apdo. 90, Santa Cruz), Guanacaste. ☎ **800/
458-4735** in the U.S., or 506/654-4242. Fax 506/654-4239. www.sugar-beach.com. E-mail:
sugarb@racsa.co.cr. 29 units. A/C. $90–$138 double, $165 suite. AE, MC, V.

As the name implies, the Hotel Sugar Beach is located on a white-sand beach—one of
the few in the area and therefore one of the most attractive, in my opinion. So far, this
hotel is the only thing out here, giving it a strong measure of seclusion and privacy.
The beach is on a small cove surrounded by rocky hills. Unfortunately, the hills
become very brown and desolate in the dry season, so don't expect the verdant tropics
if you come down here in March or April. The hotel itself is perched above the water.
Nature lovers will be thrilled to find wild howler monkeys and iguanas almost on their
doorsteps. Snorkelers should be happy here, too; this cove has some good snorkeling
in the dry season. The newest rooms are set back amid the trees and are quite large.
Tile floors, wicker furniture, beautiful carved doors, and big bathrooms all add up to
first-class comfort. The oldest rooms are the most basic, though they're in an interesting circular building. Hammocks under the trees provide a great way to while away a
hot afternoon.

   Dining: The open-air dining room is in a circular building with a panoramic vista
of ocean, islands, and hills. The menu is long and there are daily specials with entree
prices from $6 to $18.

   Amenities: There's a kidney-shaped pool, set on the hillside below the restaurant.
Scuba-diving and snorkeling trips, horseback riding, and fishing-boat charters can be
arranged. The hotel rents masks and fins, and boogie boards.

MODERATE

Hotel Bahía Potrero Beach Resort. Playa Potrero (Apdo. 45-5051, Santa Cruz), Guanacaste. ☎ **506/654-4183.** Fax 506/654-4093. 10 units. $60 double. AE, MC, V.

This little hotel is on Playa Potrero and has a view of Playa Flamingo across the bay.
A laid-back atmosphere prevails, with hammocks for dozing, a pool, and miles of nearly
deserted beach for strolling and swimming. The rooms are large and cool, though a
little dark and run-down. They all have refrigerators and small patios. This place is
popular with sport fishermen; both fishing and snorkeling trips can be arranged, and
horses are available at $15 per hour. To find this hotel, watch for the sign pointing
down a road to the left a mile or so after you pass the turnoff for Playa Flamingo. The
hotel's restaurant is a breezy, high-ceilinged room and has a nice view of green lawns,
white fence, and blue ocean. Fresh seafood and hearty steaks average $5 to $10.

INEXPENSIVE

It's possible to camp on Playas Potrero and Brasilito. At the former, contact **Maiyra's** (☎ **506/654-4213**), and at the latter try **Camping Brasilito** (☎ **506/654-4452**). Each charges around $3 per person to make camp and use the basic bathroom facilities. Each also has some basic cabins for around $10 per person.

Cabinas Conchal. Playa Brasilito, Santa Cruz, Guanacaste. ☎ **506/654-4257.** 9 units. $25 double, $30 triple, $40 quad; lower in the off-season. No credit cards.

Located on the south edge of Brasilito, Cabinas Conchal consists of several yellow buildings inside a walled compound. The stucco-and-stone construction gives the buildings a bit of character as well as added security. Some rooms have just a double bed, while others have a double and a pair of bunk beds. All are quite clean. Table fans help keep the rooms cool. The beach is about 200 meters (218 yd.) away.

Cabinas Cristina. Playa Potrero (Apdo. 121, Santa Cruz), Guanacaste. ☎ **506/654-4006.** Fax 506/654-4128. www.cabinas.nf.ca. E-mail: danielbo@racsa.co.cr. 6 units. $30–$50 double. AE, MC, V.

This little place is located on Playa Potrero across the bay from Playa Flamingo and a few kilometers north of Brasilito. Although Cabinas Cristina isn't right on the beach, it's a great value in this area of high-priced hotels. The rooms are spacious and very clean. You can opt for a simple room with a couple of beds, a desk, and a fan, or a two-bedroom apartment with kitchenette and air-conditioning. All rooms have small verandas with large rocking chairs. There's a small pool in the middle of a grassy green yard, and a thatch-roofed palapa. Playa Potrero is a 5-minute walk down a dirt road.

Hotel Brasilito. Playa Brasilito, Santa Cruz, Guanacaste. ☎ **506/654-4237.** Fax 506/654-4247. www.brasilito.com. E-mail: compes@racsa.co.cr. 15 units. $25–$35 double. V.

This hotel, right in Brasilito and just across a sand road from the beach, offers basic small rooms that are generally quite clean. There's also a bar and big open-air restaurant serving economical meals. This is still one of the best values in town. The higher-priced rooms have nice balconies and ocean views. The hotel rents snorkeling equipment, kayaks, body boards, and horses, and can arrange a variety of tours.

DINING

Amberes. Playa Flamingo near the Flamingo Marina Hotel. ☎ **506/654-4001.** Reservations recommended in high season. Main courses $6–$20. AE, MC, V. Daily 5–10pm. CONTINENTAL.

Not only is this the most upscale restaurant outside of a hotel, but it also boasts a bar, an open-air disco, and even a tiny casino. You can come for dinner and make it an evening. Though the menu changes nightly, you'll always find a wide selection of dishes, with the emphasis on seafood. Fresh fish served either meunière or Provence style are two of the best dishes here. People with sensitive ears should take note: The music can become way too loud at dinner. However, if you dine early, it should be no problem—the disco doesn't usually get cranking until 10pm.

✪ **Marie's.** Playa Flamingo near the Flamingo Marina Hotel. ☎ **506/654-4136.** Reservations not accepted. Sandwiches $3–$6, main courses $6–$17. V. Daily 6:30am–9:30pm. COSTA RICAN/SEAFOOD.

Right in the middle of all the luxury hotels at Playa Flamingo is a great little place for a snack or a full meal. The menu is primarily sandwiches and other lunch foods, but on the blackboard behind the bar you'll find daily specials, which usually feature the freshest catch, such as mahimahi (called *dorado* down here), marlin, and red snapper.

You'll also find such Tico favorites as casados and ceviche. Tables in the open-air restaurant are made from slabs of tree trunks. Be sure to try the *tres leches,* or three-milks cake (a Nicaraguan specialty), which just might be the moistest cake on earth.

PLAYA FLAMINGO AFTER DARK

If you don't head to the disco and casino at Amberes, you might want to check out the poolside bar at the **Mariner Inn** (☎ **506/654-4081**), which seems to be the liveliest spot in town. Over in Playa Potrero, the **Tucan Jungle Sports Bar** (☎ **506/ 654-4014**) is the most happening joint.

6 Playa Tamarindo & Playa Grande

183 miles (295km) NW of San José; 45 miles (73km) SW of Liberia

Tamarindo is a bit of a boomtown, perhaps too much of a boomtown. So far, the development is a mixture of predominantly small hotels in a variety of price ranges, and an eclectic array of restaurants. The most recent development seems to be creeping up the hills inland from the beach and south beyond Punta Langosta. The beach itself is a long, wide swath of white sand that curves gently from one rocky headland to another. Behind the beach are low, dry hills that can be a very dreary brown in the dry season but instantly turn green with the first brief showers of the rainy season. The dust that turns the hills brown can also make the main street through Tamarindo extremely unpleasant to walk along, so stick to the beach.

Though there's only one major resort hotel in town, the proximity to great surfing and an abundance of stylish smaller hotels have made Tamarindo one of the most popular beaches on this coast. Fishing boats bob at their moorings at the south end of the beach, and brown pelicans fish just outside the breakers. A sandy islet offshore makes a great destination if you're a strong swimmer; if you're not, it makes a great foreground for sunsets. As I said above, Tamarindo is popular with surfers, who ply the break right here or use the town as a jumping-off place for Playas Grande, Langosta, Avellana, and Negra.

Just to the north of Tamarindo lies **Playa Grande,** one of the principal nesting sites for the giant leatherback turtle, the largest turtle in the world. This beach is often too rough for swimming, but the well-formed and consistent beach break is very popular with surfers. I almost hate to mention places to stay in Playa Grande, because the steady influx of tourists and development could doom this beach as a turtle nesting site.

ESSENTIALS

GETTING THERE & DEPARTING   By Plane   Sansa (☎ **506/221-9414;** fax 506/255-2176; E-mail: reservations@flysansa.com) flies to Tamarindo from San José's Juan Santamaría International Airport daily at 5:15, 8:30, and 11:35am, and 1, 2:30, and 3:30pm. The flight takes 55 minutes. The fare is $60 each way.

Travelair (☎ **506/220-3054;** fax 506/220-0413; E-mail: reservations@travelair-costarica.com) flies to Tamarindo daily at 8:20am, 1pm, and 3:30pm from Tobías Bolaños International Airport in Pavas. The duration is 55 minutes, and the fare is $92 one-way, $152 round-trip. Whether you arrive on Sansa or Travelair, there are always a couple of cabs or minivans waiting for arriving flights. It costs around $5 for the ride into town.

Sansa flights leave Tamarindo for San José at 6:20 and 9:35am, and 12:40, 2:05, 3:35, and 4:35pm daily. Travelair flights leave for San José at 9:30am, 2pm, and 4:25pm daily.

By Bus   An express bus (☎ 506/222-2666) leaves San José daily for Tamarindo at 3:30pm, departing from Calle 14 between avenidas 3 and 5, and takes 5¹/₂ hours. The one-way fare is $5.

Alternately, you can catch a bus to Santa Cruz from the same station. Buses (☎ 506/221-7202) leave San José for Santa Cruz roughly every hour between 7am and 6pm. The trip's duration is 5 hours; the one-way fare is $4. Buses leave Santa Cruz (☎ 506/680-0392) for Tamarindo daily at 10:30am, 1:30, 3:30, and 8pm. The trip lasts 1¹/₂ hours; the one-way fare is $1.50.

A direct bus leaves Tamarindo for San José daily at 6am. Buses to Santa Cruz leave at 6 and 9am, noon, and 3pm. In Santa Cruz you can transfer to one of the frequent San José buses.

Finally, there's a new alternative: **Best Western** (☎ 506/653-0114) runs a daily shuttle leaving its San José Best Western Irazú hotel at 7:30am, arriving in Tamarindo at around noon; the return trip leaves the Best Western Vista Villas at 2pm and arrives in San José at 6pm. This shuttle costs $19 per person each way.

By Car   The most direct route is by way of the **Tempisque River Ferry** (☎ 506/ 661-8105). Take the Interamerican Highway west from San José, and 29 miles (47km) past the turnoff for Puntarenas, turn left toward the ferry. The ferry operates 24 hours a day (at approximately 20-min. intervals) and costs about $3 per car and driver, with a nominal 35¢ fee per passenger. On busy days (especially Friday nights and Saturday mornings) you may have to wait for several crossings before making it onboard. After crossing the Tempisque River, follow the signs for Nicoya and Santa Cruz. About 10 miles (16km) north of Santa Cruz, just before the village of Belén, take the turnoff for Tamarindo. In another 12¹/₂ miles (20km), take the left fork for Playa Tamarindo. The drive takes about 6 hours.

On Friday and Saturday, when beach traffic is heavy, it's often quicker to drive all the way north to Liberia and then come back south, thus avoiding the lines of cars waiting to take the ferry. This also applies if you're heading back to San José on a Sunday. See the "Driving Tip" in "Playas Flamingo, Potrero, Brasilito & Conchal," above.

ORIENTATION   The unpaved road leading into town runs parallel to the beach and dead-ends just past Cabinas Zully Mar. There are a couple of side roads off this main road that lead farther on to Playas Langosta, Avellana, and Negra. You'll find several of the newer hotels mentioned below off of these side roads.

GETTING AROUND   **Elegante Rent A Car** (☎ 506/653-0015) has an office at the Pueblo Dorado Hotel. **Alamo Rent A Car** (☎ 506/653-0727) and **Economy Rent A Car** (☎ 506/653-0728) both have offices on the beach side of the main road into Tamarindo, before the Tamarindo Diriá hotel.

FUN ON & OFF THE BEACH

Tamarindo is a long beach, and though it can sometimes be great for swimming, it's often too rough. You also have to be careful when and where you swim. There are rocks just offshore in several places, some of which are exposed only at low tide. An encounter with one of these rocks could be nasty, especially if you're bodysurfing. You should also avoid swimming near the estuary mouth, where the currents can carry you out away from the beach. That said, the best swimming is always down at the southern end of the beach, toward Punta Langosta.

If you just want to laze on the beach, you can pick up beach chairs, umbrellas, and mats at **Tamarindo Tour/Rentals** (☎ and fax 506/653-0078), located on the right as you come into town. It's open daily. There's a little storefront and gift shop here,

Para Bailar La Salsa

If you want to brush up on your Spanish or learn how to dance salsa, check in with the folks at **Wayra Instituto de Español** (☎ and fax **506/653-0359;** E-mail: spanishw@ racsa.co.cr). This place is located up a side street from Iguana Surf.

which doubles as a local information center and clearinghouse for condo and apartment rentals around the area.

Finally, if you're sore and worn out from all the activities listed below, call **Shannon Vacca** (☎ **506/653-0291**) for professional sports and/or Swedish massage. Shannon is based out of the Coral Reef, but she'll come to any hotel in the area. A 1-hour massage costs $55; half-hour, $35.

BIKING & HORSEBACK RIDING   Bikes are available for rent at **Iguana Surf** (☎ **506/653-0148;** E-mail: iguanasurf@aol.com). These folks have one shop on the main road into Tamarindo, but their main office is a little bit out of "downtown" Tamarindo, on the road to Playa Langosta.

You'll probably see plenty of horses and riders running up and down the beach. You can flag one of these down and ask about rates, or set up a riding date with **Tamarindo Tour/Rentals** or **Papagayo Excursions** (☎ **506/653-0254** or 506/653-0227; E-mail: papagayo@racsa.co.cr). Rates for horse rental, with a guide, are around $10 to $15 per hour. Both companies, as well as **Iguana Surf,** also offer boat or kayak tours of the nearby estuary for around $20 per person. Papagayo Excursions offers the widest selection of full-day and multiday trips, including excursions to Santa Cruz and Guaitíl ($45), raft floats on the Corobicí River ($85), tours to Palo Verde and Rincón de la Vieja national parks ($85), and tours to Arenal Volcano and Tabacón Hot Springs ($100).

FOUR-WHEELING   Tamarindo Adventures (☎ **506/653-0640;** www. tamarindoadventure.com; E-mail: tamquad@racsa.co.cr) has a fleet of four-wheel-drive all-terrain vehicles. They're available for the day ($75) and half day ($55). A wide range of guided tours around the region are also available. These folks also rent out snorkel equipment, surf and boogie boards, and jet skis.

GOLF   Golf has come to this region in a big way, with not one but two courses. The better course and facilities are at the **Meliá Playa Conchal Resort** (☎ **506/ 654-4123**). This Robert Trent Jones–designed course is still open to the walk-in public, but as the resort itself gets more and more popular, they may restrict public access. Currently, it will cost you $90 in greens fees for 18 holes, including a cart and a bucket of balls for the driving range. If you tee off after 1pm it's just $60. Closer to Tamarindo, in Playa Grande, you'll find **Rancho Las Colinas** (☎ **506/383-3759**), a Ron Garl–designed 18-hole course, which charges $50 in greens fees plus $20 for the cart. While this is actually a nice course, and locals love it, it's almost always deserted, and I wouldn't be surprised if they went out of business shortly.

SAILBOAT CHARTERS   The folks who run the **Finca Monte Fresco** (☎ **506/ 653-0096;** fax 506/653-0275), just outside of Tamarindo, also own the 52-foot ketch *Samonique III.* They charter this boat for anything from sunset cruises to weeklong trips out to Cocos Island. A half-day cruise costs $60 per person, and a full day is just $90 per person. This includes an open bar and snacks on the half-day cruise, lunch on the full-day trip. Beyond this, they run a sunset cruise for $45 per person, and charter rates are around $225 per person per day, including all board, and vary depending on the size of your group.

SNORKELING, SURFING & SEA KAYAKING   If you want to try any of these water sports while in Tamarindo, **Iguana Surf** (☎ **506/653-0148**) is your one-stop source for equipment. These folks are open daily and rent snorkeling equipment ($15 per day), boogie boards ($10 per day), sea kayaks ($35 per day), and surfboards ($20 per day). They have half-day and hourly rates for many of these items. You can also rent similar equipment of slightly lesser quality, and at slightly lower rates, from Tamarindo Tour/Rentals.

If you want to do any scuba diving while you're here, check in with **Agua Rica** (☎ **506/653-0094;** www.tamarindo.com; E-mail: agricadv@racsa.co.cr), which you'll find on the main road, near Cabinas Marielos. They have a full-service dive shop and offer day trips, multiday dive cruises, and the standard resort and full certification courses.

SPORTFISHING   **Papagayo Excursions** (see above), which has its office and a small gift shop in the commercial center across from the Tamarindo Diriá hotel, offers folks a chance to go after the "big ones" that abound in the waters offshore. From here it takes only 20 minutes to reach the edge of the continental shelf and the waters preferred by marlin and sailfish. Although fishing is good all year, the peak season for billfish is between mid-April and August. Alternately, you can contact **Tamarindo Sportfishing** (☎ **506/653-0090;** www.tamarindosportfishing.com), **Warren Sellers Sportfishing** (☎ **506/653-0186;** www.wssportfishing.com), or **Capullo Sportfishing** (☎ **506/653-0048;** www.capullo.com). All offer half-day trips for between $250 and $500 and full-day trips for between $400 and $1,000.

WATCHING NESTING SEA TURTLES   On nearby **Playa Grande,** leatherback sea turtles nest between late September and mid-March. The only time to see this activity is at night. During the nesting season you'll be inundated with opportunities to sign up for the nightly tours—they usually cost around $20 to $30 per person. If your hotel can't set it up for you, you'll see signs all over town offering tours. Make sure you go with someone licensed and reputable. No flash photography is allowed because any sort of light can confuse the turtles and prevent them from laying their eggs; guides must use red-tinted flashlights. In Tamarindo, there are two main organizations running the tours: a local cooperative of guides called **Coopetamarindo** (no phone; office located on the road into town) and **Papagayo Excursions** (see above). Playa Grande is just north of Tamarindo across a small river mouth. The tours either drive you around to the Playa Grande entrance or simply ferry you across the Tamarindo estuary in small *pangas* (outboard-driven boats), where you begin your trek up Playa Grande in search of a nesting mother. In both cases, you will probably be shown a brief introductory video before hitting the beach. If you are driven to Playa Grande, you will probably tour the small turtle museum there (see below).

Be forewarned, turtle nesting is a natural, unpredictable, and increasingly rare event. You may have to hike quite a ways, wait, and even accept the possibility that no nesting mothers will be spotted. Moreover, with the vast development in this area, the numbers of nesting turtles have dropped, while the number of tourists has skyrocketed. Do not expect an intimate experience.

Do-it-yourselfers can drive over to Playa Grande, where tours are offered by the **Matapalo Conservation Association.** These local folks operate out of a small shack next to the Las Tortugas Hotel. Part of the money goes to support local schools and a medical clinic. Try to arrive early (the shack opens at 6pm) to sign up for a tour ($15), because only a limited number of people are allowed on the beach at one time. The list fills up fast, and if you arrive late, you may have to wait until real late.

If the turtles are not nesting, or you've got some time to kill before your turtle tour, check out **El Mundo de la Tortuga** (☎ and fax **506/653-0471**), a small turtle museum/ exhibit at Playa Grande. Visitors take the half-hour self-guided tour by picking up a cassette player and choosing a tour cassette in English, Spanish, German, or Italian. The museum opens each afternoon at 4pm and stays open until the turtle tours are done for the night. Admission $5.

ACCOMMODATIONS
IN TOWN
Very Expensive
Hotel and Villas Cala Luna. Playa Tamarindo, Guanacaste. ☎ **506/653-0214.** Fax 506/ 653-0213. www.calaluna.com. E-mail: reservations@calaluna.com. 20 units, 21 villas. A/C TV TEL. $145 double, $300–$380 villa; slightly lower in the off-season. AE, MC, V.

If you're looking for serious luxury in Tamarindo, stay in one of the two- or three-bedroom villas here. These independent villas are the size of a small home and just as well equipped. The living rooms are huge, with high-peaked ceilings, couches, tables and chairs, satellite televisions, and complete sound systems. The full kitchen comes with a microwave oven and cappuccino machine, and there's even a washing machine. If this isn't enough, each villa has its own private swimming pool. The bedrooms are spacious and elegant with either a king or two double beds. Everything is done in soft pastels with hand-painted accents, and the red-tile roofs and Mexican tile floors add to the elegance while keeping things cool. Rooms in the hotel are similarly spacious and well done, but you'll have to share the hotel's main swimming pool with the rest of the guests. The biggest drawback is that the service falls far short of measuring up to the surroundings. The hotel isn't right on the beach; you have to cross the street and walk a short path to reach the ocean.

Dining: The **Cala Moresca** restaurant serves a selection of continental and Italian dishes.

Amenities: Aside from the villas with their private pools, there's a large free-form pool with a poolside bar. The hotel has its own boat for fishing and diving trips and can arrange a whole host of other tours around the region. Bicycle and surfboard rentals, room service, and baby-sitting are also available.

Hotel El Jardín del Eden. Playa Tamarindo, Guanacaste. ☎ **506/653-0137.** Fax 506/ 653-0111. www.jardin-eden.com. E-mail: giulio@racsa.co.cr. 18 units, 2 apts. A/C TV TEL. $125–$145 double; lower in the off-season. Rates include breakfast. AE, MC, V.

Though it isn't right on the beach, this is one of the most luxurious and comfortable hotels in Tamarindo. The Italian owners bring a touch of sophistication that's often lacking at beach hotels in Costa Rica. There are splendid views from many of the guest rooms, which are in Mediterranean-style buildings on a hill 137 meters (150 yd.) from the beach. Almost all have balconies or private terraces with views of the Pacific. The large stone-tiled terraces, in particular, give you the sense of staying at your own private villa. The honeymoon room has a large bathroom with a tub, while other rooms have showers only. The staff can help you arrange various tours and excursions.

Dining: The thatch-roofed, open-air dining room features excellent French and Italian meals with nightly specials and the occasional live band.

Amenities: There are two swimming pools, one of which has a swim-up bar. There's also a whirlpool tub. The terraces surrounding the pools and tub have thatch palapas for shade, and there's even a little artificial waterfall flowing into the pool. Just off the reception you'll find a small open-air gym. The beach is 137 meters (150 yd.) down the hill.

Expensive

Best Western Tamarindo Villas Hotel & Resort. Playa Tamarindo, Guanacaste. ☎ **506/653-0118.** Fax 506/653-0115. www.centralamerica.com. E-mail: tamvv@racsa.co.cr. 32 units. A/C TEL. $89–$99 double, $119–$179 suite. Rates include continental breakfast. AE, MC, V.

This place overwhelmingly attracts and caters to surfers. There is a wide range of accommodations here, from the simple Garden View rooms to the Tropical and Corona suites. The latter are split-level one-bedroom affairs with full kitchens, a large living room (with two couches that double as single beds), TVs with VCRs, and either a private patio or a balcony with fabulous views of the Pacific Ocean.

Dining/Diversions: There's a good restaurant here and a lively sports bar.

Amenities: There's a free-form pool with a swim-up bar and a waterfall that is sometimes turned on. The hotel runs a daily shuttle to and from San José, and can help arrange a wide variety of tours and adventures.

✪ **Hotel Capitan Suizo.** Playa Tamarindo, Guanacaste. ☎ **506/653-0353** or 506/653-0075. Fax 506/653-0292. www.capitansuizo.com. E-mail: capsuizo@racsa.co.cr. 22 units, 8 bungalows. TEL. $110–$130 double, $165 bungalow; lower in the off-season. AE, MC, V.

This luxurious beachfront hotel is located on the quiet southern end of Tamarindo. The rooms are located in a series of two-story buildings. The lower rooms have air-conditioning and private patios; the upper units have plenty of cross ventilation and small balconies. All have large bathrooms and sitting rooms with fold-down futon couches. In effect, all the rooms are really suites, with their separate sitting/living room area. The spacious bungalows are spread around the shady grounds, near the large free-form pool. These all come with a tub in the bathroom and an inviting outdoor shower among the trees. Perhaps this hotel's greatest attribute is the fact that it's just steps from one of the calmer and more isolated sections of Playa Tamarindo.

Dining: All the meals are served in the open-air rancho.

Amenities: The hotel's free-form pool is quite nice. The shallow end slopes in gradually, imitating a beach; there's also a separate children's pool. There is a small gift shop on the premises, as well as a small gym. The hotel can arrange a wide variety of tours and activities and has its own horses.

✪ **Sueño del Mar.** Playa Tamarindo, Guanacaste. ☎ and fax **506/653-0284.** www.tamarindo.com/sdmar. E-mail: suenodem@racsa.co.cr. 4 units, 1 casita. $95–$115 double, $150 suite or casita. Rates include breakfast. V.

This place is such a gem I was hesitant to let the secret out. Now it's nearly impossible to get a room. Located at the south end of Tamarindo Beach on Punta Langosta, the hotel features rooms that are a bit small. But it's the little touches and innovative design that set Sueño del Mar apart: four-poster beds made from driftwood, African dolls on the windowsills, Kokopeli candleholders, and open-air showers with sculpted angelfish, hand-painted tiles, and lush tropical plants. Fabrics are from Bali and Guatemala. Somehow, all this works well together, and the requisite hammocks nestled under shade trees right on the beach add the crowning touch.

The separate small casita has its own kitchen, veranda, and sleeping loft, while the suite is a spacious second-floor room, with wraparound screened-in windows, a delightful open-air bathtub and shower, and an ocean view. The beach right out front is rocky and a bit rough but does reveal some nice, quiet tidal pools at low tide. The newest addition here is a small swimming pool just off the main building.

Dining: Breakfasts are huge and creative and have earned local renown. In fact, co-owner Susan Money has even published her own breakfast cookbook. In 2000, Susan's daughter, Nancy Goodfellow, began cooking up dinner, and now it's a toss-up as to who gets greater acclaim. The menu varies nightly and has a creative, fusion flare. Reservations are recommended.

Amenities: Small pool, snorkel equipment, and boogie boards. Owners arrange tours and activities.

Tamarindo Diriá. Playa Tamarindo (Apdo. 476-1007, San José), Guanacaste. ☎ **506/ 653-0031.** Fax 506/653-0208. www.tamarindodiria.co.cr. E-mail: tnodiria@racsa.co.cr. 86 units. A/C TV TEL. $100–$140 double; lower in the off-season. Rates include breakfast buffet. AE, MC, V.

This is Tamarindo's oldest and largest beachfront resort. A 1997 remodeling and steady upkeep have kept the hotel in pretty good shape. Wedged into a narrow piece of land between a dusty road and the beach, the Diriá manages to create its own little world of tropical gardens and palm trees. The remodeled rooms are done in contemporary pastel colors with red-tile floors. Some rooms have separate seating areas, and most have hair dryers, clock radios, and a basket of toiletries in the small bathroom. It's the central beachfront location and attractive gardens that make this hotel a worthwhile place to stay.

Dining/Diversions: The big open-air bar/restaurant beside the pool features a different menu nightly, with prices for main dishes ranging from $5 to $12. The new **Matapalo** restaurant serves a continental menu by the beach under an immense matapalo tree. There's also a lunch buffet in the garden most days.

Amenities: There's a swimming pool, gift shop, tour desk, and game room, and both beach-equipment rentals and car rentals can be arranged on-premises. Across the street, there's a small commercial center with a minimart.

Villa Alegre. Playa Tamarindo, Guanacaste. ☎ **506/653-0270.** Fax 506/653-0287. www. tamarindo.com. E-mail: vialegre@racsa. 5 units, 2 with bathroom; 4 villas. A/C. $85–$125 double, $175 villa. Rates include full breakfast. V.

This small bed-and-breakfast on Playa Langosta is yet another well-run and homey option in Tamarindo. The owners' years of globe-trotting has inspired them to decorate each room in the theme of a different country. The Guatemalan and United States rooms share a large bathroom; however, these can easily be joined to form one larger suite. The Mexican room is wheelchair accessible. Each room has its own private patio. The villas are quite spacious and luxurious. My favorite is the Japanese unit, with it's subtle design touches and great woodwork. The Russian villa is truly wheelchair accessible and -equipped.

Dining: Breakfasts here are a full four-course affair.

Amenities: There's a small pool, horseshoe and shuffleboard courts, and the beach is about 91 meters (100 yd.) away through the trees.

Moderate

Hotel El Milagro. Playa Tamarindo (Apdo. 145-5150, Santa Cruz), Guanacaste. ☎ **506/ 653-0042.** Fax 506/653-0050. www.elmilagro.com. E-mail: elmilagro@elmilagro.com. 32 units. $55 double with fan, $60 double with A/C; lower in the off-season. Rates include breakfast buffet. AE, MC, V.

This place started out as a restaurant but has expanded into an attractive little hotel on the edge of town. It's located across the road from the beach, and the rooms are lined up in two long rows facing each other behind the restaurant. The front wall of each room is made of louvered doors that open onto small semicircular patios. Pretty gardens and some big old shade trees make El Milagro even more attractive. The restaurant serves well-prepared seafood and continental dishes, and there's a swimming pool with a swim-up bar. There's also a children's pool. Various tours and excursions can be arranged through the hotel.

Hotel Pasatiempo. Playa Tamarindo, Santa Cruz, Guanacaste. ☎ **506/653-0096.** Fax 506/653-0275. www.hotelpasatiempo.com. E-mail: passtime@racsa.co.cr. 11 units. A/C. Dec 15–May 1 $59 double; May 2–Dec 14 $49 double. A/C $10 extra. AE, MC, V.

A great value, this hotel is set back from the beach a couple of hundred yards in a grove of shady trees. The guest rooms are housed in duplex buildings, but each room has its own private patio with a hammock or chairs. There's plenty of space in every room, and some even sleep five people. Each room bears the name of a different beach, and the bedroom walls all have hand-painted murals. A small yet very inviting pool sits in the center of the five duplexes. The last time I visited, there were plans to add 10 more rooms. **Pacho's Restaurant and Bar** serves excellent fresh fish, as well as Cajun, Thai, and Tex-Mex specialties. This popular rancho-style affair also has a pool table, nightly happy hour, cable television with live sporting events, good snacks, and occasional live music. This place gets loud and lively, especially on weekends, so it may be hard to get an early night's sleep if you're staying in one of the rooms close by.

Inexpensive

In addition to the Hotel El Bucanero in Playa Grande and the cabinas listed below, there's **Tito's Camping,** located out toward the Hotel Capitan Suizo in Tamarindo. It costs $2.50 per person.

Cabinas Marielos. Playa Tamarindo, Guanacaste. ☎ and fax **506/653-0141.** 17 units. $30 double, $40 triple, $45 quad. V.

This place is located down a palm-shaded driveway across the road from the beach. Rooms are clean and fairly new, though small and simply furnished. Patios have tile floors and wooden chairs. Some of the bathrooms don't have doors, but they're clean. There's a kitchen that guests can use, and the garden provides a bit of shade. The hotel provides a laundry service and can arrange turtle tours and horseback riding; they also rent surfboards. All in all, this is probably the best budget option in town.

Cabinas Zully Mar. Tamarindo, Guanacaste. ☎ **506/653-0140** or 506/226-4732. Fax 506/653-0028. E-mail: zullymar@racsa.co.cr. 46 units. $30–$55 double, $40–$65 triple. AE, MC, V.

The Zully Mar has long been a favorite of budget travelers staying in Tamarindo. The newer rooms, which are in a two-story, white-stucco building with a wide, curving staircase on the outside, have air-conditioning and are more comfortable. The doors to these guest rooms are hand-carved with pre-Columbian motifs. These rooms also have tile floors, long verandas, overhead or standing fans, and large bathrooms. The older, less expensive rooms are smaller, darker, and have soft foam mattresses. The newest addition here is a small free-form pool, although there's not much landscaping or shade around it. Miles of beach are just across the street.

IN PLAYA GRANDE

Hotel El Bucanero. Playa Grande, Guanacaste. ☎ and fax **506/653-0480.** 8 units. $35 double, $40 triple, $45 quad. V (add 6% surcharge).

This new hotel is a good choice in Playa Grande. The rooms are all clean and cool, with tile floors and private bathrooms. The rooms come in several sizes and a mix of bed arrangements: several singles, a double and a single, two doubles—take your pick or mix and match. Three of the rooms have air-conditioning. The hotel's restaurant and bar, which is located on the second floor of the octagonal main building, serves reasonably priced seafood dishes and Tico standards, but the best part about it is the fact that it's an open-air affair and gets a nice breeze. The hotel is located about 91 meters (100 yd.) from the beach.

✪ **Las Tortugas Hotel.** Apdo. 164, Playa Grande, Guanacaste. ☎ and fax **506/ 653-0458,** or 506/653-0423. www.cool.co.cr/usr/turtles. E-mail: nela@cool.co.cr. 11 units. A/C. $70 double, $125 suite; slightly higher during peak weeks, lower in the off-season. V (add 5% surcharge).

Playa Grande is best known for the leatherback turtles that nest here, and much of the beach is now part of Las Baulas National Park, which was created to protect the turtles. However, this beach is also very popular with surfers, who make up a large percentage of the clientele at this beachfront hotel. Several of the rooms are quite large, and most have interesting stone floors and shower stalls. The upper suite has a curving staircase that leads up to its second room. The owners led the fight to have the area declared a national park and continue to do everything possible to protect the turtles. The hotel's restaurant serves well-prepared local and continental dishes. As part of the hotel's turtle-friendly design, a natural wall of shrubs and trees shields the beach from the restaurant's light and noise. There's also a small bar, a turtle-shaped swimming pool, and a Jacuzzi. A few canoes on the nearby estuary are available for gentle paddling among the mangroves. Las Tortugas also manages some nearby houses for longer stays.

DINING

In addition to the restaurants listed below, **Nogui's Sunset Café** (☎ 506/653-0029) is one of the most popular places in town—and rightly so. This simple open-air cafe is just off the beach on the small traffic circle and serves hearty breakfasts and well-prepared salads, sandwiches, and quiche for lunch. The **Blue Maxx Cafe** (☎ 506/ 653-0647), located right beside Nogui's, is a great spot for filling breakfasts, creative lunches, and a wide range of fresh fruit and fancy coffee drinks. **Stella's** (☎ 506/ 653-0127), located 183 meters (200 yd.) beyond Pasatiempo, is a local favorite for Italian food and fresh-baked pizzas. **Soda Natural,** next to Coconut Café, is also a good, inexpensive spot for breakfast and lunch. Finally, there's **Pedro's Fish Shack,** just a basic wooden shanty on the beach, just beyond Nogui's, where I've had some of the freshest fish dinners of my life. For vegetarian fare, check out **Arco Iris** (☎ 506/ 653-0330). If you're coming from Tamarindo Center, Arco Iris is located up a side street to the right just beyond Hotel Pasatiempo.

In addition, I've been getting raves about the five-course dinners being cooked up at **Sueño del Mar,** located on Playa Langosta (☎ 506/653-0284). The menu changes nightly, and you'll definitely need a reservation in the high season.

Cantina Las Olas. On the side road toward Punta Langosta before Iguana Surf. ☎ 506/ 653-0087. Reservations not necessary. Main courses $3–$8. No credit cards. Sun–Fri 6pm–midnight (kitchen closes at 9:30pm). MEXICAN.

A real bargain, this casual open-air restaurant is painted in light blue pastel, with bright geometric designs for trim. There's a large and popular bar in the back and a pool table off to the side. Dining is at one of the three wooden picnic tables or several smaller bare-wood tables. The tacos, burritos, and fajitas are all well-prepared Tex-Mex standards and come with a very spicy hot sauce on the side. There are even several vegetarian entrees. I recommend the fish burritos, but ask about the nightly specials, which might feature blackened fish tacos or shrimp enchiladas. Wash the whole thing down with some mango margaritas. Since this is a surfer hangout, you can expect surf videos and loud rock-and-roll or reggae music.

Coconut Café. On the left as you come into town. ☎ and fax **506/653-0086.** Reservations not necessary. Main courses $7–$25. V. Daily 6–11pm. INTERNATIONAL.

This is one of Tamarindo's more atmospheric restaurants. A thatch roof, wicker furniture, and fresh flower arrangements all set on a raised deck add up to a gringo fantasy of the tropics. With a host of nightly specials, the Coconut Café has long served some of the most creative food in town, including such dishes as red chicken curry, mahimahi teriyaki, shrimp brochettes, and fondue. However, I do have two caveats here: Food quality and service have been spotty on my most recent visits, and the very dusty road is only a few feet away.

Fiesta del Mar. At the end of the main road. No phone. Main courses $4–$15. No credit cards. Daily 8am–11pm. STEAK/SEAFOOD.

Another bargain spot, the Fiesta del Mar is located across the circle from the beach and specializes in steaks and seafood cooked over a wood fire. Try the grilled steak in garlic sauce for $7 or the whole fried fish for $5. The open-air dining area is edged with greenery and has a thatch roof, so it feels very tropical. There's even live music several nights a week.

✪ **La Meridiana.** About 100m (109 yd.) off the main road, turn left just before Zully Mar. ☎ and fax **506/653-0230.** Reservations recommended in the high season. Main courses $12–$24. AE, MC, V. Daily 6–11pm. ITALIAN.

Loosen your belt a notch and prepare for some very good Italian food at this elegant family-run place. The restaurant, which takes up most of the terraced outdoor patio of a large house, is surrounded by lush gardens and a pool down below. Tables are set with linen tablecloths and plenty of silverware. Ceiling fans keep things cool and the entire affair is casually elegant. The extensive menu covers all the bases with a wide range of antipasti, pasta, meat, and seafood to choose from. The fish is fresh (dorado, tuna, and snapper are usually on hand) and can be done *al limone, alla siciliana,* or *al vino bianco.* The *filetto tartufato* is a tender piece of tenderloin in a truffle-butter sauce.

But don't rush past the pastas. The house tagliatelle is a delicious seafood pasta in a light cream sauce, the gnocchi come in delicate medaillons, and the homemade ravioli with lobster is to die for. The wine list features a wide range of Italian vintages including some very high end offerings. Whether or not you choose one of the delicious desserts, you should definitely wash everything down with a glass of *grappa,* which is a contraband brew made by an uncle somewhere in northern Italy.

EN ROUTE SOUTH: PLAYA AVELLANAS & PLAYA NEGRA

As you head south from Tamarindo you will come to several as yet underdeveloped beaches, most of which are quite popular with surfers. Beyond Tamarindo and Playa Langosta are **Playa Avellanas** and then **Playa Negra,** both of which have a few basic cabinas catering to surfers.

ACCOMMODATIONS

Hotel Playa Negra. Apdo. 31, Santa Cruz, Guanacaste. ☎ **506/382-1301.** Fax 506/ 382-1302. www.playanegra.com. E-mail: playaneg@racsa.co.cr. 10 bungalows. $60 double, $70 triple, $80 quad. AE, MC, V.

This collection of thatch-roofed bungalows is right in front of the famous Playa Negra point break. Even if you're not a surfer, the beach and coast along this area are beautiful, with coral and rock outcroppings and calm tide pools. The round bungalows each have one queen and two single beds, two desks, a ceiling fan, and a private bathroom. Although they have concrete floors, everything is painted in contrasting pastels and feels quite comfortable. The restaurant is out by the oval pool in a large open-air rancho. It also serves as a social hub for guests and surfers staying at more-basic cabinas inland from the beach.

✪ **Mono Congo Lodge.** Apdo. 177-5150, Santa Cruz, Guanacaste. ☎ and fax **506/ 382-6926.** wsurf@racsa.co.cr. 6 units, 5 with bathroom. $35–$40 double, $75 guest house. No credit cards.

This overgrown jungle house has morphed into a popular surf and nature lodge. The main house is a huge three-story affair that is almost entirely open—no exterior walls—and has the feel of a giant tree house. There are ample open areas for lounging on both the second and third floors, where you'll find the basic but clean and comfortable rooms; the beds have mosquito netting. Off the main building you'll find the separate two-bedroom guest house, which is more swank, with its arched door and rounded windows, full kitchen, and tile floors. The restaurant is in the main building and serves three meals daily, with nightly dinner specials. The owners are friendly and have horses available for riding. There's even a clay tennis court here, as well as plans to put in a pool. The hotel is about a 10-minute walk from Playa Negra through Pacific dry forest.

7 Playa Junquillal

18¹/₂ miles (30km) W of Santa Cruz; 12¹/₂ miles (20km) S of Tamarindo

Playa Junquillal (pronounced Hoon-key-*al*) is a long, windswept beach that, for most of its length, is backed by grasslands. This gives it a very different feel from other beaches on this coast. There's really no village to speak of here, so if you're heading out this way, plan on getting away from it all. In fact, if you're looking to leave the maddening crowds behind and want some unfettered time on a nearly deserted beach, this is a great choice. The long beach is great for strolling, and the sunsets are superb. When the waves are up and the sea is rough, this beach can be a little dangerous for swimming. When it's calm, jump right on in

ESSENTIALS

GETTING THERE & DEPARTING   By Plane   The nearest airport with regularly scheduled flights is in Tamarindo. You can arrange a taxi from the airport to Playa Junquillal. The ride should take 45 minutes and costs about $40.

By Bus   An express bus (☎ **506/221-7202**) leaves San José daily at 2pm from the corner of Calle 20 and Avenida 3. The trip takes 5¹/₂ hours; the one-way fare is $5.

Alternately, you can take a bus to Santa Cruz (see "Playas Flamingo, Potrero, Brasilito & Conchal," earlier in this chapter, for details), and from there, take a bus to Playa Junquillal. Buses leave Santa Cruz for Junquillal at 10am, and 12:30, 2:30, and 5:30pm. The ride takes 1¹/₂ hours, and the one-way fare is $1.25.

The one express bus to San José departs Playa Junquillal daily at 5am. There are also daily buses to Santa Cruz departing at 5 and 6am, noon, and 2pm.

By Car   Take the Interamerican Highway from San José. Twenty-nine miles (47km) past the turnoff for Puntarenas, turn left toward the **Tempisque River Ferry** (☎ **506/661-8105**). The ferry operates continually (at about 20-min. intervals), 24 hours a day. The fare is $3 per car, with an additional fee of 35¢ per passenger. The ferries that ply this crossing are quite small, and on busy days you may have to wait for several crossings before making it onboard. After crossing the Tempisque River, continue north through Nicoya to Santa Cruz. In Santa Cruz, head west 8¹/₂ miles (14km) to the town of 27 de Abril, which is where the pavement ends. From here it's another rough 11 miles (18km) to Playa Junquillal.

WHAT TO DO IN JUNQUILLAL

Other than walking on the beach, swimming when the surf isn't too strong, and exploring tide pools, there isn't much to do here, which is just fine with me. This beach is ideal for anyone who just wants to relax without any distractions. Bring a few good books. The larger hotels here—**Antumalal, Iguanazul,** and **Villa Serena**—all offer plenty of activities and facilities, including volleyball, swimming pools, and/or tennis courts. Sportfishing trips can also be arranged at most hotels. At the Iguanazul, guests can rent bikes, which is a good way to get up and down to the beach; horseback-riding tours are also popular.

If you're a surfer, the beach break right in Junquillal is sometimes pretty good. I've also heard that if you look hard enough, there are a few hidden reef and point breaks around.

Finally, if you want to do some **diving,** check in with Micke and Maarten at **El Lugarcito** (☎ and fax **506/653-0436;** E-mail: lugarcito@racsa.co.cr). These folks offer day trips to the Catalina Islands as well as resort and full certification courses.

ACCOMMODATIONS & DINING

Most of the hotels listed below have their own restaurants, and guests usually take their meals right where they're staying. You can get good Italian meals, homemade pasta, and fresh seafood at **La Puerta del Sol** (☎ **506/653-0442**), which is located right in front of the beach as you come into Junquillal.

EXPENSIVE

Hotel Antumalal. Playa Junquillal (Apdo. 49-5150, Santa Cruz), Guanacaste. ☎ and fax **506/653-0425.** www.hotelantumalal.co.cr. E-mail: antumal@racsa.co.cr. 30 units. $95 double, $110 suite. AE, MC, V.

Located at the end of the road into Playa Junquillal, the Antumalal is the most extensive and oldest hotel on the beach. However, everything is well maintained. The big, old shade trees and lush gardens create a world of tropical tranquillity that's perfect for romance and relaxation. Guest rooms are all in duplex buildings with stucco walls on the outside and murals on the inside. Out front, you'll find a big patio with a hammock, while inside there are brick floors and big bathrooms. The suites are located in a large two-story building closer to the beach; each suite has a sitting room, kitchenette, and lots of space. Oddly, the views are best from those on the ground floor, at least until the many coconut palms grow a bit more. Right now, the second-floor balconies put you right at the level of the palm fronds, which largely block the view of the sea.

Dining/Diversions: The main dining room is housed under a huge high-peaked rancho that has a fascinating driftwood chandelier hanging from the ceiling. The menu includes plenty of good Italian dishes, as well as fresh seafood and Tico standards. There's a bar up in the original dining room and another beside the pool. During the high season, they sometimes crank up another restaurant/grill down near the pool area.

Amenities: The swimming pool, with its swim-up bar, is only a few steps from the beach and is beautiful at night when the underwater lights are on. There is also a tennis court, horseback riding, and boat charters for fishing and scuba diving.

MODERATE

Hotel Villa Serena. Playa Junquillal (Apdo. 37-5150, Santa Cruz), Guanacaste. ☎ and fax **506/653-0430.** E-mail: serenaho@racsa.co.cr. 12 units. $56 double; lower in the off-season. MC, V.

Villa Serena is directly across the street from the beach and has long been a popular choice in Playa Junquillal. The hotel changed owners a couple of years ago and received a major refurbishing in the process. Each of the individual bungalows is surrounded by neatly manicured lawns and gardens. The rooms are quite spacious and have ceiling fans, dressing rooms, and large bathrooms. Each has its own covered patio, and only steps away is the small pool. The hotel's main building houses the second-floor Land Ho Restaurant, which serves filling and tasty continental and Tico dishes, with an enticing view of the sea.

✪ **Iguanazul Hotel.** Playa Junquillal (Apdo. 130-1550, Santa Cruz), Guanacaste. ☎ and fax **506/653-0123,** or 506/653-0124. www.iguanazul.com. E-mail: info@iguanazul.com. 24 units. $70–$90 double, $80–$100 triple. Rates include continental breakfast. AE, MC, V.

Set on a windswept, grassy bluff above a rocky beach, Iguanazul is far from the crowds. Originally catering to surfers, this is definitely a spot for sun worshippers who like to have a good time, and the clientele tends to be young and active. The pool is large, as is the surrounding patio area, and there's a volleyball court. However, that's not to say you can't relax here. Head down to one of the quiet coves or grab a hammock set in a covered palapa on the hillside. Don't, however, expect a tropical setting; grasslands surround the hotel, which gives the area the feel of Cape Cod or the Outer Banks. Guest rooms are nicely decorated with basket lamp shades, wicker furniture, red-tile floors, high ceilings, and blue-and-white–tile bathrooms. The higher prices are for air-conditioned rooms, and two of these even have televisions.

There are plenty of things to do around here. You can rent horses, bikes, and body boards. Captain Gene runs sportfishing charters out of the hotel, and there are board games, dartboards, and table tennis for those who've had a little too much sun and sea. The hotel maintains a little gift shop. Even if you're not staying here, this is a good place to dine; the food is excellent and the sunsets are phenomenal.

INEXPENSIVE

In addition to the lodgings listed below, **Camping Los Malinches** (☎ **506/653-0429**) has wonderful campsites on fluffy grass, amid manicured gardens, set on a bluff above the beach. Camping will run you $5 per person, and the fee entitles you to bathroom and shower privileges. You'll see a sign on the right as you drive toward Playa Junquillal, a little bit beyond the Iguanazul Hotel. The campground is located about half a mile (1km) down this dirt road.

Hibiscus Hotel. Playa Junquillal (Apdo. 163-5150, Santa Cruz), Guanacaste. ☎ and fax **506/653-0437.** 5 units. $40 double, $50 triple. Rates include continental breakfast. V.

Though the accommodations here are very simple, the friendly German owner makes sure that everything is always clean and in top shape. The grounds are pleasantly shady, and the beach is just across the road. The rooms have cool Mexican-tile floors and firm beds. For years now, I've been getting glowing reports about both the service and general ambiance. A restaurant has recently been added, specializing in fresh seafood at reasonable prices.

Hotel El Castillo Divertido. Playa Junquillal, Santa Cruz, Guanacaste. ☎ and fax **506/653-0428.** 7 units. $35 double; slightly lower in the off-season. AE, MC, V.

This fanciful hotel is for people who come to Costa Rica from around the world in hopes of living out fantasy lives impossible in their home countries. Built by a young German, it's a tropical rendition of a classic medieval castle (well, sort of). Ramparts and a turret with a rooftop bar certainly grab the attention of passersby. Guest rooms here are fairly small, though rates are also some of the lowest in the area. Ask for an upstairs room with a balcony. If you don't get one of these, you'll still have a good view from the hotel's rooftop bar. The hotel is about 500 meters (545 yd.) from the beach. They've recently added a restaurant serving international cuisine, which often features live music.

8 Playa Nosara

34 miles (55km) SW of Nicoya; 165 miles (266km) W of San José

Playa Nosara is actually several beaches, almost all of which are nearly deserted most of the time. Because the village of Nosara is several kilometers from the beach, and because the land near the beach has been turned into a large spread-out resort community, Nosara has been spared the sort of ugly, uncontrolled growth characteristic of many other Guanacaste beaches. All of the hotels are spread out and most are tucked away down side roads. There is not the hotels-on-top-of-hotels feeling that you get at Playas Flamingo, Tamarindo, or Coco. In fact, on first arriving here, it's hard to believe there are any hotels around at all. Nosara has long been popular with North American retirees and a handful of Hollywood celebrities, and they too have made sure that their homes are not crammed cheek-by-jowl in one spot, hiding them instead among the profusion of trees that make Nosara one of the greenest spots on the Nicoya Peninsula. So, if you're looking for reliably sunny weather and a bit of tropical greenery, this is a good bet.

The best way to get to Nosara is to fly; however, with everything so spread out, that makes getting around once you've arrived difficult. The roads to and in Nosara are in horrendous shape, and though there has long been talk of some sections being widened and paved, it will probably still be quite a few years before the blacktop reaches here.

ESSENTIALS

GETTING THERE & DEPARTING   By Plane   Sansa (☎ **506/221-9414;** fax 506/255-2176; E-mail: reservations@flysansa.com) has one flight daily to Nosara, departing from San José's Juan Santamaría International Airport at 11:30am. Flight duration is 50 minutes; the fare is $60 each way. Taxis are waiting for every arrival; fares range between $4 and $7 to most hotels.

The return Sansa flight to San José departs Nosara daily at 12:20pm.

By Bus   An express bus (☎ **506/222-2666**) leaves San José daily at 6am from Calle 14 between avenidas 3 and 5. The trip's duration is 6¹/₂ hours; the one-way fare is $6.50.

You can also take a bus from San José to Nicoya (see "Playa Sámara," below, for details) and then catch a second bus from Nicoya to Nosara. A bus leaves Nicoya for Nosara daily at 1pm. Trip duration is 3 hours; the one-way fare is $1.25.

The bus to San José leaves daily at 12:45pm. The bus to Nicoya leaves daily at 6am. Buses leave Nicoya for San José daily at 5, 7, and 9am, noon, and 2:30 and 5pm.

By Car   Follow the directions above for getting to Playa Sámara but watch for a well-marked fork in the road a few kilometers before you reach that beach. The right-hand fork leads, after another 13¹/₂ miles (22km) of terrible road, to Nosara.

ORIENTATION   The village of Nosara is about 3 miles (5km) inland from the beach; however, most of the hotels listed here are on the beach itself.

FUN ON & OFF THE BEACH

There are several beaches at Nosara, including the long, curving **Playa Guiones, Playa Nosara,** and, my personal favorite, diminutive **Playa Pelada.** Pelada is a short white-sand beach lined with sea grasses and mangroves. However, there isn't too much sand at high tide, so you'll want to hit the beach when the tide's out. At either end of the beach there are rocky outcroppings that reveal tide pools at low tide. Surfing and bodysurfing are both good here; Playa Guiones in particular is garnering quite a reputation as a consistent and rideable beach break. Because the village of Nosara is several miles inland, these beaches are very clean, secluded, and quiet.

When evening rolls around, don't expect a major party scene. Nightlife in Nosara seems to be limited to the two bars located across from each other by the town's soccer field.

FISHING CHARTERS & OTHER OUTDOOR ACTIVITIES   Most of the hotels in the area can arrange fishing charters for $250 to $400 for a half day or $450 to $800 for a full day. These rates are for one to four people and vary according to boat size and accoutrements. You can also contact **Grand Slam Charters** (☎ 506/682-0012) or **Black Marlin Sportfishing** (☎ 506/682-0059; www.blackmarlinfishing.com) to arrange a fishing trip. This latter outfit is tied in to the new Harbor Reef Lodge, and can also arrange guided horseback and kayak tours, as well as private or group surfing lessons.

BIRD & SEA TURTLE WATCHING   Bird-watchers should explore the mangrove swamps around the estuary mouth of the Río Nosara. Just walk north from Playa Pelada and follow the riverbank; explore the paths into the mangroves.

If you time your trip right, you can do a night tour to nearby **Playa Ostional** to watch nesting olive Ridley sea turtles. These turtles come ashore by the thousands in a mass egg-laying phenomenon known as an *arribada*. These arribadas take place 4 to 10 times between July and November; each occurrence lasts between 3 and 10 days. Consider yourself very lucky if you happen to be around during one of these fascinating natural phenomena. Even if it's not turtle-nesting season, you might still want to look into visiting Playa Ostional, just to have a long, wide expanse of beach to yourself. However, be careful swimming here, as the surf and riptides can be formidable. During the dry season (mid-November through April), you can usually get here in a regular car, but during the rainy season you'll need four-wheel drive. This beach is part of Ostional National Wildlife Refuge. At the northwest end of the refuge is **India Point,** which is known for its tide pools and rocky outcrops.

ACCOMMODATIONS

Almost Paradise. Playa Nosara (Apdo. 15-5233, Bocas de Nosara), Guanacaste. ☎ and fax **506/682-0173.** www.nosara.net. E-mail: almostparadise@iname.com. 6 units. $30–$45 double. Rates includes breakfast. V.

Located on the hill above Playa Pelada, this delightful little hotel is aptly named. This older wood building is a welcome relief from all the concrete and cinder block so common in Costa Rican construction. The rooms are simple and clean and feature colorful local artwork. All have access to an inviting covered veranda with strung hammocks and an ocean view. The newest addition here is a small lap pool. The

Livin' La Vida Yoga

If you'd like to combine a stay in Nosara with a more spiritual experience, check out the **Nosara Retreat** (☎ 888/803-0580 in the U.S., or 506/682-0071; www.nosarayoga.com; E-mail: yogacr@racsa.co.cr), which is a yoga retreat run by former instructors at the Kripalu Center. Rates here run between $250 and $350 per person per day, including room and board and yoga classes.

attached restaurant and bar are perennially popular, and feature German and other international cuisines.

Cabinas Chorotega. Nosara, Guanacaste. ☎ **506/682-0129.** 8 units, 2 with bathroom. $10–$15 double. No credit cards.

Located on the outskirts of Nosara village, Cabinas Chorotega is about 3 miles (5km) from the beach, so you'll need a car if you want to go to the beach. The rooms are very basic but clean, and the rooms with private bathrooms are a particularly good value. Some rooms have more windows and are quite a bit brighter than others, so look at a couple before you settle in.

Estancia Nosara. Playa Nosara (Apdo. 37, Bocas de Nosara), Guanacaste. ☎ and fax **506/682-0178.** www.nosara.com. E-mail: estancia@nosara.com. 8 units. $35 double, $40 triple, $50 quad. Rates include breakfast. MC, V.

Although Estancia Nosara is a mile or so from the beach (located inland on the main road heading toward town and the airport), it's set amid shady jungle trees and has a swimming pool and tennis court. There's an artificial waterfall tumbling from a small hill of stones near the pool and reproductions of pre-Columbian stone statues in the lush garden. The guest rooms are in two buildings and have red-tile floors, kitchenettes, high ceilings, overhead fans, showers, and plenty of closet space. There's a large open-air restaurant that serves moderately priced meals; the hotel also rents out horses, boogie boards, snorkeling equipment, and bikes.

Hotel Villa Taype. Playa Nosara (Apdo. 8-5233, Bocas de Nosara), Guanacaste. ☎ **506/682-0188.** Fax 506/682-0187. www.villataype.com. E-mail: info@villataype.com. 12 units, 7 bungalows. A/C. $60 double, $70 triple, $80 bungalow. Rates include breakfast buffet. AE, MC, V.

This sprawling hotel is located down a side road that leads from the main road to Playa Guiones. The room decor is simple but attractive, with white-tile floors, high ceilings, overhead fans, and well-designed bathrooms. All the rooms have patios, but the bungalows are a little larger and each has its own little *ranchito,* with a sitting area and hammock. The dining room, with its wood ceiling and arched windows overlooking the pool, serves moderately priced meals; the swimming pool has a swim-up bar. There's also a tennis court here, and you can rent body boards, surfboards, tennis rackets, and snorkeling gear. Best of all, the beach is only 91 meters (100 yd.) away. During the high season, they even open a small disco here, which can get quite lively.

Nosara Beach Hotel. Playa Nosara (Apdo. 4, Bocas de Nosara), Guanacaste. ☎ **506/682-0121.** Fax 506/682-0123. www.nosarabeachhotel.com. E-mail: vailas@racsa.co.cr. 16 units. $30–$60 double. AE, DC, MC, V.

Perched high on a hill above both Playa Pelada and Playa Guiones, this hotel has the best views in the area, if not necessarily the best accommodations. In the 7 years I've been visiting, the place has always had the feeling of someone's unfinished backyard project. And it still does. There's a six-story tower with an onion-dome on top, looking something like "Gaudy-Goes-Russian-Orthodox." While this is the best place to take in the amazing sunsets, it's not yet finished. However, the large kidney-shaped pool is finally open and work is actually nearing completion on most of the rooms and surrounding landscaping. Most of the rooms have balconies overlooking either Playa Guiones or Playa Pelada. They are simple and clean, and most are quite spacious. The restaurant holds a high perch over Playa Pelada and serves good seafood and continental cuisine.

You can brush up or start up your Spanish in Nosara at the **Rey de Nosara Language School** (☎ and fax **506/682-0215;** www.nosara.com). They offer group and private lessons according to demand, and can coordinate week or multiweek packages according to your needs.

DINING

In addition to the place mentioned below, I've been getting rave reviews about the Italian food found at **La Dolce Vita** (☎ **506/682-0107**), located on the main road into town, about 1¼ miles (2km) before the sign BIENVENIDOS A PLAYAS DE NOSARA. For light meals, pizzas, and fresh baked goods, stop in at **Café de Paris** (☎ **506/682-0087;** www.cafedeparis.net), which also rents out a few rooms.

Doña Olga's. On the beach at Playa Pelada. No phone. Main courses $3–$15. No credit cards. Daily 6:30am–10pm. COSTA RICAN.

Little more than a roof over a concrete slab, with some tables in between, Olga's is still one of the most popular restaurants in Nosara. Gringos and Ticos alike hang out here, savoring fried-fish casados, sandwiches, and breakfasts that include huge helpings of bacon. On the weekends the cavernous structure beside the restaurant becomes a lively disco.

9 Playa Sámara

21½ miles (35km) S of Nicoya; 152 miles (245km) W of San José

Playa Sámara is a pretty beach on a long, horseshoe-shaped bay. Unlike most of the rest of the Pacific coast, the water here is excellent for swimming, since an offshore island and rocky headlands break up most of the surf. Because Playa Sámara is easily accessible by bus or car along a well-paved road, and because there are quite a few cheap cabinas, *sodas,* and a raging disco here, this beach is popular both with families seeking a quick and inexpensive getaway and with young Ticos out for a weekend of beach partying. In the wake of this heavy traffic, the beach can get trashed; however, the calm waters and steep cliffs on the far side of the bay make this a very attractive spot, and the beach is long and wide. Directly behind the main beach is a wide, flat valley that stretches inland and to the north.

ESSENTIALS

GETTING THERE & DEPARTING   By Plane   Sansa (☎ **506/221-9414;** fax 506/255-2176; E-mail: reservations@flysansa.com) flies to Carillo (15 min. south of Sámara) daily at 7:30 and 11:30am from San José's Juan Santamaría International Airport. The flight takes 1 hour; the fare is $60 each way.

Travelair (☎ **506/220-3054;** fax 506/220-0413; E-mail: reservations@travelair-costarica.com) flies to Carillo daily at 1pm from Tobías Bolaños International Airport in Pavas. The flight takes 50 minutes; the fare is $82 one-way, $134 round-trip.

Most hotels will arrange to pick you up in Carillo. If not, you'll have to hire a cab for between $8 and $10.

Sansa flights leave Carillo for San José at 8:40am and 12:40pm. Travelair flies out of Carillo daily at 1:50.

By Bus   An express bus (☎ **506/222-2666**) leaves San José daily at 12:30pm from Calle 14 between avenidas 3 and 5. The trip lasts 6 hours; the one-way fare is $6.

Alternately, you can take a bus from this same San José station to Nicoya and then catch a second bus from Nicoya to Sámara. Buses leave San José for Nicoya daily at 6:30, 8, and 10am and 1, 2, 3, and 5pm. The trip takes 5 hours; the fare is $4. Buses leave Nicoya for Sámara and Carillo daily at 8am, 3pm, and 4pm. The trip's duration is 1¹/₂ hours. The fare to Sámara is $1.25; fare to Carillo is $1.50.

The express bus to San José leaves daily at 4am. Buses for Nicoya leave daily at 5:30am, 7:30am, 1:30pm, and 4:30pm. Buses leave Nicoya for San José daily at 5am, 7am, 9am, noon, 2:30pm, and 5pm.

By Car   Take the Interamerican Highway from San José. Twenty-nine miles (47km) past the turnoff for Puntarenas, turn left toward the Tempisque ferry. The ferry operates 24 hours a day (at approximately 20-min. intervals) and costs about $3 per car and driver, with a nominal 35¢ fee per passenger. The ferries that ply this crossing are quite small, and on busy days you may have to wait for several crossings before making it onboard. After crossing the Tempisque River, continue north to Nicoya. In Nicoya, head more or less straight through town until you see signs for Playa Sámara. From here it's a paved road almost all the way to the beach (rumor has it that the road is paved because an important government official has a beach house here). Alternately, you can reach Nicoya via Liberia. This route is longer but comes in handy when the ferry is down or extremely busy.

ORIENTATION   Sámara is a busy little town at the bottom of a steep hill. The main road heads straight into town, passing the soccer field before coming to an end at the beach. Just before the beach is a road to the left that leads to most of the hotels listed below. This road also leads to Playa Carillo and the Guanamar Resort

FUN ON & OFF THE BEACH

Aside from sitting on the sand and soaking up the sun, the main activities in Playa Sámara seem to be hanging out in the *sodas* and dancing into the early morning hours. If you stay close to the center of town (by the soccer field), expect to stay up until the disco closes down.

You'll find that the beach is nicer and cleaner down at the south end, near **Las Brisas del Pacífico** hotel. The masses don't usually head south to **Playa Carillo,** a long, flat beach about 20 minutes from Sámara, but if you want a bit more desolation, check it out.

CAVING   Cavers will want to head 38¹/₂ miles (62km) northeast of Playa Sámara on the road to the Tempisque ferry. If you don't have a car, your best bet is to get to Nicoya, which is about half an hour away by bus, and then take a taxi to the park, which should cost about $12. Here, at **Barra Honda National Park,** there's an extensive system of caves, some of which reach more than 200 meters (218 yd.) in depth. Human remains and indigenous relics have been found in other caves, but these are not open to the public. Since this is a national park, you'll have to pay the $6 entrance fee. If you plan to descend the one publicly accessible cave, you'll also need to rent (or bring your own) equipment and hire a local guide at the park entrance station. Expect to pay around $50 to $60 per person for a visit to the Terciopelo Cave. Furthermore, the cave is open only during the dry season (mid-Nov through Apr). Inside you'll see plenty of impressive stalactites and stalagmites and enough bats to last you until the next *Batman* sequel. Even if you don't descend, the trails around Barra Honda and its prominent limestone plateau are great for hiking and bird-watching.

ACCOMMODATIONS
VERY EXPENSIVE

✪ **Hotel Punta Islita.** (Apdo. 242-1225, Plaza Mayor, San José), Playa Islita. ☎ **800/ 525-4800** in the U.S., or 506/231-6122 in Costa Rica. Fax 506/231-0715. www.hotelpuntaislita. com. E-mail: info@hotelpuntaislita.com. 37 units, 3 villas. A/C MINIBAR TV. $165 double, $220 junior suite, $275–$325 suite, $350–$500 villa. Rates include breakfast. AE, MC, V.

Set on a high bluff between two mountain ridges that meet the sea, Punta Islita is isolated and luxurious. The rooms here are done in a Santa Fe style, with red Mexican floor tiles, neo-Navajo print bedspreads, and calm adobe-colored walls offset with sky-blue doors and trim. Each room has a king-size bed, a stocked minibar, and a private patio with a hammock. The suites come with a separate sitting room and a private two-person Jacuzzi; the villas have two bedrooms, their own private swimming pools, and full kitchens. The beach below the hotel is a small crescent of gray-white sand with a calm, protected section at the northern end. It's about a 10-minute hike, but the hotel will shuttle you up and back if you don't feel like walking. There's even a small rancho bar down there for when you get thirsty. Although it's possible to drive here, most guests opt to fly into the nearby airstrip (see "Getting There," above). Punta Islita is just one beach down from Guanamar, but if you do drive, it's best to come over on the Naranjo ferry from Puntarenas and then up through Jicarral and Coyote.

Dining: Meals are all served in the large thatched rancho, which also houses the hotel's bar and sitting area. When you're this isolated, the meals better measure up, and so far Punta Islita has met the challenge. The emphasis is on fresh seafood in light nouvelle French sauces, but the steak in two-pepper sauce is also excellent

Amenities: The small tile pool and adjoining Jacuzzi are set on the edge of the bluff and create the illusion of blending into the ocean far below. The hotel also has two tennis courts, a small gym, a golf driving range, water-sports equipment, bicycle and four-by-four rentals, a conference center, a shuttle to the beach, a tour desk, a small gift shop, laundry service, and nightly turndown.

Villas Playa Sámara. Playa Sámara (Apdo. 111-1007, Centro Colón, San José), Guanacaste. ☎ **506/256-8228.** Fax 506/221-7222. E-mail: htlvilla@racsa.co.cr. 57 units. $149 double, $185–$225 quad. Off-season rates available. AE, MC, V.

Located 5 minutes south of town, right on the beach, this is the closest thing to a resort in Playa Sámara. Built to resemble a small village, the hotel consists of numerous villas varying in size from one to three bedrooms. The rooms are outfitted with bamboo furniture and have tiled bathrooms. All the villas have kitchens and patios, and some of the nicer touches include colorful bedspreads and artwork, basket lampshades, and vertical blinds on the windows. White-stucco exterior walls and red-tile roofs give the whole thing a Mediterranean look. However, this place has never been very successful, the upkeep and maintenance have been spotty, and service can be downright bad.

Dining: The open-air restaurant overlooks the pool and serves seafood, Tico, and Italian cuisine.

Amenities: Horse and bicycle rentals. A wide range of tours around the region can be arranged, as well as sportfishing and scuba diving. The swimming pool here is lit at night and has a swim-up bar and adjacent (unheated) whirlpool tub.

MODERATE

✪ **Hotel Las Brisas del Pacífico.** Playa Sámara (Apdo. 11917-1000, San José), Guanacaste. ☎ **506/656-0250.** Fax 506/656-0076. www.brisas.net. E-mail: labrisa@racsa.co.cr. 36 units. $60–$100 double. Rates lower in the off-season; higher during peak weeks. AE, MC, V.

Located on the southern end of Playa Sámara, this hotel is set amid very shady grounds right on a quiet section of the beach, and backs up on a steep hill. Most of the rooms are up a long and steep flight of stairs at the top of the hill and have large balconies and walls of glass that provide an excellent view of the bay. The third-floor rooms are the largest here, but the second-floor rooms actually have the best views. At the base of the hill, there are rooms in stucco duplexes with steeply pitched tile roofs and red-tile patios. The range in prices reflects the range in room size, location, and amenities. Some of the rooms have air-conditioning. There's a kidney-shaped pool on the hillside and another smaller one—as well as an unheated Jacuzzi—only a few steps from the beach. There are two restaurants here: The beachfront **Las Brisas** features Tico fare and international dishes at moderate prices; the hilltop **Puerta del Sol** serves up fancier Italian cuisine, fresh seafood, and stunning views.

INEXPENSIVE

In addition to the accommodations listed below, you'll find a slew of very inexpensive places to stay along the road into town and around the soccer field. Many of the rooms at these places are less accommodating than your average jail cell. As an alternative, you can pitch a tent right by the beach for a few dollars at **Camping Cocos,** where you can also use their basic showers and bathrooms. You'll find Camping Cocos about 400 meters (436 yd.) north of the center of town. It can be reached from the beach or from the main road heading north, parallel to the beach.

Hotel Giada. Playa Sámara, Nicoya, Guanacaste. ☎ **506/656-0132.** Fax 506/656-0131. www.hotelgiada.net. E-mail: htgiada@racsa.co.cr. 13 units. $40 double, $50 triple, $60 quad. Rates include breakfast. MC, V.

This neat little Italian-owned hotel is located on the left-hand side of the main road into town, about 150 meters (164 yd.) before the beach. The rooms are all very clean and comfortable and even have a small balcony. Breakfast is served in a cool, shady central gazebo. The newest additions here are a small pool and a Jacuzzi. The management is very helpful and can arrange diving or fishing expeditions and horseback-riding trips.

Hotel Marbella. Playa Sámara, Guanacaste. ☎ **506/656-0122.** Fax 506/656-0121. 14 units. $25–$40 double; weekly and off-season rates available. AE, MC, V.

Though it's about 183 meters (200 yd.) to the beach, and the immediate surroundings are none too appealing, this small German-run hotel is properly tropical in decor. You'll find the Marbella just around the corner from the road that leads down to the soccer fields and the beach. Guest rooms are fairly large and have red-tile floors and woven mats for ceilings. There are open closets and modern bathrooms with hot water. There's a small swimming pool in a gravel courtyard and a second-floor dining room with rattan chairs and a bamboo-fronted bar. All the rooms have a small balcony or porch, though not necessarily any sort of a view. The dining room serves reasonably priced Tico and international dishes. You'll also find a bar and lounge area here.

DINING

There are numerous inexpensive *sodas* in Sámara, and most of the hotels have their own dining rooms. If you want to eat overlooking the water, check out either **El Ancla** for seafood and Tico cuisine, or **El Delfin,** which serves pretty good French food. These two places are right next to each other on the beach, a little bit to the left of where the main road hits the beach. In town, try **Colocho's,** which is on the main street through town. There are four different types of ceviche, lobster dishes, paella, and plenty of shrimp plates. Prices are very reasonable and portions are large.

PLAYA SÁMARA AFTER DARK

Most of the nightlife in town is centered on the soccer field (located where the main road into town dead-ends into the sea). Here you'll find several very basic bars and a popular disco. The most popular place is **La Gondola Bar,** which has a pool table, dartboards, and board games. However, my favorite evening activity is still walking the long, wide expanse of beach and watching the stars.

10 Playa Tambor

93–104 miles (150–168km) W of San José (not including ferry ride); 12^1/$_2$ miles (20km) S of Paquera; 23^1/$_2$ miles (38km) S of Naranjo

Playa Tambor itself is a long scimitar of beach protected on either end by rocky head-lands. These headlands give the waters a certain amount of protection from Pacific swells, making this a good beach for swimming. However, the sand is a rather hard-packed, dull gray-brown color, which often receives a large amount of flotsam and jet-sam brought in by the sea. I find this beach much less attractive than those located farther south along the Nicoya Peninsula.

In 1993, Playa Tambor became the site of Costa Rica's first all-inclusive beach resort, the **Barceló Playa Tambor Beach Resort.** The original plans called for a sprawling mega-resort with several hotels. However, controversy and shifting fortunes have consistently plagued the project. In late 1999, Barceló inaugurated Los Delfines, a 60-villa condominium project and nine-hole golf course to complement its existing 402-room hotel. Despite all this development, the Tambor still has a forgotten, iso-lated feel to it.

ESSENTIALS

GETTING THERE & DEPARTING   By Plane   Sansa (☎ **506/221-9414;** fax 506/255-2176; E-mail: reservations@flysansa.com) flies twice daily to Tambor from San José's Juan Santamaría International Airport at 10am and 2:30pm. These flights depart for San José at 10:40am and 3:15pm. Flight duration is 30 minutes; the fare is $50 each way.

Travelair (☎ **506/220-3054;** fax 506/220-0413; E-mail: reservations@travelair-costarica.com) flies to Tambor daily at 11:30am from Tobías Bolaños International Airport in Pavas. Flight duration is 30 minutes; the fare is $69 one-way, $110 round-trip. The return flight leaves at 12:10pm.

By Bus & Ferry   If you're traveling from San José by public transportation, it takes two buses and a ferry ride to get to Tambor. If you miss your connections, you might have to spend the night in Puntarenas, so plan ahead and give yourself plenty of time.

Express buses (☎ **506/222-0064**) leave for Puntarenas from San José daily every 30 minutes between 6am and 9pm from Calle 16 and Avenida 12. Trip duration is 2 hours; the fare is $2.50.

From Puntarenas take the passenger launch **Paquereña** (☎ **506/661-2830**), which leaves from the pier behind the market at 6am, 11am, and 3pm. This passenger launch (*la lancha*) should not be confused with the several car ferries that also leave from Puntarenas, and you should always check the schedule before making plans. Ferry-trip duration is 1^1/$_2$ hours; the fare is $2. The bus south to Montezuma (this will drop you off in Tambor) will be waiting to meet the lancha when it arrives in Paquera. The bus ride takes about 45 minutes; the fare is $2.

When you're ready to head back, the Paquera bus, which originates in Montezuma, passes through Tambor at approximately 6am, 10:45am, and 2:45pm to meet the

Paquereña ferry, which leaves for Puntarenas at 8am, 12:30pm, and 5pm. Total trip duration is $3^1/2$ hours. Buses to San José leave Puntarenas daily every 30 minutes between 5:30am and 7pm.

By Car   Take the Interamerican Highway from San José to Puntarenas and catch either the Naranjo ferry or the Paquera ferry.

In 1998, a new company was given permission to operate a car ferry between Puntarenas and Paquera, easing some of the load on this popular route. Lines and waits are much shorter now, but I still recommend arriving a little bit early during the peak season and on weekends. **Ferries to Paquera** (Naviera Tambor: ☎ 506/661-2084; Paquera Ferry: ☎ 506/661-3674) leave daily at 5 and 8:45am and 12:30, 2, 5, and 8:15pm. The trip takes $1^1/2$ hours. The fare is around $10 for a car and driver; $1.50 for additional adults, $4 for adults in first class; $1 for children, and $2 for children in first class.

The **Naranjo ferry** (☎ 506/661-1069) leaves daily at 3, 7, and 10:50am and 2:50 and 7pm. The trip takes $1^1/2$ hours. The fare is $10 for cars, $1.50 for adults, and 75¢ for children.

The car ferry from Paquera to Puntarenas leaves daily at 6, 8, and 11:45am and 2:30, 6, and 8:30pm. The car ferry from Naranjo leaves at 5:10 and 8:50am and 12:50, 5, and 9pm.

Tambor is about 45 minutes south of Paquera and 2 hours south of Naranjo. The road from Paquera to Tambor was upgraded when the resort was built, and taking the Paquera ferry will save you time and some very rough, dusty driving. The road from Naranjo to Paquera is all dirt and gravel and in very bad shape.

ORIENTATION   Though there's a small village of Tambor, through which the main road passes, the hotels themselves are scattered along several kilometers. You'll see signs for these hotels as the road circles around Playa Tambor.

FUN ON & OFF THE BEACH

The Barceló Playa Tambor Beach Resort is an all-inclusive, full-service resort, so if you're staying here, you'll have access to all manner of beach toys. All the hotels listed below offer horseback riding and tours around this part of the peninsula and can arrange dive trips.

Curú Wildlife Refuge, 10 miles (16km) north of Tambor (☎ 506/661-2392), is a private reserve that has several pretty, secluded beaches, as well as forests and mangrove swamps. This area is extremely rich in wildlife. Howler and white-faced monkeys are often spotted here, as are quite a few species of birds. Admission for the day is $10 per person. Camping is also permitted for a nominal fee, and there are some very rustic cabins available with advance notice for around $25. If you don't have a car, you should arrange pickup with the folks who manage this refuge. Or you could hire a taxi in Paquera to take you there for around $7.

ACCOMMODATIONS

Aside from the hotels listed here, there are a few inexpensive cabinas available near the town of Tambor, at the southern end of the beach. Your two best bets are **Cabinas El Bosque** (☎ 506/683-0039) on the main road, and **Hotel Dos Largatos** (☎ and fax 506/683-0236), on the beach next to Tambor Tropical.

Barceló Playa Tambor Beach Resort. Bahía Ballena, Puntarenas (P.O. Box 771-1150, La Uruca, San José). ☎ **506/683-0303.** Fax 506/683-0304. www.barcelo.com. E-mail: tambor@ racsa.co.cr. 402 units. A/C MINIBAR TV TEL. $120–$400 double. Rates are all-inclusive. AE, MC, V.

All-inclusive beach resorts can be found all over the Caribbean, but this was Costa Rica's first. Still, the beach here is mediocre at best, and the resorts found farther north in Guanacaste would be my first choice if an all-inclusive, large resort vacation is what you're looking for. Moreover, the Playa Tambor development has been surrounded by controversy since its inception, and charges of violating Costa Rica's environmental laws, ignoring zoning regulations, and mistreating workers were leveled against the Spanish developers.

A huge complex of open-air buildings forms the lobby, theater, restaurants, and bars. The guest rooms are in attractively designed two-story buildings that are reminiscent of banana plantation houses. The rooms themselves are built to international standards, and though they have not even a hint of Costa Rican character, they're quite comfortable. About one-quarter of the rooms have "ocean views." But beware: They are mostly set back between 183 and 457 meters (200 and 500 yd.) from the beach, with lots of trees and gardens in between. Around the resort, hundreds of vacationers soak up the sun, splash in the pool and the waves, and indulge all day in the endless supply of free refreshments.

Dining/Diversions: The cost of all your meals and bar drinks is included in the room rates here, and when it comes time to eat, you can choose from a buffet at **El Tucán,** à la carte meals at **El Rancho,** or fast food from the poolside **El Palenque.** There are also a couple of different bars, a disco, an open-air theater that stages nightly entertainment revues, and a large casino.

Amenities: The free-form pool, one of the largest in the country, is surrounded by hundreds of lounge chairs and has a swim-up bar. Other facilities include lighted tennis courts, a basketball court, an outdoor exercise facility, and a whirlpool tub. Tours, cruises, jet skis, parasailing, sportfishing and sunset sailboat excursions, and scuba trips can be arranged for an additional cost. Sports equipment available for use by guests free of charge includes sailboards, sea kayaks, snorkeling gear, small sailboats (Hobie Cats and Sunfish), and boogie boards. Table tennis, croquet, and badminton are also available. The newest addition here is the neighboring Los Delfines golf course. At press time, only nine holes were open and operational, but the other nine are expected to open within a year.

✪ **Tango Mar Resort.** Tambor, Puntarenas (mailing address: SJO 684, Box 025216, Miami, FL 33102). ☎ **888/259-2965** in the U.S., or 506/289-9328. Fax 506/288-1257. www. tangomar.com. E-mail: tangomar@racsa.co.cr. 18 units, 17 suites, 4 villas. A/C MINIBAR TEL TV. $135 double, $140–$190 suite, $350–$900 villa. Rates include breakfast. AE, DC, MC, V.

Before the Playa Tambor Beach Resort was built, Tango Mar was *the* luxury resort in this neck of the woods. Today, it's still a great place to get away from it all. With only 18 rooms and scattered suites and villas, there are never any crowds. The water is wonderfully clear, and the beach is fronted by coconut palms and luxuriant lawns. If you choose to go exploring, you'll find seaside cliffs and a beautiful nearby waterfall that pours into a tide pool. The hotel rooms all have big balconies and glass walls to soak up the ocean views; some even have their own Jacuzzis. The suites are set back among shade trees and flowering vegetation. Each has a carved four-poster canopy bed and indoor Jacuzzi. The villas are all different, but all are spacious and relatively secluded. Some of the suites and villas are a bit far from the beach and main hotel, so you'll either need your own car or one of the hotel's gas-powered golf carts. My favorite suites are the five octagonal Tiki suites located close to the main lodge and beach.

Dining/Diversions: The small open-air restaurant overlooks the beach and has plenty of patio space. The varied menu includes plenty of fresh fish, with prices ranging from $9 to $18 for entrees. There's also an adjacent bar.

Amenities: There are two swimming pools. The nicest, though small, is set in a lush, secluded garden that is reached by way of a sidewalk across a frog pond. Tango Mar's nine-hole "executive" golf course ($25 greens fee) has wonderful sea views. There are also two lighted tennis courts, guided horseback rides ($40 to $50), boat and snorkeling tours ($40 to $80), fishing charters ($550 for a half day, $1,200 for a full day for up to six people), limited room service, golf club and bike rentals, and massages.

Tambor Tropical. Tambor, Puntarenas (mailing address: Public Affairs Counsel, 867 Liberty St. NE, Salem, OR 97301). ☎ **506/683-0011.** Fax 506/683-0013. E-mail: tamborcr@ racsa.co.cr. 10 units. $125–$150 double. Rates include breakfast. No children under 16. AE, MC, V.

If you're looking for upscale, adults-only, accommodations right in Tambor, this should be your first choice. The rooms here are located in five two-story octagonal cabins, and the whole place is an orgy of varnished hardwoods, with purpleheart and cocobolo offsetting each other at every turn. The rooms are enormous and come with large, complete kitchens and a spacious sitting area. The walls are in effect nothing but shuttered picture windows, which give you the choice of gazing out at the ocean or shutting in for a bit of privacy. The upstairs rooms have large wraparound verandas, while the lower rooms have garden-level decks. The beach is only steps away. Plenty of coconut palms and flowering plants provide a very tropical feel.

Dining: The restaurant serves well-prepared meals and great desserts at very reasonable prices.

Amenities: There's an inviting free-form tile pool and Jacuzzi. A wide range of tours and activities can be arranged here, from horseback riding to scuba diving, with plenty of nature hikes mixed in between.

11 Playa Montezuma

103–114 miles (166–184km) W of San José (not including the ferry ride); 22$^{1}/_{2}$ miles (36km) SE of Paquera; 33$^{1}/_{2}$ miles (54km) S of Naranjo

For years, Montezuma has enjoyed near legendary status among backpackers, UFO seekers, hippie expatriates, and European budget travelers. This fame and tourist traffic have had their price. The haphazard collection of budget lodgings that sprang up were generally pretty ratty, long-term campers were trashing the beach, and Montezuma earned a reputation for having noise, sewage, and drug problems. In recent years, local businesspeople and hotel owners have joined together and addressed most of these problems. Now the town has a well-tended feel, and there are lodgings of value and quality in all price ranges. The local community even passed an ordinance shutting down all loud discos in the town center, so it's now possible to get a good night's sleep as well.

Still, it's the natural beauty, miles of almost abandoned beaches, rich wildlife, and jungle waterfalls that first made Montezuma famous, and they are what keep this one of my favorite beach towns in Costa Rica. The water here is a gorgeous royal blue, and beautiful beaches stretch out along the coast on either side of town. Be careful, though: The waves can occasionally be too rough for casual swimming, and you need to be aware of stray rocks at your feet. Be sure you know where the rocks and tide are before doing any bodysurfing. The best places to swim are a couple hundred yards north of town in front of the El Rincón de los Monos campground, or several kilometers farther north at Playa Grande.

ESSENTIALS

GETTING THERE & DEPARTING   By Plane   The nearest airport to Montezuma is in Tambor, 10^1/$_2$ miles (17km) away. See above for flight details. Some of the hotels listed below may be willing to pick you up in Tambor for a reasonable fee. If not, you will have to hire a taxi, which could cost anywhere between $10 and $20. **Taxis** are generally waiting to meet most regularly scheduled planes, but if they aren't, you can call Gilberto Rodríguez (☎ **506/642-0241**) or Miguel (☎ **506/683-0015**) for a cab. Budget travelers can just walk the 50 meters (55 yd.) out to the main road and hitchhike or flag down the next bus.

By Bus & Ferry   If you're traveling from San José by public transportation, it takes two buses and a ferry ride to get to Montezuma. If you miss your connections, you might have to spend the night in Puntarenas, so plan ahead and give yourself plenty of time.

Express buses (☎ **506/222-0064**) leave for Puntarenas from San José daily every 30 minutes between 6am and 9pm from Calle 16 and Avenida 12. Trip duration is 2 hours; the fare is $2.50.

From Puntarenas take the passenger launch Paquereña (☎ **506/661-2830**), which leaves from the pier behind the market at 6am, 11am, and 3pm. This passenger launch should not be confused with the several car ferries that also leave from Puntarenas, and you should always check the schedule before making plans. Ferry-trip duration is 1^1/$_2$ hours; the fare is $2. The bus south to Montezuma will be waiting to meet the launch when it arrives in Paquera. The bus ride takes 1^1/$_2$ hours; the fare is $3.

When you're ready to return, the bus for Paquera leaves Montezuma daily at 5am, 10am, and 2pm and meets the Paquereña ferry, which leaves for Puntarenas at 8am, 12:30pm, and 5pm. Buses to San José leave Puntarenas daily every 30 minutes between 5:30am and 7pm.

By Car   Take the Interamerican Highway from San José to Puntarenas and catch either the Naranjo ferry or the Paquera ferry. The Paquera ferry will save you a lot of time and a lot of driving on the rough road from Naranjo to Paquera.

In 1998, a new company was given permission to operate a car ferry between Puntarenas and Paquera, easing some of the load on this popular route. Lines and waits are much shorter now, but I still recommend arriving a little bit early during the peak season and on weekends. **Ferries to Paquera** (Naviera Tambor: ☎ **506/661-2084;** Paquera Ferry: ☎ **506/661-3674**) leave daily at 5 and 8:45am and 12:30, 2, 5, and 8:15pm. The trip takes 1^1/$_2$ hours. The fare is around $10 for a car and driver; $1.50 for additional adults, $4 for adults in first class; $1 for children, and $2 for children in first class.

The **Naranjo ferry** (☎ **506/661-1069**) leaves daily at 3, 7, and 10:50am and 2:50 and 7pm. The trip takes 1^1/$_2$ hours. The fare is $10 for cars, $1.50 for adults, and 75¢ for children.

The car ferry from Paquera to Puntarenas leaves daily at 6, 8, and 11:45am and 2:30, 6, and 8:30pm. The car ferry from Naranjo leaves at 5:10 and 8:50am and 12:50, 5, and 9pm.

Montezuma is about 1^1/$_2$ hours south of Paquera and 3 hours south of Naranjo. The road from Paquera to Tambor has been upgraded with the arrival of the resort hotel. Beyond Tambor, it's approximately another 50 minutes to Montezuma. .

ORIENTATION & INFORMATION   As the winding mountain road that descends into Montezuma bottoms out, you turn left onto a small dirt road that defines the village proper. On this 1-block road, you will find the Sano Banano restaurant and across from it a small park with its own brand-new basketball court. The bus stops at the end of this road. From here, hotels are scattered up and down the beach and around the village's few sand streets.

Buses these days are met by hordes of locals trying to corral you to one of the many budget hotels. Remember, they are getting a small commission for every body they bring in, so their information is biased.

FUN ON & OFF THE BEACH

In Montezuma, mostly you just hang out at the beach, a restaurant, a bar, or in a hammock. However, if you're interested in more than just hanging out, head for the waterfall just south of town. This waterfall is one of those tropical fantasies where water comes pouring down into a deep pool. It's a popular spot, but it's a bit of a hike up the stream. There are actually a couple of waterfalls up this stream, but the upper falls are by far the more spectacular. You'll find the trail to the falls just over the bridge south of the village (on your right just past Las Cascadas restaurant). At the first major outcropping of rocks, the trail disappears and you have to scramble up the rocks and river for a bit. A trail occasionally reappears for short stretches. Just stick close to the stream and you'll eventually hit the falls.

HORSEBACK RIDING & VISITING A GREAT TIDE POOL   Several people around the village will rent you horses for around $7 to $10 an hour, though most people choose to do a guided 4-hour horseback tour for $30 to $40. The longer rides usually go to a second waterfall 5 miles (8km) north of Montezuma. This waterfall cascades straight down into a deep tide pool at the edge of the ocean. The pool here is a delightful mix of fresh- and seawater, and you can bathe while gazing out over the sea and rocky coastline. When the water is clear and calm, this is one of my favorite swimming holes in all of Costa Rica. However, the pool here is dependent upon the tides—it disappears entirely at very high tide. You can also ride a horse to Cabo Blanco (see below). Luis, whose rental place is down the road that leads from town out to the beach, is a reliable source for horses, as is "Roger the horse guy"—any local can direct you to him. However, you'll find the best-cared-for and -kept horses at **Finca Los Caballos** (☎ **506/642-0124**), which is located up the hill on the road leading into Montezuma.

OTHER ACTIVITIES   There are some rental shops in the center of the village where you can rent a bicycle by the day or hour, as well as boogie boards and snorkeling equipment (although the water must be very calm for snorkeling).

Your best one-stop resource is **Aventuras en Montezuma** (☎ and fax **506/642-0050**), which functions as a tour and information clearinghouse. Located next to El Sano Banano restaurant, Aventuras en Montezuma can arrange boat tours and rafting trips, car and motorcycle rentals, airport transfers, international phone, fax, and Internet service, and currency exchange. However, since this is pretty much the only game in town, the service can be gruff and indifferent.

Nicoya Expeditions/Cabo Blanco Divers (☎ and fax **506/642-0467**) has set up shop across the street from Chico's Bar and offers most of the same tours as Aventuras, as well as diving trips and certification classes. One of the more popular excursions is

Buy the Book . . . or Just Borrow It

If you came unprepared, or run out of reading material, check in at **Libreria Topsy** (☎ **506/642-0576**), which, in addition to selling books, also runs a lending library.

a day trip to Tortuga Island ($40, including lunch). Most hotels can also arrange most of these tours and services.

AN EXCURSION TO CABO BLANCO NATURE RESERVE: PELICANS, HOWLER MONKEYS & BEAUTIFUL BEACHES

As beautiful as the beaches around Montezuma are, the beaches at **Cabo Blanco Absolute Nature Reserve,** 6³/₄ miles (11km) south of the village, are even more stunning. Located at the southernmost tip of the Nicoya Peninsula, Cabo Blanco is a national park that preserves a nesting site for brown pelicans, magnificent frigate birds, and brown boobies. The beaches are backed by lush tropical forest that is home to howler monkeys. You can hike through the preserve's lush forest right down to the deserted, pristine beach. This is Costa Rica's oldest official bioreserve and was set up thanks to the pioneering efforts of conservationists Karen Mogensen and Nicholas Wessberg. Admission is $6; the reserve is closed on Monday and Tuesday.

On your way out to Cabo Blanco you'll pass through the tiny village of **Cabuya.** Some very basic cabinas and hotels have sprung up out here. There are nice deserted stretches of beach and very few travelers.

There are usually shared taxis heading out this way from Montezuma in the morning. The fare is around $4 per person. Taxis here are generally red four-by-fours, clearly marked. They tend to hang around Montezuma center. Some enterprising locals also function as pirate taxis. The general rule is, "Don't call us, we'll find you." However, the most dependable *taxista* is **Gilberto Rodríguez** (☎ 506/642-0241).

ACCOMMODATIONS

In addition to the places listed below, **Horizontes de Montezuma** (☎ and fax **506/642-0534;** www.horizontes-montezuma.com) is a new hotel up on the hill above the beach. This place functions at times as a language school and is a good alternative if you don't mind a long hike, or short drive, to the beach.

Now that camping on the beach is discouraged (although many folks still get away with it), most campers make do at **El Rincón de Los Monos** (no phone), which is about 91 meters (100 yd.) north of town along the beach, charges about $3 per tent, and provides showers and bathrooms. Others head south toward Cabuya and Cabo Blanco.

MODERATE

✪ **Amor de Mar.** Montezuma, Cóbano de Puntarenas. ☎ and fax **506/642-0262.** www.costaricanet.net/amordemar. E-mail: shoebox@racsa.co.cr. 11 units, 9 with bathroom. $30–35 double with shared bathroom, $40–$70 double or triple with private bathroom; slightly lower in the off-season. V.

It would be difficult to imagine a more idyllic spot in this price range. In fact, it's hard to imagine a much more idyllic spot in any price range. With its wide expanse of neatly trimmed grass sloping down to the sea, tide pools (one of which is as big as a small swimming pool), and hammocks slung from the mango trees, this is the perfect place for anyone who wants to do some serious relaxing. The rooms are all housed in a beautifully appointed two-story building, which abounds in varnished hardwoods. Most of the rooms have plenty of space, and all are very clean and receive lots of sunlight. The big porch on the second floor is a great place for reading or just gazing out to sea. Only breakfast is served here, but it's served all day and is one of the best in town; the specialties include big banana pancakes and fresh homemade whole-wheat French bread.

✪ **El Sano Banano.** Montezuma, Cóbano de Puntarenas. ☎ and fax **506/642-0068**, or ☎ 506/642-0638. www.elbanano.com. E-mail: elbanano@racsa.co.cr. 5 units, 8 bungalows, 1 apt. $60 double, $75 bungalow, $100 apt; lower in the off-season. AE, MC, V.

El Sano Banano is the sort of tropical retreat many travelers dream about. If you walk down the beach (toward your left as you face the water), after about 10 minutes you'll find it on the left. From the front porch of your cabin you can sit and listen to the waves crashing on the beach a few feet away. Please don't try to drive up the beach, even if you have a four-wheel-drive vehicle—seclusion and quiet are the main offerings of this place, and cars would ruin the atmosphere. If you don't want to carry all your bags, the hotel will be pleased to bring them to your room.

There are two types of cabins here. Most are white ferroconcrete geodesic domes that look like igloos; there's also one octagonal, hardwood Polynesian-style bungalow. Most of the showers are outdoor garden affairs, which match the surroundings perfectly. There are also two hostel-style rooms, three standard rooms, and one large apartment in a separate building. Most of the rooms have refrigerators, coffeemakers, and hot plates, enticing many guests to opt for extended stays. There's a swimming pool and the whole operation is set amid a lush garden planted with lots of banana and elephant-ear plants.

Nature Lodge Finca Los Caballos. Apdo. 22, Cóbano de Puntarenas. ☎ and fax **506/642-0124**. www.centralamerica.com. E-mail: naturelc@racsa.co.cr. 8 units, 1 apt. $60 double. No credit cards.

This new lodge is located on a high ridge about $1^3/_4$ miles (3km) above and before Montezuma. The rooms are in two separate concrete block buildings. Each room has either one double or one double and one single bed, a private bathroom, and cement floors. Spanish-style tile roofs, hardwood trim, and some nice painting accents make this place feel a lot nicer than most budget lodges. I prefer the end rooms of each building as they have open gables (screened, of course) that allow for more cross ventilation. Every room has a small patio, and there are plenty of hammocks strung around. There's a small pool here, with a wonderful view of rolling hills down to the Pacific Ocean. The restaurant serves creative, well-prepared meals using fresh and natural ingredients.

The name of the lodge translates to "horse ranch," and riding is taken seriously here. The owners have 40 acres of land and access to many neighboring ranches and trail systems. The horses are well tended and trained. The standard trips to Montezuma's waterfalls and Cabo Blanco are available, as well as a host of other adventure-tour options.

INEXPENSIVE

Hotel La Aurora. Montezuma, Apdo. 2, Cóbano de Puntarenas. ☎ and fax **506/642-0051**. E-mail: aurorapacific@hotmail.com. 10 units. $15–$30 double. Extra person $5. Lower rates in the off-season. AE, MC, V.

Just to the left as you enter the village of Montezuma, you'll see this large white house. The rooms are spread around the spacious three-story building, which also features a small library of books, some hammocks and comfortable chairs, and flowering vines growing up the walls. In fact, there are plants and vines all over La Aurora, which give it a tropical yet gothic feel. Most rooms are of average size and have wood walls that don't go all the way to the ceiling, which improves air circulation but reduces privacy. There are two rooms on the third floor with balconies and an ocean view over the treetops. Fresh coffee, tea, and hearty breakfasts are served each morning, and there are communal refrigerators located on each floor, as well as a kitchen available for guests' use.

Hotel Lucy. Montezuma, Cóbano de Puntarenas. ☎ **506/642-0273.** 10 units, all with shared bathroom. $10 double, $15 triple. No credit cards.

Situated on a pretty section of beach a bit south of town, in front of Los Mangos, this converted two-story home has the best location of any budget lodging in Montezuma. If you can snag a second-floor room with an ocean view, you'll be in budget heaven. The beach here is a bit rough and rocky for swimming, but the sunbathing and sunsets are beautiful. There's a small restaurant here serving Tico standards at very reasonable prices all day long. There's even a gift shop.

Hotel Moctezuma. Montezuma, Cóbano de Puntarenas. ☎ and fax **506/642-0058.** 18 units. $20 double; lower in the off-season. V (add 6% surcharge).

Located right in the center of the village and overlooking the small bay, the Hotel Moctezuma offers basic but clean rooms with fans, in two facing buildings. Some of the rooms are upstairs from the hotel's bar and restaurant; it may be noisy here, but you get a veranda with an ocean view. If you like to go to sleep early, try to get a room at the back of the building or across the street. The walls don't go all the way to the ceiling, which is great for air circulation, but lousy for privacy.

Los Mangos. Montezuma, Cóbano de Puntarenas. ☎ and fax **506/642-0259,** or 506/642-0076. 10 units, 6 with bathroom; 10 bungalows. $30 double without bathroom, $50 double with bathroom, $65 bungalow. Rates lower in the off-season. V.

Situated across the road from the water a bit before the waterfall on the road out toward Cabo Blanco, this place takes its name from the many mango trees under which the bungalows are built. (If mango is your passion, come in May, when they're in season.) The rooms are fairly basic, and those in the older building close to the road are a good value. However, it's the octagonal bungalows built of Costa Rican hardwoods that are the nicest accommodations here. Each has a small porch with rocking chairs, a thatched roof, a good amount of space, and ceiling fans. The swimming pool is built to resemble a natural pond—there's even an artificial waterfall flowing into it—and there's a separate Jacuzzi. The large rancho-style restaurant and bar serves reasonably priced continental dishes, with several Greek specialties.

DINING

In addition to the places listed below, you'll find several basic *sodas* and casual restaurants right in the village. For a midday break, try **La Esquina Dulce** ("The Sweet Corner") for some homemade ice cream and sorbets. There is also **The Bakery** (☎ **506/642-0458**), which serves breakfast and is a great place to pick up a snack, something sweet, or the makings of a bag lunch.

✪ **El Sano Banano.** On the main road into the village. ☎ **506/642-0272.** Reservations not accepted. Main courses $5–$9. AE, MC, V. Daily 7am–9:30pm. VEGETARIAN/INTERNATIONAL.

Delicious vegetarian meals, including nightly specials, sandwiches, and salads, are the specialty of this ever-popular Montezuma restaurant, although there's also a nightly fresh-fish dish. Lunches feature some hefty sandwiches and homemade pizzas. You can even order a sandwich with cheese from the cheese factory in Monteverde, and there are always fish and vegetarian casados available for around $5. The nightly dinner menu specials are posted on a blackboard out front early in the afternoon so you can be savoring the thought of dinner all day. Anytime at all, the yogurt fruit shakes are fabulous, but I like to get a little more decadent and have one of the mocha shakes. El Sano Banano also doubles as the local movie house. Nightly laser disc and DVD releases are projected on a large screen; there's also a library of more than 800 movies. The movies begin at 7:30pm and require a minimum purchase of $5.

Las Cascadas. On the road out of town toward Cabo Blanco. ☎ **506/642-0057.** Reservations accepted. Main courses $3–$12. V. Daily 7am–10pm. COSTA RICAN/SEAFOOD.

This little open-air restaurant is built on the banks of the stream just outside of the village and takes its name from the nearby waterfalls. The menu sometimes includes fresh-fish fillets, whole red snapper, or shrimp in salsa ranchera. Las Cascadas even added a few vegetarian items recently (as well as some budget rooms). This is one of the more enjoyable places in Costa Rica to have a meal—you can sit for hours beneath the thatched roof listening to the stream rushing past.

✪ **Playa de Los Artistas.** Across from Hotel Los Mangos. No phone. Main courses $6–$18. No credit cards. Mon–Sat 5–10:30pm. ITALIAN/MEDITERRANEAN.

If you're craving Italian food for dinner, this is the place to find it in Montezuma. The open-air restaurant is beside an old house fronting the beach, and there are only a few tables. This place is popular, so arrive early. If you don't get a seat and you feel hearty, try the low wooden table surrounded by tatami mats on the sand. Meals are served in large, broad wooden bowls set on ceramic-ringed coasters and come with plenty of fresh bread for soaking up the sauces. The menu changes nightly but always features several fish dishes. The fresh grouper in a black-pepper sauce is phenomenal. The new outdoor grill is great for grilled fish and seafood.

MONTEZUMA AFTER DARK

Montezuma has had a tough time coming to terms with its nightlife. For years, local businesses had banded together to force most of the loud and late activity out of town. This has eased somewhat and there's currently quite an active nightlife in Montezuma proper. The local action seems to base itself either at **Chico's Bar** or at the bar at the **Hotel Moctezuma.** Both are located on the main strip in town facing the water. A nicer option, however, is **Luz de Mono,** a new place nestled in some trees across from the school. This large open-air restaurant and bar has been featuring some interesting live music. I also enjoy **El Chiringuito,** which has natural wood tables set in the sand under thatch-roofed palapas and serves some hearty bocas with their drinks. You can even borrow a chess or backgammon board here. It's located in downtown Montezuma, on the same road as Chico's and Hotel Moctezuma. If your evening tastes are even mellower, **El Sano Banano** restaurant also doubles as the local movie house. See the listing under "Dining," above, for more information.

For real raging nightlife, some folks have been heading to the large disco at the **Playa Tambor Beach Resort.** Another option is **Las Manchas,** which is located about half a mile (1km) outside of town on the road to Cabo Blanco. It's open nightly during the high season, but during the off-season it has a sporadic schedule. Both Playa Tambor Beach Resort and Las Manchas have been known to offer free round-trip taxi service in order to lure the crowds.

12 Malpais & Santa Teresa

93 miles (150km) W of San José; 7¹/₂ miles (12km) S of Cóbano

Malpais translates as "badlands" and I can't decide if this is an accurate description or a deliberate local ploy to keep this place private. The beach here is a long, wide expanse of light sand dotted with rocky outcroppings. Sure, it can get rough here, but the surfers seem to like it. The road out here from Cóbano is perhaps even rougher than the surf, but this promises to keep out the madding crowds for some time to come. What you will find in Malpais and Santa Teresa are a scattering of beach hotels and simple restaurants, miles of nearly deserted beach, and easy access to some nice jungle and the nearby Cabo Blanco Reserve.

ESSENTIALS

GETTING THERE & DEPARTING   By Bus & Ferry   Follow the directions above for getting to Montezuma, but get off the Montezuma bus in Cóbano. From Cóbano there are three buses daily for Malpais and Santa Teresa at 10:30am and 2:30 and 6pm (fare: $1.50), which in theory wait for the above buses. These buses return daily to Cóbano at 7am, noon, and 4pm. Be forewarned, these bus schedules are subject to change according to demand, road conditions, and the whim of the bus company, so it pays to check with your hotel in advance.

If you miss this bus connection, you can hire a cab for around $12.

By Car   Follow the directions above to Montezuma. At Cóbano, follow the signs to Malpais and Playa Santa Teresa. It's another 7¹/₂ miles (12km) or so down a very rough dirt road that pretty much requires four-wheel-drive year-round and is sometimes impassable during the rainy season.

ORIENTATION   Malpais and Santa Teresa are two tiny beach villages. As you reach the ocean, the road will fork; Malpais is to your left; Santa Teresa is to your right. If you continue on beyond Santa Teresa, you will come to the even more deserted beaches of Playa Hermosa and Manzanillo (not to be confused with beaches of the same names to be found elsewhere in the country).

FUN ON & OFF THE BEACH

If you do decide to do anything here besides lie on or walk the beach and body-, boogie-, or board-surf, your primary options include nature hikes and horseback riding, which most hotels can help arrange.

ACCOMMODATIONS & DINING

In addition to the hotels listed below, budget travelers should probably head over to **Cabinas Bosque Mar** (☎ 506/640-0074), which is on the Malpais road and has a few basic rooms. You may also be able to pitch a tent. Look for camping signs; you should get bathroom and shower access for a few bucks.

If you venture away from the rather dependable restaurants located at the hotels listed below, you'll probably end up at **Dulce Magia** (☎ 506/640-0073), a homey Italian restaurant located across the street from Cabinas Bosque Mar, or **Frank's Place** (☎ 506/640-0096), which is located at the crossroads where you enter town. Frank's is a notch above most *sodas* and seems to be the most happening spot in town. For breakfasts and light lunches, I've been getting good reports on **Mango Café** (no phone), which is located right off the beach, near Frank's Place.

Mal País Surf Camp & Resort. Malpais, Cóbano de Puntarenas. ☎ and fax **506/ 640-0061.** www.malpaissurfcamp.com. E-mail: surfcamp@racsa.co.cr. 16 units (8 with shared bathroom). $25–$70 double, $5 per person camping. No credit cards.

There is a wide range of accommodations here, reflected in the equally wide range of prices. The most basic rooms are open-air ranchos, with gravel floors, lathe and bamboo walls, bead curtains for a door, and shared bathrooms. From here your options get progressively more comfortable, ranging from shared-bathroom bunk-bed rooms, to new deluxe poolside villas, to private houses with all the amenities. You can also pitch a tent. There's a refreshing free-form tile pool in the center of the complex, and the large open main lodge area serves as a combination restaurant, bar, lounge, and surfboard storage area. There's satellite TV and surf videos playing most of the day, as well as pool, Ping-Pong, and foosball tables. This place is run by and caters to surfers. The restaurant serves filling, fresh, and at times quite creative cuisine, depending on how accomplished the itinerant surf-chef-of-the-month is. Surf rentals, lessons, and video sessions are all available, as are fishing excursions, mountain-bike rentals and tours of the nearby Cabo Blanco Reserve.

✪ **Tropico Latino Lodge.** Playa Santa Teresa, Cóbano, Puntarenas. ☎ and fax **506/ 640-0062.** www.centralamerica.com. E-mail: tropico@centralamerica.com. 6 units. $52 double; lower in the off-season. No credit cards.

This simple hotel is still my favorite hotel in Malpais/Santa Teresa. The rooms, housed in three duplex bungalows, are massive. The king-size bamboo bed barely makes a dent in the floor space. There's also a separate sofa bed, as well as a small desk and wall unit of shelves and closet space galore. The bathrooms are modern and comfortable. Although none of the rooms have an unobstructed ocean view, they do all have private patios with a hammock; best of all, the beach is less than 100 meters (109 yd.) away. You'll find more hammocks and some chaise lounges out on the beach. The shady grounds are rich in the native pochote tree, which is known for its spiky trunk. There's a swimming pool and Jacuzzi, if the ocean is too rough. The small restaurant here has excellent fresh fish and plenty of pasta dishes, probably just to please the palate of the Italian owners. A wide range of tours and activities can be arranged, as well as transport to Cóbano or the Tambor airport.

The Northern Zone: Mountain Lakes, Cloud Forests & a Volcano

If you like your ecotourism rough and gritty but don't think you can take the heat and humidity of the Osa Peninsula (covered in chapter 8), this is the area for you. The northern zone, roughly defined here as the area north of San José and between Guanacaste province on the west and the lowlands of the Caribbean coast on the east, is a naturalist's dream come true. There are rain forests and cloud forests, jungle rivers, and an unbelievable diversity of birds and other wildlife. In addition to its reputation for muddy hiking trails and crocodile-filled rivers, the northern zone claims one of the best windsurfing spots in the world (on **Lake Arenal,** which is free of crocodiles, by the way) and Costa Rica's most active volcano. **Arenal Volcano,** when free of clouds, puts on spectacular nighttime light shows. Adding a touch of comfort to a visit to the northern zone are several hot springs and a variety of hotel options that vary in their levels of luxury.

1 Puerto Viejo de Sarapiquí

51 miles (82km) N of San José; 63¹/₄ miles (102km) E of La Fortuna

The Sarapiquí region, named for the river that drains this area, lies at the foot of the Cordillera Central mountain range. To the west is the rainforest of **Braulio Carrillo National Park,** and to the east are **Tortuguero National Park** and **Barra del Colorado National Wildlife Refuge.** In between these protected areas lie thousands of acres of banana, pineapple, and palm plantations. It's here that you can see the great contradiction of Costa Rica: On the one hand, the country is known for its national parks, which preserve some of the largest tracts of rain forest left in Central America; on the other hand, nearly every acre of land outside of these parks has been clear-cut and converted into plantations—and the cutting continues.

Within the remaining rain forests, there are several lodges that attract naturalists (both amateur and professional). Two of these lodges, La Selva and Rara Avis, have become well known for the research that's conducted on their surrounding reserves. Bird-watching is the primary attraction here, but more active types will find plenty of boating and rafting trips along the Sarapiqui River.

ESSENTIALS

GETTING THERE & DEPARTING   By Bus   Express buses (☎ 506/ 259-8571) leave San José daily at 6:30, 7, 8, 9, 10, and 11:30am, noon, and 1, 1:30, 3, 4:30, and 6pm from Avenida 9 and Calle 12. The buses will be marked RÍO FRÍO, PUERTO VIEJO, or both. There are two routes to Puerto Viejo de Sarapiquí. The faster heads out on the Guápiles Highway, through Braulio Carrillo National Park and then past Las Horquetas. The slower, but more scenic, route heads out through Heredia, Varablanca, and La Virgen, passing between the Barva and Poás volcanoes. If you're heading to La Selva, Rara Avis, or El Gavilán lodges, be sure you're on a bus going through Braulio Carrillo and Las Horquetas. The trip takes between 2 and 4 hours, depending on the route taken, the condition of the roads, and the frequency of stops; the fare is $3.

Buses for San José leave Puerto Viejo daily at 5:30, 7, 8, and 11am and 1:30, 3:30, 4:30, 5:30, and 7pm.

By Car   The Guápiles Highway, which leads to the Caribbean coast, heads north out of downtown San José on Calle 3 before heading east. Turn north before reaching Guápiles on the road to Río Frío and continue north through Las Horquetas, passing the turnoffs for Rara Avis, La Selva, and El Gavilán lodges, before reaching Puerto Viejo.

A more scenic route goes through Heredia, Barva, Varablanca, and San Miguel before reaching Puerto Viejo. This route passes very close to the Poás Volcano and directly in front of the La Paz waterfall. If you want to take this route, head west out of San José and then turn north to Heredia and follow the signs for Varablanca.

ORIENTATION   Puerto Viejo is a small town, at the center of which is a soccer field. If you continue past the soccer field on the main road and stay on the paved road, then turn right at the Banco Nacional, you'll come to the Río Sarapiquí and the dock, where you can look into arranging a boat trip.

WHAT TO SEE & DO

BOAT TRIPS   For the adventurous, Puerto Viejo is a jumping-off point for trips down the Río Sarapiquí to Barra del Colorado National Wildlife Refuge and Tortuguero National Park on the Caribbean coast. Boat trips can be arranged at most hotels in town. A boat for up to 10 people will cost you around $200 to $250 to Barra del Colorado, and $250 to $350 to Tortuguero.

Alternately, you can head down to the town dock on the bank of the Sarapiquí and see if you can arrange a less expensive boat trip on your own, by tagging on with another group, or better yet, with a bunch of locals. It's worth checking at your hotel, or with either **Oasis Nature Tours** (☎ 506/766-6108) or **Aventuras Sarapiquí** (☎ 506/766-6846). In addition to the longer trips, these two companies also offer shorter trips on the river for between $15 and $20. A trip down the Sarapiquí, even if it's for only an hour or two, provides opportunities to spot crocodiles, caimans, monkeys, sloths, and dozens of bird species.

If you want a faster, wilder ride on the river, you should check in with **Aguas Bravas** (☎ 506/292-2072; www.aguas-bravas.co.cr), a **white-water-rafting** company that has its local base at the very basic **Islas del Río Hotel** (☎ 506/766-6575). You'll find this hotel on the main road between Puerto Viejo and Chilamate on the left, a little before Selva Verde. Aguas Bravas runs trips on a variety of sections of the Sarapiquí River, ranging from Class III to Class V. Trips cost between $50 and $75 per person. Aguas Bravas also runs mountain-biking tours in the area. Located just off the main road about 1¼ miles (2km) west of La Virgen, the **Sarapiquí Outdoor Center** (☎ 506/761-1123; E-mail: sarapiquioutdoor@hotmail.com) offers similar tours at similar prices. Both companies also rent kayaks and offer kayak trips for more experienced and/or daring river rats.

The Northern Zone

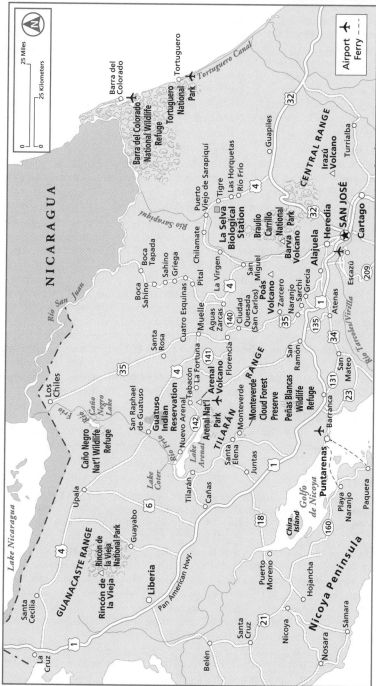

Airport ✈
Ferry - - -

25 Miles
25 Kilometers

Barra del Colorado
Tortuguero
Tortuguero Canal
Tortuguero National Park
Barra del Colorado National Wildlife Refuge

NICARAGUA

32

Guapiles

CENTRAL RANGE

Irazú Volcano
Turrialba

Las Horquetas
Río Frío

Puerto Viejo de Sarapiquí
Tigre
4

La Selva Biological Station
Braulio Carrillo National Park

SAN JOSÉ

32

Cartago

Rio Sarapiquí

Chilamate
La Virgen
Pital
San Miguel

Barva Volcano
Heredia
Alajuela
Escazú

209

Boca Tapada
Sahino
Griega
Boca Sahino
Cuatro Esquinas
Muelle
4
Aguas Zarcas
Ciudad Quesada (San Carlos)
Poás Volcano
Zarcero
Naranjo
Sarchi
Grecia
Atenas

Santa Rosa

35

San Raphael de Guatuso

4
Tabacón
La Fortuna
141
Arenal Volcano
Florencia

MONTEVERDE RANGE

San Ramón

135

34

San Mateo

131

23

Barranca

Rio San Juan

Guatuso Indian Reservation

142
Arenal Nat'l Park
TILARÁN

Nuevo Arenal
Monteverde
Santa Elena
Monteverde Cloud Forest Preserve
Peñas Blancas Wildlife Refuge

Juntas

1

Puntarenas

Caño Negro Nat'l Wildlife Refuge
Caño Negro Lake
Río Frío

Lake Coter
Lake Arenal
Tilarán
Cañas

18

Chira Island
Golfo de Nicoya
Playa Naranjo
Paquera

Los Chiles

NICARAGUA

35

Upala

6
Guayabo

GUANACASTE RANGE
Rincón de la Vieja
Rincón de la Vieja National Park
Liberia

Pan American Hwy.

21

Belén
Santa Cruz
Nicoya

Puerto Moreno
Hojancha

Nicoya Peninsula

Nosara
Sámara

160

Lake Nicaragua

Santa Cecilia
La Cruz

1

209

Another option is to take a **kayak trip** with the folks at **Rancho Leona,** in La Virgen de Sarapiquí (☎ and fax **506/761-1019;** www.rancholeona.com; E-mail: rleona@ racsa.co.cr). Rancho Leona is a small stained-glass workshop, kayaking center, and rustic guest house on the banks of the Río Sarapiquí in the village of La Virgen. (They also have a very isolated geodesic-dome cabin deep in the rain forest.) Their trips are offered as a package that includes 2 nights' lodging in simple dormitory-style accommodations and an all-day kayak trip with some basic instruction and lunch on the river. The cost for the 2-day trip is $85 per person. No experience is necessary, and the river here is very calm. Trips for experienced kayakers can be arranged.

AERIAL TRAM If you're driving to Puerto Viejo de Sarapiquí via the Guápiles Highway, you might want to stop here. You'll see the entrance to the Aerial Tram on your right, a little bit after passing through the Zurquí tunnel. For more information, see "Side Trips from San José," in chapter 4.

HIKING & GUIDED TOURS Anyone can take advantage of the 35 miles (56km) of well-maintained trails at **La Selva** (see below). If you're not staying there, however, you'll have to take a guided hike, led by experienced and well-informed naturalists.

Half-day ($20) and full-day ($40) hikes are offered daily, but you must reserve in advance (☎ **506/766-6565;** fax 506/766-6535; E-mail: laselva@sloth.ots.ac.cr). The half-day tours leave at 8am and 1:30pm daily.

My favorite hike starts off with the Cantarana ("singing frog") trail, which includes a section of low bridges over a rain-forest swamp. From here you can join up with either the near or far circular loop trails—**CCC** and **CCL.**

Finally, if you want to visit the Sarapiquí region on a day trip from San José, call either **Costa Rica Fun Adventures** (☎ **506/290-6015**) or **Ecoscapes Highlights Tour** (☎ **506/297-0664**), which run jam-packed day trips up here that combine a bus ride and stop at the La Paz waterfall, a visit to a banana plantation, a rain-forest hike, and a boat ride on the river for around $75 to $80 per person.

ACCOMMODATIONS & DINING

All of the lodges listed below arrange excursions throughout the region, including boat trips on the Sarapiquí, guided hikes in the rain forest, and horseback or mountain-bike rides.

VERY EXPENSIVE

Selva Verde Lodge. Apdo. 55, Chilamate, Sarapiquí. ☎ **800/451-7111** in the U.S. and Canada, or 506/766-6800. Fax 506/766-6011. www.selvaverde.com. E-mail: selvaver@racsa. co.cr. 40 units, 5 bungalows. $136 double; $145 triple; slightly lower during the off-season (May–Nov). Rates include 3 meals daily and taxes. MC, V.

For years, this was one of the showcase ecotourist lodges in Costa Rica. A recent remodeling included the building of a new reception area and a covered bus port for the numerous tour buses that come here. Frankly, I think the success has gone to their heads. Service, food, and personal attention have all suffered and there's an assembly-line feel to the whole operation. But you can't beat the location: It's right between the main road (a few kilometers west of Puerto Viejo) and by the Río Sarapiquí. Across the river is a large rain-forest preserve.

These are without doubt the nicest rooms in the area. They're all connected by covered walkways that keep you dry even though this area receives more than 150 inches of rain each year. The lodge buildings are all built of varnished hardwoods, inside and out, and are built on pilings so that all the rooms are on the second floor. The bungalows are located across the road and 500 meters (545 yd.) into the forest and are not nearly as comfortable as the rooms in the main compound, but they do offer somewhat more privacy. Meals are served buffet style in a beautiful large dining room that overlooks the river; they're well prepared and filling but not too creative. There are several trails on the grounds, a wonderful suspension bridge across the Sarapiquí River to more trails, and modest butterfly and botanical gardens. Excursions that can be arranged through the lodge include river trips ($25 per person), rafting trips ($45 per person), horseback riding ($20 per person), and guided walks ($15 per person).

EXPENSIVE

El Gavilán Lodge. (Apdo. 445-2010, San José), Puerto Viejo de Sarapiquí. ☎ **506/ 234-9507** or 506/383-5627. Fax 506/253-6556. www.gavilanlodge.com. E-mail: gavilan@ racsa.co.cr. 13 units. $90 double, $115 triple; lower in the off-season (May–Nov). MC, V.

Located on the banks of the Río Sarapiquí just south of Puerto Viejo on the road to Río Frío, El Gavilán is surrounded by 250 acres of forest reserve (secondary forest) and 25 acres of gardens planted with lots of flowering ginger, heliconia, orchids, and bromeliads. Guest rooms are basic and simply furnished, and I'm not sure they're really worth the recently inflated prices. Still, all have fans and hot water, and there are always fresh-cut flowers. Most have one single and one double bed, but there are variations. What El Gavilán lacks in luxurious comfort, it makes up for in friendliness and attentive service. There's a Jacuzzi in the garden and several open-air ranchos, some of which have hammocks strung up for afternoon siestas. Tico and continental meals are served buffet style, and there's always plenty of fresh fruits and juices. Breakfast will run you $7; lunch, $9; and dinner, $12. Guided hikes through the forest, horseback rides, and river trips are all offered for around $20 per person. Multiday packages, as well as day trips to the Arenal Volcano, are also available.

Rara Avis. Apdo. 8105-1000, San José. ☎ **506/253-0844** or 506/764-3131. Fax 506/ 257-0438. www.rara-avis.com. E-mail: raraavis@racsa.co.cr. 12 units, 10 with bathroom. $90 double with shared bathroom, $160 double with private bathroom. Rates include transportation from Las Horquetas (you can't get here by car), guided hikes, 3 meals daily, and taxes. MC, V.

Once the exclusive stomping grounds of scientists and students, Rara Avis was made famous by the pioneering canopy research of Dr. Donald Perry, who first erected his famous canopy cable-car system in the rain forest here. Since that time, Rara Avis has become a popular destination for people with a more casual interest in the rain forest. Though Perry's cable car is no longer here, this rain-forest research facility is still a fascinating place to visit. The Waterfall Lodge is by far the most comfortable option here. It has rustic rooms and a wraparound porch. Located 1³/₄ miles (3km) away from the main lodge, there's the more Spartan and economical El Plastico Lodge.

Rara Avis also has two individual cabins of note. The comfortable two-room honeymoon cabin is set deep in the forest beside a river, for those wanting closer communion with nature. (It's a 10-min. walk from the main lodge.) There's also a treetop cabin that requires an athletic 30-meter (100-ft.) ascent with harness and climbing gear, and then a rappel back down. You can spend the night in the beds up here, but there's no bathroom, so you must also book a room in one of the lodges.

Meals are basic Tico-style dishes with lots of beans and rice. Rara Avis is adjacent to Braulio Carrillo National Park, and together the two have many miles of trails for you to explore. Bird-watchers take note: More than 362 species of birds have been sighted here.

When making reservations, be sure to get directions for how to get to Las Horquetas, and to coordinate your ride on the lodge's tractor. The tractor leaves around 9am each day for the 3-hour/9¹/₂-mile (15km) ride to the lodge.

MODERATE

Casa Río Blanco. Apdo. 241-7210, Guápiles. ☎ **506/382-0957.** Fax 506/710-2264. 6 units. $60 double, $75 triple; lower in the off-season (May–Nov). Rates include breakfast. No credit cards.

This small nature lodge is located about 1¼ miles (2km) up a gravel road just off the Guápiles Highway. The lodge is located in a small but dense patch of rain forest on a steep hill overlooking the Río Blanco. The atmosphere here is rustic but comfortable. There are two rooms in the main lodge building and four separate cabins. The cabins, with their wood floors, clapboard walls, and private balconies, are the best bet. Numbers 1 and 4 have the best views. There are trails through the rain forest, a covered lookout point, and several swimming holes on the premises. Located close to the Aerial Tram and La Selva, and en route to the Caribbean coast, this hotel makes a good stopover point for a night or two as part of a larger itinerary.

Hotel El Bambú. Apdo. 1518-2100, Puerto Viejo de Sarapiquí. ☎ **506/766-6005.** Fax 506/766-6132. www.elbambu.com. E-mail: info@elbambu.com. 14 units. A/C TV TEL. $56 double, $66 triple, $77 quad. Rates include continental breakfast. MC, V.

This is the most luxurious hotel in Puerto Viejo, although that's not saying much. The best rooms here are up on the second floor facing away from the main road. They all have high ceilings, tile floors, and attractive bamboo furniture. Three of the rooms have air-conditioning. Downstairs, just off the lobby, you'll find the big open-air restaurant that overlooks the dense grove of bamboo for which the hotel is named. The restaurant serves basic Tico and Chinese standards. The hotel is directly across the street from the soccer field in the middle of town. Tours around the region, as well as boat trips down the Río Sarapiquí as far as Barra del Colorado and Tortuguero, can be arranged.

La Quinta de Sarapiquí Country Inn. Apdo. 11021-1000, San José), Chilamate, Sarapiquí. ☎ **506/761-1052.** Fax 506/766-6535. www.laquintasarapiqui.com. E-mail: laquinta@costarica.net. 23 units. $45 double. MC, V.

This small family-run lodge makes a good base for exploring the Sarapiquí region. Located on the banks of the Sardinal River about 15 minutes west of Puerto Viejo, La Quinta caters primarily to nature lovers and bird-watchers. The rooms are located in four buildings dispersed around the grounds among richly flowering gardens. They're simple but clean and have either two or three single beds. There are no double or queen-size beds here, so couples beware. Each room has a small patio with a sitting chair or two for gazing out into the garden. Meals are served family style in the main lodge and will run you an extra $25 per day. There's a small pool, and it's even safe to swim in the river. There's also a small gift shop, a small butterfly garden, and a reforestation project on hand. Horses are available for guests to ride free of charge, as are mountain bikes, and a host of tours around the region are offered as well. If you don't have a car, call the hotel to see if you can arrange a pickup in Puerto Viejo.

✪ La Selva Biological Station. South of Puerto Viejo (P.O. Box 676-2050, San Pedro, Costa Rica; U.S. mailing address: Interlink 341, P.O. Box 02-5635, Miami, FL 33152). ☎ **506/240-6696** or 506/766-6565. Fax 506/240-6783. www.ots.duke.edu. E-mail: reservas@ots.ac.cr. 10 units, all with shared bathroom. $60 per person double occupancy; lower rates for researchers. Rates include 3 meals daily, a half-day tour, and taxes. MC, V.

Located a few kilometers south of Puerto Viejo, La Selva Biological Station caters primarily to students and researchers but also accepts visitors seeking a rustic rain-forest adventure. The atmosphere is definitely that of a scientific research center. La Selva, which is operated by the Organization for Tropical Studies (OTS), covers 3,700 acres and is contiguous with Braulio Carrillo National Park. Researchers estimate that more than 2,000 species of flora exist in this private reserve, and 400-plus species of birds have been identified here. Rooms are basic but large, and the high ceilings help keep them cool. Most have bunk beds and all share bathrooms. The dining hall is a big, bright place where students and scientists swap data over fried chicken or fish and rice and beans.

Because scientific research is the primary objective of La Selva, researchers receive priority over casual short-term visitors. However, very informative guided tours are available most days, even if you are staying at another hotel in the area. Call the local number (☎ **506/766-6565**) at least 1 day in advance to arrange one of these. If you wish to stay overnight at La Selva, you must have a reservation with the San José office. Since there are very few rooms here, it pays to book well in advance. Direct transportation to and from La Selva can be arranged with the OTS and costs $10 each way.

INEXPENSIVE

Mi Lindo Sarapiquí. Puerto Viejo de Sarapiquí. ☎ and fax **506/766-6074**. 8 units. TV. $17 double, $27 triple. AE, MC, V.

This little family-run lodging is located in the center of town overlooking the soccer field. The rooms are on the second floor above the large restaurant and bar. Nothing fancy, but this is the most popular budget lodging around. Be warned that the bar/restaurant is popular with locals and can be noisy.

A REMOTE NATURE LODGE

✪ **La Laguna del Lagarto Lodge.** Boca Tapada (Apdo. 995-1007, Centro Colón, San José). ☎ **506/289-8163**. Fax 506/289-5295. www.adventure-costa-rica.com. E-mail: lagarto@racsa.co.cr. 20 units, 18 with bathroom. $50 double with shared bathroom, $60 double with private bathroom. V.

It's hard to get much more remote than this northern nature lodge. Located near the Nicaraguan border, La Laguna del Lagarto Lodge is bordered by over 1,200 acres of virgin rain forest that is home to a rich variety of tropical flora and fauna. The accommodations are simple yet comfortable. Most rooms open on to a balcony or veranda with sitting chairs and hammocks. Meals, which will run you around $24 per person per day, are served family style in the open-air dining room, and are filling affairs.

The hotel is named after the two man-made lagoons that sit below; canoes are available for paddling around these and several other nearby jungle waterways. There are over 6 miles (10km) of well-maintained hiking trails, and the lodge offers trips on the San Carlos and San Juan rivers ($25), touching ground briefly in Nicaragua. Over 350 species of birds have been spotted here and the hotel is involved in efforts to preserve the rare great green macaw, two of which I spotted soon after my arrival. In addition to the rain forest, the lodge also sits on a small pepper plantation and has other lands planted with palmito, pineapple, and other tropical fruits. To get here, you would head first to Pital and then continue on dirt roads to the town of Boca Tapada. It's another 4 miles (6km) to the lodge on more bumpy dirt roads. It's also possible to get here on public transportation (call for directions), or you can arrange a ride with the lodge for $75 per person round-trip.

2 Arenal Volcano & La Fortuna

87 miles (140km) NW of San José; 37³/₄ miles (61km) E of Tilarán

If you've never experienced it firsthand, the sight and sound of an active volcano erupting are awesome. In July 1968, **Arenal Volcano,** which had lain dormant for hundreds of years, surprised everybody by erupting with sudden and unexpected violence.

The nearby village of Tabacón was destroyed, and nearly 80 of its inhabitants were killed. Since that eruption 32 years ago, 5,358-foot Arenal has been Costa Rica's most active volcano. Frequent powerful explosions send cascades of red-hot lava rocks tumbling down the western slope, and during the day the lava flows steam and rumble. However, it's at night that the volcano puts on its most mesmerizing show. If you are lucky enough to be here on a clear night, you'll see the night sky turned red by lava spewing from Arenal's crater. In the past few years, the forests to the south of the volcano have been declared Arenal National Park. Eventually, this park should stretch all the way to Monteverde Biological Cloud Forest Preserve.

Lying at the eastern foot of this natural spectacle is the tiny farming community of **La Fortuna.** In recent years, this town has become a center for volcano-watchers from around the world. There is a host of moderately priced hotels in and near La Fortuna, and it's here that you can arrange night tours to the best volcano-viewing spots, which are 10¹/₂ miles (17km) away on the western slope, past Tabacón Hot Springs.

ESSENTIALS

GETTING THERE & DEPARTING   By Plane   Sansa (☎ **506/221-9414;** fax 506/255-2176; E-mail: reservations@flysansa.com) flies to La Fortuna daily at 10am from San José's Juan Santamaría International Airport. The flight's duration is 25 minutes; the fare is $50 each way.

Travelair (☎ **506/220-3054;** fax 506/220-0413; E-mail: reservations@travelair-costarica.com) flies to La Fortuna daily at 11:20am from Tobías Bolaños International Airport in Pavas. Flight duration is 25 minutes; the fare is $57 one-way, $94 round-trip.

The **airport** (☎ **506/469-1080**) is actually located in El Tanque, a few kilometers outside of La Fortuna. A taxi or airport shuttle should cost around $5 to the center of La Fortuna, around $15 to Tabacón.

By Bus   Buses (☎ **506/255-4318**) leave San José for La Fortuna daily at 6:15, 8:40, and 11:30am from the Atlantico del Norte bus station at Avenida 9 and Calle 12. The trip's duration is 4¹/₂ hours; the fare is $2.75.

Alternately, you can take a bus to Ciudad Quesada from the same location in San José and then take a local bus from Ciudad Quesada to La Fortuna. Ciudad Quesada buses leave San José roughly every hour from 5am to 7:30pm, and "roughly" is the operative word. Buses are sometimes added or canceled depending on demand, and hours may vary, though you'll never have to wait more than an hour for the next bus. If you want to be sure, call ☎ **506/255-4318.** The fare for the 2¹/₂-hour trip is $2. The bus you take may be labeled TILARÁN. Make sure it is passing through Ciudad Quesada. If it is, you're in luck, because it will also pass through La Fortuna. Local buses between Ciudad Quesada and La Fortuna run regularly through the day, though the schedule changes frequently depending on demand. The trip lasts 1 hour; the fare is $1.25.

Buses depart **Monteverde/Santa Elena** for Tilarán every day at 7am. This is a journey of only 22 miles (35km), but the trip lasts 2¹/₂ hours because the road is in such horrendous condition. Pregnant women and people with bad backs should think twice about making this trip, especially by bus. The return bus from Tilarán to Santa Elena leaves at 1pm. The fare is $1.50. Buses from Tilarán to La Fortuna depart daily at 7am and 12:30pm (hence, a person coming from Monteverde would have to wait for the 12:30pm bus) and make the return trip at 8am and 2:30pm. The trip is 3 to 4 hours; the fare is $1.75.

Boats, Horses & Taxis

You can travel between La Fortuna and Monteverde on a combination boat, horseback, and taxi trip. After a quick boat ride across the lake, participants are saddled up for a 4-hour ride up and over the mountains to the town of San Gerardo, which is just a short taxi ride from Santa Elena and Monteverde.

Be forewarned: The riding is often rainy, muddy, and steep. Many find it much more arduous than awe-inspiring. Moreover, I've received numerous complaints about the condition of the trails and the treatment of the horses, so be very careful and demanding before signing on for this trip. **Desafío Raft and Sunset Tours** (see below for phone numbers) both offer this trip for between $55 and $65 per person. They will even drive your car around for you while you take the scenic (and sore) route.

Buses depart La Fortuna for San José daily at 12:45 and 2:45pm. Buses to Ciudad Quesada leave at 5 and 8am, and 12:15, 2, and 3:30pm daily. From there, you can catch one of the hourly buses to San José.

Jacamar Tours (☎ 506/479-9456; E-mail: jacamar@racsa.co.cr) runs daily shuttles leaving La Fortuna at 8:30am for Tilarán ($10), continuing on to Liberia ($30), Monteverde ($35), and Tamarindo ($35). And another leaving at 10am for San José ($20).

By Car   There are several routes to La Fortuna from San José. The most popular is to head west on the Interamerican Highway and then turn north at Naranjo, continuing north through Zarcero to Ciudad Quesada. From Ciudad Quesada, one route goes through Jabillos, while the other goes through Muelle. The former route is more popular and was repaved in 1997. However, the severe weather and heavy traffic up here quickly take their toll, and I don't expect the smooth roads to last very long.

I personally recommend staying on the Interamerican Highway until San Ramón (west of Naranjo), then heading north through La Tigra, which is very scenic and passes the hotels Villablanca and Valle Escondido and is currently the fastest route to La Fortuna. The travel time on any of the above routes will be between 3 and 4 hours.

Finally, if you're combining your visit here with a stop at the Poás Volcano and La Paz waterfall, or if you're staying at one of the lodges closer to Aguas Zarcas, you can go first to Alajuela or Heredia and then head north to Varablanca before continuing on to San Miguel, where you turn west toward Río Cuarto and Aguas Zarcas. From Aguas Zarcas, continue west through Muelle to the turnoff for La Fortuna. This is the longest route.

ORIENTATION   As you enter La Fortuna, you will see the massive volcano directly in front of you. La Fortuna is only a few streets wide, with almost all the hotels, restaurants, and shops clustered along the main road that leads out of town toward Tabacón and the volcano. There are several small information and tour-booking offices across the street from the soccer field, as well as a Laundromat. There's a Banco de Costa Rica as you enter La Fortuna, just over the Río Burrío bridge, and a Banco Nacional in the center of town, across the park from the church. Both have ATM machines.

GETTING AROUND   If you don't have a car, you'll need to either take ⟨   ⟩r go on an organized tour if you want to visit the hot springs or view the volcar ⟨   ⟩ One alternative is to rent a car. **Elegante,** behind the Hotel San Bos⟨   ⟩ 479-8055), and **Ada,** on the main road beside the church (☎ 506/47⟨   ⟩ have offices in La Fortuna.

WHAT TO SEE & DO
EXPERIENCING THE VOLCANO

The first thing you should know is that you can't climb Arenal Volcano; it's not safe due to the constant activity. Several foolish people who have ignored this warning have lost their lives, and others have been severely injured. The second thing you should know is that Arenal Volcano borders a region of cloud and rain forests, and the volcano's cone is often socked in by fog. Many people come to Arenal and never get to see the exposed cone. Moreover, the volcano does go through periods when it is relatively quiet. Still, waiting for and watching Arenal's nearly constant eruptions is the main activity in La Fortuna and is best done at night when the orange lava glows against the starry sky. Though it's possible simply to look up from the middle of town and see Arenal erupting, the view is best from the north and west sides of the volcano along the road to Tabacón and toward the national-park entrance. If you have a car, you can drive along this road, but if you've arrived by bus, you will need to take a taxi or tour.

Arenal National Park constitutes an area of more than 7,200 acres, which include the viewing and parking areas closest to the volcano. The park is open from 8am to 10pm daily and charges $6 admission per person. However, the view from inside the park is no better than on the roads just outside it.

OTHER ADVENTUROUS PURSUITS IN THE AREA

Aside from the impressive volcanic activity, the area around Arenal Volcano is packed with other natural wonders.

HIKING & HORSEBACK RIDING   Leading the list of side attractions in the area is the impressive **Río Fortuna waterfall,** located about 3$^{1}/_{2}$ miles (5.5km) outside of town in a lush jungle setting. There's a sign in town to indicate the road that leads out to the falls. Depending on recent rainfall, you can drive or hike to just within viewing distance. Once you get to a makeshift entrance to the lookout, you'll have to pay the $3 entrance fee to actually check out the falls. It's another 15- to 20-minute hike down a steep and often muddy path to the pool formed by the waterfall. You can swim, but stay away from the turbulent water at the base of the falls—several people have drowned here. Instead, check out and enjoy the calm pool just around the bend. If this seems like too much exercise, you can rent a horse and guide for transportation.

Another good ride is up to **Cerro Chato,** a dormant volcanic cinder cone on the flank of Arenal. There's a pretty little lake up here. Either of these tours should cost around $20 to $25 per person. You can arrange either tour through your hotel, or through **Aventuras Arenal** (☎ 506/479-9133; fax 506/479-9295), or **Sunset Tours** (☎ and fax 506/479-9099; www.sunset-tours.com). In addition to the above tours, each of these companies offers most of the tours listed below, as well as fishing trips and sightseeing excursions on the lake.

CANOPY TOURS   The **Original Canopy Tour** company (☎ 506/257-5149; www.canopytour.com) has an operation set up at **Termales del Bosque** (see below) just outside of Aguas Zarcas. You strap on a climbing harness, ascend more than 100 feet up to a treetop platform, and careen from tree to tree while hanging from a pulley on a skinny cable. It's exhilarating. By press time, the same company is expected to open another such tour at the **Tabacón Resort** (see below).

WHITE-WATER RAFTING & FISHING   For adventurous tours of the area, check out **Desafio Raft** (☎ 506/479-9464; fax 506/479-9178; www.desafiocostarica.com; mail: desafio@racsa.co.cr) or **Aguas Bravas** (☎ 506/479-9025; www.aguas-bravas. E-mail: info@aguas-bravas.co.cr). Both of these companies offer daily raft rides

Taking a Soothing Soak in Hot Springs

One of the primary fringe benefits that Arenal Volcano has bestowed on the area around it are several naturally heated thermal springs. Located at the site of the former village, ✪ **Tabacón Hot Springs Resort** (☎ **506/256-1500;** www.tabacon.com) is the most extensive and luxurious spot to soak your tired bones. It feels like a playground for adults: A series of variously sized pools, fed by natural springs, are spread out among lush gardens. At the center is a large, warm, spring-fed swimming pool with a slide, a swim-up bar, and a perfect view of the volcano. One of the stronger streams flows over a sculpted waterfall, with a rock ledge underneath that provides a perfect place to sit and receive a free hydraulic shoulder massage. The resort also offers professional massages, mud masks, and other treatments at very reasonable prices.

The Ave de Paraiso restaurant here serves well-prepared Tico and international cuisine, and there is also a more informal restaurant serving burgers and sandwiches. You can sign a credit-card voucher when you enter and charge your food and drinks throughout your stay. This sure beats pulling soggy bills from your bathing suit. Entrance fees are $16 for adults and $9 for children under 9. The hot springs are open daily from 10am to 10pm. They recently instituted a policy of limiting the number of visitors at any one time, so reservations are recommended during the high season (late November through late April).

Across the street from the resort and down a gravel driveway is another bathing spot fed by the same springs. You'll find several large pools here but far more basic facilities and no view. Admission is $5. There are changing rooms and showers, but you won't find the Disneyland-like atmosphere that prevails at the Tabacón resort.

There's a popular free public spot located in a densely forested section of the road between Tabacón and the park entrance. This area has some very rudimentary dams set in a section of a warm side-stream. To find it, keep going past the Tabacón Hot Springs Resort away from La Fortuna. You'll soon enter the forested section. After a few tight turns, the path leading down to the springs is on your left. There's a small sign and this is a well-known and popular spot, so you'll usually see several cars parked on the side of the road here.

Finally, there's a new entry in the hot-springs field. **Baldi Termae,** next to the Volcano Look Disco (☎ **506/479-9651**), are the first hot springs you'll come to as you drive from La Fortuna toward Tabacón; however, the main attraction here is the swim-up bar set in the center of the circular concrete pool. I find this place far less attractive than the options you'll find a little further on down the road. Admission is $7.

If you don't have a car and are staying in La Fortuna, every hotel in town and several tour offices offer night tours of the volcano (they don't actually enter the park; rather they stop on the road that runs between the park entrance and the Arenal Observatory Lodge). Most tours, which cost $7 to $15 per person, include a stop at one of the hot springs (not Tabacón).

of Class I to II, III, and IV to V on different sections of the Peñas Blancas and Sarapiquí rivers. A half-day trip on the Peñas Blancas leaving from Fortuna costs just $37 per person; a full day of rafting costs $60 to $80 per person. Both of these companies also offer mountain biking and most of the standard local guided trips.

With Lake Arenal just around the corner, **fishing** is also a popular activity here. The big action is guapote, a South American species of rainbow bass. Most hotels and adventure-tour companies can arrange fishing excursions. Costs run around $100 to $150 for a half day, and $200 to $250 for a full day.

SIDE TRIPS AROUND LA FORTUNA

La Fortuna is a great place from which to make a day trip to the ✪ **Caño Negro National Wildlife Refuge.** This vast network of marshes and rivers is 62 miles (100km) north of La Fortuna near the town of Los Chiles. This refuge is best known for its amazing abundance of bird life, including roseate spoonbills, jabiru storks, herons, and egrets, but you can also see caimans and crocodiles. Bird-watchers should not miss this refuge, though keep in mind that the main lake dries up in the dry season (mid-April through November), which reduces the number of wading birds. Full-day tours to Caño Negro average between $40 and $60 per person.

You can also visit the Venado Caverns, a 45-minute drive away. In addition to plenty of stalactites, stalagmites, and other limestone formations, you'll see bats and cave fish. Tours here cost around $35. Desafio Raft, Aguas Bravas, Aventuras Arenal, and Sunset Tours all offer these trips. Ask at your hotel for more information.

Kids and the young at heart may enjoy the pool, fountain, and water slide at **Jungla y Senderos Los Lagos** (☎ **506/479-9126**). I personally come here more for the network of trails and small lakes that are also on this property. They've recently added a small crocodile hatchery, and hot springs are in the works. You'll find Los Lagos on the road to Tabacón a few kilometers out of La Fortuna. They charge $8 for daily use of their facilities.

ACCOMMODATIONS IN LA FORTUNA

La Fortuna is a tourist boomtown, and basic cabins have popped up here at a phenomenal rate. Right in La Fortuna you'll find a score of budget options. If you have time, it's worth walking around and checking out a couple. If you have a car, drive a little bit out of town toward Tabacón and you'll find several more basic cabins, some even with views of the volcano. **Hotel Jungla y Senderos Los Lagos** (☎ **506/ 479-9126;** fax 506/479-8009) has a campground a few minutes west of La Fortuna. This growing complex recently introduced 20 small cabins near its swimming pool, water slide, crocodile farm, and recreation area just off the main road. However, its nicest attractions are the small lakes and jungle trails located a couple of kilometers down a dirt road. This is where you'll find the campground, which charges around $5 per person for camping and has cooking and bathroom facilities.

Hotel La Fortuna. La Fortuna, San Carlos. ☎ and fax **506/479-9197.** 13 units. $10–$15 per person. Rates include breakfast. No credit cards.

Located 1 block south of the gas station, this perennial budget travelers' favorite has risen from the ashes. A 1997 fire destroyed most of the original hotel, but reconstruction was quick. Most of the rooms are on the original site, but there are three rooms in a new annex across the street. Accommodations are very basic, but what do you expect at these prices? At least the rooms are clean and have private bathrooms. There is an open-air restaurant at the front of the hotel, and the helpful owners can arrange a wide variety of tours.

Hotel Las Colinas. Apdo. 06 (150m/164 yd. south of the National Bank), La Fortuna, San Carlos. ☎ and fax **506/479-9107.** E-mail: hcolinas@racsa.co.cr. 19 units. $25 double, $35 triple. Rates include breakfast. AE, MC, V.

This three-story building in the center of town offers clean but basic rooms. You'll need to be in good shape if you stay in one of the third-floor rooms, but it's worth it if you can snag room 33, which has a private balcony and an unobstructed view of the volcano. There are a few rooms on the ground floor, but they don't even have windows to the outside and are very dark.

Hotel San Bosco. La Fortuna, San Carlos (200m/218 yd. north of the gas station). ☎ **506/ 479-9050.** Fax 506/479-9109. www.arenal-volcano.com. E-mail: fortuna@racsa.co.cr. 34 units. $40–$50 double; lower in the off-season. AE, MC, V.

Located a block off La Fortuna's main street, the San Bosco has two styles of rooms. The older rooms all received a recent face-lift and now feature tile floors and fans. Nevertheless, the newer rooms are still much more attractive, with stone walls, tile floors, air-conditioning, reading lights, and benches on the veranda in front. There's an observation deck for volcano viewing on the top floor of the hotel, and they recently added a swimming pool and Jacuzzi. The San Bosco can help you arrange a wide variety of tours and even has a small gift shop and gym.

Las Cabañitas Resort. Apdo. 5-4417, La Fortuna, San Carlos. ☎ **506/479-9400.** Fax 506/479-9408. www.cabanitas.com. E-mail: cabanita@racsa.co.cr. 32 cabins. $79 double. Rates slightly lower in the off-season (May–Nov). AE, MC, V.

Located 0.62 miles (1km) east of town, these rustic mountain cabins are spacious and clean. About half of the cabins face the volcano and have little porches where you can sit and enjoy the show by day or night. Each cabin is built of varnished hardwoods and has a beautiful floor, a high ceiling, louvered walls to let in the breezes, a modern tile bathroom down a few steps from the sleeping area, and rocking chairs on the porch. There's a small kidney-shaped swimming pool with a snack bar beside it and also a larger full-service restaurant specializing in Costa Rican cuisine. A full meal plan will run you $29 per day. Some of the rooms are wheelchair accessible. A wide variety of tours can be arranged through the hotel. For years this was a good bargain that provided the feel of an isolated nature lodge, yet was close to La Fortuna. Now, there are more, and better, choices on the road out toward Tabacón.

DINING IN LA FORTUNA

Dining in La Fortuna is nowhere near as spectacular as volcano viewing. Most folks either eat at their hotel or go to any one of a number of basic *sodas* serving Tico standards. The favorite meeting places in town are the **El Jardín Restaurant** (☎ **506/ 479-9360**), and **Lava Rocks** (no phone); both are on the main road, right in the center of La Fortuna. Other choices include **La Choza de Laurel** (☎ **506/479-9231**), **Rancho La Cascada** (☎ **506/479-9145**), and **La Pradera** (☎ **506/479-9167**). Heading out of town, you'll find your best alternative at **El Vagabundo** (☎ **506/ 479-9565**), an Italian pizza and spaghetti joint. After dark, the area's biggest attraction is the volcano, but the new **Volcano Look Disco** (☎ **506/479-9690**) on the road to Tabacón is hoping to compete. If you get bored of the eruptions and seismic rumbling, head here for heavy dance beats and mirrored light balls.

ACCOMMODATIONS & DINING NEAR THE VOLCANO

Most of the hotels below also offer full dining options.

Arenal Lodge. Apdo. 1139-1250, Escazú. ☎ **506/228-3189.** Fax 506/289-6798. www.arenallodge.com. E-mail: arenal@racsa.co.cr. 24 units, 10 chalets. $65 double, $112 junior suite, $117 chalet, $130 master suite; $140 matrimonial suite; slightly higher during peak weeks, lower in the off-season (May–Nov). Rates include breakfast. AE, MC, V. Drive west from La Fortuna past Tabacón and the National Park. About 200m (218 yd.) past the dam over Lake Arenal, you'll see a steep driveway. The lodge is a couple of kilometers up the driveway.

Located high on a hillside a mile (1.6km) from Lake Arenal, this lodge has a direct view of Arenal Volcano (some 6 miles/9.5km away) over a forested valley. Although it's not as close to the volcano as some of the other lodges mentioned below, the view is still stunning. The standard rooms, though attractively decorated, have no views at all, although it's only a few steps to a large viewing deck. If you reserve one of the huge junior suites, you can lie in bed and gaze out at the volcano through a wall of glass. These rooms have two queen-size beds, balconies, large picture windows, two sinks in the bathroom, and lots of space. Five separate buildings on a hill behind the main building house the 10 new chalet rooms. These rooms all have plenty of space and good views from their balcony or patio. The matrimonial suite comes with its own private Jacuzzi. All of the suites and chalet rooms come with small kitchenettes.

Moderately priced meals are served in a dining room with a glass wall facing the volcano. After dinner, you can retire to the library, where there's a huge stone fireplace and a pool table, or soak in the outdoor Jacuzzi. A separate lounge has a TV and VCR. The lodge provides free shuttle service to Tabacón Hot Springs, and can also arrange night tours ($15 per person), trips to the national park ($30 per person), and fishing for rainbow bass in Lake Arenal ($250 for two people with lunch and a guide). Situated on a macadamia plantation between two strips of virgin forest, the lodge has several trails that are great for bird-watching.

✪ **Arenal Observatory Lodge.** Apdo. 321-1007, Centro Colón, San José. ☎ **506/ 257-9489.** Fax 506/257-4220. www.arenal-observatory.co.cr. E-mail: arenalob@racsa.co.cr. 28 units, 23 with bathroom. $42–$98 double; slightly lower in the off-season (May–Nov). AE, MC, V.

This once-rustic lodge was originally built for the use of volcanologists from the Smithsonian Institute but has turned into my favorite lodge in the Arenal area. The hotel is only 2¹/₂ miles (4km) from the volcano and is built on a high ridge, with a spectacular view of the cone. Lying in bed at night listening to the eruptions, it's easy to think you're in imminent danger (don't worry; you're not). The superior rooms feature massive picture windows, with a direct view of the volcano. The nicest of these are the four new rooms in the Observatory Block. Room 29 even has a view of both the lake and the volcano. The most basic rooms are in the original *casona* (big house) and are located about 500 meters (545 yd.) from the main lodge; bathrooms are shared.

Surrounding the lodge is the Arenal National Park, which includes thousands of acres of forest and many kilometers of excellent trails. The lodge offers a number of guided and unguided hiking options, including a free morning trip to one of the cooled-off lava flows, as well as a wide range of other tours. Meals are served in a well-placed dining room, with a full wall of glass facing the volcano. A full meal plan will run you $34 per day. To get here, head to the national-park entrance, keep on the dirt road past the entrance, and follow the signs to the Observatory Lodge. A four-wheel-drive vehicle used to be recommended for the 5¹/₂-mile (9km) dirt road up to the lodge, but two bridges now eliminate the need to ford any major rivers, and a two-wheel-drive vehicle will usually make it in the dry season (December through April).

Monta̅ ̅ de Fuego Inn. La Palma de la Fortuna, (A.P. 82-4417) San Carlos. ☎ **506/** Fax 506/460-1455. www.montanadefuego.com. E-mail: monfuego@racsa.co.cr. ─$100 double. MC, V.

rted out as a small collection of cabins with a great view, and great prices. ty grew, the prices and a whole host of new cabins have quickly gone up. Still, these individual cabins have wonderful volcano views from their spacious glass-enclosed porches. Inside, the cabins are all varnished wood, with sparse but new appointments. Eighteen of them have air-conditioning. Be careful, a couple of the standard, or lower-priced cabins, have obstructed views. When I last visited, there were plans to add a swimming pool, Jacuzzi, and spa facilities. There's a large, glass-walled restaurant, Acuarelas, that serves overpriced international cuisine. If this place is full, check next door at the **Cabañas Arenal Paraiso** (☎ 506/479-9006), which has very similar accommodations at slightly lower prices and is run by the same family (the owners of the two lodges are brothers). Both of these hotels are located 5 miles (8km) outside La Fortuna on the road to Tabacón,

✪ **Tabacón Resort.** P.O. Box 181-1007, Centro Colón, San José. ☎ **506/256-1500.** Fax 506/221-3075. www.tabacon.com. E-mail: info@tabacon.com. 42 units. A/C TV TEL. $120 double, $150 suite; slightly lower in the off-season (May–Nov). Rates include buffet breakfast. AE, MC, V.

This new hotel is part of the Tabacón Hot Springs Resort and Spa; guests here enjoy privileges at the spa across the street. Together they pack a pretty good one-two punch. Most rooms here have excellent, direct views of the volcano; those toward the west end of the property and higher up have the best views. They're all spacious and new, with nice wooden furniture. They also have a private terrace or balcony with a couple of chairs for volcano viewing. Nine of the rooms here are truly designed to be accessible to travelers with disabilities. One of the suites is quite a bit larger and has its own Jacuzzi. The last time I visited, work was well under way on a new, large restaurant area located in the gardens behind the rooms. There will also be a spring-fed (hot) pool with a swim-up bar, not unlike the one at the more extensive spa and hot springs facilities across the street. The hotel is located on the main road between La Fortuna and Lake Arenal. As you drive along this road, you will hit the lodge on your right, and then about 91 meters (100 yd.) later, around a sharp bend, the hot springs will be on your left.

Volcano Lodge. La Fortuna de San Carlos. ☎ **506/460-6080** or 506/460-6022. Fax 506/460-6020. www.volcano-lodge.com. E-mail: info@volcano-lodge.com. 20 units. A/C. $75 double. Rate includes breakfast. MC, V.

This new lodge is a collection of 10 duplexes, across the road from and facing the volcano. All of the rooms come with two double beds, a private bathroom, two wicker chairs inside and a small terrace with a couple of wooden rocking chairs for volcano viewing outside. The appointments are simple, but the rooms get plenty of light through big picture windows. Room numbers 1 through 12 have the best views. There's a small free-form pool and Jacuzzi. A wide range of tours are available. The hotel also provides free shuttle service to La Fortuna and Tabacón Hot Springs.

ACCOMMODATIONS & DINING EAST OF LA FORTUNA

✪ **El Tucano Resort and Spa.** (Apdo. 114-1017, San José), Aguas Calientes de San Carlos. ☎ **506/460-6000** or 506/460-3141. Fax 506/460-1692. E-mail: tucano@racsa.co.cr. 100 units. TV TEL. $90 double, $110 junior suite, $150–$220 suite. AE, DC, MC, V.

Located 5¼ miles (8.5km) north of Ciudad Quesada (San Carlos) on the road to Aguas Zarcas, El Tucano is one of the most elegant spa facilities in Costa Rica, with natural hot springs, Jacuzzis, indoor and natural steam rooms, a small gym, and in-house massage therapists. There's also a pool and two tennis courts, and a miniature golf course. The resort is located in a steep-walled valley and faces a lush rain forest. The rooms are set into the hillside and are connected by narrow, winding alleys and stairways. Most rooms are carpeted and very comfortable, with attractive decorations.

The two presidential suites have private terraces, in-room Jacuzzis, and large-screen TVs. This is a great place just to kick back and relax for a day or two.

There are hiking trails on the property, and you can arrange a variety of tours around the region, including some on horseback. Just hanging around, you should see plenty of colorful toucans, the hotel's namesake, as well as many other birds. The dining room is large and formal, with excellent service and a continental menu that includes such dishes as chicken à l'orange and pasta with shrimp. The best tables here, when the weather is nice, are on an outdoor balcony overlooking the river. Room service is also available.

Hotel La Garza. (Apdo. 100-2250, Tres Ríos), Plantanar, San Carlos. ☎ **506/475-5222.** Fax 506/475-5015. E-mail: information@hotel-lagarza-arenal.com. 12 units. TEL. $89 double, $109 triple; lower in the off-season (May–Nov). AE, DC, MC, V.

This comfortable lodge is set on a large working ranch just south of Muelle. La Garza means "the egret," and you will see plenty of these birds here, as they roost nearby. Also, the ranch includes 750 acres of primary rain forest, where many other species of birds can be spotted. Built on the banks of the San Carlos River, the hotel consists of six duplex bungalows, each of which has a deck overlooking the river. Large trees provide shade, and the sound of the river lulls you to sleep at night. High ceilings and overhead fans help keep the rooms cool, and all the rooms are attractively decorated and have views of Arenal Volcano in the distance. The hotel's restaurant and bar are reached via a small suspension bridge over the lazy little river that runs through the property. Meals will run you around $32 per person per day. You can arrange tours of the region, or wander around the ranch observing the day-to-day activities. The hotel has a pool, a Jacuzzi, and even a tennis court, but the rain forest is the primary attraction.

Termales del Bosque. Ciudad Quesada, (Apdo. 243-4400) San Carlos. ☎ **506/460-4740** or 506/257-5149. Fax 506/460-1356. www.canopytour.com. E-mail: canopy@racsa.co.cr. 13 units. $45 double, $55 triple. Rates include breakfast. MC, V.

This new place packs a lot of ecotourism punch for the buck. Most of the rooms are in duplex buildings set on a small hill. Each comes with two double beds, or a double and a single, and front and back patios. The rooms are clean and spacious, but the beds are a bit soft. There is also a three-bedroom bungalow with a shared bathroom and kitchenette. Meals will run you around $20 per day.

Nowhere near as fancy as the neighboring El Tucano Resort, Termales del Bosque does have some wonderful natural hot springs set in rich rain forest. The series of sculpted pools are set on the banks of a small river. Down by the pools, there's a natural steam room (scented each day with fresh eucalyptus), a massage room, and a snack-and-juice bar. The trail down here winds through the thick forest and, if you want to keep on walking, you can take guided or self-guided tours on a network of well-marked trails. You can rent horses right at the lodge, and there's even a canopy tour. If you aren't staying here, you can use the pools and hike the trails for $8, or do the canopy tour for $45. You'll find Termales del Bosque on the road from San Carlos to Aguas Zarcas, just before El Tucano.

✪ Tilajari Hotel Resort. Muelle (Apdo. 81-4400), San Carlos. ☎ **506/469-9091.** Fax 506/469-9095. www.tilajari.com. E-mail: tilajari@tilajari.com. 76 units. A/C TV TEL. $85 double, $105 junior suite, $110 family suite; slightly lower in the off-season (May–Nov). AE, MC, V.

This sprawling 30-acre resort just outside the farming community of Muelle (17.4 miles/28km from La Fortuna) makes a good base for exploring this area. Built on the banks of the San Carlos River, the Tilajari Hotel offers some of the most luxurious accommodations in the region. Most of the rooms have views of the river (some even have balconies), while others open onto rich flowering gardens. Each suite comes with a separate living room and kitchenette. Large iguanas are frequently sighted on the grounds, and crocodiles live in the San Carlos River. There's a large open-air dining room that has both formal and informal sections and a bar. The menu consists primarily of moderately priced Tico and international dishes. There's also a swimming pool, Jacuzzi, lighted indoor and outdoor tennis courts, racquetball court, soccer field, sauna, game room with pool tables and table tennis, gift shop, orchid garden, tropical fruit-and-vegetable garden, medicinal herb garden, and well-maintained butterfly garden to keep guests busy.

The lodge arranges tours around the region, including trips to Caño Negro, Arenal Volcano and Tabacón Hot Springs, and Fortuna Falls, for around $45 per person. Trips into the nearby rain forest, either on foot, on horseback, or by tractor, can also be arranged, as can gentle floats on the Peñas Blancas River.

To reach Tilajari from San José, drive first to Ciudad Quesada; from there continue on to Florencia. In Florencia turn north on the road to Muelle (marked). In Muelle turn left (head west) toward Tanque and follow the signs for Tilajari, which will be on your right a mile (1.6km) from this last turn.

ACCOMMODATIONS & DINING SOUTH OF LA FORTUNA

Hotel Valle Escondido. San Ramón (Apdo. 452-1150, La Uruca). ☎ **506/231-0906.** Fax 506/232-9591. www.valleescondido.com. E-mail: hotel@valleescondido.com. 33 units. $70 double, $85 triple. AE, MC, V.

This modest hotel, which provides access to some of the region's rain forests, is south of La Fortuna, just off the road between San Ramón and La Fortuna. Valle Escondido (Hidden Valley) is situated on a 990-acre farm that includes primary and secondary forest as well as fields of ornamental plants grown for export. The rooms are located in long low rows of buildings, with good views over a forested valley. All are spacious and comfortable. Some are carpeted, but I prefer those with hardwood floors. In front of the rooms run long verandas where you can sit and enjoy the tranquillity of the surroundings.

The restaurant serves Tico and continental dishes, and there's also a small bar where you can wet your whistle, and a small pool and Jacuzzi where you can wet the rest of you. There are miles of well-maintained trails here. Hiking, horseback riding ($10 per hr.), mountain biking ($4 per hr.), and bird-watching are the primary activities here; a wide range of tours are available for an additional charge.

Villablanca Hotel. Apdo. 247-1250, San Ramón, Alajuela. ☎ **506/228-4603** or 506/661-1600. Fax 506/228-4004. www.villablanca-costarica.com. E-mail: info@villablanca-costarica.com. 48 units. $99 double, $119 triple, $163 family casita for up to 6. AE, DC, MC, V.

Owned and operated by a former president of Costa Rica, this lodge consists of a series of Tico-style *casitas,* or little houses, surrounded by 2,000 acres of farm and forest. Each casita is built of adobe and has traditional tile floors and whitewashed walls with deep-blue trim (this is the classic color scheme of 19th-century adobe homes throughout the country). Inside, you'll find a rounded fireplace in one corner, window seats, comfortable hardwood chairs, colorful curtains, and two twin beds covered with colorful bedspreads. The "family" casitas have two bedrooms and two baths. Most rooms come with electric teapots and some have small refrigerators. In several rooms the bathrooms have tubs that look out through a wall of windows onto lush gardens.

The dining room, which offers a simple-but-filling buffet, is in the hacienda-style main lodge. A central atrium garden, library, TV room/lounge, gift shop, and small bar round out the amenities. Villablanca is off the beaten track, but it is relatively close to San José, and if you're interested in bird-watching or exploring a cloud forest and want to avoid the crowds of Monteverde, this is a good choice.

Adjacent to the lodge are 6³/₄ miles (11km) of trails through the Los Angeles Cloud Forest Reserve. Admission to the reserve is $24 per person and includes a guided hike. You can also rent horses ($12 per hr.), or take an adventurous swing through the canopy on their new canopy tour ($39). Transportation between the lodge and San José is $30 each way. Or you can take a public bus from San José to San Ramón and then take a taxi for around $15. If you're driving, head west out of San José to San Ramón and then head north, following the signs to Villablanca.

3 Tilarán & Lake Arenal

124 miles (200km) NW of San José; 12¹/₂ miles (20km) NW of Monteverde; 43¹/₂ miles (70km) SE of Liberia

This remains one of the least-developed tourism regions in Costa Rica but not for lack of resources or charms. It does, after all, have Lake Arenal, a manmade lake with an area of 33 square miles (85.5km; making it the largest lake in Costa Rica), surrounded by rolling hills that are partly pastured and partly forested. The perfect cone of Arenal Volcano lies at the opposite (east) end of the lake from Tilarán. The volcano's barren slopes are a stunning sight from here, especially when reflected in the waters of the lake. The northwest side of Lake Arenal is a dry region of rolling hills and pastures, distinctly different from the lusher landscape near La Fortuna.

People around here used to curse the winds, which often come blasting across this end of the lake at 60 knots or greater. However, since the first sailboarders caught wind of Lake Arenal's combination of warm freshwater, steady blows, and spectacular scenery, things have been changing quickly. Although the town of Tilarán is still little more than a quiet farm community, hotels are proliferating out along the shores of the lake. Even if you aren't a fanatical sailboarder, you still might enjoy hanging out by the lake, hiking in the nearby forests, and catching glimpses of Arenal Volcano.

The lake's other claim to fame is its rainbow-bass fishing. These fighting fish are known in their native South America as *guapote* and are large members of the cichlid family. Their sharp teeth and fighting nature make them a real challenge.

ESSENTIALS

GETTING THERE & DEPARTING   By Bus   Express buses (☎ 506/222-3854) leave San José for Tilarán daily at 7:30 and 9:30am and 12:45, 3:45, and 6:30pm from Calle 12 between avenidas 7 and 9. The trip lasts from 4 to 5¹/₂ hours, depending on road conditions; the fare is $3.

There are also morning and afternoon buses from **Puntarenas** to Tilarán. The ride takes about 3 hours; the fare is $2.25. To get to Puntarenas, see the information on getting to Puntarenas in chapter 5. From **Monteverde** (Santa Elena), there is a bus daily at 7am. The fare for the 3-hour trip is $1.50. Buses from **La Fortuna** leave for Tilarán daily at 8am and 2:30pm, returning at 7am and 12:30pm. The trip is 3 to 4 hours; the fare is $1.75.

From Tilarán, direct buses to San José leave daily at 5, 7, and 7:45am and 2 and 5pm. Buses to Puntarenas leave at 6am and 1pm daily. The bus to Santa Elena (Monteverde) leaves daily at 1pm. Buses also leave regularly for Cañas, where you can catch buses north or south along the Interamerican Highway. Buses for La Fortuna, at the south end of Lake Arenal, leave daily at 7am and 3pm.

By Car   From San José, take the Interamerican Highway west toward Puntarenas and then continue north on this road to Cañas. In Cañas, turn east toward Tilarán. The drive takes 4 hours. You can also drive here from La Fortuna, in approximately 1 hour, along a scenic road that winds around the lake.

ORIENTATION   Tilarán is about 3 miles (5km) from Lake Arenal. All roads into town lead to the central park, which is Tilarán's main point of reference for addresses. If you need to exchange money, check at one of the hotels listed here, or go to the Banco Nacional. If you need a taxi to get to a lodge on Lake Arenal, call **Taxis Unidos Tilarán** (☎ 506/695-5324).

WHAT TO SEE & DO

✪ **WINDSURFING**   If you want to try windsurfing, you can rent equipment from **Tilawa Windsurfing Center** (☎ 506/695-5050), which has its facilities on one of the lake's few accessible beaches, about 5 miles (8km) from Tilarán on the road along the west end of the lake. Boards rent for $45 to $55 per day, and lessons are also available. You can also ask at **Tico Wind** (☎ 506/383-2694; www.ticowind.com; E-mail: info@ticowind.com), which sets up shop on the shores of the lake each year when the winds blow, or at **Rock River Lodge** (☎ 506/695-5644) (see "Accommodations," below), which rents equipment for $325 per week, including daily lunch. Rock River Lodge also has some high-end mountain bikes, which will run you around $35 per day.

FISHING   If you want to try your hand at fishing for rainbow bass, contact **J.J.'s Fishing and Outdoor Tours** (☎ 506/695-5825). A half-day fishing trip will cost around $175, and a full day goes for $200. J.J.'s can also arrange nonfishing boat trips out on the lake, and other outdoor tours.

HORSEBACK RIDING & HIKING   If you're looking for another way to get around on dry land, the folks at **Tilawa** or **Rock River Lodge** (see "Windsurfing," above) can arrange for you to rent a horse for around $10 to $15 per hour. If you feel like strapping on your hiking boots, there are some trails for hiking on the far side of Lake Arenal, near the smaller Coter Lake.

SWIMMING   Up above Lake Arenal on the far side of the lake from Tilarán, you'll find the beautiful little heart-shaped **Coter Lake.** This lake is surrounded by forest and has good swimming. UFO watchers also claim that this is a popular pit stop for extraterrestrials. A taxi to Coter Lake will cost around $12.

ARENAL BOTANICAL GARDENS   Continuing clockwise on the road around the lake will bring you to the town of Nuevo Arenal, where the pavement ends. If you continue another 2¹⁄₂ miles (4km) on the dirt road, you'll come to the Arenal Botanical Gardens (☎ 506/694-4273), which is open daily from 9am to 5pm and charges $8 admission. This private garden was started only in 1991, but it's already quite beautiful and extensive. Not only are there many tropical plants and flowers to be seen, but there are always butterflies and hummingbirds here.

ACCOMMODATIONS

Cabinas Mary. Apdo. 89 (on the south side of the park), Tilarán, Guanacaste. ☎ and fax **506/695-5479.** 18 units. $20 double. No credit cards.

Located right on Tilarán's large and sunny central park, Cabinas Mary is a very basic, but fairly clean, lodging. It's upstairs from the restaurant of the same name and has safe parking in back. Rooms are large, and most have plenty of windows. You even get hot water here, which is a surprise at this price. The restaurant downstairs is a popular hangout. It's open daily from 6am to 10pm; meals cost between $3 and $7.

Chalet Nicholas. Apdo. 72-5710, Tilarán, Guanacaste. ☎ and fax **506/694-4041.** E-mail: chaletnicholas@costarica.net. 3 units. $59 double. Rate includes full breakfast. No credit cards.

This friendly American-owned bed-and-breakfast is located 1^1/$_2$ miles (2^1/$_2$ km) west of Nuevo Arenal and sits on a hill above the road. There are great views from the garden, and all three rooms have a view of Arenal Volcano. This converted home is set on 15 acres and has pretty flower gardens, an organic vegetable garden, and an orchid garden. Behind the property are acres of forest through which you can hike in search of birds, orchids, butterflies, and other tropical beauties. The upstairs loft room is the largest. It even has its own private deck. No smoking is allowed in the house or on the grounds. A 3-hour horseback-riding tour costs $25 per person. Owners John and Catherine Nicholas go out of their way to make their guests feel at home, although their three Great Danes might intimidate you when you first drive up. All around, it's a really good deal.

Hotel Naralit. Tilarán, Guanacaste. ☎ **506/695-5393.** Fax 506/695-6767. 26 units. $14–17 double, $20–$25 triple. V.

This budget hotel is a good bet in Tilarán. The rooms are clean and comfortable and some even come with cable TV, albeit with very small television sets. There are three second-floor rooms that have a nice shared balcony with views of the town's church.

Hotel Tilawa. Apdo. 92-5710, Tilarán, Guanacaste. ☎ **800/851-8929** in the U.S., or 506/695-5050. Fax 506/695-5766. www.hotel-tilawa.com. E-mail: tilawa@racsa.co.cr. 28 units. TEL. $77 double, $100 triple, $148 suite. AE, MC, V.

Built to resemble the Palace of Knossos on the island of Crete, the Hotel Tilawa sits high on the slopes above the lake, has a sweeping vista down to the water, and is primarily a windsurfers' hangout. Unusual colors and antique paint effects give the hotel a weathered look; inside there are wall murals and other artistic paint treatments throughout. Rooms have dyed cement floors, Guatemalan bedspreads, and big windows. Some have kitchenettes. There's a bar/disco beside the pool, as well as a moderately priced restaurant in the main building. The most recent addition here is a refurbished windsurfing center and new grill restaurant down by the lake. Amenities include a swimming pool and a tennis court. For a fee, the Tilawa can arrange windsurfing, mountain biking, horseback riding, and fishing trips (with or without meals and/or equipment). They also offer a 5-hour boat tour across the lake, with a visit to Tabacón Hot Springs, for $47.

✪ Rock River Lodge. Apdo. 95, Tilarán, Guanacaste. ☎ and fax **506/695-5644.** http://rockriver.mastermind.net. E-mail: rokriver@racsa.co.cr. 6 units, 8 bungalows. $45–$65 double, $55–$75 triple. V.

Set high on a grassy hill above the lake, this small lodge looks as if it might have been transported from Hawaii. The rooms are in a long, low lodge set on stilts. Walls and floors are made of hardwood, and there are bamboo railings along the veranda. Wind chimes let you know when the breezes are kicking up, and there are sling chairs on the porch. Rooms are of medium size and have one double bed and a bunk bed, as well as modern tiled bathrooms. Though fairly simple in style, this is one of the most attractive lodges in the area. The newer bungalows, which are farther up the hill, offer more privacy and have sculpted bathtubs. It's a long walk down to the lake (not to mention the walk back up), so a car is recommended. Meals will cost you around $25 per person per day and are served in the spacious open-air restaurant, where there's a large stone fireplace. This hotel caters to sailboarders and other active travelers. When the wind isn't up, owner Norman List offers mountain-biking trips and horseback and hiking adventures to a nearby waterfall.

✪ **Villa Decary.** Nuevo Arenal, 5717 Tilarán, Guanacaste. ☎ **506/383-3012.** Fax 506/694-4330. www.villadecary.com. E-mail: info@villadecary.com. 4 units, 1 casita. $69 double, $79 casita. No credit cards.

Named after a French explorer (and a rare palm species he discovered and named), this small bed-and-breakfast is nestled on a hill above Lake Arenal, midway between the town of Nuevo Arenal and the Arenal Botanical Gardens (see above). Each room comes with two double beds, large picture windows, and a spacious private balcony with a lake view. The rooms get plenty of light, which, combined with the bright Guatemalan bedspreads and white-tile floors, give the place a very lively feel. The separate casita has a full kitchen and the best view on the premises. Breakfasts are extravagant and memorable, with a steady stream of fresh fruits; fresh juice; strong coffee; homemade pancakes, waffles, or muffins; and usually an excellent omelet or soufflé. You might not want to stop eating, but eventually you'll just have to call it quits and get on with your day. There's great bird-watching on the hotel grounds, and howler monkeys are common guests here as well.

DINING

There are numerous inexpensive places to eat in Tilarán, including the restaurant at Cabinas Mary, as well as **La Carreta** (☎ **506/695-6654**), a popular restaurant and bar around the corner. If you're staying outside of town, it's likely you'll eat in your hotel's dining room, since there are few restaurants around the shores of the lake. In Nuevo Arenal, try the pizzas and pastas at **Tramonti** (☎ **506/694-4282**), or the basic Tico fare at **Concha del Mar** (☎ **506/694-4169**). Also worth mentioning is **Equus BBQ,** a small open-air restaurant in front of Xiloe Lodge that has a view of the lake. It specializes in roast chicken and steaks. If you're in either Tilarán or Nuevo Arenal, try the following place.

Mystica. On the road between Tilarán and Nuevo Arenal. ☎ **506/382-1499.** Reservations not necessary. Main courses $3–$9. No credit cards. Daily 7:30am–9pm. PIZZA/ITALIAN.

This new Italian-run hotel and restaurant has a wonderful setting high on a hill overlooking the lake. The large dining room features rustic wooden chairs and tables, varnished wood floors, colorful tablecloths, and abundant flower arrangements. The most striking features, aside from the view, are the large open fireplace on one end, and the large brick oven, in the shape of a small cottage, on the other. The pizzas are baked in the oven and the pastas and delicious main dishes are authentically northern Italian. Whenever possible, Mystica uses fresh ingredients from its own garden.

4 Monteverde

103 miles (167km) NW of San José; 51 miles (82km) NW of Puntarenas

Next to Manuel Antonio, this is Costa Rica's most internationally recognized tourist destination. The fame and accompanying traffic have led me to dub it the Monteverde Crowd Forest. Nevertheless, the preserve itself and the extensive network of private reserves around it are incredibly rich in biodiversity, and a well-organized infrastructure helps guarantee a rewarding experience for first-time eco-adventurers.

Monteverde translates as "Green Mountain," and that's exactly what you'll find at the end of the steep and windy rutted dirt road that leads here. Along the way, you'll pass through mile after mile of often dry, brown pasturelands. All of these pastures were once covered with dense forest, but now only small pieces of that original forest remain.

The village of Monteverde was founded in 1951 by Quakers from the United States who wished to leave behind a constant fear of war as well as an obligation to support continued militarism through paying U.S. taxes. They chose Costa Rica primarily because it had no standing army. Although Monteverde's founders came here to farm the land, they wisely recognized the need to preserve the rare cloud forest that covered the mountain slopes above their fields, and to that end they dedicated the largest adjacent tract of cloud forest as the Monteverde Biological Cloud Forest Preserve.

Perched on a high mountain ridge, this tiny, scattered village and surrounding cloud forest are well known both among scientific researchers and eco-travelers. Cloud forests are a mountaintop phenomenon. Moist, warm air sweeping in off the nearby ocean is forced upward by mountain slopes, and as this moist air rises, it cools, forming clouds. The mountaintops of Costa Rica are blanketed almost daily in dense clouds, and as these clouds cling to the slopes, moisture condenses on forest trees. This constant level of moisture has given rise to an incredible diversity of innovative life-forms and a forest in which nearly every square inch of space has some sort of plant growing. Within the cloud forest, the branches of huge trees are draped with epiphytic plants: orchids, ferns, and bromeliads. This intense botanic competition has created an almost equally diverse population of insects, birds, and other wildlife. Monteverde Biological Cloud Forest Preserve covers 26,000 acres of forest, including several different life zones that are characterized by different types of plants and animals. Within this small area are more than 2,000 species of plants, 400 species of birds, and 100 different species of mammals. It's no wonder that the preserve has been the site of constant scientific investigations since its founding in 1972.

The preserve was originally known only to the handful of researchers who came here to study different aspects of life in the cloud forest. However, as the beauty and biological diversity of the area became known outside of academic circles, casual visitors began arriving. For many, the primary goal was a chance to glimpse the rare and elusive **quetzal,** a bird once revered by the pre-Columbian peoples of the Americas. As the number of visitors began to grow, lodges began opening, word spread, more lodges opened, and so on. Today Monteverde is a prime example of too many people chasing after the same little piece of nature. Monteverde is akin to the Yosemite Valley, only on a much smaller scale—a place of great and fragile beauty whose popularity threatens to destroy the very beauty that draws people to it. That said, and despite the hordes of ecotourists traipsing its trails, Monteverde is still a beautiful place and offers a glimpse into the life of one of the world's most threatened ecosystems. However, if your primary goal is to sight a quetzal, you should also consider visiting other cloud-forest areas around Costa Rica. In particular, the Tapantí National Wildlife Refuge, near Cerro de la Muerte, which has several specialty lodges (see chapter 7), where you'll find far fewer crowds and usually better chances of seeing the famed quetzal.

ESSENTIALS

GETTING THERE & DEPARTING   By Bus   Express buses (☎ **506/222-3854** or 506/645-5159) leave San José daily at 6:30am and 2:30pm from Calle 12 between avenidas 7 and 9. The trip takes between 3¹/₂ and 5 hours, depending on road conditions; the fare is $5.50.

There's also a daily bus that departs Puntarenas for Santa Elena, only a few kilometers from Monteverde, at 2:15pm. The bus stop in Puntarenas is across the street from the main bus station. The fare for the 2¹/₂-hour trip is $2.50.

There is a daily bus from Tilarán (Lake Arenal) at 1pm. Trip duration, believe it or not, is 2 hours (for a 25-mile/40km trip); the fare is $1.20.

Monteverde

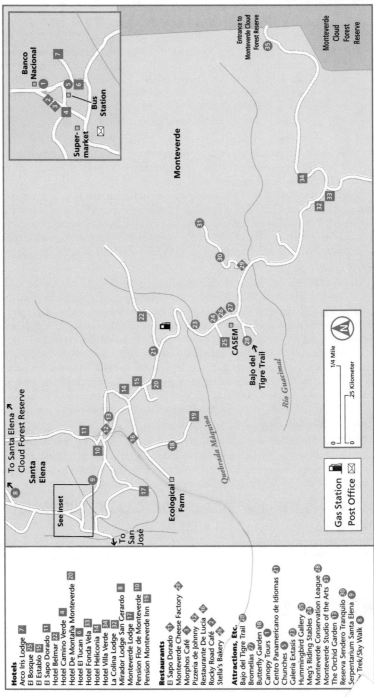

Hotels
Arco Iris Lodge 7
El Bosque 25
El Establo 15
El Sapo Dorado 11
Hotel Belmar 22
Hotel Camino Verde 4
Hotel De Montaña Monteverde 20
Hotel El Tucan 6
Hotel Fonda Vela 33
Hotel Heliconia 14
Hotel Villa Verde 34
La Colina Lodge 32
Mirador Lodge San Gerardo 8
Monteverde Lodge 17
Pension Flor de Monteverde 10
Pension Monteverde Inn 19

Restaurants
El Sapo Dorado 11
Monteverde Cheese Factory 29
Morphos Café 3
Pizzeria de Johnny 32
Restaurante De Lucia 46
Rocky Road Café 7
Stella's Bakery 26

Attractions, Etc.
Bajo del Tigre Trail 28
Bromelias 27
Butterfly Garden 18
Canopy Tours 1
Centro Panamericano de Idiomas 21
Chunches 5
Galeria Extasis 23
Hummingbird Gallery 35
Meg's Riding Stables 24
Monteverde Conservation League 28
Monteverde Studio of the Arts 31
The Orchid Garden 13
Reserva Sendero Tranquilo 30
Serpentarium Santa Elena 9
Sky Trek/Sky Walk 8

Gas Station
Post Office

1/4 Mile
.25 Kilometer

Another option is to take **Costa Rica Expeditions'** van (☎ **506/257-0766**) from San José. You must have a reservation. The fare is $40 each way.

The express bus departs for San José daily at 6:30am and 2:30pm. The bus from Santa Elena to Puntarenas leaves daily at 6am. If you are heading to Manuel Antonio, take the 6am Santa Elena/Puntarenas bus and transfer in Puntarenas. To reach Liberia, take any bus down the mountain and get off at the Río Lagarto Bridge, where you hit the paved road. You can then flag down a bus bound for Liberia (almost any bus heading north). The Santa Elena/Tilarán bus leaves daily at 7am.

By Car   Take the Interamerican Highway toward Nicaragua. About 19 miles (31km) past the turnoff for Puntarenas, watch for the signs for Monteverde, just before the Río Lagarto Bridge. It takes about 2 hours and 15 minutes to this point. From this turnoff, it's another 23¹/₂ miles (38km) and 1¹/₂ to 2 hours to Monteverde. The going is very slow because the road is so bad. Many people are told that this road is not passable without four-wheel drive, but I've been driving it in regular cars for years, albeit in the dry season. Don't try it in the rainy season (mid-April through November) unless you have four-wheel drive. Also, be careful where you turn: There's an alternate route to Monteverde that turns off the highway near the Río Sardinal (before the Río Largato), and this road is in even worse shape.

ORIENTATION   As you approach Santa Elena, take the right fork in the road if you're heading directly to Monteverde. If you continue straight, you'll come into the little village of Santa Elena, which has a bus stop, health clinic, one bank, a general store, and a few simple restaurants and budget hotels. There's a laundry located on the road out toward the preserve entrance, just beyond the Hotel Sapo Dorado.

Monteverde, on the other hand, is not a village in the traditional sense of the word. There's no center of town, only dirt lanes leading off from the main road to various farms. This main road has signs for all the hotels and restaurants mentioned here, and dead-ends at the reserve entrance.

The telephone number for the **local clinic** is ☎ **506/645-5076,** for the **Red Cross,** ☎ **506/645-6128,** and for the **local police,** ☎ **117.**

GETTING AROUND   A taxi between Santa Elena and either the Monteverde Cloud Forest Preserve or the Santa Elena Cloud Forest Reserve will cost around $8. Count on paying between $4 and $8 for the ride from Santa Elena to your lodge in Monteverde. Your lodge can call a cab for you.

EXPLORING THE MONTEVERDE BIOLOGICAL CLOUD FOREST PRESERVE

The ✪ **Monteverde Biological Cloud Forest Preserve** (☎ **506/645-5122** or 506/645-5112; www.cct.or.cr; E-mail montever@racsa.co.cr) is one of the most developed and well-maintained natural attractions in Costa Rica. The trails are clearly marked,

---

Driving Note

All roads to Monteverde are rugged, especially the one from Tilarán, which is riddled with potholes and rough gravel. Pregnant women or people with bad backs should think twice before embarking on these painful, poorly maintained roads. You can make the trip in a standard two-wheel-drive vehicle in the dry season (December through March), but you might want the extra-clearance afforded by four-wheel drive. In the rainy season (April through November), four-wheel drive is a must.

Seeing the Forest for the Trees, Bromeliads, Monkeys, Hummingbirds . . .

Since the entrance fee to Monteverde is valid for a full day, I recommend taking an early-morning walk with a guide and then heading off on your own either directly after that hike or after lunch. A guide will certainly point out and explain a lot, but there's also much to be said for walking quietly through the forest on your own or in very small groups. This will also allow you to stray from the well-traveled paths in the park.

regularly traveled, and generally gentle in terms of ascents and descents. The cloud forest here is lush and largely untouched. Still, keep in mind that most of the birds and mammals you've been reading about are rare, elusive, and nocturnal. Moreover, to all but the most trained of eyes, those thousands of exotic ferns, orchids, and bromeliads tend to blend into one large mass of indistinguishable green. However, with a guide hired through your hotel, or on one of the preserve's official guided 2- to 3-hour hikes, you can see and learn far more than you could on your own. At $15 per person, the preserve's tours may seem expensive, especially after you pay the entrance fee, but I strongly recommend that you go with a guide.

Perhaps the most famous resident of the cloud forests of Costa Rica is the quetzal, a robin-size bird with iridescent green wings and a ruby-red breast, which has become extremely rare due to habitat destruction. The male quetzal also has two long tail feathers that make it one of the most spectacular birds on earth. The best time to see quetzals is early to midmorning, and the best months are February through April (mating season).

Other animals that have been seen in Monteverde include jaguars, ocelots, and tapirs. After the quetzal, Monteverde's most famous resident was the golden toad (*sapo dorado*), a rare, native species. However, the golden toad seems to have disappeared from the forest and is feared extinct. Competing theories of the toad's demise include adverse effects of a natural drought cycle, the disappearing ozone layer, pesticides, or acid rain. Photos of the golden toad abound in Monteverde, and I'm sure you'll be as saddened as I was by the disappearance of such a beautiful creature.

ADMISSION, HOURS & TOURS   The preserve is open daily from 7am to 4pm, and the entrance fee is $9 per person, $5 for students. Because only 150 people are allowed into the preserve at any one time, you may be forced to wait for a while. Most hotels can reserve a guided walk and entrance to the preserve for the following day for you, or you can get tickets in advance directly at the preserve entrance. The trails can be very muddy, depending on the season, so ask about current conditions. If the mud is heavy, you can rent rubber boots at the preserve entrance for $1.50 per day. They may make your hike much more pleasant. Before venturing into the forest, have a look around the information center. There are several guidebooks available, as well as posters and postcards of some of the preserve's more famous animal inhabitants.

WHAT TO SEE & DO OUTSIDE THE PRESERVE
BIRD-WATCHING & HIKING
Ample bird-watching and hiking opportunities can also be found outside the preserve boundaries. You can avoid the crowds at Monteverde by heading 3 miles (5km) north from the village of Santa Elena to the **Santa Elena Cloud Forest Reserve** (☎ **506/ 645-5390**). This 900-acre reserve has a maximum elevation of 5,600 feet, which

makes it the highest cloud forest in the Monteverde area. There are 5 miles (8km) of hiking trails as well as an information center. As it borders the Monteverde Preserve, a similar richness of flora and fauna is to be found here, although quetzals are not nearly as common. The $7 entry fee at this reserve goes directly to support local schools. The reserve is open daily from 7am to 4pm. Guided tours are available for $15 per person, not including the entrance fee. Call ☎ **506/645-5390** to make a reservation for the tour.

To learn even more about Monteverde, stop in at the **Monteverde Conservation League** (☎ **506/645-5003** or 506/645-5305; E-mail: acmmcl@racsa.co.cr), which has its operations at the welcome center at the trailhead of the Bajo del Tigre trail. In addition to being a good source for information, they also sell books, T-shirts, and cards, and all proceeds go to purchase more land for the Bosque Eterno de Los Niños (Children's Eternal Forest). The **Bajo del Tigre Trail** is a 2-mile-long (3.5km) trail that's home to several different bird species not usually found within the reserve. There are several different loops you can take, lasting anywhere from one to several hours. The trail starts a little past the CASEM artisans' shop (see "Shopping," below) and is open daily from 8am to 5pm. Admission is $5 general, $2 students.

You can also go on guided 3-hour hikes at the **Reserva Sendero Tranquilo** (☎ **506/645-5010**), which has 200 acres of land, two-thirds of which is in virgin forest. This reserve is located up the hill from the cheese factory, charges $20 for its tours, and is open daily from 7am to 3pm seasonally.

CANOPY TOURS

For an elevated look at the cloud forest, check out the local branch of **Canopy Tours** (☎ **506/645-5243;** www.canopytour.co.cr), which has an office right in the center of Santa Elena. This is one of my favorite canopy tours in Costa Rica, since the ascent is made by climbing up the hollowed-out interior of a giant strangler fig. This is no educational walk through the woods. You strap on a climbing harness, clip into a pulley, and hurl yourself from tree to tree along a wire cable. In the end you rappel down. Anybody in average physical condition can do it, but it's not for the faint-hearted or acrophobic. The $2^1/2$-hour tours run three times daily and cost $45 for adults, $35 for students, and $25 for children under 12.

Another new canopy tour has opened up near the Santa Elena Reserve. The **Sky Trek/Sky Walk** (☎ **506/645-5238;** www.skywalk.co.cr) is a growing complex of aerial adventures. Like most other canopy tours in Costa Rica, the **Sky Trek** ($35 per person) consists of a series of platforms connected by cables strung through the canopy. There's no strangler-fig ascent, however, just a walk to the top of a hill.

The **Sky Walk** ($12) is a network of forest paths and suspension bridges that provides visitors with a view previously reserved for birds, monkeys, and the much more adventurous tourist. The bridges reach 130 feet above the ground at their highest point, so acrophobia is still an issue. The Sky Trek/Sky Walk is located about 2 miles (3.5km) outside of the town of Santa Elena, on the road to the Santa Elena Cloud Forest Reserve. It is open daily from 7am to 4pm. For an extra $12, a knowledgeable guide will point out the diverse flora and fauna on the Sky Walk. Reservations are recommended for the Sky Trek.

The newest entry into the aerial fray is **Aerial Adventures** (☎ **506/645-5960**), a two-person chairlift that winds through some secondary forest and open spaces for about a mile (1.6km). I find this ride a bit tacky and it is my least favorite canopy tour in the country. The cost is $12.

HORSEBACK RIDING

Meg's Riding Stables (☎ 506/645-5419) and **La Estrella Stables** (☎ 506/645-5075) are two of the more-established operators and offer guided rides for around $10 per hour. As mentioned above, there are now popular horseback/boat trips linking Monteverde and Santa Elena with La Fortuna. This is certainly an exciting and adventurous means of connecting the two popular destinations, but I've received numerous complaints about the state of the trails and the treatment of the horses, so be very careful before undertaking this trip. (See "Arenal Volcano & La Fortuna," above, for more information.)

OTHER ADVENTURES IN MONTEVERDE

Birds are not the only colorful fauna in Monteverde. Butterflies abound here, and the **Butterfly Garden** (☎ 506/645-5512), located near the Pensión Monteverde Inn, displays many of Costa Rica's most beautiful species. Besides the hundreds of preserved and mounted butterflies, there are gardens and a greenhouse where you can watch live butterflies. The garden is open daily from 9:30am to 4pm, and admission is $7 for adults and $3 for children, which includes a guided tour. The best time to visit is between 11am and 1pm, when the butterflies are most active.

If you've had your fill of birds and snakes and butterflies, you might want to stop at the **Orchid Garden** (☎ 506/645-5510), on the main road toward the preserve. This new attraction boasts more than 400 species of orchids. Admission is $5 general, $3 students.

Because the vegetation in the cloud forest is so dense, most of the forest's animal residents are rather difficult to spot. If you were unsatisfied with your sightings, even with a naturalist guide leading you, you might want to consider attending a slide show of photographs taken in the preserve. There is a host of daily slide shows around Monteverde. The longest running of these take place at the **Monteverde Lodge, El Sapo Dorado, Hotel Belmar,** and **Hummingbird Gallery** (see below for phone numbers). Dates, show times, and admissions vary, so inquire at your hotel or one of the places mentioned above.

The **Centro Panamericano de Idiomas** (☎ 800/903-8950 in the U.S. and Canada, or 506/645-5441; www.cpi-edu.com; E-mail: anajarro@racsa.co.cr) offers immersion language classes in a wonderful setting. A 2-week program, with 4 hours of class per day and a homestay with a Costa Rican family, costs $660.

Almost all of the area hotels can arrange a wide variety of other tour and activity options, including night trips to the Arenal Volcano (a grueling 4-hr. ride away) and guided night tours of the cloud forest.

SHOPPING

If you're in the mood to do some shopping, stop in at **CASEM,** on the right side of the main road, just past Restaurant El Bosque (☎ 506/645-5190). This crafts cooperative sells embroidered clothing, T-shirts, posters, and postcards with photos of the local flora and fauna, Boruca weavings, locally grown and roasted coffee, and many other items to remind you of your visit to Monteverde. CASEM is open Monday through Saturday from 8am to 5pm and Sunday from 10am to 4pm (closed Sunday from May through October). There is also a well-stocked **gift shop** at the entrance to the preserve. You'll find plenty of T-shirts, postcards, and assorted crafts here, as well as a well-stocked selection of science and natural-history books.

Perhaps the best-stocked gift shop in Monteverde is the **Hummingbird Gallery** (☎ 506/645-5030). You'll find the gallery just outside the preserve entrance. Hanging from trees around it are several hummingbird feeders that attract more than seven species of these tiny birds. At any given moment, there might be several dozen hummingbirds buzzing and chattering around the building and your head. Inside, you will, of course, find a lot of beautiful color prints of hummingbirds and other local flora and fauna, as well as a wide range of craft items, T-shirts, and other gifts. The Hummingbird Gallery is open daily from 8:30am to 4:30pm.

Over the years, Monteverde has developed a nice little **community of artists.** Around town, you'll see paintings by local artists like Paul Smith and Meg Wallace, whose works are displayed at the Fonda Vela Hotel and Stella's Bakery, respectively. You might also check out **Galería Extasis** (☎ 506/645-5548), off the main road to the reserve, which sells the intriguing wooden sculptures of artist Marco Tulio Brenes. **Bromelias** (☎ 506/645-6093), is a new gallery-cum-gift-shop-cum-coffee-shop run by the folks who own the Hummingbird Gallery. It has a good, slightly higher-end selection of artwork and crafts, housed in a wonderfully open and light two-storied building, located up the hill from Stella's Bakery.

If you are interested in taking a class or workshop with one of the many local artists, check in with the newly formed **Monteverde Studio of the Arts** (☎ 506/645-5434; www.mvstudios.com; E-mail: mstudios@racsa.co.cr).

ACCOMMODATIONS

When choosing a place to stay in Monteverde, be sure to check whether the rates include a meal plan. In the past, almost all the lodges operated on the American Plan (three meals a day), but this practice is on the wane. Check before you assume anything.

EXPENSIVE

✪ **El Sapo Dorado.** Apdo. 9-5655, Monteverde, Puntarenas. ☎ **506/645-5010** or 506/645-5184. Fax 506/645-5180 or 506/645-5181. www.cool.co.cr. E-mail: elsapo@racsa.co.cr. 30 cabin suites. $80–$90 double, $95–$109 triple; lower in the off-season (May–Nov). AE, MC, V.

Located on a steep hill between Santa Elena and the preserve, El Sapo Dorado (named for Monteverde's famous "golden toad") offers the most comfortable accommodations in Monteverde. The spacious cabins are built of hardwoods both inside and out and are surrounded by a grassy lawn. Big windows let in lots of light, and high ceilings keep the rooms cool during the day. Some of the older cabins have fireplaces, which are a welcome feature on chilly nights and during the peak parts of the rainy season. My favorite rooms are the sunset suites, which have private terraces with views to the Gulf of Nicoya and wonderful sunsets.

There's an excellent restaurant here, which is open to the public and serves three meals daily. The bar stays open until 11pm and is usually fairly quiet. The hotel has a massage room with a local therapist on call, as well as a conference room, where they sometimes show slide shows at night. Not only does El Sapo Dorado own and manage the Reserva Sendero Tranquilo, but they also have a network of well-maintained trails into primary forest. To find the hotel and restaurant, watch for the sign on the left-hand side of the main road to the preserve, just as you're leaving Santa Elena.

✪ **Monteverde Lodge.** (Apdo. 6941-1000, San José), Monteverde. ☎ **506/257-0766.** Fax 506/257-1665. www.costaricaexpeditions.com. E-mail: costaric@expeditions.co.cr. 27 units. Dec 15–Apr 30 $115 double, $132 triple; May 1–Dec 14 $100 double, $115 triple. AE, MC, V.

Operated by Costa Rica Expeditions, the Monteverde Lodge is one of the most upscale hotels in Monteverde. It's located 3 miles (5km) from the preserve entrance in a secluded setting near Santa Elena. Guest rooms are large and comfortable and have angled walls of glass with chairs and a table placed so that avid bird-watchers can do a bit of birding without leaving their rooms. The gardens and secondary forest surrounding the lodge now have some gentle groomed trails and are also home to quite a few species of birds. This lodge's most popular feature is a large hot tub in a big atrium garden just off the lobby. After hiking all day, you can soak your bones under the stars. Scheduled bus service to and from San José is available ($45 each way), as is a shuttle to the preserve ($6 each way), horseback riding, and a variety of optional tours.

The hotel's dining room offers great views, good Tico and international food, and excellent formal service provided by bow-tied waiters. Meals here run around $45 per person per day. The bar adjacent to the dining room is a very popular gathering spot. There are regular evening slide shows focusing on the cloud forest.

MODERATE

✪ **Arco Iris Lodge.** Apdo. 003-5655, Monteverde, Puntarenas. ☎ **506/645-5067.** Fax 506/645-5022. www.bbb.or.cr. E-mail: arcoiris@racsa.co.cr. 10 units. $45–$50 double. MC, V.

This is by far the nicest hotel right in Santa Elena. The rooms are spread out in eight separate buildings (so, in effect, most are individual cabins). All have wood or tile floors and plenty of wood accents. My favorite is the "honeymoon cabin," which has its own private balcony with a forest view and good bird-watching. The management here is extremely helpful, speaks five languages, and can arrange a wide variety of tours. Although they recently stopped serving lunch and dinner, there's a breakfast buffet for $5, and beer, wine, and other refreshments are available throughout the day and evening.

Hotel Belmar. Apdo. 17-5655, Monteverde, Puntarenas. ☎ **506/645-5201.** Fax 506/645-5135. www.centralamerica.com. E-mail: belmar@racsa.co.cr. 34 units. $65–$80 double; lower in the off-season (May–Nov). V.

You'll think you're in the Alps when you stay at this beautiful Swiss-chalet–style hotel. Set on the top of a grassy hill, the Belmar has stunning views of the Nicoya Gulf and the Pacific. Afternoons in the dining room or lounge are idyllic, with bright sunlight streaming in through a west-facing glass wall. Sunsets are spectacular. Most of the guest rooms are fitted with wood paneling, French doors, and little balconies that open onto splendid views. There are actually two buildings here. My favorite rooms are in the main building, those in the "Chalet" building are a bit smaller. The restaurant serves a mix of well-prepared Tico and international cuisine; a full meal plan runs around $28 per person per day. The Belmar is up a road to the left of the gas station as you come into the village of Monteverde.

Hotel de Montaña Monteverde. (Apdo. 2070-1002, Paseo Los Estudiantes, San José), Monteverde. ☎ **506/645-5046.** Fax 506/645-5320. www.ticonet.co.cr/monteverde. E-mail: monteverde@ticonet.co.cr. 34 units, 4 family cabins. $76 double, $86 family or deluxe suite, $90 master suite. AE, MC, V.

This long, low motel-style building is one of the oldest hotels in Monteverde and is frequently filled with tour groups. The hotel is surrounded by 37 acres of farm and woods, and there are horses available for rent. Older rooms are rustic and have wood paneling. Newer rooms have queen-size beds, more light, and spectacular views of the Nicoya Gulf. There are deluxe suites, and one master suite with its own whirlpool tub and a view. There is a lot of variation in room size, age, and quality. I find the newer standard rooms much nicer than some of the older suites. For family privacy, there are four cabins across the lawn from the main lodge. The rustic glass-walled dining room offers excellent views. Attached to the restaurant is a small bar that's busy in the evening, when people sit around swapping stories of their day's adventures and wildlife sightings. Meals will run you around $36 per person per day. On cold nights, you can warm up in the hotel's sauna or hot tub.

Hotel Fonda Vela. (Apdo. 70060-1000, San José), Monteverde. ☎ **506/257-1413** or 506/645-5125. Fax 506/257-1416. www.centralamerica.com. E-mail: fondavel@racsa.co.cr. 40 units. $77 double, $86 junior suite, $95 suite. AE, MC, V.

Located on the right after the La Colina Lodge, the Fonda Vela is still one of the more luxurious lodges in Monteverde. Guest rooms are in a half-dozen buildings scattered among the forests and pastures of this former farm, and most have views of the Nicoya Gulf. Lots of hardwood has been used throughout. Most of the rooms have bathtubs, which is a rarity in Costa Rica. The suites, two of which have sleeping lofts, are the most spacious accommodations available, but unfortunately, several of these do not have views. But the dining room has great sunset views, and it sometimes even features live music. There's a spacious and popular bar here, as well as a small system of private trails. Meals will run you around $34 per person per day. The hotel offers laundry service, transportation to the preserve, and horse rentals. Throughout the hotel you'll see paintings by owner Paul Smith, who also handcrafts violins and cellos and is a musician himself.

Hotel Heliconia. (Apdo. 10921-1000, San José), Monteverde. ☎ **506/645-5109.** Fax 506/645-5007. www.centralamerica.com. E-mail: heliconi@racsa.co.cr. 32 units. $75 double, $85 junior suite, $100 suite. AE, MC, V.

The Heliconia, named after one of the tropics' most fascinating flowers, is another comfortable and luxurious hotel. The new main lodge building is a three-story behemoth, located high on a hill behind the rest of the hotel's several buildings. Here you'll find most of the suites and junior suites. These immense rooms feature varnished wood walls, carpeted floors, two king-size beds, and huge private balconies. All of the rooms on the second and third floors here get great sunset views. Rooms in the older buildings down by the road are also done in floor-to-ceiling hardwoods that give them the rustic feel of a mountain resort. Some of these have large picture windows facing dense forest. All around, there are paths that lead through attractive gardens and to a hot tub in a bamboo grove. The hotel's restaurant serves standard Tico and continental cuisine. There's also a small bar, gift shop, conference room, and trails that lead from the hotel up to and through a 600-acre private reserve of virgin forest with scenic views of the Nicoya Gulf.

Hotel Villa Verde. Apdo. 16-5655, Monteverde, Puntarenas. ☎ **506/645-5025.** Fax 506/645-5115. E-mail: estefany@racsa.co.cr. 21 units. $49 double, $78 suite. Rates include breakfast. AE, MC, V.

This hotel is close to the preserve and built on a grand scale. The main lodge features a huge dining room with floor-to-ceiling windows that reach all the way to the two-story-high roof. Each suite has a living room and a fireplace and is identified not by a number but by the likeness of a specific bird carved into the door. Standard rooms are spacious and Spartan, and the textured sand bathroom walls and pale-blue tiles are an aesthetic affront. Lunch and dinner will run you an extra $18. The hotel has a small gift shop and offers a host of tour options.

Mirador Lodge San Gerardo. Apdo. 19-5655, Monteverde, Puntarenas. ☎ **506/ 645-5354** or 506/381-7277. Fax 506/645-5087. E-mail: mirador@racsa.co.cr. 7 units. $50 double, $15 for students with valid ID. Rates include full breakfast. MC, V.

This place is extremely isolated and quite basic. There are seven rooms here in four cabins. Plans for a major expansion were on hold the last time I visited and the whole operation had a run-down feel to it. The rooms are all very simply furnished, with concrete floors and soft foam mattresses. But they do have great views of Arenal Volcano (when it's clear). The Mirador is a long way from the Monteverde Biological Cloud Forest Preserve, but it's relatively close to the Santa Elena Cloud Forest Reserve. You can now reach the Mirador year-round by four-wheel-drive vehicle, so it's no longer necessary to be taken in by horseback. To get here, head out toward Santa Elena following signs to the Santa Elena Reserve and Sky Walk. As you get close to the Sky Walk, you will see the sign and turnoff for Mirador Lodge. Guided hikes are included in the rate, and the hotel also rents horses and runs tours by horseback and boat to the Arenal Volcano.

INEXPENSIVE

In addition to the hotels listed below, there are quite a few pensións and backpacker specials in Santa Elena and spread out along the road to the preserve. The best of these are **Hotel Camino Verde** (☎ and fax **506/645-5916**), **Pensión Flor de Monteverde** (☎ and fax **506/645-5236**), and **Pensión Monteverde Inn** (☎ **506/645-5156**). All three charge around $8 to $10 per person.

El Bosque. Apdo. 27-5655, Monteverde. ☎ **506/645-5221** or 506/645-5158. Fax 506/645-5129. www.bosquelodge.com. E-mail: elbosque@racsa.co.cr. 26 units. $35 double, $42 triple, $55 quad. AE, MC, V.

Hidden down the hill behind El Bosque restaurant (on the main road to the preserve) is one of Monteverde's best values. Though the rooms are very basic, they're clean and fairly large and have high ceilings, picture windows, and double beds. The cement floors and simple furnishings are what help keep the rates down. The rooms are arranged in a semicircle around a minimally landscaped garden. The setting may not be spectacular, but if you're going to spend all day in the preserve, this shouldn't bother you too much. The hotel's restaurant is 91 meters (100 yd.) up a dirt road and down a path that crosses a jungly ravine by footbridge, which turns going for breakfast into a morning bird-watching trip. Tico standards and international dishes are served here, with prices ranging from $4 to $15.

El Establo. Apdo. 549-2050, San Pedro. ☎ **506/645-5110** or 506/645-5033. Fax 506/645-5041. www.establo.com. E-mail: elestablo@racsa.co.cr. 22 units. $40 double, $50 triple, $60 quad. AE, MC, V.

Horses are an integral part of Costa Rican culture and a common sight in Monteverde. El Establo, as its name implies, is a working stable and incorporates this theme in its architectural design. Though the hotel is next to the road, there are 120 acres of farm behind it, and half of this area is in primary forest. Most of the rooms are situated off a large enclosed porch that contains plenty of comfortable chairs and a fireplace. Guest-room doors look as if they were salvaged from a stable, but inside, the rooms are carpeted and have orthopedic mattresses and modern bathrooms, though with showers only. The second-floor rooms are my favorites here, and those on the end of the hall even have a bit more light than others. There's a large new restaurant off the main hotel, by the road. Meals will run you around $25 per person per day. Of course, the hotel also has plenty of horses for rent at $10 per hour, with a guide.

Hotel El Tucan. Santa Elena, Puntarenas. ☎ **506/645-5017**. Fax 506/645-5462. 14 units, 7 with bathroom. $14 double without bathroom, $20 double with bathroom. No credit cards.

This very basic lodging is located on the edge of Santa Elena (on the back road from the village's main street that leads to Monteverde) and consequently does not have the rural feel of many of the area's other accommodations. Though the rooms without bathrooms are only slightly larger than closets, they are fairly clean. Rooms with a private bathrooms are slightly larger; some are in a separate building across the street. Very inexpensive Costa Rican–style meals are served in a very basic dining room on the ground floor. Keep in mind that this hotel is 3 miles (5km) from the preserve. If you don't have a car, transportation to and from the preserve by taxi is going to add a bit to the cost of the room.

La Colina Lodge. Monteverde. ☎ **506/645-5009.** Fax 506/645-5580. www.lacolina.com. E-mail: lacolina@racsa.co.cr. 11 units, 6 with bathroom. $35–$45 double, $45–$55 triple. Rates include breakfast. AE, MC, V.

The folks who run the La Colina bed & breakfast in Manuel Antonio have remodeled and renamed the old Pensión Flor Mar. The rooms are housed in two separate buildings. Everything is still quite simple here. Most rooms each have one double and one single bed, although a couple still have bunk beds. When I last visited there were plans to install a Jacuzzi and open a bar. Sporting events and videos are shown on a large-screen satellite TV in a lounge area. The lodge is pretty close to the reserve, which is a plus for budget travelers without a car.

DINING

Most lodges in Monteverde have their own dining rooms, and these are the most convenient places to eat, especially if you don't have a car. Because most visitors want to get an early start, they usually grab a quick breakfast at their hotel. It's also common for people to have their lodge pack them a bag lunch to take with them to the preserve, although there's now a decent little soda at the preserve entrance. If you're in the mood to eat out, there are several inexpensive restaurants scattered along the road between Santa Elena and Monteverde. One worth mentioning is the **Pizzeria de Johnny** (☎ 506/645-5066), on the road to the reserve near El Sapo Dorado, which serves excellent wood-oven–baked pizzas and assorted pasta dishes.

A good choice for lunch is **Stella's Bakery** (☎ 506/645-5560), across the road from the CASEM gift shop. Stella's is open daily from 6am to 6pm and has a small cafe and a few outdoor tables, where you can pile your plate with an assortment of fresh foods served cafeteria style. The selection changes, but might include vegetarian quiche, eggplant parmigiana, and different salads. They also have fresh-baked breads and muffins and a daily supply of other deliciously decadent baked goods.

It's also worth stopping by the **Monteverde Cheese Factory** (☎ 506/645-5136) to pick up some of the best cheese in Costa Rica (you can even see it being made). The cheese factory is open Monday through Saturday from 7:30am to 4pm and Sunday from 7:30am to noon. You can also get homemade ice cream at the Cheese Factory.

In Santa Elena, you might want to check out **Rocky Road Café** (no phone) for hefty sandwiches, excellent burgers, and a wide range of desserts. They'll also prepare you a box/bag lunch. Also in town is the **Morphos Café** (☎ 506/645-5818), which specializes in vegetarian meals, fresh-fruit juices, and ice-cream desserts.

Take a Break

If all of the activities in Monteverde have worn you out, stop in at **Chunches** (☎ **506/645-5147**), a new coffee/espresso bar and bookstore in Santa Elena, which also doubles as a Laundromat. Chunches is open Monday through Saturday from 9am to 6pm.

✪ **El Sapo Dorado.** On the left as you go from Santa Elena toward the reserve. ☎ **506/645-5010.** Reservations recommended during high season (late Nov–late Apr). Main courses $6–$15. AE, MC, V. Daily 6:30–9:30am, noon–3pm, and 6–9pm. INTERNATIONAL.

Located high on a hill above the main road, El Sapo Dorado provides great sunsets and good food. The menu is a little bit more imaginative than at most restaurants in Monteverde, which makes it well worth a visit even if you miss the sunset. A recent menu included grilled corvina in heart-of-palm sauce, fettuccine in peanut-squid sauce, and filet mignon in pepper-cream sauce. The emphasis is on fresh ingredients and healthy preparation, and there are always vegetarian and vegan options, as well. In addition to a large formal dining room, there's a patio that's a great spot for lunch or an early dinner. Taped classical music and jazz are played in the evenings.

Restaurante De Lucía. On the road down to the Butterfly Farm, on your right. ☎ **506/645-5337.** Reservations recommended during high season (late Nov–late Apr). Lunch $2.50–$6, main courses $8–$12. AE, MC, V. Daily 11am–3pm and 6–9pm. COSTA RICAN/INTERNATIONAL.

In just a few years here, De Lucía's has earned some local renown. There's really no menu, but your waiter will bring out a platter with the nightly selection of meats and fresh fish, which are then grilled to order. One of the more interesting dishes is the chicken in orange sauce. All meals come with fresh homemade tortillas and a full accompaniment of side orders and vegetables. The sweet plátanos prepared on the open grill are delicious. Service is informal and friendly. The heavy wood tables and chairs are spread comfortably around the large dining room.

7

The Central Pacific Coast: Where the Mountains Meet the Sea

The central Pacific coast is home to some of the most accessible beaches in Costa Rica. They range from the somewhat seedy Puntarenas and the cut-rate, fun-in-the-sun Jacó to the jungle-clad hillsides of Manuel Antonio and Dominical. For the most part, this coast is not as spectacular as that of the more rugged Nicoya Peninsula, but on the bright side, in the dry season, it doesn't get as brown and desolate-looking as the peninsula. The climate here is considerably more humid than farther north but not nearly as steamy as along the south Pacific or Caribbean coasts. Jacó and Manuel Antonio are Costa Rica's two most developed beaches, while Puntarenas, a former seaport, offers the most urban beach setting in the country (it's just a short day trip away from San José). If you're looking to get away from it all, without traveling too far or spending too much, Dominical should be your top choice on this coast.

This is also where you'll find some of Costa Rica's most popular and spectacular national parks and biological reserves: **Manuel Antonio National Park,** home of three-toed sloths and white-faced monkeys; **Chirripó National Park,** a misty cloud forest that becomes a barren *páramo* (a region above 10,000 ft.) at the peak of its namesake, **Mount Chirripó;** and **Carara Biological Reserve,** one of the last places in Costa Rica where you can see the disappearing dry forest join the damp, humid forests that extend south down the coast. You might even glimpse an occasional scarlet macaw.

1 Puntarenas

71 miles (115km) W of San José; 118 miles (191km) S of Liberia; 47 miles (75km) N of Playa de Jacó

Some see Puntarenas as a fallen jewel with vast potential; others see nothing more than a run-down, rough-and-tumble port town best seen through a rearview mirror. A 10-mile-long (16km) spit of land jutting into the Gulf of Nicoya, Puntarenas was once Costa Rica's busiest port, but that changed drastically when the government inaugurated nearby Puerto Caldera, a modern container port facility. After losing its port, the city survived primarily on commercial fishing. Watching the tourist boom bring big bucks to other cities, Puntarenas decided to try to grab its piece of the pie. After decades of decay and neglect, Puntarenas has recently received some long-overdue attention.

In 1998, Puntarenas initiated a large public works and renovation project that has so far yielded a new cruise-ship docking facility, a convention-and-recreation center, a modest maritime museum, and an artisans' row where visitors can stock up on regional arts and crafts.

There's a good highway leading all the way from San José, so Puntarenas can be reached (on a good day, with no traffic) in 1¹/₂ hours by car, which makes it the closest beach to San José—at least in elapsed time if not in actual mileage. Because Puntarenas is a city, a former port town, and a commercial fishing center, this beach has a very different character from any other in Costa Rica. A long, straight stretch of sand with gentle surf, the beach is backed for most of its length by the **Paseo de los Turistas** (Tourist Walk). Across a wide boulevard from the paseo are hotels, restaurants, bars, discos, and shops. The sunsets and the views across the Gulf of Nicoya are quite beautiful, and there's almost always a cooling breeze blowing in off the water. All around town you'll find unusual old buildings, reminders of the important role Puntarenas once played in Costa Rican history. It was from here that much of the Central Valley's coffee crop was once shipped, and while the coffee barons in the highlands were getting rich, so too were the merchants of Puntarenas.

If you're in Costa Rica for only a short time and want to get in some time on the beach, Puntarenas is certainly an option, though I recommend driving (or being driven) the extra hour or so that it takes to reach some of the nicer beaches farther south. Swimming here still seems more the exception than the rule, and Puntarenas is still primarily a place to spend the night during transit. It is here you must pick up the ferries to Nicoya, and many folks like to arrive the night before and get an early start. It's also a good place to break up the longer trip up to, or back from, Guanacaste. Puntarenas is most popular as a weekend holiday spot for Ticos from San José and is at its liveliest on weekends.

One final note: In 1997 and 1998, Puntarenas was the site of Costa Rica's worst outbreak of dengue fever (see chapter 2 for more information). This has subsided, but you should take precautions in Puntarenas, especially during the day, since dengue is spread by a mosquito that is active only during the daytime.

ESSENTIALS
GETTING THERE & DEPARTING   By Bus   Express buses (☎ 506/222-0064) leave San José daily every half hour between 6am and 9pm from Calle 16 and Avenida 12. Trip duration is 2 hours; the fare is $2.50.

The main Puntarenas bus station is a block east of the Hotel Imperial, which is in front of the old main dock on the Paseo de los Turistas. Buses to San José leave daily every half hour between 5:30am and 7pm. The bus to **Santa Elena** leaves daily at 2:15pm from a stop across the railroad tracks from the main bus station. Buses to **Quepos** (Manuel Antonio) leave daily at 4:30am, 10:30am, and 3pm.

By Car   Head west out of San José on the Interamerican Highway, passing the airport and Alajuela, and follow the signs to Puntarenas. The drive takes between 1¹/₂ and 2 hours.

By Ferry   See the "Playa Tambor" or "Playa Montezuma" sections of chapter 5 for information on crossing to and returning from Puntarenas from Paquera or Naranjo on the Nicoya Peninsula.

ORIENTATION   Puntarenas is built on a long, narrow sand spit that stretches 10 miles (16km) out into the Gulf of Nicoya and is marked by only five streets at its widest. The ferry docks for the Nicoya Peninsula are near the far end of town, as are the bus station and market. The north side of town faces an estuary, while the south

A Colorful Festival

If you're in Puntarenas on the Saturday closest to July 16, you can witness the **Fiesta of the Virgin of the Sea.** During this festival, a regatta of colorfully decorated boats carry a statue of Puntarenas's patron saint.

---

side faces the mouth of the gulf. The Paseo de los Turistas is on the south side of town, beginning at the pier and extending out to the point. If you need a taxi, call **Coopetico** (☎ **506/663-2020).**

WHAT TO SEE & DO

Take a walk along the Paseo de los Turistas and notice how similar this side of town is to a few Florida beach towns 50 years ago. The hotels across the street range in style from converted old wooden homes with bright gingerbread trim to modern concrete monstrosities to tasteful art-deco relics needing a new coat of paint. If you venture into the center of the city, be sure to check out the **central plaza around the Catholic Church.** The church itself is interesting, as it has portholes for windows, reflecting the city's maritime tradition. Here you'll also find the city's new cultural center, **La Casa de la Cultura** (☎ **506/661-1394)** and small **museum** (☎ **506/661-3666).**

If you want to go swimming, the ocean waters are now said to be perfectly safe (pollution was a problem for many years), although the beach is still not very attractive. Alternately, you can head out to the end of the peninsula to the **Balneario Municipal,** the public pool. It's huge, has a great view (albeit through a chain-link fence), and is surrounded by lawns and gardens. However, this place is pretty run-down and a bit seedy. Entrance is only $1 for adults and 50¢ for children. The pool is open Tuesday through Sunday from 9am to 4pm. Your best bet is to head back down the spit, and just a few kilometers out of town you'll find **Playa Doña Aña,** a popular beach with picnic tables, bath- and changing rooms, and a couple of *sodas.*

Puntarenas isn't known as one of Costa Rica's prime sportfishing ports, but there are usually a few charter boats available. Check at your hotel, near the docks, or at the **Hotel Yadran.** Rates are usually between $250 and $400 for a half day and between $400 and $700 for a full day. These rates are for up to four people.

YACHT CRUISES   The most popular water excursions from Puntarenas are yacht cruises through the tiny, uninhabited islands of the Guayabo, Negritos, and Pajaros Islands Biological Reserve. These cruises include a lunch buffet and relaxing stop on beautiful and undeveloped **Tortuga Island,** where you can swim, snorkel, and sun. The water is clear blue and the sand is bright white. However, as this trip has surged in popularity, a cattle-car element to these tours has developed. Several San José–based companies offer these excursions, with round-trip transportation from San José, but if you're already in Puntarenas, you might receive a slight discount by boarding here.

Calypso Tours (☎ **506/256-2727;** E-mail: info@calypsotours.com) is the most reputable company that cruises out of Puntarenas. In addition to Tortuga Island, Calypso Tours takes folks to their own private nature reserve at Punta Coral and even on a sunset cruise that includes dinner and some guided stargazing. Any of these cruises will run you $99 per person from San José, or $94 from Puntarenas. If you check down at the docks, you might find some other boats that ply the waters of the Nicoya Gulf. Some of these companies also offer sunset cruises with live music, snacks, and a bar. However, make sure you feel comfortable with the seaworthiness of the vessel and the professionalism of the crew—in 1997, one of these boats capsized, and two passengers drowned.

Diving Trips to Isla del Coco (Cocos Island)

This little speck of land located some 300 miles (480km) off the Pacific coast was a prime pirate hideout and refueling station (freshwater and foodstuffs). Robert Louis Stevenson most likely modeled *Treasure Island* on Cocos. Sir Francis Drake, Captain Edward Davis, William Dampier, and Mary Welch are just some of the famous corsairs who dropped anchor in the calm harbors of this Pacific pearl. They allegedly left troves of buried loot, though scores of treasure hunters over several centuries have failed to unearth more than a smattering of the purported bounty.

Today Cocos Island is far more famous for another type of treasure: the rich abundance of its massive—both in size and numbers—and varied underwater life. The clear, warm waters around Cocos are widely regarded as one of the most rewarding dive destinations on this planet.

Cocos Island lives up to its reputation as a prime place to see schooling herds of scalloped hammerhead sharks. On a recent shallow-water checkout dive—normally, a perfunctory and uninspiring affair—I spotted my first (12-ft.) hammerhead lurking just 15 feet below me within 15 seconds of flipping into the water. Soon there were more, and soon they came much, much closer.

Other denizens of the waters around Cocos Island include white- and silver-tipped reef sharks; marbled, manta, eagle, and mobula rays; moray and spotted eels; octopi; spiny and slipper lobsters; hawksbill turtles; squirrel fish, trigger fish, and angelfish; surgeon fish, trumpet fish, grouper, grunts, snapper, jack, tangs, and more. Two of the more spectacular underwater residents here include the red-lipped bat fish and the frog fish.

Most diving at Cocos is relatively deep: between 85 and 120 feet, and there are often strong currents and choppy swells to deal with—not to mention all those sharks. This is not a trip for novice divers.

The perimeter of Cocos Island is ringed by steep forested cliffs punctuated by dozens of majestic waterfalls—cascading down in stages or steady streams for hundreds of feet. The island itself has a series of trails that climb its steep hills and wind through its rain-forested interior. There are several endemic bird, reptile, and plant species here, including the ubiquitous Cocos finch, which I spotted soon after landing onshore, and the wild Cocos Island pig.

Isla del Coco was first mapped by the French in 1556 (it appears as "Ile de Coques"—"Shell" or "Nut Shell" Island). But for phonetic reasons, it became universally known as Isla del Coco. The Costa Rican flag was first raised here on September 15, 1869. Throughout its history, Cocos Island has provided anchorage and freshwater to hundreds of ships, broken the backs and spirits of treasure seekers, and entertained divers and dignitaries (Franklin Delano Roosevelt visited it three times). In 1978, it was declared a national park and protected area.

With just a small ranger station housing a handful of national-park guards, Cocos Island is essentially uninhabited. Visitors these days come on private or charter yachts, fishing boats, or one of the few live-aboard dive vessels making regular voyages out here. It's a long trip: Most dive vessels take 30 to 36 hours to reach Cocos. Sailboats are even slower.

Aggressor Fleet Limited, P.O. Box 1470, Morgan City, LA 70381-1470 (☎ **800/348-2628** or 504/385-2628; fax 504/384-0817; www.aggressor.com; E-mail: divboat@aol.com), regularly runs dive trips to Coco Island from Puntarenas.

ACCOMMODATIONS

Hotel Ayi Con. 50m (55 yd.) south of the market (Apdo. 358), Puntarenas. ☎ **506/ 661-0164** or 506/661-1477. 44 units, 22 with bathroom. $12 double without bathroom, $18 double with bathroom, $22 double with bathroom and A/C. No credit cards.

Centrally located near the market and close enough to the ferryboat docks, the Ayi Con is your basic low-budget Tico accommodation. It's above a row of shops in a very busy shopping district of Puntarenas and is frequented primarily by Costa Ricans. Backpackers will find that this is probably the best and the cleanest of the cheap hotels in Puntarenas. If you're just passing through and have to spend a night in town, this place is convenient and acceptable.

Hotel Las Brisas. Paseo de los Turistas (Apdo. 83-5400), Puntarenas. ☎ **506/661-4040.** Fax 506/661-2120. E-mail: hbrisas@racsa.co.cr. 20 units. A/C TV. $65–$80 double, $81–$95 triple; lower in the off-season. Rates include breakfast. AE, MC, V.

Out near the end of the Paseo de los Turistas, you'll find this clean hotel with large air-conditioned rooms, a small pool out front, and the beach right across the street. All the rooms have tile floors, double or twin beds, and small televisions and tables. Large picture windows keep the rooms sunny and bright during the day. The hotel's small open-air dining room serves some of the best food in town, with the emphasis on continental dishes. The bouillabaisse is excellent, and there's always a Greek-style fish special or homemade moussaka on the menu. There's complimentary coffee and a secure parking lot. The new owners have raised the prices considerably and I'm not sure it's worth it anymore.

Hotel Tioga. Paseo de los Turistas (Apdo. 96-5400), Puntarenas. ☎ **506/661-0271** or 506/ 255-3115. Fax 506/661-0127. www.hoteltioga.com. E-mail: tiogacr@racsa.co.cr. 46 units. A/C TV TEL. $45–$75 double. Rates include breakfast. AE, MC, V.

This 1950s modern-style hotel is the old standard on the Paseo de los Turistas. The beach is across the street, and there are plenty of nearby restaurants. When you walk through the front door, you enter a courtyard with a pool that's been painted a brilliant shade of blue. In the middle of the pool, there's a tiny island with a tree growing on it. Rooms vary in size and view, but all come with air-conditioning, telephone, and television. The garden-sector rooms, however, only have cold-water showers. The larger rooms are attractive, with huge closets, modern bathrooms, and private balconies with a view of the ocean. The smaller, less-expensive rooms have louvered, frosted-glass windows to let in lots of light and air while maintaining some privacy. The restaurant and bar are on the second floor, and there's a breakfast room and lounge on the fourth floor, so you can look out across the water as you enjoy your complimentary breakfast. The newest addition here is the Corona de Oro casino.

Yadran Hotel. At the end of the Paseo de los Turistas (Apdo. 14-5400), Puntarenas. ☎ **506/661-2662.** Fax 506/661-1944. 42 units. A/C TV TEL. $70–$99 double, $91–$120 triple. AE, MC, V.

Located at the far end of Puntarenas, at the tip of the spit, this is the most luxurious in-town choice, which isn't exactly saying much. I find it a bit overpriced for what you get, but because it's in town, you're close to the Paseo de los Turistas and most restaurants. Also, the car-ferry dock is only a few blocks away. The range in room prices reflects whether you get an ocean view. I like the upper-floor rooms, with a balcony and a view, but even the priciest rooms can seem a bit dreary. The hotel has two small restaurants. One is a poolside patio restaurant and the other is a slightly more formal indoor dining room with a view over the water. The seafood here is good, if a bit pricey—entrees range from $7 to $21. A small casino is open every evening from 6pm onward. The hotel's disco gets going nightly at 6pm. It's located underground, so the beat won't keep you awake if you decide not to dance the night away. The hotel also has a tour desk, bicycle rentals, and a gift shop.

DINING

Since you're in a seaport, you should be sure to try some of the local catch. **Corvina,** or sea bass, is the most popular offering and it's served in various forms and preparations. My favorite dish on a hot afternoon is **ceviche,** and you'll find that just about every restaurant in town serves this savory marinated seafood concoction. The most economical option is to pull up a table at one of the many open-air snack bars along the Paseo de los Turistas. They have names like **Soda Rio de Janeiro** and **Soda Acapulco,** and serve everything from sandwiches, drinks, and ice cream to ceviche and whole fish meals. Sandwiches are priced at around $1.50, and a fish fillet with rice and beans should cost around $4. If you want a slightly more formal atmosphere, try the open-air **Restaurant Aloha** (☎ 506/661-2375), which is also on the Paseo de los Turistas.

Jardin Cervecero. Paseo de los Turistas between calles 21 and 23. ☎ **506/661-0330.** Main courses $3–$9. AE, DC, MC, V. Wed–Mon noon–1am. SEAFOOD.

This Tico beer garden is a popular drinking spot. It also happens to serve excellent seafood. The restaurant is a huge open room with a high ceiling; louvered windows swing open and provide fresh breezes and a view of the bay. This is a good place to grab a window seat, order some ceviche, and kick back. There's beer on tap and good hearty meals.

La Caravelle. Paseo de los Turistas between calles 21 and 23. ☎ **506/661-2262.** Reservations recommended in high season and on weekends. Main courses $5.50–$15. AE, MC, V. Tues–Sun noon–2:30pm and 6–10:30pm. FRENCH.

For more than 18 years, La Caravelle has been serving fine French dinners in an eclectically decorated cafe atmosphere. The restaurant's walls are decorated with a curious assortment of paintings, as well as a carousel horse, which gives La Caravelle a very playful feel. The menu, however, is strictly traditional French, with such flavorful and well-prepared dishes as tenderloin with bourguignonne sauce or a tarragon béarnaise. There are quite a few good seafood dishes, as well as a salade Niçoise. There's a modest assortment of both French and Chilean wines to accompany your meal.

✪ **La Yunta Steakhouse.** Paseo de los Turistas. ☎ **506/661-3216.** Main courses $4–$17. AE, MC, V. Daily 10:30am–midnight. STEAKS/SEAFOOD.

This place bills itself as a steak house, but it has an ample menu of seafood dishes as well. Most of the tables are located on a two-tiered covered veranda at the front of the restaurant, overlooking the street and the ocean just beyond. There's plenty of wood trim and the whole thing has a very airy feel. The portions are immense and the meat is tender and well prepared.

2 Playa de Jacó

73 miles (117km) W of San José; 47 miles (75km) S of Puntarenas

Playa de Jacó is the closest thing Costa Rica has to Daytona Beach during spring break. This long stretch of beach is strung with a dense hodgepodge of hotels in all price categories, cheap souvenir shops, seafood restaurants, pizza joints, and even a miniature golf course. If you're looking for a cheap place not far from San José where you can spend a few days in the sun, Jacó continues to be the top choice.

However, the beach here is not particularly appealing. It's made of dark-gray sand with lots of little rocks and it's often very rough. Charter flights arrive weekly from Montréal and Toronto, and consequently many of the hotels here are owned and populated by Canadians. Jacó is also now gaining popularity with Germans and young Ticos. However, the number-one attraction is the surf, and this is definitely a surfer-dominated beach town. This is the most touristy beach in Costa Rica and is a prime example of what happens when rapid growth hits a beach town. However, on the outskirts of town and close to the beach, there's still plenty of greenery to offset the excess of cement along the town's main street. In fact, after the dryness of Guanacaste, this is the first beach on the Pacific coast to have a tropical feel. The humidity is palpable, and the lushness of the tropical forest is visible on the hillsides surrounding town. In hotel gardens, flowers bloom profusely throughout the year.

ESSENTIALS

GETTING THERE & DEPARTING   By Bus   Express buses (☎ **506/223-1109** or 506/643-3135) leave San José daily at 7:30am, 10:30am, and 3:30pm from the Coca-Cola bus terminal at Calle 16 between avenidas 1 and 3. The trip takes between $2^{1}/2$ and 3 hours; the fare is $2.50. On weekends and holidays, extra buses are often added, so it's worth calling to check.

Buses from San José to **Quepos** and Manuel Antonio also pass by Jacó (they let passengers off on the highway about half a mile/1km from town). These buses leave San José daily at 6am, 7am, 10am, noon, 2pm, 4pm, and 6pm. Trip duration is 3 hours; the fare to Jacó is $2.50 on the indirect bus to Quepos, $5 on the direct bus to Manuel Antonio. However, during the busy months, some of these buses will refuse passengers getting off in Jacó, or accept them only if they pay the full fare to Quepos or Manuel Antonio.

From **Puntarenas,** there are two buses daily to Jacó at 5am and 3pm, or you can catch Quepos-bound buses daily at 5am, 11am, and 2pm and get off in Jacó. Either way, the trip's duration is 1 hour; the fare is $1.50.

The Jacó bus station is at the north end of town, at a small mall across from the Jacó Fiesta Hotel. Buses for San José leave daily at 5am, 11am, and 3pm. Buses returning to San José from Quepos pass periodically and pick up passengers on the highway. Since schedules can change, it's best to ask at your hotel about current departure times.

By Car   There are two main routes to Jacó. The easier, though longer, route is to take the Interamerican Highway west out of San José and get off at the Puntarenas exit. From here, head south on the Costanera, the coast road. Alternately, you can take the narrow and winding, though more scenic, old highway, which turns off the Interamerican Highway just west of Alajuela near the town of Atenas. This highway meets the Costanera a few kilometers west of Orotina.

ORIENTATION   Playa de Jacó is a short distance off the southern highway. One main road runs parallel to the beach, with a host of arteries heading toward the water; it's off these roads that you'll find most of the hotels and restaurants.

GETTING AROUND   While almost everything is within walking distance in Jacó, you can rent a bicycle or scooter from several shops on the main street or call **Jacó Taxi** (☎ **506/643-3030**). For longer excursions, you can rent a car from **Economy** (☎ **506/643-1719**), **Elegante** (☎ **506/643-3224**), or **Zuma** (☎ **506/643-3207**). Expect to pay approximately $50 for a 1-day rental. You might also consider talking to any of the local taxi drivers, who would probably take you wherever you wanted to go for the same $50 per day, thus saving you some hassle and headache.

FAST FACTS   Both the **Banco Nacional** (☎ 506/643-3072) and the **Banco de Costa Rica** (☎ 506/643-3334) have branches in town on the main road and are open Monday through Friday from 8:30am to 3pm. **Farmacia Jacó** (☎ 506/643-3205), the town's pharmacy, is down the street from the Banco Nacional. There's a gas station out on the main highway, at the south end of town. The **health center** and **post office** are at the Municipal Center at the south end of town, across from El Naranjal restaurant. A **public phone office,** from which you can make international calls, is located in the ICE building on the main road. This office is open Monday through Saturday from 8am to noon and from 1 to 5pm. The **Aguamatic Laundry** (☎ 506/643-2083) is located on the main strip across from the Red Cross and is open Monday through Saturday from 8am to 6pm. Same-day service is available. Finally, there's a **Western Union office** in a small strip mall across from La Hacienda Restaurant.

FUN ON & OFF THE BEACH

Unfortunately, the water here has a nasty reputation for riptides, as does most of the water off Costa Rica's Pacific coast. Even strong swimmers have been known to drown in the power rips. At times, storms far offshore cause huge waves to pound on the beach, making it impossible to go in the water much beyond your waist. If this is the case, you'll have to be content with the hotel pool.

After you've spent some time on Playa de Jacó, you might want to visit some of the other nearby beaches. **Playa Esterillos,** 13¹/₂ miles (22km) southeast of Jacó, is long and wide and almost always nearly deserted. **Playa Hermosa,** 6.2 miles (10km) southeast of Jacó, where sea turtles lay eggs from July through December, is also well known for its great surfing waves. **Playa Herradura,** about 4 miles (6¹/₂km) northwest of Jacó, is ringed by lush hillsides. For years this was an almost deserted beach with just a few basic cabins and campgrounds. In late 1999, the 211 room Marriott Los Sueños Beach and Golf Resort opened up here. The luxury hotel and 18-hole golf course are open and work is ongoing to complete a full-service marina, as well as large condominium and vacation home projects. However, the Marriott only occupies one end of the beach here, and despite its presence, Playa Herradura still feels a lot more isolated and deserted than Jacó. All of these beaches are beautiful and easily reached by car, moped, or bicycle—if you've got a lot of energy. All are signposted, so you'll have no trouble finding them.

BIKING   You can rent a bike for around $8 per day or $1.50 per hour. Bikes are available from a slew of shops along the main road. One of the better choices is **Maravillas Naturales** (☎ 506/643-1158).

A CANOPY TOUR   **Chiclets Tree Tour** (☎ 506/643-3222) offers up a canopy adventure ($55 per person) just outside Jacó in nearby Playa Hermosa. You'll spend 3 hours in climbing gear, zipping across cables from one tree platform to another in this transitional forest, with some sweeping views of the Pacific. There's also another canopy tour at Iguana Park (see below).

HORSEBACK RIDING   Horseback-riding tours give you a chance to get away from all the development in Jacó and see a bit of nature. Contact **Fantasy Tours** (☎ 506/643-3231), **Sanchez Madrigal Bros.** (☎ 506/643-3203), **Jacó Equestrian Center** (☎ 506/643-1569), or **Hermanos Salazar** (☎ 506/643-3203) to make a reservation. Down in Playa Hermosa, check in with **Diana's Trail Rides** (☎ 506/643-3808). Tours lasting 3 to 4 hours cost around $25 to $50.

Day of the Iguana

The somewhat nearby **Iguana Park** (☎ 506/428-7776) is actually an iguana preservation project, and makes a good day trip from Jacó. Don't let the iguana burgers and tacos on sale at the restaurant here or the iguana "leather" wallets and belts on sale at the gift shop fool you. When you're not eating and buying iguana products, you can take a walk through a forest trail in an area massively repopulated with green iguanas, or visit the park's education center (where you can touch and hold iguanas).

The park is also the site of one of the original canopy-tour operations. The canopy tour here takes 3$^1/_2$ hours and costs $45, including the separate $8 entrance fee for Iguana Park. You'll find Iguana Park about 6.2 miles (10km) from Orotina. To get here from Jacó, head back toward San José via Orotina. In Orotina, follow the signs to Iguana Park, which is about 20 minutes south.

KAYAKING   Kayak Jacó (☎ 506/643-1233; www.kayakjaco.com) runs three different trips on stable, hard plastic sit-on-top kayaks. The first ($35) is a gentle float on the Tulin River. The second ($40) is a combination ocean-kayaking/snorkel trip on calm Herradura Bay. The third ($40) is for ocean kayak surfing. All options run around 4 hours and include transportation to and from the put-in, as well as fresh fruit and soft drinks during the trip.

LEARNING THE LANGUAGE   Escuela del Mundo (☎ 506/643-1064; www.speakcostarica.com; E-mail: info@speakcostarica.com) offers a variety of course options from 1 to 4 weeks in length that focus on language, culture, and even surfing. A 1-week course costs $275, with lodging an extra $75 per person, double occupancy.

A SPA   If all the activity here has worn you out, contact the **Serenity Spa** (☎ 506/643-1624), which offers massage, as well as mud packs, face and body treatments, and manicures and pedicures. The spa is located on the first floor, among a tiny little cul-de-sac of shops next to Zuma Rent-A-Car. These folks are also in charge of spa services at the new Los Sueños Marriott resort. If you want a massage down in Playa Hermosa, contact Mary at **Cabinas Las Olas** (☎ 506/643-3687).

SPORTFISHING, SCUBA DIVING & SUNSET CRUISES   With the opening of the new Los Sueños Marriott resort and the ongoing construction of their adjacent 250-slip marina, expect much of the local maritime activity to shift over here. To date, few charter captains have shifted operations here, but I expect] quite a few will shortly. If you're interested in doing some sportfishing, scuba diving, or any other waterborne activity, I'd recommend you check around Playa Herradura.

Alternatively, you can call **J. D. Watersports** (☎ 506/257-3857), which operates out of Punta Leona, or ask at **Hotel Club del Mar** (☎ 506/643-3194). A half-day fishing trip for four people will cost around $250 to $325, and a full day will cost between $450 and $800. J. D. Watersports also offers scuba-diving trips and sunset cruises.

SURFING   The same waves that make Playa de Jacó unsafe for swimming make it one of the most popular beaches in the country with surfers. Nearby **Playa Hermosa** and **Playa Escondida** are also excellent surfing beaches. Those who want to challenge the waves can rent surfboards for around $2.50 an hour or $10 per day, and boogie boards for $1.50 an hour, from any one of the numerous surf shops along the main road.

CARARA BIOLOGICAL RESERVE: A FAMOUS NESTING GROUND FOR SCARLET MACAWS & A PLACE TO SEE CROCODILES

A little over 9 miles (15km) north of Jacó is ✪ **Carara Biological Reserve,** a world-renowned nesting ground for scarlet macaws. It has several miles of trails open to visitors. There's a loop trail that takes about an hour and another trail that's open only to tour groups. The macaws migrate daily, spending their days in the park and their nights among the coastal mangroves. It's best to view them in the early morning when they arrive, or around sunset when they head back to the coast for the evening, but a good guide can usually find them for you during the day. Whether or not you see them, you should hear their loud squawks. Among the other wildlife you might see here are caimans, coatimundis, armadillos, pacas, peccaries, river otters, kinkajous, and, of course, hundreds of species of birds.

Be sure to bring along insect repellent, or, better yet, wear light cotton long sleeves and pants. I was once foolish enough to attempt a quick hike while returning from Manuel Antonio—still in beach clothes and flip-flops—not a good idea. The reserve is open daily from 8am to 4pm. Admission is $6 per person at the gate. There are several companies offering tours to Carara Biological Reserve for around $30 to $40. Check at your hotel or contact **Fantasy Tours** (☎ **506/643-3231**) for schedules and more information. You can also hike the trails independently, but my advice is to take the guided tour; you'll learn a lot more about your surroundings.

The muddy banks of the Tárcoles River are home to a healthy population of American crocodiles, and just north of the entrance to the Carara Biological Reserve is a bridge that's a prime spot for viewing both the crocs and the macaw migrations. It's worth a stop, but be careful: Thieves and pickpockets work this spot regularly. Don't leave your car or valuables unguarded, and be wary if yours is the only car parked here. Once you're in Jacó, you'll find several operators who run daily crocodile tours on the Tárcoles River. Most of these companies bring along plenty of freshly killed chicken to attract the reptiles and pump up the adrenaline. Expect to pay between $40 and $50 per person for the trip.

Finally, just beyond Carara National Park on the Costanera Sur in the direction of Jacó you'll find a turnoff for some spectacular waterfalls (including a 600-ft. fall) around the town of Bijagual. A local family here runs the **Complejo Ecologico La Catarata** (☎ **506/661-1787**), which features a basic restaurant and a campground. They charge a nominal fee to visit the falls on foot and also run horseback tours. To get here, turn off at the signs for Hotel Villa Lapas. From here you can either drive the very rough 5 miles (8km) up to the entrance to the falls, or arrange for them to pick you up at Villa Lapas.

ACCOMMODATIONS IN PLAYA DE JACÓ

Since Punta Leona, Playa Herradura, and Playa Hermosa de Jacó (not to be confused with Playa Hermosa in Guanacaste) are close by, many people choose accommodations in these beach towns as well. Selected listings for these towns follow this section.

VERY EXPENSIVE

Hotel Barceló Amapola. Apdo. 133, Playa de Jacó, Puntarenas. ☎ **506/643-2225.** Fax 506/643-3668. www.barcelo.com. E-mail: amapola@racsa.co.cr. 53 units. A/C TV TEL. $132–$182 double, $152–$202 suite, $158–$212 villa. Rates include all meals, beverages, and taxes. AE, MC, V.

This hotel was recently taken over by the Spanish Barceló chain and converted into an all-inclusive resort. While this hotel has perhaps the nicest accommodations in town, it has an unenviable location, some 500 meters (545 yd.) inland from the beach,

Organized Tours out of Jacó

If you will be spending your entire Costa Rican visit in Jacó but would like to see some other parts of the country, you can arrange tours through the local offices of **Explorica** (☎ 506/643-3586) or **Fantasy Tours** (☎ 506/643-3231). Both companies offer day tours to Arenal, Poás, and Irazú volcanoes, white-water rafting trips, cruises to Tortuga Island, and trips to Braulio Carrillo and Manuel Antonio national parks and other places. Overnight trips are also available. Rates range from $45 to $90 for day trips.

towards the southern end of Jacó. The rooms are new, cool, and comfortable, with white tile floors, two double beds, plenty of closet and shelf space, a desk and chair, and either a small patio or balcony. The bathrooms have sleek European fixtures and a bidet. The suites have an extra living/sitting room with a fold-out sofa bed and just a king-size bed in the master bedroom. The villas come with two bedrooms, living room, full kitchen, and small patio, but frankly I find the standard rooms much nicer and more comfortable.

Dining/Diversions: Near the reception area you'll find the open-air restaurant, which specializes in Italian food, as well as the hotel's small casino and bar/disco.

Amenities: There's a gift shop, a midsize pool with a swim-up bar and two Jacuzzis, and bicycles for rent.

EXPENSIVE

Best Western Jacó Beach Hotel. Playa de Jacó (Apdo. 962-1000, San José), Puntarenas. ☎ **506/643-1000.** Fax 506/643-3246. www.bestwestern.co.cr. E-mail: bwjaco@racsa.co.cr. 125 units. A/C TV TEL. Dec 20–Feb 28 $92 double or triple; Mar 1–Dec 19 $80 double or triple. AE, DC, MC, V.

This has long been Jacó's most popular Canadian charter-flight hotel. Several years ago, it was taken over by the Best Western chain. Given the above, you can be sure it'll be packed and lively throughout the high season. Situated right on the beach, this five-story hotel is just what you would expect of a tropical beach resort, although it shows its age. The open-air lobby is surrounded by lush gardens, and there are covered walkways connecting the hotel's buildings. Rooms are adequate and have tile floors and walls of glass facing onto balconies; however, not all of the rooms have good views (some face another building). Ask for a view room on a higher floor, if possible. Bathrooms tend to be a bit battered, but they do have bathtubs. If you'd like more space and a kitchen, ask about the Villas Jacó Princess, managed by the same company, and located just across the road.

Dining/Diversions: El Muelle, the hotel's open-air restaurant, overlooks the pool and serves local and international dishes in the $5-to-$20 price range. Out by the beach, there's **the Bar Guipipías,** which overlooks the water.

Amenities: Facilities include a small, crowded swimming pool, a tennis court, a volleyball court, and a gift shop. Room service; a tour desk; car, motorcycle, and surfboard rentals; laundry service; and shuttle service from San José are all available. In addition, bicycles are provided free of charge to guests.

Hotel Cocal. Apdo. 54, Playa de Jacó, Puntarenas. ☎ **506/643-3067.** Fax 506/643-3082. E-mail: cocalcr@racsa.co.cr. 43 units. A/C. $75 double; lower in the off-season (May–Nov). Rates include breakfast buffet. AE, MC, V. No children allowed.

No children are allowed at this hotel, so the atmosphere is usually very peaceful. Located right on the beach, the building is done in colonial style, with arched porticos surrounding a courtyard that contains two medium-size pools, a few palapas for shade, and a thatch-roofed bar. Each guest room is well proportioned, with a tile floor, a double and a single bed, a desk, and a porch or a balcony. The Cocal is on one of the nameless streets leading down to the beach from the main road through Jacó; watch for their sign in the middle of town.

Dining/Diversions: There are two dining rooms here (one on each floor) serving three meals a day; the one upstairs has the best view of the beach. Service is generally quite good, and so is the food. Prices range from $5 to $20 for entrees. The hotel also has a recently remodeled casino, if you have the gaming instinct.

Amenities: The hotel is right on the beach and has a small outdoor swimming pool.

MODERATE

✪ Hotel Club del Mar. Apdo. 107-4023, Playa de Jacó, Puntarenas. ☎ and fax **506/ 643-3194.** www.jacobeach.com. 18 units. $45–$90 double; 30% lower in the off-season. AE, MC, V.

This has long been my favorite Playa de Jacó hotel because of its location, friendly owners, and attractively designed rooms. The Club del Mar is at the far southern end of the beach where the rocky hills meet the sand. The best rooms are in two newer two-story shell-pink buildings, each of which has four rooms and ocean views. The rooms have green tile floors, pastel bedspreads, fascinating custom-made lampshades, tile bathroom counters, and French doors that open onto private patios or balconies. The older rooms are also attractive and have Guatemalan throw rugs, bamboo furniture, full kitchens, and glass front walls. Twelve of the rooms here have air-conditioning and all have small unstocked refrigerators. A small swimming pool is right by the beach.

However, it's the conviviality and helpfulness of owners Philip and Marilyn Edwardes, and son their Simon, that make a stay here so enjoyable. All are avid gardeners, and the hotel grounds contain many rare palms, heliconias, and flowering gingers.

Dining: The first-class restaurant on the premises (closed Tuesdays) is one of the best in town, and open to the public (with reservations). Philip Edwardes oversees the kitchen and at times personally prepares such dishes as lemon chicken and chateaubriand.

Amenities: The Edwardeses also arrange sportfishing outings, horseback rides, raft trips, and various other tours.

Hotel Copacabana. Apdo. 150, Playa de Jacó, Puntarenas. ☎ **506/643-1005.** Fax 506/ 643-3131. www.copacabanahotel.com. E-mail: hotcopa@racsa.co.cr. 30 units. $49 double, $59 double with A/C, $79–$99 suite. AE, MC, V.

This Canadian-owned hotel is right on the beach and is popular with sport fishers and sports lovers. The standard rooms are all on the second floor and each has one double and one single bed, a ceiling fan, and little bay windows with bamboo shades. On the shared veranda, strung hammocks alternate with small tables and chairs. Although they have the benefit of air-conditioning and kitchenettes, most of the suites are located on the first floor and are a bit claustrophobic. If you can get one on the second floor with an ocean view, it's worth the splurge. Most of the activity here is centered around the pool and its neighboring bar. A 24-foot satellite dish ensures a steady stream of televised sports events, and the food is surprisingly good. In addition to hearty breakfasts, the restaurant serves up a creative pasta bar, fresh seafood, and perhaps the best french fries in Costa Rica.

Pochote Grande. Apdo. 42, Playa de Jacó, Puntarenas. ☎ **506/643-3236.** Fax 506/ 220-4979. www.centralamerica.com. E-mail: pochote@racsa.co.cr. 24 units. $55 double to quad; lower in the off-season (May–Nov). AE, MC, V.

Named for a huge old pochote tree on the grounds, this well-kept and attractive hotel is located right on the beach at the far north end of Jacó. The grounds are shady and lush, and there's a small pool. All of the rooms are quite large and have white tile floors, a small fridge, and a balcony or patio. I prefer the second-floor rooms, which are blessed with high ceilings. The restaurant and snack bar serve a mixture of Tico, German, and American meals (the owners are German by way of Africa). Prices for meals range from $4 to $15. There's also a small gift shop.

INEXPENSIVE

There are several campgrounds in or near Playa de Jacó. **Madrigal** (☎ 506/ 643-3851), at the south end of town at the foot of some jungly cliffs, is my favorite. You can also try **El Hicaco** (☎ 506/643-3004), which is close to the beach but also pretty close to the Disco La Central, so don't expect to get much sleep if you stay here. Campsites run between $2 and $5 per night.

Cabinas Alice. Playa de Jacó, Puntarenas (approx. 100m south of the Red Cross). ☎ and fax **506/643-3061.** 22 units. $34 double, $50 triple or quad. AE, MC, V.

Cabinas Alice is one of the most popular budget choices in Jacó, especially with young Ticos. The rooms are in the shade of some large old mango trees, and the beach is right outside the gate. Since the rooms vary in age and upkeep, ask to take a look at a couple before accepting one. The largest rooms have kitchens and also happen to be closest to the small pool and the beach. The rooms in back each come with a carved-wood headboard and matching nightstand, a tile floor, a large shower, and potted plants. The other rooms are pretty basic, with nothing but a double and a single bed in the room. The road down to Cabinas Alice is across from the Red Cross center. Meals are served in the small attached *soda,* where you can get a fish fillet fried in garlic and butter for around $4.

Flamboyant Hotel. Apdo. 18, Playa de Jacó, Puntarenas. ☎ **506/643-3146.** Fax 506/ 643-1068. E-mail: flamboya@racsa.co.cr. 14 units. $40–$50 double, $45–$55 triple. AE, MC, V.

The Flamboyant doesn't quite live up to its name, but it's still a good value. The rooms are arranged around a small swimming pool and are only a few steps from the beach. They're all spacious, with simple furnishings, and most have kitchenettes. The newer and more expensive rooms have air-conditioning, televisions, and private balconies. You'll find the hotel down a narrow lane toward the ocean from Caliche's Wishbone Cafe, which is on the main road in the middle of Jacó.

♻ Hotel Mar de Luz. A.P. 143, Playa de Jacó, Puntarenas. ☎ and fax **506/643-3259.** 27 units. A/C TV. $50 double; lower during the off-season. No credit cards.

This is one of Playa de Jacó's best deals and a comfortable alternative to the typical string of cut-rate cabinas you'll find crowding this popular beach town. All the rooms come with air-conditioning, small kitchenettes, full-size refrigerators, room safes, and cable television. Some feature stone walls, small sitting areas, and either one or two double beds placed on a raised sleeping nook. My only complaint is that the windows are too small and mostly sealed, so you're forced to use the air-conditioning. There are two refreshing pools, with plenty of chaise lounges around, as well as a kids' pool and a Jacuzzi. In the gardens just off the pools, there are a couple of grills available for guest use. There is also a comfortable common sitting area, with a selection of magazines and books in several languages. Dutch owners Victor and Carmen Keulen seem driven to offer as much comfort, quality, and service as they can for the price. You'll find the hotel 50 meters (55 yd.) east of the Hotel Tangeri, right in the center of Jacó.

Hotel Zabamar. Playa de Jacó, Puntarenas. ☎ and fax **506/643-3174.** 20 units. $35 double, $45 triple. A/C $10 extra. MC, V.

The Zabamar is set back from the beach in a shady compound. The older rooms have red tile floors, small refrigerators, ceiling fans, hammocks on their front porches, and showers in enclosed private patios. There are also 10 newer rooms with air-conditioning. There are even *pilas* (laundry sinks) in little gravel-and-palm gardens behind the older rooms. Some have rustic wooden benches and chairs. The shallow swimming pool stays quite warm. Travelers on tight budgets will appreciate the size of the older, less-expensive rooms. Special rates can be negotiated for longer stays, and prices for all rooms are lower from April 15 to December 15. The small open-air restaurant serves breakfast and lunch at quite reasonable prices.

ACCOMMODATIONS AROUND PLAYA DE JACÓ
VERY EXPENSIVE

✪ **Los Sueños Marriott Beach & Golf Resort.** Playa Herradura (A.P. 502-4005, San Antonio de Belén). ☎ **800/228-9290** in the U.S.; 506/298-0000 or 506/630-9000 in Costa Rica. Fax 506/298-0033. www.marriotthotels.com. E-mail: costaric@marriott.co.cr. 211 units. A/C MINIBAR TV TEL. $150–$240 double, $650 suite, $1,050 presidential suite. Rates include full breakfast. AE, MC, V.

This is the newest large-scale resort on the Pacific coast and the closest to San José. The hotel is a massive, four-story horseshoe facing the beach. As at the Marriott in San José, the whole thing is done in a Spanish colonial style, with stucco walls, heavy wood doors, and red clay roof tiles. The rooms are all spacious and tastefully done. They come with either one king or two queen-size beds, a large armoire, a desk, and a sitting chair with ottoman. Every room has a balcony, but all are not created equal. Most only have small Juliet-style balconies. Those facing the ocean are clearly superior, and a few of the ocean-facing rooms even have large, comfortable balconies with chaise lounges and tables and chairs. You'll have to be specific if you want one of these.

The expansive lobby area opens out on a large terrace and the Puesta del Sol bar, with its panoramic views of the beach and the bluffs bordering Playa Herradura. The pool is a large, intricate maze built to imitate the canals of Venice (in miniature), with private nooks and grottos.

The beach here is calm and good for swimming, although it's one of the least attractive beaches on this coast, with a mix of rocks and hard-packed dark-brown sand.

Dining/Diversions: There are several dining options here. The most popular is **La Vista** restaurant, which serves up a broad mix of international and continental dishes, in a casual setting, with both indoor and outdoor seating. As its name suggests, **El Nuevo Latino** serves up modern takes on traditional Latin cooking. Entrees range from guava-glazed baby back ribs to sear & shiver Honduran tuna ceviche. This is the hotel's most formal restaurant, housed in an elegant glass-walled room that overlooks a quiet pool fed by fountains from an overhead aqueduct. There are also informal restaurants and grills both by the pool and the golf course's pro shop, as well as a gourmet coffee shop. The **Stellaris casino** is the largest and most comfortable I've found at a beach resort in Costa Rica.

Amenities: There's an 18-hole Ted Robinson–designed golf course that winds through some of the neighboring forest. There's also a large outdoor pool, health club and spa, four tennis courts, pro shop, water-sports equipment rentals, jogging trail, gift shop, beauty parlor, tour desk, car-rental desk, conference center, ballrooms, and concierge. A 250-slip marina is still under construction.

✪ **Villa Caletas.** Apdo. 12358-1000, San José. ☎ **506/257-3653** or 506/637-0505. Fax 506/222-2059 or 506/637-0303. www.hotelvillacaletas.com. E-mail: caletas@racsa.co.cr.

8 units, 21 villas. A/C TEL TV. $130 double, $160–$190 villa, $290 master suite; slightly lower in the off-season (Apr 16–Nov 30). AE, MC, V.

It's hard to find a luxury hotel in Costa Rica with a more spectacular setting. Perched 350 meters (382 yd.) above the sea, Villa Caletas enjoys commanding views of the Pacific. While the rooms are all elegantly appointed and spacious, you'll want to stay in a villa here. Each individual villa is situated on a patch of hillside facing the sea or surrounding forests. Inside, you'll find a main bedroom with a queen-size bed and a comfortable sitting room with couches that convert into two single beds. The villas feature white tile floors, modern bathrooms, and a private terrace for sitting around and soaking up the views. The junior suites are even larger, while the suites and master suites are larger still—and even come with their own private swimming pools. All of the rooms were recently equipped with telephones, cable television, and air-conditioning, although I prefer to open one of the sliding glass doors and soak in the breezes. While most guests are happy to lounge around and swim in the free-form "infinity" pool that seems to blend into the sea below and beyond, Villa Caletas also offers periodic shuttle service to its own little private beach.

Dining/Diversions: The hotel has two restaurants featuring French and continental cuisines. **The Mirador** is the most formal option and is often closed during the low season. **The Amphitheater** is nearly as elegant. Breakfasts are served in the shade of an outdoor patio. You can either grab your lunch here or have it by the pool. The hotel also has a Greek-style amphitheater where you can sometimes catch sunset concerts of jazz and classical music.

Amenities: Swimming pool, private beach, conference room, and six suites with private pools.

MODERATE

Punta Leona Beach Hotel. (Apdo. 8592-1000, San José), Punta Leona. ☎ **506/231-3131.** Fax 506/232-0791. www.hotelpuntaleona.com. E-mail: info@hotelpuntaleona. com. 108 units, 72 apts. A/C TEL TV. $66–$82 double, $70–$200 apt or suite (4–8 people). AE, DC, MC, V.

Located 6.2 miles (10km) north of Jacó, this gated resort and residential community was the first large-scale resort complex in Costa Rica. A private forest reserve, white-sand beaches (two of them), and a rocky promontory jutting out into the Pacific give Punta Leona more natural charms than anything this side of Manuel Antonio. However, due to its status as a popular Tico weekend party resort and a haphazard sense of development planning, these natural charms are often drowned out by the blare of jet skis, all-terrain vehicles, and nightly discos. The main guest rooms are not as luxurious as one would hope, and in fact some of them are downright run-down. The standard hotel rooms are in Spanish-style buildings with red tile roofs and white stucco walls. Inside, you'll find that the beds and bedspreads are a bit dated and worn, but otherwise the rooms are comfortable. In addition to these rooms, there is a variety of different apartment types, including some unusual small chalets and some converted railroad cars (which feel a lot like mobile homes).

Dining/Diversions: Restaurant Léon Marino serves a variety of Costa Rican and international dishes. Prices are moderate. There's also a more informal outdoor restaurant that serves grilled meats and typical meals, as well as two bars. The one on Playa Mantas doubles as a disco.

Amenities: Facilities include two swimming pools, 4 miles (6.5km) of beach, a tennis court, miniature golf, a boutique, a supermarket, and a conference room. There's regular daily bus service between the guest accommodations and Playa Blanca. Sportfishing, sunset cruises, and rental of sailboards, jet skis, and horses are all available. Scuba lessons and equipment rental are also offered (there's decent diving at Playa Blanca).

DINING

Playa de Jacó has a wide range of restaurants. Most cater to surfers and budget travelers. Budget travelers who really want to save money on meals can always stay at a hotel that provides kitchenettes for its guests, shop at the local *supermercado,* and fix their own meals. Even the most inexpensive lodgings have restaurants, so if you don't want to cook, you won't have to venture far.

If you end up walking the strip and want to eat in town, I've recommended some places below. In addition, the **Garden Café** (☎ **506/643-3284**), **Colonial Restaurant** (☎ **506/643-3326**), and **Pancho Villa** (☎ **506/643-3571**) are all local favorites, and **Pizzeria Terraza** (☎ **506/643-1169**) has excellent clay-oven pizzas and homemade pastas. If you're looking for simply prepared, fresh seafood, **El Recreo** (☎ **506/643-1172**) and **Restaurante Santimar** (☎ **506/643-3605**) are both good bets, serving standard Tico beach fare—fresh seafood, sandwiches, chicken, and steak. For a filling American-style breakfast, try **Chatty Cathy's** (☎ **506/643-1039**). Actually, one of the best restaurants in town is the dining room at the **Hotel Club del Mar** (☎ **506-643-3194**), which is open to the public with reservations.

On the main road to Jacó, around Tárcoles, a good place for lunch is **Steve & Lisa's** (☎ **506/637-0106**). The food here is standard Tico fare, but the ocean-side setting and views set it apart from other *sodas.*

❂ **Caliche's Wishbone Café.** On the main road in Jacó. ☎ **506/643-3406.** Reservations not necessary. Main courses $4–$8. V. Thurs–Tues 11:30am–3pm and 5:30–10pm. SEAFOOD/MEXICAN.

This is another casual eatery popular with surfers. Tex-Mex standards and homemade pizzas are the staples here. However, you can also get excellent fresh fish and seafood dishes perfectly prepared, as well as hearty stuffed potatoes and a variety of sandwiches served in homemade pita bread. The portions are huge. The nicest tables are streetside on a covered veranda. Inside there are more tables, as well as a bar with television sets showing surf videos.

Río Oasis. On the main road in Jacó. ☎ **506/643-3354.** Reservations not accepted. Main courses $3–$12. V. Wed–Mon noon–midnight. PIZZA/MEXICAN.

For years the owners of this joint ran the popular Killer Munchies. The name and location have changed, but the menu has remained basically the same. Río Oasis serves hearty burritos, simple pasta dishes, and a wide array of freshly baked wood-oven pizzas. My favorite item is the Greek pizza, with olives, feta cheese, and anchovies, but the barbecued chicken pizza is also delicious. The new location is much larger, with both indoor and terrace seating, as well as an expanded bar area, complete with pool table, dartboards, and a couple of televisions for sports events and surf videos.

PLAYA DE JACÓ AFTER DARK

Playa de Jacó is the central Pacific's party town, and the **Disco La Central** (☎ **506/643-3076**) is packed every night of the high season and every weekend during the low season. La Central is right on the beach near the south end of town. There's a huge open-air hall, which features the requisite seventies flashing lights and suspended mirrored ball, as well as a garden bar in a thatch-roofed building that serves as a slightly quieter place to have a drink. The disco charges a nominal cover charge. If you're looking for a surfer hangout, check out **La Hacienda** (☎ **506/643-3191**), a second-floor bar with a laid-back feel, a beat-up pool table, a dartboard, and surf videos on the TVs. Lately, live rock-and-roll bands perform here on weekends. La Hacienda is located on the main drag toward the north end of town. Sports freaks can catch the latest games at **Hotel Copacabana** (☎ 506/643-3131) or **El Zarpe** (☎ 506/643-3473). The latter serves up good, reasonably priced burritos, burgers, and other assorted bar food. The very late-night crowd always seems to end up at the **Pancho Villa Restaurant** (☎ 506/643-3571).

The newest addition to the after-hours scene in Jacó is the **Hollywood Nightclub** (☎ 506/643-1703). You can't miss the neon lights out on the highway just north of town. As at their sister club in San José, you can expect topless dancers, prostitutes, and very expensive drinks here. Be careful: "Working women" prey on young surfers (who figure they're just incredibly charming and sexy and lucky)—after things get going the women hit them up for moola.

EN ROUTE TO MANUEL ANTONIO: PLAYA HERMOSA

Playa Hermosa is the first beach you'll hit as you head south from Playa de Jacó. This is primarily a surfers' beach, but it is still a lovely spot to spend some beach time. In addition to the hotels listed below, **Safari Surf Cabinas** (☎ 506/643-3508) has basic rooms ($15 per person) as well as a popular restaurant/bar and equipment rental.

If you're looking for something even more remote and undeveloped, head further south to Playa Esterillos Este for the **Auberge du Pelican** (fax 506/779-9236).

ACCOMMODATIONS

Cabinas Las Olas. Apdo. 258, Jacó, Puntarenas. ☎ and fax **506/643-3687.** www. cabinaslasolas.com. E-mail: lasolas@racsa.co.cr. 4 units, 3 ranchos. $50 double, $60 triple, $80 rancho cabina (sleeps up to 5). No credit cards.

Playa Hermosa is a renowned surfing beach, and this is its most popular surfer hotel. The main building is on a hill by the road. Two of the rooms are located upstairs and have two double beds, a veranda with a hammock, and ocean views; downstairs are a couple of smaller budget rooms that are fine for a single traveler. The rooms are basic but comfortable. Closer to the beach are three A-frame cabins or ranchos, which have a roomy bedroom on the second floor (in the peak of the A), and a single bed, bunk bed, kitchenette, and bathroom on the ground floor. Perhaps the nicest room here is the new "Skybox Suite," which is located on the top floor of the main building, with a great view. This room sleeps up to four and goes for $90. Between the main building and the cabins is a pool with a small stone waterfall. Out by the ocean there's the Hard Charger's Cafe, which serves three meals daily. The breakfast burritos provide just the carbo load needed for a full day of surfing. If you don't surf, there's a thatch palapa strung with hammocks for watching the waves, the sunsets, and the surfers. The folks at Las Olas can also arrange a wide variety of tours and activities.

Terraza del Pacífico. Playa Hermosa de Jacó (Apdo. 168), Jacó, Puntarenas. ☎ **506/643-3222.** Fax 506/643-3424. www.terraza-del-pacifico.com. E-mail: terraza@racsa.co.cr. 43 units. A/C TV TEL. $80 double or triple. AE, MC, V.

Located just over the hill at the start of Playa Hermosa, this hotel has a wonderful setting on a mostly undeveloped section of beach. However, it never seemed to attract visitors and quickly fell into disrepair and decay. In the past year it's received major renovation and repairs. Rooms are built so that they all have ocean views, and in the middle of the hotel complex is a circular pool with a swim-up bar and plenty of chaise lounges for sunbathing and siestas. Red tile roofs and faux-stucco walls give the buildings a very Mediterranean look, while hardwood balcony railings add a touch of the tropics. The guest rooms each have two double beds, private bathrooms, and either a patio or balcony. The hotel's restaurant is located within a few feet of the high-tide mark and serves Costa Rican and international cuisine. The hotel offers a range of tours, including a nearby canopy tour. Surfing is still the major draw at this beach and this hotel, and Terraza has even installed klieg lights on the beach for night surfing.

PLAYA HERMOSA AFTER DARK

Most folks at Playa Hermosa find their way to **The Backyard** (☎ 506/643-3936), a lively surfer bar with a pool table, darts, and hearty food.

3 Manuel Antonio National Park

87 miles (140km) SW of San José; 43 miles (69km) S of Playa de Jacó

No other destination in Costa Rica has received more international attention than Manuel Antonio. Many first-time visitors to Costa Rica plan their vacation around seeing it, and it's no surprise why: The views from the hills overlooking Manuel Antonio are spectacular, the beaches (both inside and outside the national park) are idyllic, and its jungles are crawling with white-faced and squirrel monkeys, among other forms of exotic wildlife. The flip side is that you'll have to pay more to see it, and you'll have to share it with more fellow travelers than in other parts of this coast. Moreover, development here is leaving a noticeable footprint. What was once a smattering of small hotels tucked into the forested hillside has become a long string of lodgings along the 4¹/₄ miles (7km) of road between Quepos and the national-park entrance.

Still, this is one of the most beautiful locations in the entire country. Gazing down on the blue Pacific from high on the mountainsides of Manuel Antonio, it's almost impossible to hold back a gasp of delight. Offshore, rocky islands dot the vast expanse of blue, and in the foreground the rich deep green of the rain forest sweeps down to the water. Even cheap Instamatics regularly produce postcard-perfect snapshots. It's this superb view that the numerous hotels at Manuel Antonio sell, and that keeps people transfixed on decks, patios, and balconies.

One of the most popular national parks in the country, Manuel Antonio is also one of the smallest, covering fewer than 1,700 acres. Its several nearly perfect small beaches are connected by trails that meander through the rain forest. One of its most striking features is how quickly the mountains surrounding its beaches rise as you head inland from the water; however, the park was created to preserve not its beautiful beaches, but its forests, home to endangered squirrel monkeys, three-toed sloths, purple-and-orange crabs, and hundreds of other species of birds, mammals, and plants. Whereas once this entire stretch of coast was a rain forest teeming with wildlife, now just this small rocky outcrop of forest remains.

The popularity of Manual Antonio has brought increased development and ever-growing crowds of beachgoers. In just the last few years, these factors have turned what was once a remote and pristine spot into an area full of crowded parking areas, over-priced hotels, and noisy crowds. In many respects, Manuel Antonio has been victimized by adoring throngs, some of whom have taken to feeding the wild animals (monkeys and pizotes, in particular), which is a dangerous distortion of what ecotourism should be. On weekends, the beaches are filled with people, and the disco near the park entrance blares its music until early morning, drowning out the sounds of crickets and frogs that once lulled visitors to sleep here. A shantytown of snack shacks lines the road just outside the park, which makes the entrance road look more like a slum than a national park.

Those views that are so bewitching also have their own set of drawbacks. If you want a great view, you aren't going to be staying on the beach and, in fact, you probably won't be able to walk to the beach. This means that you'll be driving back and

Manuel Antonio

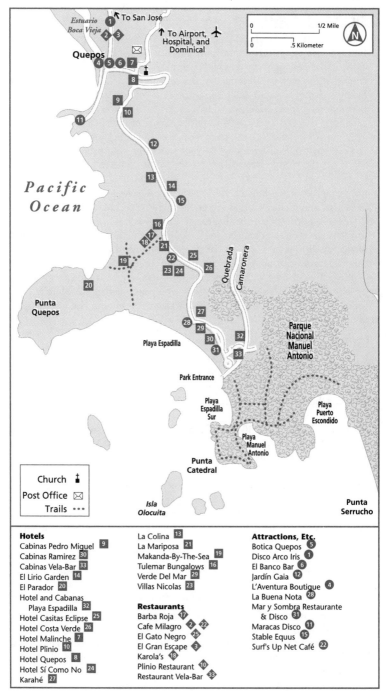

To San José

To Airport, Hospital, and Dominical

Estuario Boca Vieja

Quepos

Pacific Ocean

0 — 1/2 Mile
0 — .5 Kilometer

Punta Quepos

Quebrada Camaronera

Parque Nacional Manuel Antonio

Playa Espadilla

Park Entrance

Playa Espadilla Sur

Playa Manuel Antonio

Playa Puerto Escondido

Punta Catedral

Punta Serrucho

Isla Olocuita

Church ✝
Post Office ✉
Trails ···

Hotels
Cabinas Pedro Miguel 9
Cabinas Ramirez 30
Cabinas Vela-Bar 33
El Lirio Garden 14
El Parador 20
Hotel and Cabanas Playa Espadilla 32
Hotel Casitas Eclipse 25
Hotel Costa Verde 26
Hotel Malinche 7
Hotel Plinio 10
Hotel Quepos 8
Hotel Sí Como No 24
Karahé 27

La Colina 13
La Mariposa 21
Makanda-By-The-Sea 19
Tulemar Bungalows 16
Verde Del Mar 29
Villas Nicolas 23

Restaurants
Barba Roja 17
Cafe Milagro 2 22
El Gato Negro 25
El Gran Escape 3
Karola's 18
Plinio Restaurant 10
Restaurant Vela-Bar 33

Attractions, Etc.
Botica Quepos 5
Disco Arco Iris 1
El Banco Bar 6
Jardín Gaia 12
L'Aventura Boutique 4
La Buena Nota 28
Mar y Sombra Restaurante & Disco 31
Maracas Disco 11
Stable Equus 15
Surf's Up Net Café 22

Travel Tips _____

Despite the above caveats, Manuel Antonio is still worth visiting. If you plan carefully, you can escape many of the problems that detract from its appeal. If you steer
clear of the peak months (December through March), you'll avoid most of the
crowds. If you must come during the peak months, try to avoid weekends, when the
beach is packed with families from San José. If you stay at a hotel partway up the
hill from the park entrance, you'll have relatively easy access to the beach, you may
get a view, and best of all, you'll be out of earshot of the disco. If you visit the park
early in the morning, you can leave when the crowds begin to show up at midday.
In the afternoon, you can lounge by your pool or on your patio.

---

forth, taking taxis, or riding the public bus a lot. Also keep in mind that it's hot and
humid here, and it rains a lot. However, the rain is what keeps Manuel Antonio lush
and green, and this wouldn't be the tropics if things were otherwise.

If you're traveling on a budget, you'll likely end up staying in the nearby town of
Quepos, which was once a quiet banana port—the land to the north was used by
Chiquita to grow its bananas. Disease wiped out most of the banana plantations, and
now the land is planted with African oil-palm trees. To reach Quepos by road, you
must pass through miles and miles of these oil-palm plantations. More and more,
Quepos is filling up with a wide variety of restaurants, souvenir and craft shops, and
lively bars.

ESSENTIALS

GETTING THERE & DEPARTING   By Plane   Sansa (☎ **506/221-9414;** fax
506/255-2176; E-mail: reservations@flysansa.com) flies to Quepos daily at 7:40, 9,
10:20, and 11:20am and 1, 2, 3:35, and 4:30pm. All flights leave from San José's Juan
Santamaría International Airport. The flight's duration is 30 minutes; the fare is
$40 each way.

Travelair (☎ **506/220-3054;** fax 506/220-0413; E-mail: reservations@travelair-
costarica.com) also flies to Quepos daily at 7:45 and 9am and 1 and 4pm from Tobías
Bolaños International Airport in Pavas. Flight duration is 30 minutes; the fare is
$50 one-way, $80 round-trip.

There's an airport transfer service that charges $4 per person to any hotel in Manuel
Antonio and Quepos. Speak to a gate agent at either Sansa or Travelair to arrange a
ride. Taxis occasionally meet incoming flights as well. Expect to be charged between
$7 and $10 per car for up to four people, depending on the distance to your hotel and
your bargaining abilities.

When you're ready to depart, **Sansa** (☎ **506/777-0683** in Quepos) has daily
flights to San José leaving at 8:20, 9:40, and 11am and noon, 1:40, 2:40, 4:15, and
5:10pm.

Travelair flights leave for San José daily at 8:15 and 10:10am and 2:50 and 4:40pm.

By Bus   Express buses (☎ **506/223-5567** or 506/777-0101) to Manuel Antonio leave
San José daily at 6am, noon, and 6pm from the Coca-Cola bus terminal at Calle 16
between avenidas 1 and 3. Trip duration is 3¹/₂ hours; the fare is $5.50. These buses go
all the way to the park entrance and will drop you off at any of the hotels along the way.

Regular buses (☎ **506/223-5567**) to Quepos leave San José daily at 6, 7, and
10am, and noon, 2, 4, and 6pm. Trip duration is 4 hours; the fare is $4.50. These
buses stop in Quepos. From here, if you're staying at one of the hotels on the road to
Manuel Antonio, you must take a local bus or taxi to your hotel.

Buses leave **Puntarenas** for Quepos daily at 5am, 11am, and 2:30pm. The ride takes 3^1/$_2$ hours; the fare is $3.

Many of the buses for Quepos stop to unload and pick up passengers in **Playa de Jacó.** If you're in Jacó heading toward Manuel Antonio, you can try your luck at one of the covered bus stops out on the Interamerican Highway (see the section on Playa de Jacó, above).

From Quepos, buses leave for Manuel Antonio daily, roughly every hour, from 6am to 10pm. The fare is 40¢. The ride takes about 15 minutes.

When you're ready to depart, the Quepos bus station is next to the market, which is 3 blocks east of the water and 2 blocks north of the road to Manuel Antonio. Express buses to San José leave daily at 6am, noon, and 5pm. Local buses to San José (duration is 4 hr.) leave at 5 and 8am and 2 and 4pm.

In the busy winter months, tickets sell out well in advance, especially on weekends; if you can, purchase your ticket several days in advance. However, you must buy your Quepos-bound tickets in San José and your San José return tickets in Quepos. If you're staying in Manuel Antonio, you can buy your return ticket for a direct bus in advance in Quepos and then wait along the road to be picked up. There is no particular bus stop; just make sure you are out to flag the bus down and give it time to stop—you don't want to be standing in a blind spot when the bus comes flying around some tight corner.

Buses for **Puntarenas** leave daily at 4:30am, 10:30am, and 3pm. Any bus headed for San José or Puntarenas will let you off in Playa de Jacó.

By Car   Despite being one of the most traveled routes in Costa Rica, the roads between San José and Manuel Antonio have historically been a national disgrace. Massive repair work has left them in good shape for the start of this millennium, but it's not clear how long that will remain the case. From San José, the most popular route is to take the narrow and winding old highway, which turns off the Interamerican Highway just west of Alajuela near the town of Atenas and joins the Costanera near Orotina, just in time to catch the worst of the potholes. Just follow the many signs to hotels in either Jacó or Manuel Antonio. When you reach Jacó, it's a straight shot and another couple of hours to Manuel Antonio.

Alternately, you can take the Interamerican Highway west to the Puntarenas turnoff and head south on the Costanera, the coastal road through Jacó. This is an excellent road until south of Puerto Caldera. It is also your best bet if heading to Manuel Antonio from Puntarenas or any point north.

ORIENTATION   Quepos is a little port town at the mouth of the Boca Vieja Estuary. After crossing the bridge into town, take the lower road (to the left of the high road). In 4 blocks, turn left, and you'll be on the road to Manuel Antonio. This road winds through town a bit before starting over the hill to all the hotels and the national park.

GETTING AROUND   A taxi from Quepos to Manuel Antonio (or any hotel along the road toward the park) costs around $4. The return trip from the park to your hotel should only cost 75¢ per person. I know this system doesn't make much sense, but this is a fixed price, so watch out for drivers who try to charge more. If the taxi must leave the main road (for hotels like La Mariposa, El Parador, and Makanda), the charge is higher.

The bus between Quepos and Manuel Antonio takes 15 minutes each way, and runs roughly every half hour from 6am to 10pm daily, from the main bus terminal in Quepos, near the market. The fare is 40¢.

You can also rent a car from **Elegante Rent-a-Car** (☎ 506/777-0115) for around $50 a day. They're located in downtown Quepos, on the left just as you cross the bridge into town. With advance notice, they'll meet you at the airport with your car for no extra charge.

If you rent a car, never leave anything of value in it unless you intend to stay within sight of the car at all times. Car break-ins are commonplace here. Children will offer to watch your car for a small price when you leave it anywhere near the beach. Take them up on the offer if you want to avoid damage by thieves trying to find out what's in your trunk. Also, there is now a parking lot just outside the park entrance, which costs around $3 for the whole day—well worth it.

FAST FACTS   The **Lucimax Laundromat** is located on the edge of town on the road toward Manuel Antonio. **Botíca Quepos** is the main pharmacy in town. It's on the corner of the main street where you make the turn for Manuel Antonio (☎ 506/ 777-0038) and is open daily from 7am to 8pm. If you need to call a taxi, dial ☎ 506/ 777-1693 or 506/777-0425. The telephone number of the **Quepos Hospital** is ☎ 506/777-0922; and for the **Rural Guard** (local police), call ☎ 506/777-0196.

You can rent computer time, check your E-mail, and surf the Net at the **Surf's Up Net Café,** located in the little line of shops in front of Hotel Sí Como No (☎ 506/ 777-0777). They're open daily from 7am to 8pm.

EXPLORING THE NATIONAL PARK

Manuel Antonio is a small park with only three major trails. Most visitors come primarily to lie on one of the beaches and check out the white-faced monkeys, which sometimes seem as common as tourists. A guide is not essential here, but as I've said before, unless you're experienced in rain-forest hiking, you'll see and learn a lot more with one. A 2- or 3-hour guided hike should cost between $25 and $35 per person. Almost any of the hotels in town can help you set up a tour of the park. If you decide to explore the park on your own, a basic map is available at the park entrance.

ENTRY POINT, FEES & REGULATIONS   The park is closed on Monday, but open Tuesday through Sunday from 8am to 4pm year-round. You'll find the park entrance at **Playa Espadilla,** the beach at the end of the road from Quepos. To reach the park station, you must cross a small, sometimes polluted stream that's little more than ankle-deep at low tide but can be knee- or even waist-deep at high tide. Just after crossing the stream, you'll come to a small ranger station. You will have to pay a fee of $6 per person to enter. This is where you can pick up the small map of the park I mentioned above. The Parks Service allows only 600 visitors to enter each day, which may mean that you won't get in if you arrive in midafternoon during the high season. Camping is not allowed.

THE BEACHES   **Playa Espadilla Sur** (as opposed to Playa Espadilla, which is just outside the park; see below) is the first beach you come to within the park boundaries. It's usually the least-crowded beach in the park and one of the best places to find a quiet shade tree to plant yourself under. If you want to explore further, you can walk along this soft-sand beach or follow a trail through the forest parallel to the beach. At the far end, there's a short connecting trail to **Playa Manuel Antonio,** which is sometimes clear enough to offer good snorkeling along the rocks at either end. At low tide, Playa Manuel Antonio shows a very interesting relic: a circular stone turtle trap left by its pre-Columbian residents. From Playa Manuel Antonio, there's another slightly longer trail to the **Puerto Escondido,** where there's a blowhole that sends up plumes of spray at high tide.

THE HIKING TRAILS   From either Playa Espadilla Sur or Playa Manuel Antonio, you can take a circular hike around a high promontory bluff. The furthest point on this hike, which takes about 25 minutes round-trip, is **Punta Catedral** (Cathedral Point), where the view is spectacular. The trail is a little steep in places, but anybody in average shape can do it. I have done it in sturdy sandals, but you might want to wear good hiking shoes. This is a good place to spot monkeys, though you're more likely to see a white-faced monkey than a rare squirrel monkey.

Another good place to see monkeys is the **trail inland** from Playa Manuel Antonio. This is a linear trail, and mostly uphill, but not too taxing. It's great to spend hours exploring the steamy jungle and then take a refreshing dip in the ocean.

Finally, there is a trail that leads first to Puerto Escondido (see above) and **Punta Surrucho,** where there are some sea caves. Be careful when hiking beyond Puerto Escondido: What seems like easy beach hiking at low tide becomes treacherous to impassable at high tide. Don't get trapped. Two other trails wind their way inland from the trail between Playa Manuel Antonio and Puerto Escondido.

HITTING THE WATER

BEACHES OUTSIDE THE PARK   Playa Espadilla, the gray-sand beach just outside the park boundary, is often perfect for board surfing and bodysurfing. At times, it can be a bit rough for casual swimming, but because there's no entrance fee, it's the most popular beach with locals and visiting Ticos. There are some shops by the water that rent boogie boards, beach chairs, and beach umbrellas. A full-day rental of a beach umbrella and two chaise lounges will cost around $10 (these are not available inside the park).

BOATING, KAYAKING, RAFTING & SPORTFISHING TOURS   Iguana Tours (☎ and fax **506/777-1262;** www.iguanatours.com; E-mail: info@iguanatours.com) is the most established and dependable tour operator in the area, offering a wide range of tours, including river rafting, sea kayaking, mangrove tours, and guided hikes. These folks have an office on the main road, just as you begin to head out of Quepos toward Manuel Antonio. Tour prices range from $35 to $85.

Among my favorite tours in the area is a mangrove estuary tour of Damas Island. These trips generally include lunch, a stop on Damas Island, and roughly 3 to 4 hours of cruising the waterways. You'll see loads of wildlife. Ask at your hotel or contact **Iguana Tours** (☎ **506/777-1262**). The cost is $65.

There are several rafting companies in Quepos that ply the same rivers. Among them are **Amigos del Río** (☎ **506/777-0082;** E-mail: amigorio@racsa.co.cr) and **Iguana Tours** (☎ **506/777-1262**). All offer full-day rafting trips for around $70 to $90. Large multiperson rafts are used during the rainy season, and single-person "duckies" are broken out when the water levels drop. Both of the above companies also offer sea-kayaking trips for around $65.

Among the newer options around Quepos/Manuel Antonio are boat excursions in search of dolphins and simple sunset cruises. **Iguana Tours** (☎ **506/777-1262**), **Planet Dolphin** (☎ **506/777-1647;** www.planetdolphin.com), and **Taximar** (☎ **506/777-1647**) all offer these tours. **Waverunner Safaris** (☎ **506/777-1706**) offers 2-hour jet-ski tours for $95 per person.

Quepos is one of Costa Rica's billfish centers, and sailfish, marlin, and tuna are all common in these waters. If you're into sportfishing, try hooking up with **Blue Fin Sportfishing** (☎ **506/777-1676;** www.bluefinsportfishing.org; E-mail: bluefin@racsa.co.cr), **Blue Water II** (☎ **506/777-1596;** www.bluewaterii.com; E-mail: bluewat@racsa.co.cr), **Costa Rican Dreams** (☎ **506/777-0593;** www.crdreams.com; E-mail:

info@crdreams.com), or **Poseidon Adventures** (☎ **506/777-0935;** E-mail: cksibus@ racsa.co.cr). A full day of fishing should cost between $450 and $1,250, depending on the size of the boat. There's a lot of competition here, so it pays to shop around and investigate. Try asking at **El Gran Escape** restaurant and also down at the **Manuel Antonio Marina.**

OTHER ACTIVITIES IN THE AREA

BIKING   If you want to do some mountain biking while you're here, check in with **Cycling Estrella** (☎ and fax **506/777-1286;** E-mail: estrellatour@queposcostarica. com), which is in downtown Quepos. Well-maintained bikes rent for $20 per day. You can also do guided tours for around $40 per day, as well as multiday expeditions.

A CANOPY WALK   About 20 minutes outside of Quepos is **Rainmaker Nature Refuge** (☎ **506/777-0777;** www.rainmaker-costarica.com), a private reserve run by the folks at Hotel Sí Como No. Aside from a small network of trails and some great swimming holes, the main attraction here is a system of connected suspension bridges strung through the forest canopy, crisscrossing a deep ravine. There are eight bridges, the longest is 300 feet across. A half-day tour, including a light breakfast, buffet lunch, round-trip transportation from Quepos, and a guide costs $65 per person. Tours leave every morning.

HORSEBACK RIDING   If your tropical fantasy is to ride a horse down a beach between jungle and ocean, contact **Stable Equus** (☎ **506/777-0001**), which charges $35 for a 2-hour ride in Manuel Antonio. This stable allegedly treats its animals more humanely than other stables in the area and is also concerned with keeping horse droppings off the beaches. Full-day horseback-riding excursions to a typical Costa Rican farm are provided by **Rancho Savegre Tours** (☎ **506/777-0528**). Tours cost $50 per person and include hotel transfers, lunch, and several swimming stops. You can also take an all-day horseback tour to the Los Tucanes Waterfalls by contacting **Rancho Los Tucanes** (☎ **506/777-0290**) or **Brisas del Nara** (☎ **506/777-1493**). These tours leave from Londres, about 15 minutes outside of Quepos, include transportation to and from your hotel, breakfast, and lunch, and cost around $50 per person.

A WILDLIFE REHABILITATION CENTER   For a closer look at some exotic birds and other assorted wildlife, check out **Jardín Gaia** (☎ **506/777-0535**), a wildlife rescue center that rehabilitates and breeds injured and confiscated animals, many of them endangered. The center is located on the road between Quepos and Manuel Antonio. Jardín Gaia runs daily guided tours at 9am and 4pm. Currently, you can only visit Jardín Gaia on one of the tours. Admission is $5 for adults, $2 for children.

SHOPPING

If you're looking for souvenirs, you'll find plenty of beach towels, beachwear, and handmade jewelry in a variety of small shops in Quepos and at impromptu stalls down near the national park. For a good selection in one spot, try **La Buena Nota** (☎ **506/ 777-1002**), which is on the road to Manuel Antonio, right near the Hotel Karahé.

Yo Quiero Hablar Español

La Escuela de Idiomas D'Amore (☎ and fax **506/777-1143;** www.escueladamore. com; E-mail: damore@racsa.co.cr) runs immersion programs out of a former hotel with a fabulous view, on the road to Manuel Antonio. A 2-week conversational Spanish course, including a homestay and two meals daily, costs $980.

This shop is jam-packed with all sorts of beachwear, souvenirs, and U.S. magazines and newspapers and also acts as an informal information center for the area. They recently put in a few basic rooms upstairs, and if you'd like to find out about renting a house, this is a good place to ask.

If you're looking for higher-end gifts, check out **L'Aventura Boutique** (☎ 506/ 777-1019) on Avenida Central in Quepos. This small shop has a nice collection of woodwork by Barry Biesanz, banana-fabric works by Lil Mena, and pottery by Cecilia "Pefi" Figueres.

The Hotel Sí Como No's **Regalame** gift shop is pretty well stocked and now has two locations, one at the small shopping center in front of the hotel, and another down in Quepos, just as you cross the bridge into town.

One of my favorite hangouts in Quepos has always been the ✪ **Cafe Milagro** (☎ and fax **506/777-1707**), which is one of the few homey coffeehouses I've found in Costa Rica. The folks here roast their own beans and also have a mail-order service to keep you in Costa Rican coffee year-round. You'll find local art for sale on the walls and a good selection of Cuban cigars, too. There's another branch on the main road to Manuel Antonio right near La Mariposa.

ACCOMMODATIONS

Take care when choosing your accommodations in Quepos/Manuel Antonio. There are very few true beachfront hotels in Manuel Antonio, so you won't have much luck finding a hotel where you can walk directly out of your room and onto the beach. In fact, most of the nicer hotels here are half a mile (1km) or so away from the beach, high on the hill overlooking the ocean. If you're traveling on a rock-bottom budget, you'll get more for your money by staying in Quepos and taking the bus to the beaches at Manuel Antonio every day. The rooms in Quepos may be small, but they're generally cleaner and more appealing than those available in the same price category closer to the park.

VERY EXPENSIVE

El Parador. Apdo. 284, Quepos. ☎ **506/777-1414.** Fax 506/777-1437. www.hotelparador. com. E-mail: parador@racsa.co.cr. 69 units. A/C MINIBAR TV TEL. $262 standard, $309 deluxe, $403 junior suite, $1,167 presidential suite; slightly higher during peak weeks, lower in the off-season. Rates include breakfast. AE, MC, V.

What is luxurious opulence to one person can seem blindingly ostentatious to another. I lean toward the latter in this case. The hotel itself is spread out over more than 12 acres of land on a low peninsula, down a dirt road from La Mariposa. Its design aims to imitate Spanish Mediterranean grandeur, and the main building is loaded with antiques, including 17th-century Dutch and Flemish oil paintings, a 300-year-old carved wooden horse, and a 16th-century church and castle doors. The standard rooms, although small, are new and well appointed. All have private patios, but few have any view to speak of. Most look out on the miniature-golf course. Deluxe rooms offer slightly more space, and the second-floor units have private balconies.

The junior suites are located on the top of a hill, giving a good view of the sea and Cathedral Point in the distance. Each is equipped with a VCR, Jacuzzi, wet bar, and refrigerator. Be forewarned: It's an arduous hike up to these units, although they do offer an on-call golf-cart shuttle service. The three-bedroom presidential suite is in the main building and has the amenities of the other suites, plus a fully equipped kitchenette and decorative antiques. The hotel can arrange a wide variety of tours and activities in the area and runs a shuttle van to the national park. There's also a small secluded beach about 500 meters (545 yd.) from the hotel.

Dining/Diversions: Most of the meals are served in the main **La Galería** dining room and its adjoining terrace. Breakfast is served buffet style, while dinners are more formal, chosen from a menu that changes nightly and generally includes eight main-course selections. There are three private dining rooms of varying sizes that can be reserved for special occasions. Sunsets are best enjoyed from the **Mirador Lounge,** above and behind the main building.

Amenities: The small kidney-shaped pool has a swim-up bar and central fountain. There's also a modest fitness center, Jacuzzi, steam room, tennis court, private helipad, tour desk, and small gift shop.

✪ **Hotel Sí Como No.** Apdo. 5-6350, Quepos (mailing address in the U.S.: Mail Stop SJO 297, P.O. Box 025216, Miami FL, 33102). ☎ **506/777-0777.** Fax 506/777-1093. www. sicomono.com. E-mail: information@sicomono.com. 39 units. A/C MINIBAR. Dec 1–Apr 15 $150–$195 double; Apr 16–Nov 30 $130–$165 double. Rates include breakfast. AE, MC, V.

This small resort complex seeks to combine modern amenities with an ecologically conscious attitude. All the wood used is farm grown, and although all the rooms have air-conditioning, guests are asked to use it only when necessary. The standard rooms (housed in the hotel's main building or in the ground floor of a villa) are quite acceptable, but it's worth the small splurge for a superior or deluxe room. Most of these are on the top floors of the villas, with treetop views out over the forest and onto the Pacific. These rooms all have bedrooms, living rooms, private balconies, and either a kitchenette or a wet bar. You'll find the best views in villas 4, 6, 8, and 14. There's a new building set on a high patch of land that has a more art-deco style to it. This building features a penthouse honeymoon suite with a private outdoor Jacuzzi.

Dining/Diversions: There are two dining options here. The **Claro Que Sí** restaurant in the main building is the more formal option, with a moderately priced menu of "nouvelle Costa Rican" cuisine. Try the fish of the day in an avocado butter sauce, or the pork tenderloin with pineapple chutney. Down by the pool, you'll find the **Rico Tico Bar and Grill,** which serves excellent ceviche, fresh fish, and grilled meats, plus Mexican snacks like nachos and quesadillas.

Amenities: A free-form tile pool with waterfall, Jacuzzi, and slide; conference center and 50-seat laser-projection theater. A movie on laser disc is shown nightly. Nonguests who dine here can watch the movie for free. The hotel also has a full-time concierge, a well-stocked gift shop, an Internet cafe, and a new open-air restaurant for banquets and weddings.

La Mariposa. Apdo. 4, Quepos. ☎ **800/416-2747** in the U.S., or 506/777-0456. Fax 506/777-0050. www.lamariposa.com. E-mail: htlmariposa@msn.com. 33 units, 4 villas. A/C TV TEL. $120–$145 double, $180–$250 suite or villa. AE, MC, V.

While this is still one of Manuel Antonio's premier accommodations, I think it's been coasting on its reputation for some time. Perched on a ridge at the top of the hill between Quepos and Manuel Antonio, La Mariposa (the Butterfly) commands a mountains-to-the-sea ✪ **vista** of more than 270°. Needless to say, the sunsets here are knockouts, and the daytime views are pretty captivating themselves. La Mariposa offers spacious, attractively designed and decorated rooms, but the service and meals frequently fall far below the mark. Keep in mind that if you decide to abandon the view and the attractive little pool, it'll take either a steep hike or a short drive to get to the beach.

The nicest accommodations are the bilevel villas and suites. Each has a large bedroom and bathroom on the upper floor and a spacious living room and deck on the lower floor. There are painted tropical murals behind the two queen-size beds in the bedrooms, plus high ceilings, skylights, blue-and-white-tile counters, and shelves of plants. The bathrooms are spacious and most even have small atrium gardens. Several of these villas have recently been split into separate junior suites and deluxe rooms. The junior suites each have a Jacuzzi out on the small balcony or just inside its sliding glass door. There are also several standard rooms, most of which are quite comfortable but do not have views or much distinctive charm.

Dining/Diversions: The open-air restaurant is set on a red-tiled terrace that takes in all the views. The emphasis is on seafood. On my three most recent visits, the food has fallen far short of what one would expect at these surroundings and at these prices. There's also a small bar.

Amenities: The small swimming pool is set on its own terrace. Services include room service, a concierge, and a tour desk. The hotel provides a complimentary shuttle to and from the national park.

✪ **Makanda-by-the-Sea.** P.O. Box 29, Quepos. ☎ **506/777-0442.** Fax 506/777-1032. www.makanda.com. E-mail: info@makanda.com. 9 units. TEL. Nov 1–Apr 30 $175 studio, $230 villa; May 1–Oct 31 $135 studio, $175 villa. Rates include continental breakfast. AE, DC, MC, V.

Located halfway down the road to El Parador and Punta Quepos, Makanda is a wonderfully luxurious collection of studio apartments and private villas. Each is individually decorated, with flair and a sense of style. If you combine Villa 1 with the three studios, you get one very large four-bedroom villa, great for a family or small group. Every choice comes with a full kitchenette and either a terrace or a balcony. The grounds are well tended, intermixed with tropical flowers and Japanese gardens. A continental breakfast is delivered to your room each morning. The hotel's pool and Jacuzzi combine intricate and colorful tile work with a view of the jungle-covered hillsides and the Pacific Ocean.

Dining: Makanda's ✪ **Sunspot Bar & Grill** is one of the best restaurants in Manuel Antonio, with just a few tables set under open-sided cloth tents, serving creative continental dishes and rich desserts. Be sure to make reservations in the high season.

Amenities: Pool, Jacuzzi, laundry service, and concierge.

Tulemar Bungalows. Quepos (mailing address in the U.S.: SJO 042, P.O. Box 025369, Miami, FL 33102). ☎ **506/777-0580** or 506/777-1325. Fax 506/777-1579. www. tulemar.com. E-mail: tulemar@racsa.co.cr. 14 bungalows. A/C MINIBAR TV TEL. Dec 16–Apr 30 $220 bungalow; May 1–Dec 15 $139 bungalow. Rates include full breakfast. AE, MC, V.

These individual octagonal bungalows are some of the more enticing and exclusive accommodations in Manuel Antonio. Each bungalow has a spacious living room, full kitchenette, two queen-size beds, and 180° views over jungle and ocean. The couches in the living room fold out into beds, and extra cots for children can be placed in the rooms. The furnishings are fine but a bit sparse and lacking in style.

Dining: The hotel's poolside open-air restaurant serves local and continental cuisine. A new, larger restaurant is being built on the hillside above the bungalows, and is expected to open in 2001.

Amenities: A private road winds steeply down to a small cove and semiprivate beach where you'll find chaise lounges, kayaks, boogie boards, and a snack bar. The pool here is small yet elegant, with its infinity effect blending in with the Pacific Ocean and breathtaking view.

EXPENSIVE

Hotel Casitas Eclipse. Apdo. 11-6350, Quepos. ☎ **506/777-0408.** Fax 506/777-1738. www.casitaseclipse.net. E-mail: eclipseh@racsa.co.cr. 25 units. A/C TEL. Dec 16–Apr 15 $95–$135 double, $225 2-bedroom casita; Apr 16–Dec 15 $70–$90 double, $150 2-bedroom casita. AE, MC, V.

Located close to the top of the hill between Quepos and Manuel Antonio, these beautiful casitas are some of the most boldly styled structures in Manuel Antonio. While the villas have a distinctly Mediterranean flavor, the owner swears they're inspired by Mesoamerican and Pueblo Indian villages. Their styling makes them seem much larger than they actually are, although they're certainly plenty roomy. All are painted a blinding white and are topped with red tile roofs. Though simply furnished, the rooms are quite comfortable and attractive inside.

You can rent either the entire casita or split it up. The larger downstairs suites have tile floors, built-in banquettes, high ceilings, large patios, and full kitchens. If you don't need all that space, you can opt for the upstairs room, which has a separate entrance, private bathroom, and balcony of its own. There are three attractive tiled pools spread out among the lush grounds. Only the restaurant and a couple of villas have ocean views here, and even these are rather blocked by trees. I personally prefer the units farther from the road, where you're more likely to hear and see squirrel monkeys passing by than trucks and buses.

Dining/Diversions: The **El Gato Negro** restaurant (see "Dining," below) serves breakfast, lunch, and dinner. There's a small bar just off the restaurant, as well as the more lively Cockatoo Bar on the terrace above.

Amenities: Three swimming pools, concierge, tour desk.

MODERATE

Hotel and Cabinas Playa Espadilla. A.P. 195, Manuel Antonio, Quepos. ☎ and fax **506/ 777-0416,** or 506/777-0903. www.maqbeach.com. E-mail: spadilla@racsa.co.cr. 16 units, 12 cabinas. $50–$60 double cabina, $80 double rm. AE, MC, V.

These are actually two separate developments located across the street from each other. The newer hotel rooms all have air-conditioning and full kitchenettes. This project also has a refreshing pool, tennis court, well-tended green areas, and a bordering private reserve with a small trail system. The older cabinas are more basic, and most just have fans. Although there isn't much in the way of decor or closet space in any of them, there are enough beds to sleep up to four people comfortably (a double bed and a bunk bed). You'll find both of these places down the side road that runs inland, perpendicular to Playa Espadilla, the first beach outside the national park.

Hotel Costa Verde. Apdo. 106-6350, Quepos (mailing address in the U.S.: SJO 1313, P.O. Box 025216, Miami, FL 33102). ☎ **888/234-5565** in the U.S. and Canada, or 506/ 777-0584. Fax 506/777-0506. www.hotelcostaverde.com. E-mail: costaver@racsa.co.cr. 43 units. Dec 15–Apr 15 $79–$119 double, $144 penthouse; Apr 16–Dec 14 $55–$94 double, $119 penthouse. AE, MC, V.

The guest rooms at Costa Verde have long been one of the best values in the area. Over the years, Costa Verde has continued to add new rooms and new buildings. And today, there are rooms in a wide range of sizes and prices. While the original rooms are some of the least expensive, they're still pleasant. With their screen walls, they seem to sum up the sensual climate of the tropics—no need for walls when they only keep out the breezes. The nicest rooms here have ocean views, kitchenettes, private balconies, and loads of space. There is also a huge penthouse suite, which has a commanding view of the spectacular surroundings. There are two small pools set into the hillside, with views out to the ocean. The lodge's open-air Anaconda restaurant serves good Costa Rican and international cuisine. There's also the new roadside La Cantina Bar & Grill for more-informal drinking and dining, as well as a small gift shop. The hotel has a couple of miles of private trails through the rain forest.

I do have two caveats here: Some of the buildings are located quite a hike from the hotel's pools and restaurant, so be sure you know exactly what type of room you'll be staying in and where it's located. I've also heard that they've taken to feeding the monkeys each evening around sunset, which is a particular pet peeve of mine. Costa Verde is more than halfway down the hill to Manuel Antonio, about a 10-minute walk from the beach.

Hotel Plinio. Apdo. 71-6350, Quepos. ☎ **506/777-0055** or 506/777-0077. Fax 506/777-0558. www.hotelplinio.com. E-mail: plinio@racsa.co.cr. 13 units. Dec–Apr $60–$70 double, $75 standard suite or house, $90 deluxe suite. Lower rates available May–Nov. Rates include a breakfast buffet during the high season. AE, MC, V (6% surcharge).

The Plinio was for many years a favorite of budget travelers visiting Manuel Antonio, and although its room rates have crept up over the years, it's still a good value. The hotel is built into a steep hillside, so it's a bit of a climb from the parking lot up to the guest rooms and restaurant (roughly the equivalent of three flights of stairs). Once you are up top, though, you'll think you're in a tree house. Floors and walls are polished hardwood, and there are even rooms with tree-trunk pillars.

The hotel's suites are the best value. These are built on either two or three levels. Both have sleeping lofts, while the three-story rooms also have rooftop decks. My favorite room is known as the "jungle house" and is set back in the forest. The restaurant, which is one of the more popular places to eat in Manuel Antonio, serves a variety of good Italian and international dishes, with entree prices ranging from $4.50 to $10. Behind the hotel there's a private reserve with 9 miles (15km) of trails and, at the top of the hill, a 50-foot-tall observation tower with an incredible view. There's also a snack bar near the pool, for lunches. A lap pool, kids' pool, and recreation room with library round out the amenities.

Karahé. Apdo. 100-6350, Quepos. ☎ **506/777-0170.** Fax 506/777-0175. www.karahe.com. E-mail: reservations@karahe.com. 24 units, 9 villas. A/C TEL. $50–$100 double. Rates include continental breakfast. AE, MC, V.

The Karahé has long been one of the better beachfront hotels in Manuel Antonio, but competition is increasing, and in order to keep up, the hotel has had to lower its rates, which is good news for travelers. Note that if you opt for one of the villas (the cheapest and oldest rooms in the hotel), you'll have a steep uphill climb from the beach and won't have air-conditioning. On the other hand, you'll have a much better view. If you stay in one of the more expensive beachfront units, you'll have a new room with cool tile floors, two double beds, air-conditioning, and a small patio. All except the very cheapest rooms have balconies and full bathtubs. The gardens surrounding the upper half of the hotel are quite lush and are planted with flowering ginger that often attracts hummingbirds. The gardens are not nearly as attractive in the lower part of the hotel grounds, where you'll find the small pool, Jacuzzi, and spa. The hotel is located on both sides of the road about 457 meters (500 yd.) before you reach Manuel Antonio.

The hotel's restaurant is built at treetop level, midway between the two levels of accommodations. Entree prices range from $5 to $17, and the specialty of the house is shish kebab cooked over an indoor barbecue. There's also a snack bar near the pool, which serves lunch and doubles as the hotel's bar. The hotel can arrange a wide variety of tours and charters, including sportfishing ($800 for a full day).

✪ La Colina. Apdo. 191, Quepos. ☎ **506/777-0231.** Fax 506/777-1553. www.lacolina.com. E-mail: lacolina@racsa.co.cr. 13 units. Dec–Apr $39–$49 double, $60–$75 suite; slightly higher on peak holiday weeks. May–Nov $29–$39 double, $50–$60 suite. Rates include full breakfast. AE, MC, V.

This casual little place is operated by Colorado natives who moved to Manuel Antonio several years ago and converted their home into a B&B. Although the original rooms here are fairly small, they're decorated with style. They have black-and-white tile floors, louvered French doors, and a good writing desk. Outside each room, there's a small patio area with a few chairs. The new suites are built on the highest spot on this property and have front and back balconies with views of both the ocean and the mountains. The suites are large and comfortable and several come with cable television. All of the suites and a couple of the rooms have air-conditioning. In addition to filling breakfasts, the Sunset Grill serves up lunch and dinner, offering up a mix of international dishes with a hefty emphasis on fresh seafood. There's a two-tiered swimming pool with a swim-up bar. La Colina also rents out two fully equipped apartments and can accommodate longer-term stays. The hotel is on your right as you head toward Manuel Antonio, right at a sharp switchback on a steep hill, hence the name, La Colina (The Hill).

Verde Del Mar. Manuel Antonio (Apdo. 348-6350), Quepos. ☎ **506/777-1805** or 506/777-2122. Fax 506/777-1311. www.maqbeach.com. E-mail: verdemar@racsa.co.cr. 20 units. $55–$75 double. A/C $10 extra. AE, MC, V.

This new hotel is one of the better choices for proximity to the national park and the beach. From your room, it's just a 50-meter (55 yd.) walk to the beach (Playa Espadilla) via a raised wooden walkway. All but two of the rooms come with a basic kitchenette; six of them have air-conditioning. All have plenty of space, nice wrought-iron queen-size beds, red tile floors, a desk and chair, a fan, and a small porch. Some of the larger rooms even have two queen-size beds. The hotel has no restaurant, but there are plenty within walking distance. There's a small pool here, for when the surf is too rough. You'll find Verde del Mar on the beach side of the road just before the Mar y Sombra.

Villas Nicolas. Apdo. 236, Quepos. ☎ **506/777-0481.** Fax 506/777-0451. www.hotels.co.cr/nicolas. E-mail: nicolas@racsa.co.cr. 20 units. $59–$90 double, $105 triple, $110–$165 quad; weekly, monthly, and low-season (May–Nov) rates available. AE, MC, V.

These large villas offer bang for the buck. Built as terraced units up a steep hill in deep forest, they really give you the feeling you're in the jungle. They're spacious and well appointed, with wood floors, throw rugs, separate living rooms, and large bathrooms; some rooms even have full kitchenettes, which make longer stays comfortable. My favorite features, though, are the huge balconies, with sitting chairs and a hammock. There's also a small tiled pool and Jacuzzi. The rooms highest up the hill have views I'd be willing to pay a lot more for, and two of them even have air-conditioning.

INEXPENSIVE

Cabinas Pedro Miguel. Apdo. 17, Manuel Antonio, Quepos. ☎ and fax **506/777-0035.** E-mail: pmiguel@racsa.co.cr. 14 units. $22–$28 double; $37 quad. AE, MC, V.

Located a kilometer outside Quepos on the road to Manuel Antonio (across from Hotel Plinio), these cabinas are very basic, with cement floors and cinder-block walls, but at least they're away from the fray and surrounded by forest. The second-floor rooms are newer and cleaner and have carpeting, as well as a glimpse of the water from the common veranda. One of them is huge, with a kitchen, and a back wall made entirely of screen. From it, guests can look out over a lush stand of trees. During the high season (late November through late April), there's a breakfast buffet. In the evening you can dine at the restaurant, which serves Costa Rican standards; the owners encourage guests to participate in meal preparation. There's a postage-stamp swimming pool.

Cabinas Ramirez. Playa Manuel Antonio, Quepos. ☎ **506/777-0003.** 16 units. $18–$30 double. No credit cards.

These basic beachside cabinas are the most popular budget choices near the park, especially among young Ticos. The hotel is next door to the restaurant/bar and disco Mar y Sombra, so evenings can be loud. The rooms are basic cinder-block affairs with concrete floors. Some are quite dark and prisonlike, but all are clean. The owner also allows camping for backpackers with tents, for $3 per person.

Cabinas Vela-Bar. Apdo. 13, Manuel Antonio, Quepos. ☎ **506/777-0413.** Fax 506/777-1071. www.maqbeach.com. E-mail: velabar@maqbeach.com. 11 units. $25–$60 double, $48–$65 triple, $60–$100 quad. AE, MC, V.

You'll find this little hotel up the dirt road that leads off to the left just before the end of the road to Manuel Antonio National Park. It has a wide variety of room choices: If you're on an exceedingly tight budget, you can stay in a tiny room or, if you have a little more money to spend, you can opt for a spacious one-bedroom house that has tile floors and arched windows. There are double beds and tiled bathrooms in all rooms. The open-air restaurant/bar is deservedly popular; check the chalkboard for the day's special. Entrees range in price from $5 to $15. This is one of the best budget options in Manuel Antonio, and it's only 100 meters (109 yd.) from the beach.

El Lirio Garden. Apdo. 123, Quepos. ☎ **506/777-0403.** Fax 506/777-1182. E-mail: elirio@racsa.co.cr. 9 units. Dec–Apr $40 double; May–Nov $30 double. Rates include continental breakfast. AE, MC, V.

A Mediterranean style prevails at this budget hotel, with arches, stucco walls, and red tile floors and roofs. The rooms are basic but clean, with high ceilings and tiled bathrooms. The nicest rooms here are located in the back of the property near the swimming pool. The grounds are quiet and lush, planted with orchids and other tropical flowers and overhung by large, shady trees. You'll find the sharp turnoff for El Lirio on the left, near the top of the hill as you drive from Quepos to Manuel Antonio. From the turn it's only about 25 meters (27 yd.) to the hotel. All in all, this is an attractive, well-maintained place and a pretty good deal.

Hotel Malinche. Quepos. ☎ and fax **505/777-0093.** 24 units. $20 double, $45 double with A/C. AE, MC, V.

Another good choice for backpackers, the Hotel Malinche is located on the first street to your left as you come into Quepos. You can't miss the hotel's arched brick entrance. Inside, you'll find bright rooms with louvered windows. The rooms are small but have hardwood floors and clean bathrooms. The more expensive rooms are new and have air-conditioning and carpets.

Hotel Quepos. Quepos. ☎ **506/777-0274.** 20 units, 11 with bathroom. $12 double without bathroom, $17 double with bathroom. No credit cards.

This little budget hotel is both comfortable and clean. There are hardwood floors, ceiling fans, a large, sunny TV lounge, and even a parking lot and laundry service. The management is very friendly, and there's an interesting souvenir shop and a charter-fishing office on the first floor. This hotel is hard to miss—it's directly across from the soccer field on the way out of town toward Manuel Antonio, and it's painted hot pink with green trim.

DINING

There are scores of dining options around Manuel Antonio and Quepos, and almost every hotel has some sort of restaurant. My favorite of these is the small restaurant at **Makanda-by-the-Sea** (see "Accommodations," above).

For the cheapest meals around, try a simple *soda* in Quepos, or head to one of the open-air shacks near the side of the road just before the circle at the entrance to the national park. The standard Tico menu prevails, with prices in the $2.50-to-$8 range. Though these little places lack atmosphere, they do have views of the ocean. In Quepos, **La Marquesa** and **Restaurant Isabel,** on the main road, are good bets. At both of these places, the fish is fresh daily, the portions are large, and the prices are bargains.

If you have a room with a kitchenette, you can shop at one of several supermarkets in Quepos, or brave the cluttered stalls of its central market, right next to the bus station. For a picnic lunch, complete with cooler, check out **Pickles Deli** in the small shopping center next to Hotel Sí Como No. Another option for light meals and well-prepared sandwiches is **L'Angelo Italian Deli** in Quepos, located 1 block west of the bus terminal.

Barba Roja. Quepos–Manuel Antonio Rd. ☎ **506/777-0331.** Reservations not accepted. Main courses $5–$20, sandwiches $3–$6. V. Tues–Sun 7am–10pm, Mon 4–10pm. SEAFOOD/CONTINENTAL.

Perched high on a hill, with stunning views over jungle and ocean, the Barba Roja has long been one of the more popular restaurants in Manuel Antonio. The rustic interior is done with local hardwoods and bamboo, which gives the open-air dining room a warm glow, and there's an outdoor patio where you can sit for hours taking in the view or the stars. There's even a gallery attached to the restaurant, so if you tire of the view you can take a gander at some original art by local artists. On the blackboard, there are daily specials such as grilled fish steak served with a salad and a baked potato. Portions here are massive. The restaurant is open for breakfast and serves delicious whole-wheat French toast. For lunch, there are a number of different sandwiches, all served on whole-wheat bread. If you're in the mood to hang out and meet some locals and other fellow travelers, spend some time at the bar sipping piña coladas or margaritas.

El Gato Negro. Quepos–Manuel Antonio Rd. at Hotel Casitas Eclipse. ☎ and fax **506/ 777-1728.** Reservations recommended during high season. Main courses $8–$25. AE, MC, V. Daily 7am–3pm and 6–10pm. MEDITERRANEAN.

Perched at the highest part of the Hotel Casitas Eclipse, this place serves the best Mediterranean cuisine in the area. Fresh fillets of red snapper and dorado ($8 to $12) come either grilled or in light sauces with fresh basil or thyme. The *tagliatelle al frutti di mare* ($13) is fresh pasta piled with clams, shrimp, chunks of fish, and a half lobster, served in a light tomato sauce. There are plenty of meat and chicken choices, as well as a healthy and reasonably priced selection of wines for the area. The restaurant is an open-air affair with rattan tables and chairs, cloth tablecloths, and oil lanterns. You can also get breakfast and light lunches. Upstairs on the open terrace is the new Cockatoo Bar, which has great panoramic views of Manuel Antonio.

✪ **El Gran Escape.** On the main road into Quepos, on your left just after the bridge. ☎ **506/777-0395.** Reservations accepted. Main courses $6–$16. V. Wed–Mon 6am–11pm. SEAFOOD.

This Quepos landmark is a favorite with locals and fishermen—for good reason. The fish is fresh and expertly prepared, and the prices are reasonable. If that's not enough of a recommendation, the atmosphere is lively and the service is darn good for a beach town in Costa Rica. The popularity has translated into a major expansion, with covered outdoor seating nearly doubling the original dining capacity. Sturdy wooden tables and chairs fill up the large indoor dining room, and sportfishing photos and an exotic collection of masks fill up the walls. If you venture away from the fish, there are hearty steaks, giant burgers, and a wide assortment of delicious appetizers. El Gran Escape's Fish Head Bar is usually crowded and lively, and if there's a game going on, it will be on the television here.

⭕ **Karola's.** Quepos–Manuel Antonio Rd. ☎ **506/777-1557.** Reservations accepted. Main courses $10–$22. V. Daily 11am–11pm. SEAFOOD/CONTINENTAL.

The steep driveway leading down to this open-air restaurant is within a few feet of the Barba Roja parking lot but is easily overlooked. Watch closely when you're up at the top of the hill. The restaurant is across a footbridge from its parking lot and is set against a jungle-covered hillside. Far below you can see the ocean if you're here during the day. Grilled seafood is the specialty, but there's also a wide range of international treats including sashimi, fish burritos, and Caribbean chicken. Desserts are decadent, and you can order a variety of margaritas by the pitcher. As at the Barba Roja, there's a separate art gallery here as well.

Plinio Restaurant. 0.62 miles (1km) out of Quepos toward Manuel Antonio. ☎ **506/777-0055.** Main courses $5–$15. AE, MC, V. Daily 5–10pm. INTERNATIONAL.

This is a long-standing, popular restaurant in Manuel Antonio, located at an equally popular hotel. The open-air restaurant is about three stories above the parking lot, so be prepared to climb some steps. It's worth it, though. The basket of bread that arrives at your table shortly after you sit down is filled with delicious treats; the menu that follows is an enticing mix of international dishes. The chef uses organically grown herbs and veggies. Thai and Indonesian dishes are plentiful, and there are always vegetarian options and a nightly special. Breakfasts are served in the high season. At lunchtime, a separate chef takes over the restaurant at the poolside snack bar, preparing some wonderful lunches, with frequent Asian and Creole specials.

Restaurant Vela-Bar. 100m (109 yd.) down side road near park entrance. ☎ **506/777-0413.** Reservations accepted. Main courses $5–$12. AE, MC, V. Daily 7–11pm. INTERNATIONAL.

The Vela-Bar is a small and casual place that serves some of the more creative cuisine in Manuel Antonio. This is also the best of the restaurants closest to the park entrance. Seafood and vegetarian meals are the specialties. The most interesting dishes are almost always the specials posted on the blackboard. A typical day's choice might include fresh fish in sherry or wine sauce with curried vegetables.

MANUEL ANTONIO AFTER DARK

Discos are becoming almost as common in Manuel Antonio as capuchin monkeys. Night owls and dancing fools have their choice. The local favorite appears to be **Arco Iris** (☎ 506/777-0449), which is located just over the bridge heading out of town. Admission is usually around $2.50. Down near the beach, folks get going at the restaurant ⭕ **Mar y Sombra** (☎ 506/777-0510). This is my favorite spot—you can walk off the dance floor and right out onto the beach, and there's usually no cover. **Maracas** (no phone), which is located at the southern pier in Quepos, seems to go in and out of favor. The open-air dance floor is quite large and I personally like the setting quite a bit. Admission fees range between $1 and $5, depending on whether or not they have a live band.

The bars at the **Barba Roja** restaurant (☎ 506/777-0331) and the **Hotel Sí Como No** (☎ 506/777-0777) are also good places to hang out and meet people in the evenings. You can also hang out at the **Vela-Bar** (☎ 506/777-0413), which seems to be popular with gay men. Back in Quepos, **El Banco Bar** (☎ 506/777-0478) and the **Fish Head Bar** at **El Gran Escape** (☎ 506/777-0395) are the most popular gringo hangouts.

If you enjoy the gaming tables, the **Hotel Kamuk** (☎ 506/777-0379) in Quepos has a small casino and will even foot your cab bill if you try your luck and lay your money down. You'll also find a small casino at the **Hotel Divisamar** (☎ 506/777-0371) on the Manuel Antonio Road, across from the Barba Roja.

If you want to see a flick, check what's playing at **Hotel Sí Como No's** little theater, although you have to eat at the restaurant or spend a minimum at the bar to earn admission.

EN ROUTE TO DOMINICAL: PLAYA MATAPALO

Playa Matapalo is a long strand of flat beach that's about midway between Quepos and Dominical. It's an easy but bumpy 16 miles (26km) south of Quepos on the Costanera Sur. It's nowhere near as developed as either of those two beaches, but that's part of its charm. The beach here seems to stretch on forever, and it's usually deserted. Unfortunately, the surf is often too rough for swimming, although boogie boarding can be good. Foremost among this beach's charms are peace and quiet. Matapalo is basically a little village; the beach is about half a mile (1km) away. In addition to the hotel listed here, there's an Italian restaurant that serves economical meals, a Tico cabina with a disco, and other projects in the works.

El Coquito del Pacífico. Playa Matapalo (Apdo. 6783-1000, San José). ☎ **506/228-2228.** Fax 506/228-6484. E-mail: ecobraun@racsa.co.cr. 8 units. $45 double, 52 triple, $60 quad. No credit cards.

This little collection of cabinas is operated by the same people who run the Hotel Ritz/Pension Continental, a budget travelers' standard in San José. The cabina rooms are all quite large and have white tile floors, high ceilings, colorful sheets on the beds, and overhead fans. There's a small restaurant/bar, and guests can use the mountain bikes and boogie boards for free. The newest addition is a small swimming pool. Horseback rides can also be arranged. When you hit the beach at Matapalo, turn right, and the hotel will be a 90 meters (100 yd.) or so north.

El Silencio. Cooperativa El Silencio (A.P. 6939-1000, San José). ☎ **506/777-1938,** or ☎ and fax 506/779-9545. E-mail: cooprena@racsa.co.cr. 10 units. $40 double. Rate includes breakfast. No credit cards.

A bit before you reach Matapalo, you'll pass one of the more interesting tourism developments in Costa Rica. El Silencio is a project run by the 60 or so families of an agricultural cooperative. There are 10 simple rooms in thatch-roofed cabins here. Each comes with two single beds on the ground floor and another two in a sleeping loft. All have private bathrooms, and some even have water. This is a new, grassroots tourism venture and not many of the folks here, not even the guides, speak much English. A stay here, however, allows you to mix hikes in the forest and horseback rides with a look into the rural life of Costa Rica. El Silencio is located about 3³/₄ miles (6km) inland from the Coastal Highway, about 14¹/₄ miles (23km) south of Quepos. Volunteer stays are available.

4 Dominical

18 miles (29km) SW of San Isidro; 26 miles (42km) S of Quepos; 99 miles (160km) S of San José

This area is no longer the best-kept secret in Costa Rica, but Dominical and the coastline south of Dominical remain excellent places to find isolated beaches, spectacular views, remote jungle waterfalls, and abundant budget lodgings. The beach at Dominical itself has both right and left beach breaks, which means there are usually plenty of surfers in town. In fact, the beach in Dominical really has appeal only to surfers; it's generally too rough and rocky for regular folk. However, you will find excellent swimming, sunbathing, and strolling beaches just a little further south at **Dominicalito, Playa Hermosa,** and **Ballena Marine National Park.**

Leaving Manuel Antonio, the road south to Dominical runs by mile after mile of oil-palm plantations. However, just before Dominical, the mountains once again meet the sea. From Dominical south, the coastline is dotted with tide pools, tiny coves, and cliff-side vistas, all of which bring Big Sur, California, to mind. Dominical is the largest village in the area and has several small lodges both in town and along the beach to the south. The village enjoys an enviable location on the banks of Río Barú, right where it widens considerably before emptying into the ocean. There's good bird-watching along the banks of the river and throughout the surrounding forests.

ESSENTIALS

GETTING THERE & DEPARTING   By Plane   The nearest airport with regular service is in Quepos (see "Essentials" in the "Manuel Antonio National Park" section, above). From there you can hire a taxi, rent a car, or take the bus.

By Bus   To reach Dominical, you must first go to San Isidro de El General or Quepos. Buses (☎ **506/222-2422** or 506/771-3829) leave San José for San Isidro roughly every hour between 5am and 5pm from Calle 16 between avenidas 1 and 3. Leave no later than 9:30am if you want to catch the 1:30pm bus to Dominical. The trip takes 3 hours; the fare is $3.

From San Isidro de El General, buses (☎ **506/257-4121** or 506/771-2550) leave for Dominical at 7 and 9am and 1:30 and 4pm. The bus station for Dominical is 1 block south of the main bus station and 2 blocks west of the church. Trip duration is $1^{1}/_{2}$ hours; the fare is $1.50.

From **Quepos,** buses leave daily at 5am and 1:30pm. Trip duration is $3^{1}/_{2}$ hours; the fare is $3.50.

When you're ready to leave, buses depart Dominical for San Isidro at 7am, 2:45pm, and 3:30pm. If you want to get to San José the same day, you should catch the morning bus. Buses leave San Isidro for San José roughly every hour between 5am and 5pm. Buses to Quepos leave Dominical at approximately 7am and 1:30pm.

By Car   From San José, head south (toward Cartago) on the Interamerican Highway. Continue on this road all the way to San Isidro de El General, where you turn right and head down toward the coast. The entire drive takes about 5 hours.

You can also drive here from Manuel Antonio/Quepos. Just take the road out of Quepos toward the hospital and airport. Follow the signs for Dominical. It's a straight, albeit bumpy, shot. However, the road is slated to be paved, and if that happens, it should no longer take several hours to cover the mere 25 miles (40km).

ORIENTATION   Dominical is a small village on the banks of Río Barú. The village is to the right after you cross the bridge and stretches out along the main road parallel to the beach. As you first come into town, there's a soccer field and general store, where there's a public telephone.

FAST FACTS   You can purchase stamps and send mail from the **San Clemente Bar & Grill.** Taxis tend to congregate in front of the soccer field, or you can ask around for Beto. The gas station is located about $1^{1}/_{4}$ miles (2km) north of town on the road to Quepos.

EXPLORING THE BEACHES & BALLENA MARINE NATIONAL PARK

Because the beach in the village of Dominical is unprotected and at the mouth of a river, it's often much too rough for swimming; however, you can go for a swim in the calm waters at the mouth of the Río Barú, or head down the beach a few kilometers to the little sheltered cove at **Roca Verde.** If you have a car, you should continue driving south, exploring beaches as you go. You will first come to **Dominicalito,** a small beach and cove that shelters the local fishing fleet and can be a decent place to swim, but I recommend continuing on a bit. You will soon hit **Playa Hermosa,** a long stretch of desolate beach with fine sand. As in Dominical, this is unprotected and can be rough, but it's a nicer place to sunbathe and swim than Dominical. At the village of Uvita, 10 miles (16km) south of Dominical, you'll reach the northern end of the Ballena Marine National Park, which protects a coral reef that stretches from Uvita south to Playa Piñuela and includes the little Isla Ballena, just offshore. To get to **Playa Uvita,** turn in at the village of Bahia and continue until you hit the ocean. The beach here is actually well protected and good for swimming. At low tide, an exposed sand-bar allows you to walk about and explore another tiny island. This park is named for the whales that are sometimes sighted close to shore in the winter months. If you ever fly over this area, you'll also notice that this little island and the spit of land that's formed at low tide compose the perfect outline of a whale's tail.

HORSEBACK TOURS, RAIN-FOREST HIKES & WATERFALLS

Although the beaches stretching south from Dominical should be beautiful enough to keep most people content, there are lots of other things to do. Several local farms offer horseback tours through forests and orchards, and at some of these farms you can even spend the night. **Hacienda Barú** (☎ 506/787-0003; fax 506/787-0004; www. haciendabaru.com) offers several different hikes and tours, including a walk through mangroves and along the riverbank (for some good bird-watching), a rain-forest hike through 200 acres of virgin jungle, an all-day trek from beach to mangrove to jungle that includes a visit to some Indian petroglyphs, an overnight camping trip, and a combination horseback-and-hiking tour. They even have tree-climbing tours and a small canopy platform 100 feet above the ground. Tour prices range from $20 (for the mangrove hike) to $60 (for the jungle overnight). If you're traveling with a group, you'll be charged a lower per-person rate, depending on the number of people in your group. Hacienda Barú also has six comfortable cabins with two bedrooms each, full kitchens, and even a living room ($50 double, $60 triple). Hacienda Barú is located about a mile (1.6km) north of Dominical on the road to Manuel Antonio.

The jungles just outside of Dominical are home to two spectacular waterfalls. The most popular and impressive is the **Santo Cristo** or **Nauyaca Waterfalls,** a two-tiered beauty with an excellent swimming hole. Most of the hotels in town can arrange for the horseback ride up here, or you can call **Don Lulo** at ☎ **506/771-3187.** A half-day tour, with both breakfast and lunch, should cost around $35 to $40 per person. This site has become so popular that Don Lulo has set up a little welcome center at the entrance (just off the road into Dominical from San Isidro) and even allows camping here. **Woody Dyer** (☎ 506/388-0155), who runs Bellavista Lodge, also runs tours to these falls, although he's begun calling them the **Barú River Falls,** as there seems to have been a copyright battle over the name Nauyaca. This tour ($40) leaves from Woody's lodge up on the Escaleras road. Round-trip car transportation can be arranged for a nominal charge. It is also possible to reach these falls by horseback from an entrance near the small village of Tinamaste (you will see signs on the road). Similar tours (at similar prices) are offered to the **Diamante Waterfalls,** which are a three-tiered set of falls with a 1,200-foot drop, but not quite as spacious and inviting a pool as the one at Santo Cristo.

ACCOMMODATIONS
VERY EXPENSIVE

Villas Escaleras. Dominical, Pérez Zeledón (mailing address in the U.S.: Suite 2277 SJO, P.O. Box 025216, Miami, FL 33102). ☎ and fax **506/787-0031.** E-mail: crinfo@racsa.co.cr. 3 villas. $160–$280 villa. AE, MC, V. The lodge is 1³/₄ miles/3km up a steep road, just south of town. You must have a 4-wheel-drive vehicle to get here.

If you're looking for an isolated, luxurious getaway with breathtaking views, this place is for you. Located 1,200 feet above Dominical, these three separate villas are all meticulously crafted and finished, with combination hardwood and Mexican tile floors, Guatemalan fabrics, and interesting decorative crafts from around the world. The main three-bedroom villa sleeps up to 10 people. Its massive library/sitting room opens onto an equally spacious wraparound balcony, with tables and chairs and several hammocks for soaking in the views. When not soaking in the views, you can soak in the villa's kidney-shaped pool. The other villas are smaller but equally luxurious and oriented toward the view. There's another private pool at the newest two-bedroom villa and one planned for the "small villa." The lodge is located 1³/₄ miles (3km) up a steep road, just south of Dominical. You'll need a sturdy four-wheel-drive vehicle to get up here, and you'll have to do most of your own cooking (in the well-equipped full kitchens) or drive back down into town for meals, although catering is sometimes available on request.

EXPENSIVE

Hotel Roca Verde. Dominical. ☎ **506/787-0036.** Fax 506/787-0013. www.hotelrocaverde. com. E-mail: rocaver@racsa.co.cr. 10 units. A/C. $85 double. Rates lower in the off-season. MC, V.

This newly rebuilt hotel offers the nicest beachfront accommodations in this area. The setting is superb—on a protected little cove with rocks and tide pools. The rooms are located around the central swimming pool. Each room comes with one queen and one single bed, and a small patio. There's a large open-air restaurant and bar that keeps folks dancing most weekend nights. The rooms are a bit close to the bar, so it can sometimes be hard to get an early night's sleep. Roca Verde is located half a mile (1km) south of Dominical, just off the coastal highway.

MODERATE

Bella Vista Lodge. Dominical (c/o Selva Mar, Apdo. 215-8000, San Isidro de El General). ☎ **506/771-4582** or 506/388-0155. Fax 506/771-8841. www.bellavistalodge.com. E-mail: selvamar@racsa.co.cr. 4 units, 2 cabins. $45–$60 double. AE, MC, V. You must have a 4-wheel-drive vehicle to get here. Otherwise, you'll have to arrange pickup in Dominical.

Bella Vista means "beautiful view" and that is exactly what you get when you stay at this small rustic lodge high in the hills south of Dominical. The simple rooms have recently been renovated and each now has a private, tiled bathroom with hot-water showers. There are two separate cabins, located a little below the main lodge, both of which come with fully equipped kitchens. The owners here are friendly, the location is magnificent, and there are even plans for a swimming pool. Simple meals are served ($4 for breakfast and lunch, $5 to $7 for dinner). The favorite activity of guests is an all-day horseback ride through the rain forest to a beautiful waterfall. The price of $40 per person includes your horse, guide, breakfast, and lunch. The lodge is located 1³/₄ miles (3km) up the steep Escaleras road, just south of Dominical. You'll need a four-wheel-drive vehicle to get up here, or arrange pickup in Dominical.

Cabinas Punta Dominical. Apdo. 196-8000, Dominical. ☎ **506/787-0016.** E-mail: endpdsa@racsa.co.cr. 4 cabins. $50 double, $62 triple, $74 quad. V.

Located about $2^1/2$ miles (4km) south of Dominical on a rocky point, this place has a stony cove on one side and a sandy beach on the other. The cabins and restaurant are set among shady old trees high above the surf and have excellent views of both coves. All the cabinas have good views, but the best are to be had from the ones higher up the hill. The cabins, built on stilts and constructed of dark polished hardwood, all have big porches with chairs and hammocks. Screened and louvered walls are designed to catch the breezes. The bathrooms are large and have separate changing areas. The hotel's open-air restaurant specializes in seafood and is very reasonable, with entree prices ranging from $3 to $15.

✪ **Pacific Edge.** Apdo. 531-8000, Dominical, Pérez Zeledón. ☎ **506/771-4582** or 506/ 381-4369. Fax 506/771-8841. E-mail: pacificedge@pocketmail.com. 4 units. $45 double, $50 triple. MC, V (10% surcharge added). You'll need a 4-wheel-drive vehicle to get here.

Pacific Edge is $2^1/2$ miles (4km) south of Dominical and then another three-quarter miles (1.2km) up a steep and rocky road; four-wheel-drive vehicles are highly recommended—I'd say required. This place is a bit of a way from the beach, but the views from each individual bungalow are so breathtaking that you may not mind. Spread along a lushly planted ridge on the hillside over Dominical, these comfortable cabins have wood floors, solar-heated water, and solar reading lights. Their best feature is surely the spacious private porch with a comfortable hammock in which to laze about and enjoy the view. The restaurant serves breakfast and dinner daily, which will run you around an extra $20 per person per day. A wide range of tours and activities can be arranged here.

Villas Río Mar. Dominical, Pérez Zeledón (Apdo. 1350-2050, San José). ☎ **506/787-0052** or 506/787-0053. Fax 506/787-0054. www.villasriomar.com. E-mail: riomar@racsa.co.cr. 40 units. Dec 15–Apr 15 $80 double; Apr 16–Dec 14 $55 double. AE, MC, V.

This is the closest thing to a resort in this neck of the woods. The bamboo-accented rooms are in 20 separate thatch-roofed duplex bungalows. While the rooms themselves seem a bit overwhelmed by queen-size beds, each has a spacious and comfortable porch with several sitting chairs, a small couch, coffee table, wet bar, and mini-fridge. At night, you can drop the tulle drapes that enclose each patio for some privacy and mosquito protection. There's a large kidney-shaped pool with a small gym and Jacuzzi, as well as tennis and basketball courts. The grounds have beautiful flowering plants, and the bird-watching is excellent. Meals are served in the large open-air rancho, with an emphasis on fresh seafood. A wide range of tours are offered, including inner-tube floats on the nearby Río Barú. The hotel is located up a dirt road a few hundred meters/yards up the Río Barú, just on the right as you enter Dominical.

INEXPENSIVE

In addition to the places listed here, if you continue south another 10 miles (16km) you'll find a campground at Playa Ballena and a couple of basic cabinas in Bahia and Uvita. The most popular of these is **Cabinas El Cocotico** (no phone, $20 double), owned and operated by Jorge Díaz, a local legend and enjoyable raconteur who also arranges trips to a nearby waterfall. You'll see a sign for Cabinas El Cocotico on your left as you reach Uvita, traveling south from Dominical. Turn here; the hotel is 500 meters (545 yd.) up the dirt road. Closer to the beach, in Bahia, **Cabinas Hegalva** (no phone) offers clean, basic rooms costing $15 double.

○ **Cabinas San Clemente.** Apdo. 703-8000, Dominical, Pérez Zeledón. ☎ **506/787-0026** or 506/787-0055. Fax 506/787-0158. 21 units, 16 with bathroom. $10 double with shared bathroom, $15–$50 double with private bathroom. AE, MC, V.

In addition to running the town's most popular restaurant and serving as the social hub for the surfers, beach bums, and expatriates passing through, this place offers a variety of accommodations to fit most budgets. The cheapest rooms are all located above the restaurant, which is on the main road in the center of town. These are very basic budget affairs, with wood walls and floors, shared bathrooms, and floor or ceiling fans. A couple of miles/kilometers away, at the beach, San Clemente has much nicer rooms in two separate buildings. Some of the newer second-floor rooms have wood floors and wraparound verandas and are a real steal in this price range. The grounds are shady, and there are plenty of hammocks. The **Atardecer Restaurant** is a beach-side cafe serving up falafel, hummus and other pita sandwiches, refreshing fresh-fruit juices, and a host of other light lunch items. San Clemente also has a surf shop and board rentals, and the owner makes, bottles, and sells a very serious hot sauce.

Finca Brian y Milena. Apdo. 2-8000, San Isidro de El General. ☎ **506/771-4582.** Fax 506/771-3060. 1 cottage. $50 per person, including all meals. No credit cards. You'll need a 4-wheel-drive vehicle to get here.

This is a working farm, with only one guest cottage, and a maximum of four visitors at a time. Here you can bird-watch, explore the tropical rain forest, and visit the farm, where tropical fruits, nuts, and spices are grown. If you stay for several nights, you can visit the Santo Cristo or Diamante waterfalls by horseback or on foot. At night, you can soak in the hot tub. Horse rentals and overnight excursions (including to the owners' farm in the hills above Dominical) are additional. The hotel is located about 3.1 miles (5km) up the rugged Escaleras road (bring four-wheel drive) that heads into the hillsides, off of the Costanera Sur around Dominicalito. This same road serves Villas Escaleras and Buena Vista Lodge, and there are signs marking the turnoff.

Tortilla Flats. 200m (218 yd.) west of Rancho Coco, Dominical. ☎ and fax **506/787-0033.** 18 units. $30–$40 double or triple; lower in the off-season. AE, MC, V (7% surcharge).

This long-standing surfer hotel recently received a new set of owners and a name change. There are several styles of rooms located in a cluster of buildings, including older rooms with fans, older rooms with air-conditioning, and newer rooms with air-conditioning, skylights, carved wooden headboards, and louvered windows. I recommend the second-floor rooms with ocean views but no air-conditioning. Despite their size differences and comfort levels, all rooms come with one double and one single bed. Definitely take a look at a few of them before choosing. There's a small restaurant serving moderately priced Tex-Mex and Tico fare.

DINING

The social center of Dominical is definitely the ○ **San Clemente Bar & Grill,** a gringo/surfer hangout and sports bar specializing in massive breakfasts, nightly dinner specials (usually seafood), and a regular menu of hefty sandwiches and tasty Mexican-American food. One interesting (and sobering) thing here is the ceiling full of broken surfboards. If you break a board out on the waves, bring it in, and they'll hang it and even buy you a bucket of beer. If you head a little bit south of town, you can check out the restaurants at either Roca Verde or Punta Dominical. All of the above restaurants are moderately priced, with main courses running between $5 and $15.

Right in town, in front of the soccer field, there's the **Su Raza** (☎ 506/787-0105), which serves basic Tico meals and good seafood at great prices, and even has a nice view of the river mouth. A little farther on down the main road is the **Soda Nanyoa.** Dishes at these places range in price from $2 to $8.

DOMINICAL AFTER DARK

Don't come to Dominical expecting a raging nightlife. Most folks hang out either at the ✪ **San Clemente Bar & Grill** (☎ 506/787-0055), located right at the entrance to town beside the soccer field, or **Thrusters** (☎ 506/787-0150), a couple of hundred yards south of San Clemente about mid-way between the soccer field and the beach. Both are surfer bars with pool tables and dartboards. Occasionally there are roving discos that set up shop at one bar or another on weekends. If so, you'll hear about it—and hear it.

SOUTH OF DOMINICAL

The beaches south of Dominical are some of the nicest and most unexplored in Costa Rica. Basic cabinas and hotels are starting to pop up all along this route. This is a great area to ✪ **roam in a rental car.** The southern highway (**Costanera Sur**) is still not paved, but it is relatively well graded and maintained. One good itinerary is to make a loop from San Isidro to Dominical, down the Costanera Sur, hitting several deserted beaches and then returning along the Interamerican Highway.

Among the beaches you'll find are **Playa Ballena, Playa Piñuela, Playa Ventanas,** and **Playa Tortuga.** There's a bit of development in the area around Playa Tortuga and Ojochal, and some in the works around Playas Piñuela and Ventanas.

A REMOTE NATURE LODGE

Hotel Villas Gaia. Playa Tortuga (P.O. Box 11516-1000, San José). ☎ and fax **506/ 256-9996.** E-mail: hvgaia@racsa.co.cr. 12 units. $55 double. MC, V.

Located just off the Costanera Sur just before the town of Ojochal, this small hotel has the nicest accommodations down in this neck of the woods. All the rooms are separate wood bungalows. Each has one single and one double bed, a private bathroom, a ceiling fan, and a small veranda with a jungle view. The swimming pool was specially designed for scuba instruction—Villa Gaia hopes to lure divers with its close proximity to Isla del Caño. The pool (and a poolside bar) is up on a high hill with a good view over mangrove forests to the sea. There's a large open-air dining room down by the parking lot, which is too close to the highway for my taste. A wide range of tours is available, including Isla del Caño, Corcovado National Park, and Wilson Botanical Gardens.

5 San Isidro de El General: A Base for Exploring Chirripó National Park

74 miles (120km) SE of San José; 76 miles (123km) NW of Palmar Norte; 18 miles (29km) NE of Dominical

San Isidro de El General is the largest town in this region and is located just off the Interamerican Highway in the foothills of the Talamanca Mountains. Although there isn't much to do right in town, this is the jumping-off point for trips to Chirripó National Park. This is also the principal transfer point if you're coming from or going to Dominical, and most buses traveling the Interamerican Highway stop here.

ESSENTIALS

GETTING THERE & DEPARTING   By Bus   Two companies, **Musoc** (☎ 506/ 222-2422 or 506/771-3829) and **Tuasur** (☎ 506/222-9763 or 506/771-0419) run

Little Devils

If you're visiting this area in February, you should head out to nearby Rey Curré village for the Fiesta of the Diablitos, where costumed Boruca Indians perform dances representative of the Spanish conquest of Central America. There are fireworks and an Indian handcraft market. The date varies, so it's best to call the **Costa Rica Tourist Board** (☎ **800/327-7033**) for more information.

express buses between San José and San Isidro leaving roughly every hour between 5am and 5pm from Calle 16 between avenidas 1 and 3. Trips take 3 hours; the fare is $3. There are buses from **Quepos** to San Isidro daily at 5am and 1pm. Trip duration is 3¹/₂ hours; the fare is $3. Buses to or from **Golfito** and **Puerto Jiménez** will also drop you off in San Isidro.

Buses depart San Isidro for **San José** roughly every hour between 5am and 5pm. Buses to **Dominical** (onward to **Quepos**) leave daily at 7am and 1:30pm. Buses to **Dominical** and **Uvita** leave daily at 9am and 4pm. Buses to **Puerto Jiménez** leave San Isidro daily at 6am and noon. The San José bus to **Puerto Jiménez** passes through San Isidro at around 9am and 3pm. Buses to **Golfito** pass through San Isidro at around 10am, 2pm, and 6pm.

By Car   The long and winding stretch of the Interamerican Highway between San José and San Isidro is one of the most difficult sections of road in the country. Not only are there the usual car-eating potholes and periodic landslides, but you must also contend with driving over the 11,000-foot-high Cerro de la Muerte (Mountain of Death). This aptly named mountain pass is legendary for its dense afternoon fogs, blinding torrential downpours, steep drop-offs, constant switchbacks, and unexpectedly breathtaking views. (If you wanted adventure travel, here you go!) In other words, drive with extreme care, and bring a sweater or two—it's cold up at the top. It'll take you about 3 hours to get to San Isidro.

ORIENTATION   Downtown San Isidro is just off the Interamerican Highway. There's a large church that fronts the central park. The main bus station is 2 blocks west of the north end of the central park.

EXPLORING CHIRRIPÓ NATIONAL PARK

At 12,530 feet in elevation, Mount Chirripó is the tallest mountain in Costa Rica. If you're headed up this way, come prepared for chilly weather. Actually, come prepared for all sorts of weather: Because of the great elevations, temperatures frequently dip below freezing, especially at night. However, during the day, temperatures can soar—remember, you're still only 9° from the equator. The elevation and radical temperatures have produced an environment here that's very different from the Costa Rican norm. Above 10,000 feet, only stunted trees and shrubs survive in regions known as páramos. If you're driving the Interamerican Highway between San Isidro and San José, you'll pass through a páramo on the Cerro de la Muerte.

Hiking up to the top of Mount Chirripó is one of Costa Rica's great adventures. On a clear day (usually in the morning), you can see both the Pacific Ocean and the Caribbean Sea from the summit. You can do this trip fairly easily on your own if you've brought gear and are an experienced backpacker. While it's possible to hike from the park entrance to the summit and back down in 2 days (in fact, some daredevils even do it in 1 day), it's best to allow 3 to 4 days for the trip, to give yourself time to enjoy your hike fully and spend some time on top, since that's where the

Yo Quiero Hablar Español

If you're interested in combining your vacation with some education, the **Spanish Language and Environmental Protection Center** (☎ 506/771-1903) offers weeklong and multiweek courses that mix intensive language classes with lectures and outings.

glacier lakes and páramo are. For much of the way you'll be hiking through cloud forests that are home to abundant tropical fauna, including the spectacular quetzal, Costa Rica's most beautiful bird. These cloud forests are cold and damp, so come prepared for rain and fog.

There are several routes to the top of Mount Chirripó. The most popular, by far, leaves from San Gerardo de Rivas. However, it's also possible to start your hike from the nearby towns of Herradura and Canaan. All these places are within a mile or so of each other, reached by the same major road out of San Isidro. San Gerardo is the most popular because it's the easiest route to the top and has the greatest collections of small hotels and lodges. Information on all of these routes is available at the National Parks office in San Gerardo de Rivas.

Once you're at the summit lodge, there are a number of hiking options. The most popular is to the actual summit (the lodge itself is a bit below), which is about a 2-hour hike passing through the Valle de los Conejos (Rabbit Valley) and the Valle de los Lagos (Valley of Lakes). There are other hikes and trails leading off from the summit lodge and it's easy to spend a couple of days hiking around here. A few trails will take you to the summits of several neighboring peaks. These hikes should be undertaken only after carefully exploring an accurate map and talking to park rangers and other hikers.

ENTRY POINT, FEES & REGULATIONS   Although it's not that difficult to get to Chirripó National Park from nearby San Isidro, it's still rather remote. And to see it fully, you have to be prepared to hike. To get to the trailhead, you have three choices: car, taxi, or bus. If you choose to drive, take the road out of San Isidro, heading north toward San Gerardo de Rivas, which is some 12¹/₂ miles (20km) down the road. Otherwise, you can catch a bus in San Isidro that will take you directly to the trailhead in San Gerardo de Rivas. Buses leave daily at 5am from the western side of the central park in San Isidro. It costs 85¢ one way and takes 1¹/₂ hours. Another bus departs at 2pm from a bus station 200 meters (218 yd.) south of the park. Buses return to San Isidro daily at 7am and 4pm. A taxi from town should cost around $15 to $20. Because the hike to the summit of Mount Chirripó can take between 6 and 12 hours, depending on your physical condition, I recommend taking the earlier bus so you can start hiking when the day is still young, or, better still, arriving the day before and spending the night in San Gerardo de Rivas (there are inexpensive cabinas there), before setting out early the following morning.

Park admission is $6 per day. Before climbing Mount Chirripó, you must check in with the National Parks office in San Gerardo de Rivas. The office is open from 5am to 5pm daily. I recommend checking in the day before you plan to climb, if possible. If you plan to stay at the lodge near the summit, you must make reservations in advance, since accommodations there are limited (see "Staying at the Summit Lodge," below). Note that camping is not allowed in the park. It's possible to have your gear carried up to the summit by horseback during the dry season (December through April). Guides work outside the park entrance in San Gerardo de Rivas. They charge between $20 and $25 per pack, depending on size and weight. In the rainy season, the same guides work, but they take packs up by themselves, not by horseback. The guides like to take the packs up well before dawn, so arrangements are best made the day before.

STAYING AT THE SUMMIT LODGE   Reservations for lodging on the summit of Mount Chirripó must be made with the **National Parks office** in San Gerardo de Rivas (☎ and fax **506/771-3155** or 506/771-5116). In 1998, the old buildings were torn down and two new ones were erected. Helicopters and lots of pack horses were used in the construction. This is an increasingly popular destination, and you must reserve well in advance during the dry season. The new lodge holds only 60 people and it fills up quite frequently. There are bunk beds, bathrooms, and a common kitchen area, complete with pots, pans, plates, and silverware. There is good drinking water at the lodge and blankets, lanterns, and cook stoves for rent, although you'll certainly have to pack in your own food. Be forewarned: It gets cold up here at night and the new lodge seems to have been designed to be as cold, dark, and cavernous as possible. No consideration was made to take advantage of the ample passive solar potential. The showers are freezing. It costs $6 per person per night to stay here, in addition to the $6 park entrance fee.

WARNING   It can be dangerous for more inexperienced or out-of-shape hikers to climb Chirripó, especially by themselves. It's not very technical climbing, but it is a long, arduous hike. Such folks should just take day hikes out of San Isidro and/or San Gerardo de Rivas, and ask at their hotel about guides.

OTHER ADVENTURES IN SAN ISIDRO

If you want to undertake any other adventures while in San Isidro, contact **Brunca Tours** (☎ **506/771-3100;** fax 506/771-3033; www.ecotourism.co.cr), or **Selva Mar** (☎ **506/771-4582;** fax 506/771-8841; www.chirripo.com; E-mail: selvamar@racsa. co.cr). Brunca Tours' main operation is white-water rafting on the Río General, which has Class III and IV sections. Rafting trips run around $65 to $75 per person. Brunca Tours also offers a wide range of adventure and less-adventurous tours around the region.

Just 4¹/₂ miles (7km) from San Isidro is **Las Quebradas Biological Center** (☎ and fax **506/771-4131**), a community-run private reserve with 1³/₄ miles (2.7km) of trails through primary rain forest. Camping is permitted. There is an information center here and a small souvenir store. Admission is $5. From San Isidro, you can take a local bus to Quebradas, but you'll have to walk the last mile to the entrance. You can also take a taxi for around $8. If you're driving, take the road to Morazán and Quebradas. The center is open from 8am to 2pm Tuesday to Sunday.

ACCOMMODATIONS & DINING

The following section lists only hotels because there are no notable restaurants in San Isidro. The town has its fair share of local joints, but most visitors are content at their hotel restaurant.

Hotel Chirripó. South side of church, San Isidro de El General. ☎ **506/771-0529.** 41 units, 24 with bathroom. $9 double without bathroom, $14 double with bathroom, $20 triple with bathroom. No credit cards.

This budget hotel is fine in a pinch if you need to spend the night in San Isidro. It's located on the central square within a couple of blocks of all the town's bus stations. Rooms vary considerably, so ask to see some first. Some have windows (and street noise), and some have no windows or street noise. Stay away from the rooms in front, since these are the noisiest. There's a large, popular restaurant at the front of the lobby.

Hotel del Sur. A.P. 4-8000, San Isidro de El General. ☎ **506/771-3033.** Fax 506/771-0527. E-mail: htlsur@racsa.co.cr. 47 units, 10 bungalows. TV TEL. $50–$60 double. MC, V.

This midsize hotel is located about 3³/₄ miles (6km) south of San Isidro right on the Interamerican Highway. The hotel has far better facilities and a wider range of services than anything within several hours, but everything here has seen better days. Rooms are generally large. The nicer (and more expensive) rooms have air-conditioning, loads of space, plenty of light, and tile floors; the cheaper rooms have worn carpeting and feel cramped and dingy. The bungalows have basic kitchenettes. There's a large pool, as well as a basketball court, tennis court and pro shop, playground equipment, and Ping-Pong table. There's even a tour desk offering a host of activities. The restaurant specializes in steaks, and is popular with locals, tour groups, and folks making the longer drive south, or back to San José.

Hotel Iguazu. San Isidro de El General. Above the Super Lido department store. ☎ **506/771-2571.** 21 units, 16 with bathroom. TV. $12 double without bathroom, $18 double with bathroom. No credit cards.

This is a good, clean, safe choice in San Isidro. The rooms are basic and come in different sizes, with a different arrangement of beds, but all have small televisions. The rooms are definitely in better shape than those at the Hotel Chirripó. The hotel is a half block away from the Musoc bus station. Some may find this convenient; others might find it too noisy. The hotel is actually on the second and third floors of the Super Lido department store.

ACCOMMODATIONS CLOSER TO THE TRAILHEAD

If you're climbing Mount Chirripó, you'll want to spend the night as close to the trailhead as possible. As mentioned above, there are several basic cabinas right in San Gerardo de Rivas that charge between $5 and $10 per person. The best of these is **El Descanso** (☎ **506/771-1866**). If you're looking for a little more comfort, check out one of the two lodges listed below.

Río Chirripó Pacífico Mountain Lodge. San Gerardo de Rivas, Pérez Zeledón. No phone. 8 units. $40 double. Rate includes breakfast. No credit cards.

This new lodge is located on a beautiful bend in the Río Chirripó, just 500 meters (545 yd.) before the National Parks office. The rooms are in two side-by-side, two-story buildings. All have one single and one double bed, painted cement floors, and a small veranda, with some interesting natural wood latticework on the railings. I prefer the rooms on the second floor, as they have a slightly better view. There's a large open-air rancho that serves as the restaurant here. If you have time before or after your ascent of the big mountain, you can climb on some impressive river-polished rocks or swim in a couple of natural pools.

✪ Talari Mountain Lodge. Rivas, San Isidro (Apdo. 517-8000), Pérez Zeledón. ☎ and fax **506/771-0341.** E-mail: talaripz@racsa.co.cr. 8 units. $42 double, $58 triple. Rates include full breakfast. AE, MC, V. Closed Sept 15–Oct 31.

Rest Your Weary Muscles Here

If you're tired and sore from so much hiking, be sure to check out the small natural hot springs located a short hike off the road between San Gerardo de Rivas and Herradura. The entrance to the springs is about half a mile (1km) beyond San Gerardo de Rivas. From here you'll have to hike about 10 minutes and pay a $2 entrance fee before getting in to soak.

This small mountain getaway, though nothing fancy, is one of the nicer options right around San Isidro and also makes a good base for exploring or climbing Mount Chirripó. The eight rooms are in two separate concrete-block buildings. Most come with one double and one single bed, although one room can handle a family of four in one double and two single beds. Each of the rooms comes with a small fridge and a small patio. I prefer the four rooms that face the Talamanca Mountains. There are plenty of fruit trees around and good bird-watching right on the grounds. Hearty meals are served in the lodge's main dining room. Down by the Río General there's a small pool and separate children's pool. The hotel maintains some forest trails and has identified 179 bird species on the grounds. Talari is located 5 miles (8km) outside of San Isidro and will pick you up in town for free with advance notice. Remember, if you're here just to climb the mountain, this lodge is about 7 miles (11km) from San Gerardo de Rivas, so you'll probably also have to arrange transportation to and from the park entrance.

EN ROUTE TO SAN JOSÉ:
THREE PLACES TO SEE QUETZALS IN THE WILD

Between San Isidro de El General and San José, the Interamerican Highway climbs to its highest point in Costa Rica and crosses over the Cerro de la Muerte. This area has recently acquired a newfound importance as one of the best places in Costa Rica to see quetzals in the wild. March, April, and May are nesting season for these birds, and this is usually the best time to see them, but it's often possible to see them year-round. On one 2-hour hike here, without a guide, our small group spotted eight of these amazing birds.

All of the lodges listed below, along with some new ones, are located along a 12½-mile (20km) stretch of the Interamerican Highway, between the cities of Cartago and San Isidro. You'll probably start seeing their billboards and quetzal-painted placards long before you see any birds.

In addition to the lodges listed below, if you're looking for a rustic (although not cheap) escape on a private reserve, check in with the folks at **Genesis II Cloudforest Preserve** (☎ **506/381-0739;** fax 506/551-0070; E-mail: genesis@yellowweb.co.cr). This place recently opened a canopy tour, which combines suspension bridges and treetop platforms connected by cables (you hang from the cable as you ride from tree to tree). Day tours of the preserve cost $45 per person, including a simple lunch. You'll see signs for this place along the Interamerican Highway. The road down into Genesis is very rugged and a four-wheel-drive vehicle is necessary. If you want to stay here ($85 per person, including three meals), there are only five rooms, so reservations are highly recommended.

Albergue de Montaña Tapantí. Kilometer 62 Carretera Interamericana Sur, Macho Gaff, Cartago (Apdo. 461-1200, Pavas). ☎ and fax **506/232-0436,** or ☎ 506/231-5142. E-mail: adriandiaz@socom.net. 10 units. $55 double, $65 triple, $75 quad. Rates include breakfast. MC, V.

If you want easy access to both the highway and the cloud forest, this cross between a mountain lodge and roadside motel might be your best bet. The buildings at Tapantí are built to resemble Swiss chalets, and you may come to believe you're in Switzerland when you feel how cold it gets here at night. The lodge is at 10,000 feet and frost is not uncommon, but there's a fireplace in the lounge to warm your bones. Most of the guest rooms are actually suites with separate bedrooms and living rooms, although the furnishings are both sparse and dated. Luckily, the rooms do have heaters. The nicest rooms have private balconies that provide views of the neighboring forests. The lodge's dining room serves such Swiss specialties as beef fondue and raclette, as well as other continental dishes. Guided hikes, horseback rides, trout fishing, and bird-watching walks are all available through the lodge.

Albergue Mirador de Quetzales. Kilometer 70 Carretera Interamericana Sur, (A.P. 985-7050, Cartago). ☎ **506/381-8456.** 10 units, 8 with bathroom. $35 per person. Rate includes breakfast, dinner, a 2-hr. tour, and taxes. No credit cards.

This family-run lodge is also known as Finca Eddie Serrano. The rooms in the main lodge are quite basic, with wood floors, bunk beds, and shared bathrooms. Four newer A-frames provide a bit more comfort and a private bathroom. Meals are served family style in the main lodge. But quetzals, not comfort, are the main draw here, and if you come between December and May, you should have no trouble spotting plenty of them. There are good hiking trails through the cloud forest, and the Serrano family are genial hosts and good guides. The lodge is located about 700 meters (763 yd.) down a dirt road from the main highway.

✪ **Savegre Lodge.** Kilometer 80 Carretera Interamericana Sur, San Gerardo de Dota (Apdo. 1636), Cartago. ☎ and fax **506/771-1732.** www.ecotourism.co.cr. E-mail: ciprotur@racsa.co.cr. 26 cabins. $70 per person. Rate includes all meals and taxes. AE, MC, V. Four-wheel drive recommended.

This working apple-and-pear farm, which also has more than 600 acres of primary forest, has acquired a reputation as one of the best places in the country to see quetzals. The rustic farm has long been popular as a weekend vacation and picnicking spot for Ticos, but now people from3. all over the world are searching it out. The rooms are basic, but if you're serious about bird-watching, this shouldn't matter. In addition to the quetzals, some 150 other species have been spotted. Hearty Tico meals are served, and if you want to try your hand at trout fishing, you might luck into a fish dinner. You'll find this lodge 5^1/$_2$ miles (9km) down a dirt road off the Interamerican Highway. This road is steep and often muddy, and four-wheel drive is recommended. Some of the signs pointing to the lodge read CABINAS CHACÓN.

The Southern Zone 8

The southern zone is an area of rugged beauty, vast expanses of virgin lowland rain forest, and few cities or settlements. Lushly forested mountains tumble into the sea, streams still run clear and clean, scarlet macaws squawk raucously in the treetops, and dolphins frolic in the Golfo Dulce. The Osa Peninsula is the most popular attraction in this region, and one of the premier ecotourism destinations in Costa Rica. It's home to **Corcovado National Park,** the largest single expanse of lowland tropical rain forest in Central America.

But this beauty doesn't come easy; you must have plenty of time (or plenty of money; preferably both) and a desire for a bit of adventure. Because it is so far from San José and there are so few roads, most of the really fascinating spots can be reached only by small plane or boat, although hiking and four-wheeling will get you into some memorable surroundings as well. In many ways this is Costa Rica's final frontier, and the cities of Golfito and Puerto Jiménez are nearly as wild as the jungles that surround them. Tourism is still underdeveloped here. It is, after all, an 8-hour drive from San José to Golfito or Puerto Jiménez. Moreover, the heat and humidity are more than many people can stand. It's best to put some forethought into planning a vacation down here, and it is usually wise to book your rooms and transportation in advance.

1 Drake Bay

90 miles (145km) S of San José; 20 miles (32km) SW of Palmar

Located on the northern end of the Osa Peninsula, Drake Bay is what adventure travel is all about. Little more than a small collection of lodges catering to naturalists, anglers, scuba divers, and assorted vacationers, Drake Bay is a good place to get away from it all. Accommodations vary from tents on wooden platforms and cement-walled cabinas to very comfortable lodges that border on the luxurious. There are few conventional phones and no power lines in Drake Bay, so most lodges make do with radio and cellular phones and gas-powered electrical generators. Until 1997, there was no road into Drake Bay and no airstrip in town. Currently both exist, but how reliable they are is another story—the road is often closed by heavy rains and mud slides, and the airstrip is serviced only by charter flights. Because of the bay's remoteness, development has been very slow here. Unfortunately, it's starting to increase and it could someday change the face of this pristine destination. The town itself is starting to grow a bit, and massive logging is under way all along the road into Drake Bay and around—and even in—the national park.

The bay is named after Sir Francis Drake, who is believed to have anchored here in 1579. Emptying into the bay is the tiny **Río Agujitas,** which acts as a protected harbor for small boats and is a great place to do a bit of canoeing or swimming. It's here that many of the local lodges dock their boats. Stretching south from Drake Bay are miles and miles of deserted beaches. Adventurous explorers will find tide pools, spring-fed rivers, waterfalls, forest trails, and some of the best bird-watching in all of Costa Rica. If a paradise such as this appeals to you, Drake Bay makes a good base for exploring the peninsula.

South of Drake Bay lie the wilds of the **Osa Peninsula** and **Corcovado National Park.** This is one of Costa Rica's most beautiful regions, yet it's also one of its least accessible. Corcovado National Park covers about half of the peninsula and contains the largest single expanse of virgin lowland rain forest in Central America. For this reason, Corcovado is well known among naturalists and researchers studying rain-forest ecology, and if you come here you'll learn firsthand why they call them rain forests. Some parts of the peninsula receive more than 250 inches of rain per year. In addition to producing lush forests, this massive amount of rain produces more than a few disgruntled visitors.

ESSENTIALS

Because Drake Bay is so remote, it's highly recommended that you have a room reservation and transportation arrangements (usually arranged with your hotel) before you arrive. The lodges listed here are scattered along several kilometers of coastline, and it is not easy to go from one to another looking for a room.

A flashlight and rain gear are always useful to have on hand in Costa Rica; they're absolutely essential in Drake Bay.

GETTING THERE Depending on your temperament, getting to Drake Bay may be half the fun, or it may be torture. Despite the new road into—and airstrip in—Drake Bay, the traditional route is still the most dependable and popular. Most guests still fly first (or take a bus) to **Palmar Sur.** From here, it's a 15-minute bus or taxi ride over dirt roads to the small town of Sierpe. This bumpy ride takes you through several banana plantations and quickly past some important archaeological sites. In Sierpe you will board a small boat for a 25-mile (40km) ride to Drake Bay (see "By Taxi & Boat," below). The first half of this trip snakes through a maze of mangrove canals and rivers, before heading out to sea for the final leg to the bay. Be warned: Entering and exiting the Sierpe River mouth is often treacherous, and I've had several very white-knuckle moments here.

By Plane The airstrip in Drake Bay itself is currently operating only by charter. Most lodges include transportation in their packages, so check with them about where you will be flying into. The closest regularly serviced airport to Drake Bay is in **Palmar Sur,** a taxi and boat ride away. **Sansa** (☎ **506/221-9414;** fax 506/255-2176; E-mail: reservations@flysansa.com) flies to Palmar Sur daily at 9:30am from San José's Juan Santamaría International Airport. The flight takes 50 minutes; the fare is $60 each way. Note that Sansa frequently alters its schedule and routing; this flight may stop in Quepos on the way down and thus take slightly longer.

Travelair (☎ **506/220-3054;** fax 506/220-0413; E-mail: reservations@travelair-costarica.com) has flights to Palmar Sur that depart daily at 8:45am from Tobías Bolaños International Airport in Pavas. This flight stops at Quepos en route. Flight duration is 55 minutes; fare is $81 one-way, $132 round-trip.

The Southern Zone

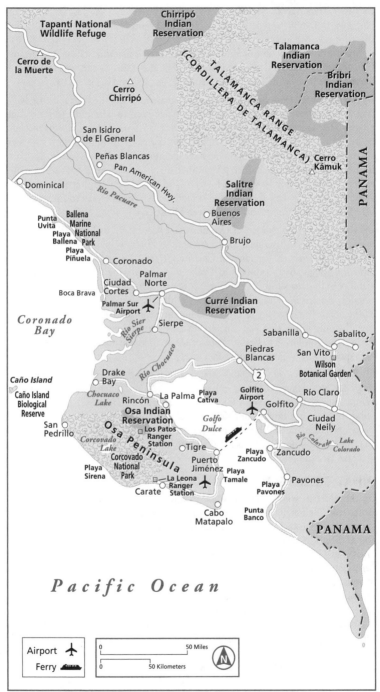

Tapantí National Wildlife Refuge

Chirripó Indian Reservation

Talamanca Indian Reservation

Bribri Indian Reservation

Cerro de la Muerte

Cerro Chirripó

TALAMANCA RANGE (CORDILLERA DE TALAMANCA)

PANAMA

San Isidro de El General

Peñas Blancas

Pan American Hwy.

Cerro Kámuk

Dominical

Río Pacuare

Salitre Indian Reservation

Punta Uvita
Ballena Marine Playa National Ballena Park
Playa Piñuela

Buenos Aires

Brujo

Coronado

Palmar Norte

Ciudad Cortes

Boca Brava

Palmar Sur Airport

Curré Indian Reservation

Coronado Bay

Río Sier Sierpe

Sierpe

Sabanilla

Sabalito

Piedras Blancas

San Vito

Wilson Botanical Garden

Caño Island

Caño Island Biological Reserve

Drake Bay

Chocuaco Lake

Río Chocuaco

Rincón

La Palma

Playa Cativa

Golfito Airport

Río Claro

Golfito

San Pedrillo

Osa Indian Reservation

Golfo Dulce

Ciudad Neily

Corcovado Lake

Los Patos Ranger Station

Tigre

Playa Zancudo

Zancudo

Río Colorado Lake Colorado

Playa Sirena

Corcovado National Park

Puerto Jiménez

Playa Tamale

Pavones

Carate

La Leona Ranger Station

Playa Pavones

Cabo Matapalo

Punta Banco

PANAMA

Pacific Ocean

Airport ✈

Ferry ⛴

0		50 Miles

0		50 Kilometers

N

By Bus   Tracopa (☎ 506/221-4214) express buses leave San José daily for Palmar Norte at 5, 7, 8:30, and 10am and 1, 2:30, and 6pm from Avenida 5 and Calle 14. Bus trips take 6 hours; the fare is $4.

You can also catch any Golfito-bound bus from this same station and get off in Palmar Norte. Once in Palmar Norte, ask when the next bus goes out to Sierpe. If it doesn't leave for a while (they aren't frequent), consider taking a taxi (see below).

By Taxi & Boat (from Sierpe)   Once you arrive at either the Palmar Norte bus station or the Palmar Sur airstrip, you'll most likely need to take a taxi to the village of Sierpe. The fare should be between $10 and $15. If you're booked into one of the main lodges, chances are your transportation is already included—via a guy named Rainer and his minibus, whom almost all the lodges use. Even if you're not booked into one of the lodges, Rainer (or another driver—there are always some hanging around) will probably have room for you (and charge you another $15). Make sure you feel confident with the boat and skipper and, if possible, try to find a spot on a boat from one of the established lodges in Drake Bay.

By Car   Driving is still not a recommended way to get to Drake Bay. But if you insist, you should drive down the Interamerican Highway, past Palmar to the turnoff for Puerto Jiménez (at the town of Chacarita; clearly marked). Then at Rincón, turn onto the rough road leading into Drake Bay. I'm getting mixed reports as to the viability of this road and I'm not sure if it remains passable during the rainy season. It certainly reaches only into the small heart of the village of Drake Bay, whereas almost all the hotels I've listed are farther out along the peninsula, where only boats reach. In fact, the only hotels that you can actually drive up to are very basic cabins in town. For the rest you'd have to find some place secure to leave your car and either haul your bags quite a way or get picked up in a boat.

DEPARTING   Have your lodge arrange a boat trip back to Sierpe for you. Be sure the lodge also arranges for a taxi to meet you in Sierpe for the trip to Palmar Sur or Palmar Norte. (If you're on a budget, you can ask around to see if a late-morning public bus is still running from Sierpe to Palmar Norte.) In the two Palmars, you can make onward plane and bus connections. At the Palmar Norte bus terminal, almost any bus heading north will take you to San José, and almost any bus heading south will take you to Golfito.

WHAT TO SEE & DO

Beaches, forests, wildlife, and solitude are the main attractions of Drake Bay. While Corcovado National Park (covered in the next section) is the area's star attraction, there's plenty to soak up in Drake Bay. The **Osa Peninsula** is home to an unbelievable variety of plants and animals: more than 140 species of mammals, 267 species of birds, and 117 species of amphibians and reptiles. While you aren't likely to see a high percentage of these animals, you can expect to see quite a few, including several species of monkeys, coatimundis, scarlet macaws, parrots, and hummingbirds. Other park inhabitants include jaguars, tapirs, sloths, and crocodiles. If you're lucky, you might even see one of the region's namesake *osas,* the giant anteaters.

Around Drake Bay and within the national park there are many miles of trails through rain forests and swamps, down beaches, and around rock headlands. All of the lodges listed below offer guided excursions into the park. It's also possible to begin a hike around the peninsula from Drake Bay.

You can do some sportfishing while you're in the area—all of the lodges listed below either run their own fishing trips or can arrange a charter boat for you.

Those Mysterious Stone Spheres

While Costa Rica lacks the great cities, giant temples, and bas-relief carvings of the Maya, Aztec, and Olmec civilizations of northern Mesoamerica, its pre-Columbian residents did leave a unique legacy that continues to cause archaeologists and anthropologists to scratch their heads and wonder. Over a period of several centuries, hundreds of painstakingly carved and carefully positioned granite spheres were left by the peoples who lived throughout the Diquís Delta, which flanks the Terraba River in southern Costa Rica. The orbs, which range from grapefruit-size to more than 7 feet in diameter, can weigh up to 15 tons, and many reach near spherical perfection.

Archaeologists believe that the spheres were created during two defined cultural periods. The first, called the Aguas Buenas period, dates from around A.D. 100 to 500. Few spheres survive from this time. The second phase, during which spheres were created in apparently greater numbers, is called the Chiriquí period, and lasted from approximately A.D. 800 to 1500. The "balls" believed to have been carved during this time frame are widely dispersed along the entire length of the lower section of the Terraba River. To date, only one known quarry for the spheres has been discovered, in the mountains above the Diquís Delta, which points to a difficult and lengthy transportation process.

Some archaeologists believe the spheres were hand-carved in a very time-consuming process, using stone tools, perhaps aided by some sort of firing process. However, another theory holds that granite blocks were placed at the bases of powerful waterfalls, and the hydraulic beating of the water eventually turned and carved the rock into these near-perfect spheres. And not a few proponents have credited extraterrestrial intervention for the creation of the stone balls.

Most of the stone balls have been found at the archaeological remains of defined settlements and are associated with either central plazas or known burial sites. Their size and placement have been interpreted to have both social and celestial importance, although their exact significance remains a mystery. Unfortunately, many of the stone balls have been plundered and are currently used as lawn ornaments in the fancier neighborhoods of San José. Some have even been shipped out of the country. The Museo Nacional de Costa Rica (see chapter 4) has a nice collection, including one massive sphere in its center courtyard. It's a never-fail photo op. You can also see the stone balls near the small airport in Palmar Sur and on Caño Island (which is located 12 miles/19km off the Pacific coast near Drake Bay).

AN EXCURSION TO CAÑO ISLAND BIOLOGICAL RESERVE

One of the most popular excursions from Drake Bay is a trip out to **Caño Island** and the **Caño Island Biological Reserve** for a bit of exploring and snorkeling or scuba diving. The island is located about 12 miles (19km) offshore from Drake Bay and was once home to a pre-Columbian culture about which little is known. A trip to the island will include a visit to one of this culture's cemeteries, and you'll also be able to see some of the stone spheres that are commonly believed to have been carved by the people who once lived in this area (see box, above). Few animals or birds live on the island, but the coral reefs just offshore teem with life and are the main reason most people come here. This is one of Costa Rica's prime scuba-diving spots. Visibility is often quite good, and there's even easily accessible snorkeling from the beach.

All of the lodges listed below offer trips to Caño Island.

ACCOMMODATIONS & DINING

Given the remote location and logistics of reaching Drake Bay, as well as the individual isolation of each hotel, almost all of the hotels listed below deal almost exclusively in package trips that include transportation, meals, tours, and taxes. I've listed the most common packages, although all of the lodges will work with you to accommodate longer or shorter stays. Where available and practical, generally at the more moderately priced hotels, I've listed nightly room rates.

VERY EXPENSIVE

Aguila De Osa Inn. Apdo. 10486-1000, San José (mailing address in the U.S.: Isla Fantasma, Interlink 898, P.O. Box 025635, Miami, FL 33102). ☎ and fax **506/296-2190** or 506/232-7722. www.aguiladeosa.com. E-mail: reserve@aguiladeosa.com. 14 units. $250–$300 double, $375–$450 triple. Rates include 3 meals daily. AE, MC, V.

The is the most expensive and luxurious lodge in Drake Bay. Situated high on a hill overlooking Drake Bay and the Pacific Ocean, the Aguila de Osa Inn offers large, attractively decorated rooms located a vigorous hike up a steep hillside. This could pose a problem for older guests, or those with heart or health problems, since the restaurant, reception, and docks are located far below, around river level. There's a bar built atop some rocks on the bank of the Río Agujitas and the dining room has a good view of the bay. Meals are simply prepared, but tasty and filling, and the kitchen leaves a fresh thermos of coffee outside each room every morning. All the guest rooms have hardwood or tile floors, ceiling fans, large bathrooms, and excellent views.

Excursions available through the lodge include hikes in Corcovado National Park ($75 per person), trips to Caño Island ($75 per person for snorkelers, $110 per person for scuba divers), horseback rides ($55 per person), and sportfishing ($450 to $800 for a full day's rental, depending on the size of the boat and the number of people in your party). Room rates generally do not include air transportation. Round-trip boat transportation from Sierpe is an additional $55 per person. Round-trip transportation between Palmar Sur and Sierpe is $50 for a four-passenger taxi and $70 for a seven-passenger van.

Dining: Meals are served in the open-air dining room. Since most folks are either fishing or on one of the organized tours, lunches are often picnic affairs on the boat, in Corcovado National Park, or on Caño Island. Dinners feature fresh fish, meat, and chicken, often prepared with a tropical or Caribbean flair.

Amenities: A fresh pot of coffee is left outside your door each morning; laundry service.

Casa Corcovado Jungle Lodge. Apdo. 1482-1250, Escazú (mailing address in the U.S.: Interlink 253, P.O. Box 526770, Miami, FL 33152). ☎ **888/896-6097** in the U.S., or 506/256-3181. Fax 506/256-7409. www.casacorcovado.co.cr. E-mail: corcovdo@racsa.co.cr. 10 units. $630 per person for 3 days/2 nights with 1 tour, $725 for 4 days/3 nights with 2 tours. Rates include round-trip transportation from San José, all meals, park fees, and taxes. AE, MC, V.

This very isolated jungle lodge is the closest accommodation to Corcovado National Park on this end of the Osa Peninsula. The rooms are all private bungalows built on the grounds of an old cacao plantation on the jungle's edge. The bungalows are all spacious, with one or two double beds (each with mosquito netting) and a large tiled bathroom. Electricity and hot water are supplied by a combination solar and hydroelectric energy system. Excellent family-style meals are served in the main lodge, although most guests take lunch with them to the beach or on one of the various tours available (including all the standard excursions, plus fishing and diving). Access is strictly by small boat here, and sometimes the beach landing can be a bit rough, so it's recommended that guests be in decent physical shape. When the sea's not too rough, the beach is great for swimming. When it is rough, it's a great place to grab a hammock in the shade and read a book.

Amenities: There's a swimming pool, nature trails, and laundry service. There's also a small conference room equipped with a TV and a VCR. A wide range of tours and activities are available.

✪ La Paloma Lodge. Apdo. 97-4005, San Antonio de Belén, Heredia. ☎ **506/239-2801,** or ☎ and fax 506/239-0954. www.lapalomalodge.com. E-mail: lapaloma@lapalomalodge. com. 4 units, 5 deluxe bungalows. Nov 16–Apr 30 $735 standard rm, $825 cabin for 4 days/ 3 nights with 2 tours; $830 standard room, $935 cabin for 5 days/4 nights with 2 tours. Rates are per-person and include round-trip transportation, all meals, park fees, indicated tours, and taxes. Lower rates May 1–Nov. 15. MC, V (6% surcharge added).

Situated on a steep hill overlooking the Pacific, with Caño Island in the distance, the individual bungalows at La Paloma offer expansive ocean views worth every huff and puff it takes to get up here. The main lodge building is a large, thatched, open-air structure with a long veranda that has a sitting area, where you can mingle with other guests. All of the cabins are built on stilts, feature private verandas, and are set among lush foliage facing the Pacific Ocean. The three older cabins are my favorites simply for their spaciousness and seclusion. Four screen walls keep you in touch with nature and let the ocean breezes blow through. The newer cabins are a little smaller, but provide amazing ocean views from their main sleeping lofts. The standard rooms, which were recently remodeled, are much smaller and less private than the cabins, but they are still quite attractive and have good views from their verandas (which, like the cabins, have hammocks).

Dining: Meals are served family style and accommodations are made for vegetarians or special needs with advance warning. Menus range from fresh fish to pasta with a shrimp/tomato sauce, along with sides of steamed vegetables, rice, mashed potatoes, and a nightly green salad. There's always delicious fresh-baked bread here.

Amenities: There's a tiled pool with superb sunset views, and the beach is down at the bottom of the hill (about a 10-min. hike away). Excursions available include hikes in the park ($75 per person), trips to Caño Island ($75 per person), horseback rides ($65 per person for a full day), scuba trips ($110 per person), and sportfishing charters ($525 for a full day's boat rental). The lodge also offers PADI resort scuba-diving certification courses. There are single and double kayaks free for guests to use.

Río Sierpe Lodge. Apdo. 85, Palmar Norte. ☎ **506/283-5573.** Fax 506/283-7655. E-mail: vsftrip@racsa.co.cr. 17 units. $130 double, $195 triple. Rates include 3 meals daily and transportation to and from Palmar. AE, MC, V (7% surcharge).

This lodge is located on the south bank of the Río Sierpe near the river mouth and is best known as a fishing lodge, with various fishing packages available. You won't be right on the beach if you stay here, but the lodge will ferry you to one of two nearby beaches. All the Drake Bay excursions are available here at comparable prices. Naturalists, anglers, and scuba divers are all catered to. Adventurous types can do a 2-day horseback trek that includes camping in the rain forest. The lodge also specializes in overnight trips into Panama. Río Sierpe is surrounded by forests, and there are hiking trails on the property. Meals in the dining room feature international cuisine with an emphasis on fresh fruits, fish, and chicken.

EXPENSIVE

Cabinas Jinetes de Osa. Drake Bay, Osa Peninsula (mailing address in the U.S.: P.O. Box 833, Conifer, CO 80433). ☎ **800/317-0333** in the U.S. and Canada, or 506/385-9541. Fax 303/838-0969 in the U.S. www.costaricadiving.com. E-mail: crventur@costaricadiving.com. 9 units, 4 with shared bathroom. $100–$120 double. Rates include 3 meals daily. Dive packages available. DISC, MC, V (6% surcharge).

This perennial budget hotel in the village of Drake Bay has been spruced up, expanded, and turned into a serious dive operation. Its wooden construction and location directly above the beach give it an edge over other lodgings in the village of Drake Bay. The hotel is pretty close to the docks on the Río Agujitas, which is nice for those traveling independently or with heavy bags. Basic Tico-style meals are served in a small open-air dining room. A wide range of tours and activities are available, as are dive packages, weekly packages, and PADI certification courses.

☉ Drake Bay Wilderness Resort. Apdo. 98-8150, Palmar Norte, Osa. ☎ and fax **506/770-8012,** or 506/284-4107; 506/256-7394 in San José. Fax 506/221-4948. www.drakebay.com. E-mail: emichaud@drakebay.com. 7 tents, all with shared bathroom; 20 units. Tents $120 double, rms $160 double. Rates include all meals. Packages available. $680 for 4 days/3 nights with 3 tours, including round-trip transportation from San José, all meals and taxes, and lodging in a cabin. MC, V.

This is one of the most convenient and best-located lodges at Drake Bay. It backs onto the Río Agujitas and fronts onto the Pacific. The resort is also one of the principal movers behind the small airstrip here, and almost all their charters fly directly to Drake Bay. The lodge offers a variety of accommodations of different ages and styles. Travelers who want to rough it a bit or economize can opt for a large tent with a double bed, small table and lamp, and nearby communal bathroom and shower. Those seeking more comfort should opt for one of the rooms, which have ceiling fans, small verandas, good mattresses on the beds, and private bathrooms. The family-style meals are filling, with an emphasis on fresh seafood and fresh fruits. My favorite treats here are the fresh-baked chocolate-chip cookies frequently served for dessert. Because it's on a rocky spit, there isn't a good swimming beach right here (it's about a 15-min. walk away), but there's a new saltwater pool in front of the bar and, depending on the tide, you can bathe in a beautiful small tide pool formed by the rocks.

Amenities: The lodge provides free use of its canoes, free same-day laundry service, and fax service for guests. Tours offered by Drake Bay Wilderness Resort include hikes within the national park ($65 per person), trips to Caño Island ($70 per person for snorkelers, $100 per person for scuba divers), horseback riding ($60 per person for a full-day), and sportfishing charters ($320 per day for one to three people). Mountain bikes are also available, as are sea kayaks. One of the new tours offered is a trip inland (by mountain bike or horse) to a private farm the owners have. The lodge runs a small butterfly farm and iguana-breeding project on some land inland from Drake Bay, and you can even spend the night here if you want.

2 Puerto Jiménez: Gateway to Corcovado National Park

21$^1/_2$ miles (35km) W of Golfito by water (56 miles/90km by road); 53 miles (85km) S of Palmar Norte

Despite its small size and languid pace, Puerto Jiménez is a double boomtown, where rough jungle gold panners mix with wealthy ecotourists, budget backpackers, and a surprising number of celebrities seeking a small dose of anonymity and escape. Located on the southeastern tip of the Osa Peninsula, the town itself is just a couple of gravel streets, with the ubiquitous soccer field, a block of general stores, some inexpensive *sodas,* a butcher shop, and several bars. Scarlet macaws fly overhead, and mealy parrots provide wake-up calls.

On first glance, it's hard to imagine anything ever happening here, but looks are often deceiving. Signs in English on walls around town advertise a variety of tours, with most of the excursions going to nearby Corcovado National Park. The national park has its headquarters here, and this town makes an excellent base for exploring this vast wilderness. If the in-town accommodations are too budget-oriented, you'll find several far more luxurious places farther south on the Osa Peninsula. However, not only the highbrow are making their way to this remote spot: You will also find a bur-geoning surfer community. It's no secret any longer—**Cabo Matapalo** (the southern tip of the Osa Peninsula) is home to several very dependable right point breaks.

If you're worried the nightlife is going to be too sleepy for you, don't forget about all those gold miners lurking about. As the home base and resupply station for miners (most of them panning illegally) seeking to strike it rich in the jungles in and around the park, Puerto Jiménez can actually get pretty rowdy at night, especially when panners cash in a find.

ESSENTIALS

GETTING THERE & DEPARTING   By Plane   Sansa (☎ **506/221-9414;** fax 506/255-2176; E-mail: reservations@flysansa.com) has flights departing for Puerto Jiménez daily at 8am and 1:30pm from San José's Juan Santamaría International Airport. The flight takes 55 minutes; the cost is $60 each way.

Travelair (☎ **506/220-3054;** fax 506/220-0413; E-mail: reservations@travelair-costarica.com) has flights to Puerto Jiménez departing from Tobías Bolaños Interna-tional Airport in Pavas at 9am and 1pm daily. The flight takes 55 minutes; the fare is $90 one-way, $152 round-trip.

Sansa flights depart Puerto Jiménez daily at 9:05am and 2:35pm. The Travelair flights leaves for San José daily at 9:55am and 2:05pm.

Note that due to the remoteness of this area and the unpredictable flux of traffic, both Sansa and Travelair frequently improvise on scheduling. Sometimes this means an unscheduled stop in Quepos or Golfito either on the way down from or back to San José, which can add some time to your flight. Less frequently it may mean a change in departure time, so it's always best to confirm.

By Bus   Express buses (☎ **506/257-4121**) leave San José daily at 6am and noon from Calle 12 between avenidas 7 and 9. The trip takes 9 hours; the fare is $8.

Buses depart Puerto Jiménez for San José daily at 5 and 11am.

By Boat   There is daily passenger launch service from **Golfito** to Puerto Jiménez at 11:30am. The boat leaves from the municipal dock. Trip duration is $1^1/_2$ hours; the fare is $4. It's also possible to charter a water taxi in Golfito for the trip across to Puerto Jiménez. You'll have to pay between $30 and $55 for an entire launch, some of which can carry up to 12 people. The return trip departs Puerto Jiménez for Golfito from the public dock at 6am; fare is $4.

By Car   Take the Interamerican Highway east out of San José (through San Pedro and Cartago) and continue south on this road. In about 3 hours, you'll pass through San Isidro de El General. In another 3 hours or so, take the turnoff for La Palma and Puerto Jiménez. This road is paved at first, but at Rincón it turns to gravel. The last 22 miles (35km) are slow and rough, and, if it's the rainy season (mid-April through November), it'll be too muddy for anything but a four-wheel-drive vehicle.

ORIENTATION   Puerto Jiménez is a dirt-lane town on the southern coast of the Osa Peninsula. The public dock is over a bridge past the north end of the soccer field; the bus stop is 2 blocks east of the center of town.

EXPLORING CORCOVADO NATIONAL PARK

Although a few gringos have, over the years, come to Puerto Jiménez to try their luck at gold panning, the primary reason for coming here these days is to visit Corcovado National Park. Within a couple of hours of the town (by four-wheel-drive vehicle) there are several entrances to the park; however, there are no roads in the park, so once you reach any of the entrances, you'll have to start hiking. Exploring Corcovado National Park is not something to be undertaken lightly, but neither is it the expedition that some people make it out to be. The weather is the biggest obstacle to overnight backpacking trips through the park. The heat and humidity are often unbearable, and frequent rainstorms cause the trails to be quite muddy. Should you choose the alternative—hiking on the beach—you'll have to plan your hiking around the tides. Often there is no beach at all at high tide and some rivers are impassable at high tide.

Because of its size and remoteness, Corcovado National Park is best explored over several days; however, it is possible to enter and hike a bit of it for day trips. The best way to do this is to book a tour with your lodge on the Osa Peninsula, from a tour company in Puerto Jiménez, or through a lodge in Drake Bay (see "Accommodations & Dining," in the Drake Bay section, above).

GETTING THERE & ENTRY POINTS   There are four primary entrances to the park, which are really just ranger stations reached by rough dirt roads. Once you've reached them, you'll have to strap on a backpack and hike. Perhaps the easiest one to reach from Puerto Jiménez is **La Leona ranger station,** accessible by car, bus, or taxi. If you choose to drive, take the dirt road from Puerto Jiménez to Carate (Carate is at the end of the road). From Carate, it's a 2-mile (3km) hike to La Leona. To travel there by bus, pick up one of the collective buses (actually a four-wheel-drive pickup truck with a tarpaulin cover and slat seats in the back) that leave Puerto Jiménez for Carate daily at 6am and 2:30pm (and return at 8am and 4:30pm). Remember, these "buses" are very informal and change their schedules regularly to meet demand or avoid bad weather, so always ask in town. One-way fare is around $7. These buses leave from the main road in town that heads out to Carate, more or less in front of the Soda Carolina, and will stop to pick up anyone who flags them down along the way. Your other option is to hire a taxi, which will charge approximately $40 each way to Carate. En route to Carate, you will pass several campgrounds and small lodges as you approach the park. If you are unable to get a spot at one of the campsites in the park, you can stay at one of these and hike the park during the day.

You can travel to **El Tigre,** about $8^3/_4$ miles (14km) by dirt road from Puerto Jiménez, where there's another ranger station. But note that trails from El Tigre go only a short distance into the park. The third entrance is in **Los Patos,** which is reached from the town of La Palma, northwest of Puerto Jiménez. From here, there's

---

Trail Distances in Corcovado National Park

It's 10 miles (16km) from La Leona to Sirena. From Sirena to San Pedrillo, it's $15^1/_2$ miles (25km) along the beach. From San Pedrillo, it's $5^1/_2$ miles (9km) to Marenco Biological Reserve. It's $11^3/_4$ miles (19km) between La Sirena and Los Patos.

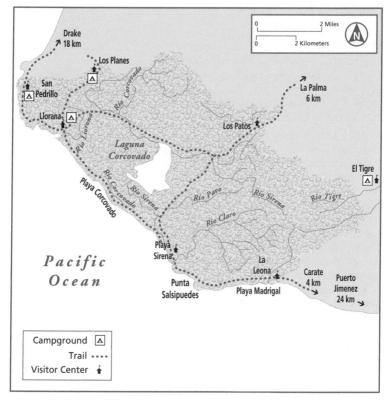

an 11³/₄-mile (19km) trail through the center of the park to Sirena, a ranger station and research facility (see "Beach Treks & Rain-Forest Hikes," below). Sirena has a landing strip that is used by charter flights. The northern entrance to the park is **San Pedrillo,** which you can reach by hiking from Sirena or by taking a boat from Drake Bay or Sierpe (see "Beach Treks & Rain-Forest Hikes," below). It's 8³/₄ miles (14km) from Drake Bay.

If you're not into hiking in the heat, you can charter a plane in Puerto Jiménez to take you to Carate, Sirena, Drake Bay, or even Tiskita Jungle Lodge (see "Accommodations & Dining" in the Playa Pavones section, later in this chapter), which is across the gulf, south of Playa Pavones. A five-passenger plane should cost between $100 and $200 one-way, depending on your destination. Contact **Alfa Romeo Aero Taxi** (☎ **506/775-1515** or 506/735-5178) for details.

FEES & REGULATIONS   Park admission is $6 per person per day. Most of the ranger stations have dormitory-style lodgings, campsites, and simple *sodas,* but all must be reserved in advance through **Osa Natural** in Puerto Jiménez (☎ **506/ 735-5440;** E-mail: osanatur@racsa.co.cr). Their office is on the main drag in Puerto Jiménez. If this doesn't work, you can try contacting the Parks Service in Puerto Jiménez (☎ **506/735-5036** or 506/735-5282). Their offices are adjacent to the airstrip. Only a limited number of people are allowed to camp at each ranger station, so make your reservations well in advance. There is an extra $2 per day fee for camping, and meals can be prepared for you at around $17 more per day, but you must also reserve your meals in advance.

VISITOR INFORMATION   If you plan to hike the beach trails from La Leona or San Pedrillo, be sure to pick up a tide table at the park headquarters' office in Puerto Jiménez. The tide changes rapidly; when it's high, the trails and river crossings can be impassable. If you plan to spend a night or more in the park, you'll want to stock up on food, water, and other essentials while you're in Puerto Jiménez, too. There's a mini-market in Carate, but the selection is limited.

BEACH TREKS & RAIN-FOREST HIKES   There are quite a few good hiking trails in the park. Two of the better-known ones are the beach routes, starting at either La Leona or San Pedrillo ranger stations. None of the hikes is easy, but the forest route from the Los Patos ranger station to Sirena, while long, is less taxing than either of the beach treks, which can be completed only when the tide is low. The route between the Los Patos/Sirena hike is 11³/₄ miles (19km) through beautiful rain forest.

Sirena is a fascinating destination. As a research facility and ranger station, it's frequented primarily by scientists studying the rain forest. One of the longest hikes, from San Pedrillo to Sirena, can be done only during the dry season. Between any two stations, the hiking is arduous and will take all day, so it's best to rest for a day or so between hikes, if possible.

Remember, this is quite a wild area. Never hike alone and take all the standard precautions for hiking in the rain forest. In addition, be especially careful about swimming in any isolated rivers or river mouths, as most rivers in Corcovado are home to crocodiles.

ACCOMMODATIONS & DINING IN THE PARK: CAMPSITES, CABINS & CANTINAS   Reservations are essential at the various ranger stations if you plan on eating or sleeping inside the park (see "Fees & Regulations," above). The **La Leona** and **San Pedrillo** ranger stations each have a campground, some very basic dormitory-style cabins, and a *soda*. There is also camping and a *soda* at **Los Patos** ranger station. **Sirena** has a modern new research facility with dormitory-style accommodations, as well as a campground, *soda,* and landing strip for charter flights. Every ranger station has potable water, but it's advisable to pack in your own; whatever you do, don't drink stream water. Campsites in the park are $2 per person per night. A dorm bed will run you $6, and meals are around $17 per day.

ACTIVE PURSUITS OUTSIDE THE PARK

Closer to Puerto Jiménez, kayaking trips around the estuary and up into the mangroves and out into the gulf are popular. Contact **Escondido Trex** (☎ **506/ 735-5210;** www.escondidotrex.com; E-mail: osatrex@racsa.co.cr), which has an office in the Soda Carolina (see "Dining in Puerto Jiménez," below). There are daily paddles through the mangroves, as well as sunset trips, where you can sometimes see dolphins. These folks also do guided rain-forest hikes and can have you rappelling down the face of a jungle waterfall. More adventurous multiday kayak and camping trips are also available, in price and comfort ranges from budget to luxury (staying at various lodges around the Golfo Dulce and Matapalo). They'll even take you gold panning (although no guarantees your panning will pay for the trip).

Osa Aventura (☎ and fax **506/735-5431;** osaave@racsa.co.cr) is another adventure outfit that offers a host of guided tours around the Osa Peninsula and into Corcovado National Park.

If you're interested in doing some **bill fishing or deep-sea fishing,** check around the public dock for notices put up by people with charter boats, or call **Marco "Taboga"**

Loaiciga (☎ 506/735-5265). Rates usually run between $350 and $700 for a full day, or between $150 and $350 for a half day, depending on the boat and tackle.

ACCOMMODATIONS IN PUERTO JIMÉNEZ
MODERATE

Doña Leta's Bungalows. Apdo. 91, Puerto Jiménez. ☎ and fax **506/735-5180.** www.hotels.co.cr/donaleta.html. E-mail: letabell@sol.racsa.co.cr. 7 units. $75 double; lower in the off-season. Rates include full breakfast. V.

This collection of individual cabins is located on a spit of land jutting out into the gulf, just east of town and the airstrip. The smaller cabins are octagonal and have just one double bed, while the larger ones each feature a sleeping loft with a double and single bed above and a double bed below. Each cabin comes with a refrigerator, two-burner stove, private bathroom, and carved-wood door. There's a small restaurant and bar here and a large central deck built under and around a large fig tree that's frequented by scarlet macaws. The grounds also include a volleyball court, a small patch of beach, and a semi-groomed trail through the mangroves. There are kayaks available free of charge for guests.

INEXPENSIVE

Agua Luna. In front of the public dock, Puerto Jiménez. ☎ **506/735-5034.** Fax 506/735-5393. 14 units. A/C TV. $30–$50 double. No credit cards.

These very reasonable rooms offer the most luxury of any of the in-town lodgings in Puerto Jiménez. Agua Luna is located right at the foot of the town's public dock and backs up to a mangrove forest. The six older rooms directly face the gulf across a fenced-in gravel parking area. The most surprising feature in each of these rooms is the bathroom, which includes both a shower and a tub facing a picture window that looks into the mangroves. The most disappointing feature is that these windows let you watch the gray water discharge directly into the mangroves. There are two double beds in each room, and on the tiled veranda out front you'll find hammocks for lounging. The newer rooms are located a half block away and are smaller and less attractive than those in the original building. The higher prices are for the larger rooms, which have tubs and mini-refrigerators.

Cabinas Oro Verde. On a cross street in the center of town, 50m (55 yd.) east of the main road, Puerto Jiménez. ☎ **506/735-5241.** E-mail: oroverde@racsa.co.cr. 10 units. $20 double; $30 triple. No credit cards.

The rooms at this budget hotel are on the second floor of a basic restaurant of the same name. The rooms are kept clean and have fans and fresh sheets. The five rooms in the front of the hotel share a narrow veranda over a sleepy street in Puerto Jiménez. The owners can help arrange a variety of tour and adventure options.

Cabinas Puerto Jiménez. 50m (55 yd.) north of Bar y Restaurant El Rancho, Puerto Jiménez. ☎ **506/735-5090** or 506/735-5152. 10 units. $12 double, $18 triple. No credit cards.

Located right on the waterfront at the north end of the soccer field, this inexpensive accommodation even offers one room with a view of the bay. The exterior of the building, with its varnished wood, is more appealing than the guest rooms. Though large, the basic rooms have cement floors, and either a floor or table fan. However, they're kept clean and are the best choice in town for travelers on a tight budget.

DINING IN PUERTO JIMÉNEZ

Bar Restaurant Agua Luna. 25m (27 yd.) north of the public pier. ☎ **506/735-5033.** Reservations not accepted. Main courses $3–$12. No credit cards. Daily 9am–10pm. COSTA RICAN.

The first restaurant you come to after arriving in Puerto Jiménez by boat is also one of the best. The restaurant is a large, mostly open building built between the dirt road and the mangroves. I recommend a table overlooking the mangroves. Seafood is plentiful and fresh, and prices for fish dinners are low even for Costa Rica. The bar and its dance floor are popular, and the music is usually loud, so don't expect a quiet, romantic dinner for two.

Soda Carolina. On the main street. ☎ **506/735-5185.** Reservations not accepted. Main courses $3–$8. No credit cards. Daily 7am–10pm. COSTA RICAN.

Set in the center of the town's main street, and otherwise known as the "Bar, Restaurante y Cabinas Carolina," this is Puerto Jiménez's budget travelers' hangout and also serves as an unofficial information center. The walls are painted with colorful jungle and wildlife scenes. As for the fare, seafood is the way to go. There's good fried fish as well as a variety of ceviches. The black-bean soup is usually tasty, and the casados are filling and cost less than $3. If you need a place to stay, there are five basic rooms with cement floors and private bathrooms behind the kitchen. The rooms cost around $10 per person and front a very unattractive yard.

ACCOMMODATIONS & DINING AROUND THE OSA PENINSULA

As with most of the lodges in Drake Bay, the accommodations listed in this section include three meals a day in their rates and do a large share of their business in package trips. Per-night rates are listed, but the price categories have been adjusted to take into account the fact that all meals are included. Ask about package rates if you plan to take several tours and stay a while: they could save you money.

In addition to the lodges listed below, there are several other options, ranging from small bed-and-breakfasts to fully equipped home rentals. Your best bet for any of the above is to contact Isabel at **Osa Tropical** (☎ 506/735-5062). In addition to being the local Sansa agent, Isabel arranges bookings via radio with a host of small remote lodges around the area.

VERY EXPENSIVE

✪ **Lapa Ríos.** Apdo. 100, Puerto Jiménez, Osa Peninsula (mailing address in the U.S.: Box 025216, SJO-706, Miami, FL 33102). ☎ **506/735-5130.** Fax 506/735-5179. www. laparios.com. E-mail: info@laparios.com. 14 units. Nov–Apr $364 double, $522 triple; May–Oct $302 double, $432 triple. Discounts for children up to 10 years old. Rates include 3 meals daily and taxes. $20 round-trip transportation from Puerto Jiménez. AE, MC, V.

If you're looking for a luxurious getaway in the jungle, this may be the place for you. However, keep in mind that there are no TVs, no telephones, no air-conditioning, no discos, no shopping, no paved roads, and no crowds. Moreover, the beach is a good 15-minute hike away, and it's not the best for swimming. In fact, other than a beautiful little pool, miles of hiking trails, and a quiet tropical bar, there is nothing around to distract your attention from the stupendous views of the forest and ocean far below.

The hotel consists of seven duplex buildings perched along three ridges. Each spacious room is totally private and oriented toward the view. Walls have open screening, and the ceiling is a high-peaked thatched roof. Mosquito nets drape languidly over the two queen-size beds. A large deck and small tropical garden, complete with outdoor shower, more than double the living space of each room. The buildings are constructed of local materials such as palm thatch, bamboo, mangrove wood, and other hardwoods. Perhaps the most appealing aspect of each room is the screen-walled shower that lets you drink in the views while you bathe. Be warned: It's a bit of a hike back and forth from the main lodge to the rooms located on the lowest ridge.

Lapa Ríos is surrounded by its own 1,000-acre private rain-forest reserve, which is home to scarlet macaws, toucans, parrots, hummingbirds, monkeys, and myriad other wildlife. For a closer look at the rain forest, hire one of the resident naturalists for guided walks or venture out on your own. If bird-watching is your thing, you need go no farther than the lodge's outdoor deck, which seems to be a popular spot with numerous avian species.

Dining: The centerpiece of the large open-air dining room is a 50-foot-tall spiral staircase that leads to an observation deck tucked beneath the peak of the building's thatched roof. Each evening there's a choice of two main entrees, with an emphasis on fresh seafood and locally available ingredients.

Amenities: Guided walks, horseback riding, boat trips, sportfishing, and sea kayaking. Day trips to Corcovado National Park, Casa Orquideas, and Wilson Botanical Gardens. Body-board and surfboard rentals. Most tours cost $20 to $30 per person, although certain activities, like sportfishing and chartered flights into Corcovado National Park, are more expensive. Facilities include a swimming pool and hiking trails.

EXPENSIVE

✪ **Bosque del Cabo Wilderness Lodge.** Osa Peninsula (mailing address in the U.S.: Interlink 528, P.O. Box 025635, Miami, FL 33152). ☎ and fax **506/735-5206,** or 506/381-4847. www.bosquedelcabo.com. E-mail: boscabo@racsa.co.cr. 8 units. $165–$182 double. Rates include 3 meals daily. $20 round-trip transportation from Puerto Jiménez. V (5% surcharge).

This secluded jungle lodge is located 500 feet above the water at the southern tip of the Osa Peninsula, where the Golfo Dulce meets the Pacific Ocean. It's surrounded by 300 acres of land that the owners purchased in order to preserve a piece of the rain forest. The cabins are all spacious and attractively furnished, have wooden decks or verandas to catch the ocean views, and are set amid beautiful gardens. The deluxe cabins come with king-size beds and slightly larger deck space. All of the cabins have indoor bathrooms, although the tiled showers are set outdoors amid flowering heliconia. Cabin 6 is my favorite for its spectacular view of the sunrise from your bed. Meals are well prepared and filling and usually feature fruit grown on the premises. These folks also rent out a separate two-bedroom house that's quite popular.

There's a trail down to a secluded beach that has some tide pools and ocean-carved caves. Another trail leads to a jungle waterfall. If you're too lazy to hike down to the beach, there's a small pool by the main lodge. Surfing is a popular activity here, as are hiking and horseback riding. The newest attraction here is a canopy platform 120 feet up a Manu tree, reached along a 300-foot zip line. Trips to the national park or fishing excursions can be arranged, as well as guided hikes, sea kayaking, and a host of other activities and tours.

✪ **Corcovado Lodge Tent Camp.** Costa Rica Expeditions, Apdo. 6941-1000, San José. ☎ **506/257-0766** or 506/222-0333. Fax 506/257-1665. www.costaricaexpeditions.com. E-mail: costaric@expeditions.co.cr. 20 tents. $135 double. Rates include 3 meals daily and all taxes. 3-day/2-night package $1,398 double, including air transportation (pickup and delivery from any San José hotel), 3 meals daily, 1 treetop/canopy tour, park entrance fee, and all taxes. Add $67 per person per day for extra days. AE, MC, V.

If you're looking for a balanced blend of comfort and adventure, check out Corcovado Lodge Tent Camp, which is built on a low bluff right above the beach. Forested mountains rise up behind the tent camp, and just a few minutes' walk away is the entrance to Corcovado National Park. Accommodations are in large tents pitched on wooden decks. Each tent has two twin beds, a table, and a couple of plastic garden chairs on the front deck. Toilets and showers are a short walk away, but there are enough so that there's usually no waiting.

Meals are served in a large open-air dining room furnished with picnic tables. A separate screen-walled building is furnished with hammocks, a small bar, a Ping-Pong table, and a few board games. Services at the lodge include guided walks and boat excursions, both into the national park and out to Caño Island. The newest addition to the lodge is a canopy platform located 120 feet up an ancient Guapinol tree. If you're truly adventurous, you can spend the night in a tent atop the platform (just don't wake up on the wrong side of the tent). Package rates that include transportation and tours are also available and are the way most people come here.

Just reaching this lodge is an adventure in itself. Most guests take a five-seat chartered plane to the gravel landing strip at Carate and then walk for around 30 minutes along the beach to the lodge. Don't worry: Your bags are hauled in on a mule-drawn cart. If you have a four-wheel-drive vehicle, you can get as far as Carate, arrange for safe parking, and then walk the remaining mile (1.6km). Once you're there, you have a real sense of being very away from it all.

3 Golfito: Gateway to the Golfo Dulce

54 miles (87km) S of Palmar Norte; 209 miles (337km) S of San José

Golfito is an odd and unlikely destination for foreign travelers. In its prime, this was a major banana port, but United Fruit pulled out in 1985 following a few years of rising taxes, falling prices, and labor disputes. Now, Ticos come here in droves on weekends and throughout December to take advantage of cheap prices on name-brand goods and clothing sold at the duty-free zone. *Be warned:* Sometimes all these shoppers make finding a room difficult. Golfito is also a major sportfishing center and a popular gateway to a slew of nature lodges spread along the quiet waters, isolated bays, and lush rain forests of the Golfo Dulce, or "Sweet Gulf." In 1998, much of the rain forest bordering the Golfo Dulce was officially declared the **Piedras Blancas National Park,** which includes 30,000 acres of primary forests, as well as newly protected secondary forests and pasturelands.

Golfito is set on the north side of the Golfo Dulce, at the foot of lush green mountains. The setting alone is enough to make this one of the most attractive cities in the country, but Golfito also has a certain charm all its own. Sure, the areas around the municipal park and public dock are kind of seedy and the "downtown" section is quite run-down, but if you go a little bit farther along the bay, you come to the old United Fruit Company housing. Here you'll find well-maintained wooden houses painted bright colors and surrounded by neatly manicured gardens. Toucans are commonly sighted. It's all very lush and green and clean—an altogether different picture from that painted by most port towns in this country. These old homes are experiencing a sort of renaissance as they become small hotels catering to shoppers visiting the adjacent duty-free shopping center.

Sportfishing cognoscenti know that Golfito's real draw is the marlin and sailfish just beyond its bay. Arguably one of the best fishing spots in Costa Rica, it provides pleasant, uncrowded surroundings in which die-hard sport fishers can indulge their greatest fantasies of landing the great one to end all great ones. Landlubbers, take heed: Golfito has great opportunities for bird-watching and is also close to some lovely botanical gardens that you can easily spend a day or more touring.

ESSENTIALS

GETTING THERE & DEPARTING   By Plane   Sansa (☎ **506/221-9414;** fax 506/255-2176; E-mail: reservations@flysansa.com) has three daily flights to Golfito departing at 6 and 9:30am and 2:15pm from San José's Juan Santamaría International

Airport. Trip duration is 1 hour; fare is $60 each way. Sansa flights return to San José daily at 7:10 and 10:40am and 3:25pm. **Travelair** (☎ **506/220-3054;** fax 506/ 220-0413; E-mail: reservations@travelair-costarica.com) has one flight to Golfito daily at 9am from Tobías Bolaños International Airport in Pavas. The flight stops in Puerto Jiménez en route, and returns to San José at 10:10am. The flight takes 1 hour and 10 minutes; the fare is $84 one-way, $144 round-trip.

By Bus   Express buses leave San José daily at 7am and 3pm from the Tracopa station at Avenida 5 and Calle 14 (☎ **506/222-2666**). The trip takes 8 hours; the fare is $6.

Buses depart Golfito for San José daily at 5am and 1:30pm from the bus station near the municipal dock.

By Boat   A passenger launch leaves **Puerto Jiménez,** on the Osa Peninsula, daily at 6am. The trip takes 1½ hours; the fare is $4. You can also hire a boat to take you across the Golfo Dulce to Golfito. However, as there are not very many available in Puerto Jiménez, you're likely to have to pay quite a bit ($30 to $55 each way) for such a service. The passenger launch departs Golfito for Puerto Jiménez daily at 11:30am.

By Car   The Interamerican Highway goes almost all the way to Golfito from San José, but even the main highway is a long and arduous trip. In the 8 hours it takes to drive the 209 miles (337km) from San José, you'll pass over the Cerro de la Muerte, which is famous for its dense fog and torrential downpours. Also, you'll have to contend with potholes of gargantuan proportions for almost the entire length of this road. Just remember, if the road is suddenly smooth and in great shape, you can bet that around the next bend there will be a bottomless pothole that you can't swerve around. Take it easy. When you get to Río Claro, you'll notice a couple of gas stations and quite a bit of activity. Turn right here and follow the signs to Golfito. If you end up at the Panama border, you've missed the turnoff by about 20 miles (32km).

GETTING AROUND   If you can't get to your next destination by boat, bus, or car, **Alfa Romeo Aero Taxi** (☎ **506/775-1515** or 506/735-5178) runs charters to most of the nearby destinations, including Carate, Drake Bay, Sirena, and Puerto Jiménez. A regular taxi ride anywhere in town should cost around 75¢.

FAST FACTS   You can **exchange money** at the gas station, or "La Bomba," in the middle of town. There is a **Laundromat** on the upper street of the small downtown that charges $3 for a 5-pound load. If you drop off your clothes in the morning, they'll be ready in the afternoon.

ACTIVE PURSUITS

BEACHES & SWIMMING   There aren't any really good swimming beaches right in Golfito. The closest spot is **Playa Cacao,** a short boat ride away, although this is not one of my favorite beaches in Costa Rica. You should be able to get a ride here for around $5 per person from one of the boat taxis down at the public docks, however, you might have to negotiate hard, as these boatmen like to gouge tourists whenever possible. If you really want some beach time, I recommend staying at one of the hotels in the Golfo Dulce (see below) or heading over to **Playa Zancudo** (see below).

SPORTFISHING & SAILBOAT CHARTERS   The waters off Golfito also offer some of the best sportfishing in Costa Rica. If you'd like to try hooking into a possible world-record marlin or sailfish, contact **Banana Bay Marina** (☎ **506/775-0838;** www.bananabaymarina.com). You could also try either **Golfito Sportfishing** (☎ **506/776-0007;** www.costaricafishing.com) or **Roy's Zancudo Lodge** (☎ **506/ 776-0008;** www.royszancudo.com). Both of these operations are based in nearby Playa Zancudo, but they can arrange pickup in Golfito. A full-day fishing trip will cost between $450 and $800.

There's no steady charter fleet here, but itinerant sailors often set up shop here for a season or so. If you're looking to charter a sailboat, you should check with the **Banana Bay Marina** (☎ 506/775-0838) or **Las Gaviotas Hotel** (☎ 506/775-0062).

GUIDED TOURS   If you're interested in having a guide for any of the above activities, or for a hike in some nearby rain forest, check in with either the **Golfo Dulce Eco-Tourist Guide Association** (☎ 506/775-1813) or **Land Sea Tours** (☎ 506/775-1614). The latter offers kayaking and camping trips out on the gulf.

VISITING BOTANICAL GARDENS

About 30 minutes by boat out of Golfito, you'll find **Casa Orquideas,** a private botanical garden lovingly built and maintained by Ron and Trudy MacAllister. Two-hour tours of the gardens (Sunday through Thursday) cost $10 per person, with a minimum of four people. During the tour, you'll sample a load of fresh fruits picked right off the trees. Most hotels in the region can organize a tour to the gardens. If your hotel can't, you'll have to hire a boat to get there, which should cost you between $55 and $75 round-trip, including the boat pilot's waiting time.

If you have a serious interest in botanical gardens or bird-watching, consider an excursion to **Wilson Botanical Gardens** (☎ 506/240-6696; fax 506/240-6783; E-mail: reservas@ots.ac.cr), located just outside the town of San Vito, about 40 miles (65km) to the northeast. The gardens are owned by the Organization for Tropical Studies and include more than 7,000 species of tropical plants from around the world. Among the plants grown here are many endangered species, which make the gardens of interest to botanical researchers. Despite the scientific aspects of the gardens, there are so many beautiful and unusual flowers amid the manicured grounds that even a neophyte can't help but be astounded. All this luscious flora has attracted at least 330 species of birds. A full day in the gardens, including lunch, will cost you $45 ($40 without lunch); a half-day walk around costs $25. Naturalist guides can be hired for around $25. If you'd like to stay the night here, there are 12 well-appointed rooms and four cabins. Rates, which include three meals, run around $60 per person; you need to make reservations beforehand if you wish to spend the night. You'll find the gardens about 3³/₄ miles (6km) before San Vito. To get here from Golfito, drive back out to the Interamerican Highway and continue south toward Panama. In Ciudad Neily, turn north. A taxi from Golfito should cost between $30 and $40 each way.

ACCOMMODATIONS IN GOLFITO

Cabinas Jardín Cervecero Alamedas. 100m (109 yd.) south of the Depósito Libre, Golfito. ☎ **506/775-1271.** 6 units. $15 double, $20 triple. No credit cards.

The six rooms here have been built across the gravel driveway from one of the more popular restaurants in the area around the free port. The rooms are clean, and each has one double, one single, and one bunk bed. I prefer the upstairs rooms, which have wood (instead of concrete) floors and more air circulation.

Complejo Turístico Samoa del Sur. 100m (109 yd.) north of the public dock, Golfito. ☎ **506/775-0233.** Fax 506/775-0573. 14 units. TV. $34–$42 double to quad. AE, MC, V.

It's hard to miss the two giant thatched spires that house this popular hotel, restaurant, and bar. The rooms are spacious and clean. Varnished wood headboards complement two firm and comfortable double beds. With red tile floors, modern bathrooms, and carved-wood doors, the rooms all share a long, covered veranda that's set perpendicular to the gulf, so the views aren't great. If you want to watch the water, you're better off grabbing a table at the restaurant. The more expensive rooms have air-conditioning.

On my last visit, there were big plans to expand and develop this hotel, adding on a full-service marina, swimming pool, tennis and volleyball courts, and more rooms.

Golfo Azul. Barrio Alameda, 300m (327 yd.) south of the Depósito Libre, Golfito. ☎ **506/775-0871.** Fax 506/775-1849. 24 units. A/C. $24 double, $27 triple, $30 quad. No credit cards.

Azul offers clean rooms and a quiet location in the most attractive part of Golfito. Most of the guests here are Ticos in town to shop at the nearby Depósito Libre (free port), and service can range from inattentive to downright rude. The smallest rooms are cramped, but there are larger rooms, some with high ceilings, making them feel even more spacious. Bathrooms are tiled and have hot water, and all rooms have air-conditioning. The hotel's restaurant only serves breakfast.

Hotel Sierra. Apdo. 37, Golfito. ☎ **506/775-0666** or 506/775-0336. Fax 506/775-0506. 72 units. A/C TV. $35 double, $40 triple. AE, MC, V.

After lying dormant in foreclosure for over a year, this hotel was recently reopened and is currently being managed by the bank—and the service and upkeep are what you'd expect from a bank. Located right beside the airstrip, the Hotel Sierra is the largest and most modern hotel in town. The Sierra is constructed to be as open and breezy as possible, though the rooms also have air conditioners. Covered walkways connect the hotel's various buildings. The rooms have pale-blue tile floors and windows on two sides to let in plenty of light. Bathrooms are large, and there are safes in all the rooms. The swimming pool is fairly large and even has a swim-up bar. Prices in the **Ara Macao restaurant** are moderate, with several lobster dishes for around $15. For light meals and snacks, there is also a casual restaurant on the far side of the pool. All in all, this place offers very good value.

Las Gaviotas Hotel. Apdo. 12-8201, Golfito. ☎ **506/775-0062.** Fax 506/775-0544. E-mail: lasgaviotas@hotmail.com. 18 units, 3 cabanas. $40–$55 double, $45–$60 triple, $84 cabana. AE, DC, MC, V.

Situated just at the start of Golfito proper—a short taxi or bus ride from the "downtown"—Las Gaviotas has long been a popular choice. The waterfront location is this hotel's greatest asset. There is a long pier that attracts the sailboat and sport-fishing crowd. For landlubbers, there's a small pool built out near the gulf. Guest rooms, which are set amid attractive gardens, all face the ocean, and though they're quite large, they're a bit Spartan and definitely show their age. There are small tiled patios in front of all the rooms, and the cabanas have little kitchens. The more expensive rooms have air-conditioning. A large open-air restaurant looks over the pool to the gulf; it's a great view, but the food leaves much to be desired. Just around the corner is a large open-air bar. In addition, there's a small gift shop.

ACCOMMODATIONS ON THE GOLFO DULCE

The lodges listed here are all located on the shores of the Golfo Dulce. There are no roads into this area, so you must get to the lodges by boat. I recommended that you have firm reservations when visiting this area, so your transportation should be arranged. If worse comes to worst, you can hire a boat taxi at the *muellecito* (little dock), which is located on the water just beyond the gas station, or "La Bomba," in Golfito, for between $25 and $35 depending on which lodge you are staying at.

✪ **Caña Blanca Beach & Rainforest Lodge.** Golfo Dulce (A.P. 48, Puerto Jiménez). ☎ **506/383-5707** or 506/735-5062. Fax 506/735-5043. canablan@racsa.co.cr. 3 units. $250 double. Rate includes all meals, drinks, daily tours, taxes, and transfers to and from either Golfito or Puerto Jiménez. 3-day minimum stay. V (with a 5% surcharge).

This small, isolated nature lodge is perfect for a romantic getaway and/or some serious relaxation. The three individual cabins are nestled on the edge of a 900-acre private reserve. All are spacious, wooden affairs, built on stilts, with private bathrooms and an outdoor-garden shower. From your balcony you can watch the waters of the Golfo Dulce lap on Caña Blanca's palm-lined black-sand beach. There are kayaks for paddling around the gulf, as well as several miles of trails and a resident naturalist guide. Gourmet meals are prepared by your hosts Earl and Carol Crews, featuring fresh fruits, herbs and vegetables, and quite often fresh fish. There are no TVs, and only an erratic cellular phone connection out here, so be prepared to get away from it all. However, the bird-watching is fabulous, and you're guaranteed to see some monkeys, pizotes, and much more of the rich local fauna.

Dolphin Quest. Apdo. 141, Golfito. ☎ **506/775-1742** or 506/735-5062. Fax 506/775-0373. www.dolphinquest.com. E-mail: dolphinquest@email.com. 6 units. $45–$100 double. Rates include 3 meals daily. No credit cards.

This expansive and rustic spread is located right by the beach, between Casa Orquideas and Golfo Dulce Lodge. There is a variety of accommodations. Each of three separate, octagonal ranchos has a roomy sleeping loft, open half-walls, cement floors, and a small kitchenette. My favorite rooms, however, are in the separate, older wooden house, which is built on stilts and has spacious front and back porches, two bedrooms, a full kitchen, and a comfortable living area. Camping is permitted ($25 per person, including meals), and there are also dormitory beds available, for those looking for a real budget stay in the Golfo Dulce. Scuba diving, snorkeling, horseback riding, and transport between the lodge and Golfito are all available. Dolphin Quest is a family-run operation. Consequently, your family is welcome, and there are discounts for children.

Golfo Dulce Lodge. Apdo. 137, Golfito. ☎ **506/222-2900.** Fax 506/222-5173. www.golfodulcelodge.com. E-mail: aratur@racsa.co.cr. 8 units. $210 double, $255 triple. Rates include 3 meals daily and transportation to and from Golfito or Puerto Jiménez. 2-night minimum stay. No credit cards.

This small Swiss-run lodge is just down the beach from Casa Orquideas and Dolphin Quest, about a 30-minute boat ride from Golfito. The five separate cabins and main lodge buildings are all set back away from the beach 500 meters (545 yd.) into the forest. The cabins are spacious, airy, and feature either a twin and a double bed or three single beds. In addition, there are large modern bathrooms, solar hot-water showers, a small sitting area, and a porch with a hammock. The rooms are all comfortable and well appointed, and even feature private verandas, but they are not nearly as nice as the cabins. Meals are served in an open thatch-roofed building beside the small swimming pool. The lodge also offers jungle hikes, river trips, and other guided tours.

✪ Rainbow Adventures. Apdo. 63, Golfito (mailing address in the U.S.: Michael Medill, 5875 NW Kaiser Rd., Portland, OR 97229). ☎ **800/565-0722** or 503/690-7750 in the U.S., or ☎ and fax 506/775-0220 in Costa Rica. Fax 503/690-7735 in the U.S. www.rainbowcostarica.com. E-mail: info@rainbowcostarica.com. 4 units, 2 cabins. $310–$350 double. Extra person $65. Rates include 3 meals daily, round-trip transportation between the lodge and Golfito, all nonalcoholic drinks, snacks, and taxes. AE, DC, MC, V.

The open architecture, varnished hardwoods, four-poster beds and scattered antiques, stained glass, and oriental rugs make this one of the more unique jungle lodges in Costa Rica. The grounds immediately surrounding the lodge are neatly manicured gardens planted with exotic fruit trees, flowering shrubs, and palms from around the world. The second-floor rooms in the main lodge are the smallest and least expensive. But for just a little more, you can have the penthouse, a large third-floor room with four open walls and treetop views of the gulf. Only slightly more expensive are the spacious cabins, which are located a hundred or so yards away from the main building and are built on stilts. Cabins have open living rooms and a large bedroom that can be divided into two small rooms. Creative and tasty meals are served either family- or buffet-style. The owner has eight more rooms in the sister lodge, Buena Vista, located several hundred meters/yards up Playa Cativa, but the level of comfort, service, and general ambiance are not as appealing there.

Days are spent lounging in hammocks, swimming, sunning, exploring the jungle, reading, bird-watching, wild-animal–watching, and maybe fishing a bit. The hotel has an air-conditioned library and reading room, with one of the most extensive collections of natural history books I've ever seen. Fishing trips (barracuda, rooster fish, snook, and red snapper are plentiful), boat charters, and guided hikes can all be arranged, as well as trips to the nearby Casa Orquideas (see "Visiting Botanical Gardens," above). The lodge has several well-maintained trails through primary rain forest, with jungle waterfalls and wonderful swimming holes. A private (albeit rocky) beach provides protected swimming and, when it's calm, there's some good snorkeling nearby (equipment is available at no charge). If neither the natural swimming holes nor Golfo Dulce appeals to you, there's also a new spring-fed pool just off the main lodge.

DINING

In addition to the restaurants listed below, **Coconut Cafe,** across from the gas station (☎ **506/775-0518**), is a popular hangout. Open for breakfast and lunch, this place specializes in espresso and exotic coffee concoctions as well as desserts. It's a good place to gather information on trips and tours around the gulf. They also offer Internet access.

Bar & Restaurant La Cubana. 150m (164 yd.) east of the gas station, on the upper road through downtown Golfito. No phone. Main courses $3–$8. No credit cards. Tues–Sun 6am–10pm. COSTA RICAN.

This small, open-air restaurant with a basic menu commands a good view of the gulf from its location on the bluff of a small hill. It serves hearty meals at rock-bottom prices. A fresh whole fish in garlic sauce costs around $4. The bar is a quiet spot to have a drink in the evening.

Jardín Cervecero Alamedas. 100m (109 yd.) south of the Depósito Libre. ☎ **506/775-1271.** Main courses $3–$12. No credit cards. Daily 7am–11pm (closed Sun–Mon during the off-season). COSTA RICAN/SEAFOOD.

This has long been one of the more popular restaurants near the Depósito Libre (Free Port). The restaurant is located underneath an old house that's built on stilts. White chairs and dark-green tablecloths provide a sort of fern-bar feel inside; outside, real tropical gardens surround the house. There are great deals on seafood here, including a long list of ceviches. The only drawback is that the stereo blasts just a little too loud.

Samoa del Sur. 100m (109 yd.) north of the public dock. ☎ **506/775-0233.** Main courses $2.50–$17. AE, MC, V. Daily 7am–midnight. CONTINENTAL.

It's hard to miss the Samoa del Sur: It's that huge twin-towered rancho just north of the public dock. This oversized jungle structure seems out of place in a town where cinder blocks are the preferred construction material, but its tropical atmosphere is a welcome change from the rather rundown ambiance that pervades the rest of this town. The restaurant's biggest surprise, however, is its extensive menu of familiar continental and French dishes (the owners are French), such as onion soup, salad

Niçςoise, fillet of fish meunière, and paella. There are also pizzas and spaghetti. The view of the gulf makes this a great spot for a sunset drink or dinner. In addition to the food, the giant rancho houses a pool table, several high-quality dartboards, and a big-screen television. The bar sometimes stays open all night.

4 Playa Zancudo

12 miles (19km) S of Golfito (by boat); 22 miles (35km) S of Golfito (by road)

Although the word has leaked out in recent years, Playa Zancudo remains one of Costa Rica's most isolated beach getaways. It's a popular backpacker hangout, which means there are plenty of cheap rooms, some cheap places to eat, and lots of young gringos and Europeans around. These factors alone are enough to keep Zancudo jumping through the winter months. The beach itself is long and flat, and because it's protected from the full force of Pacific waves, it's one of the calmest beaches on this coast and relatively good for swimming, especially toward the northern end. There's a splendid view across the Golfo Dulce, and the sunsets are hard to beat. Because there's a mangrove swamp directly behind the beach, mosquitoes and biting sand flies can be a problem, so be sure to bring insect repellent.

ESSENTIALS

GETTING THERE   By Plane   The nearest airport is in Golfito. See the Golfito section, above, for details. To get from the airport to Playa Zancudo, you can take a boat (see "By Boat," below) or a taxi (see "By Car," below).

By Boat   Water taxis can be hired in Golfito to make the trip out to Playa Zancudo; however, trips depend on the tides and weather conditions. When the tide is high, the boats take a route through the mangroves. This is by far the calmest and most scenic way to get to Zancudo. When the tide is low, they must stay out in the gulf, which can get choppy at times. Currently it costs around $10 per person for a water taxi, with a minimum charge of $20. If you can round up any sort of group, be sure to negotiate. The ride takes about 30 minutes.

Also, there's a passenger launch from the *muellecito* (little dock) in Golfito, which normally leaves twice daily at around 4:30am and noon. Because the schedule sometimes changes, be sure to ask in town (ask for "Makarela") about current departure times. The trip lasts 40 minutes; fare is $2.

If you plan ahead, you can call **Zancudo Boat Tours** (☎ 506/776-0012) and arrange for pickup in Golfito. The trips costs $10 per person each way, with a $20 minimum.

By Bus   It's possible to get to Zancudo by bus, but I recommend the above water-borne routes. If you insist, though, you can catch the 2pm Pavones bus in front of the gas station "La Bomba" in downtown Golfito and get off in the village of Conte (at around 3:30pm). A Zancudo-bound bus should be there waiting. The whole trip takes about 3 hours; the fare is $3.

By Car   If you've got a four-wheel-drive vehicle, you should be able to make it out to Zancudo even in the rainy season, but be sure to ask in Golfito before leaving the paved road. The turnoff for Playas Zancudo and Pavones is at El Rodeo, about 2¹/₂ miles (4km) outside of Golfito, on the road in from the Interamerican Highway. Pretty quickly after the turnoff, you'll have to wait and take a small diesel-operated crank ferry (fare is $2 per vehicle). A four-wheel-drive taxi will cost around $30 from Golfito. It takes about 1 hour when the road is in good condition, about 2 hours when it's not. To get here from San José, see "By Car" under "Getting There," above, in the Golfito section.

DEPARTING   The public launch to Golfito leaves twice daily at 6am and 1pm from the dock near the school, in the center of Zancudo. You can also arrange a water taxi back to Golfito, but it's best to work with your hotel owner and make a reservation at least 1 day in advance. **Zancudo Boat Tours** (☎ 506/776-0012) will take you for $10 per person with a two-person minimum. If you're heading to **Pavones** or the **Osa Peninsula** next, **Zancudo Boat Tours** is sometimes willing to make the trips to these two places. It costs around $15 per person, with a minimum charge of $30. The bus to Golfito leaves Zancudo each morning at 5:30am. You can catch the bus anywhere along the main road.

ORIENTATION   Zancudo is a long, narrow peninsula (sometimes only 91m/ 100 yd. or so wide) at the mouth of the Río Colorado. On one side is the beach; on the other is a mangrove swamp. There is only one road that runs the length of the beach, and it's along this road, spread out over several kilometers of long, flat beach, that you'll find the hotels I've mentioned here. It's about a 20-minute walk from the public dock near the school to the popular Cabinas Sol y Mar.

WHAT TO SEE & DO (OR HOW NOT TO DO ANYTHING)

The main activity at Zancudo is relaxing, and people take it seriously. There are hammocks at almost every lodge, and if you bring a few good books, you can spend quite a number of hours swinging slowly in the tropical breezes. The beach along Zancudo is great for swimming. It's generally a little calmer on the northern end and gets rougher (good for bodysurfing) as you head south. There are a couple of bars, and even a disco, but visitors are most likely to spend their time just hanging out in restaurants, meeting like-minded folks, or playing board games.

Susan and Andrew Robertson, who run Cabinas Los Cocos, also operate **Zancudo Boat Tours** (☎ 506/776-0012), which offers snorkeling trips, trips to the Casa Orquideas Botanical Garden, a trip up the Río Coto to watch birds and wildlife, and others. Tour prices are $30 per person per tour, with discounts available for larger groups.

For fishing, contact **Arena Alta Sportfishing** at Cabinas Sol y Mar (☎ 506/ 776-0120; E-mail: arenaalta@aol.com). You can also check out **Golfito Sportfishing** (☎ 506/776-0007), which, despite the name, is located in Zancudo, or **Roy's Zancudo Lodge** (☎ 506/776-0008). A full-day fishing with lunch and beer should cost between $500 and $800 per boat.

ACCOMMODATIONS
VERY EXPENSIVE

Roy's Zancudo Lodge. Apdo. 41, Playa Zancudo, Golfito. ☎ 800/515-7697 in the U.S., or 506/776-0008. Fax 506/776-0011. www.royszancudo.com. E-mail: rroig@golfito.net. 14 units. A/C. $75 per person nonfishing, $360 per person double occupancy for full-day fishing. Rates include all meals and beer. Multiday packages available. V.

Primarily a fishing lodge, this pricey hotel is located at the north end of Zancudo. All of the rooms look out onto a bright green lawn of soft grass and the small swimming pool and Jacuzzi; the beach is just a few steps beyond. The rooms are in several long row buildings on stilts. All have hardwood floors; small, clean bathrooms; ceiling fans; air conditioners; and small verandas. There are four suites that have separate sitting rooms and stocked mini-fridges.

Dining: There's an open-air restaurant that, naturally, specializes in fresh fish.

Amenities: The lodge offers many different types of fishing excursions and packages and boasts more than 20 world-record catches.

INEXPENSIVE

✪ **Cabinas Sol y Mar.** Apdo. 87, Playa Zancudo, Golfito. ☎ **506/776-0014.** Fax 506/776-0015. www.zancudo.com. E-mail: solymar@zancudo.com. 4 units. Dec 1–Apr 30 $31 double. May 1–Nov 30 $20 double. V (6% surcharge).

Although there are only four rooms here, this is the most popular lodging in Zancudo. Two of the rooms are modified geodesic domes with tile floors, verandas, and tin roofs. The bathrooms have unusual showers that feature a tiled platform set amid smooth river rocks and translucent roofs that flood them with light. The other two rooms are larger and newer but aren't as interesting. You'll have to decide between space and character. There's an adjacent open-air restaurant that's one of the most popular places to eat in Zancudo. Seafood dishes are the specialty here (the whole fried fish is good), and prices are very reasonable. There's a small gift shop, and the hotel can provide E-mail and fax services.

✪ **Los Cocos.** Apdo. 88, Golfito. ☎ and fax **506/776-0012.** www.loscocos.com. E-mail: loscocos@racsa.co.cr. 4 units. $35–$40 per night, $220–$252 per week; lower in the off-season. No credit cards.

If you've ever pondered throwing it all away and setting up shop in a simple house by the beach, these kitchen-equipped cabins might be a good place for a trial run. Set under the trees and only a few yards from the beach, the four cabins are quiet and semi-isolated from one another. Two of them served as banana-plantation housing in a former life, until they were salvaged and moved here. These wood houses have big verandas and bedrooms and large eat-in kitchens. Bathrooms are down a few steps in back and have hot water. The two newer cabins also offer plenty of space, small kitchenettes, and a private veranda, as well as comfortable sleeping lofts. If you plan to stay in Zancudo for a while, this is a perennially good choice. There are complimentary boogie boards and kayaks for guest use. The owners, Susan and Andrew Robertson, also run Zancudo Boat tours, so if you want to do some exploring or need a ride into Golfito or Puerto Jiménez, they're the folks to see.

DINING

The most popular restaurant in Zancudo has traditionally been at **Cabinas Sol y Mar** (☎ **506/776-0014**). This small open-air spot is a de rigueur hangout for resident gringos as well as travelers. You might also try the tasty Italian meals at **Restaurante Maconda** (☎ **506/776-0157**). And if you want basic Tico fare and some local company, head to **Soda Suzy** (☎ **506/776-0107**) or **Soda Catherine** (☎ **506/776-0124**).

5 Playa Pavones: A Surfer's Mecca

25 miles (40km) S of Golfito

Touted as the world's longest rideable left break, Pavones is a legendary surf spot. It takes around 6 feet of swell to get this wave cranking, but when the surf's up, you're in for a long, long ride—so long, in fact, that it's much easier to walk back up the beach to where the wave is breaking than to paddle back. The swells are most consistent during the rainy season, but you're likely to find surfers here year-round. Locals tend to be pretty possessive around here (both the wave and local properties have engendered bitter disputes), so don't be surprised if you receive a cool welcome in Pavones. Other than surfing, nothing much goes on here; however, the beach is quite nice, with some rocky areas that give Pavones a bit more visual appeal than Zancudo. If you're feeling energetic, you can go for a horseback ride or hike into the rain forests that back up this beach town, or stroll south on the beaches that stretch toward Punta Banco and beyond, all the way to the Panamanian border. Various lodges are starting to sprout up, but so far most accommodations are very basic—Pavones is a tiny village with few amenities.

For the past 20 or so years, Pavones has been the site of some fierce and ongoing land battles among locals, foreign investors, and squatters. In 1997 the conflict turned bloody, and one foreign landholder and one squatter were killed in a gun battle. The U.S. State Department quickly issued a traveler's advisory. This has since been rescinded. If you stick to tourism and stay away from wave hogging and real-estate speculation, you should have no problems.

ESSENTIALS

GETTING THERE & DEPARTING   By Plane   The nearest airport is in Golfito. See the Golfito section, above, for details. See below on how to get to Pavones from the Golfito airport.

By Bus   There are two buses (☎ 506/775-0365) to Pavones from Golfito daily at 10am and 3pm. Trip duration is 3 hours; the fare is $2. Buses to Golfito depart Pavones daily at 5am and 1pm. This is a very remote destination, and bus schedules are frequently subject to change, so it always pays to check in advance.

By Car   If you have a four-wheel-drive vehicle, you should be able to get to Pavones even in the rainy season, but be sure to ask in Golfito before leaving the paved road. The turnoff for Playas Zancudo and Pavones is at El Rodeo, about 2$^{1}/_{2}$ miles (4km) outside of Golfito, on the road in from the Interamerican Highway. Pretty quickly after the turnoff, you'll have to wait and take a small diesel-operated crank ferry (the fare is $2 per vehicle). A four-wheel-drive taxi from Golfito to Pavones will cost between $30 and $40. It takes around 2 hours.

ACCOMMODATIONS & DINING

Right in Pavones, there are several very basic lodges catering to itinerant surfers and renting rooms for between $10 and $20 per night for a double room. There are also a couple of *sodas* where you can get Tico meals. The most popular of these is **Esquina del Mar,** which is located right on the beach's edge, in front of the fattest part of the surf break.

Casa Impact. Apdo. 133, Golfito. ☎ **561/683-1429** in the U.S., or 506/775-0637. 3 units, none with bathroom. $10 per person, $38 per person with 3 meals daily. No credit cards.

Casa Impact is a favorite with itinerant surfers. The hotel is composed of two octagonal houses with simple rooms on the second floor and a communal bathroom on the ground floor. Actually, one of the houses has just one bedroom, so in effect you have a private bathroom. Most of the clientele are surfers, as is owner Ted Margraff, and, of course, there are surfboards for rent. Meals are well prepared and filling, and include fresh juices, pizzas, and freshly baked breads and cakes. The communal sitting room features a small library and satellite TV. Casa Impact is located about 46 meters (50 yd.) inland from the main road, about 1 mile (1.6km) south of the village of Pavones.

Casa Siempre Domingo. Apdo. 91, Golfito. Fax **506/775-0631.** www.casa-domingo.com. E-mail: yapada@racsa.co.cr. 4 units. $120 double. Rate includes breakfast and dinner. No credit cards.

This hillside bed-and-breakfast offers up the nicest accommodations right in Pavones. The rooms all feature high ceilings, tile floors, and two double beds (one room has two doubles and a twin). The high beds are custom-made constructions. The owner says the design helps capture every bit of breeze from the picture windows. Meals are served on picnic tables in the large interior common space, and there is also a separate sitting room with satellite TV. The nicest feature is the huge deck, with its ocean view. Casa Siempre Domingo is located several hundred meters/yards south and then several hundred more uphill from downtown Pavones.

◯ **Tiskita Jungle Lodge.** Apdo. 1195-1250, Escazú. ☎ **506/233-1511.** Fax 506/ 233-6890. www.tiskita-lodge.co.cr. E-mail: info@tiskita-lodge.co.cr. 14 units. $355 for 2 days/ 2 nights; $560 for 3 days/3 nights. Package prices are per person, based on double occupancy and including round-trip air transportation from Golfito or Puerto Jiménez, all meals, guided walks, and taxes. AE, MC, V.

This small lodge is nearly on the Panamanian border, with the beach on one side and rain-forest–clad hills behind. Originally an experimental fruit farm growing exotic tropical fruits from around the world, Tiskita has also become a great place to get away from it all. The lodge itself is set on a hill a few hundred yards from the beach and commands a superb view of the ocean. There's a dark-sand swimming beach, tide pools, jungle waterfalls, a farm and forest to explore, and great bird-watching (285 species have been sighted). The newest addition is a small refreshing pool set on a high patch of ground just off the main lodge. Of the 400 acres here, 250 are in primary rain forest, while the rest are in secondary forest, reforestation projects, orchards, and pastures.

Accommodations are in deluxe rustic cabins with screen walls and verandas. Constructed of local hardwoods, the cabins have a very tropical feel. If you're a bird-watcher, you can just sit on the veranda and add to your life list. My favorite cabin is no. 6, which has a great view and ample deck space. Some of the cabins have two or three rooms, making them great for families, but less private for couples. Most of the bathrooms are actually outdoors, although private and protected, allowing you to take in the sights and sounds as you shower and shave. Meals are served family style in the open-air main lodge. While they're not fancy, they're certainly tasty and filling, and you'll be eating plenty of ingredients straight from the gardens.

The lodge is well over 8 hours from San José by car, so most guests take advantage of the package tours, which include air transportation to Tiskita's private landing strip. If you've already driven all the way to Pavones, Tiskita is only $3^3/_4$ miles (6km) farther down the road.

The Caribbean Coast 9

Costa Rica's Caribbean coast feels a world apart from the rest of the country. The pace is slower, the food is spicier, the tropical heat more palpable, and the rhythmic lilt of patois and reggae music fill the air.

Although this was the coast Christopher Columbus landed on in 1502 and christened Costa Rica (Rich Coast), it has until recently remained terra incognita. It was not until 1987 that the Guápiles Highway opened between San José and Limón. Before that, the only routes down to this region were the famous jungle train (which is no longer in operation) and the narrow winding road from Turrialba to Siquírres. More than half of this coastline is still inaccessible except by boat or small plane. This inaccessibility has helped preserve large tracts of virgin lowland rain forest, which are now set aside as **Tortuguero National Park** and **Barra del Colorado National Wildlife Refuge.** These two parks, on the northern reaches of this coast, together form one of Costa Rica's most popular destinations with adventure and eco-travelers. Of particular interest are the sea turtles that nest along this stretch of coast. Another popular national park in this area is in Cahuita, a beach town. It was set up to preserve 500 acres of coral reef, but its palm-tree–lined beaches are stunning.

So remote was the Caribbean coast from Costa Rica's population centers in the Central Valley that it developed a culture all its own. The original inhabitants of the area included people of the Bribri, Cabécar, and Kéköldi tribes, and these groups maintain their cultures on indigenous reserves in the Talamanca Mountains. In fact, until the 1870s, there were few non-Indians in this area. However, when Minor Keith built the railroad to San José and began planting bananas, he brought in black laborers from Jamaica and other Caribbean islands to lay the track and work the plantations. These workers and their descendants established fishing and farming communities up and down the coast. Today dreadlocked Rastafarians, reggae music, Creole cooking, and the English-based patois of this Afro-Caribbean culture give this region a distinctly Jamaican flavor. Many visitors find this striking contrast with the Spanish-derived Costa Rican culture fascinating.

Over the past few years, the Caribbean coast has garnered a reputation as being a dangerous, drug-infested zone, rife with crime and danger. Part of this reputation is deserved, as there have been several high-profile crimes, and drugs such as marijuana, cocaine, and crack are rather readily available in Limón and at the beach towns here.

However, part of this reputation is exaggerated. The same crime and drug problems exist in San José and some of the more popular beach destinations on the Pacific coast. Use common sense and take normal precautions, and you should have no problems on the Caribbean coast.

1 Barra del Colorado

71 miles (115km) NE of San José

Named for its location at the mouth of the Río Colorado up near the Costa Rica–Nicaragua border, Barra del Colorado is an isolated little town, accessible only by boat or small plane. There are no roads in or to Barra del Colorado. The town itself is a small ramshackle collection of raised stilt houses, and supports a diverse population of Afro-Caribbean blacks, Miskito Indians, Nicaraguan emigrants, and transient commercial fishermen.

Visitors come here for the fishing. Tarpon and snook fishing are world-class; if this doesn't keep you busy, you can head farther offshore for some deep-sea action. Barra del Colorado shares its ecosystem with Tortuguero (see below) and, as in Tortuguero, you will find a wide abundance of wildlife and rain-forest fauna in the rivers and canals, which are accessible only by small boat. It's hot and humid here most of the year, and it rains a lot, so while some of the lodges have at times risked offering a "tarpon guarantee," they're generally hesitant to promise anything in terms of the weather.

ESSENTIALS

GETTING THERE & DEPARTING   **By Plane**   **Sansa** (☎ **506/221-9414**) has a daily flight departing at 6am for Barra del Colorado from San José's Juan Santamaría International Airport. The return flight to San José leaves Barra del Colorado daily at 6:45am. Flight duration is 35 minutes; the fare is $50 each way.

Most folks come here on multiday fishing packages, and most of the lodges in this area either operate charter flights as part of their package trips or will book you a flight.

By Boat   It is also possible to travel to Barra del Colorado by boat from **Puerto Viejo de Sarapiquí** (see chapter 6). Expect to pay $200 to $250 each way for a boat that holds up to 10 people. Check at the public dock in Puerto Viejo de Sarapiquí or ask at the Hotel El Bambú if you're interested. **Río Colorado Lodge** (☎ **800/243-9777** in the U.S. and Canada, or 506/232-4063 in Costa Rica) runs a 34-foot launch, *Colorado Queen*, between Barra del Colorado and Puerto Viejo de Sarapiquí (and sometimes between Barra and Limón), including land transportation between Puerto Viejo de Sarapiquí and San José. If you're staying at the Río Colorado Lodge, be sure to ask about this option (for at least one leg of your trip) when booking; the hotel doesn't discriminate—you can arrange transportation even if you aren't staying there. For $196 per person, you can arrange a pickup in San José, a minibus to the boat, a trip down the river to Barra, overnight accommodations at Río Colorado Lodge, and a return trip the next day, all meals and taxes included.

ORIENTATION   The Río Colorado neatly divides the town of Barra del Colorado in two. The airstrip is on the southern half of town, as are most of the lodgings. The lodges that are farther up the canals will meet you in a small boat at the airstrip.

The Caribbean Coast

0   50 Miles

0   50 Kilometers

Caribbean Sea

NICARAGUA

Río San Juan

Río Chirripó

Barra del Colorado Airport
Barra del Colorado
Boca del Río Colorado

Río Colorado

Barra del Colorado National Wildlife Refuge

Boca del Río Tortuguero

Tortuguero
Tortuguero Airport

Tortuguero National Park

To Puerto Viejo de Sarapiquí

Cariari

Río Frío

Tortuguero Canal

Río Reventazón

Río Pacuare

Boca del Río Pacuare

32 Guapiles

Braulio Carrillo National Park

Turrialba Volcano △

Guayabo National Monument

Siquírres

Playa Bonita

Moín Limón

Limón Airport

△ Irazú Volcano

CENTRAL RANGE

Turrialba

Paraiso

Tapantí National Wildlife Refuge

Río Chirripó Atlántico

Chirripó National Park

Playa Cahuita

36 Cahuita National Park

Cahuita

Puerto Viejo

BriBri

Punta Uva

Cerro de la Muerte

Cerro Chirripó

Talamanca Indian Reservation

TALAMANCA RANGE (CORDILLERA DE TALAMANCA)

San Isidro de El General

Hitoy-Cerere Biological Reserve

Bribri Indian Reservation

Gandoca-Manzanillo National Wildlife Refuge

PANAMA

FISHING, FISHING & MORE FISHING

Almost all of the lodges here specialize in fishing and fishing packages. If you don't fish, you might wonder just what in the world you are doing here. Even though there are excellent opportunities for bird-watching and touring the jungle waterways, most lodges are still merely paying lip service to ecotourists and would rather see you with a rod and reel.

Fishing takes place year-round. You can do it in the rivers and canals, in the very active river mouth, or offshore. Most anglers come in search of the tarpon, or silver king. **Tarpon** can be caught year-round, both in the river mouth and to a lesser extent in the canals, but for some reason they seem to take a little time off in July and August—the two rainiest months. And, while you might see plenty of tarpon actually rolling on their sides on the surface, they don't seem to bite very much right around the full moon. **Snook,** an aggressive river fish, peak in April, May, October, and November, while fat snook, or **calba,** run heavy from November through January. Depending how far out to sea you venture, you might hook up with **barracuda, jack, mackerel (Spanish and king), wahoo, tuna, dorado, marlin,** or **sailfish.** In the rivers and canals, fishermen regularly bring in **mojarra, machaca,** and **guapote** (rainbow bass). Following recent developments in fishing, anglers have been using traditional rod-and-reel setups, as well as fly rods, to land just about all the fish mentioned above. To fish here, you'll need both salt- ($30) and fresh- ($10) water fishing licenses. Most lodges include these in your packages or can readily provide the licenses for you. **Nonfishers** should see if their lodge has a good naturalist guide and/or canoes or kayaks for rent or use.

ACCOMMODATIONS & DINING

As I said, almost all of the hotels here specialize in package tours, including all your meals, fishing and tackle, taxes, and usually your liquor too, so rates are high. **Tarponland,** a funky collection of cabinas, closed in early 2000. It's likely that someone will either reopen this hotel or open a new option to fill this void, but to date, Barra remains a remote and difficult destination for independent and budget travelers.

VERY EXPENSIVE

Río Colorado Lodge. P.O. Box 5094-1000, San José. ☎ **800/243-9777** in the U.S. and Canada, or 506/232-4063 in Costa Rica. Fax 506/231-5987. www.riocoloradolodge.com. E-mail: tarpon@racsa.co.cr. 19 units. $1,717 per person for 7 days/6 nights/4 full days of fishing, including 2 nights' lodging in San José, all meals at the lodge, boat, guide, fuel, licenses, and taxes. Nonfishing guests $90 per person per day. AE, MC, V.

This rustic old lodge was founded and built more than 25 years ago by local legend Archie Fields. It continues to be one of the principal fishing lodges in Costa Rica. The rooms are comfortable but rustic, with some showing the wear and tear of the years. Several rooms have air-conditioning and/or televisions, and two are wheelchair accessible. There's even a "honeymoon suite," which is basically a standard room with a small mirror hung by ropes over the bed. As at Silver King Lodge, the whole complex is tied together by covered walkways. The most disappointing aspect for me here is the sad little zoo, which houses a wide range of local birds and mammals in small chicken-wire cages.

Dining/Diversions: The nicest feature is the large bar and dining area out by the river, where breakfast is served. Dinner is served family style in the second-floor dining room. There's also a large bar (where lunch is served), with satellite TV, pool table, and dartboard, as well as a conference room and well-stocked tackle shop.

Amenities: This lodge runs the *Colorado Queen* riverboat (see above) for those interested in cruising either to Puerto Viejo de Sarapiquí or Limón, as well as several other smaller launches for a variety of tours and outings. Laundry service, free coffee service all day, and free rum and soft drinks during happy hour.

✪ **Silver King Lodge.** Mailing address in the U.S.: Interlink 399, P.O. Box 02-5635, Miami, FL 33102. ☎ **800/847-3474** or 800/309-8125 in the U.S., 506/381-1403 in Costa Rica. Fax 506/381-0849. www.silverkinglodge.com. E-mail: slvrkng@racsa.co.cr. 10 units. $2,195 per person double occupancy for 4 full days of fishing, air transportation to and from Barra del Colorado from San José, all meals at the lodge, liquor, taxes, and up to 2 nights' lodging in San José; $435 per person per day, including all fishing, meals, liquor, and taxes. AE, MC, V.

This is by far the most luxurious lodge in Barra del Colorado. They take their fishing seriously here—there's a large selection of modern boats and equipment, as well as a full tackle shop—but Silver King also emphasizes comfort. The rooms are immense, with two double beds, desk and chair, luggage racks, fishing racks, an overhead fan, and a roomy closet. The floors and walls are all varnished hardwood, and the ceilings are finished in bamboo. The entire complex is built on raised stilts and connected by covered walkways (useful during one of the frequent downpours).

Dining/Diversions: The meals are truly exceptional, by far the best buffet-style lodge cooking I've ever had. Each all-you-can-eat meal is anchored with at least two main dishes and a wide variety of appetizers, salads, side dishes, and dessert. You should be eating plenty of fish during your stay—coconut-battered snook nuggets with a pineapple-wasabi dip was just one of the highlights of my culinary indulgences here. There's a comfortable bar with 24-hour-a-day service (self-service during the very off-hours), and a large satellite TV. All soft drinks, local beers, and local liquors are free, as is wine with dinner; there's a small charge for all call or specialty liquor.

Amenities: Silver King provides free daily laundry service. There's also an enclosed Jacuzzi and a small outdoor swimming pool, for those brief breaks between eating, drinking, and fishing.

MODERATE

Samay Lagoon Lodge. (Apdo. 12,767-1000, San José), Barra del Colorado. ☎ **506/384-7047.** Fax 506/383-6370. www.samay.com. E-mail: info@samay.com. 22 units. $278 per person for 3 days/2 nights, including ground and boat transportation to and from San José, meals, taxes, and several tours. AE, MC, V.

This is the only lodge in the Barra del Colorado area that doesn't specifically cater to hard-core fishermen. You can fish here, but Samay Lagoon Lodge is geared more toward backpackers and ecotourists, and is quite popular with European budget travelers and student groups. The hotel is actually about halfway between Barra and Tortuguero on a small spit of land between its namesake lagoon and the Caribbean Sea. The rooms come in a variety of shapes and sizes. The beds are all just soft foam mattresses, but they have mosquito netting. There is a separate lounge, dining room, and bar where buffet-style meals are served. The lodge has 12 canoes and several boats for tours, and overnight trips into Nicaragua are available. If that's all too active for you, there are plenty of hammocks for just hanging out.

2 Tortuguero National Park

155 miles (250km) NE of San José; 49 miles (79km) N of Limón

"Tortuguero" comes from the Spanish name for the giant sea turtles (*tortugas*) that nest on the beaches of this region every year from mid-February to mid-October. The chance to see this nesting attracts many people to this remote region, but just as many come to explore the intricate network of jungle canals that serve as the main transportation arteries. This stretch of coast is connected to Limón, the Caribbean coast's only port city, by a series of rivers and canals that parallel the sea, often running only 91 meters (100 yd.) or so from the beach. This aquatic highway is lined for most of its length with a dense rain forest that is home to howler and spider monkeys, three-toed sloths, toucans, and great green macaws. A trip up the canals is like cruising the Amazon but on a much smaller scale.

Remember the climate in this region: more than 200 inches of rain annually, so you can expect a downpour at any time of the year. Most of the lodges in the area will provide you with sturdy rain gear (including ponchos and rubber boots) but it can't hurt to carry your own.

Independent travel is difficult in this area. You'll have to rely on your lodge for boat transportation through the canals, and unless you stay at one of the accommodations on the beach side of the canal, you won't even be able to walk into town. At most of the lodges around Tortuguero, everything (bus rides to and from, boat trips through the canals, even meals) is done in big groups.

ESSENTIALS

GETTING THERE & DEPARTING **By Plane** **Travelair** (☎ **506/220-3054;** fax 506/220-0413; E-mail: reservations@travelair-costarica.com) has one flight departing daily at 6:45am for Tortuguero from Tobías Bolaños International Airport in Pavas. The flight takes 30 minutes; the fare is $51 one-way, $93 round-trip. The return flight leaves Tortuguero daily at 7:25am for San José.

Sansa (☎ **506/221-9414;** fax 506/255-2176; E-mail: reservations@flysansa.com) has a daily flight departing at 6am for Tortuguero from San José's Juan Santamaría International Airport. Flight duration is 35 minutes; the fare is $50 each way. The return flight leaves Tortuguero daily at 6:45am for San José.

It always pays to check with both Sansa and Travelair. Additional flights are often added during the high season, and departure times can vary according to weather or the whim of the airline.

In addition, many lodges in this area operate charter flights as part of their package trips.

By Car It is not possible to drive to Tortuguero. If you have a car, your best bet is to either leave it in San José and take an organized tour, or drive it to Limón and try to find a secure hotel or public parking lot and then follow the directions for arriving by boat below.

In 1996, local citizens and certain municipal officials began work on a road into Tortuguero, via the village of Cariari. A large swath was cut to within almost 0.6 miles (1km) of the village, with several kilometers of the construction passing through protected parklands. When the project was publicly discovered, it caused a minor local and regional scandal. Work was halted, and several parties are under indictment, but much of the damage is done. There are even road signs declaring TORTUGUERO at the turn-off for Cariari. Ignore them. There is no reliable road route to Tortuguero and probably won't be for some time.

By Boat Flying to Tortuguero is convenient if you don't have much time, but a boat trip through the canals and rivers of this region is often the highlight of any visit to Tortuguero. However, be forewarned: While this trip can be stunning and exciting, it can also be uncomfortable. You'll first have to ride by bus from San José to Limón; then it's 3 hours on a boat, usually with hard wooden benches or plastic seats. All of the more expensive lodges listed offer their own bus and boat transportation packages, which include the boat ride through the canals. However, if you're coming here on the cheap and plan to stay at one of the less-expensive lodges or at a budget cabina in Tortuguero, you will have to arrange your own transportation. In this case, you have a few options.

The most popular method is to get yourself first to Limón and then to the public docks in **Moín** (just north of Limón) and try to find a boat on your own. You can reach Limón easily by public bus (see "Getting There & Departing" in the Limón section, below). If you are coming by car, make sure you drive all the way to Limón or Moín. **Ignore the signs for Tortuguero** that turn off the highway near Guápiles. This will just take you to Cariari, a very secondary and infrequent embarkation point for boats to Tortuguero Village.

To get to the docks from Limón, there's a bus that runs from a stop in front of the prominent Radio Casino building, 1 block north of Limón's central market; it costs 35¢. Otherwise, you can take a taxi for around $3 (for up to four people). Once at the docks, you should be able to negotiate a fare of between $40 and $70, depending on how many people you can round up to go with you. These boats tend to depart between 8am and 10am every morning. Usually, the fare you pay covers the return trip as well, and you can arrange with the captain to take you back when you're ready to leave. Search out **Modesto Watson** (☎ **506/226-0986;** www.tortuguerocanals.com; E-mail: fvwatson@racsa.co.cr), who owns a boat named after his wife, Francesca. The couple offers overnight and multiday packages to Tortuguero. They've been doing this for a long time and are wonderful guides. The trip from **Moín** to Tortuguero takes between 3 and 4 hours. **Laura's Tropical Tours** (☎ **506/758-2410**) also offers boat tours to Tortuguero from Moín.

As I mentioned above, it is possible to get to Tortuguero by bus and boat from Cariari. This is in fact the cheapest and most adventurous means of reaching Tortuguero from San José, however it is also the least dependable. There is only one boat per day from Cariari to Tortuguero, and if you miss it or it doesn't run that day, you'll have to spend the night at some very basic cabinas in this small town, or head back toward Guápiles. To take this route, begin by catching the 9am direct bus to Cariari from the **Gran Terminal del Caribe,** on Calle Central, 1 block north of Avenida 11 (☎ **506/222-0610**). The fare is $2. In Cariari, take the noon bus to "La Geest Casa Verde." The fare is 50¢. Take this bus to the very end of the line. Tell the driver you are going to Tortuguero. A boat should be waiting to meet the bus at the dock at the edge of the river at around 1:30pm. The fare to Tortuguero is $10. This boat leaves Tortuguero every morning at 7am and makes all the return bus connections. If you have doubts, or want to check on the current state of this route, call the new **information center** in Tortuguero at ☎ 506/392-3201.

Finally, it's also possible, albeit expensive, to travel to Tortuguero by boat from **Puerto Viejo de Sarapiquí** (see chapter 6). Expect to pay $250 to $350 each way for a boat that holds up to 10 people. Check at the public dock in Puerto Viejo de Sarapiquí or ask at the Hotel El Bambú if you're interested. The ride usually takes about 3 to 4 hours and the boats tend to leave in the morning.

ORIENTATION   Tortuguero is one of the most remote locations in Costa Rica. There are no roads into this area and no cars in the village, so all transportation is by boat or foot. Most of the lodges are spread out over several kilometers to the north of the village of Tortuguero on either side of the main canal; the small airstrip is at the north end of the beachside spit of land. At the far northern end of the main canal you'll see the **Cerro de Tortuguero** (Turtle Hill), which, at some 350 feet, towers over the area. The hike to the top of this hill is a popular half-day tour and offers some good views of the Tortuguero canals and village, as well as the Caribbean Sea.

Tortuguero Village is a tiny collection of houses connected by footpaths. The village is spread out on a thin spit of land, bordered on one side by the Caribbean Sea and on the other by the main canal. At most points, it's less than 300 meters (327 yd.) wide. In the center of the village you'll find a small children's playground and a soccer field, as well as a kiosk that has information on the cultural and natural history of this area.

If you stay at a hotel on the ocean side of the canal, you will be able to walk into and explore the town at your leisure, whereas if you're across the canal, you'll be dependent on the lodge's boat transportation. However, some of the lodges across the canal have their own network of jungle trails that may appeal to naturalists.

EXPLORING THE NATIONAL PARK

According to existing records, Tortuguero National Park has hosted sea turtles since at least 1592, largely due to its extreme isolation. Over the years, turtles have been captured and their eggs harvested by local settlers, but it wasn't until the 1950s that this practice became so widespread that the turtles faced extinction. Regulations controlling this mini-industry were passed in 1963, and in 1970 Tortuguero National Park was established. Today, four different species of sea turtles nest here: the green turtle, the hawksbill, the loggerhead, and the giant leatherback. The prime nesting period is from mid-June to mid-October (with August and September being the peak months). The park's beaches are excellent places to watch sea turtles nest, especially at night. Appealingly long and deserted, however, the beaches are not appropriate for swimming. The surf is usually very rough, and the river mouths have a nasty habit of attracting sharks that feed on the turtle hatchlings and many fish that live here.

Green turtles are perhaps the most common turtle found in Tortuguero, so you're more likely to see one of them than any other species if you visit during the prime nesting season. **Loggerheads** are very rare, so don't be disappointed if you don't see one. Perhaps the most spectacular sea turtle to watch laying eggs is the **giant leatherback.** The largest of all turtle species, the leatherback can grow to 6¹/₂ feet long and weigh well over 1,000 pounds. It nests from mid-February to mid-April, predominantly in the southern part of the park.

You can also explore the park's rain forest, either by foot or by boat, and look for some of the incredible varieties of wildlife that live here: jaguars, anteaters, howler monkeys, collared and white-lipped peccaries, some 350 species of birds, and countless butterflies, among others. There are several trails that branch out from the park entrance.

ENTRY POINT, FEES & REGULATIONS   The Tortuguero National Park entrance and ranger station are at the south end of Tortuguero Village. Admission to

---

Turtle Tips

- Visitors to the beach at night must be accompanied by a licensed guide. Tours generally last around 2 hours.
- Sometimes you must walk quite a bit to encounter a nesting turtle. Wear sneakers or walking shoes, rather than sandals. The beach is very dark at night and it's easy to trip or step on driftwood or other detritus.
- Wear dark clothes. White T-shirts are not permitted.
- Flashlights, cameras, and video cameras are prohibited on turtle tours.
- Smoking is prohibited on the beach at night.

the park is $6. A 4-day pass can be purchased for $10. However, there are some caveats: Most people visit Tortuguero as part of a package tour. Be sure to confirm whether or not the park entrance is included in the price. Moreover, only certain canals and trails leaving from the park station are actually within the park. Many hotels and private guides take their tours to a series of canals that border the park, and are very similar in terms of flora and fauna, but don't require a park entrance. When the turtles are nesting, you will have to arrange a night tour in advance either with your hotel or one of the private guides working in town. These guided tours generally run between $10 and $15 and include admission to the park. Flashlights and flash cameras are not permitted on the beach at night, since the lights discourage the turtles from nesting.

ORGANIZED TOURS   Most visitors come to Tortuguero on an organized tour. All of the lodges listed below, with the exception of the most budget accommodations in Tortuguero Village, offer complete package tours that include various hikes and night tours, and this is generally the best way to visit the area. For rates, see the individual lodge listings below. In addition, there are several San José–based tour companies that offer budget 2-day/1-night excursions to Tortuguero, which include transportation, all meals, and limited tours around the region. Prices for these trips range between $100 and $200 per person, and—depending on price—guests are lodged either in one of the basic hotels in Tortuguero Village or one of the nicer lodges listed below. There are even 1-day trips that allow time for a quick tour of the canals and lunch in Tortuguero. These trips are good for travelers who like to be able to say, "Been there, done that," and generally run between $80 and $95 per person. Companies offering these excursions include **Ecole Travel** (☎ **506/223-2240;** E-mail: ecolecr@racsa.co.cr), **Caño Blanco Marina** (☎ **506/256-9444**), and **Arenas Tours** (☎ **506/221-6839**). However, if you really want to experience Tortuguero, I recommend staying for at least 2 nights and booking directly with one of the lodges.

BOAT CANAL TOURS   Aside from watching the turtles nest, the unique thing to do in Tortuguero is tour the canals by boat. Most of the lodges can arrange a canal tour for you, but you can also arrange a tour through one of the operators in Tortuguero Village. I recommend **Ernesto Castillo,** who can be reached through Cabinas Sabina or by just standing anywhere in the village and shouting his name— Tortuguero's that small. **Daryl Loth** (☎ **506/392-3201;** E-mail: safari@racsa.co.cr), who runs a small B&B in the center of the village, and **Albert Taylor,** who can be reached through Cabinas Miss Junie (☎ **506/710-0523**), are also good. If none of these guides is available, ask for a recommendation at **Paraiso Tropical Gift Shop** (no phone) or at the **Caribbean Conservation Corporation's Museum** (☎ **506/ 710-0547**). Most guides charge between $10 and $15 per person for a tour of the canals. If you travel through the park, you'll also have to pay the park entrance fee ($6 per person). Expect to pay around $10 per person for a night tour of the canals.

EXPLORING THE TOWN

The most popular attraction in town is the small **Caribbean Conservation Corpora- tion's Visitors' Center and Museum** (☎ **506/710-0547;** E-mail: ccc@cccturtle.org). While the museum has information and exhibits on a whole range of native flora and fauna, its primary focus is on the life and natural history of the sea turtles. Most vis- its to the museum include a short informative video on the turtles. There is a small gift shop here, and all the proceeds go toward conservation and turtle protection. The museum is open daily from 10am to noon and 2 to 5pm. On Sunday the museum is open only from 2 to 5pm. There's a $1 admission charge, but more-generous donations are encouraged. There's also a new information center in town across from the Catholic church. This is a good place to go if you're desperate for an Internet connection and E-mail services.

In the village, you can also rent dugout canoes, known in Costa Rica as *cayucos* or *pangas*. Be careful before renting and taking off in one of these; they tend to be heavy, slow, and hard to maneuver, and you may be getting more than you bargained for.

There are a couple of souvenir shops on the main footpath near the center of the village. The **Jungle Shop** (no phone) donates 10% of its profits to local schools and is open from 9am to 5pm. **Paraiso Tropical Gift Shop** (no phone) is open from 8:30am to 6pm.

ACCOMMODATIONS & DINING

Although the room rates below appear quite high, keep in mind that they usually include round-trip transportation from San José (which amounts to approximately $100 per person), all meals, and taxes. When broken down into nightly room rates, most of the lodges are really only charging between $40 and $80 for a double room.

Most visitors take all their meals, as part of a package, at their hotel. There are a couple of simple *sodas* and local restaurants in town. The best of these is **La Caribeña** (no phone). There's also a nice little coffee shop, **The Vine** (no phone), just across from The Jungle Shop.

EXPENSIVE

✪ **Tortuga Lodge.** Tortuguero (Apdo. 6941-1000, San José). ☎ **506/257-0766** or 506/222-0333. Fax 506/257-1665. www.costaricaexpeditions.com. E-mail: costaric@expeditions.co.cr. 24 units. $578 double for 2 days/1 night; $758 double for 3 days/2 nights. Rates include round-trip transportation (bus and boat one-way, charter flight the other) from San José, taxes, and 3 meals daily. AE, MC, V.

This is Costa Rica Expeditions' oldest hotel, but thanks to several years of renovations and additions, it's not only aged well, but improved with time. The nicest feature here is the long multilevel deck, where you can sit and dine, sip a cool tropical drink, or just take in the view as the water laps against the docks at your feet. There's also a new pool, built to create the illusion that it blends into Tortuguero's main canal. All the rooms are considered standards, with one double and one single bed, ceiling fans, and a comfortable private bathroom. I'd opt for the second-floor rooms, which feature varnished wood walls and floors and come with a small covered veranda. Despite the high rates (considerably higher than at other area lodgings), the rooms are not substantially larger or more luxurious than those at the Mawamba, Laguna, or Pachira lodges; what you're paying for is all the years of experience that Costa Rica Expeditions brings to Tortuguero. Service here is generally quite good, as are the meals.

Dining: The meals are much more creative than those you'll find at other lodges in Tortuguero. Although served family style, they go far beyond the typical rice and beans that usually define meals in this region. They include homemade bread and special treats, such as cold fresh-seafood salad.

Amenities: In addition to the small pool, there are several acres of forest behind the lodge, and a few kilometers of trails wind their way through the trees. This is a great place to look for howler monkeys and colorful poison-arrow frogs. Most packages include a couple of different tours, including boat trips through the canals, visits to Tortuguero Village, and trips to see the turtles laying eggs (in season). There are also several optional tours including fishing trips, hikes to Tortuguero Hill, and night hikes.

MODERATE

○ Laguna Lodge. Tortuguero (Apdo. 173-2015, San José). ☎ **506/225-3740.** Fax 506/283-8031. 34 units. $374 double for 2 days/1 night; $468 double for 3 days/2 nights. Rates include round-trip transportation from San José, tours, taxes, and 3 meals daily. AE, DC, MC, V.

This small lodge is a good choice, located 1¼ miles (2km) north of Tortuguero Village, on the ocean side of the main canal (which allows you to walk into town). The rooms are all very attractive, with wood walls, waxed hardwood floors, and tiled bathrooms with screened upper walls to let in air and light. Each room also has a little shared veranda. The large dining room is located on a free-form deck that extends out over the Tortuguero Canal. The restaurant serves up basic family-style meals. Another covered deck, also over the water, is strung with hammocks for lazing away the afternoons. Several covered palapa huts have also been built among the flowering ginger and hibiscus and strung with hammocks. There are two bars, and a large free-form pool with waterfall and Jacuzzi. When I last visited, plans were under way for a butterfly garden and frog-farm. All the standard Tortuguero tours are available.

Mawamba Lodge. Tortuguero (Apdo. 10980-1000, San José). ☎ **506/223-7490** or 506/223-2421. Fax 506/222-5463. www.crica.com/mawamba. E-mail: mawamba@racsa.co.cr. 54 units. $402 double for 2 days/1 night; $504 double for 3 days/2 nights. Rates include round-trip transportation from San José, 3 meals daily, taxes, and some tours. AE, MC, V.

Located about 500 meters (545 yd.) north of Tortuguero Village on the ocean side of the canal, Mawamba is a good choice for anyone who would like to be able to wander this isolated stretch of beach or walk into town at will. Rooms have varnished wood floors, twin beds, hot-water showers, ceiling fans, and verandas with rocking chairs. There are plenty of hammocks around for anyone who wants to kick back, and a beach volleyball court for those who don't. There's also a free-form pool for cooling off, which is a big plus, as the ocean here is generally not suitable for bathing. The gardens are lush and overgrown with flowering ginger, heliconia, and hibiscus.

Breakfast and dinner are served in the poolside open-air Limbo Bar & Grill, while lunch is served in the smaller, screened-in dining room, or Chelonia Restaurant. The family-style meals are above average for Tortuguero, and might include pasta with shrimp or chicken in béchamel sauce. Plus there's usually good, fresh bread. Tours included in the rates include a 4-hour boat ride through the canals and a guided forest hike. There's a small gift shop on the premises and nightly lectures and slide shows that focus on the natural history of this area. Optional tours include a night turtle hike ($10 per person) and fishing trips ($50 per person per hour).

Pachira Lodge. Tortuguero (P.O. Box 1818-1002, San José). ☎ **506/256-7080** or 506/256-6340. Fax 506/223-1119. www.pachiralodge.com. E-mail: paccira@racsa.co.cr. 40 units. $352 double for 2 days/1 night; $478 double for 3 days/2 nights. Rates include round-trip transportation from San José, 3 meals daily, taxes, and tours. AE, MC, V.

The rooms in this new lodge are in a series of buildings perched on stilts and connected by covered walkways in a dense section of secondary forest set in a little bit from the main canal. Each room is spacious and clean, with varnished wood floors, painted wood walls, two double beds, ceiling fans, and plenty of cross-ventilation. The covered walkways come in handy when it rains. Meals are served family style in a large screened-in dining room, and there's even a small gift shop here. Bilingual guides and all the major tour options are available.

INEXPENSIVE

There are several basic lodges in the village of Tortuguero, offering budget lodgings for between $7 and $15 per person. **Cabinas Miss Junie** (☎ **506/710-0523**) and

Cabinas Sabinas (no phone) are the traditional favorites, although the best of this batch is the new **Cabinas Tortuguero** (no phone), located at the south end of the village on the way to the national-park entrance. If you choose one of these, you'll likely be taking your meals at one of the several small *sodas* in town and will have to make your own arrangements for touring the canals or renting a canoe. One new option I expect to be open by press time is the **Casa Luz Denia** (☎ **506/392-3201;** E-mail: safari@racsa.co.cr), a new bed-and-breakfast run by longtime resident and guide Daryl Loth.

El Manati Lodge. Tortuguero, Limón. ☎ and fax **506/383-0330.** 8 units. $30 double. Rate includes breakfast. No credit cards.

For budget travelers looking for some of the trappings of an ecolodge experience, this is a good choice. El Manati is located across the canal from Laguna Lodge, about 1¹⁄₄ miles (2km) north of Tortuguero Village. The owners live here and have slowly built the lodge themselves over the years. They are also very active in a local project to protect the manatees that inhabit these waters. Most of the rooms are fairly basic, with cement floors and floor fans, but they're kept clean and painted. There's even hot water. Some of the cabins have several rooms, with a variety of sleeping arrangements, including bunk beds. These are a good deal for families. Lunch and dinner are available (for $5 and $8, respectively). Canal tours and turtle-watching walks run between $10 and $16 per person, and there are canoes you can rent for $5 per hour. The honor bar is housed in a separate screened-in building and features a dartboard and Ping-Pong table.

3　Limón: Gateway to Tortuguero National Park & Southern Coastal Beaches

99 miles (160km) E of San José; 34 miles (55km) N of Puerto Viejo

It was just offshore from present-day Limón, in the lee of Isla Uvita, that Christopher Columbus is believed to have anchored in 1502, on his fourth and last voyage to the New World. He felt that this was potentially a very rich land and named it Costa Rica (Rich Coast), but it never quite lived up to his expectations. The spot where he anchored, however, has proved over the centuries to be the best port on Costa Rica's Caribbean coast, so his judgment wasn't all bad. It was from here that the first bananas were shipped to North America in the late 19th century. Today, Limón is primarily a rough-and-tumble port city that ships millions of pounds of bananas northward every year.

　Limón is not generally considered a tourist attraction, and I don't recommend it except during Carnaval, or as a logistical stop in a more complex itinerary. Most travelers use it primarily as a gateway to Tortuguero to the north and the beaches of Cahuita and Puerto Viejo to the south. If you do spend some time in Limón, you can take a seat in Parque Vargas along the seawall and watch the city's citizens go about their business. There are even some sloths living in the trees here. Maybe you'll spot them. Take a walk around town if you're interested in architecture. When banana shipments built this port, many local merchants erected elaborately decorated buildings, several of which have survived the city's many earthquakes. There's a certain charm in the town's fallen grace, drooping balconies, rotting woodwork, and chipped paint. Just be careful, particularly after dark and outside of the city center—Limón has earned a reputation for frequent muggings and robberies.

A Fall Festival

The biggest event of the year in Limón, and one of the most fascinating festivals in Costa Rica, is the annual Carnaval, which is held for a week around Columbus Day (Oct 12). For 1 week of the year, languid Limón shifts into high gear for a nonstop bacchanal orchestrated to the beat of reggae, soca, and calypso music. During the revelries, residents of the city don costumes and take to the streets in a dazzling parade of color. In recent years, the central government has tried to rein in Carnaval, citing health and safety concerns, but this hasn't deterred the Limónenses. If you want to experience Carnaval, make hotel reservations early, as they fill up fast.

ESSENTIALS

GETTING THERE & DEPARTING   By Bus   Buses (☎ 506/221-2596) leave San José roughly every half hour daily, between 5am and 7pm from the new Caribbean bus terminal (Gran Terminal del Caribe) on Calle Central, 1 block north of Avenida 11. Trip duration is 2¹/₂ to 3 hours. The buses are either direct or local (*corriente*), and they don't alternate in any particularly predictable fashion. The local buses are generally older and less comfortable and stop en route to pick up passengers from the roadside. I highly recommend taking a direct bus if possible. The fare is $2.50 for the local, $3.50 for the direct.

Buses leave Limón for San José roughly every half hour between 5am and 7:30pm and similarly alternate between local and direct. The bus stop is 1 block east and half a block south of the municipal market. Buses to **Cahuita** and **Puerto Viejo** leave daily at 5, 8, and 10am and 1, 4, and 6pm. The Cahuita/Puerto Viejo bus stop is on Avenida 4, near the Radio Casino building, 1 block north of the municipal market. Buses to **Punta Uva** and **Manzanillo,** both of which are south of Puerto Viejo, leave Limón daily at 6am and 2:30pm, from the same block.

By Car   The Guápiles Highway heads north out of San José on Calle 3 before turning east and passing close to Barva Volcano and through Braulio Carrillo National Park, en route to Limón. The drive takes about 2¹/₂ hours. Alternately, you can take the old highway, which is equally scenic though slower. This highway heads east out of San José on Avenida Central and passes through San Pedro before reaching Cartago. From Cartago on, the road is narrow and winding and passes through Paraiso and Turrialba before descending out of the mountains to Siquírres, where the old highway meets the new. This route will take you around 4 hours, more or less, to get to Limón.

ORIENTATION   Nearly all addresses in Limón are measured from the central market, which is aptly smack-dab in the center of town, or from Parque Vargas, which is at the east end of town fronting the sea. The stop for buses out to Moín and Playa Bonita is located in front of the prominent Radio Casino building, just to the north of the Cahuita/Puerto Viejo bus stop.

ACCOMMODATIONS & DINING

Two of the hotels listed here are actually a few kilometers out of town toward Playa Bonita, and I recommend them over the options you'll find in Limón proper.

Cabinas Cocori. Playa Bonita, Limón. ☎ **506/758-2930.** Fax 506/798-1670. 22 units. $40–$45 double. AE, MC, V.

Located on the water just before you reach Playa Bonita, this hotel commands a fine view of the cove, small beach, and crashing surf. The grounds are in need of landscaping, and the rooms are a bit run-down. A pair of two-story peach-colored buildings house the rooms, most of which are small and basic. Ten rooms have air-conditioning, and a few more even have televisions. Those on the second floor have better sea breezes and views. A long veranda runs along both floors. The restaurant serves basic Tico fare, but has a great setting overlooking the sea.

Hotel Acon. Avenida 3 and Calle 3 (Apdo. 7300-528), Limón. ☎ **506/758-1010.** Fax 506/758-2924. 39 units. A/C TV TEL. $25 double, $30 triple. AE, MC, V.

This older in-town choice is a good bet in Limón. The rooms, all of which are air-conditioned (almost a necessity in this muggy climate), are clean and have two twin beds with bright yellow bedspreads. The architecture and decor could best be described as art-deco decay. The **restaurant** on the first floor just off the lobby is a cool, dark haven on steamy afternoons and features a wide selection of typical Tico and Chinese dishes. Prices range from $2.50 to $10. The second-floor disco is open every night and particularly lively on weekends, so if your room is anywhere near it, don't count on a quiet night.

Hotel Maribu Caribe. Apdo. 623-7300, San José. ☎ **506/758-4543,** 506/758-4010, or 506/253-1838 in San José. Fax 506/758-3541, or 506/234-0193 in San José. 52 units. A/C TEL. $78 double, $88 triple. AE, DC, MC, V.

Located on top of a hill overlooking the Caribbean and built to resemble an Indian village, the Maribu Caribe is a pleasant, if not overly luxurious, choice if you're looking to spend some time in the sun. The hotel is popular with Tico families from San José because it's easy to get to for weekend trips. The guest rooms are in circular bungalows with white-tile floors and varnished wood ceilings. The furnishings are comfortable but a bit old.

The hotel's **restaurant** has the best view in or around Limón. It's built out over the edge of a steep hill, with tide pools and the ocean below. In addition to the formal dining room, there are tables outside on a curving veranda that make the most of the view. Entree prices range from $5 to $20, and the emphasis is on seafood prepared in the continental style. There's a bar here, as well as a bar/snack bar by the pool. The Maribu Caribe can help you with tour arrangements and has a gift shop.

Park Hotel. Avenida 3, between calles 1 and 3 (Apdo. 35), Limón. ☎ **506/758-3476** or 506/798-0555. Fax 506/758-4364. 32 units. $35 double, $45 triple, $55 suite. AE, MC, V.

You can't miss this pastel peach building across the street from the fire station. It's certainly seen better years, but in Limón there aren't too many choices, and this seems to be where I often end up staying. This place is periodically painted (last year it was pink) and spruced up, but the climate and sea breezes really take their toll. Still, part of what makes this hotel memorable is the aging tropical ambiance. Try to see the room you'll be getting before putting any money down. Ask for a room on the ocean side of the hotel because these are brighter, quieter, and cooler than those that face the fire station, although they're also slightly more expensive. The suites are generally kept in much better condition and have private ocean-view balconies, air-conditioning, and

A Nearby Beach: Playa Bonita

If you want to get in some beach time while you're in Limón, hop in a taxi or a local bus and head north a few kilometers to **Playa Bonita,** a small public beach. Although the water isn't very clean and is usually too rough for swimming, the setting is much more attractive than downtown. This beach is popular with surfers.

cable television. The large, sunny **dining room** off the lobby serves standard Tico fare at very reasonable prices.

EN ROUTE SOUTH

Staying at one of the places below is a great way to combine some quiet beach time on the Caribbean coast with a more active ecolodge or bird-watching experience into one compact itinerary.

✪ **Aviarios del Caribe.** Apdo. 569-7300, Limón. ☎ and fax **506/382-1335.** E-mail: aviarios@costarica.net. 6 units. $75 double, $95 junior suite. Rates include full breakfast. AE, MC, V.

If you prefer bird-watching to beaching, this B&B, located on the edge of a small river delta, is the place to stay on this section of the Atlantic coast. As the name implies, birds are important here; the lodge's owners have spotted more than 310 species within the immediate area. You can work on your life list from the lawns, the second-floor open-air dining room and lounge, or a canoe paddling around the nearby canals. This small hotel is surrounded by a private wildlife sanctuary, comprised mainly of the estuary, mangroves, and an uninhabited island, but it also includes several well-groomed forest trails adjacent to the main building. The guest rooms are all large and comfortable and have fans, tile floors, potted plants, fresh flowers, and modern bathroom fixtures. Some rooms also have king-size beds. In the lounge area you'll find an interesting collection of mounted insects, as well as terrariums that house live snakes and poison-arrow frogs. You'll also certainly make friends with Buttercup, the resident three-toed sloth. Only breakfast is served here, so you'll have to take your other meals in Cahuita or at a roadside *soda* along the way. Aviarios is located 5¹/₂ miles (9km) north of Cahuita, just off the main road.

✪ **Selva Bananito Lodge.** P.O. Box 801-1007, San José (mailing address in the U.S.: 850 Juniper Ave., Kellogg, IA 50135). ☎ and fax **506/253-8118,** or 506/284-4278. www. selvabananito.com. E-mail: conselva@racsa.co.cr. 11 units. $160 double; lower in the off-season. Rate includes 3 meals daily and all taxes. No credit cards. You need 4-wheel-drive to get here; otherwise you can call to arrange pickup in Bananito (or San José).

This new nature lodge is a welcome addition to the Caribbean coast, allowing you to combine some rain-forest adventuring with some serious beach time in Cahuita or Puerto Viejo. The individual raised-stilt cabins are all spacious and comfortable, with an abundance of varnished woodwork. Inside you'll find two double beds, a desk and chair, and some fresh flowers, as well as a large private bathroom. Outside, there's a wraparound veranda, with a hammock and some sitting chairs. It all adds up to what I call rustic luxury. Half the cabins have views of the Bananito River and a small valley; the other half have views of the Matama Mountains, part of the Talamanca mountain range.

There are no electric lights at Selva Bananito, but each evening as you dine by candle-light, your cabin's oil lamps are lit for you. Hot water is provided by solar panels. Tasty family-style meals are served in the large, open rancho, which is also a great spot for morning bird-watching. There's a wide range of tours and activities, including rain-forest hikes and horseback rides in the jungle, tree climbing, self-guided trail hikes, and even the opportunity to rappel down the face of a jungle waterfall. The owners are very involved in conservation efforts in this area, and approximately two-thirds of the 2,100 acres here are primary forest managed as a private reserve. You'll need a four-wheel-drive vehicle to reach the lodge, or arrange pickup in Bananito beforehand. You can also arrange to be picked up in San José.

4 Cahuita

124 miles (200km) E of San José; 26 miles (42km) S of Limón; 8 miles (13km) N of Puerto Viejo

Cahuita is a sleepy Caribbean beach village and the first "major" tourist destination you'll reach heading south out of Limón. The boom going on in Puerto Viejo and the beaches south of Puerto Viejo has in many ways passed Cahuita by. Any way you cut it, Cahuita is one of the most laid-back villages you'll find anywhere in Costa Rica. After a short time, you'll find yourself slipping into the heat-induced torpor that affects anyone who ends up here. The few dirt and gravel streets here are host to a languid parade of pedestrian traffic, parted occasionally by a bicycle, car, or bus.

The village traces its roots to Afro-Caribbean fishermen and laborers who settled in this region in the mid-1800s, and today the population is still primarily English-speaking blacks whose culture and language set them apart from other Costa Ricans.

The main reason people come to Cahuita, other than its laid-back atmosphere, is its miles of pristine beaches, which stretch both north and south from town. The southern beaches, the forest behind them, and the coral reef offshore (one of just a handful in Costa Rica) are all part of Cahuita National Park. Silt and pesticides washing down from nearby banana plantations have taken a heavy toll on the coral reefs, so don't expect the snorkeling to be world-class. But on a calm day, it can be pretty good, and the beaches are idyllic every day. It can rain almost any time of year here, but the most dependably dry season is in September and October.

In recent years, the influx of visitors and an apparently robust drug trade have changed the face and feel of this quiet little town. A few notorious crimes against tourists and businesses have had a serious impact here. Local citizens and business owners have responded to the problem and even organized civilian patrols to monitor the park paths during the day (and unlit streets at night). Still, it's highly recommended that you take every possible precaution against robbery and avoid walking alone outside of downtown at night.

ESSENTIALS

GETTING THERE & DEPARTING **By Bus** Express buses (☎ 506/ 257-8129) leave San José daily at 10am, 1:30pm, and 4pm from the new Caribbean bus terminal (Gran Terminal del Caribe) on Calle Central, 1 block north of Avenida 11. The trip's duration is 4 hours; fare is $5. During peak periods, extra buses are often added. However, it's wise to check, as this bus line **(Mepe)** is one of the most fickle. Buses leave from the same station for **Sixaola** at 6am and 3:30pm and currently stop in Cahuita.

Alternatively, you can catch a bus to **Limón** (see the Limón section, above, for details) and then transfer to a Cahuita- or Puerto Viejo–bound bus in Limón. These latter buses leave daily at 5, 8, and 10am and 1, 4, and 6pm from Radio Casino, which is 1 block north of the municipal market. Buses from Limón to Manzanillo also stop in Cahuita and leave daily at 6am and 2:30pm. The trip takes 1¹/₂ hours; the fare is $1.25.

Buses departing **Puerto Viejo** and Sixaola (on the Panama border) stop in Cahuita at approximately 7, 8, 10, and 11:15am and 2, 4, and 5pm en route to San José. However, this schedule is far from precise, so it's always best to check with your hotel. Moreover, these buses are often full, particularly on weekends and throughout the high season. To avoid standing in the aisle all the way to San José, it is sometimes better to take a bus first to Limón and then catch one of the frequent Limón/San José buses. Buses to Limón leave daily at 6:30am, 9am, noon, 3pm, 4:30pm, and 6pm.

Another tactic I've used is to take a morning bus to Puerto Viejo, spend the day down there, and board a direct bus to San José at its point of origin, thereby snagging a seat.

By Car   Follow the directions above for getting to Limón, and as you enter Limón, about 500 meters (545 yd.) from the busiest section of downtown, watch for a paved road to the right (it's just before the railroad tracks). Take this road south to Cahuita, passing the airstrip and the beach on your left as you leave Limón. Alternately, there's a turn-off with signs for Sixaola and La Bomba several miles before Limón. This winding shortcut skirts the city and puts you on the coastal road several miles south of town.

ORIENTATION   There are only about eight dirt streets in Cahuita. The highway runs parallel to the ocean/coast, with three main roads running perpendicular. The northernmost of these bypasses town and brings you to the northern end of Playa Negra. It is marked with signs for the Magellan Inn and other hotels up on this end. The second road in brings you to the southern end of Playa Negra, a half-mile closer to town. Look for signs for Atlantida Lodge. The third road is the main road into town. The village's main street dead-ends at the entrance to the national park (a foot-bridge over a small stream).

Buses usually drop their passengers in front of Coco's Bar, which is still sometimes called Salon Vaz, its legendary prior incarnation. If you come in on the bus and are staying at a lodge on Playa Negra, head out of town on the street that runs between Coco's Bar and the small park. This road curves to the left and continues a mile or so out to Playa Negra.

FAST FACTS   You can wash your clothes at the self-service **Laundromat** in front of Cabinas Vaz (about 1 1/2 blocks south of the former Salon Vaz). One load in the washer or dryer will cost $1.50. The **police station** is located where the road from Playa Negra turns into town. The **post office,** next door to the police station, is open Monday through Friday from 8am to 5pm. If you can't find a **cab** in town, try calling **René** (☎ **506/755-0243**), **Wayne** (☎ **506/755-0078**), or **Dino** (☎ **506/755-0012**).

EXPLORING CAHUITA NATIONAL PARK

On arrival, you'll immediately feel the call of the long scimitar of beach that stretches south from the edge of town. This beach is glimpsed through the trees from Cahuita's sunbaked main street and extends a promise of relief from the heat. While the lush coastal forest and picture-perfect palm lines are a tremendous draw, the park was actually created to preserve the 600-acre coral reef that surrounds it. The reef contains 35 species of coral and provides a haven for hundreds of brightly colored tropical fish. You can walk on the beach itself, or follow the trail that runs through the forest just behind the beach to check out the reef.

The best place to swim is just before or beyond the **Río Peresoso** (Lazy River), several hundred yards inside Cahuita National Park. The trail behind the beach is great for bird-watching, and if you're lucky, you might see some monkeys or a sloth. The loud grunting sounds you hear off in the distance are the calls of howler monkeys, which can be heard from more than a mile away. Nearer at hand, you're likely to hear crabs scuttling amid the dry leaves on the forest floor—there are half a dozen or so species of land crabs living in this region. My favorites are the bright orange-and-purple ones.

The trail behind the beach stretches a little more than 4 miles (6.4km) to the southern end of the park at **Puerto Vargas,** where you'll find a beautiful white-sand beach, the park headquarters, and a primitive campground with showers and outhouses. The reef is off the point just north of Puerto Vargas, and you can snorkel here. However, the nicest coral heads are located several hundred yards offshore, and it's best to have a boat take you out. A 3-hour snorkel trip should cost between $15 and $20 per person with equipment. These can be arranged with any of the local tour companies listed below. Be warned: These trips are best taken when the seas are calm—for safety's sake, for visibility, and for comfort. If you don't dawdle, the hike to Puerto Vargas should take no more than 2 hours each way. Bring plenty of mosquito repellent, as this area can be buggy.

ENTRY POINTS, FEES & REGULATIONS   The in-town park entrance is just over a footbridge at the end of the village's main street. It has bathroom facilities, changing rooms, and storage lockers. This is the best place to enter if you're just interested in spending the day on the beach and maybe taking a little hike in the bordering forest. The main park entrance is at the southern end of the park in Puerto Vargas. This is where you should come if you plan to camp at the park, or if you don't feel up to hiking a couple of hours to reach the good snorkeling spots. The road to Puerto Vargas is approximately 3 miles (5km) south of Cahuita on the left. Officially, admission is $6 per person per day, but the last time I visited, the fee was being collected only at the Puerto Vargas entrance, and it was possible to enter the park from the town of Cahuita with just a voluntary contribution. The park is open from dawn to dusk for day visitors. There is an extra $1.50 per person charge for camping. The 50 campsites at Puerto Vargas stretch along for several kilometers and are either right on, or just a few steps from, the beach. My favorite campsites are those farthest from the entrance. There are basic shower and bathroom facilities at a small ranger station, but these can be a bit far from some of the campsites.

GETTING THERE   By Bus   Your best bet is to get off of a Puerto Viejo– or Sixaola-bound bus at the turnoff for the Puerto Vargas entrance (well marked, but tell the bus driver in advance). The actual guard station/entrance is only about 500 meters (545 yd.) down this road. However, the campsites are several kilometers further on, so it's a long hike with a heavy pack.

By Car   The turnoff for the Puerto Vargas entrance is clearly marked, 4¹/₂ miles (7km) south of Cahuita.

BEACHES & ACTIVE SPORTS OUTSIDE THE PARK

Outside the park, the best place for swimming is **Playa Negra.** The stretch right in front of Atlantida Lodge is my favorite spot.

If you want to take advantage of any organized adventure trips or tours while in Cahuita, there are plenty of options. I recommend **Cahuita Tours and Adventure Center** (☎ **506/755-0232;** fax 506/755-0082), on the village's main street heading out toward Playa Negra. Cahuita Tours offers glass-bottom boat and snorkeling trips ($20 per person), jungle tours ($25), white-water rafting trips ($95), and Jeep tours to the Bribri Reservation ($60). Cahuita Tours has a decent little gift shop and provides international fax and E-mail services. **Turistica Cahuita Information Center** (☎ and fax **506/755-0071**), also on the main road heading toward Playa Negra, and **Roberto Tours** (☎ **506/755-0117**), a block away from Coco's Bar toward the national park, offer similar tours at similar prices. Most of the companies offer multiday trips to Tortuguero, as well as to Bocas del Toro, Panama. **Brigitte** (watch for the sign on Playa Negra) rents horses for $7 per hour (you must have experience) and also offers guided horseback tours for $25 to $35.

Bird-watchers who have cars should head north 5¹/₂ miles (9km) to the ✪ **Aviarios del Caribe Bed-and-Breakfast Lodge** (☎ and fax **506/382-1335**), where guided canoe tours of the Estrella Estuary are available. More than 310 species of birds have been sighted in the immediate area. The $3^1/2$-hour tour costs $30 per person and leaves throughout the day, but it's best to leave very early or very late in the afternoon, and to make reservations in advance. If you would just like to walk the grounds and bird-watch from their covered deck, there's a $5 entrance fee.

SHOPPING

For a wide selection of beachwear, local crafts, cheesy souvenirs, and batik clothing, try **Boutique Coco Miko** or **Boutique Bambata,** which are both on the main road near the entrance to the park. The latter is also a good place to have your hair wrapped in colorful threads and strung with beads. Out toward Playa Negra, similar wares are offered at the gift shop at **Cahuita Tours.** Handmade jewelry and crafts are sold by local and itinerant artisans in makeshift stands near the park entrance.

Ask around town and you should be able to pick up a copy of Paula Palmer's *What Happen: A Folk-History of Costa Rica's Talamanca Coast* (Publications in English, 1993). The book is a history of the region, based on interviews with many of the area's oldest residents. Much of it is in the traditional Creole language, from which the title is taken. It makes fun and interesting reading, and you just might bump into someone mentioned in the book.

ACCOMMODATIONS

✪ **Alby Lodge.** Apdo. 840, Limón. ☎ and fax **506/755-0031.** 4 units. $40 double, $45 triple, $50 quad. Children under 12 stay free in parents' room. No credit cards.

Located about 150 yards down the winding lane to the right just before you reach the park entrance, the Alby Lodge is a fascinating little place hand-built by its German owners. Though the four small cabins are close to the center of the village, they're surrounded by a large lawn and feel secluded. The cabins are quintessentially tropical, with thatched roofs, mosquito nets, hardwood floors and beams, big shuttered windows, tile bathrooms, and a hammock slung on the front porch. You won't find more appealing rooms in this price range. There's no restaurant here, but there is a communal kitchen area if you want to cook your own meals.

Atlantida Lodge. Cahuita, Limón. ☎ **506/755-0115.** Fax 506/755-0213. www.atlantida. co.cr. E-mail: atlantis@racsa.co.cr. 30 units. $55 double, $65 triple or quad; lower in the off-season. AE, MC, V.

This quiet, comfortable retreat has a great location on Playa Negra, amid lush gardens and wide green lawns. The guest rooms are clean and comfortable, with pale-yellow stucco walls, red-tile floors, a ceiling fan, and plenty of bamboo trim. Each room also has a small patio with a bamboo screen divider for privacy, which opens onto the hotel's lush gardens. The continental-style dinners in the open rancho dining room are reasonably priced and well prepared—the lodge is run by French Canadians—but they're available only to hotel guests. There is complimentary coffee offered all day. A host of different tours can be arranged here, from snorkeling to horseback riding to white-water rafting. The beach is right across the street, and the hotel also has a conference room, a small gym, a Jacuzzi, and a nice tile pool. You'll find the Atlantida beside the soccer field on the road to Playa Negra, about a mile (1.6km) out of town.

Cabinas Arrecife. Cahuita (100m/109 yd. east of the post office), Limón. ☎ and fax **506/ 755-0081.** 12 units. $20 double, $25 triple. AE, MC, V.

Located near the water, next to Restaurant Edith (see "Dining," below), this new row of basic rooms is another excellent budget choice in Cahuita. Each room comes with a double and a single bed, table fan, and tile floors. There's not a lot of room to move around, but things are pretty clean and new for this price range. There's a shared veranda with some chairs for sitting, where you can catch a glimpse of the sea through a dense stand of coconut palms. If you want to be closer to the sea, grab one of the hammocks strung on those palms, or sit in the small open restaurant, which serves breakfast every day and dinners according to demand.

Chalet Hibiscus. Apdo. 943, Limón. ☎ **506/755-0021.** Fax 506/755-0015. E-mail: hibiscus@ racsa.co.cr. 7 units. Dec–Apr $40–$50 cabin, $50–$100 house; lower May–Nov. AE, MC, V.

If you're planning a long stay in Cahuita, I advise checking into this place. Although it's about 1¼ miles (2km) from town on the road along Playa Negra, it's well worth the journey. The largest house has two bedrooms and sleeps up to six people. There's hardwood paneling all around, a full kitchen, hot water, red tile floors, a *pila* (washbasin) for doing your laundry, and even a garage. A spiral staircase leads to the second floor, where you'll find hammocks on a balcony that looks over a green lawn to the ocean. The attractive little cabins have wicker furniture and walls of stone and wood. You're a kilometer north of Playa Negra here, but there's a tiny swimming pool for cooling off during the day. The other houses are similarly simple yet elegant, and the setting is serene and beautiful. Be sure to ring the bell outside the gate—there are guard dogs on the grounds. If the houses and cabins here are full, the owner can arrange rentals of similar accommodations nearby. The hotel now has a small second-floor bar, with a good billiards table. There is also a TV room for vegging out, and a volleyball court for getting active.

El Encanto Bed and Breakfast. Apdo. 1234, Limón (just outside of town on the road to Playa Negra). ☎ and fax **506/755-0113.** E-mail: encanto@racsa.co.cr. 5 units. $38 double, $46 triple; lower in the off-season. Rates include full breakfast. MC, V.

The individual bungalows at this new bed-and-breakfast are set in from the road, on spacious and well-kept grounds. The bungalows themselves are equally spacious and have interesting touches such as wooden bed frames, arched windows, Mexican-tile floors, Guatemalan bedspreads, and framed Panamanian molas hanging on the walls. Hearty breakfasts are served in the open dining room.

Jenny's Cabinas. Cahuita, Limón. ☎ **506/755-0256.** Fax 506/755-0096. E-mail: jennys@ racsa.co.cr. 9 units. $20–$30 double; slightly lower during the off-season. No credit cards.

Located 183 meters (200 yd.) straight ahead (toward the water) from the bus stop, Jenny's place has been popular for years, and her newer rooms are some of the best in town in this price range. Best of all, they're right on the water, so you can go to sleep to the sound of the waves. All of the rooms have shuttered windows, and there are sling chairs and hammocks on their porches. The more expensive rooms are on the second floor and have what are arguably the best views around. There's one room in an older building, which, even though it has a big porch and plenty of Caribbean atmosphere, is not quite as nice as the others.

✪ Magellan Inn. Cahuita (Apdo. 1132), Limón. ☎ and fax **506/755-0035.** www.web-span. com/tropinet. E-mail: tropinet@betaweb.com. 6 units. $69 double, $81 triple. Rates include continental breakfast. AE, MC, V.

This small inn is out at the far end of Playa Negra (about 1¼ miles/2km north of Cahuita) and is the most luxurious hotel in the area. The six large rooms are all carpeted and have French doors, vertical blinds, tiled bathrooms with hardwood counters, and two joined single beds. And while there is a ceiling fan over the bed, the rooms could use a bit more ventilation. The rooms also have a spacious tiled veranda with an overhead fan, Persian rug, and bamboo chairs. There is a casually sophisticated combination bar/lounge and sitting room that has more Persian-style rugs and wicker furniture. Most memorable of all are the hotel's sunken pool and garden, both of which are built into a crevice in the ancient coral reef that underlies this entire region—which leads to good bird-watching. Quiet breakfasts are served here, and the sister **restaurant Casa Creole** is just next door.

DINING

Coconut meat and milk figure in a lot of the regional cuisine. Most nights, local women cook up pots of various local specialties and sell them from the front porches of the two discos; a full meal will cost you around $2–$3. For snacks, there's the **Pastry Shop,** a tiny bakery on the left side of the main road as you head toward Playa Negra. The coconut pie, brownies, gingersnaps, banana bread, and corn pudding are all delicious. Prices range from 50¢ to $1.

In addition to the places listed below, **Cha Cha Cha** (☎ 506/755-0232) serves up a tasty mix of Mediterranean-influenced pasta and fresh-seafood dishes, on the main road a few blocks north of Coco's Bar.

✪ **Casa Creole.** Playa Negra Rd., 1¹/₂ miles (2.5km) north of Cahuita. ☎ **506/755-0104.** Reservations suggested during the high season. Main courses $7–$18. MC, V. Mon–Sat 6–9pm. FRENCH/CREOLE.

While the rest of Cahuita may feel like a misplaced piece of Bob Marley's Jamaica, this new restaurant takes its inspiration from islands a little farther south in the Caribbean—and far more French. The restaurant is an outgrowth of the neighboring Magellan Inn. Tables in the open first-floor dining room are set with linen tablecloths and candles in glass lanterns. The building is painted a lively pastel pink, with plenty of painted gingerbread and varnished wood trim. There's a sense of informal elegance about it all. Start with a dish of the pâté maison or a shrimp, coconut, and pineapple cocktail. The spiced shrimp martiniquaise and the jumbo coconut shrimp soup are both excellent, as is the fresh fish seasoned and baked inside a banana leaf. The emphasis here is on seafood, but the ample menu includes meat, chicken, and pasta dishes. Top it off with some fresh raspberry coulis, homemade profiteroles, or exquisite homemade fresh-fruit sherbet.

✪ **Restaurant Edith.** By the police station. ☎ **506/755-0248.** Reservations accepted. Main courses $3.50–$12. No credit cards. Mon–Sat 7am–10pm. CREOLE/SEAFOOD.

This place has become a tradition, and deservedly so. Quite some years ago, Miss Edith decided to start serving up home-cooked meals to all the hungry visitors hanging around. If you want a taste of the local cuisine in a homey sit-down environment, this is the place. While Miss Edith's daughters take the orders, Mom cooks up a storm out back. The menu, when you can get hold of it, is long, with lots of local seafood dishes and Creole combinations such as yucca in coconut milk with meat or vegetables. The sauces here have spice and zest and are a welcome change from the typically bland fare served up throughout the rest of Costa Rica. After you've ordered, it's usually no more than 45 minutes until your meal arrives. It's often crowded here, so don't be bashful about sitting down with total strangers at any of the big tables. Miss Edith's place is at the opposite end of town from the park entrance; just turn right at the police station/ post office. This place is sometimes open on Sunday.

CAHUITA AFTER DARK

Coco's Bar (formerly Salon Vaz), a classic Caribbean bar, has traditionally been the place to spend your nights (or days, for that matter) if you like cold beer and very loud reggae and soca music. **Salon Sarafina,** located just across the street, is giving Coco's a run for its money, and I personally find it slightly nicer and more hospitable. There are usually local women hanging out on the front porches of each establishment, selling fresh pati pies or bowls of rundown stew (see "That Rundown Feeling," later in this chapter). Toward the park entrance, the **National Park Restaurant** (☎ 506/755-0244) has a popular bar and disco most nights during the high season and weekends during the low season. **Sobre Las Olas** (no phone) is a restaurant-bar with a stunning location, just north of town, right on the water. However, it's gone throughowners like wildfire and I can't vouch for the most recent incarnation, yet. If you're looking for a more relaxed jungle atmosphere, check out **Topo's Baum Beiz** (☎ and fax **506/755-0105**), an open-air bar located a couple hundred meters inland from Playa Negra. If you visit during the day, you can tour the owner's frog garden; if you visit at night, you'll hear the amphibian symphony.

5 Puerto Viejo

124 miles (200km) E of San José; 34 miles (55km) S of Limón

Though Puerto Viejo is even smaller than Cahuita, it has a somewhat livelier atmosphere due to the many surfers who come here from around the country (and around the world) to ride the village's famous Salsa Brava wave. For nonsurfers, there are also some good swimming beaches, and if you head still farther south, you will come to the most beautiful beaches on this coast. When it's calm (between August and October), the waters down in this region are some of the clearest anywhere in the country, and there is some good snorkeling among the coral reefs.

This is the end of the line along Costa Rica's Caribbean coast. After the tiny town of Manzanillo, just south of Puerto Viejo, a national wildlife reserve stretches a few final kilometers to the Panamanian border.

You may notice, as you make your way into town from the highway, that there are cacao trees planted along the road. Most of these trees continue to suffer from a blight that has greatly reduced the cacao-bean harvest in the area. However, there is still a modest local harvest, and you can get delicious cocoa candies here.

ESSENTIALS

GETTING THERE & DEPARTING   By Bus   Express buses (☎ 506/257-8129) to Puerto Viejo leave San José daily at 10am, 1:30pm, and 4pm from the new Caribbean bus terminal (Gran Terminal del Caribe) on Calle Central, 1 block north of Avenida 11. The trip's duration is 5 hours; fare is $5.50. During peak periods, extra buses are sometimes added. Always ask if the bus is going into Puerto Viejo (some just drop off passengers at the turnoff for Sixaola), and if it's continuing on to **Manzanillo** (especially helpful if you're staying in a hotel south of town). Regardless, don't be surprised if it doesn't do exactly what you were told.

Buses leave from the same station for **Sixaola** at 6am and 3:30pm, and will leave you at the turnoff for Puerto Viejo (except when they decide to continue into Puerto Viejo) about 3 miles (5km) outside of town. However, be warned: There is not much traffic on this road and no taxi will likely be waiting for you. You will have to hike in, hitchhike, or wait for a bus coming from Limón to stop and pick you up.

Alternately, you can catch a bus to **Limón** (see the Limón section, above, for details) and then transfer to a Puerto Viejo–bound bus in Limón. These latter buses leave daily at 5, 8, and 10am and 1, 4, and 6pm from Radio Casino, which is 1 block north of the municipal market. Buses from Limón to Manzanillo also stop in Puerto Viejo and leave daily at 6am and 2:30pm. The trip takes 1¹/₂ hours; the fare is $1.50.

Express buses leave Puerto Viejo for San José daily at 6:30, 9, and 11am and 4pm. Buses for Limón leave daily at 6 and 9am, and 1, 4, and 5pm. Buses to **Punta Uva** and **Manzanillo** leave Puerto Viejo daily around 7am and 4pm. These buses return from Manzanillo at 8:15am and 5:15pm.

By Car   To reach Puerto Viejo, continue south from Cahuita for another 10 miles (16km). Watch for a prominent fork in the highway. The right-hand fork continues on to Bribri and Sixaola. The left-hand fork (it actually appears to be a straight shot) takes you into Puerto Viejo on 3 miles (5km) of recently paved road.

ORIENTATION   The road in from the highway runs parallel to Playa Negra, or Black Sand Beach, for a couple hundred meters before entering the village of Puerto Viejo, which has all of about six dirt streets. The sea will be on your left and forested hills on your right as you come into town. It's another 9 miles (15km) or so on a rough dirt and gravel road south to Manzanillo.

FAST FACTS   **Public phones** are located at Hotel Maritza, El Pizote lodge, the Manuel Leon general store (next to Johnny's Place), and the ATEC office. The latter is your best bet for **mailing a postcard** and obtaining **visitor information.** The nearest **bank** is in **Bribri,** about 6 miles (10km) away. There is a **Guardia rural police** post near the park on the beach. The town's main **taxi** driver is named **Bull** (☎ 506/750-0112) and he drives a beat-up old Isuzu Trooper. You might find him hanging around the *parquecito* (little park), or ask a local to point you to his house. If Bull's not around or he's busy, you could try **Juan** (☎ 506/750-0141) or **Papa** (☎ 506/750-0325).

WHAT TO SEE & DO

Most people who show up in this remote village have only one thing on their mind: surfing. Just offshore from the tiny village park is a shallow reef where powerful storm-generated waves sometimes reach 20 feet. These waves are the biggest on the Caribbean coast. Even when the waves are small, this spot is recommended only for very experienced surfers because of the danger of the reef. There are also popular beach breaks south of town on Playa Cocles. For swimming, head out to **Playa Negra** (this is not the same one I talked about in Cahuita), along the road into town, or to the beaches south of town around Punta Uva, where the surf is much more manageable.

If you aren't a surfer, the same activities that prevail in Cahuita are the norm here also. Read a book, take a nap, or go for a walk on the beach. If you have more energy, you can rent a bicycle or a horse (watch for signs), or just hike and head south toward Punta Uva. You can either follow the beach or stick to the road. After about 5 miles (8km), you'll be rewarded with some of the nicest beaches on this coast.

The **Asociación Talamanqueña de Ecoturismo y Conservacion (ATEC)** office, across the street from the Soda Tamara (☎ 506/750-0398; ☎ /fax 506/750-0191; www.greencoast.com; E-mail: atecmail@racsa.co.cr), is concerned with preserving both the environment and the cultural heritage of this area and promoting ecologically sound development and tourism in the region. In addition to functioning as the local post office, cyber cafe, and information center, ATEC runs a little shop that sells T-shirts, maps, posters, and books. They also offer quite a few different tours. There are half-day walks that focus on nature and either the local African-Caribbean culture or the indigenous Bribri culture. These walks pass through farms and forests, and along the way you'll learn about local history, customs, medicinal plants, and Indian mythology, and have an opportunity to see sloths, monkeys, iguanas, keel-billed toucans, and other wildlife. There are four different walks through the nearby Bribri Indians' Kéköldi Reserve; there are also more strenuous hikes through the primary rain forest.

ATEC also offers snorkeling trips to the nearby coral reefs, as well as snorkeling and fishing trips in dugout canoes. A half day of snorkeling or fishing will cost around $20 per person. Bird walks and night walks will help you spot more of the area wildlife; there are even overnight treks. The local guides who lead these tours have a wealth of information and make a hike through the forest a truly educational experience. Half-day walks (and night walks) are $15, and a full-day runs between $25 and $40.

ATEC can also help you arrange overnight and multiday camping trips into the Talamanca Mountains and through neighboring indigenous reserves, as well as trips to Tortuguero. Some tours require minimum groups of 5 or 10 people and several days' advance notice. The ATEC office is open Monday through Friday from 7am to 9pm, and Saturday and Sunday from 8am to noon and 4 to 8pm.

One of the nicer ways to spend a day in Puerto Viejo is to visit the local **Botanical Gardens** (☎ 506/750-0046; E-mail: jardbot@racsa.co.cr), located a couple hundred yards inland from the Black Sand Beach on a side road just north of El Pizote lodge. Hosts Peter and Lindy Kring have devoted an equal share of time and love to create this meandering collection of native and imported tropical flora. There are medicinal, commercial, and just plain wild flowering plants, fruits, herbs, trees, and bushes. Visitors get to gorge on whatever is ripe at the moment. There is also a rigorous rain-forest loop trail leaving from the grounds. The gardens are generally open Friday through Monday from 10am to 4pm, but visits can sometimes be arranged for other days with prior notice. Entrance to the garden or loop trail is $3 per person, or $9 including the guided tour.

If you're interested in organized adventure tours to Tortuguero, white-water rafting, horseback riding, or snorkeling, you can check with **Atlantico Tours** (☎ 506/750-0004). Tour options include a 3-day/2-night trip to Bocas del Toro, Panama, which costs around $125 per person, with transportation, lodging, and meals. Day trips into the jungle or snorkeling cost between $30 and $90 per person.

Finally, if you're looking for some body-mind replenishment, check in with **Samasati** (☎ 506/224-1870; fax 506/224-5032; www.samasati.com; E-mail: samasati@samasati.com), a lovely jungle yoga retreat, with spectacular hillside views of the Caribbean sea and surrounding forests. Rates here run around $65 per person per day, all-inclusive. You can also come up for yoga classes ($8), meditations ($5) or private massages ($45) with prior notice. Samasati is located a couple of kilometers before Puerto Viejo (near the turn-off for Bribri) and another half mile (1km) up into the jungle.

MANZANILLO & THE MANZANILLO-GANDOCA WILDLIFE REFUGE

If you continue south on the coast road from Puerto Viejo, you'll come to a couple of even smaller villages. **Punta Uva** is 5 miles (8km) away, and **Manzanillo** is about 9^1/$_4$ miles (15km) away. For a good day trip, you can catch the 7am bus from Puerto Viejo down to Manzanillo and then catch the 5:15pm bus back. Again, it's always wise to check with ATEC about current local bus schedules. Alternatively, it's about 2 hours

---

Factoid

If you're looking to stay in Puerto Viejo for an extended period of time and would like to contribute to the community, you can ask about volunteering at the **Asociación Talamanqueña de Ecoturismo y Conservacion (ATEC)** office (☎ 506/750-0398; ☎/fax 506/750-0191; www.greencoast.com; E-mail: atecmail@racsa.co.cr), across the street from the Soda Tamara.

each way on bicycle, with only two real hills to contend with. However, since the road and most of the bikes rented in town are rather rugged, expect your wrists and rear end to take quite a beating. It's also possible to walk along the beach from Punta Cocles to Manzanillo, a distance of about 6 miles (10km).

Manzanillo is a tiny village with only a few basic cabinas and funky *sodas*. The most popular place to eat and hang out is **Restaurant Maxi** (no phone), an open-air joint located on the second floor of an old wooden building facing the sea. There's no menu here, but a fresh fish plate will cost you between $5 and $7; lobster, in season, will cost around $12. Whatever you order will come with rice and beans, patacones, and a small side of cabbage salad.

The **Manzanillo-Gandoca Wildlife Refuge** encompasses the small village and extends all the way to the Panamanian border. Manatees, crocodiles, and more than 350 species of birds live within the boundaries of the reserve. The reserve also includes the coral reef offshore—when the seas are calm, this is the best snorkeling and diving spot on this entire coast. Four species of sea turtles nest on one $5^{1}/_{2}$-mile-long (8.9km) stretch of beach within the reserve, between March and July.

If you want to explore the refuge, you can easily find the well-maintained trail by walking along the beach just south of town until you have to wade across a small river. On the other side you'll pick up the trailhead. Otherwise you can ask around the village for local guides or check out **Aquamor** (☎ **506/391-3417;** E-mail: aquamor@racsa.co.cr), a kayak and dive operation located on the one main road in town. These folks rent kayaks for $5 per hour, and offer a variety of guided excursions for between $15 and $45 per person. Depending on tides and sea conditions, this is a great way to explore the mangroves and estuaries, visit several nearby beaches, and even snorkel or dive the nearby coral reef. A one-tank beach dive, with equipment and guide, costs $30 per person. They have a whole variety of tour and diving options, including PADI dive certification courses. Aquamor also often has a few kayaks for rent down on the beach at Punta Uva near Selvyns.

SHOPPING

Puerto Viejo attracts a lot of local and international bohemians, who seem to survive solely on the sale of handmade jewelry and painted ceramic trinkets (mainly pipes and cigarette-lighter holders). You'll find them at makeshift stands set up by the town's "little park" or *parquecito,* a few wooden benches in front of the sea between Soda Tamara and Stanford's. **The Jewelry Factory,** across the street from Cabinas Grant (☎ **506/750-0075**), sells hand-painted T-shirts, batik beachwear, and coconut-shell jewelry. Similar wares, as well as a wider selection of Bob Marley memorabilia, can be found at **Boutique Tabu,** located near the Mepe bus stop. There are also a couple of *pulperías* in the village. The **ATEC shop** is a great place to get reading materials relevant to the region. Here, you can usually pick up Paula Palmer's oral history, *What Happen: A Folk-History of Costa Rica's Talamanca Coast* (Publications in English, 1993). If you'd like to learn more about the culture of the local Bribri Indians, look for a copy of *Taking Care of Sibö's Gifts* by Paula Palmer, Juanita Sánchez, and Gloria Mayorga. ATEC itself publishes and sells *Coastal Talamanca, A Cultural and Ecological Guide,* a small booklet packed with information about this area.

ACCOMMODATIONS IN PUERTO VIEJO

In addition to the hotels listed below, true budget hounds will find a host of basic cabinas in downtown Puerto Viejo. Of these, **Hotel Pura Vida** (☎ **506/750-0002;** fax 506/750-0296) and Cabinas **Maritza** (☎ **506/750-0003;** fax 506/750-0313) are your best bets.

MODERATE

El Pizote. (Apdo. 1371-1000, San José), Puerto Viejo, Limón. ☎ **506/750-0227.** Fax 506/750-0088. www.hotels.co.cr/pizote.html. E-mail: pizotelg@racsa.co.cr. 8 units, all with shared bathroom; 6 bungalows; 4 deluxe bungalows. $45 double, $65 double bungalow, $95 double deluxe bungalow. Rates include breakfast. AE, MC, V.

El Pizote changed ownership a couple of years ago and has received a major face-lift. The big change is the addition of a new free-form tile swimming pool and poolside snack bar. There are also four new deluxe bungalows with kitchenettes, two separate bedrooms, and air-conditioning. And while there have been some improvements, the changes have obliterated much of the rustic ambiance of the old hotel. Gone are the unique oversized showerheads and stone paths connected by wooden footbridges. They've been replaced with modern plumbing (including hot water) and far too much concrete.

The most basic rooms are in a U-shaped unpainted wooden building on raised stilts. These rooms are cool, and feature polished wood walls, two double beds, ceiling fans, a shared wraparound veranda, and shared bathroom facilities. The older bungalows are similar in style, but come with their own bathrooms and private verandas. For activity, there are hiking trails in the adjacent forest and a volleyball court. There is good bird-watching here, too. The restaurant serves local cuisine at moderate prices. The bar has a pool table and is popular with locals. El Pizote is directly in front of Black Sand Beach about 274 meters (300 yd.) before you enter downtown Puerto Viejo.

INEXPENSIVE

✪ **Cabinas Chimuri.** Puerto Viejo, Limón. ☎ and fax **506/750-0428.** E-mail: atecmail@racsa.co.cr. 4 units, none with bathroom. $25 double, $40 triple or quad. $10 per person in dormitory. Discounts in the low season. AE, MC, V.

If you're an inveterate camper and don't mind being a 15-minute walk from the beach, I'm sure you'll enjoy this rustic lodge. It's built in traditional Bribri Indian style with thatch-roofed A-frame cabins in a forest setting, a short stroll up a trail from the parking lot to the lodge buildings. (There are other trails on the property as well.) This lodge is definitely for nature lovers and budget travelers who are used to roughing it. Breakfast will cost you $4, and other meals are available with advance notice. In addition to the cabins, there is a dormitory room that sleeps up to eight people in bunk beds. The lodge rents several cabins right on Black Sand Beach for around $15 per person per day, or $195 per week. Chimuri runs several different hiking trips into the rain forest and the adjacent Bribri Indian Kéköldi Reserve ($30 per person). If arriving by bus, be sure to get off at the trail to Cabinas Chimuri before the road reaches the beach.

Cabinas Jacaranda. Puerto Viejo, Limón. ☎ and fax **506/750-0069.** 7 units, 3 with bathroom. $12–$15 double without bathroom, $16–$18 double with bathroom, $20 triple with bathroom. V.

This basic backpackers' special has a few nice touches that set it apart from the others. The cement floors have recently been tiled, Japanese paper lanterns cover the lights, and mosquito nets hang over the beds. Guatemalan bedspreads add a dash of color and tropical flavor, as do the tables made from sliced tree trunks. If you're traveling in a group, you'll enjoy the space and atmosphere of the big room. If the hotel is full, the owners also rent a few nearby bungalows. From the center of town, follow the signs to The Garden Restaurant. If the latter is open, you'll be right next door to one of the best restaurants in town.

✪ **Casa Verde.** Apdo. 1115, Puerto Limón. ☎ **506/750-0015.** ☎ and fax 506/750-0047. www.greencoast.com. E-mail: casaver@hotmail.com. 14 units, 6 with bathroom. $20 double without bathroom, $30 double with bathroom. AE, MC, V.

This little hotel is located on a side street on the south side of town. The older rooms, with shared bathrooms, are in an interesting building with a wide, covered breezeway between the rooms and the showers and toilets out back. The front and back porches of this building are hung with hammocks and surrounded by lush gardens. A quiet sense of tropical tranquillity pervades this place. The newer rooms are behind the house next door and are a bit larger than the older rooms. These new rooms have high ceilings, tile floors, private bathrooms, and a veranda. There is also a small separate bungalow with a kitchenette. Everything is well maintained, and even the shared bathrooms are kept immaculate. Last time I visited, they were building a small coffee shop and souvenir shop.

ACCOMMODATIONS BETWEEN PUERTO VIEJO & MANZANILLO

All of the hotels listed below are located along the road south of Puerto Viejo heading toward Manzanillo. This is one of the most beautiful and isolated stretches of beach you'll find in Costa Rica. However, I recommend that you have a vehicle if you plan to stay at one of these hotels, since public transportation is sporadic.

In addition to the hotels listed below, budget travelers should check out **La Isla** (☎/fax **506/750-0188**), a simple hotel catering to surfers, located at the start of Playa Cocles.

EXPENSIVE

✪ **Shawandha Lodge.** Puerto Viejo, Limón. ☎ **506/750-0018.** Fax 506/750-0037. E-mail: shawanda@racsa.co.cr. 10 units. Dec 15–Apr 15 $90 double; Apr 16–Dec 14 $69 double. Rates include full breakfast. AE, MC, V.

If you're looking for a luxurious, isolated, and romantic getaway, this small collection of individual bungalows is a great choice. Set in a lush patch of forest about 183 meters (200 yd.) inland from Playa Chiquita, Shawandha has the feel of a small village. Artistic flourishes abound. The thatch-roofed, raised bungalows feature painted exterior murals, high-pitched ceilings, varnished wood floors, and either one king or a mix of queen and single beds. The bathrooms are practically works of art, each with original, intricate mosaics of hand-cut tile highlighting a large open shower. Every bungalow has its own spacious balcony, with both a hammock and a couch, where you can lie and look out on the flowering gardens. There's a large open-air restaurant and lounge, where meals and drinks are served. The menu is an eclectic mix, featuring fresh fish and meats in a variety of French, Caribbean, and Polynesian sauces. The beach is easily accessed by a private path, and a host of activities and tours can be arranged.

MODERATE

✪ **Almendros and Corales Tent Camp.** Manzanillo, Limón (Apdo. 681-2300, San José). ☎ **506/272-2024** or 506/272-4175. Fax 506/272-2220. www.geoexpediciones.com. E-mail: almonds@racsa.co.cr. 20 tents. $70 double; slightly lower during the off-season. AE, MC, V.

This isn't camping in any traditional sense, so don't expect to be roughing it. What you will find here are large raised platforms, big enough so that within the stretched-tarp roof and screened walls there's another large standing-room tent, providing protection against rain and mosquitoes. This second tent takes up about half of the platform's screened-in floor space and still leaves room for a hammock, table, chairs, and a bathroom area with a cold-water shower and toilet. Inside the tent you'll find either two single beds or one double bed, a small table, two oil lamps, and a small closet. If that sounds more luxurious than you'd like, remember that the tents are in some dense secondary forest, with nothing but screen and cloth for walls, so you'll still feel very close to nature. There are wooden walkways connecting the tents to the main lodge and dining area. Meals will run you an extra $25 per person per day. Perhaps the best part of the whole setup is the fact that Manzanillo Beach is just 183 meters (200 yd.) away through the jungle. Snorkel equipment, sea kayaks, and a variety of tours are also available.

✪ Cariblue Bungalows. Playa Cocles, Puerto Viejo de Talamanca, Limón. ☎ **506/ 750-0035,** or ☎ and fax 506/750-0057. www.cariblue.com. E-mail: cariblue@racsa.co.cr. 5 units, 5 bungalows. $50–$65 double. Rates include breakfast buffet. AE, MC, V.

This new bed-and-breakfast offers guests a lot of comfort and character. The rooms are spread around the well-tended and lush grounds. My favorites are the raised stilt wood bungalows with spacious bedrooms featuring either one king and one single bed, or two queens. The beds are covered with mosquito nets and there's a small veranda with a hammock. The nicest features here are the bathrooms with their intricate mosaic tile designs. The five newer rooms are in a couple of concrete-block buildings with high-pitched thatch roofs. They are clean and comfortable, but not quite as private and charming as the bungalows. Meals are served in the large open rancho building, which also houses a small gift shop and a bar. Cariblue is located about 91 meters (100 yd.) inland from the southern end of Playa Cocles.

Casa Camarona. Playa Cocles, Puerto Viejo, Limón (Apdo. 2270-1002, Paseo de los Estudiantes, San José). ☎ **506/283-6711** or 506/750-0151. Fax 506/222-6184. www. casacamarona.com. E-mail: camarona@mail.ticonet.co.cr. 20 units. $58 double, $77 triple. Rates include continental breakfast. AE, MC, V.

Casa Camarona is a new hotel and has the enviable distinction of being one of the few hotels in this area right on the beach—no road to cross, no path through the jungle, just a small section of shady gardens separates you from a quiet section of Playa Cocles and the Caribbean Sea. The rooms are in two separate two-story buildings. Definitely get a room on the second floor. Up here you'll find spacious rooms painted in pleasant pastels, with plenty of cross-ventilation and a wide shared veranda. Nine of the rooms have air-conditioning. I don't know who designed the first-floor rooms, but several of them have such low ceilings that it felt as if the walls were closing in on me. There's a nice open-air restaurant and bar, as well as an outdoor cigar lounge and a pretty nice gift shop. The hotel keeps some chaise longues on the beach under the shade of palm trees, and there's even a beach bar open during the day, so you barely have to leave that chaise to quench your thirst.

Hotel Punta Cocles. Puerto Viejo, Limón (Apdo. 11020-1000, San José). ☎ **506/750-0017** or 506/750-0337. Fax 506/750-0336. www.novanet.co.cr. E-mail: puntacocles@expressmail. net. 60 units. A/C TEL. $70 standard room (accommodates 4 people), $90 with kitchenette (accommodates 6 people). AE, MC, V.

Although this is one of the largest and most resortlike hotels in the area, it's not my first choice. The hotel has changed management several times in recent years and there's a general sense of chaos and disrepair. The air-conditioned rooms are large, and those that come with kitchenettes are a decent deal, especially if you're traveling with a large group or family. There's the large open-air La Iguana restaurant, which serves unmemorable meals, and the poolside Rasta Mouse Bar, which sometimes features live music. There's an adult pool, children's pool, and a Jacuzzi. There's also a small playground and game room for children, and a TV room for the whole lot. The hotel is located about 500 meters (545 yd.) inland from the beach, but there's a small shuttle to a semiprivate section of beach with chaise lounges and hammocks.

Villas del Caribe. Puerto Viejo, Limón (Apdo. 8080-1000, San José). ☎ **506/750-0202** or 506/233-2200. Fax 506/750-0203. www.villascaribe.net. E-mail: info@villascaribe.net. 12 units. $69 double, $79 triple, $89 quad. AE, MC, V.

If you want to be right on the beach and have spacious, comfortable accommodations, there isn't a better choice in this area. Villas del Caribe, built in a sort of contemporary Mediterranean style and set on a private 100-acre nature reserve, offers two-story villas with full kitchens and a choice of one or two bedrooms. The living rooms have built-in sofa beds, and just outside there is a large terrace complete with barbecue grill. The kitchens are attractively designed, with blue-and-white–tile counters, and fully equipped. Bathrooms feature wooden-slat shower doors, potted plants on a platform by the window, louvered and screened walls that let in light and air, and more blue-tile counters. Upstairs, you'll find either a large single bedroom with a king-size bed or two smaller bedrooms (one with bunk beds). Either way, there's a balcony with a hammock and an ocean view.

The water, which is usually fairly calm, is only steps away through the coconut palms, and there's some coral just offshore that makes for good snorkeling. The hotel can arrange horseback rides, fishing trips, snorkeling, and diving—even oxcart rides. There may finally be a restaurant here by the time this book goes to press—although I've been writing this for 2 years. The building's been built for some time, and it has a wonderful view of the Caribbean Sea. If it's still not open, you'll have to cook your own food, use one of the nearby basic *sodas,* or head back into Puerto Viejo.

INEXPENSIVE

Cabinas Selvyn. Punta Uva, Limón. No phone. 10 units, all with shared bathroom; 2 apts. $8–$12 double, $150–$200 per month for an apt. No credit cards.

The atmosphere here is friendly and funky. Rooms are located in two old wooden buildings behind the small open-air restaurant. There are no fans, so try for a second-floor room, which receives a bit of the sea breezes. All the rooms come with mosquito nets, but beyond that, the accommodations are Spartan. Nevertheless, the hotel is located 100 meters (109 yd.) down a dirt lane from one of the most isolated and beautiful beaches in Costa Rica, and the owner is a great cook.

Playa Chiquita Lodge. Puerto Viejo, Limón. ☎ **506/750-0408.** Fax 506/750-0062. www.playachiquita.com. E-mail: wolfbiss@racsa.co.cr. 10 units. $39 double, $49 triple; lower in the off-season. Rates include full breakfast. MC, V.

This place just oozes jungle atmosphere. Set amid the shade of large old trees a few miles south of Puerto Viejo toward Punta Uva (watch for the sign), the lodge consists of unpainted wooden buildings set on stilts and connected by wooden walkways. There are wide verandas with built-in seating and rocking chairs. The basic, spacious rooms have recently been painted, which lightens things up, but it's still hard to read in bed at night. There is a short trail that leads down to a private little swimming beach with tide pools and beautiful turquoise water. Lately, this stretch of beach has become the site of a daily 4pm volleyball game. Meals cost from $5 to $13, and choices range from spaghetti to lobster; since the management is German, you can expect a few German dishes as well. Throughout the day there are free bananas and coffee. The owners also rent out fully equipped houses for those interested in longer stays or more privacy and independence.

DINING IN PUERTO VIEJO

To really sample the local cuisine, you need to look up a few local women. Ask around for **Miss Dolly** and see if she has anything cooking. Her specialties are bread (especially banana) and ginger biscuits, but she'll also fix a full Caribbean meal for you if you ask a day in advance and she has time. **Miss Daisy** also makes *pan bon* (a local, sweet dark bread), ginger cakes, patties (meat-filled turnovers), and coconut oil (for tanning). **Miss Sam, Miss Isma,** and **Miss Irma** all serve up sit-down meals in their modest little *sodas.* Just ask around for these women and someone will direct you to them.

Puerto Viejo has become a very popular destination for Italian immigrants, and it seems there's a pretty decent Italian restaurant everywhere you turn. In addition to the places listed below, you can get very good Italian cuisine at both **Caramba** and **Marco's Pizzeria and Ristorante,** right in town. There's also good seafood to be had at **Salsa Brava** and **El Dorado.**

Finally, the Garden Restaurant, one of my all-time favorite restaurants in Costa Rica, was closed during the 2000 season. The owner has plans of reopening, with a lighter, simpler menu, and a large screen TV showing nightly movies on video and DVD. If it's open when you arrive in Puerto Viejo, go there.

✪ **Amimodo.** On the left-hand side of the main road heading south of Puerto Viejo, just after Cabinas Salsa Brava. ☎ 506/750-0257. Main courses $4–15. AE, MC, V. Mon–Wed and Fri noon–3pm and 6–11pm, Sat–Sun noon–11pm. NORTHERN ITALIAN.

This is my favorite Italian restaurant in Puerto Viejo. The dining room occupies the open-air bottom floor of a traditional local raised stilt house. It's airy and there's lots of whitewashed wood and gingerbread trim. On good days you can feel the sea breeze coming in off the ocean about 91 meters (100 yd.) away. The sturdy wood tables have hand-painted trim patterns that match the painted chairs. Be sure to begin your meal with the *bresaula de tiburon,* thin slices of home-smoked shark served on a bed of lettuce with a light avocado dressing. I also recommend the homemade ravioli stuffed with lobster in a lobster-and–cognac-based red sauce, and the gnocchi, which are some of the most melt-in-your-mouth gnocchi I've ever tasted. If you've got room for dessert, opt for the chocolate salami. There's a small bar that sometimes fills with locals and a big-screen TV that broadcasts the most important soccer games and Italian television programs.

Café Pizzeria Coral. On the road to the soccer field. ☎ 506/750-0051. Reservations not accepted. Pizza $3.50–$5, pasta $4–$5. No credit cards. Tues–Sun 7am–noon and 5:30–9:30pm. ITALIAN/PIZZA.

Although this place bills itself as a pizzeria, your best bets are the breakfasts, desserts, and fresh breads. While the pizza here is mediocre (especially compared to the local competition), the chocolate cake is a standout. The morning baskets of bread, fruit, granola plates, and giant pancakes will set you back a few colones, but they'll also set you up for most of the day. The open-air dining room is up a few steps from the street. The whole place is walled in by flowering hibiscus that attracts plenty of hummingbirds in the morning, which is why this is my favorite breakfast joint in town. You'll find the Café Pizzeria Coral about 2 blocks from the water in the center of the village.

That Rundown Feeling

Don't be discouraged by signs advertising "rundown" soup or stew. It's not what you think. Rundown (or "rondon") soup, is a spicy coconut-milk stew made with anything the cook can run down. Be sure to try this authentic taste of the Caribbean.

The Place. On a side street one-half block inland from the bus stop. No phone. Reservations not accepted. Main courses $2.50–$7. No credit cards. Daily 7am–9pm. INTERNATIONAL.

If you want a quick casual meal, check out this humble collection of tables under an open A-frame roof, located on a side street just off the bus stop. Open for breakfast, lunch, and dinner, The Place features a small menu with daily specials and excellent sandwiches. The menu is eclectic—it might feature anything from vegetarian nori rolls to the local "rondon" stew.

Soda Tamara. On the main road through the village. ☎ **506/750-0148.** Main courses $3.50–$8. AE, MC, V. Daily 7am–9pm. COSTA RICAN.

This little Tico-style restaurant has long been popular with budget-conscious travelers and has an attractive setting for such an economical place. There's a patio dining area, which is actually larger and more comfortable than the main dining room, which is a bit dark and cramped. The painted picket fence in front gives the restaurant a homey feel. The menu features standard fish, chicken, and meat entrees, served with a hefty helping of Caribbean-style rice and beans. You can also get *patacones* (fried chips made out of plantains) and a wide selection of fresh-fruit juices. Be forewarned: Service can be slow. At the counter inside, you'll find homemade cocoa candies and unsweetened cocoa biscuits made by several women in town. They're definitely worth a try. Soda Tamara recently added a second-floor open-air bar that's open nightly from 6pm until the last straggler calls it quits.

DINING BETWEEN PUERTO VIEJO & MANZANILLO

As the beaches stretching south of Puerto Viejo keep getting more and more popular, there has been a corresponding increase in the number of places to grab a meal. In addition to the restaurants listed above, **Cabinas Selvyn,** at Punta Uva, and **Elena Brown's Restaurant,** at Playa Chiquita (☎ 506/750-0265), are two very popular and dependable spots for local cuisine. **El Ranchito,** at Punta Uva (☎ 506/750-0218), is a great spot for lunch, especially if you're already on the beach at Punta Uva. If you make it as far south as Manzanillo, **Maxi's Restaurant** is your best bet. For fancier fare, check out the restaurant at **Shawandha** (☎ 506/750-0018).

PUERTO VIEJO AFTER DARK

There are two main disco-bars in town. ✪ **Johnny's Place** is near the Rural Guard station, about 100 meters (109 yd.) north of the ATEC office. You'll find **Standford's** overlooking the water out near Salsa Brava just as the main road heads south of town. Both have small dance floors with ground-shaking reggae, dub, and rap rhythms blaring. The action usually spills out from the dance floor at both joints on most nights. I like the atmosphere better at Johnny's, where they have tables and candles set out on the sand, near the water's edge. Another place I like is **El Bambú,** just beyond Stanford's on the road toward Punta Uva. It's smaller and more intimate than either of the other bars, yet still packs them in and gets them dancing on the Monday or Friday reggae nights. There's a new open-air bar on the second floor of **Soda Tamara,** which has become a casual and quiet place to gather after dark.

As in Cahuita and Limón, Puerto Viejo has had its peaceful image tarnished by a couple of rapes and other violent incidents like drug trafficking and endemic petty theft. Be careful here, especially at night, and never leave valuables unattended, *anywhere.*

Appendix A:
Costa Rica in Depth

Costa Rica is, and has been for many years, a relative sea of tranquillity in a region that has been troubled by turmoil for centuries. For more than 100 years, it has enjoyed a stable democracy and a relatively high standard of living for Latin America. The literacy rate is high, as are medical standards and facilities. Perhaps most significant, at least for proud Costa Ricans, is that this country does not have an army. When former Costa Rican president Oscar Arias Sánchez was awarded the Nobel Peace Prize for negotiating a peace settlement in Central America in 1987, Costa Rica was able to claim credit for exporting a bit of its own political stability to the rest of the region.

1 The Natural Environment

Costa Rica occupies a central spot in the isthmus that joins North and South America. For millennia, this land bridge served as a migratory thoroughfare and mating ground for species native to the once-separate continents. It was also the meeting place of Mesoamerican and Andean pre-Columbian indigenous cultures.

The country comprises only 0.01% of the earth's landmass, yet it is home to 5% of the planet's biodiversity. There are more than 10,000 identified species of plants, 850 species of birds, 800 species of butterflies, and 500 species of mammals, reptiles, and amphibians found here.

The key to this biological richness lies in the many distinct life zones and ecosystems that can be found in Costa Rica. It may all seem like one big mass of green to the untrained eye, but the differences are profound.

In any one spot in Costa Rica, temperatures remain relatively constant year-round. However, they vary dramatically according to altitude, from tropically hot and steamy along the coasts to below freezing at the highest elevations.

Costa Rica's lowland rain forests are true tropical jungles. Rainfall in them can be well over 200 inches per year, and their climate is hot and humid. Trees grow tall and fast, fighting for sunlight in the upper reaches. In fact, life and foliage on the forest floor are surprisingly sparse. The action is typically 100 feet above, in the canopy, where long vines stream down, lianas climb up, and bromeliads grow on the branches and trunks of towering hardwood trees. You can find these lowland rain forests along the southern Pacific coast and Osa Peninsula, as well as along the Caribbean coast.

At higher altitudes you'll find Costa Rica's famed cloud forests. Here the steady flow of moist air meets the mountains and creates a nearly constant mist. Epiphytes—resourceful plants that live cooperatively on the branches and trunks of other trees—grow abundantly in the cloud forests, where they must extract moisture and nutrients from the air. Since cloud forests are found in generally steep, mountainous terrain, the canopy here is lower and less uniform than in lowland rain forests, providing better chances for viewing elusive fauna. Costa Rica's most spectacular cloud forest is the **Monteverde Biological Cloud Forest Preserve** in Guanacaste province (see chapter 6).

At the highest reaches, the cloud forests give way to elfin forests and páramos. More commonly associated with the South American Andes, a páramo is characterized by a variety of tundralike shrubs and grasses, with a scattering of twisted, windblown trees. Reptiles, rodents, and raptors are the most common residents here.

In a few protected areas of Guanacaste, you will still find examples of the otherwise vanishing tropical dry forest. During the long and pronounced dry season (late November through late April), no rain relieves the unabating heat. In an effort to conserve much-needed water, the trees drop their leaves but bloom in a riot of color: purple jacaranda, scarlet poró, and brilliant orange flame-of-the-forest are just a few examples. Then, during the rainy season, this deciduous forest is transformed into a lush and verdant landscape. Because the foliage is not so dense, the dry forests are excellent places to view a variety of wildlife species, especially howler monkeys and pizotes (*coatimundi*).

Along the coasts, primarily where river mouths meet the ocean, you will find extensive mangrove forests and swamps. Around these seemingly monotonous tangles of roots exists one of the most diverse and rich ecosystems in the country. All sorts of fish and crustaceans live in the brackish tidal waters. Caimans and crocodiles cruise the maze of rivers and unmarked canals, and hundreds of herons, ibises, egrets, and other marsh birds nest and feed along the silty banks. Mangrove swamps are often havens for waterbirds: cormorants, frigate birds, pelicans, and herons. The larger birds tend to nest up high in the canopy, while the smaller ones nestle in the underbrush. The Gulf of Nicoya is particularly popular among frigate birds and brown pelicans, and all manner of terns and seagulls.

Over the last decade or so, Costa Rica has taken great strides toward protecting its rich biodiversity. Whereas 30 years ago it was difficult to find a protected area anywhere, now more than 11% of the country is protected within the national park system. Another 10% to 15% of the land enjoys moderately effective preservation as part of private and public reserves, Indian reserves, and wildlife refuges and corridors. Still, Costa Rica's precious tropical hardwoods continue to be harvested at an alarming rate, often illegally, while other primary forests are clear-cut for short-term agricultural gain. Many experts predict that Costa Rica's unprotected forests will be gone by the early part of this century.

This is also a land of high volcanic and seismic activity. There are three major volcanic mountain ranges in Costa Rica, and many of the volcanoes are still active, allowing visitors to experience the awe-inspiring sight of steaming fumaroles and intense lava flows during their stay. Two volcanoes near the capital—Poás and Irazú—are currently active although relatively quiet. The best places to see volcanic activity are farther north in **Rincón de la Vieja National Park** and at **Arenal Volcano.**

SEARCHING FOR WILDLIFE

Animals in the forests are predominantly nocturnal. When they are active in the daytime, they are usually elusive and on the watch for predators. Birds are easier to spot in clearings or secondary forests than they are in primary forests. Unless you have lots of experience in the tropics, your best hope for enjoying a walk through the jungle lies in employing a trained and knowledgeable guide. Also, if it's been raining a lot and the trails are muddy, a good pair of rubber boots come in handy. These are usually provided by the lodges or at the sites where necessary.

Here are a few helpful hints:

- **Listen.** Pay attention to rustling in the leaves; whether it's monkeys up above or pizotes on the ground, you're most likely to hear an animal before seeing one.
- **Keep quiet.** Noise will scare off animals and prevent you from hearing their movements and calls.
- **Don't try too hard.** Soften your focus and allow your peripheral vision to take over. This way you can catch glimpses of motion and then focus in on the prey.
- **Bring your own binoculars.** It's also a good idea to practice a little first, to get the hang of them. It would be a shame to be fiddling around and staring into space while everyone else in your group oohs and aahs over a quetzal.
- **Dress appropriately.** You'll have a hard time focusing your binoculars if you're busy swatting mosquitoes. Light, long-sleeved pants and shirts are your best bet. Comfortable hiking boots are a real boon, except where heavy rubber boots are necessary. Avoid loud colors; the better you blend in with your surroundings, the better your chances of spotting wildlife.
- **Be patient.** The jungle isn't on a schedule; however, you do have your best shot at seeing forest fauna in the very early morning and late afternoon hours.
- **Read up.** Familiarize yourself with what you're most likely to see. Most lodges and hotels have a copy of *Birds of Costa Rica* and other wildlife field guides, although as with binoculars it's always best to have your own copy.

2 Costa Rica Today

Costa Rica has a population of roughly $3^{1}/_{2}$ million, more than half of whom live in the Central Valley and are classified as urban. The people are ethnically the most homogeneous of Central America: Nearly 96% of the population is of Spanish or otherwise European descent, and it is not at all unusual to see blond Costa Ricans. This is largely because the indigenous population in place when the first Spaniards arrived was small and thereafter was reduced to even more of a minority by wars and disease. There are still some remnant indigenous populations, primarily on reservations around the country; the principal tribes include the Bribri, Cabécar, Boruca, and Guaymí. In addition, on the Caribbean coast there is a substantial population of English-speaking black Creoles who came over from the Antilles to work on the railroad and in the banana plantations.

In general, Costa Ricans (who call themselves Ticos, a practice that stems from their tendency to add a diminutive, either "tico" or "ito," to the ends of words to connote familiarity or affection) are a friendly and outgoing people. In conversation and interaction with visitors, Ticos are very open and helpful.

In a region plagued by internal strife and civil wars, Costa Ricans are proud of their peaceful history, political stability, and relatively high level of development. This, however, can also translate into arrogance and prejudice toward immigrants from neighboring countries, particularly Nicaraguans, who make up a large percentage of the workforce on the banana and coffee plantations.

Roman Catholicism is the official religion of Costa Rica, although freedom to practice any religion is guaranteed by the country's Constitution. More than 90% of the population identifies itself as Roman Catholic, yet there are small but visible evangelical Christian, Protestant, and Jewish communities. By and large, Ticos are relatively religious. While many city dwellers lead quite secular lives, those in small villages and towns attend mass regularly. Time also has relative meaning to Ticos. While most tour companies and other establishments operate efficiently, in general, don't expect punctuality.

Modern Costa Rica is a nation of contrasts. On the one hand, it's the most technologically advanced and politically stable nation in Central America and has the largest middle class. Even the smallest towns have electricity, the water is mostly safe to drink, and the phone system is relatively good. On the other hand, Costa Rica finds itself in the midst of a huge economic transition. Several "Free Zones" and some hi-tech investments have dramatically changed the face of Costa Rica's economy. Intel, which opened two side-by-side assembly plants in Costa Rica in 1997, currently accounts for over 35% of the country's exports—compared with traditional exports like coffee (4.5%) and bananas (9%). More importantly, while Intel and other international companies are used to trumpet a fast-growing gross domestic product, very little of the profits actually make their way into the Costa Rican economy.

Instead, the gap between rich and poor is widening. The government and banking institutions are regularly embroiled in scandal. The country's per-capita debt ranks among the world's worst. In an attempt to come to terms with decades of trade deficits and pay back its debt, there has been a move toward economic austerity and privatization, causing the country's vast network of social services, as well as its health-care system and its educational institutions, to become overburdened and underfunded. This has led to increased unemployment, lower wages, and more expensive goods and services.

Finally, tourism has quickly grown to the point of becoming the nation's true principal source of income, surpassing both cattle ranching and exports of coffee and bananas. In 1999, for the first time, one million tourists visited Costa Rica. Increasingly, Ticos whose fathers and grandfathers were farmers find themselves hotel owners, tour guides, and waiters. While most have adapted gracefully and regard the industry as a source of new jobs and opportunities for economic advancement, restaurant and hotel staff can seem gruff and uninterested at times, especially in rural areas. And, unfortunately, an increase in the number of visitors has led to an increase in crime, prostitution, and drug trafficking. Common sense and street savvy are required in San José and Limón.

3 History 101

EARLY HISTORY Little is known of Costa Rica's history before its colonization by Spanish settlers. The pre-Columbian Indians who made their home in this region of Central America never developed the large cities or advanced culture that flowered farther north in what would

Dateline

■ **13,000 B.C.** Earliest record of human inhabitants in Costa Rica.

continues

- **1,000 B.C.** Olmec people from Mexico arrive in Costa Rica searching for rare blue jade.
- **1,000 B.C.–A.D. 1400** City of Guayabo is inhabited by as many as 10,000 people.
- **1502** Columbus lands in Costa Rica in September, at what is now Limón.
- **1519–61** Spanish explore and colonize Costa Rica.
- **1563** City of Cartago is founded in the Central Valley.
- **1737** San José is founded.
- **Late 1700s** Coffee is introduced as a cash crop.
- **1821** On September 15, Costa Rica, with the rest of Central America, gains independence from Spain.
- **1823** San José is named the capital. The decision is disputed and isn't officially settled until 1835.
- **1848** Costa Rica is proclaimed an independent republic.
- **1856** Battle of Santa Rosa: Costa Ricans defeat the United States, which backed pro-slavery advocate William Walker.
- **1870s** First banana plantations are established.
- **1889** First election is won by an opposition party, establishing democratic process in Costa Rica.
- **1890** Inauguration of the railroad connecting San José with the Caribbean coast.
- **1899** The United Fruit Company is founded by railroad builder Minor Keith.
- **1941** Costa Rica's social security and health system instituted by President Rafael Angel Calderón.
- **1948** After aborted revolution, Costa Rican army is abolished.
- **1949** Women are given the right to vote.

continues

become Guatemala, Belize, and Mexico. However, from scattered excavations around the country, primarily in the northwest, ancient artifacts have been unearthed that indicate a strong sense of aesthetics. Beautiful gold and jade jewelry, intricately carved grinding stones, and artistically painted terra-cotta objects point toward a highly skilled, if not large, population. The most enigmatic of these ancient relics are carved stone balls, some measuring several yards across and weighing many tons, that have been found along the southern Pacific coast. The purpose of these stone spheres remains a mystery: Some archaeologists say that they may have been boundary markers, while others speculate that they were celestial references; still others now claim that they are not human-made at all, but rather natural geological formations.

SPAIN SETTLES COSTA RICA In 1502, on his fourth and last voyage to the New World, Christopher Columbus anchored just offshore from present-day Limón. Whether it was he who gave the country its name is open to discussion, but it wasn't long before the inappropriate name took hold.

The earliest Spanish settlers found that, unlike the Indians farther north, the native population of Costa Rica was unwilling to submit to slavery. Despite their small numbers, scattered villages, and tribal differences, they fought back against the Spanish until overcome by superior firepower and European diseases. When the fighting was finished, the settlers in Costa Rica found that there were very few Indians left to force into servitude. The settlers were thus forced to till their own lands, a situation unheard of in other parts of Central America. Few pioneers headed this way because they could settle in Guatemala, where there was a large native workforce. Costa Rica was nearly forgotten, as the Spanish crown looked elsewhere for riches to plunder and souls to convert.

It didn't take long for Costa Rica's few Spanish settlers to head for the hills, where they found rich volcanic soil and a climate that was less oppressive than in the lowlands. Cartago, the colony's first capital, was founded in 1563, but it was not until the 1700s that more cities were founded in this agriculturally rich region. In the late 18th century, the first coffee plants were introduced, and because these plants thrived in the highlands, Costa Rica began to develop its first cash crop. Unfortunately, it was a long and difficult journey transporting the coffee to the Caribbean coast and then onward to Europe, where the demand for coffee was growing.

FROM INDEPENDENCE TO THE PRESENT In 1821, Spain granted independence to its colonies in Central America. Costa Rica joined with its neighbors to form the Central American Federation, but in 1838 it withdrew to form a new nation and pursue its own interests, which differed considerably from those of the other Central American nations. By the mid-1800s, coffee was the country's main export. Land was given free to anyone willing to plant coffee on it, and plantation owners soon grew wealthy and powerful, creating Costa Rica's first elite class. Coffee plantation owners were powerful enough to elect their own representatives to the presidency.

This was a stormy period in Costa Rican history. In 1856, the country was invaded by William Walker, a soldier of fortune from Tennessee who, with the backing of U.S. President James Buchanan, was attempting to fulfill his grandiose dreams of presiding over a slave state in Central America (before his invasion of Costa Rica, he had invaded Nicaragua and Baja California). The people of Costa Rica, led by their own president, Juan Rafael Mora, marched against Walker and chased him back to Nicaragua. Walker eventually surrendered to a U.S. warship in 1857, but in 1860 he attacked Honduras, claiming to be the president of that country. The Hondurans, who had had enough of Walker's shenanigans, promptly executed him.

Until 1890, coffee growers had to transport their coffee either by oxcart to the Pacific port of Puntarenas or by boat down the Río Sarapiquí to the Caribbean. In the 1870s, a progressive president proposed a railway from San José to the Caribbean coast to facilitate the transport of coffee to European markets. It took nearly 20 years for this plan to reach fruition, and more than 4,000 workers lost their lives constructing the railway, which passed through dense jungles and rugged mountains on its journey from the Central Valley to the coast. Partway through the project, as funds were dwindling, the second chief engineer, Minor Keith, proposed an idea that not only enhanced his fortunes but also changed the course of Central American history. Banana plantations would be developed along the railway right-of-way (land on either side of the tracks). The export of this crop would help to finance the railway, and in exchange Keith would get a 99-year lease on 800,000 acres of land with a 20-year tax deferment. The Costa Rican government gave its consent, and in 1878 the first bananas were shipped from the country. In 1899 Keith and a partner formed the United Fruit Company, a business that would eventually become the largest landholder in Central America and cause political disputes and wars throughout the region.

In 1889 Costa Rica held what is considered the first free election in Central American history. The opposition candidate won the election, and the control

- **1956** Costa Rica's population tops one million.
- **1963** Cabo Blanco Reserve becomes Costa Rica's first national park.
- **1987** Pres. Oscar Arias Sánchez is awarded the Nobel Peace Prize for orchestrating the Central American Peace Plan.
- **1994** Pres. Rafael Angel Calderón hands over the reigns of government to José María Figueres, in a peaceful replay of their fathers' less amenable and democratic transfer of power in 1948.
- **1996** Claudia Poll earns Costa Rica its first Olympic Gold Medal in the 200-meter free-style swimming event at the Atlanta Summer Games.
- **1999** More than one million tourists visit Costa Rica for the first time in a single year.

of the government passed from the hands of one political party to those of another without bloodshed or hostilities. Thus, Costa Rica established itself as the region's only true democracy. In 1948, this democratic process was challenged by Rafael Angel Calderón, who had served as the country's president from 1940 to 1944. After losing by a narrow margin, Calderón, who had the backing of the Communist labor unions and the Catholic Church, refused to concede the country's leadership to the rightfully elected president, Otillio Ulate, and a civil war ensued. Calderón was eventually defeated by José "Pepe" Figueres. In the wake of this crisis, a new constitution was drafted; among other changes, it abolished Costa Rica's army so that such a revolution could never happen again.

In 1994, history seemed to repeat itself—peacefully this time—when José María Figueres took the reins of government from the son of his father's adversary, Rafael Angel Calderón.

Over 100 years of nearly uninterrupted democracy have helped make Costa Rica the most stable country in Central America. This stability, adherence to the democratic process, and staunch position of neutrality in a region that has been torn by 200 years of nearly constant strife are a source of great pride to Costa Ricans, who like to think of their country as the "Switzerland of Central America."

4 Gallo Pinto, Ceviche & Frescos: Costa Rican Food & Drink

Costa Rican food is not especially memorable. Perhaps that's why there's so much international food available throughout the country. However, if you really want to save money, you'll find that Costa Rican, or *típico*, food is always the cheapest nourishment available. It's primarily served in *sodas*, Costa Rica's equivalent of diners.

MEALS & DINING CUSTOMS

Rice and beans are the basis of Costa Rican meals—all three of them. At breakfast, they're called *gallo pinto* and come with everything from eggs to steak to seafood. At lunch or dinner, rice and beans are an integral part of a *casado* (which means "married"). A casado usually consists of cabbage-and-tomato salad, fried plantains (a starchy, bananalike fruit), and a chicken, fish, or meat dish of some sort.

Dining hours in Costa Rica are flexible, but generally follow North American customs. Some downtown restaurants in San José are open 24 hours; however, expensive restaurants tend to be open for lunch between 11am and 3pm and for dinner between 6 and 11pm.

APPETIZERS Known as *bocas* in Costa Rica, appetizers are served with drinks in most bars. Often the bocas are free, but even if they aren't, they're very inexpensive. Popular bocas include *gallos* (stuffed tortillas), ceviche (a marinated seafood salad), *tamales* (stuffed cornmeal patties wrapped and steamed inside of banana leaves), *patacones* (fried green plantain chips), and fried *yuca* (yucca).

SANDWICHES & SNACKS Ticos love to snack, and there's a large variety of tasty little sandwiches and snacks available on the street, at snack bars, and in *sodas*. *Arreglados* are little meat-filled sandwiches, as are *tortas*, which are served on little rolls with a bit of salad tucked into them. *Gallos* are tortillas piled with meat, beans, or cheese. Tacos, tamales, and *empanadas* (meat pies) also are quite common.

MEAT Costa Rica is beef country, one of the tropical nations that have converted much of their rain-forest land to pastures for raising beef cattle. Consequently, beef is cheap and plentiful, although it may be a bit tougher than it is back home. Spit-roasted chicken is also very popular here and is surprisingly tender.

SEAFOOD Costa Rica has two coasts, and as you'd expect, there's plenty of seafood available everywhere in the country. *Corvina* (sea bass) is the most commonly served fish, and it's prepared innumerable ways, including as *ceviche,* a sort of marinated salad. Be careful: In many cheaper restaurants, particularly in San José, shark meat is often sold as corvina. You might also come across *pargo* (red snapper), *dorado* (mahimahi), and tuna on some menus, especially along the coasts. Although Costa Rica is a major exporter of shrimp and lobster, both are very expensive here—that's why most are exported, causing them to be high-priced and in short supply at home.

VEGETABLES On the whole, you'll find vegetables surprisingly lacking in the meals you're served in Costa Rica—usually nothing more than a little pile of shredded cabbage topped with a slice or two of tomato. For a much more satisfying and filling salad, order *palmito* (hearts of palm salad). The heart (actually the stalk or trunk of these small palms) is first boiled and then chopped into circular pieces and served with other fresh vegetables, with a salad dressing on top. If you want something more than this, you'll have to order a side dish such as *picadillo,* a stew or purée of vegetables with a bit of meat in it. Most people have a hard time thinking of *plátanos* (plantains) as vegetables, but these giant relatives of bananas require cooking before they can be eaten. Green plantains have a very starchy flavor and consistency, but become as sweet as candy as they ripen. Fried plátanos are one of my favorite dishes. *Yuca* (manioc root or yucca in English) is another starchy staple vegetable of Costa Rica.

One more vegetable worth mentioning is the *pejibaye,* a form of palm fruit that looks like a miniature orange coconut. Boiled pejibayes are frequently sold from carts on the streets of San José. When cut in half, a pejibaye reveals a large seed surrounded by soft, fibrous flesh. You can eat it plain, but it's usually topped with a dollop of mayonnaise.

FRUITS Costa Rica has a wealth of delicious tropical fruits. The most common are mangoes (the season begins in May), papayas, pineapples, melons, and bananas. Other fruits include the *marañon,* which is the fruit of the cashew tree and has orange or yellow glossy skin; the *granadilla* or *maracuyá* (passion fruit); the *mamón chino,* which Asian travelers will immediately recognize as the rambutan; and the *carambola* (star fruit).

DESSERTS *Queque seco,* which literally translates as "dry cake," is the same as pound cake. *Tres leches* cake, on the other hand, is so moist you almost need to eat it with a spoon. Flan is a typical custard dessert. It often comes as either *flan de caramelo* (caramel) or *flan de coco* (coconut). There are many other sweets available, many of which are made with condensed milk and raw sugar.

BEVERAGES

Frescos, refrescos, or *jugos naturales* are my favorite drinks in Costa Rica. They are usually made with fresh fruit and milk or water. Among the more common fruits used are mangoes, papayas, blackberries (*mora*), and pineapples (*piña*). You will also come across *maracuyá* (passion fruit) and *carambola* (star fruit). Some of the more unusual frescos are *horchata* (made with rice flour and a lot of cinnamon) and *chan* (made with the seed of a plant found mostly in

Guanacaste—definitely an acquired taste). The former is wonderful; the latter requires an open mind (it's reputed to be good for the digestive system). Order *un fresco con leche sin hielo* (a fresco with milk but without ice) if you are trying to avoid untreated water.

If you're a coffee drinker, you may be disappointed here. Most of the best coffee has traditionally been targeted for export, and Ticos tend to prefer theirs weak and sugary. The better hotels and restaurants are starting to cater to gringo and European tastes and are serving up better blends. If you want black coffee, ask for *café negro;* if you want it with milk, order *café con leche.*

If you want to try something different for your morning beverage, ask for *agua dulce,* a warm drink made from melted sugarcane and served with either milk or lemon, or straight.

WATER   Although water in most of Costa Rica is said to be safe to drink, bottled water is readily available. *Agua mineral,* or simply soda, is sparkling water in Costa Rica. If you like your water without bubbles, be sure to request *aqua mineral sin gas.*

BEER, WINE & LIQUOR   The German presence in Costa Rica over the years has produced several fine beers, which are fairly inexpensive. Licensed local versions of Heineken and Rock Ice are also available. Costa Rica distills a wide variety of liquors, and you'll save money by ordering these rather than imported brands. The national liquor is *guaro,* a rather crude cane liquor that's often combined with a soft drink or tonic or mineral water. Imported wines are available at reasonable prices in the better restaurants throughout the country. You can usually save money by ordering a Chilean wine rather than a Californian or European one. **Café Rica** and **Salicsa** are two coffee liqueurs made in Costa Rica; the former is very similar to Kahlúa, and the latter is a cream coffee liqueur. Both are delicious.

5 Recommended Books

Some of the books mentioned below may be difficult to track down in U.S. bookstores, but you'll find them all in abundance in Costa Rica.

GENERAL   For a straightforward, albeit somewhat dry, historical overview there's *The History of Costa Rica,* by Ivan Molina and Steven Palmer (University of Costa Rica, 1998).

For a more readable look into Costa Rican society, check out the newly published ✪ *The Ticos: Culture and Social Change,* by Richard, Karen, and Mavis Biesanz (Lynne Rienner Publishers, 1999), an examination of the country's politics and culture, by the authors of the out-of-print *The Costa Ricans.*

You could pick up either *Costa Rica in Focus: A Guide to the People, Politics and Culture,* by Tjabel Daling (Interlink Books, 1998), or *Inside Costa Rica,* by Silvia Lara (Interhemispheric Resource Center, 1995).

To learn more about the life and culture of Costa Rica's Talamanca Coast, an area populated by Afro-Caribbean people whose forebears emigrated from Caribbean islands in the early 19th century, pick up a copy of *What Happen: A Folk-History of Costa Rica's Talamanca Coast,* by Paula Palmer (Publications in English, 1993). Or for a look at the perspective of the indigenous people of the Talamanca region, read Palmer, Sánchez, and Mayorga's *Taking Care of Sibpü's Gifts: An Environmental Treatise from Costa Rica's Kéköldi Indigenous Reserve* (Editorama, 1991).

If you're looking for literature, ✪ *Costa Rica: A Traveler's Literary Companion,* edited by Barbara Ras and with a foreword by Oscar Arias Sánchez (Whereabouts Press, 1994), is a collection of short stories by Costa Rican writers, organized by region of the country. If you're lucky, you might find and pick up a copy of *Stories of Tatamundo* (University of Costa Rica Press, 1998), *Years Like Brief Days* (Peter Owen, 1996) by Fabian Dobles, or *The Lonely Men's Island* by José León Sánchez (Escritores Unidos, 1997). Sánchez is Costa Rica's "Papillon," and the book details his death-defying escape from a prison island.

Costa Rica by Ricardo Zuniga (Incafo, 1999) and *Todo/All Costa Rica* by Ricardo Vilchez Navamuel (Editorial Escudo de Oro, 1999) are two bilingual coffee-table books which highlight the people, architecture, and natural beauties of Costa Rica. Other good coffee-table selections, which focus more on the flora and fauna, are ✪ *Costa Rica The Forests of Eden,* by Kevin Schafer (Rizzoli, 1996); *The Illustrated Geography of Costa Rica,* edited by Alonso Trejos (Trejos Hermanos, 1996); *Birds of the Rain Forest: Costa Rica,* by Carmen Hidalgo (Trejos Hermanos, 1996); *Portraits of the Rainforest,* by Adrian Forsyth, with photos by Michael and Patricia Fogden (Firefly Books, 1995); and ✪ *Costa Rica: Wildlife of the National Parks and Reserves,* written and with photos by Michael and Patricia Fogden (Editorial Heliconia, 1997). The Fogdens are perhaps the most prominent wildlife photographers working in Costa Rica.

Finally, anyone interested in a possible longer-term stay in Costa Rica should look at *The New Golden Door to Retirement and Living in Costa Rica* (10th edition) by Christopher Howard (Editora de Turismo Nacional, S.A., 1999) and/or *Living Overseas Costa Rica* (7th edition) by Robert Johnson (Living Overseas Books, 2000).

NATURAL HISTORY   Mario A. Boza's beautiful ✪ *Costa Rica National Parks* (INCAFO, 1998) has recently been reissued in an elegant coffee-table edition. Each of the country's national parks is represented by several color photos and a short description of the park in Spanish and English. *Costa Rica's National Parks and Preserves* by Joseph Franke (The Mountaineers, 1993) is similar but with fewer photos.

Dr. Donald Perry's fascinating *Life Above the Jungle Floor* (Don Perro Press, 1991) is an account of Perry's research into the life of the tropical rain-forest canopy. Perry is well known for the cable-car network he built through the rain-forest treetops at Rara Avis, as well as the new commercial Aerial Tram.

For an introduction to a wide range of Costa Rican fauna, there's ✪ *The Ecotraveller's Wildlife Guide: Costa Rica,* by Les Beletsky (Academic Press, 1998). This book packs a lot of useful information into a concise package, a great field guide for amateur naturalists and inquisitive tourists.

✪ *A Guide to the Birds of Costa Rica,* by F. Gary Stiles and Alexander Skutch (Cornell University Press, 1989), is an invaluable guide to identifying the many birds you'll see during your stay. It's often available for examination at nature lodges. Some serious bird-watchers also like to have *The Guide to the Birds of Panama, with Costa Rica, Nicaragua and Honduras,* by Robert S. Ridgely and John A. Gwynne (Princeton University Press, 1992), in order to have two different illustrations for identifying some of those more subtle species variations. Bird-watchers might also enjoy Dennis Rodgers's *Site Guides: Costa Rica & Panama* (Cinclus Publications, 1996), which details each country's bird-watching bounty by site and region.

Turtle enthusiasts should read pioneering turtle researcher Archie Carr's *The Sea Turtle* (University of Texas Press, 1984). *Lessons of the Rainforest,* edited by Suzanne Head and Robert Heinzman (Sierra, 1990), is a collection of essays by leading authorities in the fields of biology, ecology, history, law, and economics, who look at the issues surrounding tropical deforestation.

Other interesting natural-history books that will give you a look at the plants and animals of Costa Rica include *Sarapiquí Chronicle,* by Allen Young (Smithsonian Institution Press, 1991); *Costa Rica Natural History,* by Daniel Janzen (University of Chicago Press, 1983); the two-volume collection of *Butterflies of Costa Rica,* by Philip DeVries (Princeton University Press, 1987 and 1997); *A Field Guide to the Mammals of Central America & Southeast Mexico,* by author and illustrator Fiona A. Reid (Oxford University Press, 1998); the classic *A Neotropical Companion,* by John C. Kricher (Princeton University Press, 1997), which was recently reissued in an expanded edition with color photos; *The Monkey's Bridge: Mysteries of Evolution in Central America,* by David Rains Wallace (Sierra Club Books, 1999); and my all-time favorite book on tropical biology, ✪ *Tropical Nature,* by Adrian Forsyth and Ken Miyata (Simon & Schuster, 1984). It's a well-written and lively collection of tales and adventures by two neotropical biologists.

Appendix B: Glossary of Spanish Terms & Phrases

A Basic Spanish Phrases & Vocabulary

English	Spanish	Pronunciation
Hello	**Buenos días**	*bway*-noss *dee*-ahss
How are you?	**Como está usted?**	*koh*-moh ess-*tah* oo-*stead*?
Very well	**Muy bien**	mwee byen
Thank you	**Gracias**	*gra*-see-ahss
Good-bye	**Adiós**	ad-*dyohss*
Please	**Por favor**	pohr fah-*vohr*
Yes	**Sí**	see
No	**No**	noh
Excuse me	**Perdóne me**	pehr-*doh*-neh-may
Give me	**Deme**	*day*-may
Where is . . . ?	**Donde está . . . ?**	*dohn*-day ess-*tah* . . . ?
the station	**la estación**	la ess-*tah*-syohn
the bus stop	**la parada**	la pah-*rah*-da
a hotel	**un hotel**	oon oh-*tel*
a restaurant	**un restaurante**	oon res-tow-*rahn*-tay
the toilet	**el servicio**	el ser-*vee*-see-o
To the right	**A la derecha**	ah lah day-*ray*-chuh
To the left	**A la izquierda**	ah lah is-*kyayr*-duh
Straight ahead	**Adelante**	ah-day-*lahn*-tay
I would like . . .	**Quiero . . .**	*kyehr*-oh . . .
to eat	**comer**	ko-*mayr*
a room	**una habitación**	oo-nah ah-bee-tah-*syohn*
How much is it?	**Cuánto?**	*Kwahn*-toh?
The check	**La cuenta**	la *kwen*-tah
When?	**Cuándo?**	*Kwan*-doh?
Yesterday	**Ayer**	ah-*yayr*
Today	**Hoy**	oy
Tomorrow	**Mañana**	mahn-*yah*-nah
Breakfast	**Desayuno**	deh-sai-*yoo*-noh
Lunch	**Comida**	co-*mee*-dah
Dinner	**Cena**	*say*-nah

NUMBERS

1	**uno** (*oo*-noh)	16	**dieciséis** (dyays-ee-*sayss*)
2	**dos** (dose)	17	**diecisiete** (dyays-ee-*sye*-tay)
3	**tres** (trayss)	18	**dieciocho** (dyays-ee-*oh*-choh)
4	**cuatro** (*kwah*-troh)	19	**diecinueve** (dyays-ee-*nyway*-bay)
5	**cinco** (*seen*-koh)	20	**veinte** (*bayn*-tay)
6	**seis** (sayss)	30	**treinta** (*trayn*-tah)
7	**siete** (*syeh*-tay)	40	**cuarenta** (kwah-*ren*-tah)
8	**ocho** (*oh*-choh)	50	**cincuenta** (seen-*kween*-tah)
9	**nueve** (*nway*-bay)	60	**sesenta** (say-*sen*-tah)
10	**diez** (dee-*ays*)	70	**setenta** (say-*ten*-tah)
11	**once** (*ohn*-say)	80	**ochenta** (oh-*chen*-tah)
12	**doce** (*doh*-say)	90	**noventa** (noh-*ben*-tah)
13	**trece** (*tray*-say)	100	**cien** (syen)
14	**catorce** (kah-*tor*-say)	1000	**mil** (mil)
15	**quince** (*keen*-say)		

B Some Typically Tico Words & Phrases

Chunche Knicknack; thing—as in "whatchamacallit."

Con mucho gusto With pleasure.

De hoy en ocho In one week's time.

Diay An untranslatable but common linguistic punctuation, often used to begin a sentence.

Macha, or machita A blond woman.

Mae Translates a lot like "man"; used by teenagers as constant verbal punctuation.

Maje A lot like *mae* above, but with a slightly derogatory connotation.

Ponga la maría, por favor This is how you ask taxi drivers to turn on the meter.

Pura vida Literally, "pure life"; translates as "everything's great."

Si Dios quiere God willing. You'll hear Ticos say this all the time.

Tuanis Means the same as *pura vida* above, but is used by a younger crowd.

Una teja 100 colónes.

Un rojo 1,000 colónes.

Un tucan 5,000 colónes.

C Menu Terms

FISH

almejas	clams	**langosta**	lobster
atún	tuna	**langostinos**	prawns
bacalao	cod	**lenguado**	sole
calamares	squid	**mejillones**	mussels
camarones	shrimp	**ostras**	oysters
cangrejo	crab	**pargo**	snapper
ceviche	marinated seafood salad	**pulpo**	octopus
corvina	sea bass	**tiburón**	shark
dorado	dolphin, or mahimahi	**trucha**	trout

Spanish Terms & Phrases

MEATS

albóndigas   meatballs
bistec   beefsteak
cerdo   pork
chicharrones   fried pork rinds
chuleta   cutlet
conejo   rabbit
cordero   lamb

costillas   ribs
jamón   ham
lengua   tongue
mondongo   tripe
pato   duck
pavo   turkey
pollo   chicken

VEGETABLES

aceitunas   olives
alcachofa   artichoke
berenjena   eggplant
cebolla   onion
elote   corn on the cob
ensalada   salad
esparragos   asparagus
espinacas   spinach
hongos   mushrooms

palmito   heart of palm
papa   potato
pepino   cucumber
remolacha   beet
repollo   cabbage
tomate   tomato
vainica   string beans
yuca   yucca, or manioc
zanahoria   carrot

FRUITS

aguacate   avocado
banano   banana
carambola   star fruit
cerezas   cherries
ciruela   plum
fresa   strawberry
limón   lemon or lime
mango   mango
manzana   apple

melocotón   peach
mora   raspberry
naranja   orange
pera   pear
piña   pineapple
plátano   plantain
sandía   watermelon
toronja   grapefruit
uvas   grapes

BASICS

aceite   oil
ajo   garlic
arreglado   small meat sandwich
azúcar   sugar
bocas   appetizers
casado   plate of the day
frito   fried
gallo   corn tortilla topped with meat or chicken
gallo pinto   rice and beans
hielo   ice
mantequilla   butter

miel   honey
mostaza   mustard
natilla   sour cream
pan   bread
patacones   fried plantain chips
picadillo   chopped vegetable side dish
pimienta   pepper
queso   cheese
sal   salt
tamal   filled cornmeal pastry
tortilla   flat corn pancake

Spanish Terms & Phrases

Index

Index

FROMMER'S® COMPLETE TRAVEL GUIDES

Alaska
Amsterdam
Arizona
Atlanta
Australia
Austria
Bahamas
Barcelona, Madrid &
 Seville
Beijing
Belgium, Holland &
 Luxembourg
Bermuda
Boston
British Columbia & the
 Canadian Rockies
Budapest & the Best of
 Hungary
California
Canada
Cancún, Cozumel &
 the Yucatán
Cape Cod, Nantucket &
 Martha's Vineyard
Caribbean
Caribbean Cruises & Ports
 of Call
Caribbean Ports of Call
Carolinas & Georgia
Chicago
China
Colorado
Costa Rica
Denmark
Denver, Boulder & Colorado
 Springs
England
Europe

European Cruises & Ports
 of Call
Florida
France
Germany
Greece
Greek Islands
Hawaii
Hong Kong
Honolulu, Waikiki &
 Oahu
Ireland
Israel
Italy
Jamaica
Japan
Las Vegas
London
Los Angeles
Maryland & Delaware
Maui
Mexico
Miami & the Keys
Montana & Wyoming
Montréal & Québec City
Munich & the Bavarian
 Alps
Nashville & Memphis
Nepal
New England
New Mexico
New Orleans
New York City
New Zealand
Nova Scotia, New Brunswick
 & Prince Edward Island
Oregon
Paris

Philadelphia & the
 Amish Country
Portugal
Prague & the Best of the
 Czech Republic
Provence & the Riviera
Puerto Rico
Rome
San Antonio & Austin
San Diego
San Francisco
Santa Fe, Taos & Albuquerque
Scandinavia
Scotland
Seattle & Portland
Singapore & Malaysia
South Africa
Southeast Asia
South Pacific
Spain
Sweden
Switzerland
Thailand
Tokyo
Toronto
Tuscany & Umbria
USA
Utah
Vancouver & Victoria
Vermont, New Hampshire
 & Maine
Vienna & the Danube Valley
Virgin Islands
Virginia
Walt Disney World &
 Orlando
Washington, D.C.
Washington State

FROMMER'S® DOLLAR-A-DAY GUIDES

Australia from $50 a Day
California from $60 a Day
Caribbean from $70 a Day
England from $70 a Day
Europe from $60 a Day

Florida from $60 a Day
Hawaii from $70 a Day
Ireland from $60 a Day
Italy from $70 a Day
London from $85 a Day

New York from $80 a Day
Paris from $85 a Day
San Francisco from $60 a Day
Washington, D.C.,
 from $60 a Day

FROMMER'S® PORTABLE GUIDES

Acapulco, Ixtapa &
 Zihuatanejo
Alaska Cruises & Ports of Call
Bahamas
Baja & Los Cabos
Berlin
California Wine Country
Charleston & Savannah
Chicago

Dublin
Hawaii: The Big Island
Las Vegas
London
Maine Coast
Maui
New Orleans
New York City
Paris

Puerto Vallarta, Manzanillo
 & Guadalajara
San Diego
San Francisco
Sydney
Tampa & St. Petersburg
Venice
Washington, D.C.

FROMMER'S® NATIONAL PARK GUIDES

Family Vacations in the National Parks
Grand Canyon

National Parks of the American West
Rocky Mountain

Yellowstone & Grand Teton
Yosemite & Sequoia/ Kings Canyon
Zion & Bryce Canyon

FROMMER'S® MEMORABLE WALKS

Chicago
London

New York
Paris

San Francisco
Washington D.C.

FROMMER'S® GREAT OUTDOOR GUIDES

New England
Northern California

Southern California & Baja
Southern New England

Washington & Oregon

FROMMER'S® BORN TO SHOP GUIDES

Born to Shop: China
Born to Shop: France

Born to Shop: Italy
Born to Shop: London

Born to Shop: New York
Born to Shop: Paris

FROMMER'S® IRREVERENT GUIDES

Amsterdam
Boston
Chicago
Las Vegas

London
Los Angeles
Manhattan
New Orleans

Paris
San Francisco
Seattle & Portland
Vancouver

Walt Disney World
Washington, D.C.

FROMMER'S® BEST-LOVED DRIVING TOURS

America
Britain
California

Florida
France
Germany

Ireland
Italy
New England

Scotland
Spain
Western Europe

THE UNOFFICIAL GUIDES®

Bed & Breakfasts in California
Bed & Breakfasts in New England
Bed & Breakfasts in the Northwest
Beyond Disney
Branson, Missouri
California with Kids
Chicago

Cruises
Disneyland
Florida with Kids
Golf Vacations in the Eastern U.S.
The Great Smoky & Blue Ridge Mountains
Inside Disney

Hawaii
Las Vegas
London
Miami & the Keys
Mini Las Vegas
Mini-Mickey
New Orleans
New York City
Paris

Safaris
San Francisco
Skiing in the West
Walt Disney World
Walt Disney World for Grown-ups
Walt Disney World for Kids
Washington, D.C.

SPECIAL-INTEREST TITLES

Frommer's Britain's Best Bed & Breakfasts and Country Inns
Frommer's Britain's Best Bike Rides
The Civil War Trust's Official Guide to the Civil War Discovery Trail
Frommer's Caribbean Hideaways
Frommer's Food Lover's Companion to France
Frommer's Food Lover's Companion to Italy
Frommer's Gay & Lesbian Europe
Frommer's Exploring America by RV
Hanging Out in Europe
Israel Past & Present

Mad Monks' Guide to California
Mad Monks' Guide to New York City
Frommer's The Moon
Frommer's New York City with Kids
The New York Times' Unforgettable Weekends
Places Rated Almanac
Retirement Places Rated
Frommer's Road Atlas Britain
Frommer's Road Atlas Europe
Frommer's Washington, D.C., with Kids
Frommer's What the Airlines Never Tell You